Handbook of
Software Engineering
&
Knowledge Engineering

Vol. 3
Recent Advances

Also Published by World Scientific

Handbook of Software Engineering & Knowledge Engineering, Vol. 1
Fundamentals
ISBN 981-02-4973-X

Handbook of Software Engineering & Knowledge Engineering, Vol. 2
Emerging Technologies
ISBN 981-02-4974-8

Handbook of
Software Engineering
&
Knowledge Engineering

Vol. 3
Recent Advances

Editor

S K Chang

University of Pittsburgh, USA
and
Knowledge Systems Institute, USA

World Scientific

NEW JERSEY · LONDON · SINGAPORE · BEIJING · SHANGHAI · HONG KONG · TAIPEI · CHENNAI

Published by

World Scientific Publishing Co. Pte. Ltd.

5 Toh Tuck Link, Singapore 596224

USA office: 27 Warren Street, Suite 401-402, Hackensack, NJ 07601

UK office: 57 Shelton Street, Covent Garden, London WC2H 9HE

British Library Cataloguing-in-Publication Data
A catalogue record for this book is available from the British Library.

HANDBOOK OF SOFTWARE ENGINEERING & KNOWLEDGE ENGINEERING, Vol. 3
Recent Advances

ISBN 981-256-273-7

Typeset by Stallion Press
Email: enquiries@stallionpress.com

Printed in Singapore by B & JO Enterprise

PREFACE

The *Handbook of Software Engineering and Knowledge Engineering* is the first comprehensive handbook covering these two important areas that have become interwoven in recent years. Many international experts contribute to this Handbook. Each article is written in a way that a practitioner of software engineering and knowledge engineering can easily understand and obtain useful information. Each article covers one topic and can be read independently of other articles, providing both a general survey of the topic and an in-depth exposition of the state of the art. Practitioners will find this Handbook useful when looking for solutions to practical problems in software engineering and knowledge engineering. Researchers in turn can use the Handbook to quickly obtain background information, current trends and the most important references on a certain topic.

The Handbook consists of three volumes. Volume One covers the basic principles and applications of software engineering and knowledge engineering. Volume Two expands the coverage of basic principles and also contains many articles that specifically addresses visual and multimedia software engineering, and emerging topics in software engineering and knowledge engineering such as software patterns, data mining for software knowledge, etc. Volume Three provides a comprehensive treatment of recent new advances and also completes the coverage of basic principles such as Petri nets. The three volumes form a complete set but can be used separately for different purposes.

Turning Knowledge into Software

There is a growing awareness that the central issue in software engineering and knowledge engineering is how to turn knowledge into software. Traditionally software engineering is concerned with the specification, design, coding, testing and maintenance of software. It also implicitly deals with the issues of transforming knowledge into software in the sense that the gathering of knowledge about the problem domain is incorporated into the requirements analysis phase of the software life cycle. Often, informal techniques of knowledge acquisition are used. Thus in the past, the role of knowledge engineering in the software process is an implicit one.

However, it has long been recognized by many people that knowledge engineering plays an increasingly important role in software design. Indeed it is because of this conviction that the international conference series on Software Engineering and Knowledge Engineering (SEKE) was founded in 1988, followed by the publication of the *International Journal of Software Engineering and Knowledge*

Engineering (IJSEKE) three years later. For both the SEKE conference series and the IJSEKE journal, the basic viewpoint is that the interdisciplinary area of software engineering and knowledge engineering is concerned with the interplay between software engineering and knowledge engineering — how software engineering can be applied to knowledge engineering, and how knowledge engineering can be applied to software engineering.

This viewpoint should now be modified and expanded because, both in theory and in practice, more and more software engineers and knowledge engineers are explicitly incorporating knowledge into the software process. In editing this three-volume handbook, this expanded viewpoint — that software engineering is concerned with the transformation of knowledge into software — has been carefully taken into consideration to conceptually organize the recent progresses in software engineering and knowledge engineering.

Software Patterns

Let us start with two distinct, yet complementary, viewpoints on software engineering. The two viewpoints may seem completely different, but they are but different ways of viewing the "elephant" that is software engineering.

The first viewpoint, as stated above, is that software engineering is concerned with the transformation of knowledge into software. The second viewpoint is somewhat more technical. It says that software engineering is concerned with the specification, design, transformation, verification and validation of patterns.

Software is nothing but patterns. A program is constructed from some basic patterns, and the construction rules can in turn be expressed as other types of patterns. With grammars, formal languages and automata, there are many approaches to describe the basic patterns and how they are composed into programs.

Specifications are composed of patterns that are the basic building blocks of formal, informal or visual specifications. The specification, in the ideal case, can then be automatically transformed into programs, and verified and validated in the transformational process.

As mentioned above, knowledge used to be described informally, but now there are formal techniques and more precise ways of dealing with knowledge. With advances in object oriented methods, one comes to the inevitable conclusion that knowledge is also composed of patterns. Knowledge is first acquired, then transformed into formal/informal/visual specification, design and finally program.

Therefore, software engineering can now be viewed as the transformation of knowledge into software through the transformation of patterns. The central issue of software engineering is how to turn knowledge into software by means of the creation, composition and transformation of various types of patterns. A key question that can be asked repeatedly for any topic or sub-topic is the following: how to turn what-kind-of knowledge patterns into what-kind-of software patterns?

Overview of Volume Three

As mentioned above, the *Handbook of Software Engineering and Knowledge Engineering* is a comprehensive handbook, providing the reader with both useful overviews and detailed explanations of the methodologies, techniques and current research issues in software engineering and knowledge engineering. The seventeen chapters in this volume provide a comprehensive treatment of the following topics:

- requirements engineering;
- attacks and countermeasures in software system security;
- autonomous software and software agents;
- capability maturity for software development;
- object oriented modeling and software architecture;
- agent-oriented design patterns;
- knowledge-based consistency checking in UML models;
- model-driven ontological engineering;
- migration of legacy systems to multi-layered web-based architectures;
- Petri nets;
- program slicing;
- simulation-based software process modeling and evaluation;
- software release planning;
- software traceability;
- goal-oriented measurement;
- time/knowledge management in e-learning; and
- tool-based software project control.

In a rapidly expanding area such as software engineering and knowledge engineering, no handbook can claim to cover all the subjects of interest. However it is hoped that this Handbook is comprehensive enough to serve as a useful and handy guide to both practitioners and researchers at least for a number of years to come.

Shi-Kuo Chang
University of Pittsburgh and
Knowledge Systems Institute
April 28, 2005

CONTENTS

Preface   v

Analysis Styles for Requirements Engineering: An
Organizational Perspective   1
  Manuel Kolp, T. Tung Do and Stéphane Faulkner

Attacks and Countermeasures in Software System Security   31
  Lu Ma and Jeffrey J.P. Tsai

Autonomous Software   63
  Michael Rovatsos and Gerhard Weiss

Capability Maturity for Software Development   85
  Alfs T. Berztiss

Coexistence of Object-Oriented Modeling and
Architectural Description   119
  Tahar Khammaci, Adel Smeda and Mourad Oussalah

Introspecting Agent-Oriented Design Patterns   151
  Manuel Kolp, T. Tung Do and Stéphane Faulkner

Knowledge-Based Inconsistency Detection in UML Models   177
  Ekawit Nantajeewarawat and Vilas Wuwongse

MDA-Based Ontological Engineering   203
  *Dragan Djurić, Dragan Gašević, Violeta Damjanović and
  Vladan Devedžić*

Migrating Legacy Systems Towards Multi-Layered
Web-Based Architectures   233
  *Thierry Bodhuin, Gerardo Canfora, Aniello Cimitile
  and Maria Tortorella*

Petri Nets: A Tutorial   275
  Alfs T. Berztiss

Program Slicing   307
    Jens Krinke

Simulation-Based Software Process Modeling and Evaluation   333
    Ove Armbrust, Thomas Berlage, Thomas Hanne, Patrick Lang,
    Jürgen Münch, Holger Neu, Stefan Nickel, Ioana Rus, Alex Sarishvili,
    Sascha Van Stockum and Andreas Wirsen

Software Release Planning   365
    Günther Ruhe

Software Traceability: A Roadmap   395
    George Spanoudakis and Andrea Zisman

System Dynamics and Goal-Oriented Measurement:
A Hybrid Approach   429
    Dietmar Pfahl and Günther Ruhe

Time and Knowledge Management in E-Learning   455
    Shi-Kuo Chang

Tool-Based Software Project Control   477
    Jürgen Münch and Jens Heidrich

Index   513

ANALYSIS STYLES FOR REQUIREMENTS ENGINEERING: AN ORGANIZATIONAL PERSPECTIVE

MANUEL KOLP* and T. TUNG DO

University of Louvain,
ISYS — Information Systems Research Unit,
Place des Doyens, 1, 1348, Louvain-La-Neuve, Belgium
E-mail: {kolp, do}@isys.ucl.ac.be

STÉPHANE FAULKNER

University of Namur,
Department of Management Sciences,
Rempart de la Vierge, 8, 5000 Namur, Belgium
E-mail: Stephane.Faulkner@fundp.ac.be

Early requirements analysis is concerned with modeling and understanding the organizational context within which a software system will eventually function. This chapter proposes organizational styles motivated by organizational theories intended to facilitate the construction of organizational models. These styles are defined from real world organizational settings, modeled in *i** and formalized using the Formal Tropos language. Additionally, the chapter evaluates the proposed styles using desirable qualities such as coordinability and predictability. The research is conducted in the context of *Tropos*, a comprehensive software system development methodology.

Keywords: Organizational styles, *i**, Tropos, requirements engineering, organizational modeling.

1. Introduction

Modeling the organizational and intentional context within which a software system will eventually operate has been recognized as an important element of the requirements engineering process (e.g. [1, 6, 40]). Such models are founded on primitive concepts such as those of actor and goal. This chapter focuses on the definition of a set of organizational styles that can be used as building blocks for constructing such models. Our proposal is based on concepts adopted from organization theory and strategic alliances literature.

The research reported in this chapter is being conducted within the context of the Tropos project [3,4,30], whose aim is to construct and validate a software development methodology for agent-based software systems. The methodology adopts ideas from multi-agent system technologies, mostly to define the implementation phase of our methodology. It also adopts ideas from requirements engineering, where

---

*Corresponding author.

actors and goals have been used heavily for early requirements analysis. The project
is founded on that actors and goals are used as fundamental concepts for modeling
and analysis during all phases of software development, not just early requirements,
or implementation. More details about Tropos can be found in [4]. The present work
continues the research in progress about social abstractions for the Tropos methodology. In [23], we have detailed a social ontology for Tropos to consider information
systems with social structures all along the development life cycle. In [14,22,24], we
have described how to use this Tropos social ontology to design multi-agent systems
architectures, notably for e-business applications [7]. As a matter of fact, multi-
agent systems can be considered structured societies of coordinated autonomous
agents. In the present chapter, which is a extended and revised version of [25], we
emphasize the use of organizational styles based on organization theory an strategic
alliances for early requirements analysis, with the concern of modeling the organizational setting for a system-to-be in terms of abstractions that could better match
its operational environment (e.g. an enterprise, a corporate alliance, . . .) Throughout the chapter, we use i^* [40] as the modeling framework in terms of which the
proposed styles are presented and accounted for.

   The chapter is organized as follows. Section 2 describes organizational and
strategic alliance theories, focusing on the internal and external structure of an
organization. Section 3 details two organizational styles — the structure-in-5 and
the joint venture — based on real world examples of organizations. These styles
are modeled in terms of social and intentional concepts using the i^* framework
and the Formal Tropos specification language. Section 4 identifies a set of desirable
non-functional requirements for evaluating these styles and presents a framework to
select a style with respect to these identified requirements. Section 5 overviews the
Tropos methodology. Finally, Sec. 6 summarizes the contributions of the chapter
and overviews related work.

2. Structuring Organizations

Since the origins of civilization, people have been designing, participating in, and
sharing the burdens and rewards of organizations. The early organizations were
primarily military or governmental in nature. In the *Art of War*, Sun Tzu describes
the need for hierarchical structure, communications, and strategy. In the *Politics*,
Aristotle wrote of governmental administration and its association with culture.
To the would-be-leader, Machiavelli advocated in the *Prince* power over morality.
The roots of organizational theories, then, can be traced to antiquity, including
thinkers from around the world who studied alternative organizational structures.
Such structures consist of stakeholders — individuals, groups, physical or social
systems — that coordinate and interact with each other to achieve common goals.
Today, organizational structures are primarily studied by two disciplines: *Organization Theory* (e.g. [28, 32, 39]), that describes the structure and design of an
organization and *Strategic Alliances* (e.g. [10, 17, 29, 33]), that model the strategic

collaborations of independent organizational stakeholders who have agreed to pursue a set of agreed upon business goals.

Both disciplines aim to identify and study organizational patterns. These are not just modeling abstractions or structures, rather they can be seen, felt, handled, and operated upon. They have a manifest form and lie in the objective domain of reality as part of the concrete world. A pattern is however not solely a set of execution behaviors. Rather, it exists in various forms at every stage of crystallization (e.g. specification), and at every level of granularity in the organization. The more manifest is its representation, the more the pattern emerges and becomes recognizable, whether at a high or low level of granularity.

At the lowest level of granularity, we find *information patterns* and *service patterns* that represent the "nitty-gritty" of business that an organization must deal with on a day-to-day basis. When we move to an upper level, we find *business patterns* — the mix of products and markets that flows from organizational styles. The highest level of granularity is the *organizational styles* that addresses the mix of socio-technical context and organizational constructs: they are manifestation of organization invariants, layers of organizational constructs, organization molecules, and complex arrangements of molecules, the collection of which constitutes organizational structures.

Many organizational styles are fully formed patterns with definite characteristics as the ones we present in the rest of this section. In contrast, many other organizational styles are not very explicit, that is, not easily specified, operationalized, and measured. Michael Porter's generic strategies [31] are examples of such patterns. Each strategy type is characterized by general properties that distinguish one strategy from another. For the most part, however, the distinguishing characteristics of each style are only partially described in terms of an organization's architecture.

In this chapter, we are interested to identify and use, for requirements engineering, organizational styles that have already been well-understood and precisely defined in organizational theories. Our purpose is not to categorize them exhaustively nor to study them on a managerial point of view. The following sections will thus only insist on styles that have been found, due to their nature, interesting candidates also considering the fact that they have been studied in great detail in the organizational literature and presented as fully formed patterns.

2.1. *Organization theory*

"An organization is a consciously coordinated social entity, with a relatively identifiable boundary, that functions on a relatively continuous basis to achieve a common goal or a set of goals" [29]. Organization theory is the discipline that studies both structure and design in such social entities. Structure deals with the descriptive aspects while design refers to the prescriptive aspects of a social entity. Organization theory describes how practical organizations are actually structured, offers suggestions on how new ones can be constructed, and how old ones can change to improve effectiveness. To this end, since Adam Smith, schools of organization theory have proposed models and patterns to try to find and formalize recurring organizational structures and behaviors.

In the following, we briefly present organizational styles identified in organization theory. The structure-in-5 will be studied in detail in Sec. 3.

The Structure-in-5. An organization can be considered an aggregate of five sub-structures, as proposed by Minztberg [28]. At the base level sits the *Operational Core* which carries out the basic tasks and procedures directly linked to the production of products and services (acquisition of inputs, transformation of inputs into outputs, distribution of outputs). At the top lies the *Strategic Apex* which makes executive decisions ensuring that the organization fulfils its mission in an effective way and defines the overall strategy of the organization in its environment. The *Middle Line* establishes a hierarchy of authority between the Strategic Apex and the Operational Core. It consists of managers responsible for supervising and coordinating the activities of the Operational Core. The *Technostructure* and the *Support* are separated from the main line of authority and influence the operating core only indirectly. The Technostructure serves the organization by making the work of others more effective, typically by standardizing work processes, outputs, and skills. It is also in charge of applying analytical procedures to adapt the organization to its operational environment. The Support provides specialized services, at various levels of the hierarchy, outside the basic operating work flow (e.g. legal counsel, R&D, payroll, cafeteria). We describe and model examples of structures-in-5 in Sec. 3.

The pyramid style is the well-know hierarchical authority structure. Actors at lower levels depend on those at higher levels. The crucial mechanism is the direct supervision from the Apex. Managers and supervisors at intermediate levels only route strategic decisions and authority from the Apex to the operating (low) level. They can coordinate behaviors or take decisions by their own, but only at a local level.

The chain of values merges, backward or forward, several actors engaged in achieving or realizing related goals or tasks at different stages of a supply or production process. Participants who act as intermediaries, add value at each step of the chain. For instance, for the domain of goods distribution, providers are expected to supply quality products, wholesalers are responsible for ensuring their massive exposure, while retailers take care of the direct delivery to the consumers.

The matrix proposes a multiple command structure: vertical and horizontal channels of information and authority operate simultaneously. The principle of the unity of command is set aside, and competing bases of authority are allowed to jointly govern the work flow. The vertical lines are typically those of functional departments that operate as "home bases" for all participants, the horizontal lines represents project groups or geographical arenas where managers combine and coordinate the services of the functional specialists around particular projects or areas.

The bidding style involves competitivity mechanisms, and actors behave as if they were taking part in an auction. An auctioneer actor runs the show, advertises the auction issued by the auction issuer, receives bids from bidder actors and ensures communication and feedback with the auction issuer who is responsible for issuing the bidding.

2.2. *Strategic alliances*

A strategic alliance links specific facets of two or more organizations. At its core, this structure is a trading partnership that enhances the effectiveness of the competitive strategies of the participant organizations by providing for the mutually beneficial trade of technologies, skills, or products based upon them. An alliance can take a variety of forms, ranging from arm's-length contracts to joint ventures, from multinational corporations to university spin-offs, from franchises to equity arrangements. Varied interpretations of the term exist, but a strategic alliance can be defined as possessing simultaneously the following three necessary and sufficient characteristics:

- The two or more organizations that unite to pursue a set of agreed upon goals remain independent subsequent to the formation of the alliance.
- The partner organizations share the benefits of the alliances and control over the performance of assigned tasks.
- The partner organizations contribute on a continuing basis in one or more key strategic areas, e.g. technology, products, and so forth.

In the following, we briefly present organizational styles identified in Strategic Alliances. The joint venture will be studied in details in Sec. 3.

The joint venture style involves agreement between two or more intra-industry partners to obtain the benefits of larger scale, partial investment and lower maintenance costs. A specific joint management actor coordinates tasks and manages the sharing of resources between partner actors. Each partner can manage and control itself on a local dimension and interact directly with other partners to exchange resources, such as data and knowledge. However, the strategic operation and coordination of such an organization, and its actors on a global dimension, are only ensured by the joint management actor in which the original actors possess equity participations. We describe and model examples of joint ventures in Sec. 3.

The arm's-length style implies agreements between independent and competitive, but partner actors. Partners keep their autonomy and independence but act and put their resources and knowledge together to accomplish precise common goals. No authority is lost, or delegated from one collaborator to another.

The hierarchical contracting style identifies coordinating mechanisms that combine arm's-length agreement features with aspects of pyramidal authority. Coordination mechanisms developed for arm's-length (independent) characteristics involve a variety of negotiators, mediators and observers at different levels handling conditional clauses to monitor and manage possible contingencies, negotiate and resolve conflicts and finally deliberate and take decisions. Hierarchical relationships, from the executive apex to the arm's-length contractors restrict autonomy and underlie a cooperative venture between the parties.

The co-optation style involves the incorporation of representatives of external systems into the decision-making or advisory structure and behavior of an initiating organization. By co-opting representatives of external systems, organizations are, in effect, trading confidentiality and authority for resource, knowledge assets and support. The initiating system has to come to terms with the contractors for what is being done on its behalf; and each co-optated actor has to reconcile and adjust its own views with the policy of the system it has to communicate.

3. Modeling Organizational Styles

We will define an organizational style as a metaclass of organizational structures offering a set of design parameters to coordinate the assignment of organizational objectives and processes, thereby affecting how the organization itself functions. Design parameters include, among others, goal and task assignments, standardization, supervision and control dependencies and strategy definitions.

This section describes two of the organizational styles presented in Sec. 2: the structure-in-5 and the joint-venture.

3.1. *Structure-in-5*

To detail and specify the structure-in-5 as an organizational style, this section presents three case studies: Agate [2], Volvo Trucks Corporation [27] and GMT [16]. They will serve to propose a model and a semi-formal specification of the structure-in-5.

Agate is an advertising agency located in England that employs about seventy-five staff, as detailed in Table 1.

Table 1.

Direction	*Edition*	*IT*
1 Campaigns Director	3 Editors	1 IT manager
1 Creative Director	7 Copywriters	2 Network administrator
1 Administrative Director		2 System administrator
1 Finance Director	*Documentation*	2 Analyst
	2 Media librarian	2 Computer technician
Campaigns Management	2 Resource librarian	
3 Campaign managers	1 Knowledge worker	*Accounts*
4 Campaign marketers		2 Accountant manager
2 Editor-in-Chief	*Administration*	1 Credit controller
2 Creative Manager	4 Direction assistants	2 Accounts clerks
	6 Manager Secretaries	2 Purchasing assistants
Graphics	2 Receptionists	
10 Graphic designers	2 Clerks/typists	
4 Photographers	1 Filing clerk	

The *Direction* — four directors responsible for the main aspects of Agate's *Global Strategy* (advertising campaigns, creative activities, administration, and finances) — forms the *Strategic Apex*. The *Middle Line*, composed of the *Campaigns Management* staff, is in charge of *finding* and *coordinating* advertising campaigns (marketing, sales, edition, graphics, budget, ...). It is supported in these tasks by the *Administration and Accounts* and *IT and Documentation* departments. The *Administration and Accounts* constitutes the *Technostructure* handling administrative tasks and policy, paperwork, purchases and budgets. The *Support* groups the *IT and Documentation* departments. It defines the *IT policy* of Agate, provides *technical means* required for the management of campaigns, and ensures services for *system support* as well as information retrieval (*documentation* resources). The *Operational Core* includes the *Graphics and Edition* staff in charge of the creative and artistic aspects of *realizing campaign* (texts, photographs, drawings, layout, design, logos).

Figure 1 models Agate in structure-in-5 using the *i** strategic dependency model. *i** is a modeling framework for organizational modeling [40], which offers goal- and actor-based notions such as *actor, agent, role, position, goal, softgoal, task,*

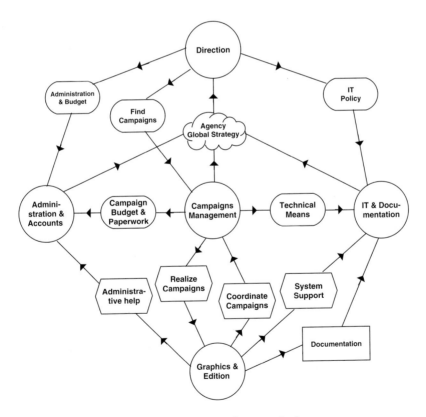

Fig. 1. Agate as a Structure-in-5.

resource, belief and different kinds of social *dependency* between actors. Its strategic dependency model describes the network of social dependencies among actors.
It is a graph, where each node represents an *actor* and each link between two
actors indicates that one actor depends on the other for some goal to be attained.
A dependency describes an "agreement" (called *dependum*) between two actors:
the *depender* and the *dependee*. The *depender* is the depending actor, and the
dependee, the actor who is depended upon. The type of the dependency describes
the nature of the agreement. *Goal* dependencies represent delegation of responsibility for fulfilling a goal; *softgoal* dependencies are similar to goal dependencies,
but their fulfillment cannot be defined precisely (for instance, the appreciation is
subjective or fulfillment is obtained only to a given extent); *task* dependencies are
used in situations where the dependee is required to perform a given activity; and
resource dependencies require the dependee to provide a resource to the depender.
As shown in Fig. 1, actors are represented as circles; dependums — goals, softgoals,
tasks and resources — are represented as ovals, clouds, hexagons and rectangles;
respectively, and dependencies have the form *depender → dependum → dependee.*

Volvo Trucks Corporation (VTC) is a subsidiary company of AB Volvo,
the automobile manufacturer. The VTC distributive network is segmented into
eight commercial divisions responsible for the production and commercialization
of trucks. These divisions take charge of the coordination of assemblage factories
attached to a geographical zone and supervise dealers' networks. Dealers are responsible for the elaboration of sales local systems that correspond to customers' needs.
Commercial divisions coordinate sales at the national or international level.

The product development division is in charge of the design of new trucks and
components models. It also provides dealers with technological training.

The marketing communication is under the supervision of a single entity. The
objective is double: to increase the coherence of the sale supports and promotion
in Europe; and to improve the efficiency and the profitability of these supports.

The audit division constitutes an independent control entity that has for objective to define administrative procedures for dealers and supervise their implementation. Finally, the financial division that collaborates with the audit division provides
the financial forecasts required by the executive committee. It also determines the
budget of commercial divisions.

Figure 2 models the VTC structure-in-5 using the i^* strategic dependency
model. The executive committee composed of three administrators responsible for
the main aspects of VTC's *General Strategy* form the *Strategic Apex.* The *Middle
Line* composed of the different *Commercial Divisions* implements the *Distributive Network Management.* It coordinates the *Operational Core* (i.e., *Dealers* and
Assemblage networks). *R&D* and *Information Divisions* constitute the *Technostructure. R&D* is in charge of the *Design* of the new models and the *Training* for
the *Operational Core.* The *Information* department defines VTC *Communication
Policy* as well as the public *Image* of the firm. It also provides the *Operational Core*
with *Sales* and *Promotion* support. The *Support* groups the *Audit* and *Financial*

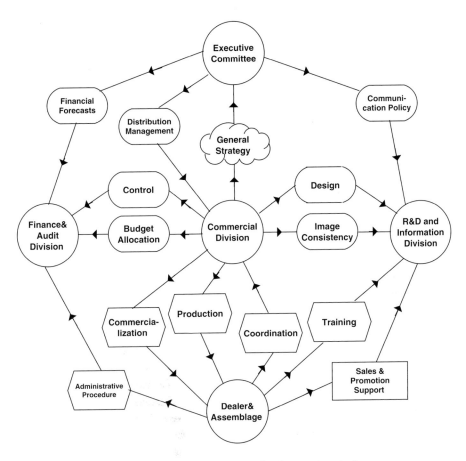

Fig. 2. Volvo trucks corporation in structure-in-5.

Divisions. The *Audit Division* defines the *Administrative Procedures* and *controls* how these are implemented. The *Financial Division* is in charge of the *Financial Forecasts* and defines the *Budget Allocations* for *Commercial Divisions*.

GMT is a company specialized in telecom services in Belgium composed of 50 employees. Its lines of products and services range from phones & fax, conferencing, line solutions, internet & e-business, mobile solutions, and voice & data management. As shown in Fig. 3, the structure of the commercial organization follows the structure-in-5. An *Executive Committee* constitutes the *Strategic Apex*. It is responsible for defining the *general strategy* of the organization. Five chief managers (*finances, operations, divisions management, marketing,* and *R&D*) apply the specific aspects of the *general strategy* in the area of their competence: *Finances & Operations* is in charge of *Budget* and Sales *Planning & Control, Divisions Management* is responsible for *Implementing Sales Strategy,* and *Marketing* and *R&D* define *Sales Policy* and *Technological Policy*.

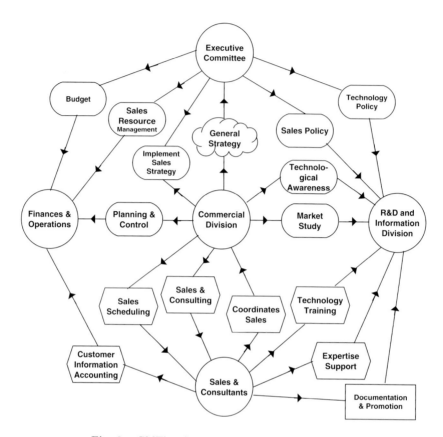

Fig. 3.   GMT's sales organization as a structure-in-5.

The *Divisions Management* groups managers that coordinate all managerial aspects of product and service sales. It relies on *Finance & Operations* for handling *Planning* and *Control* of products and services, it depends on *Marketing* for accurate *Market Studies* and on R&D for *Technological Awareness*.

The *Finances & Operations* departments constitute the *technostructure* in charge of management *control* (financial and quality audit) and sales *planning* including *scheduling* and *resource management*.

The *Support* involves the staff of *Marketing* and *R&D*. Both departments jointly define and support the *Sales Policy*. The *Marketing* department coordinates *Market Studies* (customer positionment and segmentation, pricing, sales incentive, ...) and provides the *Operational Core* with *Documentation* and *Promotion* services. The *R&D* staff is responsible for defining the technological policy such as *technological awareness services*. It also assists *Sales people* and *Consultants* with *Expertise Support* and *Technology Training*.

Finally, the *Operational Core* groups *the Sales people* and *Line consultants* under the supervision and coordination of *Divisions Managers*. They are in charge of selling products and services to actual and potential customers.

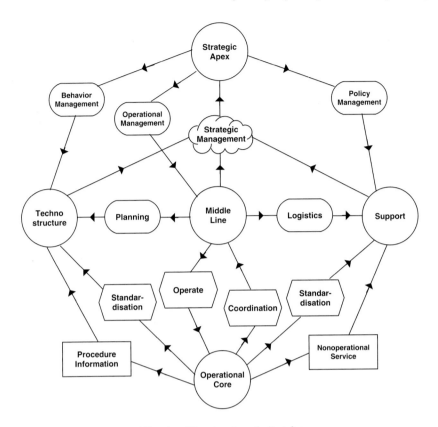

Fig. 4.   The structure-in-5 style.

Figure 4 abstracts the structures explored in the case studies of Figs. 1–3 as a structure-in-5 style composed of five actors. The case studies also suggested a number of constraints to supplement the basic style:

- the dependencies between the *Strategic Apex* as depender and the *Technostructure, Middle Line* and *Support* as dependees must be of type goal;
- a softgoal dependency models the strategic dependence of the *Technostructure, Middle Line* and *Support* on the *Strategic Apex*;
- the relationships between the *Middle Line* and *Technostructure* and *Support* must be of goal dependencies;
- the *Operational Core* relies on the *Technostructure* and *Support* through task and resource dependencies; and
- only task dependencies are permitted between the *Middle Line* (as depender or dependee) and the *Operational Core* (as dependee or depender).

To specify the formal properties of the style, we use *Formal Tropos* [12], which extends the primitives of i^* with a formal language comparable to that of KAOS [6]. Constraints on i^* specifications are thus formalized in a first-order linear-time temporal logic. *Formal Tropos* provides three basic types of metaclasses: *actor, dependency, and entity* [14]. The attributes of a *Formal Tropos* class denote relationships among different objects being modeled.

Metaclasses

    Actor := **Actor** name [attributes] [creation-properties] [invar-properties][actor-goal]
    With subclasses:
        Agent(with attributes occupies: Position, play: Role)
        Position(with attributes cover: Role)
        Role

    Dependency := **Dependency** name type mode **Depender** name **Dependee**
    name [attributes] [creation-properties] [invar-properties] [fulfill-properties]

    Entity := **Entity** name [attribute] [creation-properties][invar-properties]

    Actor-Goal := **(Goal|Softgoal)** name mode **FulFillment**(actor-fulfill-property)

Classes: Classes are instances of Metaclasses.

    In Formal Tropos, constraints on the lifetime of the (meta)class instances are given in a first-order linear-time temporal logic (see [12] for more details). Special predicates can appear in the temporal logic formulas: predicate $JustCreated(x)$ holds in a state if element x exists in this state but not in the previous one; predicate $Fulfilled(x)$ holds if x has been fulfilled; and predicate $JustFulfilled(x)$ holds if $Fulfilled(x)$ holds in this state, but not in the previous one.

    In the following, we only present some specifications for the *Strategic Management* and *Operational Management* dependencies.

Actor StrategicApex
Actor MiddleLine
Actor Support
Actor Technostructure
Actor OperationalCore

Dependency StrategicManagement
Type SoftGoal
Depender te: Technostructure, ml: MiddleLine, su: Support
Dependee sa: StrategicApex
Invariant
    $\forall dep : Dependency\ (JustCreated(dep) \rightarrow Consistent(self, dep))$
    $\forall ag : Actor - Goal\ (JustCreated(ag) \rightarrow Consistent(self, ag))$
Fulfillment
    $\forall dep : Dependency\ (dep.type = goal \wedge dep.depender = sa\wedge$
        $(dep.dependee = te \vee dep.dependee = ml \vee dep.dependee = su))\wedge$
        $Fulfilled(self) \rightarrow \blacklozenge Fulfilled(dep)$

    [Invariant properties specify, respectively, that the strategic management softgoal must be consistent with any other dependency of the organization and with any other goal of the actors in the organization. The predicate Consistent depends on the particular organization we are considering and it is specified in terms of goals' properties to be satisfied. The fulfillment of the dependency necessarily implies that the goal dependencies between the Middle Line, the Technostructure, and

the Support as dependees, and the Strategic Apex as depender have been achieved some time in the past]

Dependency OperationalManagement
Type Goal
Mode achieve
Depender sa: StrategicApex
Dependee ml: MiddleLine
Invariant

$Consistent(self, StrategicManagement)$
$\exists c : Coordination\ (c.type = task \land c.dependee = ml \land c.depender = OperationalCore \land ImplementedBy(self, c))$

Fulfillment

$\forall ts : Technostructure, dep : Dependency\ (dep.type = goal \land$
$dep.depender = ml \land dep.dependee = ts) \land Fulfilled(self))$
$\rightarrow \blacklozenge Fulfilled(dep)$

[The fulfillment of the Operational management goal implies that all goal dependencies between the Middle Line as depender and the Technostructure as dependee have been achieved some time in the past. Invariant properties specifies that Operational Management goal has to be consistent with Starategic Management softgoal and that there exists a coordination task (a task dependency between MiddleLine and Operational Core) that implement (ImplementedBy) the OperationalManagaemnt goal.]

In addition, the following structural (global) properties must be satisfied for the structure-in-5 style:

- $\forall inst1, inst2 : StrategicApex \rightarrow inst1 = inst2$

  [There is a single instance of the Strategic Apex (the same constraint also holds for the Middle Line, the Technostructure, the Support and the Operational Core)]

- $\forall sa : StrategicApex, te : Technostructure, ml : MiddleLine,$
  $su : Support, dep : Dependency$
  $(dep.dependee = sa \land (dep.depender = te \lor dep.depender = ml$
  $\lor dep.depender = su) \rightarrow dep.type = softgoal)$

  [Only softgoal dependencies are permitted between the Strategic Apex as dependee and the Technostructure, the Middle Line, and the Support as dependers]

- $\forall sa : StrategicApex, te : Technostructure, ml : MiddleLine,$
  $su : Support, dep : Dependency :$
  $(dep.depender = sa \land (dep.dependee = te \lor dep.dependee = ml \lor dep.dependee = su) \rightarrow dep.type = goal)$

  [Only goal dependencies are permitted between the Technostructure, the Middle Line, and the Support as dependee, and the Stategic Apex as depender]

- $\forall su : Support, ml : MiddleLine, dep : Dependency$
  $((dep.dependee = su \land dep.depender = ml) \rightarrow dep.type = goal)$

  [Only task dependencies are permitted between the Middle Line and the Operational Core]

- $\forall te : Technostructure, oc : OperationalCore, dep : Dependency$
  $((dep.dependee = te \land dep.depender = oc) \rightarrow$
  $(dep.type = task \lor dep.type = resource))$

  [Only resource or task dependencies are permitted between the Technostructure and the Operational Core (the same constraint also holds for the Support)]

- $\forall a : Actor, \; ml : MiddleLine,$
  $(\exists dep : Dependency(dep.depender = a \wedge dep.dependee =$
  $ml) \vee (dep.dependee = a \wedge dep.depender = ml) \rightarrow$
  $((\exists sa : StrategicApex(a = sa)) \vee (\exists su : Support(a = su)\vee$
  $(\exists te : Technostructure(a = te)) \vee (\exists op : OperationalCore$
  $(a = op))$

  [No dependency is permitted between an external actor and the Middle Line (the same constraint also holds for the Operational Core)]

This specification can be used to establish that a certain i^* model does constitute an instance of the structure-in-5 style. For example, the i^* model of Fig. 1 can be shown to be such an instance, in which the actors are instances of the structure-in-5 actor classes (e.g. *Direction* and *IT&Documentation* are instances of the *Strategic Apex* and the *Support*, respectively), dependencies are instances of structure-in-5 dependencies classes (e.g. *Agency Global Strategy* is an instance the *Strategic Management*), and all above global properties are enforced (e.g. since there are only two task dependencies between *Campaigns Management* and *Graphics&Edition*, the fourth property holds).

3.2. *Joint venture*

We describe here three alliances — Airbus and Eurocopter [10] and a more detailed one, Carsid [20] — that will serve to model the joint venture structure as an organizational style and propose a semi-formal specification.

Airbus. The Airbus Industrie joint venture coordinates collaborative activities between European aeronautic manufacturers to build and market airbus aircrafts. The joint venture involves four partners: British Aerospace (UK), Aerospatiale (France), DASA (Daimler-Chrysler Aerospace, Germany) and CASA (Construcciones Aeronauticas SA, Spain). Research, development and production tasks have been distributed among the partners, avoiding any duplication. Aerospatiale is mainly responsible for developing and manufacturing the cockpit of the aircraft and for system integration. DASA develops and manufactures the fuselage, British Aerospace the wings and CASA the tail unit. Final assembly is carried out in Toulouse (France) by Aerospatiale. Unlike production, commercial and decisional activities have not been split between partners. All strategy, marketing, sales and after-sales operations are entrusted to the Airbus Industrie joint venture, which is the only interface with external stakeholders such as customers. To buy an Airbus, or to maintain their fleet, customer airlines could not approach one or other of the partner firms directly, but has to deal with Airbus Industrie. Airbus Industrie, which is a real manufacturing company, defines the alliance's product policy and elaborates the specifications of each new model of aircraft to be launched. Airbus defends the point of view and interests of the alliance as a whole, even against the partner companies themselves when the individual goals of the latter enter into conflict with the collective goals of the alliance.

Figure 5 models the organization of the Airbus Industrie joint venture using the *i** strategic dependency model. Airbus assumes two roles (represented as a circle with a curved line): Airbus Industrie and Airbus Joint Venture. *Airbus Industrie* deals with demands from customers, *Customer* depends on it to receive airbus aircrafts or maintenance services. The *Airbus Joint Venture* role ensures the interface for the four partners (*CASA, Aerospatiale, British Aerospace* and *DASA*) with *Airbus Industrie* defining Airbus strategic policy, managing conflicts between the four Airbus partners, defending the interests of the whole alliance and defining new aircrafts specifications. *Airbus Joint Venture* coordinates the four partners ensuring that each of them assumes a specific task in the building of Airbus aircrafts: wings building for *British Aerospace*, tail unit building for *CASA*, cockpit building and aircraft assembling for *Aerospace* and fuselage building for *DASA*. Since Aerospatiale assumes two different tasks, it is modeled as two roles: *Aerospatiale Manufacturing* and *Aerospatiale Assembling*. *Aerospatiale Assembling* depends on each of the four partners to receive the different parts of the planes.

Eurocopter. In 1992, Aerospatiale and DASA decided to merge all their helicopter activities within a joint venture Eurocopter. Marketing, sales, R&D, management and production strategies, policies and staff were reorganized and merged immediately; all the helicopter models, irrespective of their origin, were marketed under the Eurocopter name. Eurocopter has inherited helicopter manufacturing and engineering facilities, two in France (La Courneuve and Marignane), one in Germany (Ottobrunn). For political and social reasons, each of them has been specialized rather than closed down to group production together at a single site. The Marignane plant manufactures large helicopters, Ottobrunn produces small helicopters and La Courneuve concentrates on the manufacture of some complex components requiring a specific expertise, such as rotors and blades.

Figure 6 models the organization of the Eurocopter joint venture in *i**. As in the Airbus joint venture, Eurocopter assumes two roles. The *Eurocopter* role handles helicopter orders from customers who depend on it to obtain the machines. It also defines marketing, sales, production and R&D strategies and policy. The *Eurocopter joint venture* role coordinates the manufacturing operations of the two partners — DASA and Aerospatiale — and depends on them for the production of small helicopters (*DASA Ottobrunn*), large ones (La Courneuve) and complex components (Marignane) such as rotors and blades. Since Aerospatiale assumes two different responsibilities, it is considered two roles: *Aerospatiale Marignane* and *Aerospatiale La Courneuve. DASA Ottobrunn* and *Aerospatiale Marignane* depends on *La Courneuve* to be supplied with complex helicopter parts.

Carsid(Carolo-Sidérurgie) is a joint venture that has recently arisen from the global concentration movement in the steel industry. The alliance, physically located in the steel basin of Charleroi in Belgium, has been formed by the steel companies Duferco (Italy), Usinor (France) — that also partially owns Cockerill-Sambre (Belgium) through the Arcelor group — and Sogepa (Belgium), a public investment

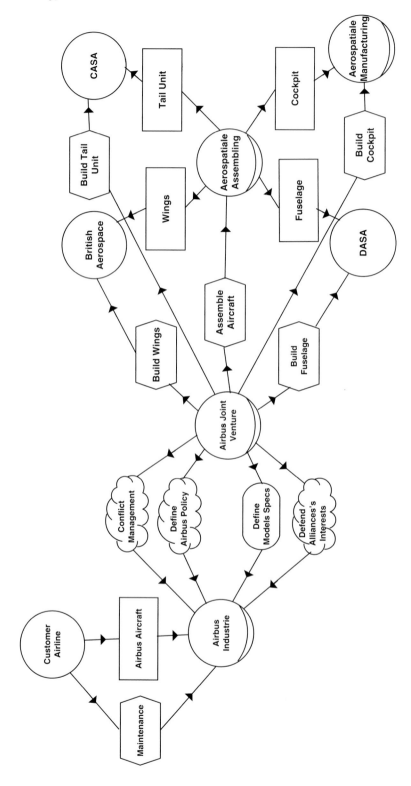

Fig. 5.   The airbus industrie joint venture.

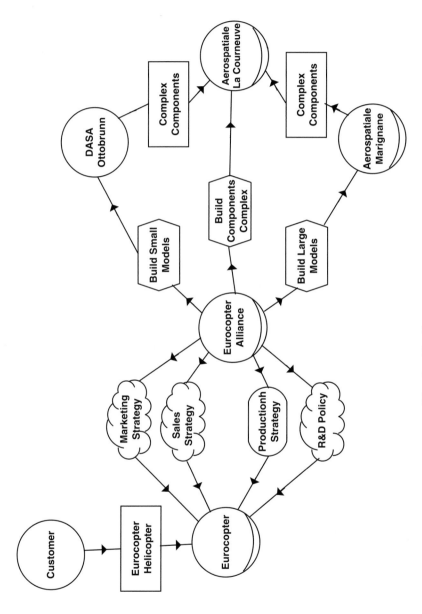

Fig. 6. The Eurocopter joint venture.

company, representing the Walloon Region Government. Usinor has also brought its subsidiary Carlam in the alliance.

Roughly speaking, the aim of a steel manufacturing company like CARSID is to extract iron from the ore and to turn it into semi-finished steel products. Several steps compose the transformation process, and each step is generally assumed by a specific metallurgic plant:

- *Sintering Plant.* Sintering is the preparation of the iron ore for the blast furnace. The minerals are crushed and calibrated to form a sinter charge.
- *Coking Plant.* Coal is distilled (i.e., heated in an air-impoverished environment in order to prevent combustion) to produce coke.
- *Blast Furnace.* Coke is used as a combustion agent and as a reducing agent to remove the oxygen from the sinter charge. The coke and sinter charge are loaded together into the blast furnace to produce cast iron.
- *Steel Making Plant.* Different steps (desulphuration, oxidation, steel adjustment, cooling, ...) are necessary to turn cast iron into steel slabs and billets. First, elements other that iron are removed to give molten steel. Then supplementary elements (titanium, niobium, vanadium, ...) are added to make a more robust alloy. Finally, the result — finished steel — is solidified to produce slabs and billets.
- *Rolling Mill.* The manufacture of semi-finished products involves a process known as hot rolling. Hot-rolled products are of two categories: flat (plates, coiled sheets, sheeting, strips, ...) produced from steel slabs and long (wire, bars, rails, beams, girders, ...) produced from steel billets.

Figure 7 models the organization of the Carsid joint venture in *i**. Carsid assumes two roles Carsid S. A. ("Société Anonyme" i.e., "Ltd") and Carsid Joint Venture.

Carsid S. A. is the legal and contractual interface of the joint venture. It handles the sales of *steel semi-finished products* (bars, plates, rails, sheets, etc. but also slabs, billets) and *co-products* (coke that does not meet blast furnace requirements, rich gases from the different plants, godroon, naphtalin, etc.) to external *industries* such as vehicle (automobile, train, boat, ...) manufacturers, foundries, gas companies, building companies, ... It is also in charge of the *proper environment policy*, a strategic aspect for steelworks that are polluting plants. Most importantly, Carsid has been set up with the help of the Walloon Region to guarantee *job security* for about two thousands workers in the basin of Charleroi. Indeed, the steel industry in general and the Walloon metallurgical basins in particular are sectors in difficulty with high unemployment rates. As a corrolar, the joint venture is committed to *improve regional economy* and maintain work in the region. Carsid has then been contractually obliged to plan *maintenance investment* (e.g. blast furnace repairing, renovation of coke oven batteries, ...) and develop *production plans* involving regional sub-contractors and suppliers. Since steelmaking is a hard and dangerous work sector, Carsid is legally committed to respect, develop and promote *accident prevention standards*.

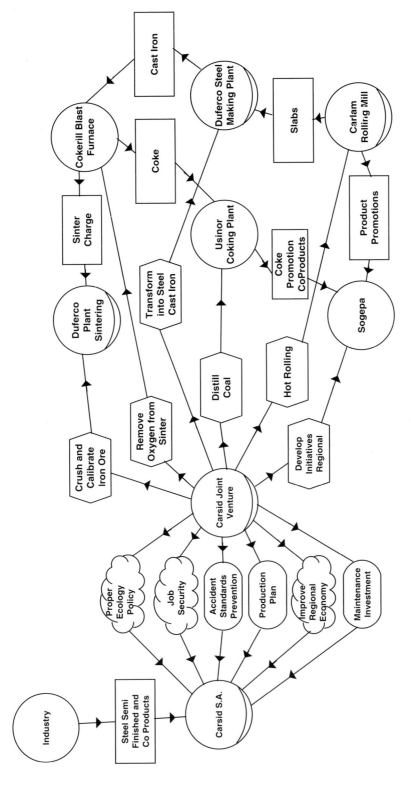

Fig. 7.   The Carsid joint venture.

The *Carsid joint venture* itself coordinates the steel manufacturing process. The sintering phase to *prepare iron ore* is the responsibility of *Duferco Sintering Plant* while *Usinor Coking Plant, distills coal* to turn it into *coke*. The *sinter charge* and *coke* are used by Cokerill Blast Furnace to produce *cast iron* by *removing oxygen from sinter. Duferco Steel Making Plant transforms cast iron into steel* to produce slabs and billets for *Carlam Rolling Mill* in charge of the *hot rolling* tasks. *Sogepa*, the public partner, has the responsibility to *develop regional initiative* to promote Carsid activities, particularly in the Walloon Region and in Belgium.

Figure 8 abstracts the joint venture structures explored in the case studies of Figs. 5–7. The case studies suggest a number of constraints to supplement the basic style:

- Partners depend on each other for providing and receiving resources.
- Operation coordination is ensured by the joint manager actor which depends on partners for the accomplishment of these assigned tasks.
- The joint manager actor must assume two roles: a private interface role to coordinate partners of the alliance and a public interface role to take strategic decisions, define policy for the private interface and represents the interests of the whole partnership with respect to external stakeholders.
- Individual partners can be decomposed in turn using another style.

Part of the Joint Venture style specification is in the following:

Role JointManagerPrivateInterface
   Goal CoordinateStyles

Role JointManagerPublicInterface
   Goal TakeStrategicDecision
   SoftGoal RepresentPartnershipInterests

Actor Partner

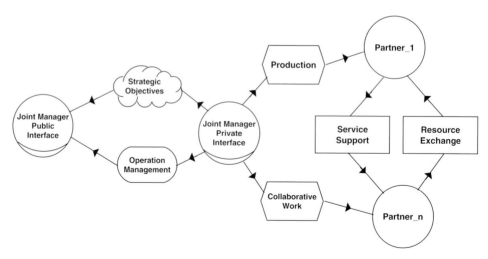

Fig. 8.   The joint venture style.

and the following structural (global) properties must be satisfied:

- $\forall jmpri1, jmpri2 : JointManagerPrivateInterface$
    $(jmpri1 = jmpri2)$

    [Only one instance of the joint manager]

- $\forall p1, p2 : Partner, dep : Dependency$
    $(((dep.depender = p1 \land dep.dependee = p2) \lor (dep.depender = p2 \land dep.dependee = p1)) \rightarrow (dep.type = resource))$

    [Only resource dependencies between partners]

- $\forall jmpri : JointManagerPrivateInterface, p : Partner,$
    $dep : Dependency((dep.dependee = p \land dep.depender = jmpri)$
    $\rightarrow dep.type = task)$

    [Only task dependencies between partners and the joint manager, with the joint manager as depender]

- $\forall jmpri : JointManagerPrivateInterface,$
    $jmpui : JointManagerPublicInterface, dep : Dependency$
    $((dep.depender = jmpri \land dep.dependee = jmpui)$
    $\rightarrow (dep.type = goal \lor dep.type = softgoal))$

    [Only goal or softgoal dependencies between the joint manager roles]

- $\forall dep : Dependency, p1 : Partner$
    $((dep.depender = p1 \lor dep.dependee = p1) \rightarrow$
    $((\exists p2 : Partner(p1 \neq p2$
    $\land(dep.depender = p2 \lor dep.dependee = p2))$
    $\lor(\exists jmpi : JointManagerPrivateInterface$
    $((dep.depender = jmpi \lor dep.dependee = jmpi))))$

    [Partners only have relationships with other partners or the joint manager private interface]

- $\forall dep : Dependency, jmpi : JointManagerPrivateInterface$
    $((dep.depender = jpmi \lor dep.dependee = jpmi) \rightarrow$
    $((\exists p : Partner((dep.depender = p \lor dep.dependee = p)))\lor$
    $(\exists jmpui : JointManagerPublicInterface$
    $((dep.depender = jmpui \lor dep.dependee = jmpui))))$

    [The joint manager private interface only has relationships with the joint manager public interface or partners]

4. Evaluation

Styles can be compared and evaluated with quality attributes [34], also called non-functional requirements [5]. For instance, the requirements seem particularly relevant for organizational structures [7, 22]:

Predictability [37]. Actors can have a high degree of autonomy [38] in the way that they undertake action and communication in their domains. It can be then difficult to predict individual characteristics as part of determining the behavior of the system at large. Generally, predictability is in contrast with the actors capabilities to be adaptive and responsive: actors must be predictable enough to anticipate and plan actions while being responsive and adaptive to unexpected situations.

Security. Actors are often able to identify their own data and knowledge sources and they may undertake additional actions based on these sources [37]. Strategies for verifying authenticity for these data sources by individual actors are an important concern in the evaluation of overall system quality since, in addition to possibly misleading information acquired by actors, there is the danger of hostile external entities spoofing the system to acquire information accorded to trusted domain actors.

Adaptability. Actors may be required to adapt to modifications in their environment. They may include changes to the component's communication protocol or possibly the dynamic introduction of a new kind of component previously unknown or the manipulations of existing actors.

Generally, adaptability depends on the capabilities of the single actors to learn and predict the changes of the environments in which they act [36], and also their capability to make diagnosis [19], that is being able to detect and determine the causes of a fault based on its symptoms. However, successful organization environments tend to balance the degree of reactivity and predictability of the single actors with their capabilities to be adaptive.

Coordinability. Actors are not particularly useful unless they are able to coordinate with other agents. Coordination is generally [21] used to distribute expertise, resources or information among the actors (actors may have different capabilities, specialized knowledge, different sources of information, resources, responsibilities, limitations, charges for services, etc.), solve interdependencies between actors' actions (interdependence occur when goal undertaken by individual actors are related), meet global constraints (when the solution being developed by a group of actors must satisfy certain conditions if it is to be deemed successful), and to make the system efficient (even when individuals can function independently, thereby obviating the need for coordination, information discovered by one actor can be of sufficient use to another actor that both actors can solve the problem twice as fast).

Coordination can be realized in two ways:

- **Cooperativity**. Actors must be able to coordinate with other entities to achieve a common purpose or simply their local goals. Cooperation can either be communicative in that the actors communicate (the intentional sending and receiving of signals) with each other in order to cooperate or it can be non-communicative [9]. In the latter case, actors coordinate their cooperative activity by each observing and reacting to the behaviour of the other. In deliberative organizations, actors jointly plan their actions so as to cooperate with each other.

- **Competitivity**. Deliberative negotiating organization [9] are like deliberative one, except that they have an added dose of competition. The success of one actors implies the failure of others.

Availability. Actors that offer services to other actors must implicitly or explicitly guard against the interruption of offered services.

Fallibility-Tolerance. A failure of one actor does not necessarily imply a failure of the whole organization. The organization then needs to check the completeness and the accuracy of information and knowledge transactions and workflows. To prevent failure, different actors can have similar or replicated capabilities and refer to more than one actor for a specific behavior.

Modularity [35] increases efficiency of service execution, reduces interaction overhead and usually enables high flexibility. On the other hand, it implies constraints on inter-organization communication.

Aggregability. Some actors are parts of other actors. They surrender to the control of the composite entity. This control results in an efficient workflow execution and low interaction overhead, however prevents the organization to benefit from flexibility.

As an illustration, we evaluate the styles with respect to coordinativity, predictability, fallibility-tolerance and adaptability. The evaluation can be done in a similar way for the other non-functional requirements.

- The **structure-in-5** improves coordinativity among actors by differentiating the data hierarchy — the support actor — from the control hierarchy — supported by the operational core, technostructure, middle line and strategic apex. The existence of three different levels of abstraction (1 — Operational Core; 2 — Technostructure, Middle Line and Support; 3 — Strategic Apex) addresses the need for managing predictability. Besides, higher levels are more abstract than lower levels: lower levels only involve resources and task dependencies while higher ones propose intentional (goals and softgoals) relationships. Checks and control mechanisms can be integrated at different levels of abstraction assuming redundancy from different perspectives and increase considerably fallibility-tolerance. Since the structure-in-5 separates data and control hierarchies, integrity of these two hierarchies can also be verified independently. The structure-in-5 separates independently the typical components of an organization, isolating them from each other and allowing then dynamic adaptability. But since it is restricted to no more than 5 major components, more refinement has to take place inside the components.

- The **joint venture** supports coordinativity in the sense that each partner actor interacts via the joint manager for strategic decisions. Partners indicate their interest, and the joint manager either returns them the strategic information immediately or mediates the request to some other partners. However, since partners are usually heterogeneous, it could be a drawback to define a common interaction background. The central position and role of the joint manager is a means for resolving conflicts and preventing unpredictability. Through its joint manager, the joint-venture proposes a central communication controller. It is less clear how the joint venture style addresses fallibility-tolerance, notably reliability. However, exceptions, supervision, and monitoring can improve its overall score with respect to these qualities. Manipulation of partners can be done easily to adapt the

structure by registering new ones to the joint manager. However, since partners can also exchange resources directly with each other, existing dependencies should be updated as well. The joint manager cannot be removed
due to its central position.

Table 2.   summarizes the strengths and weaknesses
of the reviewed styles:

	Structure-in-5	Joint-Venture
Coordinativity	++	+−
Predictability	+	+
Fallibility-Tolerance	++	+−
Adaptability	+−	+−

To cope with non-functional requirements and select the style for the organizational setting, we go through a means-ends analysis using the non-functional
requirements (NFRs) framework [5].[a] We refine the identified requirements to sub-
requirements that are more precise and evaluates alternative organizational styles
against them, as shown in Fig. 9. The analysis is intended to make explicit the space
of alternatives for fulfilling the top-level requirements. The styles are represented as
operationalized requirements (saying, roughly, "model the organizational setting of
the system with the *pyramid, structure-in-5, joint venture, arm's-length* . . . style").

The evaluation results in contribution relationships from the styles to the
non-functional requirements, labeled "+", "++", "−", "−−". Design rationale is
represented by claims drawn as dashed clouds. They make it possible for domain
characteristics (such as priorities) to be considered and properly reflected into the
decision making process, e.g. to provide reasons for selecting or rejecting possible
solutions (+, −). Exclamation marks (! and !!) are used to mark priority requirements while a check-mark "$\sqrt{}$" indicates an accepted requirements and a cross "×"
labels a denied requirement.

Relationships types (AND, OR, ++, +, −, and −−) between NFRs are formalized to offer a tractable proof procedure. AND/OR relationships corresponds
to the classical AND/OR decomposition relationships: if requirement R_0 is AND-
decomposed (respectively, OR-decomposed) into $R_1, R_2, \ldots, R_n$ then all (at least
one) of the requirements must be satisfied for the requirement R_0 to be satisfied.
So, for instance, in Fig. 9, Coordinativity is AND-decomposed into Distributivity,
Participability, and Commonality. Relationships "+" and "−" model respectively a
situation where an requirement contributes positively or negatively towards the
satisfaction of another one. For instance, in Fig. 9, Joint Venture contributes positively to the satisfaction of Distributivity and negatively to the Reliability. In addition,
relationships "++" and "−−" model a situation where the satisfaction of a requirement implies the satisfaction or denial of another goal. In Fig. 9, for instance, the

---

[a]In the NFR framework, non-functional requirements are represented as softgoals (cloudy shapes).

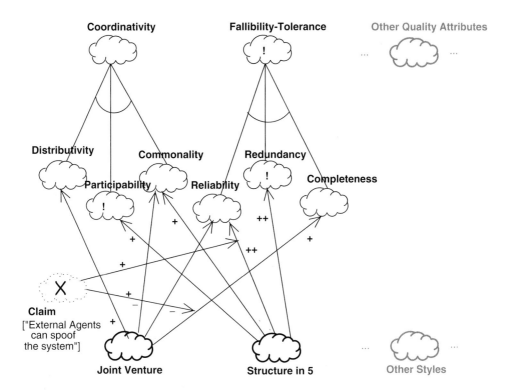

Fig. 9. Partial evaluation for organizational styles.

satisfaction of Structure-in-5 implies the satisfaction of requirements Reliability and Redundancy.

The analysis for selecting an organizational setting that meets the requirements of the system to build is based on propagation algorithms presented in [15]. Basically, the idea is to assign a set of initial labels for some requirements of the graph, about their satisfiability and deniability, and see how this assignment leads to the labels propagation for other requirements. In particular, we adopt from [15] both qualitative and a numerical axiomatization for goal (requirements) modeling primitives and label propagation algorithms that are shown to be sound and complete with respect to their respective axiomatization. In the following, a brief description of the qualitative algorithm.

To each requirement R, we associate two variables $Sat(R), Den(R)$ ranging in $\{F, P, N\}$ (full, partial, none) such that $F > P > N$, representing the current evidence of satisfiability and deniability of the requirement R. For example, $Sat(R_i) \geq P$ states there is at least a partial evidence that R_i is satisfiable. Starting from assigning an initial set of input values for $Sat(R_i), Den(R_i)$ to (a subset of) the requirements in the graph, we propagate the values through the propagation rules of Table 3. Propagation rules for AND (respectively OR) relationship are min-value

Table 3.

	$G_2 \overset{+}{\longmapsto} G_1$	$G_2 \overset{-}{\longmapsto} G_1$	$G_2 \overset{++}{\longmapsto} G_1$	$G_2 \overset{--}{\longmapsto} G_1$
$Sat(G_1)$	$min\{Sat(G_2),P\}$	N	$Sat(G_2)$	N
$Den(G_1)$	N	$min\{Sat(G_2),P\}$	N	$Sat(G_2)$

```
1      Current=Initial;
2      do
3          Old=Current;
4          for each  R_i do
5              Current[i] = Update_label(i,Old);
6          until not (Current==Old);
7          return Current;
8          for each  Rel_j s.t. target(Rel_j) == R_i do
9              sat_ij  =  Apply_Rules_Sat(i,Rel_j,Old);
10             den_ij  =  Apply_Rules_Den(R_i,Rel_j,Old);
11         return ⟨   max(max_j(sat_ij),Old[i].sat),
12                    max(max_j(den_ij),Old[i].den) ⟩;
```

Fig. 10. Schema of the label propagation algorithm.

function for satisfiability (max-value function) and max-value function (min-value function) for deniability. A dual table is given for deniability propagation.

The schema of the algorithm is described in Fig. 10. *Initial, Current* and *Old* are arrays of pairs $\langle Sat(R_i), Den(R_i)\rangle$, one for each R_i of the graph, representing respectively the initial, current and previous labeling status of the graph.

The array *Current* is first initialized to the initial values *Initial* given in input by the user. At each step, for every requirement R_i, $\langle Sat(R_i), Den(R_i)\rangle$ is updated by propagating the values of the previous step. This is done until a fixpoint is reached, that is, no updating is mode possible ($Current == Old$).

The updating of $\langle Sat(R_i), Den(R_i)\rangle$ works as follows. For each relation Rel_i incoming in G_i, the satisfiability and deniability values sat_{ij} and den_{ij} derived from the old values of the source requirements are computed by applying the rules of Table 3. Then, it is returned the maximum value between those computed and the old values.

5. A Requirements-Driven Methodology

This research is conducted in the context of the *early requirements* phase of *Tropos* [3, 4, 30], a software development methodology for building multi-agent systems which is founded on the concepts of actor and goal.

The *Tropos* methodology adopts ideas from multi-agent systems technologies, mostly to define the detailed design and implementation phase, and ideas from requirements engineering, where agents/actors and goals have been used heavily for early requirements analysis [6,40]. In particular, the *Tropos* project adopts Eric Yu's *i** model which offers actors (agents, roles, or positions), goals, and actor dependencies as primitive concepts for modelling an application during early requirements analysis. The key assumption which distinguishes *Tropos* from other methodologies is that actors and goals are used as fundamental concepts for analysis and design during *all phases of software development*, not just requirements analysis. That means that, in the light of this chapter, *Tropos* describes in terms of the same concepts and styles the organizational environment within which a system will eventually operate, as well as the system itself. *Tropos* spans four phases of software development:

- Early requirements, concerned with the understanding of a problem by studying an organizational setting; the output is an organizational model which includes relevant actors, their goals and dependencies.
- Late requirements, in which the system-to-be is described within its operational environment, along with relevant functions and qualities.
- Architectural design, in which the system's global architecture is defined in terms of subsystems, interconnected through data, control and dependencies.
- Detailed design, in which behaviour of each architectural component is defined in further detail.

6. Conclusion

Modelers need to rely on patterns, styles, and idioms, to build their models, whatever the purpose. We argue that, as with other phases of software development, early requirements analysis can be facilitated by the adoption of organizational styles. This chapter focuses on two such styles and studies them in detail, through examples, a formalization using Formal Tropos, and an evaluation with respect to desirable requirements. There have been many proposals for software patterns (e.g. [8]) since the original work on design patterns [13]. Some of this work focuses on requirements patterns. For example, [26] proposes a set of requirements patterns for embedded software systems. These patterns are represented in UML and cover both structural and behavioral aspects of a requirements specification. Along similar lines, [11] proposes some general patterns in UML. In both cases, the focus is on late requirements, and the modeling language used is UML. On a different path, [18] proposes a systematic approach for evaluating design patterns with respect to non-functional requirements (e.g. security, performance, reliability). Our approach differs from this work primarily in the fact that our proposal is founded on ideas from Organization Theory and Strategic Alliances literature. We have already described organizational styles but to be used for designing multi-agent system architectures [14, 22, 24] and e-business systems [7]. Considering real world organizations as a metaphor, systems involving many software actors, such as multi-agent systems could benefit from the same organizational models. In the present chapter, we have focused on styles for modeling organizational settings, rather than software systems and emphasized the need for organizational abstractions to better match the operational environment of the system-to-be during the early requirements analysis.

References

1. A. I. Anton, "Goal-based requirements analysis", *Proceedings of the 2nd International Conference on Requirements Analysis, ICRE'96* (1996) 136–144.
2. S. Bennett, S. McRobb and R. Farmer, *Object-Oriented Systems Analysis and Design using UML* (McGraw-Hill, 1999).
3. J. Castro, M. Kolp and J. Mylopoulos, "A requirements-driven development methodology", *Proceedings of the 13th International Conference on Advanced Information Systems Engineering, CAiSE'01*, Interlaken, Switzerland (June 2001) 108–123.
4. J. Castro, M. Kolp and J. Mylopoulos, "Towards requirements-driven information systems engineering: The Tropos project", *Information Systems*, 2002.
5. L. K. Chung, B. Nixon, E. Yu and J. Mylopoulos, *Non-Functional Requirements in Software Engineering* (Kluwer Publishing, 2000).
6. A. Dardenne, A. van Lamsweerde and S. Fickas, "Goal-directed requirements acquisition", *Science of Computer Programming* **20**, no. 1–2 (1993) 3–50.
7. T. T. Do, S. Faulkner and M. Kolp, "Organizational multi-agent architectures for information systems", *Proceedings of the 5th International Conference on Enterprise Information Systems, ICEIS'03*, Angers, France, April 2003.
8. T. T. Do, M. Kolp and A. Pirotte, "Social patterns for designing multi-agent systems", *Proceedings of the 15th International Conference on Software Engineering and Knowledge Engineering, SEKE'03*, San Francisco, USA, July 2003.
9. J. E. Doran, S. Franklin, N. R. Jennings and T. J. Norman, "On cooperation in multi-agent systems", *Knowledge Engineering Review* **12**, no. 3 (1997) 309–314.
10. P. Dussauge and B. Garrette, *Cooperative Strategy: Competing Successfully Through Strategic Alliances* (Wiley and Sons, 1999).
11. M. Fowler, *Analysis Patterns: Reusable Object Models* (Addison-Wesley, 1997).
12. A. Fuxman, M. Pistore, J. Mylopoulos and P. Traverso, "Model checking early requirements specification in Tropos", *Proceedings of the 5th International Symposium on Requirements Engineering, RE'01*, Toronto, Canada, August 2001.
13. E. Gamma, R. Helm, J. Johnson and J. Vlissides, *Design Patterns: Elements of Reusable Object-Oriented Software* (Addison-Wesley, 1995).
14. P. Giorgini, M. Kolp and J. Mylopoulos, "Multi-agent and software architecture: A comparative case study", *Proceedings of the 3rd International Workshop on Agent Software Engineering, AOSE'02*, Bologna, Italy, July 2002.
15. P. Giorgini, J. Mylopoulos, E. Nicchiarelli and R. Sebastiani, "Reasoning with goal models", *Proceedings of the 21st International Conference on Conceptual Modeling (ER 2002)*, Tampere, Finland, October 2002.
16. GMT, Gmt consulting group, 2002, *http://www.gmtgroup.com/*.
17. B. Gomes-Casseres, *The Alliance Revolution: The New Shape of Business Rivalry* (Harvard University Press, 1996).
18. D. Gross and E. Yu, "From non-functional requirements to design through patterns", *Requirements Engineering* **6**, no. 1 (2002) 18–36.

19. B. Horling, V. Lesser, R. Vincent, A. Bazzan and P. Xuan, "Diagnosis as an integral part of multi-agent adaptability", Technical Report UM-CS-1999-003, University of Massachusetts (1999).

20. M. Ibarz, M. Kolp, F. Fouss and A. Pirotte, "Steel production datawaherouse re-engineering", Technical Report IAG Working paper 85/03, IAG-ISYS Information Systems Research Unit, Catholic University of Louvain, Belgium (February 2003), *http://www.iag.ucl.ac.be/wp/*.

21. N. R. Jennings, "Coordination techniques for distributed artificial intelligence", eds. G. M. P. O'Hare and N. R. Jennings, *Foundations of Distributed Artificial Intelligence* (Wiley, 1996) 187–210.

22. M. Kolp, P. Giorgini and J. Mylopoulos, "A goal-based organizational perspective on multi-agents architectures", *Proceedings of the 8th International Workshop on Intelligent Agents: Agent Theories, Architectures, and Languages, ATAL'01*, Seattle, USA, August 2001.

23. M. Kolp, P. Giorgini and J. Mylopoulos, "Information systems development through social structures", *Proceedings of the 14th International Conference on Software Engineering and Knowledge Engineering, SEKE'02*, Ishia, Italy, July 2002.

24. M. Kolp, P. Giorgini and J. Mylopoulos, "Organizational multi-agent architecture: A mobile robot example", *Proceedings of the 1st International Conference on Autonomous Agent and Multi Agent Systems, AAMAS'02*, Bologna, Italy, July 2002.

25. M. Kolp, P. Giorgini and J. Mylopoulos, "Organizational patterns for early requirements analysis", *Proceedings of the 15th International Conference on Advanced Information Systems, CAiSE'03*, Velden, Austria, June 2003.

26. S. Konrad and B. Cheng, "Requirements patterns for embedded systems", *Proceedings of the 10th IEEE Joint International Requirements Engineering Conference, RE'02*, Essen, Germany, September 2002.

27. J. J. Lambin, *Strategic Marketing: A European Approach* (MGraw-Hill, 1993).

28. H. Mintzberg, *Structure in Fives: Designing Effective Organizations* (Prentice-Hall, 1992).

29. J. Morabito, I. Sack and A. Bhate, *Organization Modeling: Innovative Architectures for the 21st Century* (Prentice-Hall, 1999).

30. A. Perini, P. Bresciani, F. Giunchiglia, P. Giorgini and J. Mylopoulos, "A knowledge level software engineering methodology for agent oriented programming", *Proceedings of the 5th International Conference on Autonomous Agents, Agents'01*, Montreal, Canada, May 2001.

31. M. E. Porter, *Competitive Advantage: Creating and Sustaining Superior Performance* (The Free Press, New York, 1985).

32. W. R. Scott, *Organizations: Rational, Natural, and Open Systems* (Prentice-Hall, 1998).

33. L. Segil, *Intelligent Business Alliances: How to Profit Using Today's Most Important Strategic Tool* (Times Business, 1996).

34. M. Shaw and D. Garlan, *Software Architecture: Perspectives on an Emerging Discipline* (Prentice-Hall, 1996).

35. O. Shehory, "Architectural properties of multi-agent systems", Technical Report CMU-RI-TR-98-28, Carnegie Mellon University (1998).

36. G. Weiss (ed)., *Learning in DAI Systems* (Springer-Verlag, 1997).

37. S. G. Woods and M. Barbacci, "Architectural evaluation of collaborative agent-based systems", Technical Report SEI-99-TR-025, SEI, Carnegie Mellon University, Pittsburgh, USA (1999).

38. M. Wooldridge and N. R. Jennings, "Intelligent agents: Theory and practice", *Knowledge Engineering Review* **2**, no. 10 (1995).
39. M. Y. Yoshino and U. Srinivasa Rangan, *Strategic Alliances: An Entrepreneurial Approach to Globalization* (Harvard Business School Press, 1995).
40. E. Yu, "Modelling strategic relationships for process reengineering", PhD Thesis, University of Toronto, Department of Computer Science (1995).

ATTACKS AND COUNTERMEASURES IN SOFTWARE SYSTEM SECURITY

LU MA and JEFFREY J.P. TSAI

Department of Computer Science, M/C 152,
University of Illinois at Chicago,
851 S. Morgan ST,
Chicago, IL 60607
E-mail: tsai@cs.uic.edu

Security has become a major concern of software systems, especially distributed systems. The existence of various attacks should be considered in designing and developing those systems such that appropriate countermeasures could be applied. This chapter provides an overview of different types of possible attacks and countermeasures in the software security area. In addition, it discusses the security problems in mobile agent systems and introduces several related research works. This chapter also presents our research works on mobile agent system security based on Extended Elementary Object System (EEOS).

Keywords: Security, attack, confidentiality, integrity, availability, mobile agent system.

1. Introduction

With the rapid growth of networking, in particular the Internet, a large variety of information could be accessed by different users all over the world through a number of software systems. However, the development of corresponding security mechanisms does not parallel with the development of the networks and software systems. Many attacks occur and cause big losses. According to ZDNet Security News dated January 2004, "Computer virus attacks cost global businesses an estimated \$55 billion in damages in 2003, a sum that is expected to increase this year." And virus is only one kind of attacks. Therefore, security has become a major concern of today's software systems, especially distributed systems. Software security consists of lots of aspects, such as cryptography, access control and trust management, intrusion detection and tamper resistance, authentication and privacy, signature schemes, E-commerce, security analysis, mobile computing security, etc. An amount of research works has been devoted to those areas and different methods have been proposed.

In order to design and develop security mechanisms to protect software systems, different kinds of attacks and countermeasures against those attacks should be identified. In this chapter, we provide an overview of the general categories of attacks and countermeasures existing in software system security. We then emphasize on the security problems in mobile agent system, an active and promising direction in mobile computing and distributed processing, and briefly present our formal model for mobile agent system security.

The rest of this chapter is organized as follows. Section 2 introduces general security objectives a software system should meet. Section 3 discusses different types of attacks and Sec. 4 introduces possible countermeasures against attacks. Section 5 emphasizes on the security issues in mobile computing, especially in mobile agent system. Section 5 also presents our method to formally model and analyze a generic secure mobile agent system using Extended Elementary Object System (EEOS). Section 6 provides concluding remarks and presents future works.

2. General Security Objectives

It is helpful to identify security objectives before discussing various security problems in software systems. Different systems and applications have their own security objectives; while they share quite a few common ones. Generally speaking, a secure software system should meet the following security objectives, some of which are explained based on NIST definitions [24, 25] in alphabetical order below.

(1) Accountability

Accountability is the security goal that generates the requirement for actions of an entity to be traced uniquely to that entity. This objective requires that users and administrators will be held accountable for behavior that impacts the security of information. Accountability is often an organizational policy requirement and directly supports non-repudiation, deterrence, fault isolation, intrusion detection and prevention, and after-action recovery and legal action. This objective has more importance in electronic business. For example, a customer intends to buy a certain product from an online store. The user and the store have a session of communications, so that the user tells the store about his credit card to be charged, and the store gives the user a receipt. Both the user and the store should be accountable for their communications and behaviors.

(2) Assurance

Assurance grounds for confidence that other security goals (including integrity, availability, confidentiality, and accountability) have been adequately met by a specific implementation. "Adequately met" includes (1) functionality that performs correctly, (2) sufficient protection against unintentional errors (by users or software), and (3) sufficient resistance to intentional penetration or by-pass.

(3) Authentication

Authentication requires verifying the identity of a user, process, or device, often as a prerequisite to allowing access to resources in a system. This objective requires that the identity (or other relevant information) of an entity or the originator of data can be verified and assured. Satisfying this objective can prevent faking or masquerading from happening.

(4) Authorization

Authorization is to grant or deny access rights to a user, program or process. This objective requires that only legitimate users can have the rights to use certain services or to access certain resources, while unauthorized users are kept out. It is also called "access control". Authorization is often combined with authentication as the result of authentication is usually used to decide whether or not to grant a request of an entity. To achieve those security properties, digital signatures may be required in addition to password access.

(5) Availability

Availability is the security goal that generates the requirement for protection against intentional or accidental attempts to perform unauthorized deletion of data, or cause unavailability of service. This objective requires that data and system can be accessed by legitimate users within an appropriate period of time. Some attacks such as Denial of Service or instability of the system may cause loss of availability.

(6) Confidentiality

Confidentiality is the security goal that generates the requirement for protection from intentional or accidental attempts to perform unauthorized data reads. Confidentiality covers data in storage, during processing, and while in transit. This objective requires that data should be protected from any unauthorized disclosure. That is to say, it should be ensured that data can only be read by persons or machines for which it is intended. A loss of confidentiality hurts the data privacy.

(7) Integrity

Integrity can be classified into data integrity and system integrity. Data integrity is the objective that data should not be altered or destroyed in an unauthorized manner to maintain consistency. It also covers data in storage, during processing, and while in transit. System integrity is the objective that a system should be free from unauthorized manipulation when it performs its intended function in an unimpaired manner.

(8) Non-repudiation

This objective requires that either side of a communication cannot deny the communication later. Important communication exchanges must be logged to prevent later denials by any party of a transaction. This objective also relies on authentication to record the identities of entities.

Besides the objectives mentioned above, more security objectives may be identified and required in different situations. Generally speaking, accountability, availability, assurance, confidentiality and integrity are five main security objectives of a software system. These security objectives are not isolated. Instead, various relationships exist among them. Assurance is the base security objective that other objectives are built on. Confidentiality and integrity can affect and also be affected by each other. Based on them, availability and accountability can be achieved.

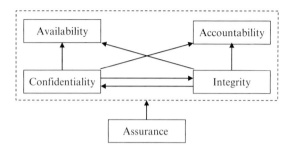

Fig. 1.   Relationship among five main security objectives.

Figure 1 shows the relationships among these five main security objectives. For a specific system, certain security objectives may conflict each other sometimes. For example, to increase the availability level, a system may have to compromise its confidentiality or integrity level. Therefore, an overall security policy is often preferred other than individual security objectives.

3. Types of Attacks

It is desired that a software system can meet all security objectives. But many issues compromise the system security. The most severe issue is the various attacks which take advantage of the weakness and vulnerability of a system, and try to breach the system. A lot of attacks have been noticed and tackled with, while more new attacks are hiding or arising. It is helpful to know how many types of attacks are there and what their characteristics are. Viewed from different aspects, attacks to a software system can be classified into different categories. In this chapter, we summarize and categorize types of attacks based on their negative effects on security objectives. Therefore, most existing attacks fall into three major categories — attacks against availability, attacks against confidentiality, and attacks against integrity. It should be noted that these categories may be overlapping since quite a few attacks have multiple targets. Since this chapter is more from the technique point of view, certain attacks and threats which involve personal factors, such as social engineering threats, are ignored here.

3.1. *Attacks against availability*

Attacks against availability mainly attempt to overload available resources or make a particular facility unavailable at a certain time for the attackers' sake. Sometimes, such attacks may not totally disable targeted resources and services, but just degrade them. Attacks in this category are usually DoS (Denial of Service) attacks.

According to CERT® Coordination Center [4], a DoS attack is characterized by an explicit attempt by attackers to prevent legitimate users from using system services, or cause delaying of time-critical operations. Time-critical may be milliseconds or hours, depending upon the service provided. Typically, DoS attacks can result in the unavailability of a particular network service or the temporary loss of all network connectivity and services. They can also destroy programming and files in a computer system. A commonly seen DoS attack on the Internet is simply to send more traffic to a network node than it is supposed to take, such that the functionality of that network node gets disabled. An example of such DoS attack is the smurf attack or a PING flood, in which a smurf attacker sends PING requests to an Internet broadcast address and spoofs the return address as the target victim's address. The victim's network line would be filled by these PING replies and its network service would be brought to its knees. SYN flood attack is another example of DoS attack using the similar strategy to PING flood.

DoS attacks come in a variety of forms and aim at a variety of services. Following are three basic modes of attacks:

(1) Consumption of scarce, limited, or non-renewable resources.
(2) Destruction or alteration of configuration information.
(3) Physical destruction or alteration of network components.

DoS attacks usually occur intentionally and maliciously, but they can also happen accidentally. DoS attacks usually do not result in the theft of information or other security loss. However, these attacks can cost the target system significant time and money.

3.2. *Attacks against confidentiality*

Attacks against confidentiality mainly attempt to reveal the contents of communications, or leak sensitive data and information of a system. Attacks in this category have different forms, while the Eavesdrop attack is a primary class.

An Eavesdrop attack is an attack where communication is monitored to reveal the secret. It usually occurs when some wiretap devices are plugged into computer networks and eavesdrop on the network traffic. Then a sniffing program lets someone listen to computer conversations. However, computer conversations consist of apparently random binary data. Therefore, network wiretap programs also come with a feature known as "protocol analysis", which allow them to decode the computer traffic and make sense of it.

Originally, the base for this type of attack is the shared principle on which the Ethernet is built, which is, all machines on a local network share the same wire. Therefore, all machines are able to "see" all the traffic on the same wire. Ethernet hardware is built with a filter that ignores all traffic that does not belong to it. A wiretap program turns off this filter, and put the Ethernet hardware into promiscuous mode. Later, networks are developed from share mode to switch mode. Electronic eavesdropping, which applies electromagnetic devices such as a frequency analyzer and a tuned antenna, emerges as well. They are often taken advantage of by amateur eavesdroppers to perform eavesdrop attack. Eavesdrop attacks usually cost the loss of confidentiality and secrecy of a system, but do not hurt integrity.

Another form of attacks against confidentiality is data aggregation, which allows an attacker to deduce classified information from unclassified information. For example, an attacker may determine a specific employee's approximate salary by looking into the department's personnel expenditure before and after hiring this employee.

Password or encryption key sniffing also do harm to system confidentiality. This kind of attack enable an attacker to gain unauthorized access to system or facilities by stealing legitimate users' passwords and masquerading as the legitimate user, or inspect encrypted files or communication messages by using encryption keys illegally. This attack usually takes advantage of the "broadcast" technology used in most networks. When a legitimate user tries to log into a system remotely, or an entity of a communication tries to request an encryption key, the attacker's computer can get those secure information if the security of the network is not strong enough. It should be noted that after a password or encryption key has been sniffed by an attacker, he/she can go ahead to perform certain attacks to hurt system integrity.

3.3. *Attacks against integrity*

Attacks against integrity mainly attempt to modify communication contents or data in a system. Attacks in this category also have many various forms.

One primary form is the Man-In-The-Middle (MITM) attack, which happens when an attacker sniffs packets from network, modifies them and inserts them back into the network. In MITM attack, an attacker is able to read and modify messages between two parties at his/her will, without letting either entity know that they have been attacked. MITM attacks remain a primary weakness of public-key based system. The introduction of signed keys by a trusted third party can help with designing a mechanism for coping with such attacks.

Another form is the Web Site Defacing and Hijacking attack. This type of attack may modify, destroy or replace some web pages of certain institutions. Visitors of those institutions are given altered information, or hijacked to other site without knowing the fact. Attackers can then request and collect certain information or gain benefits from the clients. Weaknesses of web server are always the base for this type of attacks.

Attacks on authentication usually hurt integrity as well. Such attacks generally allow an attacker to masquerade as a user with higher privilege than him/her. As we introduced in Sec. 3.2, password sniffing is used towards password-based authentication systems to perform attacks against confidentiality and integrity, while disclosure of encryption key is used towards cryptographic authentication systems. For the latter system, replay attack exists as well. A replay attack is an attack in which the attacker records data or communication contents and replays it later to deceive the recipient. For example, the initiator of a session Alice sends and receives several messages to and from the responder of this session Bob, while an intruder Elisa stores all the messages. After this session is over, Elisa may send the packages sent by Alice before to Bob again in order to impersonate as Alice in a new session. If Elisa succeeds, Bob is tricked to believe he has another session with Alice. Therefore Elisa can use Alice's privilege to access and modify information or resources of Bob.

3.4. *Attacks against miscellaneous security objectives*

Attacks are not always towards one single security objective. On the contrary, many of them have multiple security objectives as their attacking targets. Viruses, unauthorized access attacks, and code exploit attacks are to be introduced below as three examples in this category.

Viruses are self-propagating entities that move across the nodes of the Internet. The life cycle of a virus begins when it is created and ends when it is completely eradicated. Its complete life cycle contains the following stages — creation, replication, activation, discovery, assimilation, and eradication. It is not hard to understand the creation, replication and eradication. So we will only explain the rest of the three stages in more details here. A virus with damage routine will be activated when certain conditions are met, for example, on a certain day or when the infected user performs a particular action. On the contrary, a virus without damage routine does not activate. Instead, they only cause damage by stealing storage space. The "discovery" stage usually follows activation, but not necessarily. When a virus is discovered, it is sent to certain organizations for documenting and to those antivirus software developers for analysis. Then antivirus software developers modify their software so that the software can detect or kill the new virus. This stage is called "assimilation". The ability to replicate is the unique characteristic of viruses. Another commonality is that they may contain a damage routine that delivers the virus payload towards system confidentiality and system integrity. Such payload may destroy files, reformat hard drive, or cause other damages. Even if a virus does not contain a damage routine, it can still degrade the overall performance of a system to its legitimate users by consuming storage space and memory, which hurt system availability.

Unauthorized access attacks include unauthorized use of resources and illicit access of data. An attacker may impersonate as a legal user or bypass the authorization procedure which is not designed very well. The "backdoor" may be used to perform such attack. A backdoor in a computer system is a method of bypassing normal authentication or obtaining remote access to a computer, while intended to remain hidden to inspection. The backdoor may take the form of an installed program or could be a modification to a legitimate program. This type of attack may hurt system and user confidentiality as well as their integrity.

No software system is perfect. Code exploit attacks exploit software flaws to gain control of a computer, or to cause it to operate in an unexpected manner.

Such attacks often come in the form of Trojan horses, for example, non-executable media files which are disguised to function in the system. Code quality is a key point when code exploit attack is taken into consideration. Some development methodologies rely on testing to ensure the quality of any code released. But they often fail to discover extremely unusual potential exploits. According to the difference of software flaws being exploited, this kind of attack may do harm to system confidentiality, integrity and availability.

4. Countermeasures of Attacks

In order to counter various attacks, a lot of methods have been designed and proposed. Although they cannot solve all problems, they increase the security level of a software system. A countermeasure does not necessarily aim at one single attack. On the contrary, many countermeasures can provide protection against multiple attacks. These countermeasures may be applied in different layers of a computer system, such as physical layer or network layer, operating system layer which includes file system management, database management layer, or application layer. In the following, we introduce some categories of countermeasures. They are high-level techniques, and there are various concrete techniques to implement them.

4.1. *Authentication*

When considered as a countermeasure of attacks, authentication refers to the process whereby one entity proves its identity to another entity. In many situations, authentication is the most primary security service on which other security services depend. Ensuring authentication plays an important role in reinforcing those security objectives of a software system, such as accountability, authorization, confidentiality, integrity, and non-repudiation. Authentication is also a powerful shield protecting a software system from attacks towards those security objectives. In most cases, authentication establishes the identity of a human user to a computer system and is called "user-computer authentication". In other cases, authentication is also needed between computers or processes in a distributed environment. These two types of authentication are to be introduced below [22].

(1) User-Computer Authentication

User-computer authentication is often done through the checking of passwords, cryptographic token or smart card, or biometric features such as a fingerprint. Password-based authentication is the most common technique and has been widely used. But it is vulnerable to attacks since a password can be guessed and shared. It is desired that a user can choose his/her passwords intelligently and change the passwords regularly. Authentication using a cryptographic token or smart card is much stronger than using passwords, because the token or a smart card is a hardware device equipped with a cryptographic key. This key does not leave the hardware device. But the token or smart card can also be shared or stolen. Biometric authentication takes advantage of the fact that biometric features are different from person to person. It has been used for applications requiring high level security. But it is also vulnerable to replay attacks and it needs cumbersome equipments. Therefore, combination of these methods is really needed.

(2) Authentication in Distributed Systems

In a distributed system, authentication is required repeatedly when a user accesses multiple machines and uses multiple services. Typically a user logs into a workstation using his/her password and then the workstation connects to other computers in this system on the user's behalf. Authentication becomes more complicated in a distributed system. One reason is that some third party can fake by actively eavesdropping or wiretapping others' communications. Drawbacks in some communication protocols are also used by attackers to achieve this goal. Therefore, formal methods should be used to verify the correctness of those protocols before they are put into use [13].

Authentication is usually implemented using two methods, one of which is called "message authentication code"; the other is called "digital signature". A message authentication code is a short and non-transferable signature on a document. It is specific to an entity and cannot be verified by other entities. So it cannot be transferred and therefore cannot be used for contracts or receipts, which need to be saved and verified in case of a conflict. But it can be used for entities to make sure that the message they obtain is from the entity they expect. A message authentication code requires that the sender and the receiver of the authenticated message both know a symmetric secret used to generate and verify the message authentication code. This secret can be produced by one of the participants, and sent over in an encrypted form to the other, using a public key encryption method. Message authentication codes can be implemented using stream ciphers, e.g. RC5. Since a message authentication code is very efficient, it is useful for individual, small messages in interactive protocols. A digital signature is an authentication on a document and is computed using the secret key or private key of the signer on the document. A signature can be verified by anyone using the public key of the signer, the document signed, and the signature on the document. Therefore, it can be transferred and useful for contracts, receipts, etc. A digital signature is usually long, e.g. 1,024 bits, and not very quick to produce and verify. For these reasons, digital signatures should only be used when message authentication codes cannot offer the required functionalities.

4.2. *Access control*

Access control is the collection of mechanisms that permits managers of a system to exercise a directing or restraining influence over the behaviors, usage and contents of a system. It permits management to specify what users can do, which resources they can access and what operations they can perform. This technique is also known as "authorization". It is quite essential in software system security, as it grounds for higher-level security objectives such as confidentiality and integrity. Appropriate access control may prevent a software system from certain attacks, such as unauthorized access attacks.

Since access control is the process of determining whether an identity (plus a set of attributes associated with that identity) is permitted to perform some action like accessing a resource; access control usually requires authentication as a prerequisite. Authentication and access control decisions can be made at different points by different organizations. But these two are not necessarily separated. A number of security products or protocols implement these two procedures together, such as the IEEE 802.1x. It is an open-standards-based protocol for authenticating network clients or ports on a user ID basis. It takes the RADIUS methodology and separates it into three distinct groups — the supplicant, the authenticator and the authentication server. This protocol provides a means of restricting network access to authorized users.

It is necessary to make a distinction between access control policies and access control mechanisms. Policies are high level guidelines which determine how accesses are controlled and how access decisions are determined. Mechanisms are low level software and hardware functions which can be configured to implement a policy. Generally speaking, there are three access control policies [23].

(1) Mandatory Access Control

Mandatory access control (MAC) policy compares the sensitivity label at which the user is working on the sensitivity label of the object being accessed. If MAC checks are passed, the user is given the access rights on the object. If not, the access request will be refused. MAC is mandatory because the labeling of information happens automatically, and ordinary users cannot change labels unless they are authorized by an administrator.

When the security policy of a system has the following two requirements: (1) the protection decisions must not be decided by the object owner; and (2) the system must enforce the protection decisions, and thus the need for a mandatory access control (MAC) mechanism arises. MAC policy is supported by POSIX.6 standard, which provides a labeling mechanism and a set of interfaces that can be used to determine access based on the MAC policy.

(2) Discretionary Access Control

Discretionary access control (DAC) is the most common type of access control policy implemented in computer systems today. It restricts access to objects based on the identity of users and/or groups to which they belong. DAC is discretionary since a user with certain access permission is capable of passing that permission to any other user directly or indirectly. DAC controls are used to restrict a user's access to protected objects on the system. The user may also be restricted to a subset of the possible access rights available for those protected objects. Access rights are the operations a user may perform on a particular objects, e.g. read, write, execute. Since DAC restricts access to objects based solely on the identity of users who are trying to access them, the identities of both the users and objects are the key to DAC. In most systems, any program which runs on behalf of a user inherits the DAC access rights of that user. This basic principle of DAC contains a fundamental flaw that makes it vulnerable to Trojan horses.

Since the DAC permissions on system objects, usually files, can only be changed by the administrator who owns them, DAC is often used along with MAC to control access to system files.

(3) Role-Based Access Control

Role-based access control (RBAC) is receiving increasing attention as a generalized approach to access control. In a RBAC model, roles represent functions granted within a given organization and authorizations. Authorizations granted to a role are strictly related to the data objects and resources that are needed by a user in order to exercise the functions of the role. Users are thus simply authorized to "play" the appropriate roles, by acquiring the roles' authorizations. When a user logs in a system using RBAC, s/he can activate a subset of the roles s/he is authorized to play. The use of roles has several well recognized advantages. Because roles represent organizational functions, a role-based model can directly support security policies of the organization. Authorization administration is also greatly simplified. If a user moves to a new function within the organization, there is no need to revoke the authorizations s/he had in the previous function and then grant the authorizations he/she needs in the new function. The security administrator simply needs to revoke and grant the appropriate role membership. RBAC models have also been shown to be able to support multiple access control policies. In particular, by appropriately configuring a role system, a RBAC model can support MAC and DAC as well.

Different mechanisms are used to implement the access control policies introduced above, such as Access Control Lists (ACLs), capabilities, and authorization table, which are different methods to store the access matrix of a system [2]. An access matrix is a spreadsheet with columns as resources, rows as users, and items as access rights. The user in the corresponding row has over the object in the corresponding column. It is the simplest framework for describing a protection system.

(1) Access Control Lists (ACLs)

ACLs correspond to storing the access matrix by columns. They are associated with system objects and contain entries specifying the access that individual users or groups of users have to these objects. Access control lists provide a straightforward way of granting or denying access for a specified user or groups of users to a particular object. An access control list is a table that tells a computer operating system which access rights users have over a particular system object, such as a file directory or an individual file. Each object has a security attribute that identifies its access control list. The list has an entry for each system user with access privileges. The most common privileges for a file include the ability to read, write, and execute if the file is executable. Microsoft Windows NT/2000, Novell's

NetWare, Digital's OpenVMS, and Unix-based systems are among the operating systems that use access control lists. The list is implemented differently by each operating system.

(2) Capabilities

Capabilities correspond to storing the access matrix by rows. Therefore they are associated with system users and contain entries specifying the access rights each individual user or each group of users has to the system objects. Capabilities provide a straightforward way of identifying what objects can be accessed by a user or a group and how they can be accessed. Capabilities encapsulate object identity. When a process presents a capability on behalf of a user, the operating system examines the capability to determine both the object and the corresponding access. The location of the object in memory is encapsulated in the capability.

Similarly to ACLs, capabilities also aim at directly providing the relationships between subjects (users, group of users, processes on behalf of users, etc.) and objects (files, etc.). For example, both of them can answer the following two questions. The first question is "Given a subject, what objects can it access and how?" The second question is "Given an object, what subjects can access it and how?" For the first question, capabilities are the simplest way to answer while ACLs require all objects to be scanned; however, for the second question, ACLs are the simplest way while capabilities require all subjects to be scanned.

(3) Authorization table

Access table corresponds to storing the access matrix by items. It contains entries specifying which user or group of users has what access right to which object. Sorted on objects, it becomes a set of ACLs; while sorted on subjects, it becomes a set of capabilities. Therefore, it has the advantages of both ACLs and capabilities, and is more flexible than the above two. It is particularly helpful for the access control in systems with sparse access matrixes.

Besides the three mechanisms introduced above, certain other mechanisms exist as well, such as ring-based access control, locks and keys, etc. Those access control mechanism can be used to enforced system security objectives, such as availability, integrity or confidentiality, by limiting access between methods and resources to collections of users or programs. Various techniques are utilized to implement those mechanisms.

4.3. Audit and intrusion detection

Audit is *a posterior* review of practices and events versus standards for the purposes of evaluation and control. There are two types of audit — compliance audit and event audit. The definitions for compliance audit are different in different glossaries. We apply the definition from the E-Commerce PKI CA Glossary here that a "compliance audit is a review and examination of system records and activities in order to test for adequacy of system controls, to ensure compliance with established policy and operational procedures, to detect breaches in security, and to recommend any indicated changes in control, policy and procedures". Compliance audit can be classified into three common types further, which are regulatory audit, internal audit, and certified public accountant audit. Since compliance audit involves lots of social factors other than security itself, we will not go into its details here. Event audit is the process of gathering information about events happened in a system and analyzing the information to discover attacks to this system and reason about their causes. Event audit requires registration or logging of user requests and activities for later examination. Audit data is recorded in an audit trail or audit log, which varies from system to system. The auditing process can be performed both off-line and on-line. We will discuss event audit further below.

One important concept in event audit is intrusion detection. Intrusion detection is the process of monitoring the events occurring in a computer system or network and analyzing them for signs of intrusions, which are defined as attempts to compromise the confidentiality, integrity, availability of a resource, or to bypass the security mechanisms of a computer or network. Intrusion detection systems (IDSs) determine if actions perform intrusions base on one or more intrusion models. A model classifies a sequence of states or actions, or a characterization of states or actions, as "good" (no intrusion) or "bad" (possible intrusions). Modern IDSs primarily employ three models — misuse model, anomaly model and specification-based model.

Misuse detection characterizes a number of known attacks (misuse) to compromise a system and usually describes them as patterns or attack signatures, so the misuse detection is also called "signature-based intrusion detection". Misuse detection system monitors system events and is able to detect the explicit appearance or minor variations of know signatures. Misuse detection system requires a database of attack signatures and usually uses an expert system to identify intrusions based on a predetermined knowledge base. A misuse detection system has higher accuracy, but it could not detect any new intrusion without a pattern or signature. Therefore, later IDSs use adaptive methods such as neural networks and Petri Nets to improve their detection abilities. For example, Kumar and Spafford [17] have adapted colored Petri Nets to detect both attack signatures and the actions following previously unknown attacks in their system Intrusion Detection In Our Time (IDIOT).

Anomaly detection uses the assumption that unexpected behavior is evidence of an intrusion. It requires determining a baseline of normal behavior. Then it is concerned with identifying events that appear to be anomalous with respect to normal system behaviors and reports when the computed results do not match the expected measurements. An anomaly detection system may use statistical, neural network, or data mining methods of analysis. Three different statistical models are used, which are threshold metric, statistical moment, and Markov model. For example, the Next-generation Intrusion Detection Expert System (NIDES) developed by SRI contains a statistical dynamic anomaly detector [1]. Anomaly detection can identify new and previously unseen attacks. But it is difficult to determine the boundary between acceptable and anomalous behavior at some time, so it will have higher false negative and false positive rates. And an experienced intruder could train an anomaly intrusion detection system gradually to accept an intrusion as normal behavior.

Specification-based detection determines whether or not a sequence of intrusions violates a specification of how a program or system should execute. If so, it reports a potential intrusion [2]. Since the specification here is for security purpose, only those programs that may change the protection state of the system need to be specified and checked. Different from the misuse detection and anomaly detection, specification detection relies on traces or sequences of events and captures legitimate behaviors, not attack behaviors. Since it specifies the formalization of what should happen, it can detect intrusions using unknown attacks with low false alarms. However, extra efforts are needed to locate and analyze any program that may cause security problems in the system. Specification-based intrusion detection is still in its infancy. Ko, Ruschitzka, and Levitt [11] developed a specification-based intrusion detection system for the UNIX environment and applied it to monitoring program *rdist*. Uppuluri and Sekar [28] developed a declarative pattern language called Regular Expressions over Events (REE) and embedded REE into a rule-based language called Behavior Modeling Specification Language (BMSL), based on which they came up with a specification of a system and compiled the specification to produce a fast detection engine. Their experiences on 1999 Lincoln Labs offline evaluation data and 1999 AFRL online evaluation showed that this method could realize the promise of specification-based intrusion detection and was very effective.

4.4. *Cryptography*

Cryptography is the technique of data encryption and decryption. It is widely used to protection of secure-sensitive contents such as passwords, files, mutual communication, etc. When two entities need to talk or exchange some information, the initiator should encrypt the readable plain text into illegible cipher text. Then the cipher text is transmitted over the communication channel, which is most probably unsecured. When the receiver gets the cipher text, it decrypts it into readable plain text again.

Figure 2 illustrates the cryptography process.

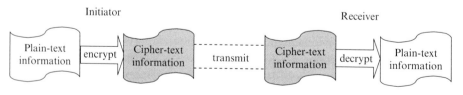

Fig. 2.   Cryptography.

Encryption and decryption are based on certain algorithms and secrets, which are called "keys". It is desired that the choice of encrypt/decrypt algorithms and keys could satisfy the following requirements: encryption procedure is easy while any attempt to decrypt without the keys is difficult. According to the characteristics of keys, we can classify cryptography into two main categories — symmetric cryptography and asymmetric cryptography [13].

(1) Symmetric Key Cryptography

Symmetric key cryptography is also called "shared-key cryptography" or "single-key cryptography". As indicated by the name, this kind of cryptography uses a common key for both encryption and decryption. Besides the initiator and the receiver, a Key Distribution Center (KDC) is often needed. The KDC sends secret keys through secure channels to the initiator, who encrypts the clear text to cipher text using the keys. On the receiver side, cipher text is decrypted using the same secret keys send by the KDC and becomes clear text.

Figure 3 illustrates this process. A drawback of this kind of cryptography is that it requires large-scale distribution of the shared keys. In addition, although it can provide confidentiality of information, it provides little authentication. Neither does it validate the integrity of the data transmitted.

(2) Asymmetric Cryptography

Asymmetric cryptography is also called "public key cryptography". In this kind of cryptography, two mathematically linked keys are applied. If one of them is used to encrypt some information, the other key must be used to decrypt the corresponding cipher text. One of the two keys is kept secret by a certain entity and is referred to as the "private key" of this entity. This private key represents the identity of its owner. The second key, which is called the "public key", is made available to the public. For instance, if the initiator Alice wants to send a message to receiver Bob, Alice will use the public key of Bob to encrypt this message and then sent the encrypted message to Bob. After Bob receives the encrypted message, he will decrypt it using his own private key. Since it is the assumption and requirement of

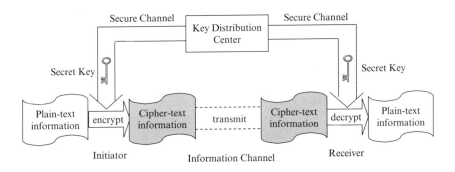

Fig. 3. Symmetric cryptography.

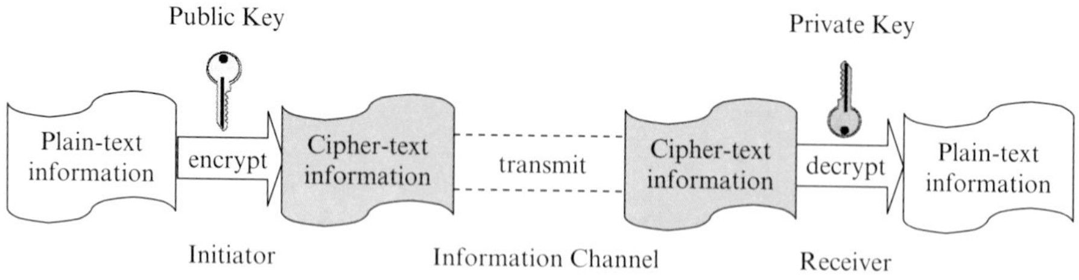

Fig. 4. Asymmetric cryptography.

asymmetric cryptography that it must be computationally infeasible to derive the private key from the public key, no one should be able to decrypt the message except for Bob. Therefore, asymmetric cryptography can provide authentication as well as confidentiality and integrity. Figure 4 illustrate the asymmetric cryptography.

(3) Encryption/Decryption Algorithms

Encryption and decryption algorithms are the foundation on which any cryptography technique is built. Therefore they are of great importance.

Data Encryption Standard (DES) is a well-known symmetric key cryptography algorithm introduced in 1977 [4]. It encrypts data through confusion and diffusion. In this algorithm, blocks of 64 bits of data is encrypted and decrypted under the control of a 64 bit key. The encryption and decryption consist of 16 iterations; in each of which a separate key of 48-bit is used. The order in which the keys are used decides the process is an encryption or a decryption. Although DES has provided the impetus for many advances in the cryptography field and been the theoretical and practical groundwork for many other ciphers, it was broken in 1999. Its successor, the Advanced Encryption Standard (AES), was proposed in 2001. The AES can use keys of 128, 192, or 256 bits and operates on blocks of 128 bits. It was specifically designed to withstand the attacks to which the DES showed weaknesses. At the same time, several other algorithms have been proposed to overcome the weaknesses in the DES, such as NewDES and IDEA.

RSA (Rivest Shamir Adelman) is a famous asymmetric cryptography algorithm and has universal acceptance. This algorithm has strong theoretical foundation of RSA Problem (RSAP), which is conjectured to be equivalent to the Integer Factorization Problem (IFP). This problem is "given a positive integer n that is a product of two distinct odd primes p and q, a positive integer e such that $gcd(e, (p-1)(q-1)) = 1$, and an integer c, find an m such that m^e is congruent to $c(\bmod n)$." No easy method has been found for the RSAP problem yet. RSA has been widely used because it can provide data and origin authentication and non-repudiation in addition to confidentiality. For instance, Alice encrypts her message using her private key. Anyone can read it with Alice's public key. However, no one can alter this message without being noticed because the altered cipher-text message cannot be decrypted correctly using Alice's public key. So if the message can be decrypted correctly, we can guarantee that this message is really encrypted by Alice based on the assumption that Alice is the only one who knows her private key and the corresponding public key bearing her name really belongs to her. RSA can also be used to provide both confidentiality and authentication simultaneously, which requires encryption with the sender's private key and the recipient's public key.

4.5. *Firewall*

A firewall is considered as the first line of defense in protecting private information. A firewall is a set of related programs or hardware devices, located at a network gateway server, which protects the resources of a private network from other networks users by allowing and disallowing certain types of access on the basis of a configured security policy. The term also implies the security policy that is used with the programs. Firewall technology provides both physical and logical protection between different networks. A firewall is often installed in front of the rest of the network so that all information flowing into this network has to be checked by this firewall and cannot get directly at private network resources. An enterprise with an intranet that allows its workers access to the Internet installs a firewall to prevent outsiders from accessing its own private data resources and for controlling what outside resources its own users have access to. Firewalls fall into three broad categories — packet filters, proxy servers, and stateful multilayer inspection firewalls [8].

(1) Packet Filtering Firewalls

Packet filtering is the most basic form of firewall security. In a packet filtering firewall, each packet is compared to a set of established rule first. Depending on the comparison results, the firewall can drop the packet, forward it, or send a message to the originator. Rules can include source and destination IP address, source and destination port number and protocol used. So the header parts of packets often get examined. Packet filtering firewalls are usually part of a router firewall. A router is a device that receives packets from one network and forwards them to another. The advantage of packet filtering firewalls is their low cost and low impact on network performance. In addition, it has general and flexible structure, and provides extra security for the sub-network. Most routers support packet filtering.

Packet filtering firewalls only work at the network layer. Although they are fairly effective and transparent to users, it is difficult to configure them. In addition, large sets of rules can be difficult to manage. Therefore, packet filtering firewalls by themselves do not support sophisticated rule-based models and they are not adequate to secure a complex network from attacks. They are also susceptible to IP spoofing.

(2) Proxy Servers

A proxy server is a firewall component that acts as an intermediary between a LAN and the internet. It monitors a session instead of examining each packet. Once a session is established, all packets in that session are allowed to cross. It can be classified into two categories according to its working layer. One is circuit-level gateway, while the other is application-level gateway.

Circuit-level gateways work at the session layer of the OSI model, or the TCP layer of TCP/IP. They monitor TCP handshaking between packets to determine whether a requested session is legitimate. Information passed to a remote computer through a circuit-level gateway appears to have originated from the gateway. This is useful for hiding information about the private network they protect. Circuit level gateways are relatively inexpensive. Besides security features, a circuit-level gateway can also act as an intermediary providing transparency to its users. When a user proposes a request, the circuit-level gateway receives it first. If the request passes filtering requirements, the circuit-level gateway looks in its local cache of previously downloaded contents. If the desired page is found, the circuit-level gateway returns it to the user directly instead of forwarding the request to the Internet. If it is not found, the circuit-level gateway acts as a client on behalf of the user and requests the page from the server on the Internet. When the page is returned, the circuit-level gateway relates it to the original request and forwards it to the user. Therefore, an enterprise can ensure security, administrative control, and caching service by using a circuit-level gateway.

Application-level gateways can filter packets at the application layer of the OSI model and are application specific. Incoming or outgoing packets cannot access services for which there is no proxy. Because they examine packets at the application layer, they can filter application specific commands, which cannot be accomplished by either packet filtering firewalls or circuit-level gateways. Application-level gateways can also be used to log user activities and logins. They offer a high level of security, but have a significant impact on network performance because context switches slow down network access dramatically. They are not transparent to end uses and require manual configuration of each client computer.

(3) Stateful Multilayer Inspection Firewalls

Stateful multilayer inspection firewalls are a hybrid combination of the other types of firewalls. They operate primarily on the network layer of the OSI model and transparently to the end users. They examine certain key parts of a packet and compare them with contents in a database of trusted information. According to the comparison results, they allow the packet to go through or discard it. They allow direct connection between client and host, alleviating the problem caused by the lack of transparency of application level gateways. They rely on algorithms to recognize and process application layer data instead of running application specific proxies. Stateful multiplayer inspection firewalls offer a high level of security, good performance and transparency to end users. However, they are expensive. In addition, if not administered by highly competent personnel, they are potentially less secure than simpler types of firewalls due to their complexity [8].

4.6. *Anti-virus software*

Anti-virus software is a class of software that looks for a virus or looks for indications of the presence of a virus in a data storage device, such as a hard drive, floppy disk, CD-ROM, etc and prevents these programs from performing their functions. Since new viruses are created and dispatched all the time, some anti-virus software should be updated periodically. The market for anti-virus software has expanded because of Internet growth and the increasing use of the Internet by businesses concerned about protecting their computer assets. It is desired that more than one antivirus software packages are installed in a system, since no single product can do everything. There are three main kinds of anti-virus programs — scanners, monitors and integrity checkers [3].

Currently, scanners are the most popular and widely used anti-virus programs. They are programs that check for viruses by scanning the executable objects, such as executable files and boot sectors, for the presence of special code sequences or strings called "signatures". Each virus recognizable by scanners has a signature associated with it. Scanners mainly consist of a searching engine and a database of virus signatures. They are widely used because they are relatively easy to maintain and update. When a new virus appears, the authors of scanners just need to pick a good signature, which is present in each copy of the virus and at the same time is unlikely to be found in any legitimate program, and add the signature to the scanner's database. This is often done very quickly. In addition to scanning for virus signatures, some scanners go a step further. For instance, the "f-prot" from Frisk Software uses a heuristic analyzer to see if executable objects contain virus-like code, such as time-triggered events, and software load trapping. Heuristics is a relatively new, but effective way to find viruses without defined signatures yet. Scanning techniques have some other variations, like virus removal programs, resident scanners, virus identifiers, and etc.

Monitors are memory resident programs, which continuously monitor computer's memory, automatically detect, and remove viruses without interrupting users' works. Once a program tries to use a function, which is considered to be dangerous and virus-like, the monitoring program intercepts it and either denies it completely or asks the user for confirmation. Unlike the scanners, the monitors are not virus-specific and therefore need not be constantly updated. But monitors have two main drawbacks which make them weaker than the scanners. One drawback is that monitors can be bypassed by the so-called "tunneling" viruses which attempt to follow the interrupt chain back down to the basic DOS or BIOS interrupt handlers and then install themselves. The other drawback is that monitors try to detect a virus by its behavior, which may cause many false alarms since viruses may use functions similar to those used by the normal programs.

Integrity checkers are programs which read the entire disk, compute some kind of checksum of the executable code in a computer system, and store the checksum in a database. The integrity checkers re-compute the checksum periodically and compare it with the stored original value to detect whether the executable code in this system have been modified. There are three main kinds of integrity checkers. The most widely used one is the off-line integrity checker, which checks the integrity of all the executable code in a computer system. Another kind is the integrity module. It can be attached to an executable file, which can check its integrity when starting its execution. The third kind is the integrity shell. It is a resident program which checks the integrity of an object only when this object is about to be executed. Integrity checkers are not virus-specific and do not need constant updating like the scanners. Currently, they are the most cost-effective and sound line of defense against the computer viruses. However, integrity checkers can only detect and report viruses, but cannot block them from infecting other files or systems. They usually cannot determine the source of infection either. Since the original checksum is considered to be the correct one for later comparison, integrity checkers must be initially installed in a virus-free system. In addition, they are prone to false positive alerts since changes they detected may be legitimate changes of a certain program. Although integrity checkers have those drawbacks mentioned above, their future is predicted as bright by specialists [3].

5. Security Issues in Mobile Computing

With the advances and development of Internet and wireless networking technology, a new paradigm of computing has emerged, which is mobile computing. Mobile computing is associated with the mobility of users, hardware, data and software in computer applications. In this section, we will focus on the security problems related with mobility of a specific kind of software, mobile agents.

Mobile agent technology has attracted great interests due to its salient merits and promising future. A mobile agent system consists of mobile agents, mobile agent platforms (platforms for short below) and other software. Mobile agents are goal-directed software agents, which can automatically suspend their execution on one platform and migrate to another platform to resume their computation. Platforms are software that can manage mobile agents in their life spans, including create, dispatch, execute, etc. Platforms run on computers connected by networks and can communicate with each other. Static agents may reside on a platform to provide services to mobile agents. A mobile agent can access a computer's resource to achieve its goal through its hosting platform on that computer.

Mobile agent technology has many distinct properties that make it a promising direction in mobile computing and distributed processing. However, it also brings significant security threats, which have become the bottleneck of the development and maintenance of mobile agent systems. In a mobile agent system, four security areas can be identified, namely: (1) inter-agent security; (2) agent-platform security; (3) inter-platform security; and (4) security between platforms and unauthorized third parties [19]. Figure 5 illustrates these areas.

Many security problems in areas (1), (3) and (4) have counterparts in conventional client-server systems. But area (2) is new and particularly important.

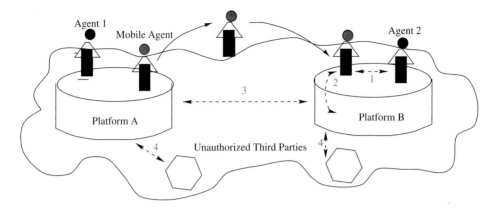

Fig. 5. Security areas in a mobile agent system.

Two sub-areas of security can be identified in agent-platform security area. On the one hand, platforms should be protected from malicious agents, known as "host security" or "mobile agent platform security." On the other hand, mobile agents should be protected from being tampered with by malicious platforms, which is known as "code security" or "mobile agent security." As a mobile agent consists of code, data and state, which are all under possible attacks; we prefer to use "mobile agent security" instead of "code security" in this chapter for clarity. Mobile agent security is notoriously difficult since a mobile agent has to expose its three areas for execution. If the platform is malicious, it can take advantage of the exposure to perform various attacks. It was once generally believed that only under hardware protection could a mobile agent be protected [5]. Recent research works have shown the incorrectness of this belief, although techniques and methods are still in great need to solve this problem.

5.1. *Malicious platform attacks*

A mobile agent has to expose its own information to the platform it migrates to so that it could be executed. In the case of strong migration, it has to expose its code, data and state. In the case of weak migration, its code and data have to be exposed. After a mobile agent arrives at a platform, it transfers control to that platform. Due to this fact, a mobile agent faces more severe security risks. A malicious platform can try to attack it in different ways. If we consider the home platform environment to be the most secure environment and try to achieve such a protection level for a mobile agent in other platform, we can classify possible malicious platform attacks to the following categories based on their targeted components of mobile agents.

(1) Leak Out/Modify Mobile Agent's Code

To get executed, a mobile agent has to expose its code to be executed to a hosting platform. This characteristic makes the attack of leaking out/modifying mobile agent's code unavoidable. A malicious platform could read and remember the instruction going to be executed and might infer the rest program based on this knowledge. Therefore, the platform could get to know the strategy and purpose of the mobile agent. The situation becomes worse if the mobile agent being attacked represents a class of mobile agents or is generated out of standard building libraries. In this case, the malicious platform can have a complete picture of a number of mobile agents' behaviors. If the malicious platform infers the physical address and has access to the code memory, it can modify the agent's code either directly or through inserting some vicious part like a virus. It could also change a mobile agent's code temporarily, execute the modified code, and resume the original code before the mobile agent leaves such that the modification of code could not be detected. This kind of attack compromise both confidentiality and integrity of a mobile agent system.

(2) Leak Out/Modify Mobile Agent's Data

This kind of attack could be very dangerous too. Since some data carried by a mobile agent are security sensitive, such as security keys, electronic cash, or social security numbers, leaking out mobile agent's data may cause leak of privacy or loss of money. If a malicious platform knows the physical location of data, it may modify the data in accordance with the semantics of data. Therefore it can result in very severe consequences. In some cases, even if the data being leaked is not that sensitive, a malicious platform can still take advantage of those data and perform attack. For example, if a malicious platform gets to know the traveling date of a person, it may leak it to some thief. Both confidentiality and integrity of a mobile agent system could be hurt by this kind of attack.

(3) Leak Out/Modify Mobile Agent's Execution Flow

If a malicious platform knows a mobile agent's code, data and the physical location of its program counter, it can infer what instruction of the mobile agent's code will be executed next. Moreover, it can deduce the state of that mobile agent. Then it might change the execution flow according to its will to achieve its goal. For example, it may get to know that the mobile agent first compares the price of a product or service provided by the platform with the expected price of the agent itself, and decides whether or not to order the product or service. A malicious platform might force the mobile agent to ignore the result of the comparison and accept its product or service directly by making the execution flow jump to a certain point. A malicious platform can also take advantage of its ability to modify the mobile agent's execution to deliberately execute agent's code in a wrong way. Confidentiality and integrity are also the victim security objectives of this kind of attack.

(4) Denial of Service

A malicious platform can perform the DoS attack to an incoming mobile agent by simply not executing the mobile agent or putting the mobile agent into a waiting list thus causing delay to that mobile agent. This attack may bring very bad consequence as well. If a mobile agent can finish its execution on that platform in time and travel to other platforms, it may catch some good chances. But DoS attack can make the mobile agent lose such chances. For example, a mobile agent is trying to book an air ticket. A malicious platform on behalf of an airline company may deliberately delay the process of the mobile agent's request for ticket price information, such that after this mobile agent gets the information, declines the prices, and then travels to another platform of a different airline company, the promotion from that company has been over. This attack hurts the availability of a mobile agent system.

(5) Masquerade

A malicious platform may disguise itself as another platform, to which a mobile agent will migrate, or even as the home platform when the mobile agent returns. If the malicious platform succeeds, it can get the secrets of the mobile agent by cheating and at the same time hurt the reputation of the original platform. For example, a malicious platform may pretend to represent a specific airline company and give a mobile agent a faked ticket after it gets the money. But the mobile agent cannot really use the ticket and may have dispute with the real airline company being faked. It hurts the authentication, and probably the confidentiality and integrity of the system.

(6) Leak Out/Modify the Interaction Between a Mobile Agent and Other Parties

A malicious platform may eavesdrop the interaction between a mobile agent residing on it and other entities, such as another agent or another platform. From the information it gets, it may infer some secrets about the mobile agent and the other entity. Moreover, if it can alternate the content of the interaction, or disguise itself as part of the interaction, or direct the interaction to other unexpected third party, it may perform attacks to the mobile agent and the other entity party as well. Confidentiality and integrity are security objectives that are targeted and hurt by this kind of attack.

5.2. *Countermeasures for malicious platform attacks*

A lot of research has been done to protect a mobile agent from those attacks or detect the attacks to a mobile agent. There are six main directions listed below in this area.

(1) The organizational approach by General Magic Inc. It eliminates the problem by allowing only trustworthy institutions to run mobile agent systems. This security mechanism stems more from the viewpoint that hardware protects software. Although it may be a secure way to protect mobile agent system, it cannot support an open system [5].

(2) The trust/reputation approach by Farmer, Guttmann and Swarup [6, 7]. They discussed achievable security goals for mobile agents and proposed an

architecture to achieve those goals. A unique point of their work is a specific mechanism called "state appraisal", which protects users and hosts from attacks via state modifications. This mechanism also provides users with flexible control over the authority of their agents. Their mechanism focuses on the state information and makes efforts to prevent the mobile agent's state from being modified by other parties. But this mechanism cannot detect the situation in which a mobile agent's code is modified.

(3) The manipulation detection approach by Vigna [32, 33]. This method is based on "cryptographic tracing", which can detect manipulations of agent data or the execution of code. The proposed method does not require dedicated tamper-proof hardware of trust between parties. But this mechanism might produce traces with huge size. Cryptographic tracing has been extended by Tan and Moreau [26, 27] to protect mobile code from denial-of-service and state tempering attacks. They introduced a trusted verification server, to undertake the verification of execution traces on behalf of the agent owner. They used model checking method to verify the security properties of their protocol.

(4) The blackbox protection approach by Hohl [9, 10]. This method aims to generate a blackbox out of agent code by using code obfuscating techniques. Since the attackers must spend some time to analyze the blackbox code before they perform attacks, this mechanism can protect a mobile agent from most of the attacks for a certain interval. After that period, the agent itself and the data it transports will become invalid to avoid attacks. But the security mechanism costs extra time when a mobile agent is created, transmitted, and executed.

(5) The CEF (Computing with Encrypted Functions) approach by Sander and Tschudin [20–22]. They used encrypted functions and the method of hiding the signing function to make digital signatures "undetachable". In this way, they can prevent the abuse of signing procedure for signing arbitrary documents. They only identified a special class of functions — polynomials and rational functions. There is still a gap between those functions and general programs. Kotzanikolaou *et al* [12] extended the CEF approach and proposed a RSA-based method to solve the open problem on undetectable signatures in Sander's work.

(6) The sixth direction takes advantage of the benefits provided by formal methods. SEAL Calculus is one example, which is based on π-calculus and extended by Vitek *et al* for distribution, mobility and security [34, 35]. It incorporates a resource access control for a platform based on linear revocable capabilities called "portals" and enforces a hierarchical protection model, while agents can protect themselves by controlling visibility and access to their own resources. Although the security properties proven in [34, 35] only relate to protecting a platform, it was claimed that a protocol would be devised to provide some guarantees to mobile agents as well.

5.3. *Our research work — An EEOS model of a secure mobile agent system*

The above works solve some problems in mobile agent security from different perspectives. However, most of them do not have a formal method basis. It is not easy to formally prove or analyze the characteristics, including the security features, of the mobile agent systems using these techniques. The sixth direction using formal method based on calculus is an exception, but it is not intuitive and hard to read and understand.

We proposed a formal model of a generic mobile agent system based on Extended Elementary Object System (EEOS) extended from the original Elementary Object System (EOS), which is a kind of Object Petri Net (OPN) [29–31]. Petri Nets have become a widely accepted technique in mainstream software engineering, because they can be used simultaneously as a graphical representation, a mathematical description, and a simulation tool for the system under study. Using Petri Nets also eliminates errors which may occur from modeling to implementation because modeling and simulation of a system happen at the same time. Our EEOS extends EOS in several aspects so as to capture mobile agent mobility, the most distinct characteristic of a mobile agent, and supports security features as well. Our EEOS model takes security into its basic consideration for both mobile agent migration and execution, which distinguishes our work from most other works using Petri Nets to model mobile agent systems. Different from the analysis methods based on mathematical deduction or theorem proving, we performed simulation-based analysis, which is generally more intuitive and practical and can be used to solve real problems. Since our research works have been introduced in details in our other papers [14–16], they will only be discussed briefly here.

Firstly, we extended the original EOS in the following six aspects: multiple system nets, multiple layers, token pool, internal/external places/transitions, two new arcs, and extended interaction relations, such that the Extended Elementary Object System (EEOS) can both naturally capture the characteristics of a mobile agent system, such as the mobility of mobile agents, but also supports security considerations.

Based on EEOS, we built a generic secure mobile agent system model, which is abstracted into three layers: mobile agent platform layer, mobile agent layer and security mechanism layer. The platform layer is the base layer consists of mobile agent platforms and the token pool, modeled as system nets. In this layer, mobile agents are tokens that can be transported among system nets via the token pool. The detailed structures and behaviors of mobile agents can be modeled in the upper layer, i.e., mobile agent layer. In this layer, mobile agents are system nets while the security mechanisms equipped with mobile agents are tokens. A platform could have security mechanisms represented by token nets in the security mechanism layer as well. The structure of the security mechanisms is modeled in the top layer, and the security mechanism layer.

Mobile agent platform layer is the bottom layer and consists of two parts: mobile agent platforms and the token pool. A mobile agent platform is responsible for managing, transporting and executing mobile agents in their life spans. In our EEOS model for a mobile agent platform shown in Fig. 6, five functionality modules exist. The "external communication process" module manages the communications between this mobile agent platform and other mobile agent platforms or the trust server in the token pool. The "internal communication process" module manages the communications between this mobile agent platform and those agents residing on it. The "mobile agent receiving and authentication" module is responsible for receiving a mobile agent from the outside world and authenticating its identity. The "mobile agent execution" module is responsible to execute mobile agents. And the "mobile agent dispatching" module is used to dispatch a mobile agent to the outside network upon its request or at this mobile agent platform's will. A mobile agent platform is also equipped with its own knowledge base and security base for the correct and secure management and execution of mobile agents.

The token pool is a place connecting all platforms and represents the network environment for traveling mobile agent token nets. To ensure that a mobile agent transfer is secure and reinforce other security features such as non-repudiation, we introduce a trust server (abbreviated as TS below) into the token pool. A simplified view of the TS is illustrated in Fig. 7.

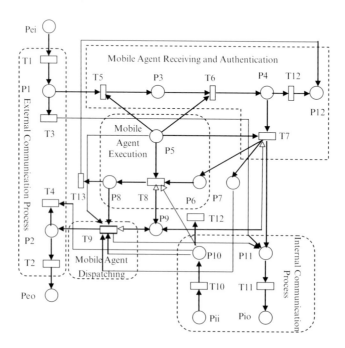

Fig. 6.   Simplified EEOS model of a mobile agent platform.

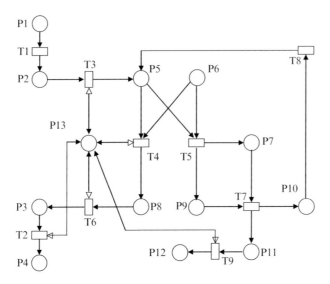

Fig. 7.   Trust server in the token pool.

Mobile agent layer is the middle layer and consists of mobile agents only. A mobile agent is capable to perform certain actions (including reactive actions, autonomous actions, and move actions) intelligently or reactively. It can also authenticate a mobile agent platform's identity which it arrives at, and record the current location and its itinerary path. It can communicate with a mobile agent platform through its In/Out communication channels. It is equipped with a knowledge base which stores all its knowledge and goals this mobile agent has, and a security base which aims to provide security mechanisms for the security of this mobile agent. The most distinct characteristic of a mobile agent is its automatic mobility, which means a mobile agent can decide WHEN and WHERE to go by itself. From this aspect, a mobile agent transfer is an active migration instead of a passive dispatch. On the other hand, since the home platform of a mobile agent has the right to ask a mobile agent to go somewhere on its behalf, transferring a mobile agent can also be initiated by the mobile agent platform. There are two kinds of mobility for a mobile agent, weak mobility and strong mobility. For the former, only the code and data of a mobile agent transfers, while for the latter the state of a mobile agent also transfers. Our model supports both because different applications require different mobility. Figure 8 illustrates a simplified EEOS model for a mobile agent.

In order to achieve secure mobile agent execution, both mobile agents and mobile agent platforms should be equipped with certain security mechanisms, which are token nets in the mobile agent layer and mobile agent platform layer, and whose structures and behaviors may be detailed in the security mechanism layer. Since there might be different security mechanisms for various attacks, the structures of security mechanism token nets are not fixed.

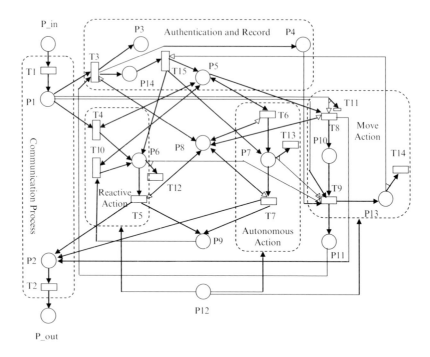

Fig. 8.   Simplified EEOS model of a mobile agent.

In the mobile agent platform layer and mobile agent layer of our EEOS model, a mutual authentication mechanism is designed based on public key cryptography to achieve the authentication between mobile agents and mobile agent platforms, as well as support secure mobility of mobile agents. A "remove-restore" mechanism is also proposed and integrated in the model to support strong mobility. In addition, dynamic and secure communications between mobile agents and mobile agent platforms are also achieved in our model. We also proposed a "synchronous firing security mechanism" to detect malicious mobile agent platform attacks to the code or execution flow of the mobile agents being executed on those platforms. Our EEOS model of a generic secure mobile agent system can meet the security objectives such as authentication, authorization, accountability, confidentiality, and non-repudiation.

Simulation and simulation-based analysis provide a thorough view of the system behaviors and characteristics. Since our EEOS stems from CPN, we simulated our EEOS model of a generic secure mobile agent system in Design/CPN, the most widely used package for CPN. We can prove formally several features concerning mobile agent mobility, mobile agent execution, and communications. For example, the simulation-based analysis show that the concurrent traveling of mobile agents can be achieved; strong mobility of mobile agents is supported; mobile agents can only be executed under their hosting platforms' supervision; and the communications between a mobile agent and other platforms must be forwarded and monitored by its hosting platform. The details of the proofs of those features can be found in [15, 16].

6. Conclusion and Future Works

Security is a major concern in modern software systems. In particular, mobile computing has emerged with the rapid growth of the Internet. Security has become a bottleneck to the development and maintenance of mobile agent system, a promising and challenging direction in mobile computing. This chapter presents general security objectives that a software system should meet, reviews various types of possible attacks and countermeasures in software security area, and then focuses on the security problems in a mobile agent system. It also introduces our research work — an intuitive and formal EEOS model of a generic secure mobile agent system.

Attacks and countermeasures in software system security are a pair of contradictions which may never disappear. New attacks keep on being created and new countermeasure keep on being developed. Immune computer system is one of the future directions on protecting a computer system from attacks. Immune computer systems become their own security experts, adapting to threats as they unfold and staying one step ahead of the action. A number of research projects are headed in that direction. For example, intrusion-detection methods that mimic biological immune systems are developed at the University of New Mexico in Albuquerque. Biometric technology will be more widely integrated into system security area. Besides fingerprints, iris and retina scanning, voice printing and signature verification are also under research. Since no security measure works perfectly, another direction is to employ multiple layers of protection effectively for a software system. In addition, since hackers recognize that humans are often the weakest link in system security and exploit this using social engineering tactics, every IT person is expected to be educated accordingly.

Acknowledgment

This research was supported in part by the National Science Foundation under Grants CCR-9988361 and CCR-0098120 and National Research Council under Grant NSC 92-2213-E-468-001, R.O.C.

References

1. D. Anderson, T. F. Lunt, H. Javitz, A. Tamaru and A. Valdes, "Detecting unusual program behavior using the statistical component of the Next-generation Intrusion Detection Expert System (NIDES)", SRI International Computer Science Laboratory Technical Report SRI-CSL-95-07, May 1995.
2. M. Bishop, *Computer Security — Art and Science* (Addison-Wesley, ISBN 0-201-44099-7, 2002).
3. V. Bontchev, "Possible virus attacks against integrity programs and how to prevent them", *http://vx.netlux.org/lib/static/vdat/epposatt.htm.*

4. CERT Coordination Center Denial of Service, *http://www.cert.org/tech_tips/denial_of_service.html*.

5. D. Chess, C. Harrison and A. Kershenbaum, "Mobile agents: Are they a good idea?" IBM Research Report, J. Watson Research Center, March 1995.

6. W. M. Farmer, J. D. Guttmann and V. Swarup, "Security for mobile agents: Authentication and state appraisal", *Proceedings of the Fourth European Symposium on Research in Computer Security*, no. 1146 (1996) 118–130.

7. W. M. Farmer, J. D. Guttmann and V. Swarup, "Security for mobile agents: Issues and requirements", *Proceedings of the 19th National Information Systems Security Conference* **2** (1996) 591–597.

8. Firewall Software White Paper, *http://www.firewall-software.com/firewall_faws/types_of_firewall.html*.

9. F. Hohl, "A model of attacks of malicious hosts against mobile agents", *4th Workshop on Mobile Object Systems (MOS'98): Secure Internet Mobile Computations*.

10. F. Hohl, "Time limited blackbox security: Protecting mobile agents from malicious hosts", *Mobile Agents and Security, Lecture Notes in Computer Science 1419* (1998) 92–113.

11. C. Ko, M. Ruschitzka and K. Levitt, "Execution monitoring of security-critical programs in distributed system: A specification-based approach", *Proceedings of the 1997 IEEE Symposium on Security and Privacy* (May 1997) 175–187.

12. P. Kotzanikolaou, M. Burmester and V. Chrissikopoulos, "Secure transactions with mobile agents in hostile environments", *ACISP 2000, Lecture Notes in Computer Science 1841* (2000) 289–297.

13. L. Ma and J. J. P. Tsai, "Formal verification techniques for computer communication security protocols", *Handbook of Software Engineering and Knowledge Engineering* (2001) 23–45.

14. L. Ma, J. J. P. Tsai, Y. Deng and T. Murata, "Extended elementary object system model for mobile agent security", *Proceedings of 2003 World Congress on Integrated Design and Process Technology* (December 3–6, 2003) 169–178.

15. L. Ma and J. J. P. Tsai, "Trust server and secure mobility in mobile agent systems", submitted to *15th IEEE International Symposium on Software Reliability Engineering (ISSRE)*, 2004.

16. L. Ma, J. J. P. Tsai and Z. Yu, "Modeling and analysis of a secure mobile agent system using extended elementary object system", submitted to *IEEE Transaction on Software Engineering*.

17. S. Kumar and E. Spafford, "A pattern matching model for misuse intrusion detection", *Proceedings of the 17th National Computer Security Conference* (October 1994) 11–21.

18. V. C. Ramasami, "Security, authentication and access control for mobile communications", *http://www.ittc.ku.edu/~rvc/documents/865/865_securityreport.pdf*.

19. K. Rothermel, F. Hohl and N. Radouniklis, "Mobile agent systems: What is missing?" *Distributed Applications and Interoperable Systems (DAIS'97)*.

20. T. Sander and C. F. Tschudin, "Towards mobile cryptography", *1998 IEEE Symposium on Security and Privacy*.

21. T. Sander and C. F. Tschudin, "Protecting mobile agents against malicious hosts", *Mobile Agents and Security, Lecture Notes in Computer Science 1419* (1998) 44–60.

22. T. Sander and C. F. Tschudin, "On the cryptographic protection of mobile code", *Workshop on Mobile Agents and Security*, October 1997.

23. R. S. Sandhu and P. Samarati, "Authentication, access control, and intrusion detection", *The Computer Science and Engineering Handbook* (CRC Press, 1997) 1929–1948.

24. G. Stoneburner, C. Hayden and A. Feringa, "Engineering principles for information technology security — A baseline for achieving security", *NIST (National Institute of Standards and Technology) Special Publication 800-27*, June 2001.

25. G. Stoneburner, "Underlying technical models for information technology security", *NIST Special Publication 800-33*, December 2001.

26. H. K. Tan and L. Moreau, "Extending execution tracing for mobile code security", *Proceedings of Second International Workshop on Security of Mobile MultiAgent Systems (SEMAS'2002)* (2002) 51–59.

27. H. K. Tan and L. Moreau, "Trust relationships in a mobile agent system", *Mobile Agents, Lecture Notes in Computer Science 2240* (2001) 15–30.

28. P. Uppuluri and R. Sekar, "Experiences with specification-based intrusion detection", *Recent Advances in Intrusion Detection (RAID)*, October 2001.

29. R. Valk, "Petri nets as token objects — An introduction to elementary object nets", *19th International Conference on Application and Theory of Petri Nets (ICATPN'98), Lecture Notes in Computer Science 1420* (1998) 1–25.

30. R. Valk, "Concurrency in communicating object petri nets", *Concurrent Object-Oriented Programming and Petri Nets, Advances in Petri Nets* (2001) 164–195.

31. R. Valk, "Relating different semantics for object petri nets — Formal proofs and examples", *Technical Report FBI-HH-B-226*, University of Hamburg, Department for Computer Science, April 2000, pp. 1–50.

32. G. Vigna, "Protecting mobile agents through tracing", *3rd ECOOP Workshop on Mobile Object Systems*.

33. G. Vigna, "Cryptographic traces for mobile agents, mobile agents and security", *Lecture Notes in Computer Science 1419* (1998) 137–150.

34. J. Vitek and G. Castagna, "Towards a calculus of secure mobile computations", *Proceedings of Workshop on Internet Programming Languages*, Chicago, Illinois, 1998.

35. J. Vitek and G. Castagna, "Seal: A framework for secure mobile computations", *Internet Programming Languages, Lecture Notes in Computer Science 1686*, 1999.

AUTONOMOUS SOFTWARE

MICHAEL ROVATSOS*

*Centre for Intelligent Systems and their Applications,
School of Informatics, The University of Edinburgh,
Edinburgh EH8 9LE, United Kingdom
E-mail: mrovatso@inf.ed.ac.uk*

GERHARD WEISS

*Institut für Informatik, Technische Universität München,
85748 Garching, Germany
E-mail: weissg@in.tum.de*

Industrial-strength software is reaching a level of inherent complexity which tends to make an effective development, deployment and administration impossible. This has led to a rapidly growing interest in the notion of autonomous software, that is, software which takes over, and encapsulates, action choice and responsibility from its users and operators so that it can handle its complexity on its own. A key condition for the broad acceptance of autonomous software is the availability of a clear notion of autonomy as a software property upon which precise specification schemes for autonomous software systems can be built. There are diverse approaches available in computer science that are useful in this respect. This chapter describes a generic autonomy specification framework which gives an integrated view of these approaches and of the state of the art in specifying autonomy as a software property.

Keywords: Agent-oriented modeling, agent-oriented software engineering, intelligent agents and multiagent systems, autonomy-oriented computation.

1. Introduction

Advances in information technology and growing expectations on the functionality of computer-based information processing systems form the basis for a fundamental change in the software landscape. Characteristic to this change is the rapidly increasing importance of industrial, commercial and scientific software systems which operate and are tightly embedded in open, distributed, networked, dynamic, and hardly predictable socio-technical environments. Despite the impressive progress achieved in software engineering during the past decades, this kind of software systems tend to possess an extraordinarily high level of inherent complexity which makes it practically impossible to develop, administrate and deploy them effectively in terms of time and costs. This serious problem has led to the

---

*Corresponding author.

much-attended vision of autonomous software, that is, software being able to handle its complexity on its own. The spectrum of primary attributes associated with autonomous software is broad and ranges from self-diagnosing and self-structuring over self-managing and self-governing to self-repairing and self-adapting.[a] The key idea underlying these attributes is to have software equipped with action and decision choice so that it can fulfil its tasks even under critical and unexpected circumstances (e.g. changes in the technological infrastructure or in the application-specific user demands) *without* requiring human support, feedback or intervention.

Autonomy orientation may be viewed as a natural next step in the evolution of generic software models [21]. In the course of this evolution, the basic building blocks of software — monolithic programs, modules, procedures, objects and components — gained increasing degrees of localization and encapsulation of data processing and state control. What is common to all traditional building blocks is that their invocation happens through *external* events, such as start directives by users and call statements or messages by other software entities. Autonomous software exceeds this limitation of "external-only invocation" by additionally encapsulating invocation control. In other words, autonomous software significantly differs from traditional software in that it takes over responsibility for deciding (in accordance with the demands of its users and administrators) when and under what conditions to become active and to react on external events. Because of this difference, the step toward autonomous software is also a highly challenging one which cannot be realized casually by adding some lines of code, but one which deeply impacts all phases of software development, from early requirements capturing over implementation to integration with legacy systems.

Putting the vision of autonomous software into practice requires, first and foremost, a clear notion of software autonomy upon which precise schemes for autonomy specification can be built. In the computer science literature — especially in the literature on autonomic computing (e.g. [34]), agent and multiagent technology (e.g. [18, 40, 43]), and agent-oriented software engineering (e.g. [23, 41]) — diverse approaches have been proposed which are useful in this respect.[b] This chapter describes a generic, domain- and application-independent autonomy specification

---

[a] Among these attributes, self-governing is most closely related to the original sense of the Greek term "auto+nomos" ("self+law"). As noted in [2], in European languages the word autonomous is commonly used to refer to something that is capable of self-government, while in American English its usage is stronger associated with self-directedness and independence from outside.

[b] Autonomic computing is a technological effort initiated by IBM that aims at building autonomous computing systems. There are related efforts by other IT leaders, such as Sun's N1 initiative [39], HP's adaptive enterprise initiative [16] and Microsoft's dynamic systems initiative [27]. In the area of agent and multiagent technology autonomy is viewed as a key characteristic of computational agents [44]. In fact, it is often through the aspect of autonomy (in the sense of self-governance without external intervention) that agents can be best distinguished from other software or hardware components, such as objects, modules, etc. Generally, in that area the term "agent" is commonly used to refer to a computational entity capable of autonomous and flexible action and interaction, and this notion of an agent is also essential to agent-oriented software engineering.

framework which brings these approaches and their key concepts together in a coherent whole. This framework comprises two parts: an autonomy matrix which gives a static view of software autonomy; and an autonomy transformation loop which captures the dynamic aspects of software autonomy. These two parts taken together provide the vocabulary necessary for talking about autonomous software. To our knowledge, they constitute the first comprehensive conceptual framework that allows for an *analysis* of computational autonomy that is crucial for engineering autonomous systems.

It should be stressed that autonomous software *is still a vision*, at least as far as the self-responsible carrying out of complex tasks without human intervention or feedback is concerned. With this respect, the framework presented in this paper should rather be understood as an "instruction manual" for dealing with autonomy issues that will arise in the future rather than a representative description of aspects of present-day software. Also, in many cases, full autonomy is not even desirable, as human designers or users want to be able to control the system at any point in time.

However, we will show that many *aspects* of autonomy already appear in existing applications (even if we cannot speak of "full" autonomy yet), and that the class of software applications in which autonomy plays a role is becoming increasingly important.

The chapter structure is as follows. First, Sec. 2 introduces an exemplary system and application which is used to illustrate the various concepts relevant to autonomy specification. Next, Secs. 3 and 4 describe the autonomy matrix and the autonomy transformation loop, respectively. Finally, Sec. 5 concludes with considerations on urgent open issues raised by autonomous software.

2. An Illustrative Example

Before we embark on a description of the key characteristics of autonomous software, it is useful to introduce an exemplary system that can be used to illustrate the concepts we suggest. The Link Exchange Simulation System LIESON [35] is a fully implemented system that is highly suitable for this purpose.

LIESON is a distributed, agent-based software simulator in which agents representing Web site owners manage the linkage (via hyperlinks) between their own site and others' on behalf of the Web site owners. These agents pursue two goals: Firstly, they seek to maximize the traffic attracted to their own(er's) site. Secondly, they want those most popular sites to express similar opinions as they do themselves, i.e., they aim at a link-based dissemination of their opinion. To further these goals, the agents negotiate with each other over linkage actions (such as laying a link, deleting it or labeling it with a positive/negative comment).

The system was primarily built as a simulation testbed for socially intelligent agents that are able to use a set of pre-defined interaction patterns when communicating with others in a goal-oriented way [36]. Apart from this social reasoning functionality, of course, they also have a rational, goal-oriented reasoning and decision-making apparatus that enables them to reason about the information they obtain about the current linkage network, to project future states, to assess the desirability of these states and to plan towards the achievement of these goals.

In the following sections, we will use LIESON as an example of a software system that is complex enough to incorporate the different kinds of autonomy we describe. More particularly, it is characterized by key features common among those software applications in which autonomy can be seen to play a crucial role:

- *Spatial distribution of data and control*: The different Web site owners who deploy agents are stakeholders with potentially incompatible motives. Typically (i.e., unless a distributed system is deployed by a single stakeholder for the purpose of distributing a complex task among "strictly co-operative" units), different parts (here: agents) of the software follow their own design objectives and are not necessarily concerned with meeting global coherence.
- *Mutual observation*: Since agents have no access to each other's internal design, there is a need for monitoring others' behaviors and reacting appropriately to it. As we shall see below, this is very important in terms of the observer perspective that is assumed when modeling the autonomy of a piece of software.
- *Complex application environment*: The Web linkage domain is an application environment characterized by constant evolution and uncertainty regarding the current status of the global network of hyperlinks due to the impossibility of constantly monitoring all Web sites and their links. Typically, such environments require that agents self-responsibly decide to prioritize their "goals" and to reason about possible paths of computation. Quite obviously, if this entails that program behavior may deviate from what was expected by its user or designer, then we are dealing with — at least partial — autonomy of the software.

While LIESON is a very particular application, we shall show below that many of these features are also present in other kinds of software. In particular, we will argue that they do not only occur in agent-based software systems.

3. Software Autonomy — The Static View

3.1. *Autonomy and agency*

In the above discussion of LIESON as a typical application in which autonomy analysis makes sense, the concept of *agents* was used in accordance with common usage, to refer to a software unit that is able to pursue its design objectives autonomously, flexibly and in interaction with humans and other agents (e.g. [31]).

The design of LIESON heavily draws upon *agent* and *multiagent* technology (see Sec. 1). Therefore, it will sometimes be convenient in the following to refer to the software artefacts that represent Web site owners as "agents" and, more generally, to speak of agents whenever we mean autonomous software components that interact with each other and their environment. However, it should by no means be inferred from this that our discussion of autonomy only applies to agent-based approaches. Instead, we make use of the notion of agency as a *design metaphor* that emphasizes autonomy (but also a certain amount of sophistication with respect to functionality, adaptiveness and the ability to operate in dynamic and/or uncertain environments, etc.) rather than in the sense of a set of technologies adopted from agent/multiagent system research (such as agent architectures, interaction protocols, agent communication languages, coordination mechanisms, etc.).

Also, what matters for our analysis when we picture a piece of autonomous software as an agent is the role of the *observer* perspective in autonomy modeling and analysis: By looking at an agent "from the outside", we put a great deal of emphasis on the process of *ascribing* autonomy qualities to software, and the agent notion supports this view (in contrast to concepts such as "unit", "program", "module" or "component").

Our analysis is based on the insight that this "ascribing" aspect of modeling autonomy is relevant for a variety of "conventional" software applications that are built without employing agent technology. As in the case of LIESON, this class of applications is characterized by the distribution of data and control, mutual observation, and complexity of the application environment. The most suitable examples of such systems are applications in which different software (and hardware) components belong to different stakeholders and are not controlled by a central coordinating instance, such as

- peer-to-peer systems for distributed management and exchange of information,
- *ad hoc* networks for routing and communication between mobile devices,
- supply chain management systems which cater for flexible and loosely coupled B2B interactions,
- electronic marketplaces, auctions and trading platforms,

and many others of a similar flavor. For this kind of systems that encapsulate components with a certain degree of autonomy — whether referred to as agents or not — we will next lay out a basic typology of different autonomy types.

3.2. *The autonomy matrix*

The autonomy matrix provides the basic vocabulary for analyzing and modeling autonomy in terms of different autonomy types, and thus is foundational to our understanding of autonomy, at least as far as the *static* view of autonomy is concerned. This means that the autonomy matrix describes what kinds of autonomy a piece of software may possess, while disregarding the dynamics that may alter this autonomy status (these will be dealt with in Sec. 4).

Table 1.   The autonomy matrix

Range	Perspective	
	Internal	External
performative	*capability*	*dependency*
deliberative	*motivation*	*control*
normative	*commitment*	*expectation*

What this typology achieves is to break down the abstract notion of autonomy into a set of concepts the existence of which can be more easily identified and assessed in a concrete software system. This not only enables us to focus on the autonomy perspective of a system, but it also constitutes an important step towards *dealing* with the different kinds of autonomy that a system may exhibit.

The matrix itself is shown in Table 1, and it distinguishes six types of autonomy and thus allows for a fine-grained specification of the autonomy status a software system might possess. The distinction made results from applying two different dimensions of autonomy: The *perspective of observation* and the *range* (or *scope*) of activity. In the following, first these two dimensions are explained, then the six autonomy types are described, and finally a basic autonomy specification pattern is presented.

3.3. *The perspective of observation*

The perspective of observation specifies the viewpoint of the observer who is describing an autonomous software component. Two kinds of perspectives can be distinguished, as they result in essentially different characterizations of the autonomy owned by a software system: The perspective of what can be called an internal observer, and the perspective of what is called here an external observer. An *internal* observer is an observer who is able to cross the boundary between the software and its environment and hence to obtain information about internal aspects of the agent that is not readily available when observing interaction with the environment. In particular, the autonomous software artefact itself is an internal observer of its own autonomy. An *external* observer, on the other hand, can only use what he perceives of the interaction of the software with its environment. Typical examples of external observers are users of a computer system or of a piece of software (who have not implemented the system themselves), market analysts who monitor the external activities of a company but are not provided with internals, etc.

Note that for both kinds of observer perspectives, several additional factors come into play that determine how the observer assesses the autonomy of the software under analysis. These are, *inter alia*,

- the *accuracy* of information about the (internal and external) behavior of a component or system,

- the *processability* of this information (e.g. if its amount exceeds the capacities of the observer), and
- the *precision* of the information (i.e., the level of detail that is provided).

Also, of course, mixed-perspective observation is possible (and very common in practice). For example, software components with a social ability are usually capable of assuming the role of other components when observing themselves. Or, a person who has implemented a software system has access to the internals on the system, but is also externally observing its behavior when testing it.

3.4. *The range of activity*

The range of activity that must be determined to gain a full understanding of the autonomy of an software entity has to do with whether its actions make it autonomous in behaving as an *individual* or in relation to its *social context*, and also whether we are referring to autonomy in terms of *actions* or in terms of *internal state*. With this respect, three categories can be distinguished.

The *performative* range of autonomy defines what actions a piece of software *can* take in principle, i.e., how it can influence its environment and the standing of others by taking action. In specifying performative autonomy, we typically identify

- the "primitives" of action the software disposes of (i.e., what changes it can effect in its physical/computer/network environment),
- the reliability with which it can employ them (a program is not really "capable" of performing some action if this action fails regularly),
- by the resources it can access (data, CPU time, network bandwidth, reasoning resources (representations, heuristics, algorithms, etc.),
- and by the complexity of "agendas" it can pursue while acting (e.g. how long or conditionally branched the action sequences are that it can pursue once it has decided on them).

If the autonomous software is ascribed mental qualities [26], (which is often the case, for instance, in agent-based approaches), certain "mental" activities can be seen as belonging to this class, but only in a low-level sense, e.g. adding and retracting facts to and from one's beliefs.

The *deliberative* range of activity has to do with the motivations that guide the behavior of a software component, it describes what it *wants* to do. Unlike the performative range, this level is not concerned with the "what" of software activity, but rather with the "why" that stands behind an observed behavior. Deliberation explains the goals and needs of an entity rather than its direct actions (by which the environment is manipulated or it communicates with other agents), i.e., it provides the reasons for a certain behavior. The activities that deliberation is aimed at are, quite naturally, only mental actions, such as generating and revising goals, adopting intentions or commitments [42] etc.

The *normative* range, finally, defines what the software is *supposed* to do. Of course, this largely depends on *who* expects the software to do something: If it has a model of e.g. its own anticipated behavior, the agent *itself* might have such normative expectations. More commonly, though, designer, the users, and other autonomous components it interacts with have a picture of what the agent "should" do. The difference to the performative view is that autonomy here is not framed by ability, but by the reactions of some other entity — it does not constrain anything the software artefact might do in principle. For example, a digital assistant who purchases goods on behalf of its owner on the Internet may be expected to pay for them at a normative level, while it may be at the same time able to commit fraud at the performative level. The difference between normative and deliberative autonomy, on the other hand, is that expectations have nothing to do with the current motives. For example, an agent may commit itself to something it does not want, and then it will certainly restrict his own autonomy by normative means of influence exerted upon itself [10].

Obviously, it is not possible to identify the latter two ranges (deliberative and normative) in just about any kind of software system, and it requires assuming a *knowledge-level* [28] outlook on computational systems that allows for ascribing mental qualities to them [26]. However, it will become clear from the description of the suggested individual types of autonomy below that assuming such a perspective is possible and reasonable in many situations.

Again, mixtures of these three different ranges are possible and do often occur in practice. For example, all deliberative and normative activities must have a physical counterpart since we are talking about physical software components, and this physical counterpart is always a performative activity.

3.5. *Different types of autonomy*

We will now discuss the six types of autonomy in more detail.

Capability — internal performative autonomy: Internal performative autonomy is defined by the capabilities of a software component, i.e., by the capacity it has to influence its environment. It is an internal view, because the software can only perform actions it knows of, and must choose from these actions. A strongly related notion is that of resources, i.e., of cognitive or environmental aspects used to effect changes on the environment. Key concepts that are related to this autonomy category are *skill, ability, competence, expertise, learning,* and *knowledgeability.*

Example. In LIESON, agents' capabilities are given by (i) the physical action options they have depending on their knowledge and their environment, and, (ii) at a more abstract level, by their reasoning resources.

At the level of physical actions they can freely modify the outgoing links of their owner's Web site, as long as they have the required knowledge to "think of" these actions. For example, they can only lay a link to a site if they have found the site on the Web before and if they have obtained feedback from their human owner as to how much he likes the respective site. Also, they can execute special actions to explore new regions of the Web and they can visit known sites to update their knowledge about the outgoing links of that site.

Their autonomy is also restricted by reasoning resources, such as the number of future linkage states they can anticipate in each iteration to consider as a goal, by the number of goals they can schedule for future attainment, by the fact that they can only entertain a single conversation at a time, and by the time they need to wait for a response during a communicative encounter. In this respect, it is also a significant limitation that they can never really "catch" up with changes to the linkage network — assuming that each agent can execute a single action (visiting a site *or* sending a message to another agent *or* modifying an outgoing link) in each iteration, the global link configuration can change much faster than the agent can perceive these changes by visiting sites.

Dependency — external performative autonomy: From an external point of view, not knowing what the internal capabilities of a component are, we can only observe the *dependencies* between the software and its environment (this relational aspect is emphasized in [7,9]). The degree to which we ascribe autonomy to a piece of software in this sense depends on how closely its behavior is coupled to that of its environment. For example, if an agent always performs an action after some specific event in the environment, it is very probable that this agent somehow depends on the effects of the environment (not necessarily in a physical sense, though; in the case of two deliberative agents it may also be the case that the action of one agent is spawned by the actions of the other through, e.g. a goal that arises from it).

Here, central concepts are *influence*, *distribution of scarce resources*, *compatibility* and *complementarity* of activities. The dependencies perspective of analysis is often assumed in coordination science, which sees coordination itself as the process of *managing* dependencies [25].

Example. LIESON agents mainly depend on each other by virtue of (i) the prescriptive force of communication patterns and (ii) correlations between agent capabilities and their utility functions.

As for (i), agents have to comply with the admissible message sequences prescribed by existing protocols, so that the range of potential responses is limited by communication patterns. This entails that any utterance will be followed by a fixed set of possible responses. Note that, although in principle any communicative message can be uttered in any situation the design of LIESON does not allow agents to dispose of certain communicative options at the deliberative level in this case, so that it is performative autonomy that is actually restricted here.

With (ii), the most basic autonomy constraint is that agents can only lay links towards existing sites, i.e., appearance or deletion of a site affects their action capabilities. With respect to utility scores, agents depend on the links others lay toward them, in the sense that they are not free to assign themselves any desired utility. (At a more abstract level, of course, this is a dependency stemming from the designer who defined the utility function and not from the actions of other agents.)

Motivation — internal deliberative autonomy: Deliberative autonomy is strongly related to "freedom of will". Unlike capabilities who merely described what the software can do, motivation explains what it wants to do. A highly autonomous software component is self-motivated, and it is able to derive the justification for his actions through inference from first principles at any point in time. Adopting others' instructions, "commands", valuations or preferences, on the other hand, severely restricts this kind of autonomy.

We shall not ponder more deeply on the issue of whether perfect motivational autonomy is possible, since this is a fundamental philosophical problem that is not of much relevance to practical software engineering (the reader may have noticed that it sounds strange to speak of what the software "wants"). For the purposes of our analysis, we will always assume that there are some underlying explicitly implemented first principles that the software component follows and that set the scene for its range of activity. We will speak of autonomy in terms of motivation if, based on these principles, the autonomous software entity has the freedom to prioritize goals, to decide on whether these are fulfilled or unachievable, and to generate plans for achieving these goals.

Key issues that arise in this type of autonomy are related to questions of *goal selection* and *goal revision, intention, preference,* and *initiative.* One area in which these phenomena are studied is that of Belief-Desire-Intention agency [33], which deals with rational (i.e., goal-oriented) practical reasoning models for computational agents.

Example. The LIESON system allows agents to deliberate regarding linkage configurations they want to achieve. In each reasoning cycle, they randomly generate possible future states of the link network, make utility predictions for these states and schedule them according to these predictions in a rank-based "goal queue" (that is bounded in size) for future achievement. Then, the top option from this queue is selected as a current goal and de-queued, a plan is generated for its achievement and this plan is subsequently executed. Thereby, goals that cannot be achieved anymore or have already been achieved are simply skipped. The range of envisioned future states depends on the agent's knowledge of the linkage environment. Thus, an agent who knows more about existing sites and links can generate more future options and hence has a wider choice of possible goals.

If a plan that has to be executed to achieve a goal involves others' actions, communication processes are initiated to persuade the respective actions to contribute to the plan. Likewise, the agent itself might be asked to participate in a joint plan, and LIESON agents are implemented in a way that forces them to at least consider cooperating with others. This limits motivational autonomy in a sense since it forces agents to treat potential future states suggested by other agents the same way as they would had they "thought" of these possible goals themselves. However, this is not too severe a limitation, since agreement to adopt such a goal still ultimately depends on whether it serves the private goals of the agents. But at least, he will have to deal with the suggestion, which may delay other decision-making steps.

Control — external deliberative autonomy: From an external point of view, self-motivation is self-control, and loosing the autonomy of which goals to choose is perceived (if it is perceived at all) in the form of an external control. The crucial difference to dependency is that dependency need not be "realized", just the statement of a relationship between several entities. Control, on the other hand, must be *exerted* to become visible. Of course, the two notions are connected, though, since larger dependency can lead to higher controllability. Note, however, that these two kinds of autonomy need not be unidirectional: From a dependency point of view, a manager is often more dependent on his staff than the other way round, if we measure dependence by "the number of people that have to support you" (in a simplified world, the manager needs the support of the majority of the staff, while each staff member needs only the manager's support). On the other hand, the staff exerts much less control on the manager than the other way round, because they are (more or less) following his instructions (and the background of company objectives/culture) in making decisions, while he is supposed to make decisions himself.

The central concepts here are *power* [5], *opponent modeling* [4], and *regulation* of behavior.

Example. In LIESON, the utility function that agents use to project the expected payoff of a possible future linkage situation is contingent on the current linkage situation (or, to be more precise, on agents' incomplete and possibly incorrect knowledge thereof). So if, for example, an agent with high popularity influences the utility values of others to a great degree, he has implicit power in the agent society, since his actions will entail a series of reactions on the side of "weaker" agents via changes to their utility scores. Note that this kind of control is different from (performative) dependencies, because the powerful agent affects the way in which agents select their *goals* rather than their capabilities to perform actions: Agents still have the same action repertoire, but the set of actions that they consider *relevant* has changed.

From an external perspective, the autonomy restriction imposed on agents by the obligation to process others' requests is not observable. However, external observers can verify whether actions that have been requested of an agent are actually performed by that agent. So (although this need not hold in LIESON in general) situations may occur in which agents obey others' "commands" with such regularity that a relationship of control manifests itself.

Commitment — internal normative autonomy: For an autonomous entity to exhibit a certain behavior that is not arbitrary with respect to its capabilities, it must *commit* itself to doing something particular. Thus, from the internal viewpoint, it sees its autonomy (possibly only temporarily) constrained by commitments it makes. The simplest kind of such commitments are intentions [11], which simply "shift" certain actions from the core reasoning components to the environment, so that they almost become part of the environment themselves (they will be executed without further reasoning, unless intention revision — which can be seen as an almost "external" interaction with those intentions — makes them undone). Much more interesting, however, are *social commitments* [6,37,38], which stem from interaction with others and constrain this kind of autonomy. It is important to note that these (internal) commitments are very different from the societal view of commitments because they only infringe autonomy if *adopted* by the individual [10,12].

Frequently used concepts of this category are *(dis)obedience*, *submission*, and *benevolence*.

Example. We observe both social and non-social commitment-relevant autonomy restrictions in LIESON.

The main social autonomy restriction is that agents have to adhere to a set of pre-defined communication patterns during inter-agent dialogues. Therefore, once they choose a "path" in the set of possible response strategies, they commit themselves to the restrictions imposed by the hard-coded patterns. So, for example, if they agree to execute an action they actually internally commit to executing it. However, they are able to learn from experience which of the given patterns to apply in a given situation in a strategic (i.e., utility-maximizing) way. This ensures that such social commitments are not generated if they contradict the agent's private interests, and, in fact compensates them for the above loss of utility by providing a mechanism of choice at the next level.

At the non-social level, agents commit to the goals they have selected, and will maintain these goals unless they have been achieved or become inachievable. This commitment is different from a motivation, because it does not *spawn* a certain kind of activity. Instead, it serves to *maintain* such activity without further rational, goal-oriented reasoning.

Expectation — external normative autonomy: The final category is that of *expectations*. Expectations are formed externally and concern interaction of the agent with its environment. They are normative in the sense that they express the rights, duties, obligations an agent is subject to, and possibly also the sanctions it has to face if it breaks these expectations. However, such expectations need not be *a priori* deontic claims made by the designer of the system, a social system, etc. They can also express the "image" of an agent that has been formed through its past behavior by expecting a similar behavior from it in the future [3].

Typical concepts in this category are *norm, convention* [13, 20], role [22, 32], *obligation* [37], *institution* [1, 15], and social order [8, 14].

Example. For this last category, the internal commitments of agents do not matter, since they cannot be observed. Still, we can infer the existence of expectations in LIESON from the fact that when agents plan their strategic communication behavior, they employ decision-theoretic utility maximization over the set of admissible continuations of the dialogue. This is only possible because they can expect the agent to adhere to the given protocols. For example, if there are only three alternative responses A, B and C that the other agent can use and probabilities for these have been derived from previous experience, the expected utility of the whole conversation can be easily computed. If, on the other hand, the other agent were allowed to produce *any* reply, the utility calculation would be very imprecise.

Additionally, the fact that the agents use previous experience to infer the future behavior of other constitutes an expectation-based strategy by itself: Each agent expects that others will behave in a similar way in the future as they did in the past.

3.6. *A pattern for autonomy status descriptions*

Based on the six types of autonomy, we can present a semi-formal pattern for *autonomy status descriptions* that specify the autonomy situation of an agent (at this point, we do not deal with groups of agents but only with single agents — most of the concepts carry over, however, if groups are viewed as collective actors):

> Component A is T-autonomous with respect to the influence of B in context C from the perspective of an observer O because it acts according to model M' rather than according to the model M that O expected.

A set of such status descriptions characterizes which autonomy situation A is in.
  For example, saying that

> *Agent 1* is control-autonomous with respect to the influence of *Agent 4* in the context of *adding a link from Agent 1 to Agent 2* from the perspective of *Agent 4* because it *adds the link to Agent 2 regardless of Agent 4's plea to refrain from this action*

allows us to make a rather precise statement regarding a specific type of autonomy in the behavior of a particular LIESON agent.

It is important to note that this kind of description focuses on the relationship between *autonomy* and *determination*, i.e., that autonomy is always identified by observing a deviation from a behavior that would have resulted from adhering to some assumed model. In other words, M is an assumption regarding the factors B that determine A's behavior in situation C, and after observing the actual behavior of A (either from the inside or from the outside), we have to overthrow M in favor of some different model M'. In the following sections, we will turn to the dynamic nature of autonomy, where this modeling activity plays an important role in reasoning about autonomy in a complex system composed of autonomous software artefacts.

4. A Dynamic View of Software Autonomy — The Autonomy transformation loop

Specifying autonomy with the above categories helps to define precisely the capabilities, motivations and social comportment of an autonomous software component with respect to a particular environment (that may contain other such components). In particular, the autonomy of an entity is always a relative notion that refers to a second entity: Whenever there is a lack of *auto*nomy, there must be *hetero*nomy, i.e., someone else must "hold" the autonomy that the first component lacks. Such autonomy specifications provide a rather *structural* specification a system that is made up of several autonomous components, a "snapshot" of who can, wants and has committed himself to doing what at some specific point in time. What is amiss is a *dynamic* view that explains how autonomy owned by a computational entity such as a software system evolves, that is, how it transformed from one status into another.

4.1. *Transformation through interaction and communication*

From the work on adjustable computational autonomy, it is known that *interaction* is an essential process that can change the status of autonomy. This implies that there is a basic feedback loop between autonomy and interaction, as shown in Fig. 1. Here, the concept of interaction is understood in the most encompassing sense, i.e., as interaction with the environment, the user, the designer, etc. The general intuition is that while interaction is unfolding, the range of possible behaviors undergoes constant changes. For example, when LIESON agents explore the environment, they may discover a new site which alters their *capability* repertoire since new linkage actions become relevant. At the same time, their link configurations may change because of the actions of others, so that different *goals* appear promising or achievable, while others may have to be disregarded. Or, a promise to maintain a link to someone else may have caused a *commitment* that they must now be held or at least considered. From an external point of view, the changes in the above example may result in autonomy status changes, depending on who is observing the respective autonomous entity and how he is modeling it.

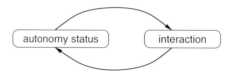

Fig. 1.   Basic autonomy transformation loop.

Looking at the process of autonomy transformation through interaction more closely, the simple feedback loop of Fig. 1 can be further refined, if we make the assumption that the observer or participating agent is *reasoning about autonomy* himself (i.e., the interesting case). Under this assumption, the *decision-making* process of interacting parties is preceded by *modeling* and *decision-making* processes that take the autonomy status into account.

Modeling autonomy consists of identifying dependencies, analyzing the distribution of resources and the control flow between components and possibly also building models of others' modeling processes.

This modeling activity only makes sense if it has the potential to influence the decision-making process of the actor. Of course, decision-making procedures also depend on other aspects such as objectives, general domain knowledge, etc. The less predictable the behaviors of other parts of the system are, the more important the aspect of autonomy becomes.

As shown in Fig. 2, *communication* plays a special role in mediating between modeling and decision making. This insight follows as a natural consequence once we discriminate between "physical" actions that can be taken and which modify the environment and purely communicative action. This is because communication allows for obtaining information about the current autonomy status before making decisions. This information feeds into the autonomy modeling processes of interacting parties, and, even more importantly, it can be used to anticipate and plan future autonomy configurations in a system. For example, if a component is informed of something that contradicts prior belief and decides to revise its belief, it is increasing its dependency on the knowledge of the informer. The informer, on the other hand, is submitting himself to the expectation that he tells the truth, and unless he states something like "I am not sure" or "I say X but won't be held responsible if it is not accurate" he implicitly agrees to be labeled as "liar" if others find out he did not tell the truth. In other words, he is restricting his own normative autonomy by committing himself to truthfulness. As another example, consider a boss who is

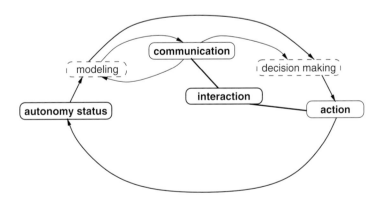

Fig. 2.   Extended autonomy transformation loop.

assigning a task to his employee and tells him "if you can't cope with this, you're fired". Through this statement, he is increasing the employee's dependency on him by threatening with loss of employment (rather than just with criticism or conflict). At the same time, delegation of the task restricts the deliberative autonomy of the employee; he must now "want" to complete the task more than anything else (at least at his workplace). If the boss also says, "Smith and Miller are going to help you in this, they are at your command", he is increasing the employee's performative autonomy, because the employee is endowed with additional resources that may increase his productivity.

It is the capacity of allowing autonomous entities to predict future autonomy states that makes communication highly suitable for *coordinating* future behaviors. In a way, engaging in communication means seeking to reduce the contingencies inherent to the behavior of other autonomous components in the system.

4.2. *Examples of autonomy transformation*

Theoretically, any interaction can increase or decrease any of the six autonomy types in our autonomy matrix at the same time. Usually, though, interactions hardly affect more than two autonomy range types at the same time, and the effects are analyzed from both an internal and an external perspective at the same time.

Let us look at some examples in the LIESON application domain, where we are going to discuss how the autonomy status of certain parts of a system can be influenced, viewed from three perspectives: (1) the designer of the overall system, (2) a human user that is using a LIESON agent to manage linkage from and to his Web site, and (3) a LIESON agent seeking to maximize the dissemination of his opinion. In these examples, we are going to mark each autonomy transformation by a combination of pairs of letters (e.g. **pi** for performative-internal (capability), **ne** for normative-external (expectation), etc.) and a + or − symbol for increase and decrease in the respective autonomy type, respectively (such that, for example, +**pi**−**ne** stands for "increase in capabilities, increase in others' expectations (decrease in "expectation-related autonomy")"). If different aspects of a single autonomy category are affected by a transformation (or if we want to express the autonomy changes of different parties at the same time), of course, this would have to be accounted for by using a more elaborate syntax.

System designer perspective: The system designer has access to the internals of the agent design, so that he can, in theory, explain whatever is happening in the deployed system, if he is given information about the preferences of the human users, and if we assume that these users would not manipulate the code of the LIESON application.

So, for example, if the designer knows the knowledge base contents of a LIESON agent, he can derive the capabilities of this agent, and the transformations +**pi** and −**pi** that occur when an agent obtains new information about sites or links (knowing the internal design, **pi** autonomy is identical to **pe** autonomy). However, the motivation of agents, although in principle regulated by a specific goal prioritization scheme, is not entirely predictable. This is because agents randomly generate possible future linkage states in each round that they will consider in determining their goals. Here, the random generator is a source of uncertainty, so that the designer cannot tell whether a new, interesting alternative has been found in a specific reasoning iteration that would modify (+**di**/−**di**) the agents autonomy in choosing a goal. However, the designer may certain +**de** and −**de** changes, e.g. when a new site is created that makes it theoretically possible for the agent to have optimal linkage with this site as a goal or when that site disappears again. As for normative autonomy, the designer knows that, by its design, the agent can only use the prescribed communication protocols, which implies that other agents can expect it to answer in a fairly predictable way. So if the designer observes, for example, that the agent is committing himself a certain linkage action in the process of communication, this reduces both its internal and external normative autonomy (−**ni**−**ne**).

As a final example, let us assume the designer is observing the system in operation and finds out that agents are acting in an overtly aggressive and deceptive fashion, so that linkage is highly sub-optimal from a global perspective. In the system as it is, the only measures the designer could take would be to re-implement the system or to insert additional agents into the running system that are programmed in a more cooperative fashion in the hope that LIESON agents (who are adaptive in the sense that they learn from communication experience) would adopt the more cooperative interaction behavior exhibited by new, "friendly" agents.

This nicely illustrates the potential dangers associated with autonomous systems, and the importance of taking appropriate precautions at design time.

Human user perspective: Typically, a human Web site owner is only given a rough description of the internal design of his LIESON agent, i.e., he knows something about the general reasoning and communication mechanisms employed by the agent but not much about the details of goal prioritization, communication learning, future utility estimation etc.

For the human user, agent autonomy is largely dependent on the feedback the user provides regarding his preferences over others' Web sites. The more complex the preference profile, the fewer profitable future link constellations will the LIESON agent be able to identify, and the smaller will his goal repertoire be (−**di**), but not knowing the internal design of the agent, it is questionable whether the user would be aware of a corresponding −**de** transformation.

Also, the human user has the ability to inspect the linkage network himself, so he will notice −**de** and −**ne** changes in his agent's autonomy caused by some other agent becoming very powerful, once these transformations become manifest in agent's actions (e.g. striving to obtain a link from the powerful site or obeying the requests of this powerful site).

Obviously, the human designer is also able to check what the action options of his agent are, i.e., $+$**pe** and $-$**pe** changes can also be observed, although they need not coincide with the respective $+$**pi** and $-$**pi** transformations, because the agent may have incomplete and/or incorrect knowledge of the network.

LIESON agent perspective: From an autonomy standpoint, an agent is only an external observer of another agent, so most of the above observations are carried over to agent observers. What is really interesting from an agent perspective are transformations that concern normative autonomy and that are caused by communication. In fact, it is *only* by communicating that agents can influence each other's autonomy status deliberately, as they do not have direct access to the capabilities and motivations of others.

Depending on the nature of the communication protocols that are used and on the physical action consequences that result from them, there exists a variety of possible autonomy transformations. Examples include:

- A promise to execute some action or a complex series of actions in the context of a distributed plan. This causes the expectation ($-$**ne**) that the agent will adhere to the promise, unless the promise is cancelled. On the side of the *debtor* of this commitment, such a promise constitutes an increase in capability ($+$**pi**), since the agent is capable of evoking an action he cannot perform itself.
- A reciprocal long-term agreement, for example, making a contract to pay a fixed amount of money every month to "rent" an ingoing link from someone else. The agent who is "renting" the link is loosing the capability of disposing of a certain amount of money, while he gains the possibility of achieving goals with a higher utility, and he is expected to make regular payments ($-$**pi** $+$ **di**$-$**ne**).
- A threat to sanction a certain behavior of the other. This imposes normative expectations (to refrain from the behavior and to implement the sanction, respectively) on both sides, but, if successful, the threatening agent will have a larger autonomy in predicting future states of the linkage network, as it can rule out certain behaviors of others ($-$**pi**$-$**ne**).

These examples nicely illustrate that a thorough planning of the communication and social reasoning functionality is essential in the process of designing distributed systems that are able to handle autonomy issues effectively.

5. Conclusion

Since its inception in the 1960s, software engineering has targeted at the development of software whose functionality and structure is, directly or indirectly (via other software entities), under full control of its users and administrators. With the advent of autonomous software, this situation changes fundamentally: Taking autonomy as a software property seriously means to hand action choice and invocation control over to the software itself. In the ultimate vision, autonomous software is able to take on any responsibility needed for the successfully running of an application under self-control and, thus, to fully hide its complexity and the complexity of its environment from users and administrators. This obviously is a long-term vision, although today software products (especially in the area of data and server management, see e.g. [19]) and research results (especially in the area of agent and multiagent technology, see e.g. [24, 29] and the two recent collections [17, 30]) are already available which indicate that this vision is much closer to reality than skeptics might think. We envisage that over the years software systems will appear which exhibit increasing levels of autonomy. This is not to say that autonomy orientation will replace other software models such as object orientation and component orientation; what autonomy orientation does is to provide a qualitatively new level of abstraction on top of existing models.

In the light of the state of the art in developing autonomous software, currently the most urgent issue is to provide developers with engineering techniques — methods, formalisms, tools, and so forth — which enable them to appropriately tailor the type and extent of autonomy a software system should own. Thereby "appropriately" means that software autonomy is neither unnecessarily cut down (as this would result in software being not remarkably distinct from traditional software), nor unnecessarily admitted (as this would result in an increased risk of undesirable or even chaotic system behavior). To tailor software autonomy appropriately without any supportive techniques is a highly complicated task even in the case of relatively simple applications such as LIESON (the LIESON case studies provided throughout this chapter prove this). The specification framework introduced in this chapter can serve as a guideline for devising such techniques. In particular, the framework presented in this chapter shows that it is possible to break down the abstract notion of autonomy into a set of concepts such as dependency and expectation which are sufficiently concrete to be processable at the level of software engineering. Once such techniques are available, other important questions can be addressed precisely, for instance: How to identify the need for autonomous software in a particular application? How to validate and verify autonomy as a software property? How to make sure that software adapts its autonomous behavior appropriately during run time? Questions like these require considerable research efforts to be answered, but these efforts are worthwhile in the light of the tremendous benefits autonomous software offers.

References

1. W. Balzer and R. Tuomela, "Social institutions, norms, and practices", eds. R. Conte and C. Dellarocas, *Social Order in Multiagent Systems* (Kluwer Academic Publishers, Norwell, MA, Amsterdam, The Netherlands, 2001) 161–180.
2. J. M. Bradshaw *et al*, "Adjustable autonomy and human-agent teamwork in practice: An interim report on space applications", eds. H. Hexmoor, C. Castelfranchi and R. Falcone, *Agent Autonomy* (Kluwer Academic Publishers, 2003) 243–280.

3. W. Brauer, M. Nickles, M. Rovatsos, G. Weiß and K. F. Lorentzen, "Expectation-oriented analysis and design", *Proceedings of the 2nd Workshop on Agent-Oriented Software Engineering (AOSE-2001) at the Autonomous Agents 2001 Conference, Lecture Notes in Artificial Intelligence 2222*, Montreal, Canada (Springer-Verlag, Berlin, 29 May 2001).

4. D. Carmel and S. Markovitch, "Learning models of intelligent agents", *Thirteenth National Conference on Artificial Intelligence* (AAAI Press/The MIT Press, CA, 1996) 62–67.

5. C. Castelfranchi, "Social power. A point missed in multi-agent, DAI and HCI", eds. Y. Demazeau and J. P. Muller, *Decentralized A.I.* (Elsevier Science Publishers, 1990) 49–62.

6. C. Castelfranchi, "Commitments: From individual intentions to groups and organizations", *Proceedings of the First International Conference on Multi-Agent Systems (ICMAS-95)* (1995) 41–48.

7. C. Castelfranchi, "Guarantees for autonomy in cognitive agent architecture", eds. M. J. Wooldridge and N. R. Jennings, *Intelligent Agents: Proceedings of the First International Workshop on Agent Theories, Architectures and Languages (ATAL-94)* (Springer-Verlag, 1995) 56–70.

8. C. Castelfranchi, "Engineering social order", *Working Notes of the First International Workshop on Engineering Societies in the Agents' World (ESAW-00)*, 2000.

9. C. Castelfranchi, "Founding agent's "Autonomy" on dependence theory", *Proceedings of the 14th European Conference on Artificial Intelligence (ECAI-2000)* (2000) 353–357.

10. C. Castelfranchi, F. Dignum, C. M. Jonker and J. Treur, "Deliberate normative agents: Principles and architecture", *Proceedings of the Sixth International Workshop on Agent Theories, Architectures, and Languages (ATAL-99)*, Orlando, FL, 1999.

11. P. R. Cohen and H. J. Levesque, "Intention is choice with commitment", *Artificial Intelligence* **42** (1990) 213–261.

12. P. R. Cohen and H. J. Levesque, "Teamwork", *Noûs* **35** (1991) 487–512.

13. R. Conte and C. Castelfranchi, "From conventions to prescriptions: Toward an integrated theory of norms", *Proceedings of the ModelAge-96 Workshop*, Sesimbra, Italy, January 1996.

14. R. Conte and C. Dellarocas (eds.), *Social Order in Multiagent Systems* (Kluwer Academic Publishers, Norwell, MA, Amsterdam, The Netherlands, 2001).

15. S. E. S. Crawford and E. Ostrom, "A grammar of institutions", *American Political Science Review* **89**(3) (1995) 582–599.

16. Hewlett-Packard. Adaptive enterprise initiative, 2003, *http://www.hp.com/large/globalsolutions/ai.html?jumpid=go/adaptive*.

17. H. Hexmoor, C. Castelfranchi and R. Falcone (eds.), "Agent autonomy", *Series on Multiagent Systems, Artificial Societies, and Simulated Organizations (MASA) 7* (Kluwer Academic Publishers, Boston, 2003).

18. M. N. Huhns and M. P. Singh (eds.), *Readings in Agents* (Morgan Kaufmann, San Francisco, CA, 1998).

19. ICAC-2004, *First International Conference on Autonomic Computing*, 2004, *http://www.autonomic-conference.org/*.

20. N. R. Jennings, "Commitments and conventions: The foundation of coordination in multi-agent systems", *The Knowledge Engineering Review* **8**(3) (1993) 223–250.

21. N. R. Jennings, "On agent-based software engineering", *Artificial Intelligence* **117** (2000) 277–296.

22. E. A. Kendall, "Agent roles and role models: New abstractions for multiagent system analysis and design", *International Workshop on Intelligent Agents in Information and Process Management*, 1998.

23. M. Luck, R. Ashri and M. D'Inverno, *Agent-based Software Development* (Artech House, Inc, Norwood, MA, 2004).

24. M. Luck and M. d'Inverno, "A formal framework for agency and autonomy", *Proceedings of the First International Conference on Multi-Agent Systems (ICMAS-95)* (1995) 254–260.

25. T. Malone and K. Crowston, "The interdisciplinary study of coordination", *ACM Computing Surveys* **26**(1) (1994) 87–119.

26. J. McCarthy, "Ascribing mental qualities to machines", ed. V. Lifschitz, *Formalizing Common Sense: Papers by John McCarthy* (Ablex Publishing Corporation, Norwood, NJ, 1990).

27. Microsoft. Dynamic systems initiative, 2003, *http://www.microsoft.com/presspass/press/2003/mar03/03-18dynamicsystemspr.asp*.

28. A. Newell, "The knowledge level", *Artificial Intelligence* **18**(1), 1982.

29. M. Nickles, M. Rovatsos and G. Weiß, "A schema for specifying computational autonomy", *Proceedings of the Third International Workshop on Engineering Societies in the Agents' World (ESAW-02), Lecture Notes in Computer Science 2577* (Springer-Verlag, 2002) 82–95.

30. M. Nickles, M. Rovatsos and G. Weiss (eds.), *"Agents and Computational Autonomy", Lecture Notes in Computer Science 2969* (Hot Topics Subseries) (Springer-Verlag, Berlin, Germany, 2004).

31. H. S. Nwana, "Software agents: An overview", *The Knowledge Engineering Review* **11**(3) (1996) 205–244.

32. O. Pacheco and J. Carmo, "A role based model for the normative specification of organized collective agency and agents interaction", *Journal of Autonomous Agents and Multi-Agent Systems* **6**(2) (2003) 145–184.

33. A. S. Rao and M. P. Georgeff, "An abstract architecture for rational agents", eds. W. Swartout C. Rich and B. Nebel, *Proceedings of Knowledge Represenation and Reasoning (KR&R-92)*, 1992.

34. IBM Research, Autonomic computing, 2003, *http://www.research.ibm.com/autonomic/*.

35. M. Rovatsos, LIESON — User's Manual and Developer's Guide, 2002–2004, *http://www7.in.tum.de/~rovatsos/lieson/users-manual.pdf*.

36. M. Rovatsos, G. Weiß and M. Wolf, "An approach to the analysis and design of multi-agent systems based on interaction frames", eds. M. Gini, T. Ishida, C. Castelfranchi and W. L. Johnson, *Proceedings of the First International Joint Conference on Autonomous Agents and Multiagent Systems (AAMAS-02)*, Bologna, Italy (ACM Press, 2002).

37. M. P. Singh, "Multiagent systems as spheres of commitment", *ICMAS-96 Workshop on Norms, Obligations, and Conventions*, 1996.

38. M. P. Singh, "An ontology for commitments in multiagent systems: Toward a unification of normative concepts", *Artificial Intelligence and Law* **7** (1999) 97–113.

39. Sun, N1 initiative, 2003, *http://www.sun.com/software/solutions/n1/index.html*.

40. G. Weiß (ed.), *Multiagent Systems. A Modern Approach to Distributed Artificial Intelligence* (The MIT Press, Cambridge, MA, 1999).

41. G. Weiß, "Agent orientation in software engineering", *Knowledge Engineering Review* **16**(4) (2002) 349–373.

42. M. J. Wooldridge (ed.), *Reasoning About Rational Agents* (The MIT Press, Cambridge, MA, 2000).
43. M. J. Wooldridge, *An Introduction to Multiagent Systems* (John Wiley & Sons Ltd, Baffins Lane, 2002).
44. M. J. Wooldridge and N. R. Jennings, "Agent theories, architectures, and languages: A survey", eds. M. J. Wooldridge and N. R. Jennings, *Intelligent Agents, Lecture Notes in Artificial Intelligence 890* (Springer-Verlag, Berlin, 1995) 1–39.

CAPABILITY MATURITY FOR SOFTWARE DEVELOPMENT

ALFS T. BERZTISS

Department of Computer Science, University of Pittsburgh
Pittsburgh, PA 15260, USA
E-mail: alpha@cs.pitt.edu

Software development should be a disciplined activity, which means that it is to be driven by well-defined processes. An organization that is to be effective in defining such processes must acquire certain capabilities, and, as it acquires the capabilities, the organization becomes more mature. Capability models define the capabilities and assign them to capability levels. This chapter centers on the Software Capability Maturity Model (SW–CMM) and Capability Maturity Model Integration (CMMI), developed by the Software Engineering Institute. Inspired by the SW–CMM, specialized capability models have been developed for individual parts of the software process and specific application domains. Two such models, for requirements engineering and information systems development, are examined in some detail.

Keywords: SW–CMM, CMMI, capability, software process, requirements engineering, information system, agile programming.

1. Introduction

Software is performing ever more complex tasks, and software systems have become increasingly large. Effective development of such systems requires highly developed management and engineering capabilities. Here our primary concern will be with efforts that have led to the identification of such capabilities, and with suggestions of how capability maturity is to be acquired in an organized manner. In other words, we shall examine capability maturity models, abbreviated to CMMs. Of particular importance is a generic software development process from which specialized development processes can be derived. Although we shall not define such a process here, it will be an implicit focus for what follows. It has to be realized that having a generic process is not enough. Such a process can be a valuable resource for an organization, but only if there are additional resources and capabilities that allow effective use to be made of the process. Moreover, the generic process itself will have to be modified as experience in its use is gained.

We note that in the software development domain there are five kinds of processes, and that they need to be clearly distinguished. The first is a process that introduces the development process into an organization. This process is a management responsibility. Second is the generic development process. Third, an adaptation process is needed to transform the generic process into a process that responds to the specialized needs of an application. Fourth is this specialization. Finally, we

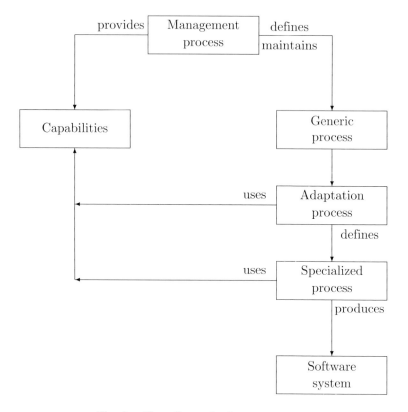

Fig. 1. The software development process.

have the target software systems which implement applications that are themselves processes. Our interest will not be in the processes as such, but in the capabilities that an organization is to possess to support this five-process structure.

Figure 1 shows the processes and how they are related: There is the generic process, its specializations, and the adaptation phase that converts the generic process into a specialization based on the requirements for the specific software system to be developed. The management process is responsible for creating and maintaining the generic process and the adaptation process, and for providing capabilities. The capabilities support the adaptation phase and operation of the specialized software processes. They also assist in maintenance of the generic software development process and the adaptation process.

To illustrate the relationship between the general and specialized processes, consider fulfillment of purchase orders. Three of the special features of this application are (i) interaction with customers and suppliers, (ii) the fact that inventory shortages can stretch out an instance of the process over a considerable time period, and (iii) that the process involves warehouses that can be far from the office that manages order fulfillment. The generic process has to be transformed into a specialized development process that makes allowance for these features. Further specialized features that may have to be taken into account are the use of existing components, with or without modification, and the geographic distribution of the development and testing teams.

In the early 1980s, software development was generally a rather haphazard activity characterized by crises caused by cost and schedule overruns. Total project failures were frequent. Watts Humphrey realized that the software process had to become a disciplined activity. In [1], he defined five levels of achievement. They constitute a standard against which an organization can measure its capabilities. More importantly, they encourage an organization to improve its capabilities and thus advance upward through the level structure. The Software Engineering Institute (SEI) took these levels as the basis for a Software Capability Maturity Model, abbreviated to SW–CMM.

Section 2 provides motivation for SW–CMM, and gives a brief outline of it. Its level structure is examined in some detail in Sec. 3, and Sec. 4 gives some indication of what distinguishes organizations that have reached the upper levels of SW–CMM. Additional capability models developed at SEI and alternatives to SW–CMM are looked at in Sec. 5. The new Capability Maturity Model Integration (CMMI) concept is introduced in Sec. 6, and in Sec. 7, we look at two components of this model in some detail. The SW–CMM has been used as a framework for capability models for some rather specialized activities. Such models are examined in Sec. 8. Section 9 is mainly a rebuttal of criticisms of SW–CMM. Some of the criticisms deal with appraisals, i.e., the determination of the level on which an organization finds itself. In Sec. 10, we look at what direction capability models can be expected to take in the future.

We are not providing an exhaustive bibliography. Our references are not even extensive. Instead we point to a good collection of references in "A Software Process Bibliography". It is available online at

www.sei.cmu.edu/activities/cmm/docs/ biblio.pdf

Two chapters of Volume 1 of this handbook already contain some material on SW–CMM [2,3]. Our contribution is a more detailed description of SW–CMM, an introduction to CMMI, and a demonstration of how the structure of SW–CMM can be adapted for specialized activities.

2. What is SW–CMM?

The initial stimulus for the SW–CMM (initially called just CMM) came in the late 1980s. The United States military services were in need of guidance in the selection of software contractors, and SEI was asked to develop a model that would allow the capabilities of potential contractors to be evaluated. The first draft of SW–CMM was released in March 1990. Public release as an SEI report followed in February 1993, and SW–CMM was published as a book in 1995 [4]. An update had been planned, but this effort lost support of its sponsors. Instead, in August 2002, SEI released a document defining a new concept, Capability Maturity Model Integration (CMMI) [5]. This we shall look at in Secs. 6 and 7. The SW–CMM is being phased out, with CMMI becoming its replacement.

A CMM serves several purposes. First and foremost, it identifies strengths and weaknesses in an organization. In this, special attention is to be given to process and product quality. Second, it provides management with a well-defined plan for improvement. Third, by advancing to higher maturity levels, an organization can fulfill its purposes much more efficiently, which translates into higher profitability. In the SW–CMM context an organization is not necessarily an entire enterprise. In a company it can be any unit that undertakes software projects, and it is not unusual that different units of the same company are on different maturity levels.

The SW–CMM has three guiding principles. First, the success of software projects depends primarily on a sound management structure. Therefore, initial emphasis in trying to improve software development should be on management issues. Second, the software development process for a specific project is to be adapted from a generic process, along the lines of Fig. 1. Third, as its name shows, it is concerned with the capabilities needed by an organization to support a process rather than with the internal structure of such a process. Note that the SW–CMM interpretation of "capability" differs somewhat from that taken here — there software process capability is taken to describe the range of expected results that can be achieved by following a software process. We take a capability to be any method, tool, or piece of knowledge that supports software development. Of course, these capabilities will affect the range of expected results achieved by the process.

The SW–CMM has a level structure, and there are five levels. Level 1 is the ground level, and an organization moves upward from this level by satisfying well-defined requirements expressed as Key Process Areas (KPAs). Nothing needs to be done to be on Level 1 of SW–CMM. This "initial" level is merely a starting point. There are some organizations on Level 1 that are doing quite well, but their success is based on efforts of outstanding individuals. Collapse is likely if these individuals were to leave the organization. The SW–CMM aims at institutionalizing good practices so that the success of an organization no longer depends on the brilliance of exceptional developers, but on the competence of the entire workforce.

Level 2 is called "repeatable". There is tracking of costs and schedule, and requirements are being traced, i.e., management checks that all software products are consistent with their requirements. An organization should be able to predict cost and schedule for projects similar to those it has completed earlier. In terms of Fig. 1, a Level 2 organization is unlikely to have a generic software process, and, if it has, is unlikely to know how to use it in cost and schedule estimation.

A Level 3 organization has a "defined" process. Now a generic process is in place, the ability exists to transform it into a specialized process, and dependable cost and schedule estimates can be made for a variety of projects. Good practices have become institutionalized, which means that both management and engineering practices are documented, that the existence of the documentation is well known throughout the organization, and that the documents are readily accessible. This is knowledge management applied to software development (on knowledge management refer to, for example [6,7]).

Level 4 is "managed". To reach this level the organization must have maintained a process and project database over a number of years. A Level 4 organization knows what to do with these data: There is a quantitative understanding of the data, and the understanding is used in effective control of the process structure of Fig. 1. On reaching the "optimizing" Level 5 an organization has to be able to improve the generic process and the adaptation process of Fig. 1 on the basis of past experience. In addition it must follow developments in software engineering. For example, there is continuing discussion of what form peer reviews should take to be most effective [8]. A Level 5 organization may perform experiments on its own to determine the form that best suits its needs.

As a general characterization, Levels 2 and 3 deal primarily with management and project aspects, Levels 4 and 5 with engineering and process aspects. It seems that the hardest transitions are to Levels 2 and 4. In order to reach Level 2, an organization has to adopt a process-oriented attitude, which may meet with resistance from some managers, resulting in inadequate resources being allocated to the improvement effort. To reach Level 4, an organization must have collected project and process data, which necessarily takes at least two to three years. Moreover, it has to make good use of the data. This requires competence in statistics, but such competence cannot be acquired overnight.

In the next section we shall look at the SW–CMM in some detail. If, as noted earlier, SW–CMM is to be phased out, why are we still concerned with it? First, CMMI is not finalized. For example, three areas for Level 3 of the software oriented CMMI (CMMI–SW, Staged Version) seem to have been added as an afterthought in [5], but the table of contents has not been modified to reflect this. Moreover, the Continuous Version, which should have the same process areas as the Staged Version (see p.17 of [5]) does not even contain them. Second, since the form and structure of SW–CMM is simpler than that of CMMI, it may help to use the former as preparation for a study of the latter. Bamberger, who participated in the development of SW–CMM has written "I am finding that the CMM is one of the most misunderstood pieces of technical literature in existence" [9]. The potential for misunderstanding is higher for CMMI. Our purpose is to advocate strongly the concept of capability modeling without being greatly concerned with the details. A simpler model better serves this purpose. Third, there exists considerable literature that expounds and evaluates SW–CMM, and documents experience with this model. Indeed, fairly recent publications still relate to SW–CMM (see, e.g. [10,11]). Nothing comparable exists for CMMI. Fourth, the structure of SW–CMM has been used to support capability models for diverse specialized areas. Of course, it will be possible to make use of CMMI in the same way, but this has not happened yet.

We feel that these reasons justify our preference for the SW–CMM. But benefits can certainly be gained from CMMI, and we are not disregarding it. Most importantly, CMMI integrates software engineering with systems engineering. This can significantly reduce cost and development time for embedded and distributed systems where far too often hardware and software developers are hardly aware of each other's needs, and tend to make changes to their side of a product without informing the other side. This should not happen if sufficient attention were given to Intergroup Coordination (a Level 3 KPA of SW–CMM), but an explicit integration of software engineering and systems engineering emphasizes to a greater extent their interdependence. As a minor, but still important matter, if SW–CMM had been updated, which had been the intention at SEI, Software Subcontractor Management, a Level 2 KPA, would have included consideration of COTS (Commercial Off-The-Shelf) software [12]. Instead, this is now part of Supplier Agreement Management in CMMI. Attention to other aspects of software development that have gained importance comparatively recently can be found throughout CMMI.

3. Components of the SW–CMM

As noted in the preceding section, SW–CMM has five maturity levels. Each maturity level is defined in terms of Key Process Areas (KPAs). Each KPA has a number of goals it is to achieve, and a list of activities that are to be performed to achieve the goals. In addition, there is a "commitment to perform", which is essentially a policy statement committing the organization to the satisfaction of these goals, and an "ability to perform" statement, which lists the resources that have to be allocated. Unfortunately, there elements make [4] rather boring to read. To take just one example, under "ability to perform" you can read eighteen times, once for each KPA, that "Adequate resources and funding are provided for (whatever the KPA relates to)". It should be obvious that if resources and funding are not adequate, where "adequate" has to mean "sufficient to ensure satisfaction of the goals of the particular KPA", then the organization will not satisfy the goals.

For each KPA there is also an indication of what process measurements are to be made, and to what review procedures the activities of the KPA are to be subjected. Both are very important. Gathering and interpreting process measurements is the only objective way of telling what does and what does not work, and for evaluating the precise effect of a particular action. However, as we discuss in Sec. 9, sometimes it may be technically impossible to determine precise cause-effect relations for process activities. The review procedures ensure that the activities of the KPAs are indeed performed.

3.1. *Outlines of Key Process Areas*

We shall give capsule descriptions of all the KPAs, but only one KPA, Requirements Management, will be examined in some detail. Figure 2 provides an overview of the levels of SW–CMM. The labels "Management" and "Engineering" are not to be taken literally. They merely relate to an overall orientation. Level 2 has a very strong management emphasis, but Level 3 deals with both management and engineering.

Management   Engineering

Level 3
Org. process focus
Org. process definition
Training Program
Integrated Management
Product Engineering
Intergroup Coordination
Peer Reviews

Level 5
Defect Prevention
Technology Change
Process Change Management

Level 2
Requirements Management
Project Planning
Tracking and Oversight
Subcontractor Management
Quality Assurance
Configuration Management

Level 4
Quant. Process Management
Quality Management

Fig. 2.   Level structure of the SW–CMM.

Requirements Management (Level 2). This KPA is examined in the next subsection.

Software Project Planning (Level 2). Planning is to be based on a documented organizational policy. The plan is to include cost and schedule estimates, as well as potential risks.

Software Project Tracking and Oversight (Level 2). This KPA is to ensure that actual results and performance agree with the software plan, and, if they do not, corrective actions are to be taken. These actions may include modification of the initial plan.

Software Subcontractor Management (Level 2). With large projects some of the work is subcontracted. Subcontractor selection is to be based on their capabilities. Contractual obligations must be formulated, and there has to be tracking to ensure that these obligations are being satisfied.

Software Quality Assurance (SQA) (Level 2). This KPA requires the setting up of a SQA group whose purpose is to review software engineering activities and audit software work products. The SQA group also verifies that the corrective actions proposed as part of Project Tracking and Oversight are indeed carried out.

Software Configuration Management (SCM) (Level 2). The purpose of SCM is to prevent inconsistencies between different representations of a software product — requirements, architecture, detailed design, code, documentation. Strict control has to be exercised over change requests and problem reports, and for any change made to some representation of a particular version of the product, corresponding changes have to be made to other representations belonging to this version. See [13] for a survey of SCM. (Author's note: Internal consistency is to be ensured for user and maintenance manuals — the table of contents, page and section references, and the index must relate to the current version of a manual.)

Organizational Process Focus (Level 3). Focus means that all software process development and improvement activities become the responsibility of the entire organization.

Organizational Process Definition (Level 3). A standard process (the generic process of Fig. 1) is to be developed and maintained by a software engineering process group. In addition, the group develops process tailoring guidelines (the adaptation process of Fig. 1), and establishes a software process database. The database is essential for the quantitative aspects of the KPAs of Levels 4 and 5.

Training Program (Level 3). Although even a Level 1 organization is likely to give some thought to training, the establishment of a training program ensures that training needs are identified in an organized manner as and when required, and training appropriate to the needs is provided.

Integrated Software Management (ISM) (Level 3). Management activities and engineering activities have to be integrated into a single standard (or generic) software process, and the integration has to extend to the adaptation and specialized processes of Fig. 1.

Software Product Engineering (Level 3). Although ISM seeks to combine management and engineering activities, some activities relate specifically to engineering. For example, risk assessment is an engineering activity, but the determination whether the level of risk justifies continuation of a project is a management decision. Both aspects should be part of an integrated process, but the specialized capabilities required for risk assessment are covered here. Similarly, management defines a test completion criterion based on its view of what is an acceptable risk, but the actual software tests are designed and carried out by software engineers.

Intergroup Coordination (Level 3). A product may consist of more than just software. A determination has to be made as to which functionalities of the product are to be implemented as software, and close cooperation is to be established between the software engineering group and other groups. In particular, critical interfaces between their respective work products need to be identified, and it must be ensured that the total system continues to satisfy the requirements relating to these interfaces.

Peer Reviews (Level 3). The purpose of peer reviews is to remove defects from software work products at an early stage. The products reviewed may be requirements and design documents, code, or user and maintenance manuals. The generic software process itself may have to be subjected to periodic peer reviews. Peer reviews are discussed in [8]; [14] is an extensive survey.

Quantitative Process Management (QPM) (Level 4). Here the purpose is to control quantitatively the performance of the software process used in a software project. This is achieved by measuring process performance, analyzing measurements, and making adjustments that are to keep process performance within acceptable limits. Some of the measurements: Accuracy of initial estimates of software size, cost, and schedule compared to actual data; coverage and efficiency of peer reviews; test efficiency; number and severity of defects found in requirements, design, code, the test plan, and manuals.

Software Quality Management (SQM) (Level 4). Whereas SQA (at Level 2) involves little more than checking that the software project plan is being followed, SQM sets quantitative quality goals for software products. Measurements determine whether the goals are being reached, and these measurements may be used in QPM to adjust the software process so as to improve quality.

Defect Prevention (Level 5). Here the purpose is to classify defects, prioritize the defect classes according to the severity of the defects, identify the causes of the defects, and take appropriate action to prevent the recurrence of the defects.

Technology Change Management (Level 5). New technologies have to be identified, their relevance to the software development process of the organization is to be determined, and, if relevant, they are to be introduced into the software process. The technologies can be classified into tools, methods, and processes. For example, a new tool may automate parts of software configuration management, a new methodological approach may improve the effectiveness of peer reviews, and a process based on agile programming may reduce costs.

Process Change Management (Level 5). Process change management aims at improving software quality, increasing productivity, and decreasing cycle time for product development, This is to be achieved by setting process improvement goals, and being continuously engaged in process improvement.

3.2. *KPA: Requirements management*

We have selected this KPA for more detailed examination so that it can be used as base against which to compare a CMM designed specifically for requirements engineering (see Sec. 8.1). Requirements Management is defined by two goals, a single commitment to perform, four abilities to perform, three activities, a single measurement and analysis component, and three verification statements. The goals are modest: Software requirements are controlled to establish a baseline for engineers and managers, and software plans, products, and activities are kept consistent with the software requirements.

The commitment requires the project to follow a written organizational policy for managing the software requirements. The policy should require documentation of the requirements, and their review by software managers and other affected groups, such as the SQA group and the testers. Whenever the software requirements change, the policy specifies that corresponding changes are to be made to the software plan and the work products under development.

The ability to perform statements are fairly standard for all KPAs. The first statement: For each project, responsibility is established for analyzing the system requirements and allocating them to hardware, software, and other system components. The other abilities: Software requirements are documented, adequate resources and funding are provided, and adequate training is provided.

Now to the activities. First, the software requirements are reviewed before becoming incorporated into the software project. Second, the requirements are to be the basis for software plans, work products, and activities. Third, changes to the software requirements are reviewed and incorporated into the software project.

As regards to measurements, they are to determine the status of the activities for managing the software requirements. An example: Counts are to be maintained of changes to requirements. Author's note: Actually current practice tends to go further; as a change request goes through the stages of being proposed, evaluated (approved or rejected), and, if approved, made part of the requirements, the date on which it reaches each stage is stored in the project database.

Under verification, the requirements management activities are to be reviewed periodically by senior management, and periodically or on an event-driven basis by the manager of the project. The SQA group is to review both activities and work products. This includes review of the requirements, resolution of problems, and determination that appropriate changes have been made in all work products affected by a requirements change.

The attention of SW–CMM to software requirements does not stop here. Activity 2 of Software Product Engineering (Level 3) deals with the development of software requirements. It may be asked why the software requirements should be managed on Level 2 before they have been developed on Level 3. This level assignment is a result of the development philosophy that underlies SW–CMM. Level 2 deals primarily with management issues, and engineering issues begin to be addressed in the KPAs of Level 3. Requirements development is an engineering activity.

A problem with Requirements Management as seen by Barry Boehm [15] is that it does not go far enough. He takes issue with an amplification of its first Ability-to-Perform statement: "Analysis and allocation of the system requirements is not the responsibility of the software engineering group but is a prerequisite for their work." Boehm interprets this as showing strong academic bias — instead of involving software engineers as active participants in the allocation process, software engineers are seen primarily as mere programmers who turn requirements into code. Actually, the KPA does provide for interaction between software engineers and system engineers, but this interaction occurs after allocation of requirements to software has already taken place. For example, an allocation change would be negotiated if the software requirements as allocated are found to be inappropriate for implementation as software.

4. Paths to Upper Levels of the SW–CMM

The SEI maintains a list of high maturity organizations [16]. At the time of writing this chapter (November 2003), the list had last been updated in October 2002. It lists 72 Level 4 and 74 Level 5 organizations. The geographic concentration is interesting: 77 of the 146 high-level organizations are in India, and 59 are in USA. The list is not exhaustive in that some high maturity organizations do not wish to be listed. As regards to the organizations listed, the earliest assessments with high-level outcomes were made in November 1989 (Level 5, Space Shuttle Onboard Software Project, described in [4]) and in November 1993 (Level 5, Motorola India Electronics). Actually the Shuttle Project had achieved high maturity before SW–CMM existed, but it uses SW–CMM to guide its continuing improvement efforts [17]. It should be noted that although SEI personnel have participated in assessment teams, SEI does not itself certify organizations with respect to maturity levels, and it does not confirm the accuracy of the maturity levels reported to it.

Most experience reports by organizations that have reached high maturity levels have been published in *Crosstalk: The Journal of Defense Software Engineering*. This journal, though unclassified, may be difficult to find in a library, but online access via

www.stsc.hill.af.mil/crosstalk/

is possible. More readily available case studies detail experience at different divisions of Motorola [11,18], at Raytheon [19,20], and at Computer Sciences Corporation [21].

Paulk [17] examines at considerable length the practices of high maturity organizations. He summarizes them as six principles, which we paraphrase as follows:

(1) The organization understands *why* each task is performed.
(2) It does not overreact to problems when they arise, but looks for common causes for the problems.
(3) It error-proofs its processes to protect against human error.
(4) It converts errors and problems into process improvements.
(5) It balances team and individual empowerment with management controls.
(6) It measures and predicts the additional effort needed to reach defined goals.

A survey of 13 high-level organizations finds that the majority has the following tools, methods, or approaches in common use, or have standardized them [17]:

- cost models, such as COCOMO;
- lines-of-code metric;
- critical path method or PERT;
- earned value metric;
- evolutionary life cycle models, e.g. the spiral model;
- systematic risk management;
- independent SQA group;
- SQA functions embedded in the process;

- independent test group;
- Web-based process deployment;
- CASE tools;
- systematic reuse;
- trend charts and control charts;
- Pareto analysis.

It is also interesting to note what is not used by most or all of the organizations:

- function points;
- cost of quality analysis;
- Cleanroom;
- process simulation ("what if") models;
- reliability engineering models;
- the Personal Software Process (see Sec. 5.1);
- the Team Software Process (see Sec. 5.1).

Eickelmann [11] identifies three problems that are hardest to deal with in moving to high maturity levels:

- Lack of commitment or sponsorship from top management, which results in inadequate investment of resources.
- Failure to understand that in moving from Level 3 to Level 4, the organization has to undergo a major cultural change — qualitative sporadic improvements become quantitative continuous improvement.
- The belief that an organization can ease off on reaching a high maturity level. Instead of serving as ends in themselves, the SW–CMM levels have to be seen as means to improved business results.

5. Extensions and Alternatives to the SW–CMM

The SW–CMM has provided a framework in which to build extensions and specialization. Alternatives to SW–CMM have also been formulated — they are its precursors, or they respond to the different needs of different developer communities. An extension or alternative falls into one of four categories:

(1) It considers issues that SW–CMM does not deal with. We call a model of this type an adjunct.
(2) It addresses the needs of an organization that does not satisfy the assumptions underlying SW–CMM. For example, it is of a smaller size or it follows an agile development process. This we call a tailored model.
(3) It has been developed before or in parallel with the SW–CMM, and it may have a different emphasis. This is is an alternative model.
(4) It examines in detail an individual phase of the overall software process, such as requirements engineering, or takes into account the special features of a domain for which the software is being developed, such as the domain of embedded software. The result is an adaptation.

Here we consider the first two categories, and briefly touch on the third. Adaptations will be looked at in Sec. 8.

5.1. *Adjunct models*

The SEI has developed four adjunct models. These models deal, respectively, with people, software acquisition, systems engineering, and integrated product development. The People CMM (P–CMM) aims at improving the capabilities of individuals and raising the effectiveness of teams. It combines the best practices in fields such as knowledge management and organizational principles. It was released in 1995. A book dealing with P–CMM was published in 2002 [22].

A text by Humphrey [23] introduces a Personal Software Process (PSP), which refers to the role of individuals in the P–CMM, taking software development for its context. A later text [24] investigates the team aspect, and defines the Team Software Process (TSP). The PSP is closely linked to SW–CMM: 12 of the 18 KPAs of SW–CMM are applicable in the PSP [25]. In our opinion, the PSP should form the basis for any curriculum of software engineering. Engineering projects require technical competence, cost and schedule consciousness, and, above all, disciplined time management and attention to product quality. All this, the PSP deals with. A textbook exists [26]. The PSP is credited with reducing errors in size and schedule estimates by 26% and 40%, respectively, testing time by 43% and defects by 60% [25]. However, as noted in Sec. 4, neither the PSP nor the TSP are being used in high-level organizations.

The Software Acquisition CMM (SA–CMM) relates to the capabilities that need to be developed by people and organizations involved in planning and managing the acquisition of software. The model organizes and refines the best practices for software acquisition that have been developed primarily by various defense organizations.

Both the P–CMM and SA–CMM are based on the five-level structure of SW–CMM. The P–CMM can be followed even by organizations that do not develop software, and an organization that acquires software is not necessarily involved in software engineering. Hence P–CMM and SA–CMM can continue to function as stand-alone models. The CMMs for systems engineering (SE–CMM) and integrated product development (IPD–CMM), on the other hand, are closely related to software engineering. It is therefore natural that they have become absorbed into CMMI.

5.2. *Tailored models*

Paulk [27] lists a number of environments in which SW–CMM has to be given special interpretation, and needs to be tailored to the special circumstances:

- very large systems;
- virtual projects and organizations;
- geographically distributed projects;

- rapid prototyping projects;
- research and development organizations;
- software services organizations;
- small projects and organizations.

Here we shall consider tailoring with respect to small organizations and extreme programming. Some of the items on Paulk's list we consider as adaptations. Examples of adaptations will be found in Sec. 8.

5.2.1. The SW–CMM for small organizations

The design of SW–CMM was influenced by the needs of organizations with large personnel resources, and this is reflected in [4]. For example, under SCM (Level 2), the organization is to establish a software configuration control board, a software configuration management group (SCMG) for each project, and designate a manager specifically responsible for SCM. Although the SCMG may be just one individual assigned part-time to configuration management, the board–group–manager structure may be interpreted as too complex for a small organization. Humphrey began work on the PSP in response to requests made to the SEI for guidance on how to apply SW–CMM to small projects.

Another characteristic of small organizations is that their managers have the perception that immense amounts of documentation are required for most KPAs, and consider this as being beyond their resources. Actually SW–CMM allows flexibility, but this could have been stated more clearly (see pp.73–74 of [4]). Paulk [27] clarifies: "Keep the process simple because we live in a rapidly changing world ... A 1–2 page process definition may suffice ..." Documents need not be lengthy, but some documentation is essential: (1) documents serve as a repository of organizational knowledge; (2) in principle, their writers should understand what they are writing about; (3) they standardize work practices; (4) they reduce duplication of effort. The number of small organizations that base their process improvement on SW–CMM has been growing. As reported by SEI [28], of the 1,342 organizations appraised between 1999 and September of 2003, about half had less than 100 employees.

Kelly and Cullerton [29] survey the approaches their organization, Silicon & Software Systems (S3), with around 150 software engineers, had taken in their approach to Level 2 compliance. It is important to note that S3 has already achieved a reasonable degree of maturity — it is a subcontractor to a Level 4 organization, and their quality system had become ISO 9001–compliant. Their approach was to measure, on a scale of 10, the degree of compliance with the KPAs of Level 2. Between September 1997 and June 1998, their average score for the KPAs applicable to them had risen from approximately 5.2 to approximately 7.3. Their view is that an organization should not seek formal certification before it has a score of 9 for all applicable KPAs.

Here we summarize and amplify the findings of [28]. The negative aspect of formal software process improvement in a small organization is the initial cost. The overload, which does not greatly depend on the number of employees, has to be spread over a smaller employee base. On the other hand, in large organizations, decisions that affect the software engineering group are often made without input from the group, and excessive separation of concerns can lead to impaired communications. The smaller organization has the advantage of coherence — there is a culture of involvement, with everybody in the organization involved to some extent in nearly all aspects of systems and software engineering. Another advantage possessed by small organizations is that work teams tend to be more productive because there is less communication overhead.

5.2.2. *The SW–CMM and extreme programming*

For some software, development time is the defining concern. Moreover, requirements may change constantly and radically during development. Examples are operating systems and e-commerce interfaces. This has led to an interest in agile processes, which include extreme programming (XP). On XP see, for example [30]. The manifesto for agile software development [31]:

- Individuals and interactions are valued over processes and tools.
- Working software is valued over comprehensive documentation.
- Customer collaboration is valued over contract negotiations.
- Responding to change is valued over following a plan.

Although the manifesto does not deny the value of the items on the right, it assigns greater value to the items on the left. This appears to negate most of what the SW–CMM stands for, but appearances can deceive. The manifesto is supported by a set of twelve principles [32]. We list four of them that are entirely consistent with the intent of SW–CMM: continuous attention to technical excellence and good design enhances agility; at regular intervals, the team reflects on how to become more effective, then tunes and adjusts its behavior accordingly; working software is the primary measure of progress; our highest priority is to satisfy the customer early through an continuous delivery of valuable software. The approach is often regarded as a fairly recent development, but it is not entirely new. The daily build approach practices at Microsoft (see, e.g. [33]) exemplifies many of the approaches of XP.

Paulk [34] relates the principles of XP to SW–CMM, and finds that XP largely addresses six of the KPAs of SW–CMM, partially addresses another five, but does not address the remaining seven. His conclusion is that SW–CMM and XP are complementary. Whereas SW–CMM is a capability model, i.e., a process requirements model, the XP is a set of how-to-do practices. It is interesting to note that some organizations with Level 3 certification are shifting to XP, but that organizations practicing XP find it difficult to get SW–CMM certification [35]. It does not appear that this problem will be resolved by CMMI.

An exchange of views between Boehm and DeMarco [36] extends the debate regarding the relationship between SW–CMM and XP to a broader examination of the relevance of SW–CMM to the problems of today. DeMarco criticizes the activities of the SEI, but cannot entirely support his criticism. He claims that individual skill building is neglected at the expense of organizational competence. But the PSP [25] addresses skill building, and it is hard to see how organizational competence could be achieved except by effective use of individual skills. The documentation bloat issue is brought up, but, in addition to Paulk's rebuttal of the bloat complaint [27], Boehm points out that since SW–CMM Level 5 requires continuous process improvement, reduction of paper work may be just such an improvement. Of course, the improvement can start at Level 2 — if the amount of documentation becomes counterproductive, reduce it. An agile process will try to optimize the level of documentation.

5.3. *Alternative models*

Sheard [37] examines what she calls a framework quagmire. Her Fig. 1 shows 29 frameworks still in use in 2001, 11 that were obsolete, and dependencies between the frameworks. We shall not deal with these frameworks because an expert survey of the more relevant can be found in Vol. 1 of this handbook [3].

We merely note that the CMMI project combines three source models: The SW–CMM, the Electronic Industries Alliance Interim Standard (EIA/IS) 731, and the Integrated Product Development CMM (IPD–CMM) of the SEI. In addition, CMMI was designed to be compatible with ISO/IEC 15504 (Technical Report for Software Process Assessment). ISO/IEC 15504 is the result of the SPICE (Software Process Improvement and Capability dEtection) project, which was started in 1991. The main difference between the ISO/IEC standard and SW–CMM is explicit consideration of maintenance and reuse in the standard. On the other hand, the standard does not emphasize the Level 4 and Level 5 activities of SW–CMM.

An interesting recent paper by Zhiying [38] introduces the Taiji (sometimes written as t'ai-chi) concept into capability modeling. A Taiji interpretation of world evolution is based on a relationship between two opposite poles, which in the software development context represent human actions and automation, respectively. Taking advantage of this polarization results in what Zhiying calls CMM–Taiji.

6. Capability Maturity Model Integration

Unlike SW–CMM, the CMMI is not a single document. Instead it is referred to as the CMMI Product Suite. To quote from [5], it "contains and is produced from a framework that provides the ability to generate multiple models and associated training and appraisal material." Here we will be concerned with the software CMMI, which is in direct correspondence with SW–CMM, and is denoted by CMMI–SW. When combined with systems engineering, the model becomes CMMI–SE/SW. Inclusion of Integrated Product and Process Development results in CMMI–SE/SW/IPPD, and, when Supplier Sourcing is added in as well, we get CMMI–SE/SW/IPPD/SS.

In addition, each of the four models has two representations: Staged and continuous. Both representations are to have the same Process Areas (PAs, counterparts of KPAs in SW–CMM), but the primary mode of their organization differs. The staged representation takes over the maturity level structure of SW–CMM, and this provides for easy migration into CMMI from SW–CMM. Under the continuous representation the process areas form four groups. There are also six "capability levels", numbered 0 through 5: Incomplete, performed, managed, defined, quantitatively managed, optimizing. Organizations that have been using EIA/IS 731, and have been guided by ISO/IEC 15504 with regard to assessment, will prefer the continuous representation.

Figure 3 shows the PAs assigned to Maturity Levels 2 through 5 of the Staged Representation of CMMI–SW. We also show the group to which a PA belongs under the continuous representation. An asterisk (*) indicates that the PA does

Level 5	Proc.Group
Causal Analysis and Resolution	Support
Organizational Innovation and Deployment	ProcMgt
Level 4	
Organizational Project Management	ProjMgt
Organizational Process Performance	ProcMgt
Level 3	
Organizational Environment for Integration	Support*
Decision Analysis and Resolution	Support
Integrated Supplier Management	ProjMgt*
Integrated Teaming	ProjMgt*
Risk Management	ProjMgt
Integrated Project Management for IPPD	ProjMgt
Organizational Training	ProcMgt
Organizational Process Definition	ProcMgt
Organizational Process Focus	ProcMgt
Validation	Eng
Verification	Eng
Product Integration	Eng
Technical Solution	Eng
Requirements Development	Eng
Level 2	
Configuration Management	Support
Process and Product Quality Assurance	Support
Measurement and Analysis	Support
Supplier Agreement Monitoring	ProjMgt
Project Monitoring & Control	ProjMgt
Project planning	ProjMgt
Requirements Management	Eng

Fig. 3.   Level structure of CMMI.

not appear in the continuous representation document, but has been allocated to a group in the staged representation document. The groups are Project Management (ProjMgt), Process Management (ProcMgt), Engineering, and Support.

The structure of a PA does not differ greatly from that of a KPA in SW–CMM. There are goals, but now they are partitioned into specific and generic goals. The specific goals are to be reached by following a set of specific practices. The generic goals address Commitment to Perform, Ability to Perform, Directing Implementation, and Verifying Implementation. The only difference from SW–CMM is that Measurement and Analysis has become the broader Directing Implementation.

Some data exist on the effectiveness of CMMI-based process improvement [39]. Specifically there are case studies that demonstrate cost reduction overall and with respect to defect localization and removal, decreased time to complete tasks and increased predictability in meeting schedules, reduced defect rates, increase in customer satisfaction, and positive return on investment in CMMI-based process improvement.

7. Examples of Process Areas in CMMI

We shall look at only two PAs. They correspond to the Requirements Management KPA of SW–CMM, and to a major section of the Software Product Engineering KPA.

7.1. *Level 2 process area: Requirements management*

The major differences between this PA and the corresponding KPA of the SW–CMM are its emphasis on stakeholder participation, and detailed attention to traceability of requirements. The aim is to facilitate the identification of inconsistencies between requirements and the product in its different stages of development. This implies that requirements and all changes in the requirements, as well as the rationale for such changes, have to be documented.

An important part of the definition of this PA in [5] is a compact list of six related PAs (there are references to four related KPAs in the definition of the Requirements Management KPA in [4], but they are scattered). This list is followed by one specific and two general goals. The goals give rise to five specific and twelve generic practices. The generic practices relate to process institutionalization, and are similar for all PAs. Examples: Provide resources, assign responsibility, train people. The specific practices list typical work products and subpractices. The work products may again be interpreted as creating a documentation overload, but good judgement will tell what are to be formal documents, what are to be entries in a project database, and what are to be working notes of no permanency. We list now the five specific practices with the subpractices for one of them.

- Obtain an understanding of requirements.
- Obtain commitment to requirements.

- Manage requirements changes.

    — Capture all requirements and requirements changes that are given to or generated by the project.
    — Maintain the requirements change history with the rationale for the changes.
    — Evaluate the impact of requirement changes from the standpoint of relevant stakeholders.
    — Make the requirements and change data available to the project.

- Maintain bidirectional traceability of requirements.
- Identify inconsistencies between project work and requirements.

7.2. *Level 3 process area: Requirements development*

In SW–CMM requirements development is just one component of the Software Product Engineering KPA. Its establishment as a separate PA indicates a growing awareness of the importance of proper requirements development. In contrast to SW–CMM, now there is much greater emphasis on customer and stakeholder needs. The PA deals with three kinds of requirements — customer, product, and component. Customer requirements express the needs of the customer. They are the primary input to the requirements development process. Under a process of refinement, customer requirements, together with product and process constraints, are turned into product requirements. If appropriate, components of the product may be specified by their own individual requirements.

Here we merely list the three specific goals of this PA, and allocate the ten specific practices to the goals.

- Develop customer requirements:

    — Elicit needs.
    — Develop the customer requirements.

- Develop product requirements:

    — Establish product and product–component requirements.
    — Allocate product–component requirements.
    — Identify interface requirements.

- Analyze and validate requirements:

    — Establish operational concepts and scenarios.
    — Establish a definition of required functionality.
    — Analyze requirements.
    — Analyze requirements to achieve balance.
    — Validate requirements with comprehensive methods.

8. Adaptations of the SW–CMM

The SW–CMM has inspired a number of models that address the specific capabilities needed for specialized applications. Thus, CMMs have been defined for reuse [40] and formal specification [41]. We have presented models for e-commerce [42], knowledge management [43], and requirements quality [44]. A model for information systems is being introduced here. An investigation of how to adapt the SW–CMM for such non-traditional projects as product-line development, data base development, and schedule-driven development has also been undertaken [45]. A complete model needs to contain much detail. A dissertation by Kajko-Mattsson [46], which deals with just the problem management phase of corrective maintenance runs to 290 pages. It should be noted, however, that Kajko-Mattsson is dealing with the entire problem management process, not just a set of capabilities.

An adaptation of SW-CMM, as defined in Sec. 5, either examines in detail an individual phase of the software process, or is adapted to the special needs of an application domain. We can speak of a phase-related or a domain-related model. A second classification relates to the method of model building. One approach is to define a generic process in broad outline, and use this outline as a guide for defining capabilities. Under another approach, capabilities drive the model construction from the start. We speak accordingly of process-based and capability-based models. We will describe two models, developed by ourselves. One is for requirements engineering (RE–CMM), the other for information systems (IS–CMM). The RE–CMM is phase-related and process-based; the IS–CMM is domain-related and capability-based.

8.1. *CMM for requirements engineering*

Sommerville and Sawyer [47] have identified 66 key practices for requirements engineering (RE). They also assign the practices to a three-level maturity model [48], but the model bears little resemblance to SW–CMM. Our RE-CMM differs from this in that we follow the KPA structure of SW–CMM very closely, put much emphasis on management aspects, and were guided by an actual process model. We want to stress the dependence of the quality of requirements on good management practices. First and foremost, management is not to insist on unrealistic schedules that lead to hastily generated substandard requirements. Management must also provide adequate resources, and ensure that the RE team has access to client representatives and other stakeholders on a regular basis. In terms of the Continuous Representation of CMMI, the two PAs that deal with requirements are assigned to the Engineering Process group. Actually RE has to contain a strong management component: Throughout the RE process, management must decide whether to proceed with the project as is, or to scale it down, or to terminate it. A project that is unlikely to succeed should be stopped as early as possible, and requirements engineering supplies the data for the decision. As we noted earlier, engineering provides the data, and management makes the decision.

8.1.1. *A generic RE process*

In this section, we give a skeletal outline of a generic requirements engineering process we have developed. Greater detail is given in [49]. Software development processes can themselves be software [50]. It follows that approaches found effective for application software should also be effective for software processes. The form of the generic process here was determined by our experience with student projects in which students developed large applications from generic requirements documents. For example, a car-rental system was developed from a generic requirements document for rentals in general. We found the approach surprisingly effective [51], which leads us to believe that RE driven by a generic RE process model should be affective as well. Steps of the model now follow.

Purpose and Environment Definition. This establishes the class of the system that is to be developed, and the environment in which the system is to operate.

Feasibility Study. An initial cost-risk estimation is performed. A management decision is made whether to proceed with the project.

Requirements Gathering Format. A decision is made on how system requirements are to be obtained.

Stakeholder Identification. Techniques as outlined in [52] are used to identify stakeholders.

Change Control. Change control has to be clearly defined. In some cases volatility even at the requirements stage cannot be tolerated. In other cases requirements volatility is the defining characteristic of the project. Traceability becomes then the most important aspect of RE.

Task Identification. This is a modularization phase. The tasks can be used cases determined by means of scenarios [53–55].

Task Refinement and Review. Capsule descriptions of the tasks in natural language are produced, and subjected to a peer review. This implies selection of a format for the peer review. Participation by a broad range of stakeholders is particularly important for this phase.

Specialization of Tasks. Each generic task is adapted for the specific project, and is elaborated. The presentation is still in natural language, but a standard format is to be followed.

Specialized Requirements. Some systems have highly special requirements, such as the ability to be used by physically handicapped people. These special requirements need to be incorporated into the requirements document where appropriate.

Review of the Specialization. The set of elaborated tasks is subjected to a peer review. Again, a broad participation of stakeholders should be aimed at.

Formalization. If required or warranted, the tasks can be translated into the schemas of a formal specification language.

It is neither necessary nor advisable to follow the sequence of steps as given above. For example, it may not be possible to get a meaningful cost-risk estimate before all tasks have been identified. Hence the decision of whether to proceed with the project may have to be delayed until the Task Identification phase, but, of course, if a decision is to be made not to proceed with a project, the earlier this decision is reached, the greater the savings for the organization. We do not by any means claim that our generic process is complete, appropriate for all classes of software, or that it lends itself well to tailoring in all situations. An organization should create its own generic RE process that corresponds best to its needs and capabilities.

8.1.2. *The RE–CMM*

Let us now adapt the KPAs of SW–CMM to RE. This will require some changes in the titles of the KPAs, and some KPAs of SW–CMM will be combined. For orientation, the KPAs of the RE–CMM are shown in Fig. 4.

Requirements Management (Level 2). In SW–CMM, this KPA should cover most of what we wish to establish for RE. However, it is lacking in detail, which emphasizes the need for a specialized RE–CMM. Our KPA corresponding to this KPA of SW–CMM relates to the capabilities needed to implement the Purpose and Environment Definition, and the Feasibility Study components of our generic process. In particular, there have to be capabilities for early cost and risk estimation.

Planning (Level 2). The information relating to purpose and environment of a product has to be converted into a requirements engineering plan. The required capability addresses the selection of a requirements gathering format most appropriate for the product, i.e., the matching of the proposed attributes of the

Management	Engineering
Level 3	**Level 5**
Organization Process	Defect Prevention
Training Program	Technology Change
Integrated Process	Process Change
Product Engineering	
Intergroup Coordination	
Peer Reviews	
Level 2	**Level 4**
Requirements Management	Quantitative Management
Planning	Quality Management
Tracking and Oversight	
Subcontractor Management	
Quality Assurance	

Fig. 4.   Level structure of RE–CMM.

product to a requirements gathering format. There also has to be effective capability for identifying all persons having an interest in the product, i.e., the project stakeholders.

Tracking and Oversight and *Configuration Management* (Level 2). The format of the requirements statement should enforce compliance with requirements throughout product development, but actual requirements tracing is unlikely to be the responsibility of the RE team (on requirements tracing see, for example [56] and the special issue of December 1998 of *Communications of the ACM*). However, changes will arise during the RE process. In particular, a change may be made, and later the change may be reversed. It is therefore necessary to have a capability of keeping track of all changes to requirements, the reasons for the changes, and who authorized and who carried out the changes. In other words, a database of requirements and their changes is to be maintained, *and consulted*, so that the products of all phases of the software process are consistent with the requirements.

Subcontractor Management (Level 2). When more than one organization is responsible for the development of a software product, two strategies can be followed. Suppose three organizations are involved. One develops requirements, another (which may be offshore) codes, a third does the testing. Under one strategy, the client negotiates with the three organizations separately. Under a different strategy the RE organization is the primary contractor, and it has to supervise the other two organizations. The outline given on pp. 159–171 of [4] can be followed with little or no change.

Quality Assurance (Level 2). In our context this is a particularly important KPA. Quality Assurance (QA) tasks include review of RE activities and of the requirements document to verify that both the RE process and guidelines for the format and content of the requirements document are being followed. There has to be a QA plan, and the capability to decide when the different QA tasks are to be performed, who will perform them, and how management is to be appraised of the results of QA reviews.

Organization Process Focus and *Organization Process Definition* (Level 3, denoted by Organization Process in Fig. 3). The "focus" in our context indicates that all RE activities are to be performed with reference to a process. Quoting from [4], "The software processes used by the projects are appropriately tailored from the organization's standard software process." Substituting "RE" for "software" we get precisely the motivation for our generic RE process. This KPA is to provide the capabilities for executing the Task Identification, Task Refinement and Review, and Specialization of Tasks steps of the generic process.

Training Program (Level 3). The capabilities defined by the other KPAs have to be acquired in some way, and their acquisition is the most efficient if there is an organizational training infrastructure in place. This relates in particular to the Level 5 KPA of technical change management. If requirements have to be expressed as a formal specification, extensive training in the use of the specification language must be provided.

Integrated Process Management (Level 3). A process has managerial and technical components. Far too often the technical staff is unaware of management concerns, and management makes promises that the technical staff cannot fulfill. In setting up the requirements document, there has to be close interaction between technical and managerial staffs, and such interaction requires the capability of both sides understanding each other's language and concerns.

Product Engineering (Level 3). In terms of RE this relates to technical aspects in the preparation of the requirements document. Resources have to be provided, such as tools and facilities for group decision making. Joint Application Development [57] and Participatory Design [58] are approaches to RE that need such resources. A capability for using the tools and facilities has to be developed.

Intergroup Coordination (Level 3). In the RE context we can distinguish four groups of participants: External stakeholders, management, the RE team, and the group to which the RE team hands on the requirements document. Channels of communication between these groups have to be established and maintained. In particular, the RE team has to have guaranteed and easy access to external stakeholders, and participation in requirements development by the groups that are to use the requirements should be encouraged.

Peer Reviews (Level 3). The requirements document has to be extensively checked. Although the effectiveness of peer reviews conducted as face-to-face group sessions has been questioned, some form of review is needed to detect omissions and inconsistencies. This KPA relates to the task refinement and review of specialization steps of the generic process.

Quantitative Process Management (Level 4). The basis for improvement of all engineering activities is measurement. Thus, measurements are used to improve processes. For example, the effectiveness of peer reviews specifically in the RE setting can be determined by trying different formats, and comparing measurement data obtained with the different formats.

Quality Management (Level 4). Whereas QA merely ensures that established procedures are in fact being followed, Quality Management (QM) sets a quantitative quality goal for the requirements document. Software reliability engineering (see [59]) typically establishes a qualitative reliability goal for a software product, and testing stops when this goal is reached. The faults discovered during testing can be classified as being due to poor coding, faulty design, or defective requirements. The task of QM with respect to RE is then to institute capabilities that will lead to (a) reduction of the proportion of faults due to requirements, and (b) reduction of overall failure rates by formulating requirements in a way that permits their validation to be more effective, and leads to greater automation of the design and coding processes.

Defect Prevention (Level 5). This KPA is to establish procedures that allow defects to be traced back to their causes, and its aim is to eliminate the causes in the future. With regard to RE, there are two classes of defects to be considered: Those detected by reviews, and those that make their appearance later in software development, but can be traced back to faulty requirements. Prevention of the second type of defect is particularly important. This KPA is closely related to the Quality Management KPA.

Technology Change Management (Level 5). The RE team must be constantly aware of new developments in tools and techniques. This requires monitoring of the technical literature, such as journals, conference proceedings, and books. Appropriate web sites should also be accessed on a regular basis, but care must be taken in the evaluation of their contents, which have rarely undergone professional review. It is most important that there be close interaction between the people who monitor the technical literature and the people responsible for training.

Process Change Management (Level 5). There is no clear dividing line between technology change and process change. For example, the generic RE process and its specializations can be approached in two different ways. Our preferred mode has been to create a new specialization from the generic process. Another possibility is to find an existing similar specialization and to adapt it to the new situation. Both the location and adaptation can be carried out by means of case-based reasoning (CBR) techniques (for a survey of CBR see [60]). Now, if a change were made to the CBR approach, would this be a technology change or a process change? Whatever the answer to this question, as an organization improves its capabilities, the RE process should become richer, which means that there will be process changes, and these changes have to be managed.

8.2. *CMM for information systems*

There have been lengthy arguments about the "best" programming language. Essentially the argument is whether a procedural or a declarative approach is best. Although at times a specific programming language may be better for a particular application, we contend that both the procedural and the declarative approaches are equally good, but that they are not equally good for all people. For some the declarative approach holds greater appeal, for others it is the procedural approach. It is well-known that the so-called "left brain/right brain" dominance greatly affects the preferences and capabilities of people — see, e.g. [61] for experimental evidence. The dominance may be marked to a greater or lesser extent, and even a fairly narrow field may attract people with differences in dominance. It is highly likely that the preference for a declarative or a procedural approach is determined by differences in dominance.

In the development of ISs the declarative approach is exemplified by Entity-Relationship diagrams [62,63]; examples of representations of a procedural process are data flow diagrams [64] and Petri nets [65]. In IS development the declarative approach concentrates initially on data; the procedural on events. This difference raises the question of whether there should be two generic processes or just one. However, since the required capabilities are going to be the same irrespective of whether one or two models are proposed, we do not have to answer this question here. An IS differs from most other software systems in that its usefulness grows with time: The more information it gathers and organizes, the greater its value to the organization. As the growth happens, the IS of an organization may become the most important asset of the organization.

In describing the adaptation of the KPAs of SW–CMM to IS purposes we will follow an approach similar to that of our conversion of SW–CMM into RE–CMM. First show a diagram in which the KPAs of the adaptation are assigned to levels, and then describe these IS–CMM KPAs. Again there will be a need for some changes in the titles of the KPAs. It may seem that we go into too much technical detail. Although the intent is not to emphasize IS development as such, we have to introduce enough detail to suggest how the approach could be used in other domains.

Requirements Management (Level 2). The purpose of an IS has to be clearly understood by the entire organization. The very first step is to set up an IS-group that is to monitor the information needs of the organization, and is to work toward the satisfaction of these needs by institutionalization of requirements management procedures. A major purpose of a CMM is the distribution of capabilities throughout an organization so that the organization is no longer dependent on single individuals for particular capabilities. The knowledge needs can be expressed as requirements, i.e., statements of *what* is needed without the details of *how* the needs are to be satisfied. An important part of requirements determination is the identification of stakeholders, i.e., people who will authorize, develop, use, and be affected by a particular product, and therefore need to be consulted in its requirements management stage. In our case, the stakeholders are gatherers and organizers of information, and people who will benefit from the information.

IS Planning (Level 2). We noted that the development of an IS can start with a data-orientation or a process-orientation. The planning phase will depend on the orientation that has most adherents in the project team.

Tracking and Oversight and Configuration Management (Level 2). This KPA differs very little from the corresponding KPA of the RE–CMM: Compliance with requirements is to be enforced and changes are to be traced.

Quality Assurance (Level 2). This is a particularly important KPA. Quality Assurance (QA) tasks include review of IS development activities and of the requirements document to verify that IS development is consistent with the requirements document. There has to be a QA plan, and the capability to decide when the different QA tasks are to be performed, who will perform them, and how management is to be appraised of the results of QA reviews.

Internal Information Acquisition (Level 2). We distinguish between internal and external information. Internal information resides in an organization itself, in the form of databases and data warehouses, and, most importantly, the skills of people. External information is gathered via personal contacts and communication media.

Uncertainty Awareness (Level 2). In [66], we put considerable emphasis on uncertainty. All information is subject to uncertainty of greater or lesser degree.

Management

Engineering

Level 3
Information Representation
Training Program
Intergroup Coordination
KE techniques
User Access and Profiling
Peer Reviews

Level 5
Technology Change
Quantitative Cost/Benefits

Level 2
Requirements Management
IS Planning
Tracking and Oversight
Quality Assurance
Internal Info Acquisition
Uncertainty Awareness

Level 4
Integrated Process
External Info Acquisition
Qualitative Cost/Benefits

Fig. 5.   Level structure of IS–CMM.

To begin with, at least the IS-Group has to understand the issues relating to this. Specifically, it should see to it that degrees of uncertainty are assigned to particular items of information.

Information Representation (Level 3). Various representations of information or knowledge have been studied in different contexts. This is a very broad topic, and the details are irrelevant to us here.

Training (Level 3). The institutionalization of a training program is another priority task for the IS-Group. Everybody in an organization affected by an IS is to be informed about the purposes of this IS, and how the IS will affect them. Specialized training needs will become apparent as ISs become more sophisticated, particularly with respect to knowledge engineering techniques, and the IS-Group has to provide appropriate training opportunities.

Intergroup Coordination (Level 3). We can distinguish four groups of participants in IS development: External stakeholders, over-all management, which we take to include the IS-group, the IS development team or teams, and managers of information repositories, i.e., databases, data warehouses, and knowledge bases. Channels of communication between these groups have to be established and maintained. In particular, IS development teams have to have guaranteed and easy access to external stakeholders.

Knowledge Engineering (KE) techniques (Level 3). These techniques have been developed for extracting knowledge from different representations. Specialized KE techniques include the design of data warehouses so as to facilitate knowledge extraction, data mining, data filtering, and the management of uncertainty. Note that management of uncertainty differs from uncertainty awareness, a KPA of Level 2. Management of uncertainty means that attempts are made to estimate uncertainty quantitatively by, for example, statistical techniques. Knowledge management has become an important aspect of management of enterprises — [67] is a collection of articles dealing with knowledge management from an organizational perspective.

User Access and Profiling (Level 3). Experience shows that there can be strong resistance to the introduction of knowledge-based ISs [68]. A common cause of this resistance is that users have to go through very complex access procedures and extensive searches to arrive at items of information they are looking for. Moreover, users who could benefit from information that has been collected by an organization are often unaware of its existence. The setting up of user profiles that reflect the interests of users in some detail would allow the matching of information needs and information availability.

Peer Reviews (Level 3). The requirements document and later representations of an IS have to be extensively checked. This KPA relates in particular to a review of how a specialization has been derived from a generic process, but reviews can be extended to the design of data warehouses, data quality control procedures, etc.

Integrated Process (Level 4). This relates particularly to the case where two teams have been developing an IS, and one team has a data orientation, while the other has a process orientation. In terms of UML diagrams, they would have worked with different diagram classes. An integration of their work requires thorough understanding of both representations. We put this KPA at Level 4 because the integration requires much experience. This KPA is a refinement of Intergroup Coordination (Level 3).

External Information Acquisition (Level 4). Organizations operate in their environments — the environment is the context for the operation, and it is customary to denote the context as $< w, t >$, where w is a slice of the "world" at time t. As the context evolves over time, an organization has to respond to the changes. This, of course, has to happen even at Level 1, but our KPA requires that a thorough analysis is undertaken to determine how much of w is relevant, and how this relevant component is to influence the operation of the organization.

Qualitative Cost–Benefit Analysis (Level 4). We should be able to measure costs, and we should also be aware of improvements (or the lack of them) in the operation of an organization. The difficult part is to discern cause–effect relationships. In other words, what benefits arise from a particular expenditure of resources. The goal of this KPA is to identify cause–effect relationships. The appropriate tools are being developed [69].

Quantitative Cost–Benefit Analysis (Level 5). The next stage in cost–benefit analysis is to make it quantitative. This requires extensive measurements relating to the IS development process. What is to be measured, which measurements can contribute to cost–benefit analysis in particular instances of benefits, and how a cause–effect relation is to be expressed in quantitative terms only experience can tell.

Technical Change Management (Level 5). This is where a transition is made from state-of-the-practice to state-of-the-art. New developments arise, e.g. data mining on the Web, or data mining applied to data streams, allowing, for example, instant response to real-time trends in data from sales registers. The IS-Group must monitor research developments, and be ready to introduce new techniques after a careful cost–benefit analysis.

9. Evaluation and Criticisms of SW–CMM

Numerous success stories relating to both CMMI and SW–CMM, as referenced in [39], document the benefits of process improvement, but there has also been criticism. One kind of criticism has resulted from a misunderstanding of the purpose and nature of SW–CMM. Rebuttals by SEI personnel have clarified most of the issues raised. An article by Bamberger [9] is a short, but effective exposition of what SW–CMM stands for. Armour [70] recounts an experience he had at an organization that builds new products all the time. A claim was made that a "repeatable" process (the label for Level 2) is not for them because they never repeat anything. But the point is that "repeatable" is just a label — it tells that the benefits of the management structures of Level 2 would be most clearly visible in an organization that specializes in one type of product, but the structures should benefit any organization.

However, the adoption of a process-oriented development discipline carries with it an initial overhead: Resources have to be provided and an initial drop in productivity is to be expected while the organization adjusts itself to the new approach. Even the costs of transition from SW–CMM to CMMI are not trivial [39]. At the PRC Systems Integration unit, which in July 1996 was evaluated to be at Level 3, process improvement was estimated to cost about $1,000,000 each year, which translated to $470 per software engineer, and the move from Level 1 to Level 3 took 39 months [71]. At that time, the industry median was 26.5 months for the move to Level 2, and 24 months for the move from Level 2 to Level 3 [72]. The latest data for organizations that begun their software process improvement in 1992 or later put the median times for transition to the next higher level at 22, 21, 25, and 13 months, respectively [28]. Unfortunately management often takes a short-term view of costs, and an improvement process that is spread out over years, and does not show immediate returns is not always popular.

The second kind of complaint relates to software capability appraisals. An organization can always perform self-evaluations, and in Sec. 5.2, we looked at the approach taken at the S3 company. They determined internally their degree of compliance with the KPAs of Level 2 of SW–CMM. But often there is external pressure for a formal appraisal: An organization is required to be at a particular level (typically Level 3) to be eligible to bid for a government contract. Eligibility determination was the initial motivation for the SW–CMM. But this has changed.

Of the appraisals carried out since 1999, only 25.9% related to government agencies or contractors [28]. The appraisals resulted in 13% of the organizations remaining on Level 1, 44% moving to Level 2, 26% to Level 3, 8% to Level 4, and 9% to Level 5. An organization that misses out is tempted to blame the appraisal process and the appraisal team. But there is another side. Organizations have been known to mislead the appraisers. An appraisal is normally performed by a team of about six over a period of a week. There is not enough time to verify the accuracy of all materials supplied by the organization. In one instance [73], the team was given an elaborate process diagram for peer reviews, consisting of twelve boxes with impressive labels, and as many connecting arrows, but the actual process was a simple three-step sequence — (1) find a group of technical people, (2) give each person a copy of the code, (3) get opinions and decide what to do next.

A third source of discontent is still the "military bias" of SW–CMM, and the misconception that SW–CMM is only for large organizations. Data cited in Sec. 5.2 show that small organizations are increasingly making use of SW–CMM appraisals, but the "military bias" is another matter. A fighter plane takes many years to develop, so that the avionics software associated with the aircraft can be developed over a long period of time. The software plan is not likely to change much over time so that appropriate milestones can be defined at the very start, and progress measured in terms of the milestones. Level 3 competence is adequate under such conditions, and advancement to higher levels need not be difficult because the Level 3 process is already close to optimal.

To put it another way, SW–CMM and CMMI are best suited for stable environments. In rapidly changing fields, such as telecommunications, the environment is not stable, and, as Conradi and Fuggetta [74] point out, the CMM level that a telecommunications organization has reached has no relation to its business success. In a study of a number of organizations in Scandinavia and Italy, they found that "short-term priorities, combined with business and market turbulence, may severely prevent, hamper, and even abort well-planned ... software process improvement efforts".

Despite the claims that SW–CMM has brought about quantitative improvements in cost and schedule estimation, and defect reduction, the question remains whether this is actually due to the KPAs of the SW–CMM. Even quantitative data of experimental software engineering are very difficult to interpret, as shown by the still current controversy regarding the effectiveness of different approaches to technical reviews. Experimental determination of the effectiveness of different capabilities is much more difficult. It would require experiments with control groups, which for large-scale projects would be prohibitively expensive. Even with small projects, the assumption of independence, essential for reasonably straightforward statistical analysis, rarely applies to capabilities. What capabilities are needed, what form they should take, and how they contribute to the quality of software is therefore a largely subjective judgement. What we are facing are problems of self-selection and spotlighting. On self-selection, an organization that elects to participate in a process improvement program is likely to have already some kind of process focus, and this means that gains in performance need not be a direct result of SW–CMM. Spotlighting means that an organization under any kind of scrutiny, even if it is self-imposed, will try to improve its performance. Both these phenomena make the determination of cause–effect relationships even more difficult.

10. Future Directions

Despite the difficulty to determine which KPAs of SW–CMM have contributed to its success, SW–CMM and now CMMI–SW have undoubtedly improved software development in many organizations. Just the number of organizations that have been formally appraised shows the popularity of the models. But what of the future in which business environments are expected to be increasingly characterized by rapid change? Organizations that have coped best with change are unlikely to satisfy appraisal requirements. For CMMI to be accepted by organizations that find it irrelevant in its present form, the appraisal requirements have to become more flexible.

Process improvement is not the only use to which SW–CMM can be put. In Sec. 8, we gave examples of how its structure has been adapted to specific applications. As the body of knowledge that defines software engineering continues to grow, specialization has to increase. The specialized processes can benefit from CMMs defined for them. For example, a specialized CMM for verification and validation could be useful. Both are Level 3 PAs of CMMI, but management aspects of verification and validation could be introduced in Level 2, and improvements in the verification and validation process belong to Levels 4 and 5.

Another useful application is the measurement of emerging methodologies against the SW–CMM (or CMMI) as a benchmark. In an evaluation of the Rational Unified Process against Levels 2 and 3 of SW–CMM, support of the key practices of individual KPAs was found to range from 0% to 86% [10]. Such data can identify blind spots in a methodology.

Specialized models for different application domains are an important extension. Software engineers developing software for a particular application domain have to have some understanding of the domain, and in this context advancement in the level structure means that the understanding grows, allowing the development of increasingly more sophisticated systems. Examples are the design of graphical user interfaces, process visualization, workflow systems, and data mining. We expect such specializations to become the most important application of the CMM approach.

References

1. W. S. Humphrey, *Managing the Software Process* (Addison-Wesley, 1989).
2. S. T. Acuña, A. DeAntonio, X. Ferré, L. Maté and M. López, "The software process: Modeling, evaluation and improvement", *Handbook of Software Engineering and Knowledge Engineering: Fundamentals*, Vol. 1 (World Scientific, 2001) 193–237.

3. Y. Wang, "Software engineering standards: Review and perspectives", *Handbook of Software Engineering and Knowledge Engineering: Fundamentals*, Vol. 1 (World Scientific, 2001) 277–303.
4. M. C. Paulk *et al*, *The Capability Maturity Model: Guidelines for Improving the Software Process* (Addison-Wesley, 1995).
5. CMMI Product Team, Capability maturity model integration, Version 1.1 (CMMI–SW, V1.1) Staged representation, CMU/SEI-2002-TR-029 (August 2002).
6. G. Ruhe, "Learning software organizations", *Handbook of Software Engineering and Knowledge Engineering: Fundamentals*, Vol. 1 (World Scientific, 2001) 663–677.
7. R. Kneuper, "Supporting software processes using knowledge management", *Handbook of Software Engineering and Knowledge Engineering: Emerging Technologies*, Vol. 2 (World Scientific, 2002) 579–606.
8. A. T. Berztiss, "Technical reviews", *Handbook of Software Engineering and Knowledge Engineering: Fundamentals*, Vol. 1 (World Scientific, 2001) 157–166.
9. J. Bamberger, "Essence of the capability maturity model", *Computer* **30**, no. 6 (June 1997) 112–114.
10. L. V. Manzoni and R. T. Price, "Identifying extensions required by RUP (Rational Unified Process) to comply with CMM (Capability Maturity Model) Levels 2 and 3", *IEEE Transactions on Software Engineering* **29** (2003) 181–192.
11. N. Eickelmann, "An insiders view of CMM Level 5", *IEEE Software* **20**, no. 4 (July/August 2003) 79–81.
12. M. C. Paulk, "Software process appraisal and improvement: Models and standards", *Advances in Computers* **46** (1998) 1–33.
13. L. Bendix, A. Dattoli and F. Vitaly, "Software configuration management in software and hypermedia engineering: A survey", *Handbook of Software Engineering and Knowledge Engineering: Fundamentals*, Vol. 1 (World Scientific, 2001) 523–547.
14. O. Laitenberger, "A survey of software inspection technologies", *Handbook of Software Engineering and Knowledge Engineering: Emerging Technologies*, Vol. 2 (World Scientific, 2002) 517–555.
15. B. Boehm, "Unifying software engineering and systems engineering", *Computer* **33**, no. 3 (March 2000) 114–116.
16. *www.sei.cmu.edu/cmm/high-maturity/HighMatOrgs.pdf.*
17. M. C. Paulk, "Practices of high maturity organizations", *Proceedings of the 11th Software Engineering Process Group Conference* (March 1999).
18. M. Diaz and J. Sligo, "How software process improvement helped Motorola", *IEEE Software* **14**, no. 5 (September/October 1997) 75–81.
19. R. Dion, "Process improvement and the corporate balance sheet", *IEEE Software* **10**, no. 4 (July/August 1993) 28–35.
20. T. J. Haley, "Raytheon's experience in software process", *IEEE Software* **13**, no. 6 (November/December 1996) 34–41.
21. F. McGarry and B. Decker, "Attaining Level 5 in CMM process maturity", *IEEE Software* **19**, no. 6 (November/December 2002) 87–96.
22. B. Curtis, W. E. Hefley and S. A. Miller, *The People Capability Maturity Model: Guidelines for Improving the Workforce* (Addison-Wesley, 2002).
23. W. S. Humphrey, *A Discipline for Software Engineering* (Addison-Wesley, 1995).
24. W. S. Humphrey, *Introduction to the Team Software Process* (Addison-Wesley, 2000).
25. P. Ferguson, W. S. Humphrey, S. Khajenoori, S. Macke and A. Matvye, "Results of applying the Personal Software Process", *Computer* **30**, no. 5 (May 1997) 24–31.
26. W. S. Humphrey, *Introduction to the Personal Software Process* (Addison-Wesley, 1997).

27. M. C. Paulk, "Using the software CMM in small organizations", *Joint Proceedings 1998 Pacific Northwest Software Quality Conference and Eighth International Conference on Software Quality*, 350–361.

28. *http://www.sei.cmu.edu/sema/pdf/SW-CMM/2003sepSwCMM.pdf*.

29. D. P. Kelly and B. Cullerton, "Process improvement for small organizations", *Computer* **32**, no. 10 (October 1999) 41–47.

30. K. Beck, *Extreme Programming Explained: Embrace the Change* (Addison-Wesley, 2000).

31. *http://www.agilemanifesto.org*.

32. *http://www.agilemanifesto.org/principles.html*.

33. M. A. Cusumano and R. W. Selby, *Microsoft Secrets* (Free Press, 1995).

34. M. C. Paulk, "Extreme programming from a CMM perspective", *IEEE Software* **18**, no. 6 (November/December 2001) 19–26.

35. D. J. Reifer, "XP and the CMM", *IEEE Software* **20**, no. 3 (May/June 2003) 14–15.

36. T. DeMarco and B. Boehm, "The agile methods fray", *Computer* **35**, no. 6 (June 2002) 90–92.

37. S. A. Sheard, "Evolution of the frameworks quagmire", *Computer* **34**, no. 7 (July 2001) 96–98.

38. Z. Zhiying, "CMM in uncertain environments", *Communications of the ACM* **46**, no. 8 (August 2003) 115–119.

39. D. R. Goldenson and D. L. Gibson, "Demonstrating the impact and benefits of CMMI: An update and preliminary results", CMU/SEI–2003–SR–009 (October 2003).

40. T. Davis, "The reuse capability model: A basis for improving an organization's reuse capability", *Advances in Software Reuse* (IEEE CS Press, 1993) 126–133.

41. M. D. Fraser and V. K. Vaishnavi, "A formal specifications maturity model", *Communications of the ACM* **40**, no. 12 (December 1997) 95–103.

42. A. T. Berztiss, "Capabilities for e-commerce", *Proceedings of the Thirteenth International Workshop on Database and Expert Systems Applications (DEXA'02)* (IEEE CS Press, 2002) 875–879.

43. A. T. Berztiss, "Capability maturity for knowledge management", *Proceedings of the Thirteenth International Workshop on Database and Expert Systems Applications (DEXA'02)* (IEEE CS Press, 2002) 162–166.

44. A. T. Berztiss, "Capability maturity for requirements quality", *Proceedings of the Workshop REFSQ'02*, Essen (September 2002).

45. D. L. Johnson and J. G. Brodman, "Applying CMM project planning practices to diverse environments", *IEEE Software* **17**, no. 4 (July/August 2000) 40–47.

46. M. Kajko–Mattsson, *Corrective Maintenance Maturity Model: Problem Management*, PhD Thesis, Department of Computer and System Sciences, Stockholm University/Royal Institute of Technology, Report 01-015 (2001).

47. I. Sommerville and P. Sawyer, *Requirements Engineering — A Good Practice Guide* (Wiley, 1997).

48. P. Sawyer, I. Sommerville and S. Viller, "Capturing the benefits of requirements engineering", *IEEE Software* **16**, no. 2 (March/April 1999) 78–85.

49. A. T. Berztiss, "Requirements engineering", *Handbook of Software Engineering and Knowledge Engineering: Fundamentals*, Vol. 1 (World Scientific, 2001) 121–143.

50. L. Osterweil, "Software processes are software too", *Proceedings of the 9th International Conference of Software Engineering* (IEEE CS Press, 1987) 2–12.

51. A. T. Berztiss, "Failproof team projects in software engineering courses", *Proceedings of the 27th Frontiers in Education Conference* (IEEE CS Press, 1997) 1015–1019.

52. H. Sharp, A. Finkelstein and G. Galal, "Stakeholder identification in the requirements engineering process", *Proceedings of the Tenth International Workshop on Database and Expert Systems Applications (DEXA'99)* (IEEE CS Press, 1999) 387–391.
53. K. Weidenhaupt, K. Pohl, M. Jarke and P. Haumer, "Scenarios in system development: Current practice", *IEEE Software* **15**, no. 2 (March/April 1998) 34–45.
54. C. B. Achour, "Guiding scenario authoring", *Information Modelling and Knowledge Bases X* (IOS Press, 1999) 152–171.
55. N. A. M. Maiden, G. Rugg and P. Patel, "Guidelines for better scenarios: Supporting theories and evidence", *Proceedings of the Tenth International Workshop on Database and Expert Systems Applications (DEXA'99)* (IEEE CS Press, 1999) 352–356.
56. F. A. C. Pinheiro and J. A. Goguen, "An object-oriented tool for tracing requirements", *IEEE Software* **13**, no. 2 (February/March 1996) 52–64.
57. J. Wood and D. Silver, *Joint Application Development*, 2nd edn. (Wiley, 1995).
58. D. Schuler and A. Namioka (eds.), *Participatory Design: Principles and Practice* (Lawrence Earlbaum, 1993).
59. A. T. Berztiss, "Software reliability engineering", *Handbook of Software Engineering and Knowledge Engineering: Fundamentals*, Vol. 1 (World Scientific, 2001) 145–156.
60. K.-D. Althoff, "Case-based reasoning", *Handbook of Software Engineering and Knowledge Engineering: Fundamentals*, Vol. 1 (World Scientific, 2001) 549–587.
61. A. Beaton, *Left Side, Right Side* (Yale UP, 1986).
62. P. P. Chen, "The entity-relationship model: Toward a unified view of data", *ACM Transactions on Database System* **3** (1976) 9–36.
63. B. Thalheim, *Entity–Relationship Modeling* (Springer, 2000).
64. R. B. France, "Semantically extended data flow diagrams: A formal specification tool", *IEEE Transactions on Software Engineering* **18** (1992) 329–346.
65. A. T. Berztiss, *Software Methods for Business Reengineering* (Springer, 1995).
66. A. T. Berztiss, "Dimensions of the knowledge management process", *Twelfth International Workshop on Database and Expert Systems Applications (DEXA'01)* (IEEE CS Press, 2001) 437–441.
67. D. Morey, M. Maybury and B. Thuraisingham, *Knowledge Management: Classic and Contemporary Works* (MIT Press, 2000).
68. R. Kay and D. Cecez-Kecmanovic, "When knowledge becomes information: A case of mistaken identity", *Proceedings of the Eleventh International Workshop on Database and Expert Systems Applications (DEXA'01)* (IEEE CS Press, 2000) 1128–1133.
69. J. Pearl, *Causality: Models, Reasoning, and Inference* (Cambridge University Press, 2000).
70. P. G. Armour, "Matching process to types of teams", *Communications of the ACM* **44**, no. 7 (July 2001) 21–23.
71. C. Hollenbach, R. Young, A. Pflugrad and D. Smith, "Combining quality and software improvement", *Communications of the ACM* **40**, no. 6 (June 1997) 41–45.
72. J. Herbsleb, D. Zubrow, D. Goldenson, W. Hayes and M. Paulk, "Software quality and the capability maturity model," *Communications of the ACM* **40**, no. 6 (June 1997) 30–40.
73. E. O'Connell and H. Saiedian, "Can you trust software capability evaluations?" *Computer* **33**, no. 2 (February 2000) 28–35.
74. R. Conradi and A. Fuggetta, "Improving software process improvement", *IEEE Software* **19**, no. 4 (July/August 2002) 92–99.

COEXISTENCE OF OBJECT-ORIENTED MODELING AND ARCHITECTURAL DESCRIPTION

TAHAR KHAMMACI, ADEL SMEDA and MOURAD OUSSALAH

University of Nantes, Laboratoire d'Informatique de Nantes Atlantique (LINA),
CNRS FRE 2729,
2, Rue de la Houssinière, B.P. 92208,
F–44300, Nantes, France
E-mail: {khammaci, smeda, oussalah}@lina.univ-nantes.fr
Tel: 00-33-2-51-12-58-34

Complex software systems require expressive notations for representing their software architectures. There are at least two different approaches to describe and to model a software system and the interconnections among its components, either by using object-oriented notations or by using architectural description notations. Thanks to the unification of most of the object-oriented modeling notations under UML, object-oriented modeling has become widely used and appreciated by the industry. UML is becoming the standard language for specifying, visualizing, constructing, and documenting all the artifacts of a software system. Meanwhile, architectural description is much more visible as an important and explicit design activity in software development. During the last decade, the software architecture research community has proposed a number of Architecture Description Languages (ADLs) specifically designed to represent software and system architectures. However, it remains an open question as to how well the two approaches coexist. In this chapter, we present the two approaches focusing on the similarities and the differences between them and some perspectives to best coexist the two approaches.

Keywords: Software architecture, object-oriented modeling, architectural description, component-based software architecture, object-based software architecture, component-object based software architecture.

1. Introduction

There are at least two different modeling techniques: Object-oriented modeling notations [10, 29, 58] and architectural description [47]. Object-oriented modeling has become the *de facto* standard in the early phases of software development process during the last decade. Thanks to the unification of most of the object-oriented modeling notations under UML (Unified Modeling Language) [11], object-oriented modeling has become widely used [18] and appreciated by the industry. Initially software architectural description was largely an *ad hoc* affair. It relied on informal box-and-line diagrams, which were rarely maintained once a system was constructed. In the last decade, architectural description is much more visible as an important and explicit design activity in software development. During the last decade, the software architecture research community has proposed a number of Architecture

Description Languages (ADL) specifically designed to represent software and system architectures [47]. However, the two approaches of modeling systems are very akin, in fact the two are based on the same concept, which is abstraction and components interactions. In spite of that, each one of them has its advantages and also its flaws. It must be noted that the two perspectives (Object-Oriented Modeling and Architectural description) are approaches of describing software architecture, that is why sometimes object-oriented approach is called Object-Based Software Architecture (OBSA) and architectural description approach is called Component-Based Software Architecture (CBSA) [23, 48].

The remainder of this chapter is organized as follows: Section 2 presents the basic concepts of object-orientation and object-oriented modeling. Section 3 presents the architectural description and architecture description languages in detail. Section 4 summarizes the similarities and differences between the object-oriented modeling and architectural description. Section 5 gives some perspectives to coexist object-oriented modeling and architectural description by modeling software architectures using object notations, selecting UML modeling constructs to representing architectural elements, modeling architectural views or combining the two approaches in order to benefit from the qualities of each one of them. Section 6 concludes this chapter and Sec. 7 gives resources for further reading.

2. Object-Oriented Modeling Approach

Prior to object-orientation, a typical application was viewed as a logical procedure that takes input data, processes it, and produces output data. The programming challenge was seen as how to write the code logic. Although code logic is still important, object orientation focuses on the objects wanted to be manipulated rather than the logic required to manipulate them. Object-orientation is an approach (not a specific tool) that is organized around objects rather than actions, data, or logic. Much of the art of object-oriented programming is determining the best way to divide a program into an economical set of classes. In addition to speed development time, proper class design results in far fewer lines of code, which translates to less bugs and lower maintenance costs. Figure 1 shows a meta-model of the basic concepts of object-orientation, where the focus is in classes, objects, and their relations; the figure also shows mechanisms such as inheritance and composition.

2.1. *Object-oriented modeling concepts*

The concept of object-orientation is mainly based on entities to abstract and encapsulate functionality called classes, which are the encapsulation of data and methods serving them through interfaces. A class can be instantiated to have objects. An object (instance) has a property and behavior (attributes). Objects of different classes interact with each other via message calls.

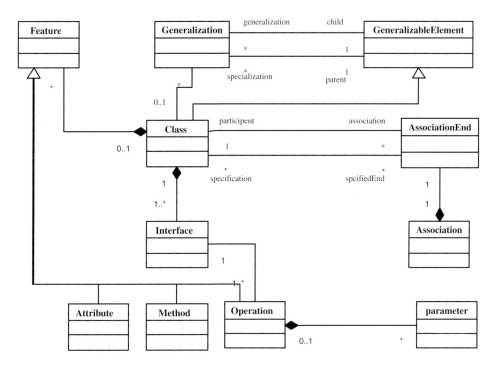

Fig. 1.   A meta-model shows the basic concepts and mechanisms of object-orientation.

- Classes: A class is a "template" describing a (possible) set of objects with similar properties (attributes), common behavior (operations), common relationships to other objects, and common semantics. It is an abstraction of a set of things from the real world in a way that: All the things in the real world that are part of a class have the same characteristics and all the objects follow the same "rules".
- Objects: Objects share two characteristics, they all have state and they all have behavior. A software object maintains its state invariable and implements its behavior with methods.
- Attributes: Two basic aspects of real-world objects are properties and behavior. The same is true for computer objects. An attribute is the abstraction of a single characteristic possessed by all the entities of an object.
- Operations and Methods: An operation is a function or transformation that may be applied to or by objects in a class. A method is the implementation of an operation for a class. All objects in a class share the same operations.
- Message calls: In object-oriented systems objects communicate with each other using message calls. Methods and properties are message calls. The parameters of a method are the message content.

2.2. *Object-oriented modeling languages*

Object-oriented modeling is a systematic technique used to observe, analyze and communicate the behavior of a system. Behavior is described in terms of the objects found in the system, their structure and how they interact with each other. Thus, behavior embodies both individual object behavior as well as the behavior of many objects interacting with each other. In the early 1990, there were three main object-oriented methods: OMT [58], Booch [10], and OOSE [29]. However, many users of these methods had trouble finding complete satisfaction in any one of these methods, fueling the "method war". In 1995, the three amigos — Grady Booch, James Rumbaugh, and Ivars Jacobson — combined their three methods in a sole but comprehensive modeling language that they called Unified Modeling Language (UML) [11,57]. UML has become the standard language for specifying, visualizing, constructing, and documenting all the artifacts of a software system, as well as for business modeling and other non-software systems. It has dominated the object-oriented modeling field. The UML represents a collection of the best engineering practices that have been found to be successful in the modeling of large and complex systems. The UML is rich and full of notations. These notations consist of two major subdivisions. There are notations for modeling the static elements of a design such as classes, attributes and relations. There are also notations for modeling the dynamic elements of a design such as objects' behavior, messages, and finite state machines. These notation models are presented in diagrams such as class diagram, use case diagram, behavior diagram and implementation diagrams (component and deployment diagrams). Recently, UML designs have been improved using automatic design patterns detection in order to assist programmers and software architects [8].

The UML uses mostly graphical notation to describe structural, dynamic, and functional aspects of a system. However, the graphical notation is inherently limited when specifying complex constraints. Thus, the UML uses Object Constraint Language, or OCL [74], to define constraints and regulations. OCL allows to attach constraints to UML models. These constraints can be defined at meta-model level as well as model level. OCL allows for the design of richer and more precise models. It can be used to specify constraints on elements in class diagrams, to specify derived attributes and derived associations. OCL is a formal language but does not require strong mathematical background.

Finally, with the release of the last version of UML (UML 2.0 [71]), UML improved the definition of components and their interfaces by introducing the notion of ports and separating provides services from required services of a component. However, UML 2.0 still defines the interactions among components implicitly and has not yet introduced the notion of connectors. Therefore, in UML 2.0, interactions remain the properties of components.

2.3. *Agent-oriented modeling*

The concept of agent was introduced by John McCarthy in the mid-1950s and established by Oliver G. Selfridge several years later [31]. In the early years, though many researchers investigated different aspects of the agent technology, it was still not considered as mainstream research within the artificial intelligence community. However, since the late 1980s, there has been a resurgence of interest in agent technology, and currently we are seeing a proliferation of agent-based applications [7, 75], particularly on the Web. To be an agent, the following three properties are needed in the modeling approach:

(1) Autonomy: An agent can make decisions about what to do based on its own state, without the direct intervention of humans.
(2) Adaptation: An agent can perceive its environment, and respond to changes in the environment in a timely fashion.
(3) Cooperation: An agent can interact with other agents through a particular agent-communication language, and typically has the ability to engage in collaborative activities to achieve its goal.

Kim *et al* [33] proposed an agent-oriented modeling process. In their mode, the authors assumed that agents in that domain have the following characteristics:

- Objects and agents can coexist, and have mutual relationships.
- An active object can be regarded as an agent.
- Agents act asynchronously.
- Interactions among agents take place through message exchanging.

Based on the above assumption, they proposed an agent-oriented modeling process. This modeling process consists of the following four steps: (a) UML based Problem Domain Analysis, (b) Agent Elicitation, (c) Intra Agent Modeling, and (d) Inter Agent Modeling. UML based Object-Oriented Analysis Method is used for the problem domain analysis. Since the utility of UML has been extensively validated in different industries, the UML based approach will provide an objective view of the domain in the early stage of Agent Elicitation. It also provides deep understanding of the problem domain with static and dynamic aspects of the system. After analyzing the problem domain, objects that can be "agentified", as well as the agents that need to be added are determined by agent selection rules. These objects and agents that are derived from the domain analysis are assimilated and represented in an Agent-Class Diagram. This diagram depicts the relationships between the various objects and agents. Once the agents are identified, their internal characteristics are captured in the intra-agent modeling step. The inter-agent modeling step involves developing the agent mobility model, as well as the agent communication model.

Agents are similar to objects, but they also support structures for representing mental components, i.e., beliefs and commitments. In addition, agents support high-level interaction (using agent-communication languages) between agents based on the "speech act" theory as opposed to *ad hoc* messages frequently used between objects [38]. Another important difference between agent-oriented programming and object-oriented programming is that objects are controlled from the outside (white-box control), as opposed to agents that have autonomous behavior which cannot be directly controllable from the outside (black-box control). In other words, agents have the right to say "no" [38].

3. Architectural Description Approach

Architectural description [6, 15, 32] concerns with constructing software systems based on components (encapsulation of functionality) and connectors (encapsulation of communication) are as shown in Fig. 2.

By doing this, it shifts our focus of developing a software system from line-of-code to a higher level, which is a coarser-grained architecture element [47]. As in Component-Based Software Engineering (CBSE) [26], there are many benefits of this such as improving reusability, enhancing understandability and reducing costs. Architectural description concepts and notations are similar (generally speaking) to object-oriented modeling notations. In this section, we present them through a meta-model that is shown in Fig. 3.

3.1. *Architectural description concepts*

Although there is considerable diversity in the capabilities of different ADLs, all share a similar conceptual basis, or ontology [30], that determines a common foundation of concepts and concerns for architectural description. The main elements of this ontology are:

- Components: Components represent the computational elements and data stores of a system and they correspond to box in box-and-line description. Hence, an explicit description of its interface is essential; the use of objects and the communication messages are not sufficient. Moreover, the components can be typified, to have a formal or abstract semantics, to export operational requirements, to allow the evolution or to present non-functional properties. Each component may have multiple interfaces called ports. Each interface consists of a set of points of interactions between the component and the external world that allow the invocation of the services.

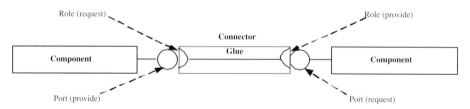

Fig. 2.   Architectural description of component-based systems.

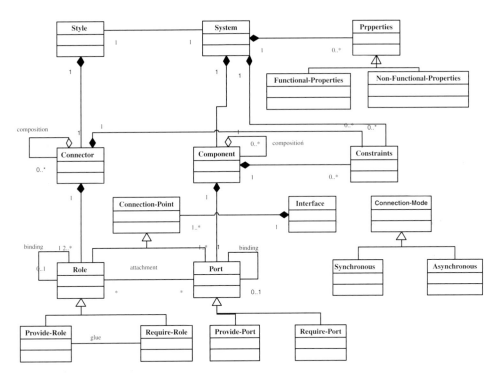

Fig. 3. A meta-model shows the basic concepts of ADL.

This interface consists of a set of ports provided with a sensitivity and is attached to a service which defines the behavior to be carried out at the time of its invocation. The ports' sensitivity determines the part that the data, which are directed to these ports, will play. These data could, for example, be translated into events that start the execution of the service or simply to be used like data shared between several components.

- Connectors: Connectors are architectural building blocks used to model interactions among components and rules that govern those interactions. They correspond to the lines in box-and-line descriptions. Hence, they are architectural entities that bind components together and act as a mediator between them. In this way, connectors separate a component interfacing requirements from its functional requirements. Examples include simple forms of interaction, such as pipes, procedure calls and event broadcast. Connectors may also represent complex interactions, such as a client-server protocol or an SQL link between a database and an application. Unlike components, connectors may not correspond to compilation units in an implemented system. As such, connector specifications in an ADL may also need to contain hints for implementing a particular kind of connector.

- Interfaces: In software architecture interfaces are first-class entities. They provide connection points between a component and a connector, consequently between that component and another component. Likewise, they define how the communication between two components can take place. Software architecture distinguishes between a component's interface (which is called port) and a connector's interface (which is called role). Both interfaces (component's interface and connector's interface) should support the two modes of communication: Synchronous mode and asynchronous mode.

- Ports: Components' interfaces are defined by a set of ports. Each port identifies a point of interaction between the component and its environment. A component may provide more than one interface by using different types of ports. The "in port" of a component is called request port and the "out port" is called provide port, where the former imports services from the environment to the component and the latter exports services from the component to its environment.

- Roles: A role is an interface to a connector; it is defined by the connector itself. Roles denote a set of roles that specific named entities for a component to play. The roles describe the expected local behavior of each of the interacting parties. How these behaviors are combined to form a communication, is described by what is called glue.

- Systems: Systems (also called architecture configurations [47]) represent graphs of components and connectors. In general, systems may be hierarchical: Components and connectors may represent subsystems that have internal architectures called representations. When a system or part of a system has a representation, it is also necessary to explain the mapping between the internal and external interfaces. The elements of this mapping are referred to as bindings.

- Constraints: Constraints define certain rules and regulations that should be met in order to ensure adherence to intended component's/connector's uses. ADLs differ in type and number of constraints they have. An example of constraints is the restriction on the number of components that can interact through a connector. A common constraint is the usage of a component by specifying its interfaces as the only legal means of interaction. Constraints also concern with architectural style regulations.

- Properties: Properties represent additional information (beyond structure) about the parts of an architectural description. Although the properties that can be expressed by different ADLs vary considerably, typically they are used to represent anticipated or required extra-functional aspects of an architectural design. For example, some ADLs allow one to calculate system throughput and latency based on performance estimates of the constituent components and connectors. In general, it is desirable to be able to associate properties to any architectural element in a description (components, connectors, systems, etc.). There are two types of properties: Functional properties and non-functional properties.

— Functional properties: Functions that relate to the semantics of a system and represent the requirements are called functional properties. They influence directly the performance of the system.

— Non-functional properties: Non-functional properties represent additional requirements. They can be directly derived from the specification of system semantics. Properties such as support for static and dynamic analysis, performance, safety, security, schedulability, portability, conformance to standards, reliability, and aid in project management [23] are needed to enhance the performance.

- Styles: An architectural style defines a design vocabulary of components, connectors, constraints and how that vocabulary can be used and combined, and semantic assumptions about that vocabulary. For example, Pipe and Filter style might define vocabulary in which a component has a set of inputs to read streams of data and a set of outputs to produce streams of data. Components produce streams of data by applying a local transformation to the input stream and computing incrementally so output begins before input is consumed, so components are data transformers (filters). Connectors guide the streams of data and transmit outputs of one filter to inputs of another; hence connectors are pipes [20]. Other common styles include object-oriented style, event-based style, layered style, client-server style, and blackboard style. Each style is appropriate for certain design. For instance, a pipe and filter style could be used for a data manipulating and passing applications but it is not appropriate for handling interaction applications, and a blackboard style might be used for applications in which there is a shared data access. In [21], Garlan argued that the use of architecture styles has a number of practical benefits, summarized in five points. First, it promotes design reuse: Routine solutions with well-understood properties can be reapplied to new problems with confidence. Second, it can lead to significant code reuse: Often the invariant aspects of an architectural style lend themselves to shared implementations. Third, it is easier for others to understand a system's organization if conventionalized structures are used. For example, even without giving details, characterization of a system as a "client-server" organization immediately conveys a strong image of the kinds of pieces and how they fit together. Fourth, by constraining the design space, an architectural style often permits specialized, style-specific analyses. For example, it is possible to analyze pipe-filter systems for schedulability, throughput, latency and deadlock-freedom. Such analyses might not be meaningful for an arbitrary, *ad hoc* architecture, or even one constructed in a different style. Fifth, it is usually possible to provide style-specific visualizations: This makes it possible to provide graphical and textual renderings that match engineers' domain-specific intuitions about how their designs should be depicted.

3.2. *Architecture description languages*

Architecture description languages are formal languages that can be used to represent the architecture of a software system. As architecture becomes a dominating theme in large systems development and acquisition, methods for unambiguously specifying an architecture will become indispensable. By architecture, we mean the components that comprise a system, the behavioral specifications for those components, the patterns and mechanisms for interactions among them (connectors), and a model defining the topology of a system (configuration). Note that a single system is usually composed of more than one type of components: Modules, tasks, functions, etc. An architecture can choose the type of component most appropriate or informative to show, or it can include multiple views of the same system, each illustrating different view of the same system.

A great number of architecture description languages were proposed. In the following, we present the most well known ones:

- Rapide [40,41] is an executable architecture description language, although it has many of the features of present-day event-based simulation languages. It also provides new features to represent system architecture.
- Aesop [22] is an ADL that is used for the specification of architectures in specific styles.
- MetaH [9,73] was presented to define the architecture of the systems in the guidance, navigation, and control (GN&C) domain.
- UniCon [63] is an ADL with glue code generation for interconnecting existing components using a set of predefined build-in connectors.
- Darwin [42] is an ADL with a support of components and no means of defining connectors. It is used for describing architectures of highly-distributed systems whose dynamisms is guided by strict formal underpinnings.
- Wright [3,4] is an ADL with a support of components, connectors, component nesting and architecture styles. It focuses on behavior specification of components and connectors via a CSP-based notation at design time.
- C2 [46] is a component and message-based style designed to support the particular needs of applications that have a graphical user interface aspect, with the potential for supporting other types of applications as well.
- SOFA [54,55] is a project aiming to provide a platform for software components. In the SOFA component model, applications are viewed as a hierarchy of nested components.

- Fractal ADL [12, 16] is an XML-based ADL that can be used to describe Fractal component configurations. A simplified ADL, not based on XML, can also be used, and other ADLs can be created if needed (indeed these ADLs are not part of the Fractal component model itself: They are just tools based on this model).
- ArchJava [1, 2] is an extension to Java that allows programmers to express the architectural structure of an application within the source code. To allow programmers to describe architectural structure, ArchJava adds new language constructs to support components, connections, and ports.
- COSA (Component-Object based Software Architecture) [52, 68] is an architecture description approach based on architectural description and object-oriented modeling. It describes systems in terms of classes and instances. Components, connectors, and configurations are classes that can be instantiated to build different architectures. COSA separates architecture description from deployment, hence it is possible to deploy a given component architecture in several ways, without rewriting the configuration/deployment program.
- ACME [23, 24] is an interchange language that is intended to support mapping of architectural specifications from one ADL to another and, hence, enable integration of support tools across ADLs [47].

Several works have been undertaken to establish a general and precise standard of an ADL [14, 35, 41, 47, 64, 72]. Clements [14] and Kogut [35] provide a wide classification of existing ADLs. This classification is based on a questionnaire of the ADL characteristics supplemented by the design teams. They used field analysis techniques to determine the characteristics that an ADL must contain. They carried out an evaluation of the existing languages by respecting these characteristics. The work of Vestal *et al* [72] was based on the analysis of four ADLs (LILEANNA, MetaH, Rapide and QAD) in order to identify their common properties. This work showed that each ADL supports with various degrees the following concepts: Component, connector, hierarchical composition, computation paradigm i.e., semantic, nonfunctional constraints and properties, communication paradigm, formal model and modeling, analysis, evaluation checking tool supports. In their work, Medvidovic and Taylor [47] tried to determine the fields that have been considered by an ADL. The study of these fields includes the characteristics of an ADL. Indeed, these authors showed that each ADL supports a set of fields. A better comprehension of these fields guides the development of rising generations of ADL. The analysis of these fields helps the architect in his choice of an ADL. Also, these authors proved that an ADL describes architecture on four levels of abstractions: Internal component semantics, component interfaces, component interconnections, and architectural style rules. Luckham and Vera [41] established a list of requirements for an ADL. These are component abstraction, communication abstraction, communication integrity, capacity to model a dynamic architecture, hierarchical composition, and capacity to connect behaviors between architectures. Shaw and Garlan [64] have given a list of properties that an ADL must provide: Composition, abstraction, re-use, configuration, heterogeneity, and analysis. In another work [63], Shaw *et al* also identified that an ADL must verify some properties like architectural information presentation, instance construction, instance composition, choice between design and implementation, checking of coherence between specification and implementation, and analysis.

Finally, several works have been done in using UML as an architecture description language [27, 43, 59]. All these works are based on extending UML to support ADL notations using UML extension mechanisms [56] and the Object Constraint Language [74].

4. Similarities between Object-Oriented Modeling and Architectural Description

Object-oriented modeling and architectural description have many things in common. In fact the two have been built based on similar concepts, which are abstraction and components interaction. In architectural description, components and connectors are the foci of the system, where components are the abstraction of modules and connectors are the description of the communication and the interactions among those components. While in object-oriented systems, classes are given as an abstraction of data, and functions serve as interfaces to that data, also associations are provided to describe the relations and the communications among classes and their objects. In terms of architecture in general the similarity between the two fields is obvious [24]. In terms of intentions, the two fields are aimed toward reducing costs of developing applications and increasing the potential for related product family, hence encouraging reusability and component based programming [53, 66]. The two have their focus shifted from lines of code to coarser grained architecture elements and their overall interconnection structure.

Given these similarities, it is worth asking the question: What are the important differences between the two fields? We will answer to this question by giving the advantages and limitations of each one of them compared to the other.

4.1. *Object-oriented modeling*

- Object-orientation is well known by a broad community of engineers and developers and supported by commercial tools. ADLs remain an *ad hoc* concept known only to academic communities.
- Object-orientation has many methods to develop systems starting from a whole of needs.
- Software architecture provides only high-level models, without ways to relate those models to source code. As noted in [24] such a link is important

to preserve the integrity of the design. Object-oriented modeling offers such a linkage, e.g. in UML we can convert a diagram to C++ or Java code.

- Object-orientation offers multi-views of a system like the different diagrams in UML (class diagram, object diagram, interaction diagram, component diagram, ...), multiple views are not clearly supported by ADL. Such views are important since different aspects of a system (e.g. behavior versus structural) need different requirements for description.
- The object-oriented programming community has presented UML as a standard notation for most of the object-oriented modeling notations. The architecture community is much less cohesive, leading to a different number of notations and approaches (and may contradictable).

4.2. *Architectural description*

- In software architecture connectors are first-class entities of interactions described explicitly through ports and roles. They go beyond simple function calls (used in object-orientation), permitting description of complex forms of communication description as new component integration mechanisms [24, 62].
- Software architecture supports non-functional properties such as performance, safety, security, schedulability, portability, conformance to standards, and reliability not only desirable but also necessary. For architectural design such properties are as important as what is being computed. Object-orientation does not provide a direct support to analyze non-functional properties.
- Software architecture has a stronger hierarchical representation compared to object-orientation. It supports associating more detailed representations (or models) with the individual parts of architecture.
- Software architecture styles define a design vocabulary and specify a set of constraints on how that vocabulary can be used. Styles allow the architect to specialize a design task to specific domains, and provide improved opportunities for system analysis (for more details see [22]). Object-orientation lacks common well defined styles.
- Object-orientation specifies the service supplied by a component implementation, but it does not define the requirements of a component.
- But the most important point is that object-orientation does not allow the definition of a system global architecture before completing the construction of its components (implementation).

4.3. *Similarities and differences in terms of basic concepts*

Figure 4 shows the similarities and the differences between object-oriented modeling and architectural description in terms of basic concepts.

Basic elements	Architectural Description	Object-Oriented
Entities to encapsulate functionality	Component	Class
Entities to encapsulate communications	Connector	Function calls buried in classes
Communication among entities	Ports and roles	Message calls
System structure	Systems and representations	Programs and packages
Interface	Component/Connector Interface	Class interface
Properties	Functional and non-functional	Attributes (functional only)

Fig. 4.   Concepts available for the two approaches.

5. Coexisting Object-Oriented Modeling and Architectural Description

From the previous comparison it can be noted that neither the object-oriented approach nor the architectural description approach is without drawbacks and each one of them has its own qualities. Therefore, the question "what is the best way to coexist the two approaches?" remains open. There are a number of work conducted to coexist the two approaches [17,25,27,37,48,59,61,68]. In the following, we present some perspectives to respond to this question. Note that, the first perspective has focused on the non-structural aspects of architectures (behaviors, interactions and constraints), the second perspective has focused on the structural aspects of architectures (components, connectors, . . .), the third perspective has focused on modeling architectural views and the last perspective on the operational mechanisms of software architectures.

5.1. Modeling software architectures using object-oriented notations

In this perspective, the intention is to investigate the possibility of using the Unified Modeling Language [11] as a starting point for bringing architectural modeling into wider, industrial use [48]. The primary goal of this study is an assessment of UML's expressive power for modeling software architectures in the manner in which existing ADLs model architectures. In this context, the authors have defined a set of requirements for objectively evaluating UML ability to represent software architectures effectively [47]. This set of requirements are: (1) UML should be well suited to model the structural concerns of a system, (2) UML should be able to capture a variety of stylistic issues addressed both explicitly and implicitly by ADLs, (3) UML should be able to model the different behavioral aspects of a system focused upon by different ADLs, (4) UML should be able to support modeling of a wide range of component interactions paradigms, and (5) UML should be able to capture any constraints arising from a system's structure, behavior, interactions, and styles.

Three possible strategies for modeling software architectures using UML have been initially suggested: (1) using UML "As Is", (2) constraint the UML meta model using UML's built-in extension mechanisms and (3) extend the UML meta-model to directly support the needed architectural concepts. Each approach has certain potential advantages and disadvantages. An evaluation of these approaches has permitted to eliminate the third approach because it violates the key require-ment that the resulting notation must be conformed to the UML standard and could become compatible with UML-compliants tools. Therefore, we discuss in the following section only the two first strategies.

5.1.1. *UML as an architecture description language*

The goal of this strategy is to assess the support provided by UML for the needs of architectural modeling and to compare directly the modeling power provided by UML to that of an ADL. To demonstrate this strategy, Medvidovic *et al* have used an example application representing a simplified version of the meeting scheduler problem, initally described by [19] and have modeled this example in C2 archi-tectural style and its accompanying ADL [70]. It demonstrated that, to a large extent, C2-style architecture is modeled sucessfully in UML because many archi-tectural concepts are found in UML (interfaces, components,...). However, this strategy does not fully satisfy the structural needs of architectural description for two reasons: UML does not provide specialized constructs for modeling architec-tural artifacts and the rules of a given architectural style are directly reflected in its corresponding ADL and maintained by the accompanying toolset, whereas those rules must be applied mentally by the software architect who chooses to use UML.

5.1.2. *Constraining UML to model software architectures*

This strategy for modeling architectures in UML involves using OCL [74] to specify constraints on existing meta classes of UML's meta model. This strategy involves selecting one or more existing meta classes from the UML meta model in which to situate a given ADL modeling construct or capability and to define a stereotype that can be applied to instances of those meta classes in order to constrain their semantics to that of the associated ADL feature. This strategy treats UML as a core notation that is extended in order to support specific architectural concerns. To demonstrate this strategy, Medvidovic *et al* have provided examples of UML extensions for three ADLs: C2, Wright, and Rapide. The extensions based on these ADLs allow a broad assessment of UML's suitability for architecture modeling.

In C2 extension, constraining UML to enforce the rules of C2 style has been fairly straightforward because many C2 concepts are found in UML. However, each C2 concept had to be carefully and explicitly specified in UML. In the extensions based on Wright, the language does not enforce the rules of a particular style, but it is applicable to multiple styles. However, it still places certain topological constraints on architectures. Thus, certain stereotypes for Wright have been defined in much the same way for C2. Components and connectors are modeled as stereotypes classes, and their valid compositions in an architecture as stereotyped associations. Finally, in the extensions based on Rapide, some of the limitations of this strategy have been encountered. These limitations stem from weaknesses and ambiguities in the semantics of UML itself, especially in its semantics for state diagrams.

5.2. *Selecting UML modeling constructs to representing architectural elements*

Another perspective to coexist architectural description and object-oriented modeling has been conducted by Garlan *et al* [25]. The goal of this perspective is to enumerate and evaluate different options an architect has in selecting UML modeling constructs to represent architectural structure (i.e., components, connectors, systems, and styles). In this study, the authors investigate four strategies for modeling architectural elements: (1) UML classes as component types and component objects as their instances (2) UML classes as component types and UML classes as component instances, (3) UML components as component types and UML component instances as component instances and (4) UML subsystems as component types and subsystem instances as component instances. Also, [24] has considered the UML Real-Time Profile [60] as a particular variant on these strategies, based on the mapping of ADL concepts to UML Real-Time [13]. This study shows that, while each of the fourth choices has its merits, none of them is an ideal fit for the needs of software architectures in terms of semantic match, understandability, or completeness.

5.3. *Representing architectural views in UML*

In this perspective, the intention is to model architectural views by constraining UML [27]. This perspective focuses on the software architecture research community approach based on views [36,69]. Kruchten [36] presents the 4+1 view model of software architectures. The four main views are the logical, process, development, and physical views. Together, these views capture a software system's architecture. Soni *et al* [69] identify four structural categories of software architectures — conceptual, module interconnection, execution and code. The different views address different engineering concerns, and separation of such concerns helps the architect make sound decisions about design trade-offs. Each of the four views has particular elements that need to be described. The conceptual view describes the architecture in terms of domain elements. The module interconnexion view is a refinement of the conceptual view; it provides a functional and layered decomposition of the system. The execution view and code views closely correspond to Kruchten's dynamic and static views respectively. Hofmeister *et al* [27] concludes that the UML is deficient in describing some software architecture constructs like ports on components, correspondences between elements in different views, protocols, dynamic aspects of the structure and general sequences of activities. On the contrary, UML worked well for describing the static structure of the architecture, variability of a structure and a particular sequence of activities.

5.4. *Combining object-oriented modeling and architectural description*

In this perspective, the intention is to combine the two fields in a sole approach benefits from the qualities of each one of them in order to propose a hybrid (but still easy to understand) approach called Component-Object based Software Architecture (COSA) [34, 67]. It describes a system as a collection of components, with well-defined interfaces, that interact which each other using elements with well-defined interfaces and behavior called connectors. Figure 5 shows a meta-model of the COSA approach. Components and connectors in COSA are at the same level of abstraction and defined explicitly. This is not the case on the other approaches, where components are defined as first-class entities, however connectors are left tangled.

Obliging components to communicate via connectors has a number of significant benefits including increasing reusability (the same component can be used in a variety of environments, each of them providing specific communication primitives), direct support for distribution, location transparency and mobility of components in a system, support for dynamic changes in the system's connectivity, improving system's maintenance. In additional, various applications can be modeled more easily by using an approach in which components and connectors explicitly separated, e.g. distributed systems.

This approach separates a connector's interfaces (roles) from its behavior (glue). A glue specification describes the behavior that is expected from the interacted parties. It could be just a simple protocol linking the roles or it could be a complex protocol which does various operations including, in addition to linking, conversion of data format, transformation, adapting,.... In general, the glue of a connector represents the connection type of that connector [67].

5.5. *COSA's operational mechanisms*

There are some similarities between the operational mechanisms used in the object-oriented modeling approach and the mechanisms used in the architectural description approach. However, there are differences in the number of the mechanisms supported by each field and how they are supported. For example, object-orientation

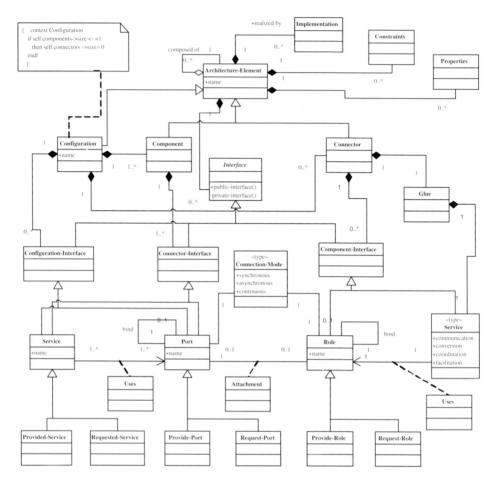

Fig. 5.   A meta-model shows the basic concepts of COSA approach.

allows the instantiation of classes only, meanwhile architectural description allows the instantiation of not only components but also connectors because they are also considered first-class entities. Another example is inheritance; inheritance in object-orientation is always non-selective, while in architectural description inheritance should be selective and non-selective. There are mechanisms that exist in one field and do not exist in the other. A mechanism like access control (data protection) exists in object-orientation only, whereas refinement and architecture styles exist in architectural description only.

It is obvious that there is an ambiguity in defining these mechanisms; there is also a mix of what is necessary and what is complementary. In what follows we define these mechanisms in a rigorous way that allows them to be used effectively in software architecture in general and in Component-Object based Software Architecture (COSA) in particular.

5.5.1. *Instantiation*

Software architecture distinguishes between component types and connector types, where component types are abstractions that encapsulate functionality into reusable blocks, and connector types are abstractions that encapsulate component communication, coordination, and mediation decisions [25, 45]. A component type can be instantiated multiple times in a single system. Regarding connectors, only ADLs that model connectors as first-class entities support their instantiations. ADLs such as Darwin [42], MetaH [73], and Rapide [40], which do not model connectors as first-class entities, do not support connectors' instantiations. ADLs' instantiation is similar to object-oriented instantiation. Figure 6 shows a system built using types (component and connector types) and instances of those types. The system example-instance is built using types (client, server and client-server-connector) and their instances (C1, S1, C1-S1).

5.5.2. *Inheritance and subtyping*

Inheritance and subtyping are two different ways of reusing models. Inheritance permits the reuse of a model itself; meanwhile subtyping supports the reuse of objects of a model. In this section, we present successively inheritance and typing to software architecture.

```
Style Example {
       Component server {
             Port provide {provide protocol;}
             Properties {properties;}
                    }
       Component client {
             Port request {request protocol;}
             Properties {properties;}
                    }
       Connector client-server-connector {
             Role server {server Role protocol;}
             Role client {client Role protocol;}
             Properties {properties;}
                    }
       }
System example-instance {
       S1= server;
       C1= client;
       C1-S1= client-server-connector;
             Attachments {
                    C1.request to C1-S1.client;
                    S1.provide to C1-S1.server;
                          }
       }
```

Fig. 6. An example of instantiation in COSA.

- Inheritance: Booch defines inheritance as a representation of abstractions' hierarchy, in which a submodel inherits from one or more supermodels. Typically, a submodel augments or redefines the existing structure and behavior of its supermodel [10]. Inheritance provides a natural classification for kinds of models and allows for the commonality of models to be explicitly taken advantage of in constructing complex systems. It is a powerful tool for evolution by allowing an inherited model to be modified by adding, deleting, or changing its internal structure. A relation of inheritance akin to that available in object-oriented languages will be very appreciated in architectural description. Inheritance improves reusability and evolution, allowing the replacement of components and connectors within the system by specialized versions, which maintain some of the properties of the original ones. It refers to a relation among components/connectors by which a component/connector inherits the properties of its parents and it can extend them by adding its own properties. The interface of a subcomponent/subconnector includes those of its parents. In architectural description, a system is composed of components that interact with each other via connectors. Each component defines its interfaces by a set of ports [23]. Each port identifies a point of interaction between the component and its environment. A component may use different ports for different interaction processes. Ports could be provided (export data) or required (import data). A component's port describes the interaction of that component specifically. Hence, if a component inherits another component, the subcomponent should redefine the supercomponent's ports to make sure that they correspond to its interactions. Regarding connectors, they also include interfaces defined by a set of roles. Each role of a connector defines a participant of the interaction represented by the connector [23]. Therefore, inheriting a connector requires modifying its roles in the heir (subconnector) to guarantee its functionality.

  Inheritance in software architecture should be selective and dynamic. Selective by using keywords such as and, not, and extend, to ensure that one can have different combinations (e.g. interface not behavior, interface and implementation, etc.). Dynamic by allowing subcomponents and subconnectors to modify what they inherit. Also, inheritance could be multiple, where a subcomponent (or subconnector) can inherit from more than one component (or connector). For example, an interface from one component, a behavior from another component, and an implementation from a third. Figure 7 gives an example of inheriting components and connectors in architectural description.

- Subtyping: Subtyping and supertyping can be defined by the following rule: A type x is a subtype of type y if values of type x can be used in any context where type y is expected without introducing errors [39]. In one word, subtyping is where an object of one type may safely be substituted where another type was expected [5]. The difference between subtyping

```
Style example1 {
    Component client {
      Ports {client-ports;}
      Properties {properties;}
      Behavior {client-behavior;}
      }
    Component client1 inherits client {
                        // inheriting component
      Ports {client1-ports;}
                        // redefine client's port
      }
    Connector link {
      Roles {link-roles;}
      Properties {properties;}
      Behavior {link-behavior;}
      }
    Connector con1 inherits link (not behavior) {
    //inheriting connector, excluding its behavior
      Roles {con-roles;} //redefine link's role
      Behavior {con1-behavior;} }
      }
```

Fig. 7.   An example of inheritance in COSA.

and subclassing is that in subtyping the component is a more specific type, but behaves exactly like the more general expectations. Meanwhile, in subclassing the component is a more specific type and behaves in ways that exceed the more general expectations. Components' and connectors' specifications are architecture types. Architectural types are distinguished from basic types (e.g. integers, characters, arrays, etc.). In object-oriented, objects communicate by passing around other objects. This is not the case in architectural description where components are distinguished from the data they exchange. A component has a name, a set of interfaces with direction indicator (provided or required), an associated behavior, and an implementation [44]. Given these definitions of a component, it is possible to specify its subtyping relationships. We can see three different component's subtyping relationships: Interface subtyping, behavior subtyping, and implementation subtyping [46]. Interface subtyping (Int) requires that if a component C1 is an interface subtype of another component C2, then C2 must specify at least the provided and at most the required interface elements from C1. Behavior subtyping (Beh) requires that each provided operation of the supertype must have a corresponding provided operation in the subtype. Finally, implementation subtyping (Imp) may be established with a syntactic check if the operations of the subtype have identical implementations as the corresponding operations of the supertype. Finally, it should be noted that in component-based systems typing must be preferred to inheritance. As noted in [26], inheritance is problematic for component composition because it breaks encapsulation. Inheritance is an

```
LayoutManager_SkyBlue is_subtype
    all ← all LayoutManager (int and beh);
    object ← all SkyBlue (int and imp);
end_subtype;
```

Fig. 8.   An example of subtyping in COSA.

open relation, where the submodel usually has full access to the internals of the supermodel. In object-oriented a mechanism called access control has been introduced to overcome this problem by indicating what parts of a subclass can be seen and what must be hidden. This mechanism should be used in component-based systems. Figure 8 describes how subtyping methods are used in COSA; this example is inspired from C2.

Some ADLs do not support inheritance and rely on underlining languages. A number of ADLs model components as inherently static, for instance, MetaH [73] and UniCon [22] support inheritance but do not allow evolution of the inherited components. Whereas, ADLs like ACME [23] support strictly subtyping using its extends feature. Rapide [40] uses object-oriented inheritance. C2 [46] supports multiple subtyping by offering a mechanism to select what parts of a component can be changed (behavior, interface, implementation) and what cannot, using keys such as "and", "or", and "not". SADL [50] provides features for refining inherited components, with respect to certain constraints, similar to object-oriented extending inherited class mechanism. Medvidovic and Taylor argued that ADLs subtyping is a form of refinement and it is similar to object-oriented extending features [47]. Only ADLs that do not model connectors as first-class elements do not provide a mechanism to inherit them. These include ADLs such as Darwin, MetaH, and Rapide. Several ADLs such as ACME, SADL, and C2 support connectors' inheritance using mechanism identical to components inheritance.

Hence, it can be noted that ADLs vary in their way of dealing with inheritance. There is mix of different types of inheritance; there are ADLs that support inheritance statically (i.e., MetaH and UniCon), in contrary, ADLs like SADL allows an inherited components or connectors to be modified. We can find selective inheritance in ADLs like C2. Some ADLs such as Darwin, MetaH, and Rapide support components' inheritance only. Meanwhile, ADLs like ACME allows not only the inheritance of components and connectors but also the inheritance of systems.

5.5.3. *Templates*

Templates refer to the ability to parameterize types. Instantiation provides no facility to parameterize instantiated types. As a result, common structures in complex system descriptions need to be repeatedly specified. Take, for example, instantiating clients and servers in a client-server system, although there is a significant common structure underlying each of the clients and the servers in a design, the definition of clients or servers in a system is different from one to another (from one client to another client and from one server to another server) and each instance of a client (or a server) need to be parameterized specifically. ADLs such as ACME, SADL, and Wright [3] make explicit use of a component/connector interface signatures parameterization, while Darwin and Rapide support components parameterization only because they do not define connectors as first-class entities. For instance, ACME includes Templates [23], a typed, parameterized facility for the specification of reusing patterns. ADLs' Templates are similar to object-oriented's Templates, which are used with classes that require source code modification in order to reuse them effectively. Figure 9 illustrates the use of Templates in COSA; this example is inspired from ACME.

Style client-server {
  Component Template client (rpc-call-ports : Ports)
    {
    Ports {rpc-call-ports;}
    Properties {responsetime : $float$ = 10.00;}
    }
  Component Template server (rpc-receive-ports : Ports)
    {
    Ports {rpc-receive-ports;}
    Properties {responsetime : $float$ = 20.00;}
    }
  Connector Template rpc (caller_port, callee_port :
          Ports) defining (conn : Connector)
    {
    conn = Connector {
        Roles {caller, callee}
        Properties {synchronous : boolean = true;
            max-roles : integer = 2; }
            }
    Attachments {conn.caller to caller_port;
            conn.callee to callee_port; }
    }

System complex_cs {
    c1 = client(send-request); c2 = client(send-request);
    c3 = client(send-request);
    s1 = server(receive-request);
    s2 = server(receive-request);
    rpc(c1.send-request, s1.receive-request);
    rpc(c2.send-request, s1.receive-request);
    rpc(c3.send-request, s2.receive-request);
    }

Fig. 9. An example of templates in COSA.

```
Component composite1 {
    provide provserv;
    require reqserv;
    Inst
        C1: Comptype1;
        C2: Comptype2;
    Bind
        provserv – C1.prov;
        C2.req – reqserv;
    }
```

Fig. 10.   An example of compositionality in COSA.

5.5.4. *Compositionality*

Compositionality is the ability to describe a system as a composite of sub-systems of existing components. It allows architects to describe software systems at different levels of details [47]. However, this mechanism requires that the *components/connectors* have well-defined interfaces since their internals are unknown. Because models are treated only as "black boxes" (the internal structure of a *component/connector* is hidden and its interface is the only seen part), this type of reuse is often called black-box reuse [51]. In architectural description components and connectors can be either simple or composite. A composite *component/connector* contains several *subcomponents/subconnectors*. Figure 10 shows how to describe a component composed of two components; the component Composite1 is composed of component C1 and component C2, the binding between the composites and the components' interfaces should be crisply defined.

Most ADLs provide explicit features to support composition of components [51]. Some ADLs (e.g. Wright) allow both composite components and connectors. In fact, ADLs that do not have a mechanism to model system architecture use composition to model architectures as a composite components. Examples of these ADLs include Darwin and UniCon, both model architectures as composite components.

5.5.5. *Refinement*

Architectural models may need to be specified at several levels of abstraction. Refinement of architectures consists of representing a high-level abstraction architectural model to subsequently lower levels of abstraction and eventually to executable systems. As stated by Medvidovic [47], refining architectural description is a complex task whose correctness and consistency cannot be guaranteed by formal proof, but adequate tool support can give architects increased confidence in this respect. Moriconi *et al* [50] have introduced the notion of an architecture refinement pattern as the principal vehicle for codifying reusable solutions to routine architectural design problems. In their language (SADL), refinement patterns enable correct refinement across styles [49]. However, this language does not take

```
arch_map MAPPING FROM arch_L1 TO arch_L2
     BEGIN
        comp → (new_comp)
        conn → (new_conn)
        port → (new_port)
        ...        END
```

Fig. 11. An example of refinement in COSA.

the final refinement step from architectural descriptions to source code. Another form of mapping between architectures has been developed for the Rapide architecture description language [40]. Two architectures are related by mapping concrete events to abstract events. Event mappings provide the basis for comparative simulation, a technique that complements static modeling. In C2 [46], architecture is refined into a partial implementation that contains completion guidelines for developers derived from the architectural description. C'2 does not provide executable language constructs but specifies, for example, a precondition and a post condition in each method generated by the language. Thus, the developer must only ensure their satisfaction when implementing the method and need not worry about the rest of the system. To support hierarchical descriptions of architectures, the ACME language [23] permits any component or connector to be represented by one or more detailed lower-level descriptions. Thus, to associate multiple representations with a design element (component or connector, for example), this language encodes multiple views of this element. Therefore, the correspondence between different descriptions is defined by the notion of representation-map (rep-map). A rep-map can be simple or complex. In the simplest case, a rep-map provides an association between internal ports and external ports of a component. Finally, only SADL [50] and Rapide [40] provide tool support for refining architectures across multiple levels of abstraction and specificity. SADL tool checks automatically whether any two architectures described in the two styles adhere to the mapping. Rapide tool compiles the event maps between architectures and the constraint checker part can verify that the events generated during simulation of the concrete architecture satisfy the constraints in the abstract architecture. Figure 11 describes a refinement mapping adapted from [47]; arch_L1 and arch_L2 are two levels of architecture.

5.5.6. *Traceability*

Software architecture consists of multiple views and may be modeled at multiple levels of abstraction. Traceability of architecture concerns with how to reflect correctly a change in a particular view of the architecture at a given level of abstraction to another view of the architecture at another level of abstraction. This mechanism is the one in which most existing ADLs are lacking. However ADLs commonly provide support for tracing changes between textual and graphical views, in a way that

Operational Mechanisms	Architectural description	Object-Oriented	COSA
Architectural styles	Client-Server, Pipe and Filters, Event-based, ...	———	Client-Server, Pipe and Filters, Event-based, ...
Instantiation	Components, connectors	Classes	Components, Connectors, Configurations
Inheritance and typing	Static and dynamic, selective and non-selective	Static and dynamic, selective and non-selective	Static and dynamic, selective and non-selective
Data protection	———	Public, Private, Protected	Public, Private, Protected
Templates	Templates (only in ACME)	Generics	Generics
Compositionality	Composition	Aggregation and composition	Composition and Aggregation
Refinement and traceability	Mapping and patterns	———-	———-

Fig. 12.   Operational mechanisms available for the three approaches.

insures changes in one view are automatically reflected in the other; yet, it may be less clear how the data flow view should affect the process view [45].

5.6. *Summary of the mechanisms and their availability on object-oriented, architectural description and COSA approaches*

Figure 12 summarizes the similarities and the differences between the object-oriented modeling, architectural description and COSA approaches in terms of operational mechanisms.

6. Conclusion and Future Work

Complex systems require expressive notations to representing their software architecture. Object-oriented notations (UML) and specialized notation for architecture (ADL) are two techniques that have emerged to describe such complex systems [25]. Object-oriented is sometimes called Object-Based Software Architecture (OBSA) whereas architectural description is sometimes called Component-Based Software Architecture (CBSA).

In this chapter, we have presented two software architecture approaches that are based on the construction of software from encapsulated entities that provide well-defined interfaces to a set of services. From an architectural perspective, architectural description approach defines architectural styles that are predominantly object-oriented. Modeling software architectures using notations, selecting UML modeling constructs to representing architectural elements, representing architectural views and combining object-oriented modeling and architectural description are some perspectives to coexist object-oriented and architectural description. Each one of these approaches focus on some aspects of software architectures. We think that the Component-Object based Software Architecture (COSA) approach is probably the best approach to the future of software architecture where it benefits from the qualities of the two approaches (object-oriented modeling and architectural description).

7. Resources

There are no journals or conferences dedicated completely to the coexistence of object oriented modeling and software architecture but there are some journals dedicated to object-oriented modeling only. As software architecture is a software engineering area, the Working IFIP Conference on Software Architecture (WICSA) and the International Software Architecture Workshop (ISAW) are the major venue on this area. The WICSA-4 is an ECOOP workshop and will be held in Oslo, Norway, 2004. Other conferences that address the theme of software architecture are: *The International Conference on Software Engineering (ICSE)*, *The European Software Engineering Conference (ESEC)* and *The ACM SIGSOFT Symposium on the Foundations of Software Engineering*.

The IEEE Transactions on Software Engineering has published a Special Issue on Software Architecture in April 1995. This special issue was forwarded by D. Garlan and D. E. Perry. Other journals that edit articles on software architecture are: *The ACM Transactions on Software Engineering and Methodology*, *The ACM Transactions on Programming Languages and Systems*, *The ACM Computing Surveys*, *The IEEE Software*, *The International Journal of Software Engineering and Knowledge Engineering (IJSEKE)*, World Scientific Publishing Company.

Pointers for further readings on software architecture can be found in *http://www.sei.cmu.edu/ata/ata_init.html* and some definitions of software architecture can be found in *http://www.sei.cmu.edu/architecture/definitions.html*. Other pointers can be found in the IEEE standard [28] and in [76].

References

1. J. Aldrich, C. Chambers and D. Notkin, "ArchJava: Connecting software architecture to implementation", *Proceeding of the 24th International Conference on Software Engineering (ICSE'02)*, Orlando, USA (May 2002) 187–197.
2. J. Aldrich, V. Sazawa, C. Chambers and D. Notkin, "Language support for connector abstractions", *Proceeding of 2003 European Conference on Object-Oriented Programming (ECOOP 2003)*, Darmstadt, Germany (July 2003).

3. R. Allen, "A formal approach to software architecture", PhD Thesis, CMU Technical Report CMU-CS-97-144, Carnegie Mellon University, Pennsylvania, Pittsburgh (May 1997).

4. R. Allen and D. Garlan, "A formal basis for architectural connection", *ACM Transactions on Software Engineering and Methodology* **6**, no. 3 (July 1997) 213–249.

5. J. Anthony and H. Simons, "The theory of classification, Part 1: Perspectives on type compatibility", *Journal of Object Technology* **1**, no. 1 (May–June 2002) 55–61, *http://www.jot.fm/issues/issue_2002_05/column5.*

6. L. Bass, P. Clements and R. Kazman, *Software Architecture in Practice* (Addison Wesley, 1998).

7. F. Bergenti and A. Poggi, "Agent-oriented software construction with UML", *Handbook of Software Engineering and Knowledge Engineering*, ed. S. K. Chang **2** (World Scientific Publishing Company, Singapore, 2002) 757–770.

8. F. Bergenti and A. Poggi, "Improving UML designs using automatic design pattern detection", *Handbook of Software Engineering and Knowledge Engineering*, ed. S. K. Chang **2** (World Scientific Publishing Company, Singapore, 2002) 771–784.

9. P. Binns, M. Englehart, M. Jackson and S. Vestal, "Domain specific software architectures for guidance, navigation and control", *International Software Engineering and Knowledge Engineering Journal* **6**, no. 2 (1996).

10. G. Booch, *Object Oriented Design with Applications* (The Benjamin/Cummings Publishing Company, Redwood City, California, 1991).

11. G. Booch, J. Rumbaugh and I. Jacobson, *The Unified Modeling Language User Guide* (Addison-Wesley Professional, Reading, Massachusetts, 1998).

12. E. Bruneton, "Developing with fractal", The ObjectWeb Consortium (2004), *http://fractal.objectweb.org/tutorial/.*

13. S. Cheng and D. Garlan, "Mapping architectural concepts to UML-RT", *Proceedings of the Parallel and Distributed Processing Techniques and Applications* (June 2001).

14. P. Clements, "A survey of architecture description languages", *Proceedings of the Eighth International Workshop on Software Specification and Design*, Schloss Velen, Germany (March 1996).

15. P. Clements, F. Bachmann, L. Bass, D. Garlan, J. Ivers, R. Little, R. Nord and J. Stafford, *Documenting Software Architectures: Views and Beyond* (Addison Wesley, 2003).

16. T. Coupaye, E. Bruneton and J. B. Stefani, "The fractal composition framework", Proposed Final Draft of Interface Specification Version 0.9, The ObjectWeb Consortium (June 2002).

17. A. Egyed and P. Kruchten, "Rose/Architect: A tool to visualize architecture", *Proceedings of the 32nd Annual Hawaii International Conference on Systems Sciences (HICSS'99)* (1999).

18. G. Engels and S. Sauer, "Object-oriented modeling of multimedia applications", *Handbook of Software Engineering and Knowledge Engineering*, ed. S. K. Chang **2** (World Scientific Publishing Company, Singapore, 2002) 21–52.

19. M. S. Feather, S. Fickas and A. van Lamweerde, "Requirements and specification exemplars", *Automated Software Engineering Journal* **4**, no. 4 (1997) 419–438.

20. D. Garlan and M. Shaw, "An introduction to software architecture", *Advances in Software Engineering and Knowledge Engineering*, eds. V. Ambriola and G. Tortora **1** (World Scientific Publishing Company, Singapore, 1993) 1–39.

21. D. Garlan, "What is style", *Proceedings of Dagshtul Workshop on Software Architecture*, Saarbruecken, Germany (February 1995).

22. D. Garlan, "An introduction to the AESOP system" (July 1995), *http://www.cs.cmu. edu/afs/cd/project/able/www/aesop/html.*

23. D. Garlan, R. Monroe and D. Wile, "ACME: An architecture description interchange language", *Proceedings of CASCON 97*, Toronto, Canada (November 1997) 169–183.

24. D. Garlan, "Software architecture and object-oriented systems", *Proceedings of the IPSJ Object-Oriented Symposium 2000*, Tokyo, Japan (August 2000).

25. D. Garlan, S. Cheng and J. Kompanek, "Reconciling the needs of architectural description with object-modeling notations", *Science of Computer Programming Journal* **44** (Elsevier Press, 2001) 23–49.

26. W. Hasselbring, "Component-based software engineering", *Handbook of Software Engineering and Knowledge Engineering*, ed. S. K. Chang **2** (World Scientific Publishing Company, Singapore, 2002) 289–306.

27. C. Hofmeister, R. L. Nord and D. Soni, "Describing software architecture with UML", *Proceedings of the First Working IFIP Conference on Software Architecture*, San Antonio, Texas (IEEE Computer Society Press, February 1999) 145–160.

28. IEEE Draft for Standard, IEEE P1471 Draft Recommended Practice for Architectural Description (October 1999).

29. I. Jacobson, *Object-Oriented Software Engineering: A Use Case Driven Approach* (Addison-Wesley, New York, 1992).

30. Y. Kalfoglou, "Exploring ontologies", *Handbook of Software Engineering and Knowledge Engineering*, ed. S. K. Chang **1** (World Scientific Publishing Company, Singapore, 2001) 863–887.

31. A. Kay, "Computer software", *Scientific American* **251**, no. 3 (1984) 53–59.

32. R. Kazman, "Software architecture", *Handbook of Software Engineering and Knowledge Engineering*, ed. S. K. Chang **1** (World Scientific Publishing Company, Singapore, 2001) 47–67.

33. M. Kim, S. Lee, I. Park, J. Kim and S. Park, "Agent-oriented software modeling", *Proceedings of the Sixth Asia Pacific Software Engineering Conference*, Takamatsu, Japan (1999) 318–325.

34. T. Khammaci, A. Smeda and M. Oussalah, "Active connectors for component-object based software architecture", *Proceedings of the International Conference on Software Engineering and Knowledge Engineering (SEKE'04)*, Banff, Alberta, Canada (June 2004) 346–349.

35. P. Kogut and P. Clements, "Features of architecture description languages", CMU-SEI Technical Report, Carnegie Mellon University, Pennsylvania, Pittsburgh (December 1994).

36. P. B. Kruchten, "The 4+1 view model of architecture", *IEEE Software* **12**, no. 6 (November 1995) 42–50.

37. P. B. Kruchten, B. Selic and W. Kozaczynski, "Describing software architecture with UML", *Proceedings of the 23rd International Conference on Software Engineering (ICSE'01)* (2001) 715–716.

38. J. Lind, "Issues in agent-oriented software engineering", *Proceedings of the First International Workshop on Agent-Oriented Software Engineering (AOSE-2000)* (2000).

39. B. Liskov, "Data abstraction and hierarchy", *ACM SIGPLAN Notices* **23**, no. 5 (1988) 17–34.

40. D. C. Luckham, L. M. Augustin, J. J Kenny, J. Vera, D. Bryan and W. Mann, "Specification and analysis of system architecture using Rapide", *IEEE Transactions on Software Engineering* **21**, no. 4 (April 1995) 336–355.

41. D. C. Luckham and J. Vera, "An event-based architecture definition language", *IEEE Transactions on Software Engineering* **21**, no. 9 (September 1995) 717–734.

42. J. Magee, N. Dulay, S. Eisenbach and J. Kramer, "Specifying distributed software architectures", *Proceedings of the Fifth European Software Engineering Conference (ESEC'95)*, Barcelona, Spain (September 1995).

43. M. Mancona and A. Strohmeier, "Towards a UML profile for software architecture descriptions", *Proceedings of UML'2000 — The Unified Modeling Language: Advancing the Standard, Third International Conference, Lecture Notes in Computer Science 1939* (Springer, October 2000) 513–527.

44. N. Medvidovic, P. Oreizy, J. E. Robbins and R. N. Taylor, "Using object-oriented typing to support architecture design in the C2 style", *Proceedings of the Fourth ACM SIGSOFT Symposium on the Foundations of Software Engineering (FSE'96)*, San Francisco, CA (October 1996) 24–32.

45. N. Medvidovic and D. S. Rosenblum, "Domains of concern in software architectures and architecture description languages", *Proceedings of the USENIX Conference on Domain-Specific Languages*, Santa Barbara, CA (October 1997) 199–212.

46. N. Medvidovic, D. Rosenblum and R. Taylor, "A language and environment for architecture-based software development and evolution", *Proceedings of the 21st International Conference on Software Engineering*, Los Angeles, CA, USA (May 1999) 44–53.

47. N. Medvidovic and R. N. Taylor, "A classification and comparison framework for software architecture description languages", *IEEE Transactions on Software Engineering* **26**, no. 1 (January 2000) 70–93.

48. N. Medvidovic, D. S. Rosenblum, J. E. Robbins and D. F. Redmiles, "Modeling software architecture in the unified modeling language", *ACM Transactions on Software Engineering and Methodology* **11**, no. 1 (January 2002) 2–57.

49. M. Moriconi, X. Qian and R. A. Riemenschneider, "Correct architecture refinement", *IEEE Transactions on Software Engineering* **21**, no. 4 (April 1995) 356–372.

50. M. Moriconi and R. A. Riemenschneider, "Introduction to SADL 1.0: A language for specifying software architecture hierarchies", Technical Report SRI-CSL-97, SRI International, Menlo Park, CA (March 1997).

51. K. Ostermann and M. Mezini, "Object-oriented composition untangled", *Proceedings of OOPSLA 2001*, Tampa Bay, Florida (November 2001) 283–299.

52. M. Oussalah, A. Smeda and T. Khammaci, "An explicit definition of connectors for component-based software architecture", *Proceedings of the IEEE International Conference on the Engineering of Computer Based Systems (ECBS'04)*, Brno, Czech Republic (IEEE CS Press, May 2004) 44–51.

53. D. Perry and A. Wolf, "Foundations for the study of software architectures", *ACM SIGSOFT Software Engineering Notes* **17**, no. 4 (October 1992) 40–52.

54. F. Plasil, D. Balek and J. Radovan, "SOFA/DCUP: Architecture for component trading and dynamic updating", *Proceedings of ICCDS 98*, Annapolis, Maryland, USA (IEEE CS Press, 1998) 43–52.

55. F. Plasil, M. Besta and S. Visnovsky, "Bounding component behavior via protocols", *Proceedings of Technology of Object-Oriented Languages and Systems (TOOLS'99)*, Santa Barbara, USA (1999) 387–398.

56. Rational Software Corporation and IBM, "Object constraint language specification", Object Management Group document ad/97-07-05 (July 1997), *http://www.omg.org/docs/*.

57. Rational Partners, "UML semantics", Object Management Group document ad/97-08-04, September 1997, *http://www.omg.org/docs/ad/97-08-04.pdf*.

58. J. Rumbaugh, M. Blaha, W. Premerlani, F. Eddy and W. Lorenson, *Object-Oriented Modeling and Design* (Prentice-Hall, Englewood Cliff, NJ, 1991).

59. B. Rumpe, A. Radermacher and A. Schurr, "UML + ROOM as a standrad ADL?", *Proceedings of the 5th IEEE International Conference on Engineering of Complex Computer Systems*, Las Vegas, Nevada (October 1999) 43–53.

60. B. Selic, "Turning clockwise: Using UML in the real-time domain", *Communications of the ACM* **42**, no. 10 (October 1999) 46–54.

61. B. Selic and J. Rumbaugh, "Using UML for modeling complex real-time systems", ObjectTime white paper, June 2000, *http://www.objectime.com*.

62. M. Shaw, "Procedure calls are the assembly language of software interconnection: Connectors deserve first-class status", CMU-CS-94-107 Technical Report, Carnegie Mellon University, Pennsylvania, Pittsburgh (January 1994).

63. M. Shaw, R. DeLine, D. V. Klein, T. J. Ross, M. Young and G. Zelesnick, "Abstractions for software architecture and tools to support them", *IEEE Transactions on Software Engineering* **21**. no. 4 (April 1995) 314–335.

64. M. Shaw and D. Garlan, "Formulations and formalisms in software architecture", *Computer Science Today, Recent Trends and Development* (Springer-Verlag, UK, 1995) 307–323.

65. M. Shaw, D. Garlan, R. Allen, D. Klein, J. Ockerbloom, C. Scott and M. Schumacher, "Candidate model problems in software architecture", November 1995, *http://www.cs.cmu.edu./afs/cs/project/compose/www/html/ModProb/*.

66. M. Shaw and D. Garlan, *Software Architecture: Perspectives on an Emerging Discipline* (Prentice Hall, New York, 1996).

67. A. Smeda, M. Oussalah and T. Khammaci, "Software connectors reuse in component-based systems", *Proceedings of the 2003 IEEE International Conference on Information Reuse and Integration*, Las Vegas, Nevada (October 2003) 473–500.

68. A. Smeda, M. Oussalah and T. Khammaci, "A multi-paradigm approach to describe complex software systems", *WSEAS Transactions on Computers* **3**, no. 4 (October 2004) 936–941.

69. D. Soni, R. L. Nord and C. Hofmeister, "Software architecture in industrial applications", *Proceedings of the 17th International Conference on Software Engineering (ICSE'17)*, Seattle, WA, USA (1995) 196–207.

70. R. N. Taylor, N. Medvidovic, K. M. Anderson, E. J. Whitehead Jr., J. E. Robbins, K. A. Nies, P. Oreizy and D. L. Dubrow, "A component- and message-based architectural style for GUI software", *IEEE Transactions on Software Engineering* (June 1996) 390–406.

71. URL: *http://www.omg.org*.

72. S. Vestal, "A cursory overview and comparison of four architecture description languages", Technical Report, Honeywell Technology Center, Minnesota, USA (February 1993).

73. S. Vestal, "MetaH programmer's manual", Version 1.09, Technical Report, Honeywell Technology Center, Minnesota, USA (April 1996).

74. J. B. Warmer and A. G. Kleppe, *The Object Constraint Language: Precise Modeling with UML* (Addison-Wesley, Reading, 1998).

75. M. Wooldridge and P. Ciancarini, "Agent-oriented software engineering", *Handbook of Software Engineering and Knowledge Engineering*, ed. S. K. Chang **1** (World Scientific Publishing Company, Singapore, 2001) 507–522.

76. R. Youngs, D. Redmond-Pyle, P. Spaas and E. Kahan, "A standard for architecture description", *IBM Systems Jounal* **38**, no. 1 (1999) 32–50.

INTROSPECTING AGENT-ORIENTED DESIGN PATTERNS

MANUEL KOLP* and T. TUNG DO

University of Louvain,
ISYS — Information Systems Research Unit,
Place des Doyens, 1, 1348, Louvain-La-Neuve, Belgium
E-mail: {kolp, do}@isys.ucl.ac.be

STÉPHANE FAULKNER

University of Namur,
Department of Management Sciences,
Rempart de la Vierge, 8, 5000 Namur, Belgium
E-mail: Stephane.Faulkner@fundp.ac.be

Multi-Agent Systems (MAS) architectures are gaining popularity over traditional ones for building open, distributed, and evolving software required by today's corporate IT applications such as eBusiness systems, Web services or enterprise knowledge bases. Since the fundamental concepts of multi-agent systems are social and intentional rather than object, functional, or implementation-oriented, the design of MAS architectures can be eased by using *social patterns*. They are detailed agent-oriented design idioms to describe MAS architectures as composed of autonomous agents that interact and coordinate to achieve their intentions, like actors in human organizations. This chapter presents social patterns and focuses on a framework aimed to gain insight into these patterns. The framework can be integrated into agent-oriented software engineering methodologies used to build MAS. We consider the *Broker* social pattern to illustrate the framework. The mapping from system architectural design (through organizational architectural styles), to system detailed design (through social patterns), is overviewed with a *data integration* case study. The automation of patterns design is also overviewed.

Keywords: Social structures, design patterns, agent-oriented software engineering, multi-agent architectures.

1. Introduction

The meteoric rise of Internet and World Wide Web technologies has created overnight new application areas for enterprise software, including eBusiness, web services, ubiquitous computing, knowledge management and peer-to-peer networks. These areas demand software that is robust, can operate within a wide range of environments, and can evolve over time to cope with changing requirements. Moreover, such software has to be highly customizable to meet the needs of a wide range of users, and sufficiently secure to protect personal data and other assets on behalf of its stakeholders.

---

*Corresponding author.

Not surprisingly, researchers are looking for new software designs that can cope with such requirements. One promising source of ideas for designing such business software is the area of multi-agent systems. Multi-agent system architectures appear to be more flexible, modular and robust than traditional including object-oriented ones. They tend to be open and dynamic in the sense that they exist in a changing organizational and operational environment where new components can be added, modified or removed at any time.

Multi-agent systems are based on the concept of agent which is defined as "a software component situated in some environment that is capable of flexible autonomous action in order to meet its design objective" [1]. An agent exhibits the following characteristics:

- Autonomy: An agent has its own internal thread of execution, typically oriented to the achievement of a specific task, and it decides for itself what actions it should perform at what time.
- Situateness: Agents perform their actions in the context of being situated in a particular environment. This environment may be a computational one (e.g. a Web site) or a physical one (e.g. a manufacturing pipeline). The agent can sense and affect some portion of that environment.
- Flexibility: In order to accomplish its design objectives in a dynamic and unpredictable environment, the agent may need to act to ensure that its goals are achieved (by realizing alternative plan). This property is enabled by the fact that the agent is autonomous in its problem solving.

An agent can be useful as a standalone entity that delegates particular tasks on behalf of a user (e.g. a personal digital assistant and e-mail filter [2], or a goal-driven office delivery mobile device [3]). However, in the overwhelming majority of cases, agents exist in an environment that contains other agents. Such environment is a multi-agent system (MAS).

In MAS, the global behavior derives from the interaction among the constituent agents: They cooperate, coordinate or negotiate with one another. A multi-agent system is then conceived as a society of autonomous, collaborative, and goal-driven software components (agents), much like a social organization. Each role an agent can play has a well defined set of responsibilities (goals) achieved by means of an agent's own abilities, as well as its interaction capabilities.

This *sociality* of MAS is well suited to tackling the complexity of today's organization software systems for a number of reasons:

- It permits a better match between system architectures and its organizational operational environment, for example, a public organization, a corporation, a non-profit association, a local community, ... (See the chapter titled *Analyzing Styles for Requirements Engineering: An Organizational Perspective* in the same book.)

- The autonomy of an agent (i.e., the ability an agent has to decide what actions it should take at what time [1]) reflects the social and decentralized nature of modern enterprise systems [2] that are operated by different stakeholders [4].
- The flexible way in which agents operate to accomplish its goals is suited to the dynamic and unpredictable situations in which business software is now expected to run [5,6].

MAS architectures become rapidly complicated due to the ever-increasing complexity of these new business domains and their human or organizational actors. As the expectations of the stakeholders change day after day, and as the complexity of the systems, communication technologies and organizations increases continually in today's dynamic environments, developers are expected to produce architectures that must handle more difficult and intricate requirements that were not taken into account ten years ago, thus making architectural design a central engineering issue in modern enterprise information system life-cycle [1].

An important technique that helps to manage this complexity when constructing and documenting such architectures is the reuse of development experience and know-how. Over the past few years, *design patterns* have significantly contributed to the reuse of design expertise, improvement application documentation and more flexible and adaptable designs [7–9]. The idea behind a pattern is to record the essence of a solution to a design problem so as to facilitate its reuse when similar problems are encountered [10–12].

Considerable work has been done in software engineering on defining design patterns [7–9]. Unfortunately, they focus on object-oriented [13] rather than agent-oriented systems. In the area of MASs, little emphasis has been put on social and intentional aspects. Moreover, the proposals of agent patterns that could address those aspects (see e.g. [1,14,15] are not aimed at the design level, but rather at the implementation of lower-level issues like agent communication, information gathering, or connection setup. For instance, the FIPA [16] (Foundation for Intelligent Physical Agents) identified and defined a set of agent's interaction protocols that are only restricted to communication.

Since there is a fundamental mismatch between the concepts used by the object-oriented paradigm (and other traditional mainstream software engineering approaches) and the agent-oriented approach [17], there is a need to develop high level patterns that are specifically tailored to the development of (multi-)agent systems using agent-oriented primitives.

Design patterns are generally used during the *detailed design* phase of software methodologies. Agent-oriented methodologies such as TROPOS [3], GAIA [18], MASE [19] and MESSAGE [20]) span the following steps of software engineering:

- Early requirements, concerned with the understanding of a problem by studying an organizational setting; the output is an organizational model which includes relevant actors, their goals and their interdependencies.

- Late requirements, where the system-to-be is described within its operational environment, along with relevant functions and qualities.
- Architectural design, where the system architecture is defined in terms of subsystems, interconnected through data, control, and dependencies.
- Detailed design, where the behavior of each architectural components is defined in detail.

The catalogue of social patterns proposed in [21] constitutes a contribution to the definition of agent-oriented design patterns. This chapter focuses on these patterns, conceptualizes a framework to explore them and facilitate the building of MAS during detailed design as well as the generation of code for agent implementation. It models and introspects the patterns along different complementary dimensions.

The chapter is organized as follows. In Sec. 2, we describe the patterns. Section 3 proposes the framework and illustrates its different modeling dimensions through the Broker pattern. A *data integrator* case study that illustrates the mapping from organizational styles (architectural design phase) to social patterns (detailed design phase), is presented in Sec. 4. The automation of social patterns is overviewed in Sec. 5 while Sec. 6 overviews related work on software patterns. Finally, Sec. 7 points to some conclusions.

2. Social Patterns

Social patterns can be classified into two categories. The *Pair* patterns describe direct interactions between negotiating agents. The *Mediation* patterns feature intermediate agents that help other agents to reach agreement about an exchange of services.

In the following, we briefly model patterns using i* [22] and AUML [2] sequence diagrams respectively to represent the social and communicational dimensions of each pattern. In i*, agents are drawn as circles and their intentional dependencies as ovals. An agent (the *depender*) depends upon another agent (the *dependee*) for an intention to be fulfilled (the *dependum*). Dependencies have the form *depender* → *dependum* → *dependee*. Note that i* also allows to model other kind of dependencies such as resource, task or strategic ones respectively represented as rectangles, hexagons and clouds as we will see in Fig. 12. AUML extends classical sequence diagrams for agent oriented modeling. For instance, the diamond symbol indicates alternative events.

The broker, as well as the subscription and call-for-proposal patterns that are both part of the broker pattern, will be modeled in detail to explain the framework in Sec. 3.

2.1. *Pair patterns*

The **Booking** pattern (Fig. 1) involves a client and a number of service providers. The client issues a request to book some resource from a service provider. The

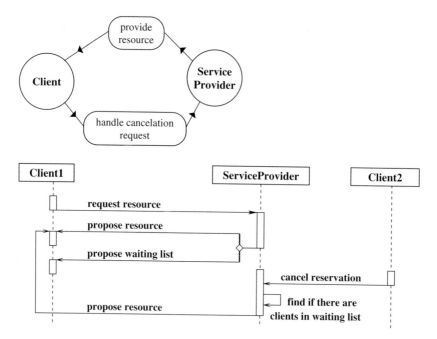

Fig. 1.   Social and communicational diagrams for the booking pattern.

provider can accept the request, deny it, or propose to place the client on a waiting list, until the requested resource becomes available when some other client cancels a reservation.

The **Subscription** pattern involves a yellow-page agent and a number of service providers. The providers advertise their services by subscribing to the yellow pages. A provider that no longer wishes to be advertised can request to be unsubscribed.

The **Call-For-Proposals** pattern involves an initiator and a number of participants. The initiator issues a call for proposals for a service to all participants and then accepts proposals that offer the service for a specified cost. The initiator selects one participant to supply the service.

The **Bidding** (Fig. 2) pattern involves a client and a number of service providers. The client organizes and leads the bidding process, and receives proposals. At every iteration, the client publishes the current bid; it can accept an offer, raise the bid, or cancel the process.

2.2. *Mediation patterns*

In the **Monitor** pattern (Fig. 3), subscribers register for receiving, from a monitor agent, notifications of changes of state in some subjects of their interest. The monitor accepts subscriptions, requests information from the subjects of interest, and alerts subscribers accordingly.

In the **Broker** pattern, the broker agent is an arbiter and intermediary that requests services from providers to satisfy the request of clients.

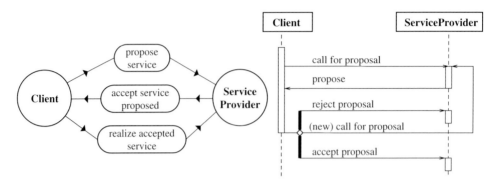

Fig. 2.   Social and communicational diagrams for the bidding pattern.

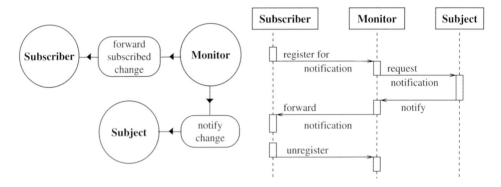

Fig. 3.   Social and communicational diagrams for the monitor pattern.

In the **Matchmaker** pattern (Fig. 4), a matchmaker agent locates a provider for a given service requested by a client, and then lets the client interact directly with the provider, unlike brokers, who handle all interactions between clients and providers.

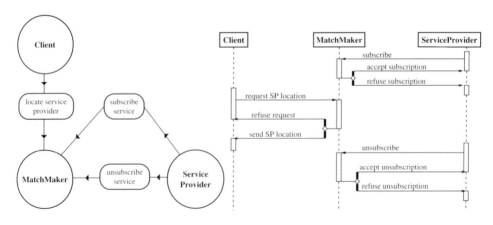

Fig. 4.   Social and communicational diagrams for the matchmaker pattern.

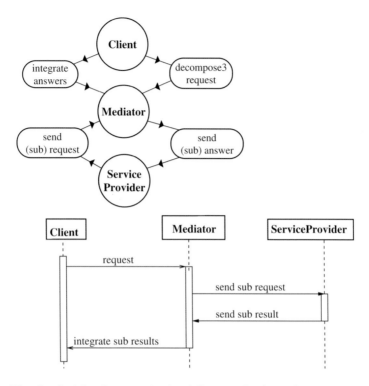

Fig. 5. Social and communicational diagrams for the mediator pattern.

In the **Mediator** pattern (Fig. 5), a mediator agent coordinates the cooperation of service provider agents to satisfy the request of a client agent. While a match-maker simply matches providers with clients, a mediator encapsulates interactions and maintains models of the capabilities of clients and providers over time.

In the **Embassy** pattern, an embassy agent routes a service requested by an external agent to a local agent. If the request is granted, the external agent can submit messages to the embassy for translation in accordance with a standard ontology. Translated messages are forwarded to the requested local agent and the result of the query is passed back through the embassy to the external agent.

The **Wrapper** pattern (Fig. 6) incorporates a legacy system into a multi-agent system. A wrapper agent interfaces system agents with the legacy system by acting as a translator. This ensures that communication protocols are respected and the legacy system remains decoupled from the rest of the agent system.

3. A Social Patterns Framework

This section describes a conceptual framework based on five complementary modeling dimensions to investigate social patterns. The framework has been applied in

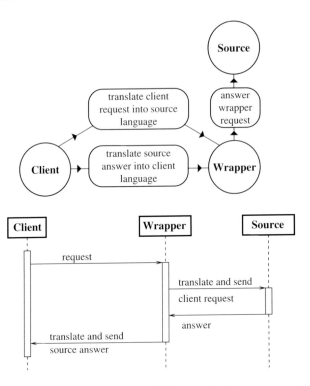

Fig. 6.   Social and communicational diagrams for the wrapper pattern.

the context of the Tropos development methodology [3]. Each dimension reflects a particular aspect of a MAS architecture, as follows.

- The *social dimension* identifies the relevant agents in the system and their intentional interdependencies.
- The *intentional dimension* identifies and formalizes services provided by agents to realize the intentions identified by the social dimension, independently of the plans that implement those services. This dimension answers the question: "What does each service do?"
- The *structural dimension* operationalizes the services identified by the intentional dimension in terms of agent-oriented concepts like beliefs, events, plans, and their relationships. This dimension answers the question: "How is each service operationalized?"
- The *communicational dimension* models the temporal exchange of events between agents.
- The *dynamic dimension* models the synchronization mechanisms between events and plans.

The social and the intentional dimensions are specific to MAS. The last three dimensions (structural, communicational, and dynamic) of the architecture are also relevant for traditional (non-agent) systems, but we have adapted and extended them with agent-oriented concepts. They are for instance the modeling dimensions used in object-oriented visual modeling languages such as UML.

The rest of this section details the five dimensions of the framework and illustrates them through the Broker pattern [23].

This pattern involves an arbiter intermediary that requests services from providers to satisfy the request of clients. It is designed through the framework as follows.

3.1. *Social dimension*

The social dimension specifies a number of agents and their intentional interdependencies using the i* model [22]. Figure 7 shows a social diagram for the Broker pattern.

The Broker pattern can be considered as a combination of (1) a Subscription pattern (shown enclosed within dashed boundary (a)), that allows service providers to subscribe their services to the Broker agent and where the Broker agent plays the role of a yellow-page agent, (2) one of the other pair patterns — Booking, Call-for-Proposals, or Bidding — whereby the Broker agent requests and receives services from service providers (in Fig. 12, it is a Call-for-Proposals pattern, shown enclosed within dotted boundary (b)), and (3) interaction between the broker and the client: the Broker agent depends on the client for sending a service request and the client depends on the Broker agent to forward the service.

To formalize intentional interdependencies, we use Formal Tropos [24], a first-order temporal-logic language that provides a textual notation for i* models and

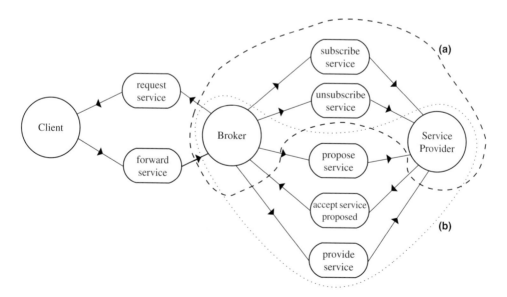

Fig. 7. Social diagram for the broker pattern.

allows to describe dynamic constraints. A *forward service* dependency can be defined in Formal Tropos as follows.

Dependum Forward Service

Mode: Achieve

Depender: Client *cl*

Dependee: Broker *br*

Fulfillment:

    ($\forall$ *sr*: ServiceRequest, *st*: ServiceType)

    request(*cl, br, sr*) $\land$ provide(*br, st*) $\land$ of Type(*sr, st*) $\rightarrow \Diamond$ received(*cl, br, st*)

[Broker *br* successfully provides its service to client *cl* if all requests *sr* from *cl* to *br*, that are of a type *st* that *br* can handle, are eventually satisfied.]

3.2. *Intentional dimension*

While the social dimension focuses on interdependencies between agents, the intentional dimension aims at modeling agent rationale. It is concerned with the identification of *services* provided by agents and made available to achieve the intentions identified in the social dimension. Each service belongs to one agent. Service definitions can be formalized by its fulfillment condition.

The following table lists several services of the Broker pattern with an informal definition. With the FindBroker service, a client finds a broker that can handle a given service request. The request is then sent to the broker through the SendServiceRequest service. The broker can query its belief knowledge with the QuerySPAvailability service and answer the client through the SendServiceRequest-Decision service. If the answer is negative, the client records it with its Record-BRRefusal service. If the answer is positive, the broker records the request (RecordClientServiceRequest service) and then broadcasts a call (CallForProposals service) to potential service providers. The client records acceptance by the broker with the RecordBRAcceptance service.

Service Name	Informal Definition	Agent
FindBroker	Find a broker that can provide a service	Client
SendServiceRequest	Send a service request to a broker	Client
QuerySPAvailability	Query the knowledge for information about the availability of the requested service	Broker
SendService RequestDecision	Send an answer to the client	Broker
RecordBRRefusal	Record a negative answer from a broker	Client
RecordBRAcceptance	Record a positive answer from a broker	Client
RecordClient ServiceRequest	Record a service request received from a client	Broker
CallForProposals	Send a call for proposals to service providers	Broker
RecordAndSend SPInformDone	Record a service received from a service provider	Broker

The Call-For-Proposals pattern could be used here, but this presentation omits it for brevity.

The broker then selects one of the service providers among those that offer the requested service. If the selected provider successfully returns the requested service, it informs the broker, that records the information and forwards it to the client (RecordAndSendSPInformDone service).

Services can be formalized in Formal Tropos as illustrated below for the Find-Broker service.

Service FindBroker (*sr*: ServiceRequest)

Mode: Achieve

Agent: Client *cl*

Fulfillment:

$(\exists\ br$: Broker, *st*: ServiceType$)$

provide(*br*, *st*) $\land$ ofType (*sr*, *st*) $\rightarrow \Diamond$ known(*cl*, *br*)

[*FindBroker* is fulfilled when client *cl* has found (*known* predicate) *Broker br* that is able to perform (*provide* predicate) the service requested.]

3.3. *Structural dimension*

While the intentional dimension answers the question "What does each service do?", the structural dimension answers the question "How is each service operationalized?". Services are operationalized as *plans*, that is, sequences of actions.

The knowledge that an agent has (about itself or its environment) is stored in its *beliefs*. An agent can act in response to the *events* that it handles through its plans. A plan, in turn, is used by the agent to read or modify its beliefs, and send events to other agents or post events to itself.

The structural dimension is modeled using a UML style class diagram extended for MAS engineering.

The required agent concepts extending the class diagram model are defined below.

3.3.1. *Structural concepts*

Figure 8 depicts the concepts and their relationships needed to build the structural dimension. Each concept defines a common template for classes of concrete MAS (for example, Agent in Fig. 8 is a template for the Broker agent class of Fig. 9).

A **Belief** describes a piece of the knowledge that an agent has about itself and its environment. Beliefs are represented as tuples composed of a key and value fields.

Events describe stimuli, emitted by agents or automatically generated, in response to which the agents must take action. As shown in Fig. 8, the structure of an event is composed of three parts: Declaration of the attributes of the event, declaration of the methods to create the event, declaration of the beliefs and the

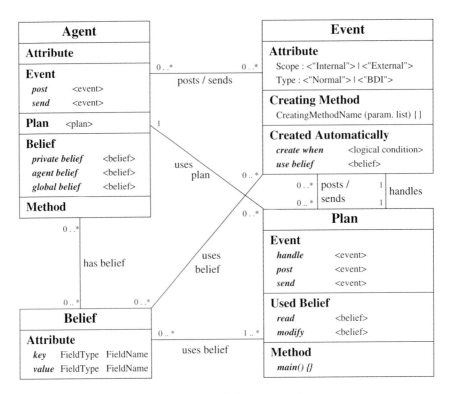

Fig. 8.   Structural diagram template.

condition used for an automatic event. The third part only appears for automatic events. Events can be described along three dimensions:

- *External or internal* event: External events are sent to other agents while internal events are posted by an agent to itself. This property is captured by the *scope* attribute.
- *Normal or BDI* event: An agent has a number of alternative plans to respond to a BDI (Belief-Desire-Event) event and only one plan in response to a normal event. Whenever an event occurs, the agent initiates a plan to handle it. If the plan execution fails and if the event is a normal event, then the event is said to have failed. If the event is a BDI event, a set of plans can be selected for execution and these are attempted in turn. If all selected plans fail, the event is also said to have failed. The event type is captured by the *type* attribute.
- *Automatic or nonautomatic* event: An automatic event is automatically created when certain belief states arise. The *create when* statement specifies the logical condition which must arise for the event to be automatically created. The states of the beliefs that are defined by *use belief* are monitored to determine when to automatically create events.

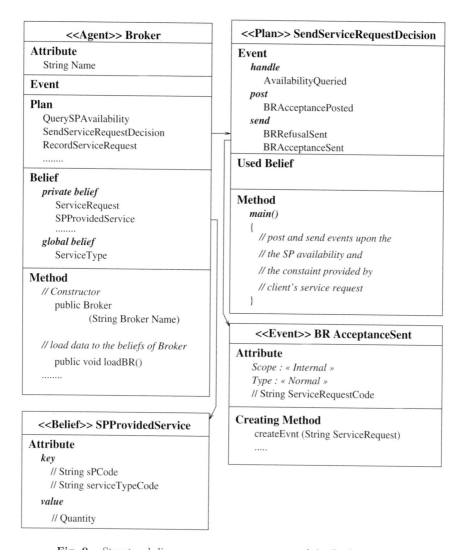

Fig. 9. Structural diagram — some components of the Broker pattern.

A **Plan** describes a sequence of actions that an agent can take when an event occurs. As shown in Fig. 8, plans are structured in three parts: The Event part, the Belief part, and the Method part. The Event part declares events that the plan handles (i.e., events that trigger the execution of the plan) and events that the plan produces. The latter can be either posted (i.e., sent by an agent only to itself) or sent (i.e., sent to other agents). The Belief part declares beliefs that the plan reads and those that it modifies. The Method part describes the plan itself, that is, the actions performed when the plan is executed.

The **Agent** concept defines the behavior of an agent, as composed of five parts: The declaration of its attributes, of the events that it can post or send explicitly (i.e., without using its plans), of the plans that it uses to respond to events, of the beliefs that make up its knowledge, and of its methods.

The beliefs of an agent can be of type *private*, *agent*, or *global*. A *private* access is restricted to the agent to which the belief belongs. *Agent* access is shared with other agents of the same class, while *global* access is unrestricted.

3.3.2. *Structural model for the broker pattern*

Figure 9 depicts the Broker pattern components. For brevity, each construct described earlier is illustrated only through one component. Each component can be considered as an instantiation of the (corresponding) template in Fig. 8.

Broker is one of the three agents composing the Broker pattern. It has plans such as QuerySPAvailability, SendServiceRequestDecision, etc. When there is no ambiguity, by convention, the plan name is the same as the name of the service that it operationalizes. The private belief SPProvidedService stores the service type that each service provider can provide. This belief is declared as private since the broker is the only agent that can manipulate it. The ServiceType belief stores the information about types of service provided by service providers and is declared as global since it must be known both by the service provider and the broker agent.

The constructor *method* allows to give a name to a broker agent when created. This method may call other methods, for example loadBR(), to initialize agent beliefs.

SendServiceRequestDecision is one of the plans that the broker uses to answer the client: The BRRefusalSent event is sent when the answer is negative, BRAcceptanceSent when the broker has found service provider(s) that may provide the requested service. In the latter case, the plan also posts the BRAcceptance Posted event to invoke the process of recording the service request and the "call for proposals" process between the broker and services providers. The SendServiceRequest Decision plan is executed when the AvailabilityQueried event (containing the information about the availability of the service provider to realize the client's request) occurs.

SPProvidedService is one of the broker's beliefs used to store the services provided by the service providers. The service provider code sPCode and the service type code serviceTypeCode form the belief key. The corresponding quantity attribute is declared as value field.

BRAcceptanceSent is an event that is sent to inform the client that its request is accepted.

At a lower level, each plan could also be modeled by an activity diagram for further detail if necessary.

3.3.3. *Communication dimension*

Agents interact with each other by exchanging events. The communicational dimension models, in a temporal manner, events exchanged in the system.

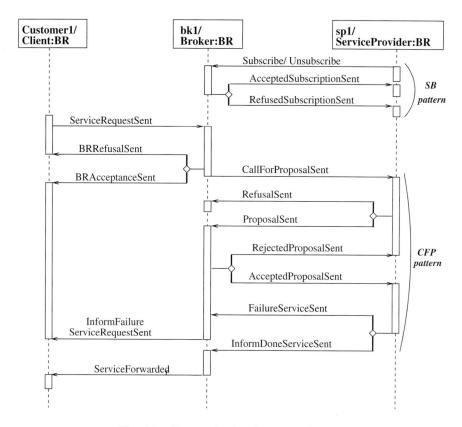

Fig. 10. Communication diagram — Broker.

We adopt the sequence diagram model proposed in AUML [2] and extend it: *agent_name/role:pattern_name* expresses the role (*role*) of the agent (*agent_name*) in the pattern; the arrows are labeled with the name of the exchanged events.

Figure 10 shows a sequence diagram for the Broker pattern. The client (customer1) sends a service request (ServiceRequestSent) containing the characteristics of the service it wishes to obtain from the broker. The broker may alternatively answer with a denial (BRRefusalSent) or a acceptance (BRAcceptanceSent).

In the case of an acceptance, the broker sends a call for proposal to the registered service providers (CallForProposalSent). The call for proposal (CFP) pattern is then applied to model the interaction between the broker and the service providers. The service provider either fails or achieves the requested service. The broker then informs the client about this result by sending a InformFailureServiceRequestSent or a ServiceForwarded, respectively.

The communication dimension of the subscription pattern (SB) is given at the top-right and the communication dimension of the call-for-proposals pattern (CFP) is given at the bottom-right part of Fig. 10. The communication specific for the broker pattern is given in the left part of the figure.

3.3.4. *Dynamic dimension*

As described earlier, a plan can be invoked by an event that it handles and it can create new events. Relationships between plans and events can rapidly become complex. To cope with this problem, we propose to model the synchronization and the relationships between plans and events with activity diagrams extended for agent-oriented systems. These diagrams specify the events that are created in parallel, the conditions under which events are created, which plans handle which events, and so on.

An internal event is represented by a dashed arrow and an external event by a solid arrow. As mentioned earlier, a BDI event may be handled by alternative plans. They are enclosed in a round-corner box. Synchronization and branching are represented as usual.

We omit the dynamic dimension of the Subscription and the CFP patterns, and only present in Fig. 11 the activity diagram specific to the Broker pattern. It models

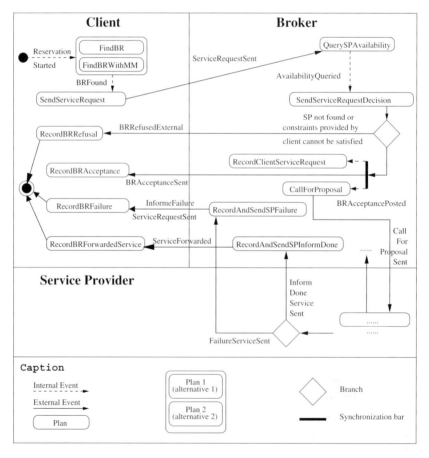

Fig. 11.   Dynamic diagram — Broker.

the flow of control from the emission of a service request sent by the client to the reception by the same client of the realized service result sent by the broker. Three swimlanes, one for each agent of the Broker pattern, compose the diagram. In this pattern, the FindBroker service described in Sec. 3.2.2, is either operationalized by the FindBR or the FindBRWithMM plans (the client finds a broker based on its own knowledge or via a matchmaker).

4. From Organizational Architectural Styles to Social Design Patterns

A key aspect to conduct MAS architectural design is the specification and use of *organizational styles* [3,21,25] that are socially-based architectural designs inspired from models and concepts from organization theory (e.g. [26–28]) and strategic alliances (e.g. [29–31]) that analyze the structure and design of real-world human organization. These are, for instance, the structure-in-fives, the matrix, the joint-venture, the hierarchical contracting, . . . (See also the chapter titled *Analysis Styles for Requirements Engineering: An Organizational Perspective* in the same book).

As described in [3,6], in MAS architectural design, organizational styles are used to give information about the system architecture to be: Every time an organizational style is applied, it allows to easily point up, to the designer, the required organizational actors and roles. Then the next step needs to detail and relate such (organizational) actors and roles to more specific agents in order to proceed with the agent behavior characterization. Namely, each actor in an organization-based architecture is much closer to the real world system actor behavior that we consequently aim to have in software agents. As a consequence, once the organizational architectural reflection has figured out the MAS global structure in terms of actors, roles, and their intentional relationships, a deepener analysis is required to detail the agent behaviors and their interdependencies necessary to accomplish their roles in the software organization. To effectively deal with such a purpose, developers can be guided by social patterns proposed in this chapter.

Social patterns offer a microscopic view of the MAS at the *detailed design* phase to express in deeper detail organizational styles during the architectural design. To explain the necessary relationship between *styles* and *patterns* we consider an original *data integrator* case study and overview on how a MAS designed from some style at the architectural level is decomposed into social patterns at the detailed design level.

The **data integrator** allows users to obtain information that come from different heterogeneous and distributed sources. Sources range from text file systems agent knowledge bases. Information from each source that may be of interest is extracted, translated and filtered as appropriate, merged with relevant information from other sources to provide the answer to the users' queries [32].

Figure 12 shows a MAS architecture in i* for the data integrator that applies the *joint-venture* style [3, 25] at the architectural design level. In a few words,

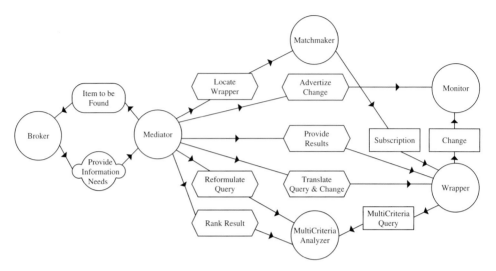

Fig. 12. A joint-venture MAS architecture expressed in terms of social patterns — a data integration example.

the joint venture organizational style is a meta-structure that defines an organizational system that involves agreement between two or more independent partners to obtain the benefits of larger scale, shared investment and lower maintenance costs. A specific joint management actor coordinates tasks and manages the sharing of resources between partner actors. Each partner can manage and control itself on a local dimension and may interact directly with other partners to exchange resources, such as data and knowledge. However, the strategic operation and coordination of such a system, and its actors on a global dimension, are the only responsibility of the joint management actor in which the original actors possess equity participations.

Joint-venture's roles at the architectural design level are expressed in the detailed design level in terms of patterns, namely the broker, the matchmaker, the monitor, the mediator and the wrapper. The *joint management private interface* is assumed by a mediator, the joint-venture partners are the *wrapper*, the *monitor*, the *multi-criteria analyzer* and the *matchmaker*. The *public interface* is assumed by the *broker*.

The system works as follows. When a user wishes to send a request, she contacts the *broker* agent which is an intermediary to select one or many *mediator(s)* that can satisfy the user information needs. Then, the selected mediator(s) decomposes the user's query into one or more subqueries to the sources, synthesizes the source answers and return the answers to the broker.

If the mediator identifies a recurrent user information request, the information that may be of interest is extracted from each source, merged with relevant information from other sources, and stored as knowledge by the mediator. This stored information constitutes a materialized view that the mediator will have to maintain up-to-date.

A *wrapper* and a *monitor* agents are connected to each information source. The *wrapper* is responsible for translating the subquery issued by the mediator into the native format of the source and translating the source response in the data model used by the mediator.

The *monitor* is responsible for detecting changes of interest (e.g. change which affects a materialized view) in the information source and reporting them to the mediator. Changes are then translated by the wrapper and sent to the mediator.

It may be also necessary for the mediator to obtain the information concerning the localization of a source and its connected wrapper that are able to provide current or future relevant information. This kind of information is provided by the *matchmaker* agent which then lets the mediator interacts directly with the correspondent wrapper.

Finally, the *multi-criteria analyzer* can reformulate a subquery (sent by a mediator to a wrapper) through a set of criteria in order to express the user preferences in a more detailed way, and refine the possible domain of results.

5. Automation

The main motivation behind design patterns is the possibility of reusing them during system detailed design and implementation. Numerous CASE tools such as Rational Rose [33] and Together [34] include code generators for object-oriented design patterns. Programmers identify and parameterize, during system detailed design, the patterns that they use in their applications. The code skeleton for the patterns is then automatically generated and programming is thus made easier.

For agent-oriented programming, SKwyRL [22], for instance, proposes a code generator to automate the use of social patterns introduced in Sec. 2. Figure 13 shows the main window of the tool. It has been developed in Java and produces code for JACK [35], an agent-oriented development environment built on top of Java. JACK extends Java with specific capabilities to implement agent behaviors. On a conceptual point of view, the relationship of JACK to Java is analogous to that between C++ and C. On a technical point of view, JACK source code is first compiled into regular Java code before being executed.

In SKwyRL's code generator, the programmer first chooses which social pattern to use, then the roles for each agent in the selected pattern (e.g. the E_Broker agent plays the *broker* role for the Broker pattern but can also play the *initiator* role for the CallForProposals pattern and the *yellow page* role for the Subscription pattern in the same application). The process is repeated until all relevant patterns have been identified. The code generator then produces the generic code for the patterns (.agent, .event, .plan, .bel JACK files).

The programmer has to add the particular JACK code for each generated files and implement the graphical interface, if necessary.

Figure 14 shows an example of the (e-business) broker for the data integrator presented in Sec. 4. It was developed with JACK and the code skeleton was

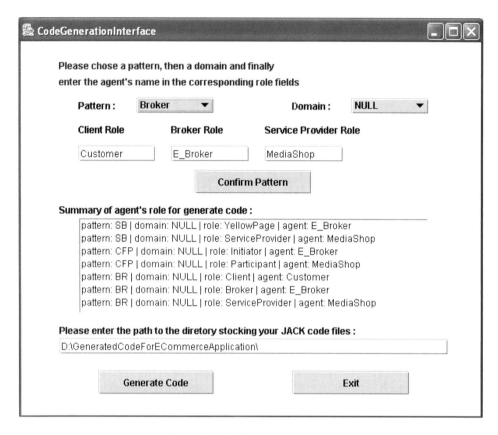

Fig. 13.   JACK code generation.

generated with SKwyRL's code generator using the Broker pattern explained in the chapter. The bottom half of the figure shows the interface between the customer and the broker. The customer sends a service request to the broker asking for buying or sending DVDs. He chooses which DVDs to sell or buy, selects the corresponding DVD titles, the quantity and the deadline (the time-out before which the broker has to realizes the requested service). When receiving the customer's request, the broker interacts with the media shops to obtain the DVDs. The interactions between the broker and the media shops are shown on the bottom-right corner of this figure. The top half of the figure shows the items that are provided by each media shop.

6. Related Work

As already said, a lot of work has been devoted to software patterns these last fifteen years. Patterns for software development are one of software engineering problem-solving discipline that has its roots in a design movement in contemporary architecture and the documentation of best practices and lessons learned in

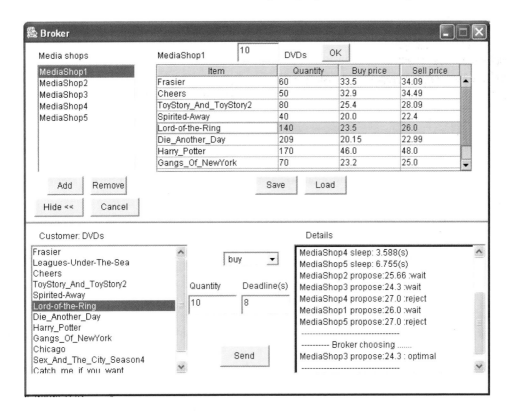

Fig. 14. An E-business Broker.

all vocations. The goal of patterns is to create a body of literature to help software developers resolve recurring problems encountered throughout all of software development. Patterns help create a shared language for communicating insight and experience about these problems and their solutions.

Ward Cunningham and Kent Beck developed a small set of five patterns [36], for guiding Smalltalk programmers to design user interface. Jim Coplien introduced a catalog for C++ patterns, called *idioms* [37]. Software patterns then became popular with the wide acceptance of the Gang of Four or GoF (Erich Gamma, Richard Helm, Ralph Johnson, and John Vlissides) book [7].

However, the patterns in the GoF book are only one kind of pattern — the object-oriented *design patterns*. There are many other kinds of patterns. For example, Martin Fowler's "*Analysis Patterns*" [38] describe the models of business processes that occur repeatedly in the analysis phase of software development; *organizational patterns* [39] are about software-development organizations and about people who work in such organizations. *Process patterns* [40] relate to the strategies that software professionals employ to solve problems that recur across organizations. Frank Buschmann, Regine Meunier, Hans Rohnert, Peter

Sommerlad, and Michael Stal, helped popularize these kinds of patterns (organizational and process patterns) [8].

Contrary to pattern that represents a "best practice", an *anti-pattern* represents a "lesson learned". There are two kinds of "anti-patterns": Those that describe a bad solution to a problem which resulted in a bad situation and those that describe how to get out of a bad situation and how to proceed from there to a good solution. Anti-pattern is initially proposed by Andrew Koenig [41]. Anti-patterns extend the field of software patterns research into exciting new areas and issues, including: Refactoring, reengineering, system extension, and system migration [42–45].

Recent popularity of autonomous agents and agent-oriented software engineering has led to the discovery of agent patterns [1,14,15,25,46] that capture good solutions to common problems in agent design in many aspect such as security, architecture, organization, etc. However, as pointed out earlier, little focus has been put on social and intentional considerations and these agent patterns aim rather at the implementation level. The framework presented in the chapter should add more detail to the design process of agent oriented software engineering [22,25].

7. Conclusion

Nowadays, software engineering for new enterprise application domains such as eBusiness, knowledge management, peer-to-peer computing or web services is forced to build up open systems able to cope with distributed, heterogeneous, and dynamic information issues. Most of these software systems exist in a changing organizational and operational environment where new components can be added, modified or removed at any time. For these reasons and more, Multi-Agent Systems (MAS) architectures are gaining popularity in that they do allow dynamic and evolving structures which can change at run-time.

An important technique that helps to manage the complexity of such architectures is the reuse of development experience and know-how. Like any architect, software architects use patterns to guide system development. Over the years, patterns have become an attractive approach to reusing architectural design knowledge in software engineering. Patterns describe a problem commonly found in software designs and prescribe a flexible solution for the problem, so as to ease the reuse of that solution.

As explored in this chapter, MAS architectures can be considered social structures composed of autonomous and proactive agents that interact and cooperate with each other to achieve common or private goals. Since the fundamental concepts of multi-agent systems are intentional and social, rather than implementation-oriented, social abstractions could provide inspiration and insights to define patterns for designing MAS architectures.

This chapter has focused on social patterns. With real-world social behaviors as a metaphor, social patterns are agent-oriented design patterns that describe MAS as composed of autonomous agents that interact and coordinate to achieve their intentions, like actors in human organizations.

The chapter has described such patterns, a design framework to introspect them and formalize their "code of ethics", answering the question: What can one expect from a broker, mediator, embassy, etc. It aims to be used during the detail design phase of any agent-oriented methodology detailing the patterns following different point of views.

References

1. Y. Aridor and D. B. Lange, "Agent design patterns: Elements of agent application design", *Proceedings of the 2nd International Conference on Autonomous Agents (Agents'98)*, St Paul, Minneapolis, USA, 1998.
2. B. Bauer, J. P. Muller and J. Odell, "Agent UML: A formalism for specifying multi-agent interaction", *Proceedings of the 1st International Workshop on Agent-Oriented Software Engineering (AOSE'00)*, Limerick, Ireland, 2001.
3. J. Castro, M. Kolp and J. Mylopoulos, "Towards requirements-driven information systems engineering: The Tropos project", *Information Systems* **27** (Elsevier, Amsterdam, The Netherlands, 2002).
4. V. Parunak, "Go to the ant: Engineering principles from natural agent systems", *Annals of Operations Research* **75** (1997) 69–101.
5. F. Zambonelli, N. R. Jennings, A. Omicini and M. Wooldridge, "Agent-oriented software engineering for internet applications", *Coordination of Internet Agents: Models, Technologies and Applications* (Springer-Verlag, Heidelberg, Germany, 2000) 326–346.
6. F. Zambonelli, N. R. Jennings and M. Wooldridge, "Organizational abstractions for the analysis and design of multi-agent systems", *Proceedings of the 1st International Workshop on Agent-Oriented Software Engineering* (2000) 243–252.
7. E. Gamma, R. Helm, R. Johnson and J. Vlissides, *Design Patterns: Elements of Reusable Object-Oriented Software* (Addison-Wesley, 1995).
8. F. Buschmann, R. Meunier, H. Rohnert, P. Sommerlad and M. Stal, *Pattern-Oriented Software Architecture — A System of Patterns* (John Wiley & Sons, 1996).
9. J. Bosch, "Design patterns as language constructs", *JOOP Journal of Object-Oriented Programming*.
10. A. Cockburn, "The interaction of social issues and software architecture", *Communication of the ACM* **39**, no. 10 (1996) 40–49.
11. W. Pree, *Design Patterns for Object Oriented Development* (Addison-Wesley, 1994).
12. D. Riehle and H. Züllighoven, "Understanding and using patterns in software development", *Theory and Practice of Object Systems* **2**, no. 1, (1996).
13. E. B. Fernandez and R. Pan, "A pattern language for security models", *Proceedings of PLoP*, 2001.
14. D. Deugo, F. Oppacher, J. Kuester and I. V. Otte, "Patterns as a means for intelligent software engineering", *Proceedings of the International Conference on Artificial Intelligence (IC-AI'99)*, CSRA, **II** (1999).
15. S. Hayden, C. Carrick and Q. Yang, "Architectural design patterns for multiagent coordination", *Proceeding of the 3rd International Conference on Agent Systems (Agents'99)*, Seattle, USA, 1999.
16. Foundation for Intelligent Physical Agent (FIPA), *http://www.fipa.org/*.
17. N. R. Jennings and M. Wooldridge, "Agent-oriented software engineering", *Handbook of Agent Technology* (AAAI/ MIT Press, 2001).
18. M. Woodridge, N. R. Jennings and D. Kinny, "The Gaia methodology for agent-oriented analysis and design", *Autonomous Agents and Multi-Agent Systems* **3**, no. 3 (2000) 285–312.

19. M. Wood, S. A. DeLoach and C. Sparkman, "Multi-agent system engineering", *International Journal of Software Engineering and Knowledge Engineering* **11**, no. 3 (2001).
20. J. Caire *et al*, "Agent-oriented analysis using MESSAGE/UML", *Proceedings of the 2nd International Workshop on Agent-Oriented Software Engineering Lecture Notes in Computer Science 2222* (Springer-Verlag, 2002).
21. M. Kolp, P. Giorgini and J. Mylopoulos, "Information systems development through social structures", *Proceedings of the 14th International Conference on Software Engineering and Knowledge Engineering (SEKE'02)*, Ishia, Italy, 2002.
22. T. T. Do, M. Kolp, T. T. Hang Hoang and A. Pirotte, "A framework for design patterns for tropos", *Proceedings of the 17th Brazilian Symposium on Software Engineering (SBES 2003)*, Maunas, Brazil, October 2003.
23. E. Yu, "Modeling strategic relationships for process reengineering", PhD thesis, University of Toronto, Department of Computer Science, Canada (1995).
24. A. Fuxman, M. Pistore, J. Mylopoulos and P. Traverso, "Model checking early requirements specifications in Tropos", *Proceedings of the 5th IEEE International Symposium on Requirements Engineering (RE'01)*, Toronto, Canada, 2001.
25. T. T. Do, S. Faulkner and M. Kolp, "Organizational multi-agent architectures for information systems", *Proceedings of the 5th International Conference on Enterprise Information Systems (ICEIS 2003)*, Angers, France, April 2003.
26. H. Mintzberg, *Structure in Fives: Designing Effective Organizations* (Prentice-Hall, 1992).
27. W. R. Scott, *Organizations: Rational, Natural, and Open Systems* (Prentice-Hall, 1998).
28. M. Y. Yoshino and U. Srinivasa Rangan, *Strategic Alliances: An Entrepreneurial Approach to Globalization* (Harvard Business School Press, 1995).
29. P. Dussauge and B. Garrette, *Cooperative Strategy: Competing Successfully Through Strategic Alliances* (Wiley and Sons, 1999).
30. J. Morabito, I. Sack and A. Bhate, *Organization Modeling: Innovative Architectures for the 21st Century* (Prentice-Hall, 1999).
31. L. Segil, *Intelligent Business Alliances: How to Profit Using Today's Most Important Strategic Tool* (Times Business, 1996).
32. J. Widom, "Research problems in data warehousing", *Proceedings of the Fourth International Conference on Information and Knowledge Management* (ACM Press, 1995).
33. Rational Rose, *http://www.rational.com/rose/*.
34. Together, *http://www.togethersoft.com/*.
35. JACK Intelligent Agents, *http://www.agent-software.com/*.
36. K. Beck and W. Cunningham, "Using pattern languages for object-oriented programs", *Workshop on the Specification and Design for Object-Oriented Programming (OOPSLA)*, 1987.
37. O. Coplien, *Advanced C++ Programming Styles and Idioms* (Addison-Wesley International, 1991).
38. M. Fowler, *Analysis Patterns: Reusable Object Models* (Addison-Wesley, 1997).
39. J. Coplien and D. Schmidt (eds.), *Pattern Languages of Program Design* (Addison-Wesley, 1995).
40. S. Ambler, *Process Patterns: Building Large-Scale Systems Using Object Technology* (Cambridge University Press, 1998).
41. *http://www.research.att.com/info/ark*.
42. W. F. Opdyke, "Refactoring object-oriented frameworks", PhD Thesis, University of Illinois at Urbana-Champaign (1992).

43. B. F. Webster, *Pitfalls of Object Oriented Development* (John Wiley & Sons Inc., 1995).
44. W. J. Brown, R. C. Malveau, H. W. McCormick and T. J. Mowbray, *AntiPatterns: Refactoring Software, Architectures, and Projects in Crisis* (John Wiley & Sons, 1998).
45. T. Love, *Object Lessons* (Cambridge University Press, 1997).
46. H. Mouratidis, P. Giorgini and G. Manson, "Modelling secure multiagent systems", *Proceedings of the 2nd International Joint Conference on Autonomous Agents and Multiagent Systems*, Melbourne-Australia (ACM Press, July 2003).

KNOWLEDGE-BASED INCONSISTENCY
DETECTION IN UML MODELS

EKAWIT NANTAJEEWARAWAT* and VILAS WUWONGSE

*IT Program, Sirindhorn International Institute of Technology,
Thammasat University, P.O. Box 22, Thammasat Rangsit Post Office,
Pathumthani 12121, Thailand
Tel: 662-501-3505-20 ext 2008
E-mail: ekawit@siit.tu.ac.th

Computer Science and Information Management Program,
School of Advanced Technologies, Asian Institute of Technology,
P.O. Box 4, Klongluang, Pathumthani 12120, Thailand
E-mail: vw@cs.ait.ac.th

Interaction among expressive modeling constructs in different parts of complex diagrams
may lead to implicit consequences that are not readily recognized, and may cause various
forms of redundancies and inconsistencies. It is desirable to equip existing CASE tools
with automated reasoning capabilities that facilitate analysis of relevant properties of
models. This article presents two knowledge-based approaches to detection of inconsistencies in UML models. The first approach is based on Description Logics. It is typically
suitable for formalizing the structural part of a model and analyzing the semantic consistency thereof; however, its application to other parts of the model is limited due to
the restricted ability of these logics to handle queries and rules. The second approach
complements the first by providing extensive rule-oriented facilities, based on the XML
Declarative Description theory, for reasoning with model elements of all kinds that are
encoded in the XML Metadata Interchange format, a standard text-based format for
UML. Since most tools supporting UML export models in this format, this approach
works directly with existing available information sources and can thus be regarded as
a lightweight formal method.

Keywords: Consistency checking, UML models, description logics, XML declarative
descriptions, knowledge representation.

1. Introduction

The Unified Modeling Language (UML) [11, 48] is widely accepted as a standard
notation for analysis and design of software-intensive systems. Sophisticated CASE
tools supporting UML are available on the market, e.g. ArgoUML, Together, Poseidon, Rational Rose;[a] they provide user-friendly graphical environments for editing, storing, and accessing multiple UML diagrams. However, the expressiveness of
UML constructs and their interaction in different parts of a model often lead to

---

*Corresponding author.
[a]*http://argouml.tigris.org, http://www.borland.com/together, http://www.gentleware.com, http:
//www.rational.com/products/rose*, respectively.

implicit consequences of various kinds, some of which are not easily detected, and may bring about various forms of redundancies and inconsistencies. It is desirable to equip existing CASE tools with automated reasoning capabilities that facilitate analysis of relevant properties of models.

This article presents two complementary knowledge-based approaches to analysis of implicit consequences and detection of inconsistencies in UML models. The first approach is based on Description Logics (DLs) [6] — a family of logics that are specifically designed for conceptual representation of the structure of an application domain in terms of classes and relationships between them — and, as such, is well suited for formalization and analysis of UML class diagrams. Basically, a class diagram can be encoded as a set of DL intensional assertions; as a result, currently existing DL systems readily offer their deductive services as analysis tools, e.g. for verifying the semantic consistency of the structural part of a model. In contrast to their strength regarding representation and reasoning in the conceptual level, the capabilities of DLs with respect to individuals are rather limited; in particular, analysis of properties of several kinds demands more extensive ability to express queries and rules involving relations between diagram components than that typically provided by DLs. The second approach complements the first in this regard. Exploiting the XML Declarative Description (XDD) theory [56, 57] as its foundation, it provides extensive rule-oriented facilities for reasoning with UML diagrams encoded in the XML Metadata Interchange (XMI) format [47], a standard text-based format for UML. Rules are represented as XDD clauses — definite-clause-style assertions that use XML expressions as their underlying data structure, equipped with the capability to specify constraints and aggregates. Inasmuch as it works directly with readily available information, i.e., XMI documents representing UML models, the second approach can also be characterized as a lightweight formal method [26, 38].

To start with, Sec. 2 reviews several dimensions of inconsistencies that may occur in UML models. Sections 3 and 4 present the DL-based approach and the XDD-based approach, respectively. Section 5 discusses related works, and Sec. 6 draws conclusions.

2. Classification of Consistency

Consistency in UML models can be considered in several different dimensions. Four types of consistency classification will be reviewed: (i) Intra-consistency and inter-consistency [33], (ii) horizontal consistency and vertical consistency [23, 34, 46, 49], (iii) consistency classified according to model layers [50, 51], and (iv) syntactic consistency and semantic consistency [5, 23]. Not only each of these types but also a combination thereof yields a class of consistency problems.

- *Intra-consistency and inter-consistency*: The former refers to the consistency within an artifact (i.e., it is a property of an artifact), while the latter refers to that between different artifacts (i.e., it is a relation between artifacts). An artifact can be a model, part of a model, a diagram, or a diagram component. Intra-inconsistencies of an artifact may arise from inter-inconsistencies between artifacts contained in it; for example, a class diagram may be intra-inconsistent due to a conflict between the multiplicity of an association class and that of its parent association class.

- *Horizontal consistency and vertical consistency*: The former refers to the consistency of artifacts at the same level of abstraction (e.g. at the same stage of model development), while the latter refers to that at different abstraction levels, most of the time due to refinement (e.g. the consistency between two subsequently elaborated specifications) or transformation (e.g. from design to implementation). Horizontal inconsistency may stem from either intra-inconsistency or inter-inconsistency, or both. Transformation of a consistent artifact into another consistent artifact may result in vertical inconsistencies; for example, a design-level diagram may be in conflict with a given original analysis-level diagram, whereas each of them alone may be consistent.

- *Consistency characterized according to model layers*: Four layers of models are specified by the Model-Driven Architecture (MDA) framework [10], i.e., the instance level, the model level, the metamodel level, and the meta-metamodel level.[b] The UML foundation, behavioral elements, and model management packages as well as UML profiles belong to the meta-model level since they define model elements of UML. User-defined models themselves all belong to the model level; however, they may describe things in the model level or the instance level. A user-defined class diagram, for example, provides model-level description since its elements (e.g. classes and associations) serve as definitions for objects and links referred to by object diagrams and sequence diagrams, which provide instance-level description. In addition to model-level inconsistencies, conflicts may occur at the instance level (e.g. incompatible object behaviors), between the metamodel and model levels (e.g. ill-formed diagrams with respect to the abstract syntax defined by a metamodel), and between the model and instance levels (e.g. classless instances, dangling feature reference, and instance definition missing of other kinds).

- *Syntactic consistency and semantic consistency*: The former is concerned with the syntax and well-formedness of models and model elements, while the latter refers to the consistency with respect to their meanings defined by the UML semantics. Conflicts between the metamodel and model levels typically cause syntactic inconsistencies in a model. Between the model and instance levels, semantic inconsistency exists, for example, between a class

---

[b]The meta-metamodel level (M3) contains Meta-Object Facility (MOF) models defining meta-models. The metamodel level (M2) contains any kind of metamodel, including the UML meta-model and the IDL metamodel. The model level (M1) contains any model with a corresponding metamodel from M2, e.g. UML models and IDL interfaces. Finally, the instance (concrete) level (M0) contains any real situation, unique in space and time, described by a given model from M1.

diagram and an object diagram if no possible legitimate interpretation of the class diagram contains the objects and links specified by the object diagram. Semantic inconsistency may also occur at the instance level; for example, when the behavior of an object described by a state diagram and that described by an interaction diagram are incompatible.

3. Inconsistency Detection Using Description Logics

Description Logics (DLs) [6] are a family of logics that are tailored towards representing knowledge in terms of concepts (classes) and relationships between them. They are a well behaved fragment of first-order logic equipped with decidable reasoning. A DL is formed by three basic components: First, a *description language*, which specifies how to construct complex concepts and (binary) relations from a set of atomic symbols by applying suitable constructors; secondly, a *knowledge specification mechanism*, which specifies how to construct a DL knowledge base in terms of assertions about properties of concepts, relations and individuals; and, thirdly, a set of *automatic reasoning procedures*, which provides logical inferences of several kinds. The set of allowed concept constructors and relation constructors characterizes the expressive power of a DL. Various description languages have been considered by the DL community, and the relationships between their expressiveness and computation complexity of reasoning have been investigated in depth in numerous articles (see [21, 22] for a survey). DLs have found application in areas such as natural languages, configuration management, and database management (e.g. the use of DLs for database modeling was illustrated in [12, 14, 20]).

A DL knowledge base consists of two parts, traditionally called a *TBox* and an *ABox*. The TBox contains *intensional knowledge* in the form of terminology, and is built through assertions stating general properties of concepts and relations. A TBox assertion has either the form $C \sqsubseteq D$ or the form $R \sqsubseteq S$, where C, D are concepts and R, S are relations, and it is intended to mean "the extension of the concept C (respectively, the relation R) is always a subset of that of the concept D (respectively, the relation S)". A pair of assertions $C \sqsubseteq D$ and $D \sqsubseteq C$ (respectively, $R \sqsubseteq S$ and $S \sqsubseteq R$) is denoted by $C \equiv D$ (respectively, $R \equiv S$). The ABox contains *extensional knowledge* consisting of assertions about properties of individuals and relations between them. An ABox assertion has either the form $a\colon C$ or the form $R(a, b)$, where a, b are individuals, C is a concept and R is a relation, and it is intended to mean "the individual a (respectively, the ordered pair (a, b) of individuals) belongs to the extension of the concept C (respectively, the relation R)". For basic description languages and the formal semantics of DL knowledge bases the reader is referred to [7].

Subsection 3.1 reviews a translation of class diagrams into DL knowledge bases and how the semantic consistency of a class diagram can be analyzed through reasoning services of DLs. Subsection 3.2 discusses the possibility of applying DLs to detection of inconsistencies in other diagrams.

3.1. *Detecting semantic inconsistencies in class diagrams*

The major role of a class diagram in modeling is to describe the structure of a domain in terms of classes (of objects) and relationships between them. DLs play essentially the same role in knowledge representation. Formalizing a class diagram as a DL knowledge base and exploiting the deductive capabilities of DLs as tools for analyzing its properties is therefore a natural approach.

$\mathcal{DLR}_{ifd}$ [16, 17], which is one of the most expressive DLs, was developed with the aim of capturing conceptual data models and object-oriented models; as such, it provides means to represent n-ary relations, identification constraints (i.e., keys), and functional dependency constraints on relations. Translation of UML class diagrams into $\mathcal{DLR}_{ifd}$ knowledge bases (with empty ABoxes) was proposed in [8,9,15]. The translation fully captures the semantics of any given class diagram, i.e., the models of the resulting $\mathcal{DLR}_{ifd}$ knowledge base (the interpretations that satisfy all the assertions in it) are exactly the possible instantiations of the given class diagram. Consequently, reasoning on class diagrams can be reduced to reasoning on $\mathcal{DLR}_{ifd}$ knowledge bases. However, not all constructs of $\mathcal{DLR}_{ifd}$ are supported by current state-of-the-art DL systems [40]; in particular, dealing with functional dependencies and identification constraints requires very advanced forms of reasoning on individuals [17], which are still problematic from an implementation point of view.

Resorting to a simpler expressive DL, called $\mathcal{ALCQI}$ [6], which is basically the most expressive DL that currently existing DL systems can support, is demonstrated in [8,9]. As an illustration, considering the class diagram in Fig. 1, the generalization between Publication and its child classes (with the disjointness constraint among them), the association between Publication and Copy (with its multiplicity),

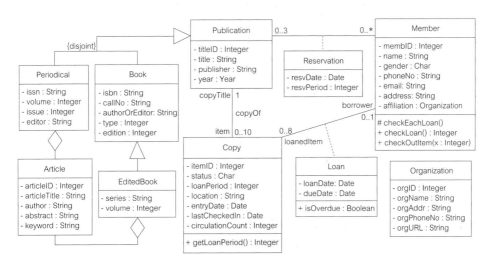

Fig. 1.   A UML class diagram.

Book	⊑	Publication
Periodical	⊑	Publication
Periodical	⊑	¬Book
item	≡	copyTitle$^-$
⊤	⊑	∀copyTitle.Publication ⊓ ∀item.Copy
Copy	⊑	(≥ 1 copyTitle.⊤) ⊓ (≤ 1 copyTitle.⊤)
Publication	⊑	(≤ 10 item.⊤)
Loan	⊑	∃loanedItem.Copy ⊓ (≤ 1 loanedItem) ⊓
		∃borrower.Member ⊓ (≤ 1 borrower)
Loan	⊑	∀loanDate.Date
Loan	⊑	∀dueDate.Date
Copy	⊑	(≤ 1 loanedItem$^-$.Loan)
Member	⊑	(≤ 8 borrower$^-$.Loan)

Fig. 2. $\mathcal{ALCQI}$ assertions corresponding to a part of the class diagram in Fig. 1.

and the association class Loan (with its attributes and multiplicity) are encoded as the $\mathcal{ALCQI}$ TBox assertions in Fig. 2. Translation into $\mathcal{ALCQI}$, while not preserving entirely the semantics of UML class diagrams, preserves enough of it to keep UML reasoning tasks that do not involve functional dependencies and identification constraints sound and complete. Such reasoning tasks include verification of the semantic consistency of a class and that of a class diagram.

- *Semantic consistency of a class*: A class c occurring in a class diagram D is semantically consistent if D admits an instantiation in which c has a nonempty set of instances, i.e., if c can be populated without violating the requirements imposed by D. Through translation into $\mathcal{ALCQI}$, the semantic consistency of the class c can be verified by checking the satisfiability of the corresponding concept of c in the DL knowledge base representing the class diagram D (i.e., checking whether the knowledge base representing D admits a model in which the corresponding concept of c has a nonempty extension).
- *Semantic consistency of a class diagram*: A class diagram D (as a whole) is semantically consistent if it admits an instantiation, i.e., if some class occurring in D is semantically consistent. Through translation into $\mathcal{ALCQI}$, the semantic consistency of a class diagram can be verified by checking the satisfiability of the DL knowledge base representing it (i.e., checking whether the knowledge base representing it admits a model in which at least one class has a nonempty extension).

Consider, for example, the class diagram in Fig. 3, which is obtained from a fragment of the diagram in Fig. 1 by adding a generalization between Periodical and Book. This modification makes Periodical semantically inconsistent since the only set that can be disjoint from and, at the same time, included by an extension of Book is the empty set. However, the class diagram in Fig. 3 as a whole is semantically

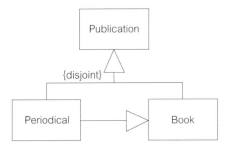

Fig. 3. A class diagram containing a semantically inconsistent class.

consistent since it can be instantiated in such a way that Publication and Book have nonempty extensions. When the size and the complexity of a class diagram increase, interaction of various types of constraints often makes semantic consistency difficult to check manually.

Checking the satisfiability of a knowledge base and that of a concept are basic reasoning services of DLs. Two of the best-known state-of-the-art DL reasoning systems that support $\mathcal{ALCQI}$ entirely are FACT[c] [35,36], developed at the University of Manchester, and RACER[d] [31,32], developed at the University of Hamburg. Besides automatic verification of the semantic consistency of classes and class diagrams, reasoning capabilities of DL systems can be employed to check implicit properties of a class diagram, e.g. implicit multiplicity of an association and class equivalence. Determination of such implicit consequences is useful, on the one hand, to reduce the complexity of a class diagram by removing parts that implicitly follow from others, and, on the other hand, it can be used to make properties explicit, thus enhancing the readability of the diagram [15].

3.2. *Detecting inconsistencies in other diagrams*

In [50–52], translation similar to that in the preceding subsection is applied to class diagrams at the metamodel level, rather than those at the model level, so as to formalize the abstract syntax of sequence diagrams and state diagrams. For example, the portion shown in Fig. 4 of the metamodel-level class diagram defining state machines is encoded as the TBox assertions in Fig. 5. In addition to the abstract syntax, some well-formedness rules, which are normally specified in OCL, can also be expressed as TBox assertions, for example, the rule stating that "a final state always has no outgoing transition" can be encoded as

$$\text{FinalState} \sqsubseteq \text{State} \sqcup \neg\exists\text{outgoing.Transition.}$$

User-defined diagrams are then represented in an ABox. Figure 7 illustrates the ABox assertions representing the fragment in Fig. 6 of a state diagram for the

---

[c]Fast Classification of Terminologies.
[d]Renamed ABox and Concept Expression Reasoner.

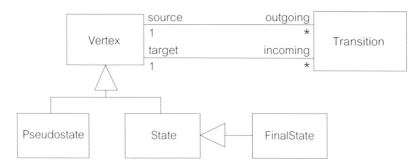

Fig. 4. A fragment of a class diagram in the UML state machines package.

$$
\begin{aligned}
\text{State} &\sqsubseteq \text{Vertex} \\
\text{Pseudostate} &\sqsubseteq \text{Vertex} \\
\text{FinalState} &\sqsubseteq \text{State} \\
\text{source} &\equiv \text{outgoing}^{-} \\
\text{target} &\equiv \text{incoming}^{-} \\
\top &\sqsubseteq \forall\text{outgoing.Transition} \sqcap \forall\text{source.Vertex} \\
\text{Transition} &\sqsubseteq (\geq 1\ \text{source.}\top) \sqcap (\leq 1\ \text{source.}\top) \\
\top &\sqsubseteq \forall\text{incoming.Transition} \sqcap \forall\text{target.Vertex} \\
\text{Transition} &\sqsubseteq (\geq 1\ \text{target.}\top) \sqcap (\leq 1\ \text{target.}\top)
\end{aligned}
$$

Fig. 5. TBox assertions corresponding to the meta-level class diagram in Fig. 4.

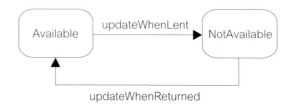

Fig. 6. A fragment of a state diagram for the class Copy.

Available : State
NotAvailble : State
outgoing(Available, updateWhenLent)
incoming(NotAvailable, updateWhenLent)
outgoing(NotAvailable, updateWhenReturned)
incoming(Available, updateWhenReturned)

Fig. 7. ABox assertions corresponding to the fragment in Fig. 6 of a state diagram.

class Copy.[e] The syntactic consistency of the encoded diagrams with respect to the encoded abstract syntax and well-formedness rules can then be verified by checking whether the resulting ABox is consistent with respect to the obtained TBox, which is a basic reasoning task of DL systems.

In principle, in addition to analysis of syntactic consistency, consistency of other kinds between the model and instance levels as well as that at the instance level can be checked using queries on the ABox. For example, classless instances can be checked by retrieving all objects participating in an interaction diagram, and then checking whether retrieval of their base classes fails with respect to the class diagram encoded in the ABox. Similarly, coarse-grained analysis of dangling operation calls can be performed by retrieving the messages received by each object in an interaction diagram, followed by checking whether the operation of each obtained message matches any operation declared in the base class of the message receiver with respect to the diagrams encoded in the ABox. These types of consistency checking often require a highly expressive ABox query language. Furthermore, the ability to define rules for derivation of implicit model elements as well as implicit relations between diagram components is often needed, especially for detailed consistency analysis. For example, more precise detection of dangling operation calls necessitates consideration of not only the operations declared in a class but also the operations that the class inherits, and rules for deriving operations of the latter kind are required.

However, based on the experience with the DL system RACER [31, 32], it is pointed out in [52] that detection of inconsistencies in UML models by means of ABox queries demands a more extensive query language than that RACER currently offers. In general, the inadequacy of their ABox query languages is a serious shortcoming of state-of-the-art DL systems [29, 40, 53]. Even conjunctive queries — the least expressive query language usually considered in database research — are often not supported [13].[f] Typically, their query languages only support instance checking (i.e., checking whether an individual a is an instance of a concept C) and instance retrieval (i.e., retrieving all individuals that are instances of a given concept), and the latter is normally performed by iterative application of the former. The reason for this weakness is that, in expressive DLs, all reasoning tasks are reduced to that of determining knowledge base satisfiability. In particular, instance checking is reduced to knowledge base (un)satisfiability by transforming a given query into its negated assertion (i.e., an assertion $a: C$ is inferred if a knowledge base of interest is unsatisfiable when $a: \neg C$ is added to its ABox). However, this technique cannot be used for queries involving relations between individuals since DLs do not support role negation (i.e., given an assertion $r(a, b)$, one cannot construct $\neg r(a, b)$).

---

[e]For reason of clarity, it is assumed that a state and a transition are identified by its name and its label, respectively.

[f]Basic techniques for supporting conjunctive queries in DL systems were developed only recently [37, 53]. However, for expressive DLs much less is known from an implementation standpoint [40].

Apart from the deficiency in their ABox query languages, the expressive power of DLs in representing rules involving relations between individuals is also inherently restricted. The restriction is due in large part to the necessity of preserving the tree model property [54], without which the decidability of DLs may be lost [18, 19]. This requirement severely constrains the way variables and quantifiers can be used, e.g. it is impossible to describe classes whose instances are related to anonymous individuals via different property paths [29]. Accordingly, some rules that can be simply represented in the Horn fragment of first-order logic cannot be asserted in DLs.[g]

In the experiments reported in [50–52], UML models were manually translated into DL assertions. However, as suggested in [51], it is possible to implement an automatic translation of UML models that are encoded in the XMI format into DL assertions by using XSL Transformations (XSLT).[h]

4. Inconsistency Detection Using XML Declarative Descriptions

While DLs are well suited for representing the structure of a domain, their capabilities with respect to individuals are rather limited. This area is a stronghold of rules, which offer extensive facilities for representing and reasoning with individuals and relations between them. Such facilities are required by consistency analysis of several kinds. This section presents an application of the framework for rule-based knowledge representation in the domain of UML proposed in [44], based on the XML Declarative Description (XDD) theory [56,57], to inconsistency detection. UML diagrams are represented in the XML Metadata Interchange (XMI) format [47] — a standard text-based representation for UML — and rules are represented as XDD clauses. Of central importance to this approach, such clauses use XML expressions as their underlying data structure; consequently, they can seamlessly specify information to be extracted as well as implicit information to be derived from diagram components represented in XMI. Since virtually every tool supporting UML is capable of reading and writing models using XMI, this approach can be characterized as a lightweight formal method [26,38]; i.e., as opposed to traditional use of formal methods, which often requires a massive investment of preparatory work, the approach works directly with existing available information sources.

Subsection 4.1 illustrates XMI representation of UML models. Subsection 4.2 introduces XDD descriptions and XDD clauses, and presents their application.

4.1. *Representing UML diagrams in XMI: Examples*

Refer to the class diagram in Fig. 1. Each predefined primitive data type is encoded in XMI as a DataType-element, and each class as a Class-element; the namespace

---

[g]As illustrated in [29], it is impossible, for example, to assert in DLs that individuals who live and work at the same location are "HomeWorkers", while this can be asserted using a simple Horn rule, e.g. $(HomeWorker(X) \leftarrow work(X,Y) \wedge live(X,Z) \wedge locate(Y,W) \wedge locate(Z,W))$.
[h]*http://www.w3.org/TR/xslt.*

```
<UML:DataType xmi.id="G.55" name="Integer"
       visibility="public" isSpecification="false"
       isRoot="false" isLeaf="false" isAbstract="false"/>
```

Fig. 8. Representing a data type in XMI.

```
<UML:Class xmi.id="S.26" name="Copy"
       visibility="public" isRoot="true" isLeaf="true" isAbstract="false">
    <UML:Classifier.feature>
       <UML:Attribute xmi.id="S.27" name="itemID" visibility="private" type="G.55">
          <UML:StructuralFeature.multiplicity>
             <UML:Multiplicity>
                <UML:MultiplicityRange lower="1" upper="1"/>
             </UML:Multiplicity>
          </UML:StructuralFeature.multiplicity>
       </UML:Attribute>
       <UML:Attribute xmi.id="S.28" name="status" visibility="private" type="G.57">
          . . .
       </UML:Attribute>
          . . .
       <UML:Operation xmi.id="S.34" name="getLoanPeriod" visibility="public">
          <UML:BehavioralFeature.parameter>
             <UML:Parameter xmi.id="XX.9" name="getLoanPeriod.Return"
                   kind="return" type="G.55"/>
          </UML:BehavioralFeature.parameter>
       </UML:Operation>
    </UML:Classifier.feature>
</UML:Class>
```

Fig. 9. Representing a class in XMI.

UML is used. The primitive type Integer and the class Copy are represented by the XML elements in Figs. 8 and 9 respectively. An attribute and an operation of a class are represented by an Attribute-element and an Operation-element, respectively. For instance, the first Attribute-subelement in Fig. 9 describes the attribute itemID of the class Copy, e.g. it specifies the type of itemID by referring to the DataType-element representing Integer and details the multiplicity of this attribute using a Multiplicity-subelement. The Attribute-subelement representing the attribute status is shown only partially, and those representing other attributes of Copy are not shown in the figure.

Each association is represented by an Association-element, and each generalization by a Generalization-element. The Association-element representing the association copyOf is given in Fig. 10. Each of its enclosed AssociationEnd-elements represents one endpoint of copyOf and details the adornments of the association at the endpoint; for instance, the second AssociationEnd-element indicates that Copy is at one endpoint of copyOf by referring, via the attribute type, to the identifier, S.26, of the Class-element in Fig. 9, and describes the navigability and multiplicity of copyOf at this endpoint using the attribute isNavigable and a Multiplicity-subelement, respectively. Assuming that the identifiers of the

```
<UML:Association xmi.id="G.13" name="copyOf" visibility="public">
  <UML:Association.connection>
    <UML:AssociationEnd xmi.id="G.14" name="copyTitle" type="S.16"
        visibility="public" isNavigable="true" aggregation="none">
      <UML:AssociationEnd.multiplicity>
        <UML:Multiplicity>
          <UML:MultiplicityRange lower="1" upper="1"/>
        </UML:Multiplicity>
      </UML:AssociationEnd.multiplicity>
    </UML:AssociationEnd>
    <UML:AssociationEnd xmi.id="G.15" name="item" type="S.26"
        visibility="public" isNavigable="true" aggregation="none">
      <UML:AssociationEnd.multiplicity>
        <UML:Multiplicity>
          <UML:MultiplicityRange lower="0" upper="10"/>
        </UML:Multiplicity>
      </UML:AssociationEnd.multiplicity>
    </UML:AssociationEnd>
  </UML:Association.connection>
</UML:Association>
```

Fig. 10.   Representing an association in XMI.

```
<UML:Generalization xmi.id="G.60" visibility="public" child="S.1" parent="S.16"/>
<UML:Generalization xmi.id="G.61" visibility="public" child="S.7" parent="S.1"/>
<UML:Generalization xmi.id="G.62" visibility="public" child="S.21" parent="S.16"/>
```

Fig. 11.   Representing a generalization taxonomy in XMI.

Class-elements representing the classes Publication, Periodical, Book and EditedBook are S.16, S.21, S.1 and S.7, respectively, the three Generalization-elements in Fig. 11 collectively represent the generalization relationship among the four classes.

An association class, e.g. Loan in Fig. 1, is regarded as both a class and an association and is represented in XMI by an AssociationClass-element, the structure of which subsumes the structure of a Class-element and that of an Association-element; e.g. an AssociationClass-element representing Loan contains two AssociationEnd-elements describing the endpoints loanedItem and borrower, two Attribute-elements describing the attributes loanDate and dueDate, and an Operation-element describing the operation isOverdue.

Figure 12 illustrates the XMI representation of the UML sequence diagram in Fig. 13, which describes a normal scenario of the use case "lending a copy". Each object participating in the sequence diagram is described by a ClassifierRole-subelement; for example, by referring to the identifier, S.26, of the Class-element in Fig. 9 via the attribute base, the ClassifierRole-subelement with the identifier G.30 specifies that item is an instance of Copy. A message in the sequence diagram is encoded as a Message-subelement, which specifies the sender, the receiver,

```
<UML:Collaboration xmi.id="S.69">
  <UML:Namespace.ownedElement>
    <UML:ClassifierRole xmi.id="G.17" name="" base="S.66"/>
    <UML:ClassifierRole xmi.id="G.19" name="" base="S.67"/>
    <UML:ClassifierRole xmi.id="G.22" name="m" base="S.36"/>
    <UML:ClassifierRole xmi.id="G.27" name="" base="S.47"/>
    <UML:ClassifierRole xmi.id="G.28" name="newLoan" base="S.47"/>
    <UML:ClassifierRole xmi.id="G.30" name="item" base="S.26"/>
    <UML:ClassifierRole xmi.id="G.31" name="" base="S.68"/>
  </UML:Namespace.ownedElement>
  <UML:Collaboration.interaction>
    <UML:Interaction.message>
      <UML:Message xmi.id="G.35" name="memberIdentified(membID)"
          sender="G.17" receiver="G.19" action="XX.50"/>
      <UML:Message xmi.id="G.36" name="retrieveMember(membID)"
          sender="G.19" receiver="G.31" predecessor="G.35" action="XX.51"/>
      <UML:Message xmi.id="G.37" name="Member()"
          sender="G.31" receiver="G.22" predecessor="G.36" action="XX.52"/>
          ...
      <UML:Message xmi.id="G.51" name="storeLoan(newLoan)"
          sender="G.22" receiver="G.31" predecessor="G.50" action="XX.66"/>
      <UML:Message xmi.id="G.52" name="updateWhenLent()"
          sender="G.22" receiver="G.30" predecessor="G.51" action="XX.67"/>
      <UML:Message xmi.id="G.53" name="updateCopy(item)"
          sender="G.30" receiver="G.31" predecessor="G.52" action="XX.68"/>
    </UML:Interaction.message>
  </UML:Collaboration.interaction>
</UML:Collaboration>
```

Fig. 12. Representing a sequence diagram in XMI.

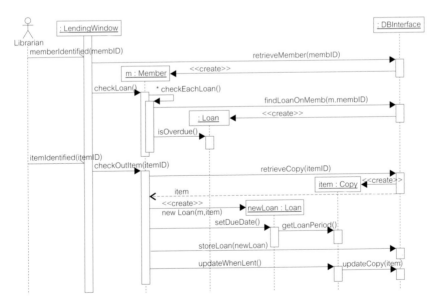

Fig. 13. A UML sequence diagram.

the predecessor and the action of the message. The Message-subelement with the identifier G.52 in Fig. 12, for example, represents the message updateWhenLent() that the object m sends to the object item.

4.2. *XDD clauses as rules for inconsistency detection*

The XML Declarative Description (XDD) theory [56, 57] is developed based on Akama's theory of declarative descriptions (DD theory) [1] — an axiomatic theory that purports to generalize the concept of conventional logic programs to cover a wider variety of data domains and has provided a template for developing formal semantics for declarative descriptions with atomic formulae of various forms, including atomic conceptual graphs [58] and typed feature terms [42]. An *XDD description* is a set of *XDD clauses*, each of which is a formula of the form

$$H \leftarrow B_1, \ldots, B_m, \beta_1, \ldots, \beta_n,$$

where $m, n \geq 0$, H and the B_i are XML-expressions, and the β_j are constraints. H is called the *head*, and $\{B_1, \ldots, B_m, \beta_1, \ldots, \beta_n\}$ the *body* of the clause. *XML expressions* are XML elements that are extended by incorporation of variables. A variable is used for a dual purpose: It denotes a specialization wildcard (i.e., a variable can be specialized into an XML expression or a part thereof) and, at the same time, specifies an equality constraint (i.e., any occurrence of a variable within the same scope must be instantiated in the same way). Variables of several kinds, with different syntactical usage and different instantiation characteristics, are employed. They include name-variables (N-variables), string-variables (S-variables), attribute-value-pair-variables (P-variables), and XML-expression-variables (E-variables). Intuitively, an N-variable will only be instantiated into either a tag name or an attribute name, an S-variable into a string, a P-variable into zero or more attribute-value pair(s), and an E-variable into zero or more XML expression(s). It is assumed that an N-variable, an S-variable, a P-variable and an E-variable are prefixed with $N:, $S:, $P: and $E:, respectively. A *constraint* is an expression that specifies certain restriction on XML elements or their components. The reader is referred to [57] for the formal semantics of XDD descriptions.

Figure 14 illustrates an XDD clause representing a rule for detecting dangling operation calls in a sequence diagram. Its body consists of two XML expressions, i.e., a Collaboration-expression and a Class-expression, and one constraint, i.e., a *notFoundIn*-constraint. For the sake of readability, a variable that specifies an equality constraint, i.e., a variable with more than one occurrence in a clause (such as $S:CollabID and $S:ReceiverID in the figure), will be underlined. The Prolog notation for anonymous variables is adopted; i.e., a variable suffixed with the underscore symbol (such as $E:_ and $P:_) is regarded as an anonymous variable (different occurrences of which are unrelated). The first XML expression in the body

```
<PossibleConflict type="Dangling operation call" collaboration=$S:CollabID
    instance=$S:ReceiverID operation=$S:CallActName class=$S:ClassID/>
  ←  <UML:Collaboration xmi.id=$S:CollabID>
        <UML:Namespace.ownedElement> $E:_
          <UML:ClassifierRole xmi.id=$S:ReceiverID base=$S:ClassID/> $E:_
        </UML:Namespace.ownedElement>
        <UML:Collaboration.interaction>
          <UML:Interaction.message> $E:_
            <UML:Message name=$S:CallActName receiver=$S:ReceiverID $P:_/> $E:_
          </UML:Interaction.message>
        </UML:Collaboration.interaction>
      </UML:Collaboration>,
      <UML:Class xmi.id=$S:ClassID $P:_>
        <UML:Classifier.feature> $E:Features </UML:Classifier.feature>
      </UML:Class>,
      notFoundIn($S:CallActName, UML:Operation, $E:Features)
```

Fig. 14. A rule for detection of dangling feature reference.

can match a Collaboration-element, say E_{Coll}, representing a sequence diagram, by instantiating

- the S-variable $S:CollabID into the identifier of E_{Coll},
- the S-variables $S:ReceiverID and $S:ClassID into the identifier and value of the attribute base, respectively, of the ClassifierRole-element, say E_{Crol}, enclosed by E_{Coll},
- the S-variables $S:CallActName and $S:ReceiverID into the values of the attributes name and receiver, respectively of a Message-element, say E_{Mes}, enclosed by E_{Coll},
- each occurrence of the anonymous variable $E:_ into zero or more sub-element(s), and each occurrence of the anonymous variable $P:_ into zero or more attribute-value pair(s).

Likewise, the second XML expression matches the Class-element, say E_{Cl}, referred to by the attribute base of the ClassifierRole-element E_{Crol}, thereby instantiating the variable $E:Features into the immediate subelements, say ES, of the feature-element enclosed by E_{Cl}. The *notFoundIn*-constraint then checks whether the name of the Message-element E_{Mes} corresponds to the name of some Operation-element in ES, and the constraint is true if this is not the case. For example, when the body of this XDD clause is instantiated in such a way that the Message-subexpression matches the Message-subelement having the identifier G.52 in Fig. 12 and the Class-expression matches the Class-element in Fig. 9, the *notFoundIn*-constraint will be true, i.e., the operation updateWhenLent is missing in the class Copy, and, as specified by its head, the clause will generate a PossibleConflict-element reporting the identifiers of the collaboration, the instance, the operation and the class in conflict.

```
<InheritedFeature receiver=$S:ReceiverID supplier=$S:SupplierID>
   <$N:Feature $P:OtherAttrs> $E:SubElements </$N:Feature>
</InheritedFeature>
   ←  <UML:Generalization child=$S:ReceiverID parent=$S:SupplierID $P:_/>,
      <UML:Class xmi.id=$S:SupplierID $P:_>
         <UML:Classifier.feature> $E:_
            <$N:Feature visibility=$S:Visibility $P:OtherAttrs>
               $E:SubElements
            </$N:Feature> $E:_
         </UML:Classifier.feature>
      </UML:Class>,
      notEqual($S:Visibility, "private")
```

Fig. 15. A rule for deriving an inherited feature from a feature declared in a parent class.

```
<InheritedFeature receiver=$S:ReceiverID supplier=$S:SupplierID>
   $E:InheritedElement
</InheritedFeature>
   ←  <UML:Generalization child=$S:ReceiverID parent=$S:ParentID $P:_/>,
      <InheritedFeature receiver=$S:ParentID supplier=$S:SupplierID>
         $E:InheritedElement
      </InheritedFeature>
```

Fig. 16. A rule for deriving an inherited feature from a feature inherited by a parent class.

As mentioned in subsec. 3.2, finer-grained analysis of dangling feature reference can be obtained by taking inherited features into account. The XDD clauses in Figs. 15 and 16 define rules for deriving inherited features. The first clause asserts that every non-private feature declared in a parent class is inherited by a child class — in particular, the clause finds each subelement (which can be an Attribute-element or an Operation-element), say E_{Fea}, of the Classifier.feature-element of a parent class, and, if the visibility-attribute of E_{Fea} is not private, creates an InheritedFeature-element containing a copy of E_{Fea}, the visibility-attribute and its value excluded, as the only subelement. The second clause asserts that every feature inherited by a parent class is further inherited by its child class. Analogously, the XDD clauses in Figs. 17 and 18 define rules for deriving available features of a class — an available feature of a class is either a non-private feature declared in the class or a feature that the class inherits from its ancestor.

Coupled with the rules in Figs. 15–18, the rule for detecting dangling operation calls in Fig. 14 can be refined by replacing the Class-expression in its body with a set-aggregate used for collecting all available features of a class of interest; the resulting rule is shown in Fig. 19. A set-aggregate is a special-purpose formula, encoded as an xdd:Aggregate-expression, that specifies a pattern of XML elements of interest and collects all derivable XML elements of the specified pattern. In particular, the set-aggregate in the body of the rule in Fig. 19 collects all avaliable features of the class referred to by a ClassifierRole-element (via the

```
<AvailableFeature class=$S:ClassID>
  <$N:Feature $P:OtherAttrs> $E:SubElements </$N:Feature>
</AvailableFeature>

  ←  <UML:Class xmi.id=$S:ClassID $P:_ >
        <UML:Classifier.feature> $E:_
          <$N:Feature visibility=$S:Visibility $P:OtherAttrs>
          $E:SubElements
          </$N:Feature> $E:_
        </UML:Classifier.feature>
     </UML:Class>,

     notEqual($S:Visibility, "private")
```

Fig. 17. A rule for deriving an available feature from a declared feature.

```
<AvailableFeature class=$S:ClassID> $E:InheritedElement </AvailableFeature>

  ←  <InheritedFeature receiver=$S:ClassID $P:_> $E:InheritedElement </InheritedFeature>
```

Fig. 18. A rule for deriving an available feature from an inherited feature.

```
<Conflict type="Dangling operation call" collaboration=$S:CollabID
      instance=$S:ReceiverID operation=$S:CallActName class=$S:ClassID/>

  ←  <UML:Collaboration xmi.id=$S:CollabID>
        <UML:Namespace.ownedElement> $E:_
          <UML:ClassifierRole xmi.id=$S:ReceiverID base=$S:ClassID/> $E:_
        </UML:Namespace.ownedElement>
        <UML:Collaboration.interaction>
          <UML:Interaction.message> $E:_
            <UML:Message name=$S:CallActName receiver=$S:ReceiverID $P:_/> $E:_
          </UML:Interaction.message>
        </UML:Collaboration.interaction>
     </UML:Collaboration>,

     <xdd:Aggregate>
       <xdd:set> $E:AllAvailableFeatures </xdd:set>
       <xdd:pattern>
         <AvailableFeature class=$S:ClassID> $E:_ </AvailableFeature>
       </xdd:pattern>
     </xdd:Aggregate>

     notFoundInSet($S:CallActName, UML:Operation, $E:AllAvailableFeatures)
```

Fig. 19. A rule for detection of dangling (inherited) feature reference.

attribute base), and instantiates the *E*-variable in its xdd:set-subexpression into the obtained collection. The *notFoundInSet*-constraint in the body then checks whether an operation call of interest does not correspond to any available operation is the collection.

Many other types of model-level, instance-level, and model-instance inconsistency can be specified using XDD clauses; among other things, they include dangling association reference, violations of well-formedness rules, generalization cycles, conflicts due to multiple inheritance, and conflicts between an ordered collection of stimuli in a sequence diagram and the sequence of call events in a state diagram. For many of detected inconsistencies one can provide rules to automatically resolve them. For example, by means of XDD clauses, when a dangling operation call is found in a sequence diagram, one can derive an Operation-subelement corresponding to the call and add it to the Class-element representing the base class of the receiver of the call.

XDD clauses can also be used for deriving various kinds of implicit consequence of a model, e.g. call dependency between classes and implicit multiplicity of an association. Besides, the framework can be applied in the area of forward engineering, e.g. representation of mapping rules for automatic generation of relational database schemas from UML class diagrams using XDD clauses is demonstrated in [43].

The Equivalent Transformation (ET) computation model [2,3] is employed as a basis for computation with XDD clauses. Reasoning in this model is typically goal-directed: A query-answering process consists in successive reduction of queries using meaning-preserving transformation with respect to a given knowledge base. An inference engine, called the *XML Equivalent Transformation* (*XET*) engine [4], has been developed for materializing equivalent transformation of XDD descriptions. An XDD clause is encoded as a well-formed XML element, called an *XET rule*, and constraints occurring in a clause are realized through built-in procedures of the XET engine. Figure 20 shows the XET rule corresponding to the XDD clause in Fig. 14. In order to satisfy the well-formedness rules of XML, an *S*-variable, a *P*-variable and an *E*-variable in an XET rule are prefixed with Svar-, Pvar- and Evar-, respectively, instead of $S:, $P: and $E:. The XET engine works directly with XML/XMI elements representing UML diagrams and this form of XET rules. The reader is referred to [4] and the XET Web site (*http://kr.cs.ait.ac.th/xet*) for further details of XET-related tools.

5. Related Works

Another lightweight and declarative approach was proposed in [30, 46], based on a generic tool for checking the consistency of distributed XML documents, called xlinkit [45]. The xlinkit framework comprises an XML-based first-order-logic rule language, for defining consistency rules, a document management system, and an engine for consistency verification. The xlinkit rule language uses XPath[i] for selection of elements from XML documents. Constraints of several types can be naturally expressed as xlinkit rules; for example, the well-formedness rule stating that "association ends must have a unique name within an association" can be represented by the xlinkit rule in Fig. 21. The xlinkit engine applies the XPath expressions in a rule to extract relevant elements from a given set of XML documents, and generates diagnostic information in the form of a collection of hyperlinks between

---

[i] *http://www.w3c.org/TR/1999/REC-xpath-19991116.*

```
<xet:Rule name = "Detecting possible dangling operation calls">
   <xet:Head>
      <PossibleConflict type="Dangling operation call"
            collaboration="Svar-CollabID" instance="Svar-ReceiverID"
            operation="Svar-CallActName" class="Svar-ClassID"/>
   </xet:Head>
   <xet:Body>
      <UML:Collaboration xmi.id="Svar-CollabID">
         <UML:Namespace.ownedElement> Evar-1
            <UML:ClassifierRole xmi.id="Svar-ReceiverID" base="Svar-ClassID"/> Evar-2
         </UML:Namespace.ownedElement>
         <UML:Collaboration.interaction>
            <UML:Interaction.message> Evar-3
               <UML:Message name="Svar-CallActName" receiver="Svar-ReceiverID"
                     Pvar-1="Null"/> Evar-4
            </UML:Interaction.message>
         </UML:Collaboration.interaction>
      </UML:Collaboration>
      <UML:Class xmi.id="Svar-ClassID" Pvar-2="Null">
         <UML:Classifier.feature> Evar-Features </UML:Classifier.feature>
      </UML:Class>
      <xet:notFoundIn>
         <xet:arg1> Svar-CallActName </xet:arg1>
         <xet:arg2> UML:Operation </xet:arg2>
         <xet:arg3> Evar-Features </xet:arg3>
      </xet:notFoundIn>
   </xet:Body>
</xet:Rule>
```

Fig. 20.   An XET rule corresponding to the XDD clause in Fig. 14.

```
<description>
      Association ends must have a unique name within an association
</description>
<forall var="a" in="//Foundation.Core.Association">
   <forall var="x" in="$a/Foundation.Core.Association.connection/
                        Foundation.Core.AssociationEnd">
      <forall var="y" in="$a/Foundation.Core.Association.connection/
                           Foundation.Core.AssociationEnd">
         <implies>
            <equal op1="$x/Foundation.Core.ModelElement.name/text()"
                   op2="$y/Foundation.Core.ModelElement.name/text()"/>
            <same op1="$x" op2="$y"/>
         </implies>
      </forall>
   </forall>
</forall>
```

Fig. 21.   An xlinkit rule.

consistent elements as well as those between inconsistent elements with respect to the constraint specified by the rule. In comparison with the approach based on the XDD theory, in which a derivable XML element produced by one XDD clause can be consumed seamlessly by other XDD clauses, xlinkit rules work separately, i.e., given a set of XML documents, consistent links and inconsistent links with respect to a rule are generated independently of those possibly generated with respect to other rules, and, as a consequence, inference through rule chaining is not readily realizable using xlinkit.

DL, XDD, and xlinkit have a common characteristic: Each of them provides a declarative language for representing knowledge and a mechanism for making inferences with respect to the declarative meaning of a knowledge base. As opposed to these declarative approaches, application of an OPS5-heritage production system to inconsistency detection was presented in [39]. Components of a UML model are converted into a collection of attribute-value-list assertions (working memory elements), and a knowledge base is expressed as a set of condition-action production rules. Operational semantics, rather than declarative semantics, is associated with rules: The antecedent part of a rule specifies patterns used to match working memory elements, and the consequence part specifies actions to be performed (e.g. addition, removal, or modification of working memory elements) when the rule fires. The production rule in Fig. 22, for instance, creates a working memory element indicating inconsistency when it finds two different attributes with the same name within a class. Inference with production rules is made through a data-driven incremental forward chaining algorithm. A rule engine for the Java platform, called Jess,[j] is employed in [39]. By using the Rete Algorithm [27] — an efficient method for comparing a large collection of patterns to a large collection of objects — for matching rules against working memory elements, Jess determines active rules in one execution cycle by considering only the changes made to working memory in the previous cycle. This makes it feasible to use a production system running in the background of a UML editor for checking inconsistency in real time while a model is being modified. Such data-driven real-time inconsistency detection, however, requires incorporation of cleanup rules into a knowledge base for removing inconsistency elements that are no longer valid with respect to the latest state of a model; i.e. for every inconsistency production rule r, there must be an associated

IF   (attribute (id: x) (name: z) (parentId: p))
        (attribute (id: $y \wedge \{\neq x\}$) (name: z) (parentId: p))
THEN ADD (inconsistency (id: [newId()]) (ruleid:"uml-1")
                        (location: ((attribute x) (attribute y)))
                        (msg: "Attributes must be unique within a class."))

Fig. 22.   A production rule for detection of inconsistency.

[j]$http://herzberg.ca.sandia.gov/jess.$

IF   (attribute (id: x) (name: z) (parentId: p))
          (attribute (id: y) (name: $w \land \{\neq z\}$) (parentId: p))
          (inconsistency (location: $\{\ni$ (attribute $x)\} \land \{\ni$ (attribute $y)\}$) (ruleid:"uml-1"))

THEN REMOVE 3

Fig. 23. A cleanup production rule.

cleanup rule that checks whether r is no longer active but an inconsistency element generated by r still exists, and, if it is the case, the cleanup rule removes that inconsistency element. Figure 23 shows the cleanup rule associated with the production rule in Fig. 22.

In contrast to inference driven by changes incrementally made to a model, reasoning in DL as well as that in XDD may go through the entire collection of diagram components, and, as such, is typically suitable as a means for conducting static consistency verification at the end of a certain development stage, in particular, verification that requires thorough analysis of a model, rather than real-time inconsistency detection. Using the DL-based approach, for example, one may perform consistency verification that requires semantic analysis of a class diagram as a whole. Likewise, using the XDD-based approach, one may check a certain type of conflict that may arise from certain implicit consequences of a model. Although it is also possible to invent production rules for generating working memory elements representing implicit properties of a model, the data-driven reasoning scheme in a production system would generate a large number of such working memory elements, most of which may not be relevant to the type of inconsistency of interest, not to mention the burden of devising cleanup rules for removing expired elements of this kind.[k]

With the aim of developing UML as a precise modeling language, the Z notation [55] has been used in [24, 25, 28, 41] to describe the abstract syntax of a subset of UML diagrams and define interpretation structures for associating meanings with well-formed modeling elements. Based on these interpretation structures, inference rules for transforming diagrams into some of their logical consequences have been introduced in [24, 41] as tools for proving properties of UML models and reasoning with diagrams. These inference rules can be represented as XDD clauses and regarded as axioms in an XDD knowledge base. The XDD clauses in Figs. 15–18, for example, are obtained from inference rules given in [41].

6. Conclusions

Formalization and analysis of the structural part of a domain are among the key features of DLs. Once a UML class diagram is represented as the TBox of a DL

---

[k]ET-based reasoning in XDD is goal-directed, as opposed to data-driven inference, and cleanup rules are not required in the XDD-based approach.

knowledge base, automated reasoning services of DLs lend themselves to verification of its semantic consistency. When DLs are applied to the metamodel-level class diagrams that define the abstract syntax of UML, they also enable automated verification of the syntactic consistency of user-defined diagrams, encoded as ABox assertions. Application of DLs to consistency problems of other types, however, is hindered by their restricted capabilities with respect to queries and rules involving ABox assertions. The XDD theory, by contrast, offers extensive rule-oriented facilities and is readily applicable to UML diagrams of all kinds that are encoded in the XMI format. It provides the capability of examining diagram components in tandem with analyzing implicit consequences of a model, which can enhance the possibility and the quality of inconsistency detection.

References

1. K. Akama, "Declarative semantics of logic programs on parameterized representation systems", *Advances in Software Science and Technology* **5** (1993) 45–63.
2. K. Akama, Y. Shigeta and E. Miyamoto, "Solving logical problems by equivalent transformation — A theoretical foundation", *Journal of the Japanese Society for Artificial Intelligence* **13** (1998) 928–935.
3. K. Akama, T. Shimizu and E. Miyamoto, "Solving problems by equivalent transformation of declarative programs", *Journal of the Japanese Society for Artificial Intelligence* **13** (1998) 944–952.
4. C. Anutariya, V. Wuwongse, K. Akama and V. Wattanapailin, "Semantic web modelling and programming with XDD", *The Emerging Semantic Web, Series: Frontiers in Artificial Intelligence* **75** (IOS Press, 2002) 79–97.
5. E. Astesiano and G. Reggio, "An algebraic proposal for handling UML consistency", *Proceedings of the Second Workshop on Consistency Problems in UML-based Software Development* (2003) 62–70.
6. F. Baader, D. Calvanese, D. McGuinness, D. Nardi and P. F. Patel-Schneider, *The Description Logic Handbook: Theory, Implementation and Applications* (Cambridge University Press, 2003).
7. F. Baader and W. Nutt, "Basic description logics", in [6], pp. 43–95.
8. D. Berardi, D. Calvanese and G. De Giacomo, "Reasoning on UML class diagram using description logic based system", *Proceedings of the KI-2001 Workshop on Applications of Description Logics, CEUR Electronic Workshop Proceedings* **44**, 2001, *http://ceur-ws.org/Vol-44/*.
9. D. Berardi, "Using DLs to reason on UML class diagrams", *Proceedings of the KI-2002 Workshop on Applications of Description Logics, CEUR Electronic Workshop Proceedings* **63**, 2002, *http://ceur-ws.org/Vol-63/*.
10. J. Bézivin and N. Ploquin, "Tooling the MDA framework: A new software maintenance and evolution scheme proposal", *Journal of Object-Oriented Programming*, December 2001, *http://www.adtmag.com/joop/*.
11. G. Booch, J. Rumbaugh and I. Jacobson, *The Unified Modeling Language User Guide* (Addison Wesley, 1998).
12. A. Borgida, "Description logics in data management", *IEEE Transaction on Knowledge and Data Engineering* **7** (1995) 671–682.
13. A. Borgida, "On the relative expressiveness of description logics and predicate logics", *Artificial Intelligence* **82** (1996) 353–367.

14. A. Borgida, M. Lenzerini and R. Rosati, "Description logics for databases", in [6], pp. 462–484.
15. A. Cali, D. Calvanese, G. De Giacomo and M. Lenzerini, "A formal framework for reasoning on UML class diagrams", *Proceedings of the Thirteenth International Symposium on Methodologies for Intelligent Systems* (2002) 503–513.
16. D. Calvanese, G. De Giacomo and M. Lenzerini, "On the decidability of query containment", *Proceedings of the Seventeenth ACM SIGACT SIGMOD SIGART Symposium on Principles of Database Systems* (1998) 149–158.
17. D. Calvanese, G. De Giacomo and M. Lenzerini, "Identification constraints and functional dependencies in description logics", *Proceedings of the Seventeenth International Joint Conference on Artificial Intelligence* (2001) 155–160.
18. D. Calvanese, G. De Giacomo, M. Lenzerini and D. Nardi, "Reasoning in expressive description logics", eds. A. Robinson and A. Voronkov, *Handbook of Automated Reasoning* (Elsevier Science Publisher, 2001) 1581–1634.
19. D. Calvanese and G. De Giacomo, "Expressive description logics", in [6], pp. 178–218.
20. D. Calvanese, M. Lenzerini and D. Nardi, "Description logics for conceptual data modeling", eds. J. Chomicki and G. Saake, *Logics for Databases and Information Systems* (Kluwer Academic Publisher, 1998) 229–264.
21. F. M. Donini, M. Lenzerini, D. Nardi and A. Schaerf, "Reasoning in description logics", ed. G. Brewka, *Principles of Knowledge Representation, Studies in Logic, Language and Information* (CSLI Publications, 1996) 193–238.
22. F. M. Donini, "Complexity of reasoning", in [6], pp. 96–136.
23. G. Engels, J. M. Küster and L. Groenewegen, "Consistent interaction of software components", *Journal of Integrated Design & Process Science* **6**, no. 4 (2002) 2–22, *http://www.sdpsnet.org/vol6-4.htm*.
24. A. S. Evans, "Reasoning with UML class diagrams", *Proceedings of the Second IEEE Workshop on Industrial-Strength Formal Specification Techniques* (1998) 102–113.
25. A. S. Evans, R. France, K. Lano and B. Rumpe, "The UML as a formal modeling notation", *Proceedings of the First International Workshop on the Unified Modeling Language, Lecture Notes in Computer Science 1618* (Springer, 1998) 336–348.
26. M. S. Feather, "Rapid application of lightweight formal methods for consistency analyses", *IEEE Transactions on Software Engineering* **24** (1998) 949–959.
27. C. L. Forgy, "Rete: A fast algorithm for the many patterns/many objects match problem", *Artificial Intelligence* **19** (1982) 17–37.
28. R. France, A. S. Evans, K. Lano and B. Rumpe, "Developing the UML as a formal modeling notation", *Computer Standards and Interfaces* **19** (1998) 325–334.
29. B. N. Grosof, I. Horrocks, R. Volz and S. Decker, "Description logic programs: Combining logic programs with description logic", *Proceedings of the Twelfth International WWW Conference* (2003) 48–57.
30. C. Gryce, A. Finkelstein and C. Nentwich, "Lightweight checking for UML based software development", *Proceedings of the First Workshop on Consistency Problems in UML-based Software Development* (2002) 124–132.
31. V. Haarslev and R. Möller, "RACER system description", *Proceedings of the International Joint Conference on Automated Reasoning, Lecture Notes in Artificial Intelligence 2083* (Springer, 1998) 701–705.
32. V. Haarslev and R. Möller, "High performance reasoning with very large knowledge bases: A practical case study", *Proceedings of the Seventeenth International Joint Conference on Artificial Intelligence* (2001) 161–168.
33. B. Hnatkowska, Z. Huzar, L. Kuzniarz and L. Tuzinkiewicz, "A systematic approach to consistency within UML based software development process", *Proceedings of the*

First Workshop on Consistency Problems in UML-based Software Development (2002) 16–29.

34. B. Hnatkowska, L. Kuzniarz, Z. Huzar and L. Tuzinkiewicz, "Refinement relationship between collaborations", *Proceedings of the Second Workshop on Consistency Problems in UML-based Software Development* (2003) 51–57.

35. I. Horrocks, "The FaCT system", *Proceedings of the Second International Conference on Analytic Tableaux and Related Methods, Lecture Notes in Computer Science 1397* (Springer, 1998) 307–312.

36. I. Horrocks and P. F. Patel-Schneider, "Optimizing description logic subsumption", *Journal of Logic and Computation* **9** (1999) 267–293.

37. I. Horrocks and S. Tessaris, "A conjunctive query language for description logic ABoxes", *Proceedings of the Seventeenth National Conference on Artificial Intelligence* (2000) 399–404.

38. D. Jackson and J. Wing, "Lightweight formal methods", *Computer* (April 1996) 21–22.

39. W. Liu, S. Easterbrook and J. Mylopoulos, "Rule-based detection of inconsistency in UML models", *Proceedings of the First Workshop on Consistency Problems in UML-based Software Development* (2002) 106–123.

40. R. Möller and V. Haarslev, "Description logic systems", in [6], pp. 282–305.

41. E. Nantajeewarawat and R. Sombatsrisomboon, "On the semantics of unified modeling language diagrams using Z notation", *International Journal of Intelligent Systems* **19** (2004) 79–88.

42. E. Nantajeewarawat and V. Wuwongse, "Defeasible inheritance through specialization", *Computational Intelligence* **17** (2001) 62–86.

43. E. Nantajeewarawat, V. Wuwongse, S. Thiemjarus, K. Akama and C. Anutariya, "Generating relational database schemas from UML diagrams through XML declarative descriptions", *Proceedings of the Second International Conference on Intelligent Technologies* (2001) 240–249.

44. E. Nantajeewarawat, V. Wuwongse, C. Anutariya, K. Akama and S. Thiemjarus, "Toward reasoning with unified modeling language diagrams based on extensible markup language declarative description theory", *International Journal of Intelligent Systems* **19** (2004) 89–98.

45. C. Nentwich, L. Capra, W. Emmerich and A. Finkelstein, "xlinkit: A consistency checking and smart link generation service", *ACM Transactions on Internet Technology* **2** (2002) 151–185.

46. C. Nentwich, W. Emmerich and A. Finkelstein, "Flexible consistency checking", *ACM Transactions on Software Engineering and Methodology* **12** (2003) 62–86.

47. Object Management Group, XML Metadata Interchange (XMI) Specification 1.2, January 2002, *http://www.omg.org/technology/xml/*.

48. J. Rumbaugh, I. Jacobson and G. Booch, *The Unified Modeling Language Reference Manual* (Addison Wesley, 1999).

49. J. L. Sourrouille and G. Caplat, "A pragmatic view on consistency checking of UML models", *Proceedings of the Second Workshop on Consistency Problems in UML-based Software Development* (2003) 43–50.

50. R. Van Der Straeten, T. Mens, J. Simmonds and V. Jonckers, "Using description logic to maintain consistency between UML models", *Proceedings of the Sixth International Conference on the Unified Modeling Language, Lecture Notes in Computer Science 2863* (Springer, 2003) 326–340.

51. R. Van Der Straeten, T. Mens, J. Simmonds and V. Jonckers, "Maintaining consistency between UML models using description logic", *Proceedings of the Second Workshop on Consistency Problems in UML-based Software Development* (2003) 71–77.

52. R. Van Der Straeten, J. Simmonds and T. Mens, "Detecting inconsistencies between UML models using description logic", *Proceedings of the 2003 Description Logic Workshop, CEUR Electronic Workshop Proceedings 81*, 2003, *http://ceur-ws.org/Vol-81/*.
53. S. Tessaris, "Questions and answers: Reasoning and querying in description logic", PhD Thesis, Department of Computer Science, University of Manchester (2001).
54. M. Y. Vardi, "Why is model logic so robustly decidable", eds. N. Immerman and P. Kolaitis, *Descriptive Complexity and Finite Models* (American Mathematical Society, 1997) 149–184.
55. J. Woodcock and J. Davies, *Using Z Specification, Refinement and Proof* (Prentice Hall, 1996).
56. V. Wuwongse, C. Anutariya, K. Akama and E. Nantajeewarawat, "XML declarative description: A language for the semantic web", *IEEE Intelligent Systems* (May/June 2001) 54–65.
57. V. Wuwongse, K. Akama, C. Anutariya and E. Nantajeewarawat, "A data model for XML databases", *Journal of Intelligent Information Systems* **20** (2003) 63–80.
58. V. Wuwongse and E. Nantajeewarawat, "Declarative programs with implicit implication", *IEEE Transactions on Knowledge and Data Engineering* **14** (2002) 836–849.

MDA-BASED ONTOLOGICAL ENGINEERING

DRAGAN DJURIĆ, DRAGAN GAŠEVIĆ,
VIOLETA DAMJANOVIĆ and VLADAN DEVEDŽIĆ

FON — School of Business Administration, University of Belgrade,
Department of Physics, Stockholm University,
POB 52, Jove Ilića 154, 11000 Belgrade, Serbia and Montenegro
E-mail: dragandj@gmail.com, gasevic@yahoo.com,
vdamjanovic@gmail.com, devedzic@fon.bg.ac.yu
Tel: +381-11-3950853

The chapter presents a concept of approaching two ongoing technologies, ontological engineering and OMG's Model Driven Architecture (MDA), which are developing in parallel, but by different communities. Our main intention is to show recent efforts to provide software engineers to use and develop ontologies. Many authors have so far stressed this problem and have proposed several solutions and some of them are analyzed in this chapter. The result of these efforts is the recent OMG's initiative for defining an ontology development platform. The ontology platform should be defined using MDA-based standards and it should consist of: Ontology Definition Metamodel, Ontology UML Profile, and a set of transformations. We depict our proposal for an MDA-based ontology development platform in order to illustrate this OMG's effort as it is in a very initial stage and a formal recommendation has not been adopted yet.

Keywords: Model-driven architecture, ontologies, Semantic Web, metamodels, XML.

1. Introduction

The Semantic Web and its eXtensible Markup Language (XML) based languages are the main directions of the future Web development. Domain ontologies [30] are the most important part of the Semantic Web applications. They are formal organization of domain knowledge, and in that way enable knowledge sharing between different knowledge-base applications. Artificial intelligence (AI) techniques are used for ontology creation, but those techniques are more related to research laboratories, and they are unknown to wider software engineering population.

The integration of the ongoing software engineering efforts with the concept of the Semantic Web is not a new idea [13, 40]. The main question is how to develop the Semantic Web ontologies using well-accepted software engineering languages and techniques in order to provide the wider practitioner population to develop and use ontologies in real-world applications. Many researchers have previously suggested using UML in order to solve this problem. However, UML is based on object oriented paradigm, and has some limitation regarding ontology development. Hence, we can only use UML in initial phases of an ontology development. We believe that these limitations can be overcomed using UML's extensions (i.e., UML profiles) [19], as well as other OMG's standards (e.g. Model Driven Architecture — MDA). Additionally, if we want to provide solution consistent with MDA proposals, we should also support automatic generation of completely operational ontology definitions (e.g. in OWL language) that are model driven [50]. The most important direction toward this goal is the Special Interest Group (SIG) within Object Modeling Group (OMG) that will converge many different proposals regarding this problem [44]. The result of this effort should be a standard language (i.e., metamodel) based on the MDA standards [42] and the W3C's Web Ontology Language (OWL) recommendation [6].

The next section contains an overview of the ontologies and the Semantic Web, while Sec. 3 describes the Semantic Web languages and OWL. Section 4 defines OMG's MDA initiative and related concepts: Meta-Object Facility (MOF), UML Profiles, and XML Metadata Interchange (XMI). In Sec. 5, we give an overview of current work using MDA-based solutions for ontology development. In Sec. 6, we give a framework for the ontology language metamodel in the context of the OMG's effort. Section 8 shows the ontology metamodel definition in detail while Sec. 9 gives description of Ontology UML Profile (OUP). The last section contains the final conclusions. This work is part of the effort of the GOOD OLD AI research group (*http://goodoldai.org.yu*) in developing AIR — a platform for building intelligent information systems.

2. An Overview of the Ontologies and the Semantic Web

Ontologies have been around for quite some time now. Since the early 1990s researchers in the domain of artificial intelligence and knowledge representation have studied ontologies as means for knowledge sharing and reuse among knowledge-based systems. However, even an early survey of the field of ontologies [24] has identified a number of application classes that benefit to a large extent from utilizing ontologies although some of them are not necessarily knowledge-based systems in the traditional sense. Some of the application classes it mentioned include natural language processing, library science, intelligent information retrieval (especially from the Internet), virtual organizations, and simulation and modeling. Later on, researchers have recognized explicitly that ontologies are not just for knowledge-based systems, but for all software systems — all software needs models of the world, hence can make use of ontologies at design time [11]. Nowadays, ontologies and ontological engineering span such diverse fields as qualitative modeling, language engineering, database design, information retrieval and extraction, knowledge management and organization, ontology-enhanced search, possibly the largest one, e-commerce (e.g. Amazon.com, Yahoo Shopping, etc.), and configuration [41].

2.1. *Definitions and background*

There are at least a dozen definitions of ontologies in the literature. A recent one says that ontology provides the basic structure or armature around which a knowledge base can be built [52]. Another one specifies that ontology should provide a set of knowledge terms, including the vocabulary, the semantic interconnections, and some simple rules of inference and logic for some particular topic or service [32]. Although informal, these definitions capture the central idea of ontologies — they are structured depictions or models of known (and accepted) facts about some topics. Ontologies appear most effective when the semantic distinctions that humans take for granted are crucial to the application's purpose [15].

Each ontology provides the vocabulary (or names) for referring to the terms in a subject area, as well as the logical statements that describe what the terms are, how they are related to each other, how they can or cannot be related to each other, as well as rules for combining terms and relations to define extensions to the vocabulary. Hence, ontologies represent a common machine-level understanding of topics that can be communicated between users and applications, i.e., domain semantics independent of reader and context. For a more recent comprehensive discussion of ontologies, see [36].

2.2. *Semantic Web*

One of the central roles of ontologies is to establish further levels of interoperability, i.e., semantic interoperability, between agents and applications on the emerging Semantic Web [8], as well as to add a further representation and inference layer on top of the Web's current layers [14, 32]. When put on the Web, ontologies specify standard terms and machine-readable definitions. The Semantic Web is based on the idea of numerous ontologies providing vocabularies, definitions, and constraints that information resources, agents, and Web-based applications can commit to in order to reuse data and knowledge effectively [31]. This way, ontology conveys the same meaning of its terms to any two or more sources that commit to it. Any source, agent, or application can commit to any ontology or create a new one. Thus, the Semantic Web is essentially a distributed approach to creating standard vocabularies.

2.3. *Ontological engineering*

The engineering part of developing ontologies comprises a complex set of activities that are conducted during conceptualization, design, implementation and deployment of ontologies. Ontological engineering covers a whole range of topics and issues, such as the basics (philosophical and metaphysical issues and knowledge representation formalisms), methodology of ontology development, recent Web technologies such as XML [7] and its relatives [38], business process modeling, commonsense knowledge, systematization of domain knowledge, Internet information retrieval, standardization, evaluation, ontology integration with agents and applications, and many more [16]. It also gives us design rationale of a knowledge base, helps us define the essential concepts of the world of interest, allows for a more disciplined design of a knowledge base, and enables us to accumulate knowledge about it. The disciplines tightly interwoven with ontological engineering include modeling, metamodeling, and numerous fields of software engineering.

2.4. *Ontology building tools*

An important aspect of building ontologies is the use of specific software tools that enable ontology conceptualization, representation, construction, and use. There are a number of such tools today. Most of them have resulted from efforts of research groups and university labs, and are currently free. However, these tools can differ to a large extent in terms of support they provide to the ontology development process, the format(s) used for storing ontologies, the number of format converters supported for translating ontologies to/from other formats, the way(s) other applications can interoperate with ontology tools, the tool stability and maturity, support for querying information about an ontology, and so on [29].

3. An Overview of the Semantic Web Tools and Languages

There were several efforts so far to develop a comprehensive classification of ontology development tools, as well as to compare and evaluate a number of different tools. The most comprehensive among such approaches to date is the one proposed by OntoWeb Consortium [29]. The approach starts from grouping all ontology-based software tools into the following large categories:

- ontology development tools — the tools, environments and suites that can be used for building a new ontology from scratch or reusing existing ontologies;
- ontology merge and integration tools — the tools helping to solve the problem of merging or integrating different ontologies on the same domain;
- ontology evaluation tools — support tools that enable getting insight into the level of quality of ontologies and their related technologies;
- ontology-based annotation tools — the tools enabling the users to insert ontology-based markups in Web pages;
- ontology storage and querying tools — the tools that allow using and querying ontologies easily; and
- ontology learning tools — the tools used to (semi) automatically derive ontologies from natural language texts.

A similar, though much more narrowly focused study by M. Denny, covered ontology editors only [15]. Ontology browsers without an editing focus and other types of ontology building tools were not included. The study was still very useful because it helped identify a cross-section of ontology editing tools.

Another group of comparative studies is focused on ontology development languages only. A good example coming from an academic environment is the study of languages for the Semantic Web [28]. The study has identified three levels of abstraction of such languages and has included only the languages based on XML technologies.

Ontology learning tools	Tools employing machine learning
Ontology-development environments	Integrated graphical tools
Ontology-representation languages (The Semantic Web languages)	Languages of different expressive power and based on different representation paradigms (regardless of the underlying technology)
XML/RDF	XML/XMLS, RDF/RDFS and the corresponding development tools

Fig. 1. Hierarchy of ontology development tools.

We propose a suitable, practically oriented, and simple framework/hierarchy that can be used for an easy, yet very informative categorization of ontology development tools. It is drawn based on informal criteria of the tools' sophistication and usability. Despite the fact that these may appear as rather subjective criteria, they do allow for a rough hierarchical categorization of all currently available ontology development tools. The framework is characterized by:

- a wider focus than that of ontology editors alone, used in [15];
- yet, a more narrow focus than that of covering all ontology-related tools as in [29] — our framework concentrates on ontology development tools only;
- ontology development languages themselves are included, although much less formally than in [28, 48];
- ontology learning tools are included, since ontology learning is also a way of *building* ontologies.

Figure 1 describes the framework/hierarchy graphically.

3.1. *The Semantic Web languages*

Common data interoperability in present applications is best achieved by using XML. XML is a meta-language used to define other languages. It describes a class of data objects called XML documents and partially describes the behavior of computer programs which process them [9]. XML defines neither the tags nor grammar, which makes it completely extensible. It only requires that document must be well-formed in a tree structure, so it could be parsed by standard XML tools. Hence, one can view XML technologies and languages, as well as their corresponding development tools, as constituting the core of ontology development tools. Ontologies represent semantics and meanings of topics and subject areas in a declarative form.

XML syntax suitable for ontology representation because it is human readable, simple to parse, well defined, and widely used. Fundamental XML-based languages — XML itself, XMLS, Resource Description Framework (RDF) and RDF Schema (RDFS) — can express some semantics themselves.

Whereas in pure HTML the tags are fixed, in XML they are arbitrary and are described in a Document Type Definition (DTD) or in an XMLS document. Having custom tags in a document adds context and gives meaning to data and let people meaningfully annotate text [6]. Using XMLS to prescribe the data structure, XML can encode all kinds of data that is exchanged between computers. This brings an extensible and easy-to-use syntax for describing Web data, though just a minimum semantics. With respect to the Semantic Web technology, it is important to stress a role of an XML Metamodel Interchange (XMI) as a standard for stream-based model interchange. The main purpose of XMI [46] is to enable easy interchange of metadata between modeling tools (based on the Object Management Group (OMG) Unified Modeling Language (UML)) and between tools and metadata repositories (OMG Meta Object Facility (MOF)) in distributed heterogeneous environments. XMI integrates three key industry standards:

(i) **XML** — a W3C standard;
(ii) **UML** — an OMG modeling standard; and
(iii) **MOF** — Meta Object Facility and OMG modeling and metadata repository standard.

The integration of these three standards into XMI marries the best of OMG and W3C metadata and modeling XMI technologies allowing developers of distributed systems to share object models and other metadata over the Internet. XMI standardizes the exchange of metamodels, models, as well as object instances between applications [46].

Apart from the XML, there are other languages attempt to achieve semantic interoperability. Such languages are Ontology Interchange Language (Ontology Inference Layer) (OIL), DARPA Agent Markup Language (DAML+OIL), RDF, RDFS, and Web Ontology Language (OWL).

OIL is a proposal for a joint standard for describing and exchanging ontologies. OIL permits semantic interoperability between web resources. OIL is not just another new language but reflects a certain consensus among the specialists in the areas such as description logic (DL) and frame-based systems. OIL is a significant source of inspiration for the ontology language DAML+OIL [21].

DAML+OIL is an ontology language specifically designed for use on the Web, as a joint effort to create a standard language for the Semantic Web. DAML+OIL uses existing standards (XML and RDF), adding the familiar ontological primitives of object-oriented and frame-based systems, and the formal rigor of a very expressive DL [34]. DAML+OIL is built on top of W3C standards such as RDF and RDFS, and extends these languages with richer modeling primitives [33].

RDF and RDFS cannot be considered as ontology specification languages, but rather as general languages for the description of metadata on the Web [12]. It is important to stress that they are a W3C standard for the Semantic Web. RDF is a framework for representing metadata, i.e., a model for representing data about resources on the Web. Each RDF description is basically a list of *object* (resource) — *attribute* (property) — *value* (resource or free text) triples, i.e., statements. This RDF data model is equivalent to the semantic network formalisms, which consist of three object types: properties, resources, and statements.

RDFS are used to define an RDF document vocabulary (domain-specific properties and classes of resources to which those properties can be applied), and are referred to in RDF documents through namespaces. It is important to stress that RDFS uses modeling primitives like *class, subclass-of, property, domain* and the like, with much higher expressive power than those used in XMLS. These allow for specifying higher-level semantics and can be used for basic ontology modeling.

The Web Ontology Language (OWL) is a semantic markup language for publishing and sharing ontologies on the WWW. OWL is developed as a vocabulary extension of RDF and is derived from the DAML+OIL Web Ontology Language. OWL is designed for use by applications that need to process the content of information instead of just presenting information to humans. OWL facilitates greater machine interpretability of Web content than that supported by XML, RDF and RDFS by providing additional vocabulary along with a formal semantics. OWL has three variants [6]:

- OWL Lite is intended mostly to support classification hierarchy and simple constraint features. It is a good starting point for tool builders. OWL Lite can be useful in migrations of existing taxonomies to OWL.
- OWL DL enables maximum expressiveness and guarantees computational completeness (all entailments are guaranteed to be computed) and decidability (all computations will finish in finite time). It includes all OWL Full constructs, and appends some constraints. The most significant constraints are that a class cannot be an individual or a property, or that a property cannot be an individual or a class. OWL DL has a good formal background since it is based on description logics.
- OWL Full provides maximum expressiveness and syntactic independence of RDF, but does not provide any computational guarantees. The main characteristic of OWL Full in comparison to OWL DL and OWL Lite is that one class, which is, by definition, a collection of individuals, can be an individual itself, like in RDF(S). This approach can lead to models that need infinite time to compute.

OWL Full is an extension of OWL DL, which is an extension of OWL Lite, thus every OWL Lite ontology is OWL DL and OWL Full ontology and every OWL DL ontology is OWL Full ontology. The place of OWL in described architecture is shown in Fig. 2.

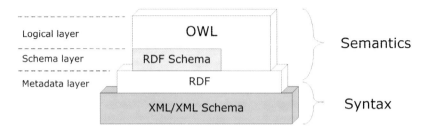

Fig. 2.   OWL in the Semantic Web architecture.

Since the World Wide Web is almost unconstrained, OWL must support open world assumption and allow importing and mixing various ontologies. Some of them may be even contradictory, but new information can never retract existing information, it can only add to it.

4. An Overview of Model Driven Architecture and Meta-Object Facility

If we look back at the history of software development, we can see a notable increase of models abstraction. Modeling becomes more and more separate from underlying platforms, making models of real world more reusable and easy to create by domain experts, requiring less knowledge of specific computer systems. This places software modeling closer to knowledge acquisition in knowledge engineering and vice versa. Current stage in that evolution is OMG's Model Driven Architecture [42].

4.1. *MDA basics*

MDA defines three viewpoints (levels of abstraction) from which a system can be seen. From a selected viewpoint, a representation of a given system (viewpoint model) can be defined. These models are (each corresponding to the viewpoint with the same name): *Computation Independent Model* (CIM), *Platform Independent Model* (PIM) and *Platform Specific Model* (PSM). CIM is a view of a system that does not show the details of a system structure. In software engineering, it is also known as a domain model, which is specified by domain experts. It is similar to the concept of ontology. PIM is the model that is computation dependent, but it is not aware of specific computer platform details. In other words, it is targeted for technology-neutral virtual machine. Specification of complete computer system is completed with PSM. The goal is to move human work from PSM towards CIM and PIM and let the specific platform detail implementations be generated as much as possible by automated tools which will do the transformation from PIM to PSM.

All metamodels, standard or custom, defined by MOF are positioned at the M2 layer. One of these is UML, a graphical modeling language for specifying, visualizing and documenting software systems. With UML profiles, basic UML concepts (Class, Association, etc.) can be extended with new concepts (stereotypes) and adapted to specific modeling needs. The models of the real world, represented by concepts defined in the corresponding metamodel at M2 layer (e.g. UML metamodel) are at M1 layer. Finally, at M0 layer are instances of concepts modeled at M1 layer. An example would be: MOF Class (at M3) is used to define UML Class (M2), which is used to define real-world describing concept, class Person (M1) that can have instances: Tom, Dick, Harry (M0).

Another standard that this architecture is based on is XMI, a standard that defines mapping from MOF-defined metamodels to XML documents and Schemas. XML, which is well-supported in various software tools, gives XMI strength to enable sharing of meta-metamodel, metamodels and models.

Present software tools support for MDA is concentrated primarily on UML as a graphical notation, with no concern of metamodeling layers [26]. UML CASE tools (e.g. Rational Rose, Borland Together, Magic Draw, Poseidon for UML, etc.) have good support for modeling at M1 layer and for code generation in certain programming languages. Using appropriate UML profile they can generate databases, XML Schemas, EJBs, etc. But, they lack support for M2 and M3 layers as well as a unified serialization to XMI. It is expected from future tools to support UML 2, which will enable common XMI representation of UML models, and MOF-compliant model repositories at M2 and M3 layers; all this will provide a good support for metamodeling.

4.2. *Modeling: Instance layers versus ontological layers*

MOF is a self-defined language intended for defining metamodels. In term of MDA a metamodel makes statements about what can be expressed in the valid models of a certain modeling language. In fact, a metamodel is a model of a modeling language [49]. Examples of the MDA's metamodels are UML and CWM. The MDA's metamodel layer is usually marked as M2. At this layer, we can define a new metamodel (e.g. modeling language) that would cover some specific application domains (e.g. ontology development). The next layer is the model layer (M1) — a layer where we develop real-world models (or domain models). In terms of the UML models that means creating classes, their relations, states, etc. This layered architecture, also shown in Fig. 3 is often difficult to understand for less experienced modelers, so we should explain the bottom-most layer, the instance layer (M0) in more depth. There are two different approaches about this question, and we note both of them:

(1) The instance layer contains instances of the concepts defined at model (M1) layer (e.g. objects in programming languages).
(2) The instance layer contains things from our reality — concrete (e.g. Mark is instance of the Person class, Lassie is a instance of the Dog class, etc.) and abstract (e.g. UML's classes — Dog, Person, etc.) [3].

In this chapter, we advocate the second approach, but we should give more details about its impact on UML. In UML, both classes and objects are at the same

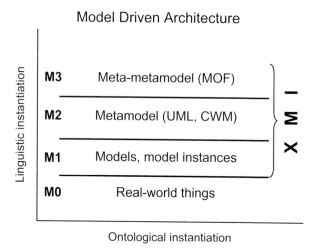

Fig. 3. The four-layer Model Driven Architecture and its orthogonal instance-of relations: linguistics and ontological.

layer (model layer) in the MDA four-layer architecture. Actually, MDA's layers are called linguistic layers. On the other side, concepts from the same linguistic layer can be at different ontological layers. Hence, UML classes and objects are at different ontological layers, but at the same linguistic layer.

4.3. Specific MDA metamodels and UML profiles

One possible solution for using MDA capacities in some specific domains is to develop a metamodel, which would be able to model relevant domain concepts. That means, creating a domain language (i.e., metamodel) using metamodeling, and these languages are created using MOF. Having defined a domain specific metamodel we should develop suitable tools for using that metamodel. However, it is rather expensive and time consuming so we try to use well-developed tools. Practically, present software tools do not implement many of the MDA basic concepts. However, most of these applications, currently primarily oriented toward UML and the M1 (i.e., model) layer [26]. Generally, UML itself is a MOF-defined general-purpose language (i.e., metamodel) that contains a set of core primitives. The problem of tools can be overcome using UML Profiles — a way for adapting UML for specific purposes. UML Profiles extend the UML metamodel with application-specific primitives (through stereotypes, tagged values, and constraints), and hence these primitives can be used as the regular UML concepts. Having understood UML Profiles in this way one can count UML as a family of languages [19].

A very important question is about the palace of UML Profiles in the MDA's four-layer architecture. The UML specification states that UML Profiles are defined at the metamodel layer (M2), and thus they are meta-concepts. Here we use a definition of UML Profiles in a strict metamodeling framework [1, 2] where UML Profiles are placed at both the metamodel layer (M2) and the model layer (M1).

5. Current Trends: Using UML and MDA-Based Languages in Ontological Engineering

In this section, we describe existing efforts to enable usage of UML, present UML tools, as well as MDA-based standards in ontological engineering. Our goal is to explain formal background of each approach, and their mappings into ontology languages. In Table 1, we give an overview of the analyzed solutions, their formal definition, kinds of model interchange description they use, proposals for mapping implementation, and target ontological languages.

The idea to use UML in ontological engineering has firstly been in Cranefield's papers [13]. He has found connections between the standard UML and ontologies concepts: Classes, relations, properties, inheritance, etc. However, there are some dissimilarities between them, and the most important one is related to the property concept — in the UML an attribute has a class scope, while in ontology a property is a first-class concept that can exist independently of a class. This approach suggests using UML class diagrams for the development of ontology taxonomy and relations between ontological concepts, whereas UML object diagrams were intended to be used for modeling ontology instances (i.e., body of knowledge) [11]. Also a practical software support was provided in the form of two XSLTs that were developed to enable transformation of the UML XMI format to RDFS and Java classes. However, we have noted some limitations (that are also propagated to generated

Table 1. An overview of present UML and MDA-based ontology development frameworks and their transformations to the Semantic Web languages.

Approach	Metamodel	Model Description	Transformation Mechanism	Generated Ontology Language
Cranefield	Standard UML	UML XMI	XSLT	RDFS, Java classes
Backlawski et al	UML Profile, MOF-based ontology language	(Not given — UML) XMI, and MOF XMI can be used	—	DAML
Falkovych et al	Standard UML	UML XMI	XSLT	DAML+OIL
Protégé	Protégé metamodel	Protégé XMI	Programmed	OWL, RDF(S), DAML+OIL, XML, UML XMI, Protégé XMI, ...
	Standard UML	UML XMI		
DUET	UML Profile	Rational Rose, ArgoUML	Programmed	DAML+OIL
Xpetal	standard UML	Rational Rose mdl files	Programmed	RDFS

languages): One cannot conclude whether the same property was attached to more than one class, one cannot create a hierarchy of properties, and target RDFS ontology description does not have advanced restriction concepts (e.g. multiplicity).

Backlawski and his colleagues have introduced two approaches for ontology development. The first one extends the UML metamodel by introducing new metaclasses [4]. For instance, these metaclasses define a property as a first class concept, as well as a restriction on a property. In this way, they have solved the "property problem" in UML. This solution is mainly based on the DAML+OIL ontology language [41]. In order to enable usage of standard UML tools, they propose an UML profile and its mapping to DAML+OIL. The authors realized that this solution was fairly awkward because it introduced some new concepts in the UML metamodel. Therefore, they have developed an independent ontology metamodel using the MOF, which they named the Unified Ontology Language (UOL) [5]. This metamodel was also inspired by DAML+OIL. We have been unable to find any practical software solution that would be able to map these two MDA-based ontology languages into a Semantic Web language.

Falkovych and her associates [20] do not extend the standard UML metamodel in order to enable transformation of UML models into equivalent DAML+OIL descriptions. They use a UML-separated hierarchy to define kinds of ontology properties. A practical mapping from UML models to DAML+OIL is implemented using XSLT. The main limitations of this solution are: (1) lack of mechanisms for formal property specification (e.g. defining property inheritance, or inverseOf relation between properties), (2) it is based on UML class diagrams, which contain only graphical artifacts of real UML elements included in a model (e.g. they assume all association that has the same name as the same property, even though each association is a distinct model element in UML). Of course, this diagram problem can be partly overcome with XMI for UML 2.0 that supports diagram representation.

Protégé is the leading ontological engineering tool [23]. It has a complex software architecture, easily extensible through plug-ins. Many components that provide interfaces to other knowledge-based tools (Jess, Argenon, OIL, PAL constraint, etc.) have been implemented in this way, as well as support for different ontology languages and formats like XML, DAML+OIL (backends), and OIL (tab). In fact, Protégé has a formally MOF-defined metamodel. This metamodel is extensible and adaptable. This means, Protégé can be adapted to support a new ontology language by adding new metaclasses and metaslots into a Protégé's ontology. Introduction of these new metamodeling concepts enable users to add necessary ontology primitives (e.g. the Protégé class has different features from OWL class). In that way it can, for instance, support RDFS [22] or OWL (*http://protege.stanford.edu/plugins/owl-plugin*). It is especially interesting that Protégé has backends for UML and XMI. These two backends use the NetBeans' MetaData Repository (MDR — *http://mdr.netbeans.org*). The first backend exchanges UML models (i.e., classes, and their relations) using the standard UML XMI format, while the second one uses the XMI format that is compliant with the Protégé MOF-defined metamodel. It is obvious that one can share ontologies through the Protégé (e.g. import an ontology in the UML XMI format and store it in the OWL format). However, Protégé has one limitation in its UML XMI support — it does not map class relations (i.e., associations) into a Protégé's ontology (i.e., does not attach instance slots to classes). But, this limitation was expected since Protégé imports UML models without any extension (i.e., a UML Profile).

The software tool called DUET (*http://codip.grci.com/Tools/Tools.html*), which enables importing DAML ontologies into Rational Rose and ArgoUML, as well as exporting UML models into the DAML ontology language [21], has been developed in order to support ontological engineering. This tool uses a quite simple UML Profile that contains stereotypes for modeling ontologies (based on UML package) and properties (based on UML class). Additionally, DUET uses an XSLT that transforms RDFS ontologies into equivalent DAML ontologies. In that way, a RDFS ontology can be imported into UML tools through the DAML language. Of course, this tool has constraints similar to approaches we have already discussed (e.g. Falkovych *et al*) since it has no ability to define advanced class and property relations (e.g. *inverseOf*, *equivalentProperty*, *equivalentClass*, etc.). On the other hand, this is the first UML tool extension that enables ontology sharing between ontology language (i.e., DAML) and a UML tool in both directions.

Xpetal (*http://www.langdale.com.au/styler/-xpetal*) is another tool implemented in Java that transforms Rational Rose models from the *mdl* format to RDF and RDFS. This tool has limitations similar to those that we have already mentioned while discussing Cranefield's software (i.e., XSLT), since it uses the standard UML and does not provide a convenient solution for representing properties, their relations, advanced class restrictions, etc. Actually, this tool is more limited than the Cranefield's one, since it is oriented to the Rational Rose, in contrast to the Cranefield's XSLT that is applicable to every UML XMI document and independent of UML tools.

Our opinion is that all these approaches we have explored above are useful, but none of them gives a full solution that contains: A formal description of the new MDA-based ontology language, a related UML profile and necessary transformations between these two languages, as well as transformations to contemporary Semantic Web languages (i.e., OWL) [44]. We believe that full usage of the recent OMG's effort — MDA [42] provides us with considerable benefits when defining metamodeling architecture and enables us to develop new languages (i.e., ontology language). Actually, there is a RFP at OMG that should enclose all these requirements, but it is still in its initial stage.

6. The Ontology Modeling Architecture

Currently, there is a RFP (Request for Proposal) within OMG that tries to define a suitable language for modeling Semantic Web ontology languages in the context

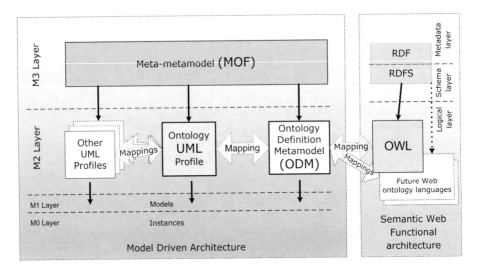

Fig. 4.   Ontology modeling in the context of MDA and Semantic Web.

of MDA [44]. According to this RFP, we developed an ontology development architecture [17]. Of course, we do not claim that this solution is either the best one, or widest accepted one, but we only want to illustrate one of possible solutions for the OMG's initiative. One can reach other similar solutions at the OMG Ontology SIG homepage: *http://ontology.omg.org*. In our approach to ontology modeling in the scope of MDA, which is shown in Fig. 4, several specifications should be defined:

- Ontology Definition Metamodel (ODM).
- Ontology UML Profile — a UML Profile that supports UML notation for ontology definition.
- Two-way mappings between OWL and ODM, ODM and Ontology UML Profile and from Ontology UML Profile to other UML profiles.

Ontology Definition Metamodel (ODM) should be designed to comprehend common ontology concepts. A good starting point for ODM construction is OWL since it is the result of the evolution of existing ontology representation languages, and is going to be a W3C recommendation. It is at the Logical layer of the Semantic Web [8], on top of RDF Schema (Schema layer). In order to make use of graphical modeling capabilities of UML, an ODM should have a corresponding UML Profile [51]. This profile enables graphical editing of ontologies using UML diagrams as well as other benefits of using mature UML CASE tools. Both UML models and ODM models are serialized in XMI format so the two-way transformation between them can be done using XSLT. OWL also has representation in the XML format, so another pair of XSLTs should be provided for two-way mapping between ODM and OWL. For mapping from the Ontology UML Profile into another technology-specific UML Profiles, additional transformations can be added to support usage of ontologies in design of other domains and vice versa. We have so far implemented an XSLT that transforms the Ontology UML Profile to OWL (for details see [27]). This XSLT can be understood as an extension of present UML tools for ontology development. However, here we do not show implementation details of this transformation, but our main focus is on the MDA-compliant ontological languages.

6.1. *Metamodeling: MDA versus Functional architecture*

Before we start with more detailed description of ODM, we must clarify differences between metamodeling based on MDA, and functional architecture which is used for Web ontology languages definition. RDFS, as a schema layer language, has a non-standard and non-fixed-layer metamodeling architecture, which makes some elements in model have dual roles in the RDFS specification [47]. Therefore, it is difficult to understand by modelers, lacks clear semantics (by assigning dual roles to some elements) and propagates "layer mistake" problem to languages it defines, in our case to OWL. MDA, on the other side, has fixed and well-defined four-layer architecture. It has separate metamodeling primitives on meta-metamodel and metamodel layer that are separated from ontology language (or some other MOF-defined language) primitives, which can have infinite layers, as in the case of OWL Full.

In OWL DL, functional architecture's problems are partially solved by introducing new modeling elements (`owl:Class`, for example) that are used for defining ontologies. In this case, `rdfs:Class` is used only for defining `owl:Class`, `owl:ObjectProperty` and other ontology-modeling primitives. It is not used for modeling ontologies, which is done using ontology-modeling primitives. On the other hand, OWL Full allows unconstrained use of RDFS constructs, which means that it completely inherits RDFS' problems. ODM that supports OWL Full cannot be modeled directly using MOF if we want to preserve fixed-layer architecture.

Accordingly, ODM will be designed primarily to support OWL DL. Support for OWL Full will be included partially, for concepts that do not introduce significant problems or break fixed-layer architecture.

A brief comparative description of the most important metamodeling constructs in MOF and RDF(S), which will make reading the next sections easier, is shown in Table 2. Detailed description of MOF can be found in OMG's MOF specification document [43]. RDF, RDFS and their concepts are described in detail in W3C documents [10].

7. Essential Ontology Definition Metamodel Concepts

This section briefly overviews the basic ODM concepts; for a more detailed description, see [17, 18]. OWL is built on top of RDFS, which is used as both modeling and metamodeling language. On the other hand, the corresponding ODM concepts are modeled by MOF. Since RDFS and MOF have numerous differences (non-fixed

Table 2.   A brief description of basic MOF and RDF(S) metamodeling constructs.

MOF Element	Short Description	RDF(S) Element	Short Description
ModelElement	ModelElement classifies the elementary, atomic constructs of models. It is the root element within the MOF Model.	rdfs:Resource	Represents all things described by RDF. Root construct of majority of RDF constructs.
DataType	Models primitive data, external types, etc.	rdfs:Datatype	Mechanism for grouping primitive data.
Class	Defines a classification over a set of object instances by defining the state and behavior they exhibit.	rdfs:Class	Provides an abstraction mechanism for grouping similar resources.
Classifier	Abstract concept that defines classification. It is specialized by Class, DataType, etc.		In RDF(S), rdfs:Class also have function that is similar to a MOF concept of Classifier.
Association	Expresses relationships in the metamodel between pairs of instances of Classes,	rdf:Property	Defines relation between subject resources and object resources.
Attribute	Defines a notional slot or value holder, typically in each instance of its Class.		
TypedElement	The TypedElement is an element that requires a type as part of its definition. A TypedElement does not itself define a type, but is associated with a Classifier. Examples are object instances, data values etc.		In RDF(S), any rdfs:Resource can be typed (via the rdf:type property) by some rdfs:Class.

versus fixed metamodeling architecture [47]), OWL concepts cannot be directly copied to ODM concepts. They need some degree of adaptation.

7.1. *Resource*

OWL is built on top of RDF; thus it inherits its concepts, such as Resource, Property, metamodeling capabilities, etc. Resource is one of the basic RDF concepts; it represents all things described by RDFS and OWL. It may represent anything on the Web: A Web site, a Web page, a part of a Web page, or some other object named by URI. Compared to ontology concepts, it can be viewed as a root concept, the Thing. In RDFS, Resource is defined as an instance of rdfs:Class; since we use MOF as a meta-metamodeling language, Resource will be defined as an instance of MOF Class. It is the root class of most other basic ODM concepts that will be

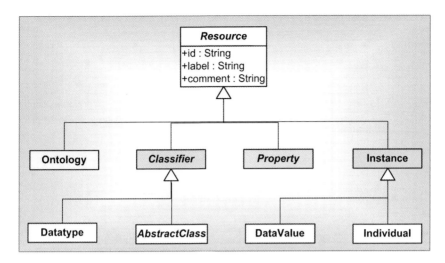

Fig. 5. The hierarchy of basic ontology concepts.

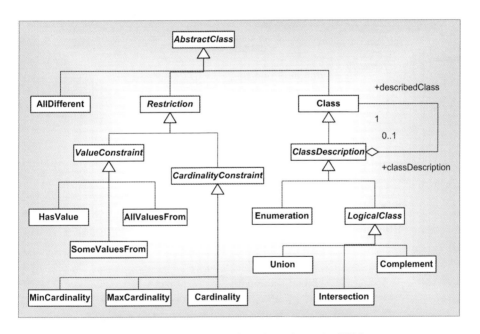

Fig. 6. The hierarchy of ontology classes in ODM.

described: Ontology, Classifier, Property, Instance, etc. The root of this hierarchy is shown on Class Diagram in Fig. 5. Other class diagrams (shown in Figs. 6–8) will depict these concepts in more detail.

Ontology is a concept that aggregates other concepts (Classes, Properties, etc.). It groups instances of other concepts that represent similar or related knowledge. Classifier is the base class of concepts that are used for classification — AbstractClass and DataType. Instance is the base class of

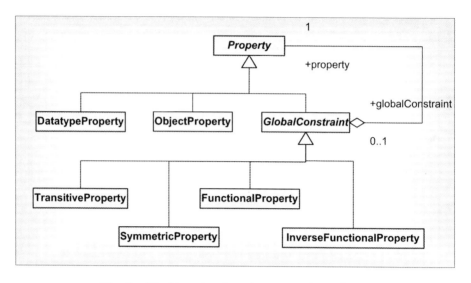

Fig. 7. The hierarchy of ontology properties in ODM.

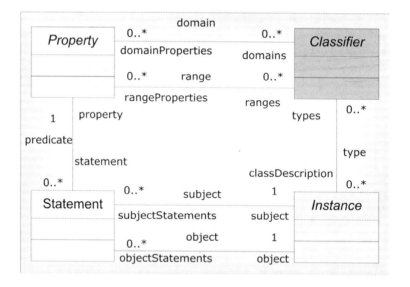

Fig. 8. Key relationships among ontology concepts.

concepts that are classified by Classifiers — concrete Individuals and concrete DataValues. Property is used to represent relationships between other concepts.

For example, Person is an AbstractClass (more precise — a Class) that classifies many Individuals: Tom, Dick, Harry, etc. All Persons have Properties — name and occupation. These Properties can have values that are of certain type; name can be a String (an example of DataType), occupation can be Profession (another example of AbstractClass).

Then, `Profession` classifies concrete professions (its `instances`): `Musician`, `Writer`, `Mechanic`, `Astronaut`, etc.

7.2. *Classifier*

In RDFS and OWL, Class (`rdfs:Class` and `owl:Class`) represents a concept for grouping resources with similar characteristics. This concept of Class (we can also call it Ontology Class) is not completely identical as a concept of Class that is defined in UML and object oriented programming languages. Every `owl:Class` is a set of individuals, called class extension. These individuals are instances of that class. Two classes can have the same class extension but still be different classes. Ontology classes are set-theoretic, while traditional classes are more behavioral. Unlike a traditional class, an OWL class does not directly define any attributes or relations with other resources, and there is no any concept similar to methods. Attributes and relations are defined as Properties. In ODM, a Class concept corresponding to `rdfs:Class` is defined as Classifier — an instance of MOF `Class` that inherits `Resource`. A concept that complies with `owl:Class` is ODM's `AbstractClass`.

OWL further introduces six ways of defining a Class — class descriptions:

(i) A class can be defined by a class identifier (an URI reference) — for example, a Class `Person`.

(ii) As an exhaustive enumeration of individuals that form the instances of a Class. For example, individuals `Mick`, `Keith`, `Ron`, `Bill` and `Charlie` form an Enumeration — `TheRollingStones`. Note that they are also members of a Class `Person`.

(iii) As a property restriction — Class of all individuals that have the same restriction on some of their characteristics.

(iv) As an intersection — A Class of all individuals that are members of all Classes that form an intersection. An intersection of Classes `TheWailers` and `TheRollingStones` is a Class that does not have any member, since no musician has played in both bands.

(v) As a union — A Class of all individuals that are members of any Class that forms a union. A union of `TheWailers` and `TheRollingStones`, has twelve individuals, all musicians from both bands.

(vi) As a complement — A Class of all individuals that are not members of other, complement class. A complement of `TheRollingStones` is a Class that has about six billion members — all Persons that are not members of `TheRollingStones`.

(vii) `AllDifferent` is a helper class, which states that all of its instances have different identity.

The first concept, named class is modeled as ODM `Class`. Other five species are defined in OWL as subclasses of `owl: Class`, and are shown in Fig. 6. If we define class descriptions as simple subclasses of `Class`, like it is defined in OWL, we will have some problems related to the differences between RDFS and MOF concept of a class and the open-world assumption of the Semantic Web. While in RDFS some class instance can be easily defined to be a member of many class extensions at the same time, in MOF it can be instance of exactly one class. The open-world assumption might demand some flexibility, i.e., that class which was a `Union` becomes an `Intersection`, which is not possible to model in MOF, since each instance can be the instance of only one `Class`, i.e., dynamic classifiers are not allowed. To solve this problem, we used the idea captured in the *Decorator* design pattern [25]. In Fig. 6, we define `ClassDescription` as a subclass of `Class` which can encapsulate a `Class`. In that way, we can have a chain of additions to the starting definition of `Class` (i.e., speaking in software engineering terms, we can add further responsibilities to the original concept of `Class`). For example, if we have some simple `Class`, we can define union by decorating that class with `Union`, and change it later to intersection, by removing the union decorator and decorating the class with `Intersection`.

7.3. *Property*

Ontology Class attributes or associations are represented through properties. A property is a relation between a subject resource and an object resource. Therefore, it might look similar to a concept of attribute and association in traditional, object oriented sense. However, the important difference is that Property is stand-alone; it does not depend of any Class (or resource) as associations or attributes are in UML. In ontology languages, a property can be defined even with no classes associated to it. In ODM, `Property` is an instance of MOF `Class` that inherits `Resource`.

In addition to the concept of `rdf:Property`, which is defined in RDF, OWL distinguishes two types of properties: `owl:ObjectProperty`, whose range can only be an `Individual`, and `owl:DatatypeProperty`, whose range can only be `DataValue`. In ODM, these concepts are instances of MOF `Class` that inherit `Property`. OWL also defines additional concepts, global cardinality constraints on a `Property` that can further refine the `Property`. These concepts are also represented as instances of MOF `Class`.

In OWL, various types of global property constraints are defined as subclasses of `Property`. Here we have the same problem we had with OWL classes, since some property might have multiple global constraints, for example, symmetric and transitive. In this case, we also apply the Decorator design pattern, just like we did with Class Descriptions. The resulting class diagram is shown in Fig. 7. If we want to define, for example, symmetric property, we will decorate `ObjectProperty` with `SymmetricProperty`, and if we later decide that this property also should be transitive, we can simply decorate it again with `TransitiveProperty`.

7.4. *Properties predefined in RDFS and OWL*

We have seen how predefined concepts, which are defined in OWL as instances of `rdf:Class`, are defined in ODM as instances of MOF `Class` with some changes in the hierarchy. RDF(S) and OWL have some predefined concepts that are instances of `rdf:Property`. These predefined properties are used to make relationships between concepts in OWL metamodel. In ODM, they are modeled as MOF `Associations` or as MOF `Attributes`.

Predefined properties of RDF(S) and OWL and their ODM counterparts are not completely identical. For example, the predefined property `rdf:type` states that a `rdfs:Resource` is an instance of a `rdfs:Class`. In ODM, it is represented as an `Association` between `Classifier` and `Instance`, as shown in Fig. 8, which is obviously a narrower usage than is defined in RDF. Recall that `Classifier` is further specialized in `AbstractClass` and `DataType`, and that `Instance` is specialized in `Individual` and `DataValue`. Such differences are caused by differences between MDA and Functional architecture. In RDF, `rdf:type` property is used as both metamodeling and modeling concept while in MDA, MOF is used for metamodeling, and ODM for modeling. Since ODM type association is not used for metamodeling, it is a narrower concept than `rdf:type`, thereby they are not equal.

A `Classifier` describes some general concept that has its `Instances` (`Individuals` and `DataValues`). On the other hand, a `Property` describes some generic characteristic that can describe that `Classifier` and possibly other `Classifiers`. Through `domain` we state that a `Property` can be used to describe a `Classifier`, and through `range` a characteristic's type. For example, a `Property nationality` can be assigned to a `Class Person` (through domain) with possible values which type is a `Class Country` (through range). In ODM, these relations are modeled as associations, as shown in Fig. 8.

7.5. *Statement*

A Statement is a Subject-Predicate-Object triple that expresses some fact in a way similar to the way facts are expressed in English. A fact that some `Individual`, `Bob` for example, has some nationality, `Jamaican`, is expressed through a Statement, which links the `Instance Bob` as the *subject*, the `nationality` property as the *predicate*, and the `Instance Jamaica` as the *object*. Thus, Statement can be viewed as some kind of `Property`'s instance. In ODM, Statement is an instance of MOF `Class` that is linked with `Instance` by *subject and object* associations and with `Property` by *predicate* association (Fig. 8). ODM Statement slightly differs from the Statement defined in RDF (`rdf:subject` and `rdf:object` link `rdf:Statement` with `rdfs:Resource`). The difference arises from the fact that ODM is not intended for metamodeling as RDF is, similarly to the case with `rdf:type`.

8. Ontology UML Profile Essentials

In order to customize UML for modeling ontologies, we define UML Profile for ontology representation, called *Ontology UML Profile*. UML Profile is a concept used for adapting the basic UML constructs to some specific purpose. Essentially, this means introducing new kinds of modeling elements by extending the basic ones, and adding them to the modeler's tools repertoire. More details about UML extension mechanisms can be found in [35, 45]. Coherent set of extensions of the basic UML model elements, defined for specific purposes or for a specific modeling domain, constitutes a UML profile.

Since stereotypes are the principle UML extension mechanism, one might be tempted to think that defining Ontology UML Profile is a matter of specifying a couple of stereotypes and using them carefully in a coherent manner. In reality, however, it is much more complicated than that. The reason is that there is a number of fine details to take care of, as well as the existence of some conceptual inconsistencies between MDA and UML that may call for alternative design decisions. The following subsections describe the most important Ontology UML Profile concepts in detail.

8.1. *Ontology classes*

Class is one of the most fundamental concepts in ODM and Ontology UML Profile. As we noted in the discussion about the essential ODM concepts, there are some differences between traditional UML Class or OO programming language Class concept and ontology class as it is defined in OWL (owl:Class). Fortunately, we are not trying to adopt UML as stand-alone ontology language, since that might require changes to UML basic concepts (Class and other). We only need to customize UML as a support to ODM.

In ODM, Ontology Class concept is represented as an instance of MOF Class, and has several concrete species, according to the class description: Class, Enumeration, Union, Intersection, Complement, Restriction and AllDifferent. These constructs in the Ontology UML Profile are all inherited from the UML concept that is most similar to them, UML Class. But, we must explicitly specify that they are not the same as UML Class, which we can do using UML stereotypes. An example of Classes modeled in Ontology UML Profile is shown in Fig. 9.

ODM Class identified by a class identifier will have the stereotype ≪OntClass≫, AllDifferent — ≪AllDifferent≫ and Restriction — ≪Restriction≫. In ODM, Enumeration, Intersection, Union and Complement are descendants of ODM Class; in Ontology UML Profile they have stereotypes ≪Enumeration≫, ≪Intersection≫, ≪Union≫ and ≪Complement≫. The ≪OntClass≫ stereotype would be extended by each of these new stereotypes.

Figure 9 shows various types of ontology classes modeled in UML. The Class Person is an example of an ontology Class that is identified by a class identifier, TheRollingStones and TheWailers are enumerations, StonesWailersIntersection is an intersection, and StonesWailersUnion is a union. There is one unnamed class that represents complement of TheWailers — all individuals that are not members of TheWailers. AllDifferent is an auxiliary class whose members are different individuals. Also shown is an ≪OntClass≫ Human and the Dependency ≪equivalentClass≫, which means that Person

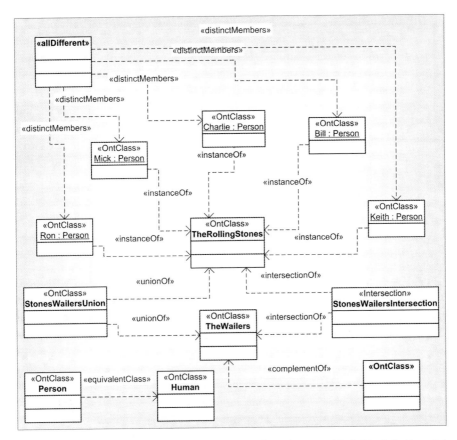

Fig. 9. Class diagram showing relations between ontology classes and individuals in the ontology UML profile.

and Human are classes that have the same class description (i.e., all Persons are Humans and vice versa).

8.2. *Individuals*

In ODM, an instance of an AbstractClass is called Individual. In UML, an instance of a Class is an Object. ODM Individual and UML Object have some differences, but they are similar enough, so in Ontology UML Profile, Individual is modeled as UML Object, which is shown in Fig. 9. The stereotype for an object must match the stereotype for its class (≪OntClass≫ in this case). Stating that some Individual has some type is done in three ways:

  (i) by using an underlined name of an Individual followed by ":" and its ≪OntClass≫ name (for example, Mick:Person is an Individual whose type is Person. This is the usual UML method of stating an Object's type.

(ii) by using a UML Dependency's stereotype ≪instanceOf≫ between an Individual and its ≪ontClass≫. This method is also allowed in standard UML. For example, Mick is an instance of TheRollingStones.

(iii) indirectly — through logical operators on ≪OntClass≫. If some ≪OntClass≫ is a union, intersection or complement, it is a class of Individuals that are not explicitly defined as its instances. For example, Mick is not explicitly defined as a member of StonesWailersUnion, but it is its member since he is a member of TheRollingStones, which is connected with StonesWailersUnion through a ≪unionOf≫ connection.

8.3. *Ontology properties*

Property is one of the most unsuitable ontology concepts to model with object-oriented languages and UML. The problem arises from the major difference between Property and its similar UML concepts — Association and Attribute. Since Property is an independent, stand-alone concept, it cannot be directly modeled with Association or Attribute, which cannot exist on their own.

Since Property is a stand-alone concept it can be modeled using a stand-alone concept from UML. That concept could be the UML Class' stereotype ≪Property≫. However, Property must be able to represent relationships between Resources (Classes, Datatypes, etc. in the case of UML), which the UML Class alone is not able to do. If we look at the ODM Property definition more closely, we will see that it accomplishes relation representation through its range and domain. According to the ODM Model, we found that in the Ontology UML Profile, the representation of relations should be modeled with UML Association's or UML Attribute's stereotypes ≪domain≫ and ≪range≫. In order to increase the readability of diagrams, the ≪range≫ association is unidirectional (from a Property to a Class). ODM defines two types (subclasses) of Property — ObjectProperty and DatatypeProperty. ObjectProperty, which can have only Individuals in its range and domain, is represented in Ontology UML Profile as the Class' stereotype ≪ObjectProperty≫. DatatypeProperty is modeled with the Class' stereotype ≪DatatypeProperty≫.

An example of a Class Diagram that shows ontology properties modeled in UML is shown in Fig. 10. It contains four properties: Two ≪DatatypeProperty≫s (name and socialSecurityNumber) and two ≪ObjectProperty≫s (nationality and colleague) UML Classes. In cooperation with ≪domain≫ and ≪range≫ UML Associations, or ≪domain≫ and ≪range≫ UML Attributes, they are used to model relationships between ≪OntClass≫ UML Classes. Tagged values describe additional characteristics, for example, ≪ObjectProperty≫ colleague is symmetric (if one Person is a colleague of another Person, the other Person is also

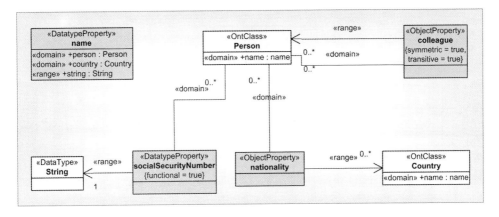

Fig. 10.   Ontology properties shown in UML class diagram.

a colleague of the first Person) and transitive (if the first Person is a colleague of the second Person, who is a colleague of the third Person, the first and
third Person are colleagues). In ODM, these characteristics are added to an ODM
Class applying the Decorator Design Pattern [25]. The transformation that maps
an Ontology UML Profile model to an ODM model should create one decoration
of an ODM Property per attribute of Ontology UML Profile ≪ObjectProperty≫
or ≪DatatypeProperty≫.

8.4. *Statement*

ODM Statement is a concept that represents concrete links between ODM
instances — Individuals and DataValues. In UML, this is done through
Link (an instance of an Association) or AttributeLink (an instance of
an Attribute). Statement is some kind of instance of a Property, which
is represented by the UML Class' stereotype (≪ObjectProperty≫ or
≪DatatypeProperty≫). Since in UML a Class' instance is an Object,
in Ontology UML Profile Statement is modeled with Object's stereotype
≪ObjectProperty≫ or ≪DatatypeProperty≫ (stereotype for Object in
UML must match the stereotype for its Class' stereotype). UML Links are used
to represent the subject and the object of a Statement. To indicate that a Link
is the subject of a Statement, LinkEnd's stereotype ≪subject≫ is used, while
the object of the Statement is indicated with LinkEnd's stereotype ≪object≫.
LinkEnd's stereotype is used because in UML Link cannot have a stereotype.
These Links are actually instances of Property's ≪domain≫ and ≪range≫.
Briefly, in Ontology UML Profile Statement is represented as an Object with
two Links — the subject Link and the object Link, which is shown in Fig. 11.
The represented Persons Mick and Keith are colleagues. They both have
UK (Great Britain) nationality.

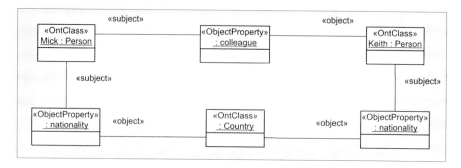

Fig. 11.   Individuals and statements shown in a UML object diagram.

9. Conclusions

The use of software engineering techniques and standards for ontology development still requires a lot of research and work in both Semantic Web and MDA communities in order to achieve an official recommendation that will be adopted by OMG. The main task is to converge all proposed solutions that are either submitted to OMG's SIG for ontologies or published as research papers [4, 13, 17, 20]. Taking into account experience from the UML 2.0 standardization (which should be finished in 2001 [39], but it is not done yet) this can be a very long process and the date of the final recommendation is difficult to predict. On the other hand, the Semantic Web community adopted the OWL recommendation [6], and currently we have many applications that are based on ontological engineering [37].

We hope that the observation given in this chapter can be useful for the researchers from the Semantic Web community who are trying to benefit ontology development with the MDA's standards. Apart of the defined solutions for MDA-based ontology languages (Ontology Definition Metamodel and Ontology UML Profile) the practitioners need software tools that will support all these theoretical efforts. One of main tasks toward this direction is the support for transformations between Ontology UML Profile (i.e., the UML XMI format) and Ontology Definition Metamodel (i.e., the ODM specific XMI format), as well as between OWL and Ontology Definition Metamodel. In this way, we will have an entire metamodeling platform compliant to the OMG's ontology initiative. Until we get the formal OMG recommendation industrial engineers can use current implementations [13, 20, 27].

References

1. C. Atkinson and T. Kühne, "Rearchitecting the UML infrastructure", *ACM Transactions on Modeling and Computer Simulation* **12**, no. 4 (2002) 290–321.
2. C. Atkinson and T. Kühne, "Profiles in a strict metamodeling framework", *Science of Computer Programming* **44**, no. 1 (2002) 5–22.
3. C. Atkinson and T. Kühne, "Model-driven development: A metamodeling foundation", *IEEE Software* **20**, no. 5 (2003) 36–41.

4. K. Baclawski, M. Kokar, J. E. Smith, E. Wallace, J. Letkowski, M. R. Koethe and P. Kogut, "Extending the Unified Modeling Language for ontology development", *International Journal Software and Systems Modeling (SoSyM)* **1**, no. 2 (2002) 142–156.

5. K. Baclawski, M. Kokar, J. E. Smith, E. Wallace, J. Letkowski, M. R. Koethe and P. Kogut, UOL: Unified Ontology Language, *Assorted papers discussed at the DC Ontology SIG meeting*, 2002, *http://www.omg.org/cgi-bin/doc?ontology/2002-11-02*.

6. S. Bechhofer, F. van Harmelen, J. Hendler, I. Horrocks, D. L. McGuinness, P. F. Patel-Schneider and L. A. Stein, OWL Web Ontology Language Reference, *W3C Recommendation*, 2004, *http://www.w3.org/TR/2004/REC-owl-ref-20040210/*.

7. A. Bergholz, "Extending your markup: An XML tutorial", *IEEE Internet Computing* **4**, no. 4 (2000) 74–79.

8. T. Berners-Lee, J. Hendler and O. Lassila, "The semantic web", *Scientific American* **284**, no. 5 (2001) 34–43.

9. T. Bray, J. Paoli, C. M. Sperberg-McQueen and E. Maler (eds.), Extensible markup language (XML) 1.0 (Second edition) *W3C Recommendation*, 2000, *http://www.w3.org/TR/2000/REC-xml-20001006/*.

10. D. Brickley and R. V. Guha, (eds.), RDF Vocabulary Description Language 1.0: RDF schema, *W3C Recommendation*, 2004, *http://www.w3.org/TR/2000/CR-rdf-schema-20000327*.

11. B. Chandrasekaran, J. R. Josephson and V. R. Benjamins, "What are ontologies, and why do we need them?", *IEEE Intelligent Systems* **14**, no. 1 (1999) 20–26.

12. O. Corcho, M. Fernández-López and A. Gómez-Pérez, Technical roadmap v1.0, *OntoWeb Consortium Deliverable D11*, 2001, *http://www.ontoweb.org/download/deliverables/D11_v1_0.pdf*.

13. S. Cranefield, "Networked knowledge representation and exchange using UML and RDF", *Journal of Digital Information* **1**, no. 8 2001, *http://jodi.ecs.soton.ac.uk*.

14. S. Decker, S. Melnik, F. van Harmelen, D. Fensel, M. Klein, J. Broekstra, M. Ederman and I. Horrocks, "The semantic web: The roles of XML and RDF", *IEEE Internet Computing* **4**, no. 5 (2000) 63–74.

15. M. Denny, "Ontology building: A survey of editing tools", 2002, *http://www.xml.com/pub/a/2002/11/06/ontologies.html*.

16. V. Devedžić, "Understanding ontological engineering", *Communications of the ACM* **45**, no. 4 (2002) 136–144.

17. D. Djurić, D. Gašević and V. Devedžić, "Ontology modeling and MDA", *Journal on Object Technology* **4**, no. 1 (2005), forthcoming.

18. D. Djurić, "MDA-based ontology infrastructure", *Computer Science and Information Systems* **1**, no. 1 (2004), forthcoming.

19. K. Duddy, "UML2 must enable a family of languages", *Communications of the ACM* **45**, no. 11 (2002) 73–75.

20. K. Falkovych, M. Sabou and H. Stuckenschmidt, "UML for the semantic web: Transformation-based approaches", eds. B. Omelayenko and M. Klein, "Knowledge transformation for the semantic web", *Frontiers in Artificial Intelligence and Applications* **95** (IOS Press, 2003) 92–106.

21. D. Fensel, F. van Harmelen, I. Horrocks, D. L. McGuinness and P. F. Patel-Schneider, "OIL: An ontology infrastructure for the semantic web", *IEEE Intelligent Systems* **16**, no. 2 (2001) 38–45.

22. N. Fridman-Noy, R. W. Fergerson and M. A. Musen, "The knowledge model of Protégé-2000: Combining interoperability and flexibility", *Proceedings of the 12th International Conference on Knowledge Engineering and Knowledge Management*, Juan-les-Pins, France (2000) 17–32.

23. N. Fridman-Noy, M. Sintek, S. Decker, M. Crubézy, R. W. Fergerson and M. A. Musen, "Creating semantic web contents with Protégé-2000", *IEEE Intelligent Systems* **16**, no. 2 (2001) 60–71.

24. N. Fridman-Noy and C. D. Hafner, "The state of the art in ontology design: A survey and comparative review", *AI Magazine* **18**, no. 3 (1997) 53–74.

25. E. Gamma, R. Helm, R. Johnson and J. Vlissides, *Design Patterns: Elements of Reusable Object-Oriented Software* (Addison-Wesley, Reading, 1995).

26. D. Gašević, V. Damjanović and V. Devedžić, "Analysis of the MDA standards in ontological engineering", *Proceedings of the Sixth International Conference of Information Technology*, Bhubaneswar, India (2003) 193–196.

27. D. Gašević, D. Djuric, V. Devedžić and V. Damjanović, "Converting UML to OWL ontologies", *Proceedings of the 13th International WWW Conference*, New York, USA (2004).

28. A. Gómez-Pérez and O. Corcho, "Ontology languages for the semantic web", *IEEE Intelligent Systems* **17**, no. 1 (2002) 54–60.

29. A. Gómez-Pérez (coord.), "A survey of ontology tools", *OntoWeb Consortium Deliverable 1.3*, 2002, *http://ontoweb.aifb.uni-karlsruhe.de/About/Deliverables/D13_v1-0.zip*.

30. T. R. Gruber, "A translation approach to portable ontology specifications", *Knowledge Acquisition* **5**, no. 2 (1993) 199–220.

31. J. Hefflin and M. N. Huhns, "The zen of the web", *IEEE Internet Computing* **7**, no. 5 (2003) 30–33.

32. J. Hendler, "Agents and the semantic web", *IEEE Intelligent Systems* **16**, no. 2 (2001) 30–37.

33. I. Horrocks and F. van Harmelen (eds.), "Reference description of the DAML+OIL ontology markup language", 2000, *http://www.daml.org/2000/12/reference.html*.

34. I. Horrocks, "DAML+OIL: A description logic for the semantic web", *IEEE Bulletin of the Technical Committee on Data Engineering* **25**, no. 1 (2002) 4–9.

35. J. Juerjens, *Secure Systems Development with UML* (Springer-Verlag, Berlin, 2003).

36. Y. Kalfoglou, "Exploring ontologies", ed. S. K. Chang, *Handbook of Software Engineering and Knowledge Engineering, Vol. I – Fundamentals* (World Scientific Publishing Co., 2001) 863–887.

37. M. Klein and U. Visser, "Guest editors' introduction: Semantic web challenge 2003", *IEEE Intelligent Systems* **19**, no. 3 (2004) 31–33.

38. M. Klein, "Tutorial: The semantic web — XML, RDF, and relatives", *IEEE Intelligent Systems* **16**, no. 2 (2001) 26–28.

39. C. Kobryn, "UML 2001: A standardization odyssey", *Communications of the ACM* **42**, no. 10 (1999) 29–37.

40. P. Kogut, S. Cranefield, L. Hart, M. Dutra, K. Baclawski, M. Kokar and J. Smith, "UML for ontology development", *The Knowledge Engineering Review* **17**, no. 1 (2002) 61–64.

41. L. McGuinness, "Ontologies come of age", eds. D. Fensel, J. Hendler, H. Lieberman and W. Wahlster, *Spinning the Semantic Web: Bringing the World Wide Web to Its Full Potential* (MIT Press, Boston, 2002) 171–194.

42. J. Miller and J. Mukerji (eds.), MDA guide version 1.0, *OMG Document: omg/2003-05-01* , 2003, *http://www.omg.org/mda/mda_files/MDA_Guide_Version1-0.pdf*.

43. Meta Object Facility (MOF) Specification v1.4, *OMG Document formal/02-04-03*, April 2002, *http://www.omg.org/cgi-bin/apps/doc?formal/02-04-03.pdf*.

44. Ontology Definition Metamodel Request for Proposal, *OMG Document ad/ 2003-03-40*, 2003, *http://www.omg.org/cgi-bin/doc?ad/2003-03-40*.

45. OMG Unified Modeling Language Specification v1.5, *OMG Document formal/03-03-01*, 2003, *http://www.omg.org/cgi-bin/apps/doc?formal/03-03-01.zip*.

46. OMG XMI Specification, v1.2, *OMG Document formal/02-01-01*, 2002, *http://www.omg.org/cgi-bin/doc?formal/2002-01-01*.

47. J. Pan and I. Horrocks, "Metamodeling architecture of web ontology languages", *Proceedings of the First Semantic Web Working Symposium*, Stanford, USA (2001) 131–149.

48. M. Ribière and P. Charlton, "Ontology overview", *Motorola Labs Paris*, 2002, *http://www.fipa.org/docs/input/f-in-00045/f-in-00045.pdf*.

49. E. Seidewitz, "What models mean", *IEEE Software* **20**, no. 5 (2003) 26–32.

50. B. Selic, "The pragmatics of model-driven development", *IEEE Software* **20**, no. 5 (2003) 19–25.

51. J. Siegel, "Developing in OMG's model-driven architecture", Rev. 2.6, *Object Management Group White Paper*, 2001, *ftp://ftp.omg.org/pub/docs/-omg/01-12-01.pdf*.

52. W. Swartout and A. Tate, "Guest editors' introduction: Ontologies", *IEEE Intelligent Systems* **14**, no. 1 (1999) 18–19.

MIGRATING LEGACY SYSTEMS TOWARDS MULTI-LAYERED WEB-BASED ARCHITECTURES

THIERRY BODHUIN, GERARDO CANFORA,
ANIELLO CIMITILE and MARIA TORTORELLA*

*RCOST - Research Centre on Software Technology,
Department of Engineering, University of Sannio,
Via Traiano, Palazzo ex-Poste – 82100, Benevento, Italy
E-mail: {bodhuin,canfora,cimitile,tortorella}@unisannio.it*

Integrating legacy systems into a Web-based architecture is a complex and challenging task. Nevertheless, it is often a prerequisite for achieving migration toward Web technologies. This chapter presents a method for migrating legacy systems towards a Web-based architecture. The method addresses both decomposable and non-decomposable systems with two complementary strategies. For decomposable systems, a conceptual model is recovered from code and wrappers are generated for retargeting the system's architecture using the Model-View-Controller (MVC) design pattern. For non-decomposable systems, a less invasive strategy is used that consists of redirecting requests to the legacy system by using screen and database proxies.

A toolkit was implemented to support and automate the method. Whilst the method is language independent in all its steps, the toolkit is language dependent in two composing tools: The code analyzer and the translator of the analyzed legacy system in the target programming language. This chapter discusses the toolkit architecture and the technological solutions adopted.

Finally, this chapter discusses a number of case studies in which the migration method and supporting toolkit were applied to migrate both decomposable and non-decomposable COBOL systems.

Keywords: Legacy systems, software migration, reverse engineering, multi-layer Web-based architecture, Model-View-Controller design pattern.

1. Introduction

The wide use of the Internet and the World Wide Web as an infrastructure for enterprise information systems calls for the integration, or substitution, of old, centralized, mainframe-based systems. However in most cases, legacy systems cannot be simply discarded, because they are mission critical for the business they support and encapsulate a great deal of knowledge and expertise about the application domain. Often, the legacy code is the only source of domain knowledge and provides the only reliable description of the actual business rules of an organization. The high costs and risks of developing new replacement systems from scratch motivate the choice for incremental migration strategies based on reverse engineering,

---

*Corresponding author.

architectural retargeting, wrapping, GUI reimplementation, and the gradual introduction of newly developed, replacement components [22].

This chapter proposes a migration method that exploits wrapping to allow new object-oriented applications to coexist with legacy components. A wrapper implements an interface that makes new applications to access legacy components through message passing. The messages received by a wrapper are converted into calls to the system components performing the required service.

The method addresses both decomposable and non-decomposable legacy systems with two different strategies. If the system is decomposable, the strategy requires the application of reverse engineering and re-engineering techniques to decompose the legacy system and identify an object model. Reverse engineering is focused on persistent data and the separation of the user interface components. Techniques of automatic migration of the user interface components towards new technologies and wrapping of the individuated objects are applied. The target architecture of the migration method is based on the Model-View-Controller (MVC) design pattern [23, 58]. If the legacy system is non-decomposable, the identification of its object model is generally excessively costly and risky, if not impossible. Therefore, an alternative strategy is exploited that leaves the control flow of the legacy system unchanged and uses proxies to redirect requests of input/output operations to/from the system. This permits the use of the legacy system in a Web-based environment and the management of its data with a modern relational DBMS.

A toolkit supporting the overall migration method was developed. Whilst the method is language independent for all the steps, the toolkit needs to be targeted to the specific language, used in the implementation of the legacy systems, in two tools that, due to their nature, are language dependent. The two tools are the legacy code analyzer and a translator of the legacy code in the target programming language. In particular, this chapter describes the instantiation of the toolkit to the COBOL programming language and to the target platform Java 2 Enterprise. The method and supporting toolkit were empirically assessed within a number of case studies concerned with the migration of COBOL legacy systems. In particular, the case studies comprise one decomposable and two non-decomposable systems. For comparative purposes, the decomposable system was additionally treated as a non-decomposable one.

The rest of this chapter is organized as follows. Section 2 discusses related work and Section 3 illustrates the migration method and target architectures for decomposable and non-decomposable legacy systems. Section 4 presents the toolkit in general terms and illustrates its instantiation to the COBOL language and its application, while the case studies and their results are discussed in Sec. 5. Section 6 provides concluding remarks.

2. Related Work

This section frames the legacy system migration problem within the wider area of software maintenance and provides general definitions and concepts useful for defining and identifying migration approaches. In particular, this section is composed of three sub-sections dealing with the most relevant concepts concerning the relationship existing between migration and maintenance, the terminology and additional definitions on migration strategies.

2.1. *Software migration within the software maintenance area*

Software maintenance is a very broad activity often defined as including all work carried out on a software system after it becomes operational [66]. This covers the correction of errors, enhancements, deletion and addition of capabilities, adaptation to changes in data requirements and operation environments, the improvement of performance, and so on. The IEEE definition of software maintenance is as follows [54]: *Software maintenance is the process of modifying a software system or component after delivery to correct faults, improve performance or other attributes, or adapt to a changed environment.*

This definition sees software maintenance as a post-delivery activity, which starts when a system is released to the customer and encompasses all activities keeping the system operational and meeting the user's needs. Several authors disagree with this definition and affirm that software maintenance should start before a system becomes operational [71, 73, 74]. This view is consistent with the approach to software maintenance taken by ISO in its standard on software life cycle processes [56]. It definitively dispels the image that software maintenance is all about fixing bugs or mistakes.

Across the years, several classifications of maintenance activities have been defined. In particular, Lientz and Swanson [61] divide maintenance into three components: *Corrective, adaptive,* and *perfective* maintenance. Subsequently, the IEEE has redefined these categories [55] and added also the category *emergency maintenance*. Software migration involves adaptive and perfective maintenance. The ISO-12207 standard [56] defines migration as follows: *Migration happens when software systems are moved from one environment to another. It is required that migration plans be developed and the users/customers of the system be given visibility of them, the reasons why the old environment is no longer supported, and a description of the new environment and its date of availability. Other tasks are concerned with the parallel operations of the new and old environment and the post-operation review to assess the impact of moving to the new environment.*

This chapter is focused on the migration of legacy systems. These systems have been developed over the past 20/30 years, in a mainframe environment, using nonstandard development techniques and, nowadays, obsolete programming languages. The structure was often degraded for changes and adaptations, and consistent documentation and adequate test suites are not available. Nevertheless, these systems are crucial to the business they support and encapsulate a great deal of knowledge and expertise of the application domain. Sometimes the legacy code is the only place where domain knowledge and business rules are recorded, and this entails their recovery even when the development of a new replacement system is considered. In short, legacy systems have been identified as *large software systems that we do not know how to cope with but that are vital to our organization* [13]. Similarly, Brodie and Stonebraker [22] define a legacy system as *an information system that significantly resists modifications and evolution to meet new and constantly changing business requirements.*

There are a number of options available to manage legacy systems. Typical solutions include [14]: Discarding the legacy system and building a replacement system; freezing the system and using it as a component of a new larger system; carrying on maintaining the system for another period, and; modifying the system to give it another lease of life. The solution analyzed in this chapter is the migration to a modern Web-based architecture.

2.2. *Terminology*

In this section, the main concepts related to the migration field will be introduced. In particular, reverse engineering and re-engineering play an important role in migration theory and practice and their definitions and key applications are discussed.

Reverse engineering is *the process of analyzing a subject system to identify the system's components and their inter-relationships and to create representations of the system in another form or at a higher level of abstraction* [33]. Accordingly, reverse engineering is a process of examination, not a process of change, and therefore it does not involve changing the software under examination. Although software reverse engineering originated in software maintenance, it is applicable to many problem areas. Chikofsky and Cross II [33] identify six key objectives of reverse engineering: Coping with complexity, generating alternate views, recovering lost information, detecting side effects, synthesizing higher abstractions, and facilitating reuse. The IEEE-1219 standard [55] recommends reverse engineering as a key supporting technology to deal with systems that have the source code as the only reliable representation. Examples of problem areas where reverse engineering has been successfully applied include identifying reusable assets [28], finding objects in procedural programs [29, 47], discovering architectures [59], deriving conceptual data models [18], detecting duplications [53], transforming binary programs into source code [34], renewing user interfaces [67], parallelizing sequential programs [15], and translating [24], migrating [31], and wrapping legacy code [77]. Reverse engineering principles have also been applied to business process re-engineering to create a model of an existing enterprise [52].

Reverse engineering activities are generally followed by re-engineering tasks, for the encapsulation of the identified components in the software modules. Chikofsky and Cross II's taxonomy [33] defines re-engineering as *the examination and alteration of a subject system to reconstitute it in a new form and the subsequent implementation of the new form.* The same chapter indicates renovation and reclamation as possible synonyms; renewal is another commonly used term. Arnold [10] gives a more comprehensive definition as follows: *Software Re-engineering is any activity that: (1) improves one's understanding of software, or (2) prepares or improves the software itself, usually for increased maintainability, reusability, or evolvability.* Software re-engineering has proven important for several reasons. Arnold [10] identifies seven main reasons that demonstrate the relevance of re-engineering, as follows: *It can help reduce an organization's evolution risk; it can help an organization recoup its investment in software; it can make software easier to change; it is a big business; its capability extends CASE toolsets; it is a catalyst for automatic software maintenance; it is a catalyst for applying artificial intelligence techniques to solve software re-engineering problems.* Examples of scenarios in which re-engineering has proven useful include migrating a system from one platform to another [21], downsizing [80], translating [24, 35], reducing maintenance costs [76], improving quality [7], and migrating and re-engineering data [5]. The IEEE-1219 standard [55] highlights that re-engineering cannot only revitalize a system, but it can also provide reusable material for future development, including frameworks for object-oriented environments.

Reverse engineering and re-engineering activities are performed for modularizing a legacy system and facilitating the migration process. The modularization of a legacy system consists of replacing a single large program with a functionally equivalent collection of smaller units [30]. From a general point of view, it can be required for different reasons, as, for instance, improvement of maintainability, construction of a repository of reusable components [28], or downsizing from mainframe to a distributed environment [80]. The motivation used in this chapter is the identification of the legacy system components to be incrementally considered in a migration process. Modularization can take place by identifying notable components implementing abstractions in the legacy code and defining their reciprocal interactions. To fulfill this purpose, many techniques have been proposed. These can be classified into three main categories [30]. The first category regards methods based on metrics [25, 51]. Another category groups methods required for the specification of the module to be identified. Some of these methods consider test cases [49], or pre- and post-conditions analysis [4, 43, 50, 86]. The last category groups the techniques required for the type of abstractions to be identified, such as data abstractions [27, 29, 41, 62, 63, 64, 91], functional abstractions [17, 32, 36, 37, 44, 65, 83, 86, 88] or control abstractions [46]. A survey of modularization methods was introduced by Wiggerts [89], while a unified framework based on graphs to express and classify the different clustering methods, introduced in literature, was defined by Lakhotia [59].

One of the problems to be tackled during migration processes is the coexistence of migrated software components and legacy ones. To fulfill this problem, gateways can be used. A gateway is *a software module introduced between operational software components to mediate between them* [22]. It has the key roles of: Insulating certain components from changes being made to other components; translating requests and data between the mediated components; coordinating between mediated components for query and update consistency. Three different kinds of gateways can be defined: Database gateway, placed between the application modules and the legacy database service; application gateway, placed between the interface and the rest of the system; and system gateway, encapsulating an entire legacy system that cannot be decomposed.

To facilitate the integration of a legacy code with new code, it is possible to build wrappers. A wrapper is *code which is combined with another piece of code to determine how that code is executed. The wrapper acts as an interface between its caller and the wrapped code* [87]. Wrappers are used to encapsulate existing applications into modules allowing their reuse and/or definitive replacement later in the time [77]. In particular, an object wrapper around a bulk of existing code enables it to interact with a new part of a system by message passing [48]. In this way, it is possible to safeguard the knowledge and experience preserved in the legacy system without moving the software components outside their native environment. This gradual process helps the restructuring of the system in a modular form that can better react in response to software changes. The wrapping of a legacy system can interest different architectural levels: It is possible to encapsulate entire applications, or only some functionalities, some objects, some interface components, or just the data management.

2.3. *Migration strategies*

Many migration strategies have been proposed in literature. From a general point of view, at the end of the migration process the organization will have a new information system, comparable to the old one in terms of functionality and data managed. Migration strategies can be classified with reference to the process that is applied and to the structure of the legacy system they address.

With reference to the process, two main typologies of strategies for migrating legacy systems can be identified [22]: One step and incremental. The former considers the rewriting of the legacy system from scratch to produce the target system using modern software techniques and the hardware of the target environment. Therefore, the legacy system is definitively dismissed when the target system is ready to offer full functionality. An example of the one-step process is the Cold Turkey approach proposed by Brodie and Stonebraker [22]. Conversely, the incremental process involves the migration of the legacy system by small incremental steps until the desired long-term objective is reached. Each step requires a relatively small resource allocation and little time and produces a specific small result (called increment) toward the desired goal. Examples of incremental strategies are the Chicken Little approach [22] and the Butterfly approach [90].

The two kinds of strategies greatly differ in risk and benefits. In particular, the one-step strategy is an indecomposable approach and involves high risk. The complete rewriting of the system involves a vast resource requirement, a multiyear development, and one massive result. If there is a failure, the entire project fails.

Conversely, the incremental approach manages the complexity of a whole large software system by splitting the original whole problem into sub-problems, with a smaller complexity and thus easier to solve. If an incremental step fails, only the failed step must be repeated. A gradual and incremental approach to migration is more appropriate as it permits the distribution of the needed investments over a period of time, even if this distribution could lead to greater costs and migration time.

With reference to the structure of legacy systems, migration strategies can be classified on the basis of the kind of system they can migrate. In particular, the structure of a legacy system can be: Decomposable, semi-decomposable and non-decomposable. In [22], the decomposable structure is defined as follows: *The best architecture for migration purposes, in which the interfaces, applications, and database services can be considered as distinct components with well-defined interfaces. For an architecture to be decomposable, the application modules must be independent of each other, that is, have no hierarchical structure, and interact only with the database service.*

Conversely, the worst legacy system architecture for migration is a non-decomposable one. *Such a system is composed of black boxes since no functional components are separable. End users interact directly with one, apparently unstructured, component or module* [22]. The intermediate situation is represented by the semi-decomposable systems where only user interfaces and system interfaces are separate modules. Brodie and Stonebraker affirm that [22]: *However often the architecture of a legacy system is not strictly decomposable, semi-decomposable or non-decomposable. During its decades-long evolution, a legacy system may have had parts added that fall into each architectural category, resulting in a hybrid architecture.* A non-decomposable software system can be transformed into a semi-decomposable one by applying isolation techniques, even if they can be expensive in terms of cost and time.

Many migration strategies discussed in literature address decomposable software systems with the interface components separated from the business logic and the data model components. In these cases, the interface component can be re-implemented, while the other components are encapsulated into software wrappers.

Sneed [77] proposes a method for software component encapsulation at different levels of granularity, including batch processes, online transactions, programs, and modules. Each component can be accessed from foreign environments by message passing through wrappers. The same author [79] describes the tools and techniques for encapsulating host COBOL programs behind an XML interface. An approach based on XML is also proposed in [16], where drawbacks of the Netron Fusion toolkit [70] are analyzed for proposing an approach based on wrapping and migration techniques. Thiran and Hainaut [82] present a wrapping method for legacy data system reuse supported by an operational CASE-tool, and in [81], a technique based on XML is described for constructing wrappers for Web applications. Aversano *et al* [12] present a pilot project for the migration of a legacy COBOL system to a Web-based architecture, using user interface reengineering and wrapping techniques. The user interface components are isolated and re-implemented using Microsoft Active Server Pages and the VBScript scripting language. The legacy program wrappers are implemented as dynamic loaded libraries written in MicroFocus Object COBOL [68]. Classen *et al* [38] present an integrated tool environment based on static analysis of character-based panels for the identification of dialog entities. The environment supports the migration of character-based panels of a mainframe application to graphical user interfaces in a client/server application. Antoniol *et al* [8] propose an approach for reengineering BASIC PC legacy code into modern graphical systems in C++ code. The approach is based on the conceptual representation of the original code in terms of abstract graphical objects and callbacks.

Screen scraping techniques [11, 39] may be used when the system is non-decomposable. Screen scraping is a common technique for user interface modernization that consists of wrapping old, text-based interfaces with new graphical interfaces. The old interface is often a set of text screens running in a terminal. In contrast, the new interface can be a PC-based, graphical user interface, or a set of HTML pages. Several commercial tools [1, 57, 84] permit the integration of legacy applications in Web or windows-based environments without modifying the source code. The problem with these tools is that they assume that the legacy system is written in a certain programming language and can be executed only within a specific software environment.

Merlo *et al* [67] define a process for reverse-engineering user interfaces to obtain a structural and behavioral specification and discuss its application to convert the user interface of a COBOL/CICS application program. Moore *et al* [69] present a restructuring process for user interface components, for migrating legacy applications toward the Web. They use the MORPH method during the understanding and analysis phases. The proposed process is based on the identification of the user interface components and their transformation towards HTML forms. It keeps on the server side the remaining part of the system and interacts with it by using the Common Gateway Interface (CGI). The user interface functionalities are decomposed into two parts: One is used for creating the HTML forms usable for the presentation, and the second is used for processing the input field in the HTML forms and for communicating with the legacy system components that use the CGI interface. Csaba presents [40] an approach for user interface reengineering, in order to transform DOS screens into Windows user interfaces. The approach uses specific MicroFocus COBOL applications based on ADIS libraries for the management of the user interface input/output operations. It is based on the transformation of the user interface instructions into calls to functions of a C library for windows user interface.

The approach proposed in this chapter integrates many of the concepts discussed above for migrating a software system toward a multi-layered Web-based architecture. In particular, it exploits an incremental approach after executing reverse engineering and re-engineering activities for modularizing the considered legacy system. The aim of the modularization process is the construction of the object model of the program, and it is based on clustering techniques, preceded by slicing activities for the isolation of the functionalities. For supporting the migration process, gateways are considered for allowing the interaction of migrated and legacy software components, and user-interface wrapping is used for facilitating the interaction through the Web. The proposed approach has been extended for supporting the migration of non-decomposable legacy systems, when isolation activities cannot be executed due to high cost.

The strength of the approach proposed consists of its ability to integrate different approaches and experiences to support different kinds of legacy systems written in different programming languages. Likewise, the toolkit that has been implemented simplifies the migration of a legacy software system and the automatic generation of the new components of the target architecture with low resources in terms of cost and time. In addition, both strategy and toolkit propose different alternatives on the basis of the decomposability level of the analyzed software system.

3. Migration Strategies and Target Architectures

The migration strategy and the target architecture depend on the decomposability of the legacy system to be migrated. For decomposable systems, the data access and user interface layers are decoupled from the components that implement the business logic, and business objects may be individually wrapped. For non-decomposable legacy systems, a coarse grained strategy is used that leaves the structure of the legacy code largely unchanged and uses proxies to manage user interface requests and data accesses. Of course, the latter strategy can also be applied to decomposable systems to obtain a Web-based version in a very short space of time.

3.1. *Migrating decomposable legacy systems*

The target architecture of the migration strategy is based on the Model-View-Controller (MVC) design pattern [23, 45, 58]. Figure 1 shows the target architecture, consisting of three main components:

- the Model component implements the business rules. It is composed of objects managing the business logic and interacting with the persistent data store;
- the View component generates the user interface for interacting with the user;
- the Controller component intercepts the user requests (http requests), interprets them, and interacts with the Model component by message exchange in order to satisfy the requests, as well as with the View component to visualize the answers.

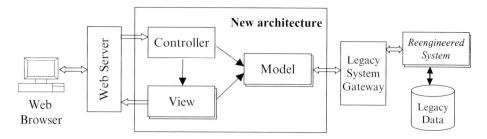

Fig. 1.   The target migration architecture for decomposable systems.

The MVC design pattern allows one to keep the business logic and data files of the original legacy system. In particular, the data files can continue to be accessed as in the original system and do not need to be immediately migrated. With this strategy all programs accessing data files can remain unchanged.

The Legacy System Gateway in Fig. 1 achieves the integration of new architecture components with the re-engineered legacy components [19]. It acts as a communication bridge and supplies methods for calling the legacy components of the Reengineered System that has to communicate with the new application architecture. The component of the new architecture that is involved in the interaction with the legacy system is the Model. It contains the objects (wrappers) encapsulating the system functionalities and possessing the capabilities for exchanging messages with the legacy system through the Legacy System Gateway.

Migrating the legacy system toward the target platform implies its decomposition and the re-engineering of the identified components. With this in mind, the migration method includes a number of steps aimed at analyzing the legacy code, restructuring it, identifying objects that can be reused in the migrated system, and generating the wrappers [3]. Six steps have been identified:

(1) Code Restructuring: The considered legacy system can be unstructured and contain instructions that can make the application of the following steps difficult. In fact, a program can include GOTO statements making the code unstructured. These statements must be removed in order to facilitate software system comprehension and the identification of software components implementing methods of the objects to be defined in the following steps. For example, a COBOL program may include CICS instructions that have to be translated by using a CICS pre-processor [75, 85], and GO TO and GO TO DEPENDING ON instructions that have to be eliminated for restructuring the flow of control.

(2) Static Analysis: The source code is analyzed and all the information useful for the following steps is extracted. In particular, this task is intended to identify in the code those objects modeling fundamental concepts of the legacy system application domain. This set of objects will represent the basis for developing the architecture of the new software system. All the information identified is stored in a repository.

(3) Program Decomposition: The segments of code implementing the interaction between user and system are identified and extracted by applying slicing techniques [26]. This task allows the user to select the components to be located on the client side. Moreover, the slicing techniques are also used for isolating functionalities implemented in just one program component and refining the segments of code managing only one persistent data store.

(4) Object Model Abstraction: An object model of the system is constructed by applying reverse engineering activities to the code modified in the first step. The approach applied is based on the analysis of persistent data stores (data file and database tables) accessed by the system. It provides a basis for defining potential persistent objects. A segment of code is associated to a persistent object on the basis of its exclusive access to a data store [26]. Techniques based on the dominance relation [37] are applied for identifying all the code fragments needed for implementing the method.

(5) Reengineering: The user interface functions and the methods of the objects identified in the previous phases are encapsulated in new programs. To effectively perform this task, the step must identify the set of parameters, representing the interfaces of each new program, and the local variables. In fact, the selected component may use global variables for information exchange. Therefore, data flow analysis algorithms have to be applied at both intra-procedural and inter-procedural levels [2, 26] for identifying the global variables a program component uses and defining new input/output parameters to be added in its interface. This task requires also the re-definition of the call instructions to each modified program component. These interventions are particularly required for programs written using programming languages like COBOL, where sections and paragraphs do not include parameters. In this case, it is necessary to identify the set of variables to be declared in the LINKAGE SECTION [26], and those that have to be declared in the other sections of the DATA DIVISION [32] of each new program. This goal is achieved by identifying the input/output parameters of each COBOL legacy component, which is either a paragraph, a set of paragraphs implementing the object methods, a section or a program.

(6) Wrapping and GUI Re-implementation: The identified objects have to be encapsulated behind wrappers to allow the interaction between the legacy and the new components, so that the user interface re-implementation can take advantage of Web technologies. Subsequently, user interface components identified during the decomposition phase have to be re-implemented using Web client-side technologies [78]. Wrappers and user interface components are organized in the new architecture which is composed of three major elements: Presentation (View), domain concepts (Model), dispatch of request and control (Controller).

The retargeted system architecture is a base for incremental replacement as it allows the coexistence of new and legacy components.

The technologies chosen in the approach for the target architecture are Java and Web-based. Java was chosen for its portability and easy integration with Web technologies. The Web technologies were chosen in order to make the user interact with the migrated system through the Web. In particular, Java Server Pages (JSPs) were used for the View component, Java Servlet was used for the Controller component and Java Beans were exploited for the Model component.

Figure 2 integrates the steps of the approach above and the target architecture, shown in greater detail. The top part of the figure depicts the approach, while the box in the bottom part illustrates the new architecture of the migrated legacy system. In particular, it highlights that the user can interact with the migrated legacy system through the Web. Particular emphasis is given in the figure to the Wrapping and GUI Re-implementation step for redefining the user interface, while the first steps are grouped in the Re-engineering activities box. Once the analysis and re-engineering activities are executed and all the extracted and abstracted information is stored in a repository, the last step defines the wrappers of the legacy system components at the Model, View and Controller levels, and integrates them into a MVC architecture. In Fig. 2, dashed lines, representing the generation of new code, link the generation activities, depicted at the top, to new architecture components at the bottom. Solid lines in the figure represent either use relations or message exchanges between various components.

The Wrapper Generation and GUI Re-implementation step necessitates the execution of four tasks, each of which aims at generating a specific component of the new architecture [19]. As shown in Fig. 2, three generation tasks are used for generating the Model component, which will contain three kinds of packages: Persistent Data Wrappers, Program Wrappers and User Interface Beans. Each task is described below with its input and output.

The View Generation task generates the JSP pages of the View component and their related User Interface Beans in the Model component, implemented as a collection of Java Beans. One JSP page will implement a HTML form corresponding to a character-based screen of the legacy system. The old screen and new HTML form have to be similar in terms of information displayed and available actions. The correspondence between the HTML interface form components and the legacy ones will be statically determined. The View generation task is performed by analyzing the information regarding the legacy user interface, retrieved during the static analysis phase and stored in the repository.

The Program Wrapper Generation task generates the Program Wrappers encapsulating the files of the legacy program system. The input to the tool consists of the information on the user interface components and the persistent data store the legacy system manages. A generated Program Wrapper object will exhibit the following functionalities: To interpret browser requests sent by the controller component; to load form content into the corresponding User Interface Bean; to serve the request by calling a program wrapper method; and to return to the Controller the JSP page representing the response to the user with the associated data stored in the User Interface Bean.

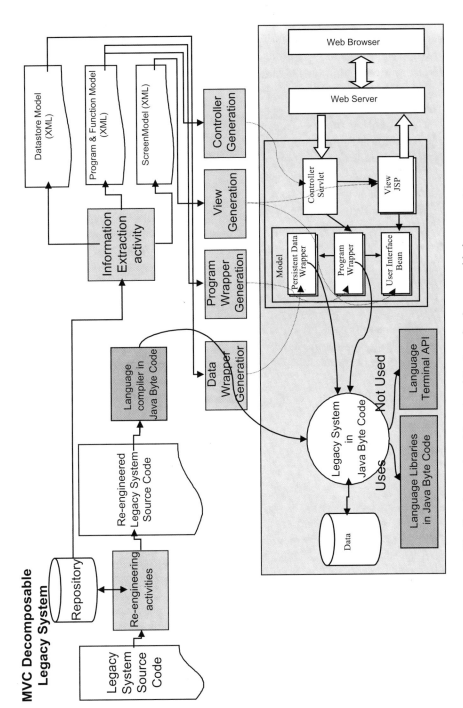

Fig. 2. Approach and target architecture for decomposable legacy systems.

By analyzing the information extracted during the static analysis phase, the Controller Generation task generates the Controller component of the new architecture as a Java Servlet implementing the following functions: To intercept the browser Web request; to interpret the request; to send the request to the program wrapper of the Model component; and to return the response to the browser.

The Data Wrapper Generation task generates the Persistent Data Wrappers, which will be wrappers of the objects identified in the Object Model Abstraction phase of the migration process. The input of the tool consists of the information about the data flow structure stored in the Repository. The Persistent Data Wrapper will map the data record structure to the fields of the data store.

The newly generated architecture has to interact with the legacy software system and its data. This is achieved by translating the legacy system components, not yet migrated, into Java Byte Code facilitating the interaction with both the legacy data and the new architecture components. Many commercial tools exist for supporting the translation of software systems written in a programming language into Java Byte Code.

3.2. Migrating non-decomposable legacy systems

For non-decomposable systems, building an object model and decoupling the user interface and data store components from the business logic can be excessively costly and risky, if not impossible, which makes steps 2 to 5 unpractical. Therefore, for accessing the legacy system in a Web-based environment and managing its data by using a modern DBMS, it can be convenient to operate at the instruction level, leaving the control flow of the legacy system unchanged. A coarse grained wrapping strategy can be applied consisting of redirecting the requests of input/output operations to the legacy system by using proxies processing them [20]. In particular, the requests can come from the screen or they can regard the interaction with the file system. Figure 3 illustrates that a Screen Proxy is introduced for the

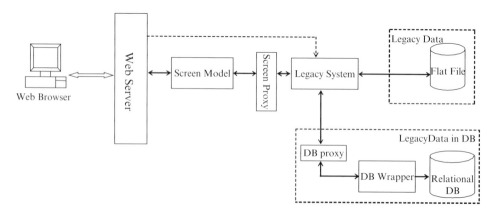

Fig. 3.   The target migration architecture for non-decomposable systems.

management of the requests from/to the user interface, while a Database Proxy is used for managing the operations accessing the persistent data.

The input/output requests from the screen (input/output instructions, e.g.: ACCEPT/DISPLAY in COBOL) are redirected to the Screen Proxy that permits communication between the legacy system and a generalized Screen Model. The Screen Model has the purpose of keeping in its state a representation of the screen and provides the needed functionalities for communicating with the Web Server. In particular, it generates a representation of the screen in HTML format and manages the interaction between the Web Server and the legacy application, mainly for recovering the HTML form input fields in a Web request and sending them to the legacy system. Additionally, the instructions of the legacy system for accessing the persistent data are transformed into calls to the Database Proxy. Interacting with a Database wrapper, permits the operations to access the relational database. The two sections of Fig. 3 contained in the dashed rectangles represent two alternative solutions for accessing the legacy data. In fact, the legacy system can continue to access the legacy persistent data store up to the point when the migration of the legacy data toward a relational database is completed and the database proxy and wrapper are implemented. At this point, the second solution can be adopted. The two solutions can also coexist if two reciprocally independent sets of legacy data are identified and only one is migrated toward a relational database.

Figure 4 shows the strategy integrated with the Web target architecture for non-decomposable legacy systems. Re-engineering activities should ensure the compilation of the legacy system source code with the language compiler in the Java Byte Code. The source code is then processed by the Screen Proxy Code Conversion activity by identifying the input and output instructions from or towards the screen, recovering all the related information (e.g. display position on the screen, color, . . .), and replacing each of them with an instruction that calls some Screen Proxy method with appropriate parameters. The new architecture of the legacy system is depicted at the bottom of Fig. 4.

The View Screen Model is composed of different classes, each of which represents the model of a character-based screen; it contains also the methods for communication between the Web browser and the Model Screen Proxy. The Model Screen Proxy implements the communication between the screen proxied legacy system and the View Screen Model. The Controller represents the communication between the Web browser and the Screen Model. The legacy system is executed together with the Screen Proxy in a separate Thread, different from the Controller Thread, thus allowing several users to potentially use the legacy application at the same time. The Controller and the legacy system are synchronized on the input of the Screen Model. Each user of the legacy system sends an HTTP request to the Web Server that manages, by using the Controller, a Web session associated with the user. A Screen Model instance is associated to each session and to a Thread that executes a path of execution to the legacy system. After the connection of a user, the Controller creates an association between a user session and an execution Thread

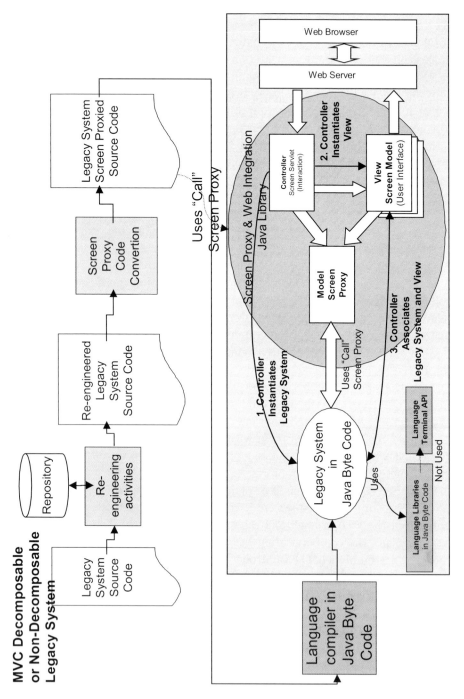

Fig. 4.   Approach and target architecture for non-decomposable legacy systems.

of the legacy system. Then, the Controller blocks itself and waits for a notification from the View Screen Model. When, during the execution of the legacy system, an output instruction to the Screen Proxy is met, the content of the View Screen Model is updated. If an input instruction from the Screen Proxy is met, the View Screen Model blocks the legacy system Thread and unblocks the Controller Thread; then, the Controller sends back to the Web Browser the HTML page, and waits until a notification is received. The sent HTML page contains a form text input field and several other HTML components simulating the function keys and/or other non-textual input, i.e., F1 key, ESC, etc. The user inserts the textual input in the HTML form and sends it to the Web Server. Therefore, the Web Server transfers the data to the View Screen Model that notifies the legacy system Thread at the end of the input instruction and blocks again the Screen Servlet in favor of the execution of the legacy system.

4. A Supporting Toolkit

In this section, a toolkit that supports the application of the proposed migration method is described. Figure 5 illustrates the architecture of the toolkit, its component tools, and their mutual interactions. In the figure, solid edges represent information exchange while dotted edges depict the control flow. All the toolkit tools are implemented in the Java programming language.

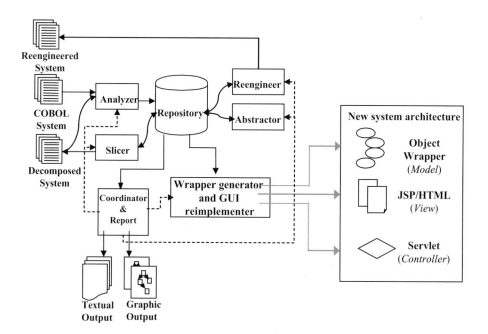

Fig. 5. The toolkit architecture.

A large part of the toolkit tools is programming language independent. Therefore, the toolkit supports the migration of legacy systems written in different languages. Its specialization to a specific programming language is performed only in the first tool, which is the Analyzer whose used technologies are tightly connected to the programming language in which the source software system is implemented. Additionally, the last step can be language specific only in the translation of the legacy components in the Java Byte Code. A brief description of the individual tools follows.

The Analyzer tool performs the static analysis of the source code. A parser and lexical analyzer [9] have to be implemented and the information it produces has to be stored so that the other tools can use it. As already cited, this tool is one of the tools specific to the programming language.

The Repository stores the information recovered by the analyzer and the results produced by the other toolkit tools. It is implemented as a relational database accessed using the JDBC API. It can be any relational database for which there is either a JDBC or an ODBC driver.

The Coordinator & Report tool has the twofold role of producing graphic and textual reports by processing the information in the Repository and that of coordinating the execution of the other tools. Figure 6 shows some examples of the graphics the tool visualizes, referring to different views of the analyzed legacy system; textual reports provide some statistical information about the legacy system under analysis.

By applying a slicing algorithm based on control dependence analysis [26], the Slicer tool decomposes the programs that are either interactive or access more than one input/output data store. It identifies and clusters in each new program component either exclusively user interface statements or exclusively I/O statements on one and only one persistent data store. The new obtained program components can be classified in one of the following three categories: User-interface components; components for managing only one persistent data store; and components that are not in the previous two categories, and therefore are candidates for contributing to the implementation of the business logic. The output produced by the Slicer consists of a re-modularized version of the legacy system, where each program is exclusively composed of components belonging to one of the categories above. The tool requires some user interaction in order to guide the extraction of the slices.

The Abstractor tool identifies in the legacy system the objects associated with the data stores. Each object corresponds to a data store containing attributes that are associated to its data structure, while its methods are modules composed of program components having exclusive access to those attributes. To identify the modules, the Abstractor uses the dominance relation [37] and groups two program components if they are of the same category and are connected by a strong and direct dominance relation.

The Reengineer tool identifies all the data managed in the new program components containing the extracted methods. In particular, the data information to

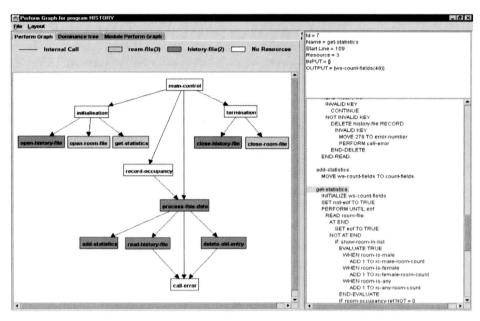

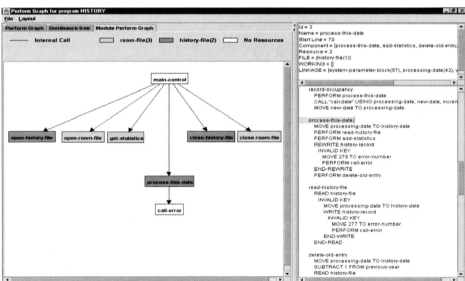

Fig. 6. Visualization of differet views of the legacy system.

be identified is: The local variables, the description of the data structure of the corresponding data store, the local variables the program component uses, and the formal parameters needed by the program components to exchange information with other components.

The following three steps are executed to define the local variables and formal parameters:

- identification of the input/output variables for each program unit;
- definition of the local variable for each module; and
- identification of the interface parameters for each module.

The goal of the Wrapper Generator and GUI Re-implementer tool is the generation of a new system architecture for the legacy system based on object-oriented and Web technologies. With reference to Fig. 2, the Wrapper Generator is composed of four generators, each corresponding to a generation task. They are: Data Wrapper Generator, Program Wrapper Generator, View Generator and Controller Generator.

In a typical scenario, the tools are used in the following order: The Analyzer parses the source code and records the information extracted in the Repository; then, the Controller evaluates the need to decompose the program and, in this case, the Slicer is performed. The results of the Slicer consist of the definition of new program components with the slices identified; this requires the re-execution of the Analyzer for updating the content of the Repository. The Abstractor identifies the objects and their methods by collecting the needed information from the Repository. The Reengineer extracts the program and method parameters and stores them in the repository. The GUI Re-implementer generates new user interface components for the system by using Java Server Pages (JSP) and HTML technologies. The Wrapper Generator generates the object and program wrappers in the Java language for accessing the legacy system.

The generation of the migrated software system is automatic. Human intervention may be needed for the Slicer component as the identification of the different functions implemented in a legacy component may be a guided process. Likewise, a human concept assignment activity, useful for recognizing selected code components, may be required. Anyway, the human resources required for the application of the strategy and toolkit is really minimal compared to those needed if a software system equivalent to the legacy one has to be re-implemented.

With reference to Fig. 4, if the analyzed software system is non-decomposable, the Wrapper generator and GUI Re-implementer tool is replaced by the Screen Proxy Code Converter. Besides the Language compiler in Java Byte Code, this tool is also specific to a particular programming language as the input/output instructions in the code have to be converted to Screen Proxy call instructions. In this case, the supporting toolkit tool can be applied in a completely automatic manner, guaranteeing the generation of a Web-based application with no resources except those required for running purposes.

4.1. *Instantiating the toolkit to COBOL software systems*

The language specific components of the toolkit were implemented in the COBOL programming language. First a specific Analyzer tool was developed for COBOL using the ANTLR environment [6, 72], a Java re-implementation of the Purdue Compiler Construction Tool Set that automatically generates a recursive-descent LL(k) parser and a predicated-LL(k) lexer from Extended BNF specification.

The tools supporting the intermediate steps are language independent. In the case of the COBOL code, the program sections that are analyzed for defining the object methods are paragraphs and sections. Likewise, the re-engineering activities define the following for each new defined programs: The FILE SECTION for modeling the file structures; WORKING STORAGE SECTION for declaring the local data; and the LINKAGE SECTION for defining the formal parameters.

With reference to the Wrapper Generator and GUI Re-implementer tool, the four generators are intended to work in the following way: The Data Wrapper generator analyses the information representing the COBOL FILE SECTION stored in the repository and automatically generates the Persistent Data Wrapper in the MVC Model component; the Program Wrapper Generator analyzes information related to the COBOL Program & Function Model and automatically generates the Program Wrappers to encapsulate the COBOL program files; the View Generator analyses the information stored regarding the COBOL SCREEN SECTION and automatically generates the JSP pages of the MVC View component and their related User Interface Bean of the MVC Model component; finally, the Controller generator analyzes the information stored regarding the COBOL Program & Function Model and automatically generates the MVC Controller component as a Java Servlet. The Program Wrapper generator may need human intervention for deriving the mapping between the fields referred in the legacy user interface, those referenced in the migrated one and the related referred fields in the model component, when it is not possible to recover this mapping from naming conventions.

The tool PERCOBOL^{TM} [60] was used to permit the interaction between the newly generated architecture and the re-engineered COBOL system and its data. The commercial COBOL compiler PERCOBOL translates a COBOL program into the Java code. The usage of a COBOL compiler permits access to the legacy data without performing a data migration process. PERCOBOL creates a Java class for each COBOL file. The Java class contains a method for each section/paragraph in the COBOL program and some internal classes implementing the FILE SECTION, the WORKING STORAGE SECTION and the LINKAGE SECTION of the DATA DIVISION.

Figure 7 shows the correspondence between the COBOL file sections and the Java classes generated by PERCOBOL. The Java version makes it possible to set/get the COBOL variable values and to execute a single paragraph code by calling the relative Java proxy method.

The parameters of the re-engineered COBOL program modules identified during the Re-engineering phase are indispensable for defining the interface of the wrapper methods, since PERCOBOL cannot automatically identify input/output parameters.

A Persistent Data Wrapper is defined for each object which has been identified in the first phase of the migration strategy for each data store the COBOL system

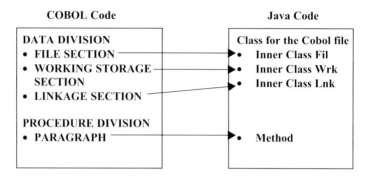

Fig. 7.   Relations between the COBOL source and the Java code generated from PERCOBOL.

manages. The attributes of the Persistent Data Wrapper consist of a set of fields of String type, each of which corresponds to a field in the associate record structure. The set and get methods are defined for each field. For each method associated with the identified objects, a method in the Persistent Data Wrapper is defined, to act as an interface with the corresponding COBOL program. The Data Wrapper Generator performs this task automatically, by considering the methods' input/output parameters identified via the Reengineer tool [19].

To better explain the generation of a Persistent Data Wrapper method, a hypothetic object wrapper called ObjWrapper is considered. Table 1 shows the ObjWrapper object. In Table 1(b), program1_inst is an instance of the Java class program_1 generated by using PERCOBOL by translating the PROGRAM-1.CBL file. program_1 contains the attributes wrk, lnk, fil, which implement the WORKING STORAGE, LINKAGE and FILE SECTIONS, respectively, of the file PROGRAM-1.CBL.

As shown in Table 1 (a), the ObjWrapper class contains the attributes, one for each unstructured field in the FILE SECTION, of the persistent data store associated with the ObjWrapper and their set/get methods. For example, if par_1 is a parameter in the FILE SECTION, the methods getPar1 and setPar1 are defined. A more complex example is provided by the method_1 method that implements a function in the paragraph/section named section-1 of the COBOL program PROGRAM-1. It is assumed that in the Re-engineering phase three parameters are identified for section-1:

- par_1, an output parameter of section-1 coded in the FILE SECTION;
- par_2, an input-output parameter of section-1 coded in the LINKAGE SECTION; and
- par_3, an input parameter of section-1 coded in the WORKING STORAGE SECTION.

Moreover, par_3 is assumed to be a sub-field of the field-1 structured field. The first two instructions, in the method_1 method, to operate on program1_inst implement the passage of parameters to the program1_inst object, while the following instruction permits the execution of the section-1 COBOL section. The fillAttribute

Table 1. Structure of the ObjWrapper object.

```
.......
public class ObjWrapper {
  program_1 program1_inst;
    ...........
// class attribute composed of field of the file
// data structure defined in the FILE SECTION
String par_1;
    ...........
public String getPar_1 (){
    return (par_1);
}
private void setPar_1(String par_1){
    this.par_1 = par_1;}
    ...........
public void method_1(String par_2, String par_3){
    synchronized (program1_inst) {
      program1_inst.lnk.par_2.move(par_2);
      program1_inst.wrk.par_3_OF_field_1.move(par_3);
      program1_inst.section_1();
      fillAttribute();
    }
}
    ..............
private void fillAttribute(){
    par_1=(program1_inst.fil.par_1).toString();
    ..................
}}
                    (a)
```

```
..................
program_1 program1_inst = new program_1();
ObjWrapper obj_wrapper = new ObjWrapper();
obj_wrapper.setProgramWrapper(program1_inst);
String par_1, par_2 = ......, par_3 = ......;
obj_wrapper.method_1(par_2, par_3);
par_1= obj_wrapper.getPar_1();
par_2=(program1_inst.lnk.par_2).toString();
ManageOutput mo = new ManageOutput(par_1, par_2);
    ..............
                    (b)
```

method updates the ObjWrapper's par1 attributes with the value of the corresponding COBOL FILE SECTION parameter.

Table 1(b) shows the Java code that has to be performed by an object to invoke the method_1 method and to pass the results to another object, for example, a hypothetical object ManageOutput. The code in Table 1(b) represents an example of a wrapper for providing external access to the functionality of a COBOL program related to the persistent data object ObjWrapper. This code creates a new instance of ObjWrapper, sets to it a pointer to the program1_inst object (instance of class generated by PERCOBOL) and calls its method method_1 with input parameters par_2 and par_3. After the method execution, par_1 and par_2 (modified by method_1) are sent to the ManageOutput object.

With reference to non-decomposable systems, Re-engineering activities prepare the legacy code for compilation with the PERCOBOL compiler. The code is then processed by the Screen Proxy Code Converter in order to identify the COBOL ACCEPT and DISPLAY instructions, recovering all the related information (e.g.

Table 2. Code conversion example produced by the Code Converter tool.

```
..............                    .................
PROCEDURE DIVISION.                PROCEDURE DIVISION.
..............                    .................
DISPLAY (1 1) " " ERASE.           CALL "screenProxy" USING "DISPLAY LINE_COL 1 1 ERASE" " ".
DISPLAY (2 1) PARAM-1.             CALL "screenProxy" USING "DISPLAY LINE_COL 2 1" PARAM-1.
..............                    .................
ACCEPT (3 1) PARAM-2 WITH          CALL "screenProxy" USING "ACCEPT LINE_COL 3 1 AUTO-SKIP
    AUTOSKIP UPDATE.                   UPDATE" PARAM-2.
..............                    .................
```

```
import com.synkronix.cobol.callableProgram;
import com.synkronix.cobol.parameterList;

public class CalledFromCobol implements callableProgram {
    public void call(){
    }

    public void call(parameterList params){
        ...................
    }

    public void cancel(){
    }

    public String redirectCall(){
        return null;
    }
}


IDENTIFICATION DIVISION.
PROGRAM-ID. CALLJAVA.
ENVIRONMENT DIVISION.
DATA DIVISION.
WORKING-STORAGE SECTION.
01   PARAM-1    PIC X(6).
01   PARAM-2.
        02   SUB-1    PIC 99.
        02   SUB-2    PIC 999.
...................
PROCEDURE DIVISION.
MAIN-PARAGRAPH.
...................
CALL "CalledFromCobol" USING PARAM-1 PARAM-2.
...................
END-PARAGRAPH.
STOP RUN.
```

Fig. 8. Call example from COBOL to the Java code using the PERCOBOL compiler.

display position on the screen, color, input and output parameters, . . .), and replacing each of them with a CALL instruction to the Screen Proxy with the appropriate parameters. Table 2 shows a fragment of the COBOL code and its converted version produced by the Screen Proxies Code Converter; an example of an actual connection between the COBOL legacy code and the Java methods of a proxy is depicted in Fig. 8.

5. Case Studies

The proposed method and toolkit were applied to a set of case studies. In particular, one decomposable legacy system, named HARRIS (Halls, Residences Record and Information System), was migrated to the Web by applying both the strategies for decomposable and non-decomposable systems migration. The other two proposed case studies, due to their non-decomposable characteristic, were migrated by applying only the second strategy.

5.1. *A case study for migrating a decomposable legacy system*

HARRIS is a decomposable system designed for the management of a college's halls and residences. The system was implemented in the ANSI COBOL 85 with MicroFocus extensions. It is composed of 101 COBOL programs and 88 COBOL COPY files, for a total number of more than 38.000 lines of code.

The static analysis of the code produced statistical data [3] that is partially discussed here. The system contains 144 dead paragraphs that is approximately 4% of the code. The total number of CALL instructions is 824, while the number of PERFORM instructions is 2,692.

Table 3 illustrates the results of a classification of all the system programs made on the basis of the types and number of resources they use. The Slicer tool was applied to the programs referencing more than one resource. The table shows that they are in total 54; in fact, 48 programs contain both user interface and persistent data flow management instructions and 6 programs manage more than one persistent data flow.

Figure 9 shows the information regarding the components identified in the re-modularized version of the system and their classification in terms of user interface (UI) and data store management (I/O) components. The number of paragraphs increased due to the slicing process. For reasons of space, Fig. 9 contains the analytical data only for some identified objects, while the total and mean lines refer to the entire system.

Figure 10 presents a subset of the automatically detected objects, and, for each of them, the name of the resources referred, the number of modules associated, the number of paragraphs the modules group, and the number of programs containing the paragraphs. A total of 55 objects are detected. Objects are associated with persistent data managed by the system and contain on average 17 candidate methods. This large number is caused by the presence of similar methods in one

Table 3.   Program characterization.

I/O AND UI PROGRAM	ONLY UI PROGRAM	I/O PROGRAM WITH MORE THAN ONE DATA FLOW	I/O PROGRAM WITH ONLY ONE DATA FLOW	OTHER PROGRAM
48	14	6	8	25

PROGRAM NAME	PARAGRAPH NUMBER	COMP. NUMBER	I/O COMP.	UI COMP.	OTHER COMP.
UPDATE	1	1	0	0	1
UPPER	28	26	18	6	2
VALDATE	1	1	0	0	1
VALIDATE	20	16	15	0	1
VERIFY	20	11	3	4	4
WITHIN	45	42	40	0	2
ZCONFIG	59	46	31	10	5
TOTAL 101	1995	1402	989	220	193
MEAN		19.75	13.88	9.79	2.17	1.91

Fig. 9. Report on the modules found in the software system.

OBJECT ID	RESOURCE NAME	METHOD NUMBER	PARAGRAPH NUMBER	PROGRAM NUMBER
50	user-file	17	26	7
51	archive-file	9	9	3
52	temp-archive	5	5	1
53	room-file	83	102	16
54	deposit-file	6	6	2
55	history-file	5	9	3
TOTAL		989	1306	206
MEAN		17.35	22.91	3.61

Fig. 10. Report on the objects found in the software system.

object. Concept assignment helps to reduce the number of methods associated to each object. For example, the election and reengineering activities for the object associated to the persistent data store named user-file permits the selection of 9 of the 17 methods, which are candidate as methods of the object. They are composed of paragraphs belonging to 7 different programs. For the sake of completeness and in order to provide an example of the full migration process some detail is provided with reference to a section of the system.

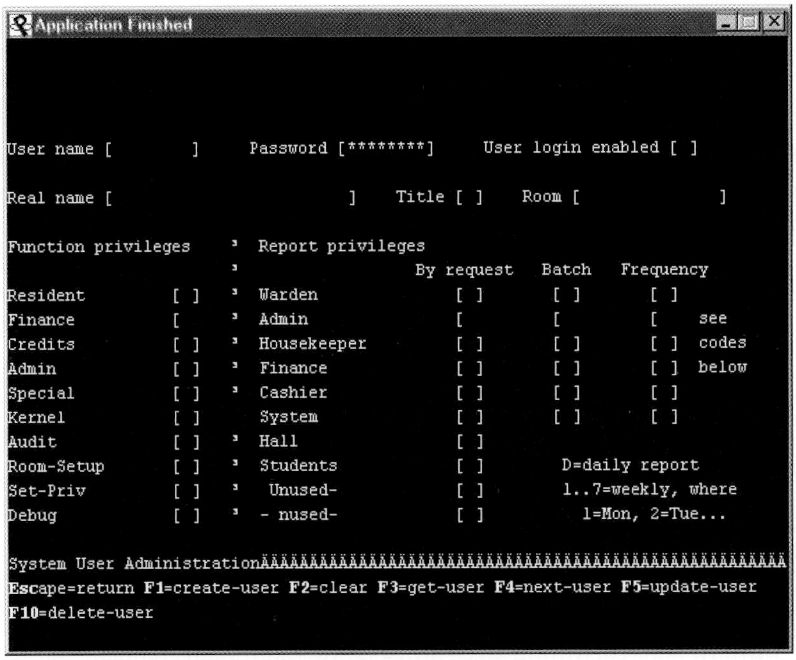

(a) Character-based interface.

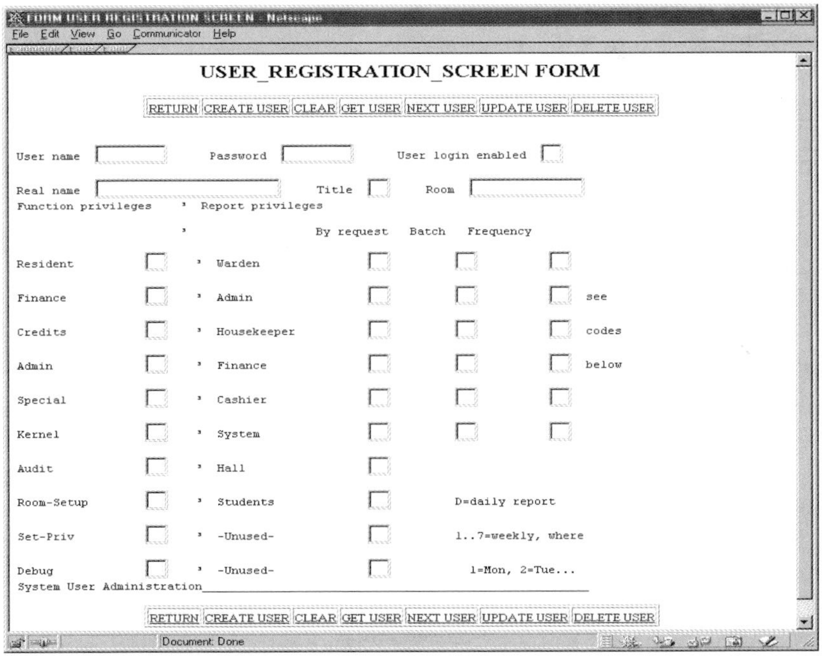

(b) Web interface.

Fig. 15. User interface for the COBOL program SYSADM.CBL.

The screen in Fig. 15(b) includes, with reference to the Report privileges —
Frequency fields, the sentence "see code below" to indicate a legend that describes
the values to be used for filling them. The interaction can be improved by modifying
the JSP page generated, in order to replace these fields with combo boxes with the
possible values.

The detailed discussion above described how a COBOL system can be migrated
toward a Web-based architecture. The reliability and efficiency of the migrated
system are comparable in terms of execution time to that of the legacy one. Moreover, the time needed for obtaining the migrated system depends on the system's
quality and available documentation. Anyway, as the supporting toolkit requires
few human interventions and, almost fully automatically, generates a Web-based
application that is equivalent, in terms of functionality and data managed, to the
legacy one, the proposed strategy is highly recommended instead of redevelopment
if a quick solution is required.

5.2. *Non-decomposable legacy systems*

Two COBOL systems implemented in different COBOL dialects and used in
real contexts were migrated by using the second strategy. The legacy systems,
named **Polizze** and **Terminal,** were provided by the Italian company Serinf S.r.l.,
which is in charge for the management of the processes of the Italian enterprise
Amoruso S.p.A., which operates as a container transport company in the port of
Salerno, in Italy. In addition, the HARRIS system was also migrated with the non-
decomposable system strategy to assess the effectiveness of the strategy when used
with decomposable systems.

Despite the different COBOL dialects, the strategy and toolkit behaved in a
similar manner producing the same kind of results. In all the cases the migrated
systems have an efficiency that is comparable to that of the legacy one. Furthermore, as for non-decomposable systems, human intervention is not required, as the
generation of the migrated Web-based application is completely automatic and the
time it employs is only that needed for running the toolkit.

5.2.1. *The Polizze system*

The **Polizze** system is designed for the management of insurance contracts for
ship containers which transport goods. It is implemented in the Microsoft COBOL
dialect and comprises 66 COBOL programs and 116 COBOL COPY files, for a
total number of more than 30 thousand lines of code. The analysis of the COBOL
system architecture demonstrated that the **Polizze** application is not decomposable
in terms of the Model, View, and Controller components and is not structured, as
it contains in the code several GO TO and ALTER statements.

Figure 16(a) shows the original screen dump of the character-based COBOL
application, while Fig. 16(b) depicts the **Polizze** application migrated towards the
Web. The user interface is the same as the original one, except for the fact that

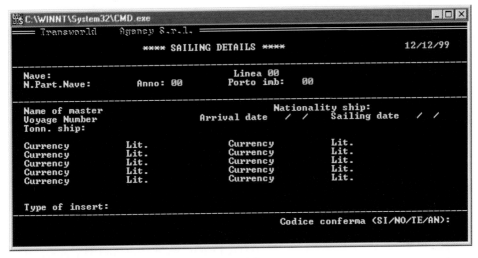

(a)

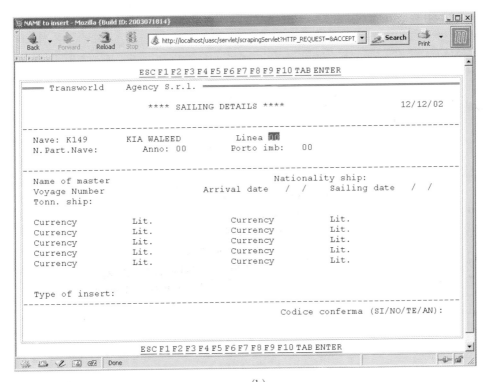

(b)

Fig. 16. Old and new user interface from the "Polizze" system.

it is hosted in a Web browser. As the special keys (e.g. function keys and ESC) that are present in the legacy interface are not available natively within the Web Browser interaction, the functionalities accessed through the special keys in the legacy application are accessed by using a set of links appearing at the top and bottom of the HTML page.

Another difference between the two screen dumps regards the current date visualized in the top right-hand part of the screen. This is because the original application was not year 2000 compatible and the data on the legacy screen shot is blocked in year 1999. The text input field in the Web screen was JavaScript-enhanced for automatically sending the HTML form to the Web Server when the field is fully filled and AUTO-SKIP is used.

5.2.2. *The Terminal system*

The **Terminal** system is used for managing ship containers in the port terminal of Salerno. It is implemented in the RM/COBOL 85 dialect and is composed of 15 COBOL programs and 23 COBOL COPY files, for a total number of more than 10 thousand lines of code. Even in this case, the preliminary analysis of the system architecture revealed that the application was not decomposable.

The migration strategy had to be tailored to manage peculiarities of the RM/COBOL 85 dialect. As an example, the input termination uses a proprietary clause for the ACCEPT instruction:

```
ON EXCEPTION identifier NEXT SENTENCE
```

This clause permits the assignment to a field (identifier) of the code of a function that terminates the current input. This behavior was mimed by means of a parameter "identifier" passed to the "callProxy" instruction:

```
CALL "callProxy" USING "ACCEPT LINE_COL 2 1" PARAM-1
identifier.
```

Another peculiarity of the RM/COBOL 85 dialect is "Pop-up" windows managed by using the CONTROL clause of the DISPLAY instruction. This clause creates or destroys pop-up screen windows, using specific parameters of the DISPLAY instruction to define the position, size, border, and title. This characteristic was managed by adding to the Screen Model a pool of children windows with the same features plus some additional more specific parameters. In this way, each DISPLAY instruction with the CONTROL clause was transformed into a special call to the proxy with the exchange of parameters related to the structure of the window. In response to this instruction, the Proxy constructs a suitable window on the Screen Model that is considered the current output for the next instructions.

Figure 17 shows the screen dumps of the Web migrated COBOL application of the **Terminal** COBOL system. Even in this case, the screen dumps of the Web application are identical to the original ones. The figure exhibits the "pop-up" windows of RM/COBOL dialect.

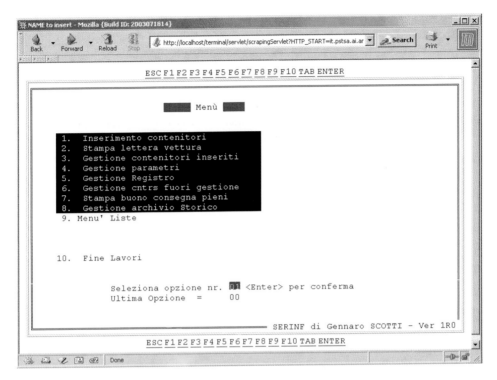

Fig. 17.   Web User Interface for the "Terminal" system.

5.2.3. *The HARRIS system*

Even the Microfocus COBOL, used for implementing HARRIS, presented some peculiarities that required an intervention on the code before applying the migration strategy. In fact, for managing the input termination, the Microfocus COBOL dialect uses "CRT STATUS IS KEY-STATUS" in the SPECIAL-NAMES paragraph, permitting the definition of a data structure, KEY-STATUS, in the WORKING STORAGE SECTION. Thanks to the ADIS module, this aspect was automatically updated with the function key code ending the last input instruction on the screen.

Likewise, the clause "CRT STATUS" for Microfocus COBOL is managed by using the call statement "CALL "callProxy" USING "ACCEPT KEY" identifier" after every instruction of input type. In this manner, the COBOL system requests the code of the terminator keys ending the current ACCEPT statement to the Screen Model. The migration process led to the same results obtained for the previous case studies. In fact, even in this case, it was possible to obtain a user interface similar to the original one but with which it is possible to interact through the Web.

6. Conclusions

Traditionally, software systems have been developed using a centralized architecture. Nowadays, the explosion of the Internet and the need to have Web-based applications obliges companies to migrate their systems to Web-based and open architectures in order to provide competitive business solutions.

However, the Internet and the Web are only new communication and interaction media. In order to quickly and cheaply integrate the new technologies into the existing business environment, a feasible solution is to integrate the new technologies through migration and wrapping instead of re-developing entire systems. This also avoids the risks associated with new development.

In this chapter a method and a toolkit for migrating legacy systems toward a technological modern platform has been proposed. The chapter faces the problem regarding the decomposability of the analyzed legacy systems. It proposes a method including two alternative strategies to be applied on the basis of the decomposability level of the system to be migrated. The strategy to migrate legacy decomposable systems decouples presentation and data access layers from business logic and individually wraps the objects that define the business rules: This permits the incremental replacement of a legacy system's components. The strategy to deal with non-decomposable systems is similar to screen scraping [39, 68]. It is not oriented toward a specific software environment, as in [1, 57, 84], and does not require reverse engineering of the user interface as in [38, 42].

For supporting the application of the method, a toolkit was implemented with reference to the COBOL programming language.

The toolkit components regarding the migration of decomposable systems are more numerous than those supporting the process for non-decomposable systems. In both cases, some difficulties were faced. The main problem met for implementing the tools supporting the migration of decomposable systems was the completely automatic generation of the bridge between the new user interface, obtained by analyzing the screen components, and the data model. In the end the structure of this bridge was automatically generated inside the Model component of the MVC design pattern and extended manually to call the suitable business logic. Furthermore, the main problems encountered for implementing the other strategy were connected to the many different input/output instructions, and their dependence on the programming language, requiring knowledge of both syntax and semantics of those instructions.

The application of each of the strategies presents some advantages and some disadvantages. In fact, the migration process of decomposable systems is more difficult and longer than that for non-decomposable systems. The time it requires depends on the software system's quality and complexity and the availability of good documentation. In addition, the intervention of a software engineer is partially required in order to guide the activities of slicing, object model abstraction and re-engineering. On the contrary, the process for migrating a non-decomposable software system is completely automatic and, if a suitable parser is available, the needed time for obtaining the migrated application is only related to the automatic generation process. Anyway, the results obtained in the first case are more attractive than those obtained by applying the second strategy, and they better address the gradual substitution of the legacy system with a completely new one.

In brief, the lessons learned are the following:

- The construction of a migration strategy does not necessarily require the definition of new methods and techniques, but literature is a precious source permitting the definition of a new strategy assembling process components previously proposed. In this case, methods and techniques can be required for supporting the classification and integration of process components proposed in literature.
- A migration strategy and supporting toolkit are not universally applicable but they may need to be instantiated to the analyzed software system on the basis of its internal characteristics, and require the introduction of completely new process components. Therefore, the strategies that are defined have to be as generic and independent as possible from the language binding characteristics.
- It is important that all the intermediate steps and tools of a strategy do not interact directly with the code of the analyzed software system, but work on an intermediate representation of it, so that the dependence on the programming languages can be located only in a limited number of methodological and technological components. This facilitates the instantiation of the strategy and toolkit to different applications.
- A migration process can vary in terms of time and costs needed for its implementation and the most expensive solutions do not always refer to the migration of low quality legacy systems.
- Even if the legacy system is decomposable, the customer may require a solution that permits the obtainment of its migration in a short space of time and with low cost. In this case, the strategy for migrating a non-decomposable system can be applied to decomposable systems.
- The enterprises need to reorganize their internal business processes by introducing Web technologies. The availability of a toolkit that economically and quickly generates a Web-based software system that is equivalent, in terms of functionality, to the legacy one, may be a precious means for accelerating business process re-engineering. In fact, employees may continue to use software systems that are familiar to them, even if Web-based, without waiting for new systems to be developed.

References

1. J. Abbott, "MicroFocus extends Web services to mainframes", 2002, *http://www.microfocus.com/press/news/20020930.asp* (18 June 2004).
2. A. V. Aho, R. Sethi and J. D. Ullmann, *Compilers: Principles, Techniques and Tools* (Addison-Wesley, Reading, MA, 1986), 500 pp.

3. C. Albanese, T. Bodhuin, E. Guardabascio and M. Tortorella "A toolkit for applying a migration strategy: A Case Study", *Proceedings of IEEE Conference on Software Maintenance and Reengineering (CSMR 2002)* (IEEE Computer Society, 2002) 154–163.

4. R. Al-Ekram and K. Kontogiannis, "Source code modularization using lattice of concept slices", *Proceedings of Conference on Software Maintenance and Reengineering (CSMR 2004)* (IEEE Computer Society, 2004) 195–203.

5. A. Andrusiewicz, A. Berglas, J. Harrison and W. M. Lim, "Evalution of the ITOC information systems design recovery tool", *The Journal of Systems and Software* **44**, no. 3 (Elsevier, 1999) 229–240.

6. Antlr, ANTLR release 2.7.1, 2000, *http://www.antlr.org/* (18 June 2004).

7. P. Antonini, G. Canfora and A. Cimitile, "Re-engineering legacy systems to meet quality requirements: An experience report", *Proceedings of the International Conference on Software Maintenance (ICSM 1994)* (IEEE Computer Society, 1994) 146–153.

8. G. Antoniol, R. Fiutem, E. Merlo and P. Tonella, "Application and user interface migration from BASIC to Visual C++", *Proceedings of International Conference on Software Maintenance (ICSM 1995)* (IEEE Computer Society, 1995) 76–85.

9. A. W. Appel, *Modern Compiler Implementation in Java* (Cambridge University Press, 1998).

10. R. S. Arnold, "A road map to software re-engineering technology", *Software Re-engineering — A tutorial* (IEEE Computer Society, 1993) 3–22.

11. Attachmate Corporation, *White Paper: Repurposing Legacy Applications for the Web: Screen-Based Access in Perspective*, 2000, *http://www.attachmate.com/article/ 0,1012,3485_1_4970,00.html* (18 June 2004).

12. L. Aversano, A. Cimitile, G. Canfora and A. De Lucia, "Migrating legacy systems to the web", *Proceedings of the 5th European Conference on Software Maintenance and Reengineering (CSMR 2001)* (IEEE Computer Society, 2001) 148–157.

13. K. H. Bennett, "Legacy systems: Coping with success", *IEEE Software* **12**, no. 1 (January 1995) 19–23.

14. K. H. Bennett, M. Ramage and M. Munro, "Decision model for legacy systems", *IEE Proceedings on Software* **146**, no. 3 (1999) 153–159.

15. S. Bhansali, J. R. Hagemeister, C. S. Raghavendra and H. Sivaraman, "Parallelizing sequential programs by algorithm-level transformations", *Proceedings of Workshop on Program Comprehension (IWPC '94)* (IEEE Computer Society, 1994) 100–107.

16. Y. Bi, M. E. C. Hull and P. N. Nicholl, "An XML approach for legacy code reuse", *The Journal of Systems and Software* **61**, no. 2 (Elsevier, 2002) 77–89.

17. D. Binkley and K. B. Gallagher, "Program slicing", ed. M. Zelkowitz, *Advances in Computers* (Academic Press, 1996).

18. M. R. Blaha and W. J. Premerlani, "An approach for reverse engineering of relational databases", *Communications of the ACM* **37**, no. 5 (1994) 42–49.

19. T. Bodhuin, E. Guardabascio and M. Tortorella, "Migrating COBOL systems to the WEB by using the MVC design pattern", *Proceedings of Working Conference on Reverse Engineering (WCRE 2002)* (IEEE Computer Society, 2002) 329–338.

20. T. Bodhuin, E. Guardabascio and M. Tortorella "Migration of non-decomposable software system to the Web using screen proxies", *Proceedings of Working Conference on Reverse Engineering (WCRE 2003)* (IEEE Computer Society, 2003) 175–184.

21. R. N. Britcher, "Re-engineering software: A case study", *IBM Systems Journal* **29**, no. 4, (1990) 551–567.

22. M. L. Brodie and M. Stonebraker, *Migrating Legacy Systems — Gateway, Interfaces & Incremental Approach* (Morgan Kaufmann Publishers, 1995) 210 pp.

23. F. Buschmann, R. Meunier, H. Rohnert, P. Sommerlad and M. Stal, *Pattern-Oriented Software Architecture* (Wiley & Sons, 2000) 476 pp.

24. E. J. Byrne, "Software reverse engineering: A case study", *Software — Practice and Experience* **21**, no. 12 (John Wiley & Sons, 1991) 1349–1364.

25. A. Caldiera and V. R. Basili, "Identifying and qualifying reusable software components", *IEEE Software* **8**, no. 2 (August 1991).

26. G. Canfora, A. Cimitile, A. De Lucia and G. A. Di Lucca, "Decomposing legacy programs: A first step towards migrating to client-server platforms", *Proceedings of International Workshop on Program Comprehension (IWPC '98)* (IEEE Computer Society, 1998) 136–144.

27. G. Canfora, A. Cimitile and M. Munro, "A reverse engineering method for identifying reusable abstract data types", *Proceedings of Working Conference on Reverse Engineering (WCRE '93)* (IEEE Computer Society, 1993) 73–82.

28. G. Canfora, A. Cimitile and M. Munro, "RE^2: Reverse engineering and reuse reengineering", *Journal of Software Maintenance: Research and Practice* **6**, no. 2 (Wiley & Sons, 1994) 53–72.

29. G. Canfora, A. Cimitile and M. Munro, "An improved algorithm for identifying reusable objects in code", *Software — Practice and Experiences* **26**, no. 1 (Wiley & Sons, 1996) 24–48.

30. G. Canfora, A. Cimitile and G. Visaggio, "Assessing modularisation and code scavenging techniques", *Journal of Software Maintenance* **7**, no. 5 (Wiley & Sons, 1995) 317–331.

31. G. Canfora, A. De Lucia and G. A. Di Lucca, "An incremental object-oriented migration strategy for RPG legacy systems", *International Journal of Software Engineering and Knowledge Engineering* **9**, no. 1 (World Scientific, 1999) 5–25.

32. G. Canfora, A. R. Fasolino and M. Tortorella, "Towards reengineering in reuse reengineering processes", *Proceedings of the International Conference on Software Maintenance (ICSM '95)* (IEEE Computer Society, 1995) 147–156.

33. E. J. Chikofsky and J. H. Cross II, "Reverse engineering and design recovery: A taxonomy", *IEEE Software* **7**, no. 1 (January 1990) 13–17.

34. C. Cifuentes and K. J. Gough, "Decompilation of binary programs", *Software — Practice and Experience* **25**, no. 7 (Wiley Interscience, 1995) 811–829.

35. C. Cifuentes, D. Simon and A. Fraboulet, "Assembly to high-level language translation", *Proceedings of International Conference on Software Maintenance (ICSM '98)* (IEEE Computer Society, 1998) 228–237.

36. A. Cimitile, U. De Carlini, and A. De Lucia, "Incremental migration strategies: Data flow analysis for wrapping", *Proceedings of Working Conference on Reverse Engineering (WCRE '98)* (IEEE Computer Society, 1998) 59–68.

37. A. Cimitile and G. Visaggio, "Software salvaging and the call dominance tree", *The Journal of System and Software* **28**, no. 2 (Elsevier, 1995) 117–127.

38. I. Classen, K. Hennig, I. Mohr and M. Schulz, "CUI to GUI migration: Static analysis of character-base panels", *Proceedings of Euromicro Conference on Software Maintenance and Reengineering (CSMR '97)* (IEEE Computer Society, 1997) 144–149.

39. S. Comella-Dorda, K. Wallnau, R. Seacord and J. Robert, *Survey of Legacy System Modernization Approaches*, CMU/SEI, 2000, *http://www.sei.cmu.edu/publications/documents/00.reports/00tn003.html* (18 June 2004).

40. L. Csaba, "Experience with user interface reengineering transferring DOS panels to windows", *Proceedings of Conference on Software Maintenance and Reengineering (CSMR '97)* (IEEE Computer Society, 1997) 150–156.

41. M. F. Dunn and J. C. Knight, "Automating the detection of reusable parts in existing software", *Proceedings of International Conference on Software Engineering (ICSM '93)* (IEEE Computer Society, 1993) 381–390.

42. M. El-Ramly, P. Iglinski, E. Stroulia, P. Sorenson and B. Matichuk, "Modeling the system-user dialog using interaction traces", *Proceedings of Working Conference on Reverse Engineering (WCRE 2001)* (IEEE Computer Society, 2001) 208–217.

43. C. Fox, M. Harman, R. M. Hierons and S. Danicic, "Backward conditioning: A new program specialisation technique and its application to program comprehension", *Proceedings of International Workshop on Program Comprehension (IWPC 2001)* (IEEE Computer Society, 2001) 89–97.

44. K. B. Gallagher and M. Harman (ed.), *Information and Software Technology* **40**, no. 11–12, Special issue on Program Slicing (Elsevier, 1998).

45. E. Gamma, R. Helm, R. Johnson and J. Vlissides, *Design Patterns: Elements of Reusable Object Oriented Design* (Addison-Wesley Professional, October 1994) 395 pp.

46. C. Ghezzi, M. Jazayeri and D. Mandrioli, *Fundamentals of Software Engineering* (Prentice Hall Pub., 1991) 624 pp.

47. J. F. Girard and R. Koschke, "A comparison of abstract data types and objects recovery techniques", *Science of Computer Programming* **36**, no. 2–3 (Elsevier, 2000) 149–181.

48. I. Graham, *Migrating to Object Technology* (Addison Wesley, 1994) 552 pp.

49. R. J. Hall, "Automatic extraction of executable program subsets by simultaneous program slicing", *Journal of Automated Software Engineering* **2**, no. 1 (Kluwer Academic, 1995) 33–53.

50. M. Harman, R. Hierons, C. Fox, S. Danicic and J. Howroyd, "Pre/Post conditioned slicing", *Proceedings of International Conference on Software Maintenance (ICSM 2001)* (IEEE Computer Society, 2001) 138–147.

51. D. H. Hutchens and V. R. Basili, "System structure analysis: Clustering with data binding", *IEEE Transaction on Software Engineering* **11**, no. 8 (August 1985) 749–757.

52. I. Jacobson, M. Ericsson and A. Jacobson, *The Object Advantage — Business Process Re-engineering with Object Technology* (Addison-Wesley, 1995) 368 pp.

53. K. Kontogiannis, R. De Mori, E. Merlo, M. Galler and M. Bernstein, "Pattern matching for clone and concept detection", *Journal of Automated Software Engineering* **3** (Kluwer Academic, 1996) 77–108.

54. IEEE Std. 610.12, *Standard Glossary of Software Engineering Terminology* (IEEE Computer Society, 1990).

55. IEEE Std. 1219-1998, *Standard for Software Maintenance* (IEEE Computer Society, 1998).

56. ISO/IEC 12207, *Information Technology — Software Life Cycle Processes* (1995).

57. Jacada, *Terminal Emulation — A Simple Approach to Web-to-Host*, 2002, *http://www.jacada.com/Products/ Jacada_Terminal_Emulator/* (18 June 2004).

58. G. E. Krasner and S. T. Pope, "A cookbook for using the model-view-controller user interface paradigm in Smalltalk-80^{TM}", *Journal of Object-Oriented Programming* **1**, no. 3 (ACM Press, 1988) 26–49.

59. A. Lakothia, "A unified framework for expressing software subsystem classification techniques", *Journal of Systems and Software* **36**, no. 3 (Elsevier, 1997) 211–231.

60. J. Legacy, PERCOBOL, 2004, *http://www.legacyj.com/lgcyj_perc1.html* (18 June 2004).

61. B. P. Lientz and B. E. Swanson, *Software Maintenance Management* (Addison-Wesley, 1980) 160 pp.

62. S. Liu and N. Wilde, "Identifying objects in a conventional procedural language: An example of data design recovery", *Proceedings of Conference on Software Maintenance (CSM '90)* (IEEE Computer Society, 1990) 266–271.

63. P. E. Livadas and T. Johnson, "A new approach to finding objects in programs", *Journal of Software Maintenance: Research and Practice* **6** (Wiley & Sons, 1994) 249–260.

64. P. E. Livadas and P. K. Roy, "Program dependence analysis", *Proceedings of Conference on Software Maintenance (CSM '92)* (IEEE Computer Society, 1992).

65. L. Markosian, P. Newcomb, R. Brand, S. Burson and T. Kitzmiller, "Using an enabling technology to reengineer legacy systems", *Communications of the ACM* **37**, no. 5 (ACM Press, 1994) 58–70.

66. J. Martin and C. Mc Clure, *Software Maintenance — The Problem and Its Solutions* (Prentice Hall, 1983).

67. E. Merlo, P. Y. Gagnè, J. F. Girard, K. Kontogianis, P. Panangaden and R. De Mori, "Re-engineering user interface", *IEEE Software* **12**, no. 1 (January 1995) 64–73.

68. Micro Focus, *Micro Focus COBOL Language Reference — Additional Topics*, 2000, *http://docs.hp.com/cgi-bin/doc3k/BB243390048.15065/2* (18 June 2004).

69. M. M. Moore and L. Moshkina, "Migrating legacy user interfaces to the internet: Shifting dialogue initiative", *Proceedings of Working Conference on Reverse Engineering (WCRE 2000)* (IEEE Computer Society, 2000) 52–58.

70. Netron Inc., Netron Vision, *http://www.netron.com* (18 June 2004).

71. W. M. Osborne and E. J. Chikofsky, "Fitting pieces to the maintenance puzzle", *IEEE Software* **7**, no. 1 (January 1990) 11–12.

72. T. Parr, J. Lilly and P. Wells, *ANTLR Reference Manual*, 2000, *http://www.antlr.org/doc/index.html* (18 June 2004).

73. T. M. Pigoski, *Practical Software Maintenance — Best Practices for Managing Your Software Investment* (Wiley & Sons, 1997) 400 pp.

74. N. F. Schneidewind, "The state of software maintenance", *IEEE Transactions on Software Engineering* **13**, no. 3 (March 1987) 303–310.

75. A. Sellink, H. Sneed and C. Verhoef, "Restructuring of COBOL/CICS legacy system", *Proceedings of Conference on Software Maintenance and Reengineering (CSMR '99)* (IEEE Computer Society, 1999) 72–81.

76. M. Slovin and S. Malik, "Re-engineering to reduce system maintenance: A case study", *Software Engineering* (Research Institute of America, 1991) 14–24.

77. H. M. Sneed, "Encapsulating legacy software for use in client/server systems", *Proceedings of Working Conference on Reverse Engineering (WCRE '96)* (IEEE Computer Society, 1996) 104–119.

78. H. M. Sneed, "Program interface reengineering for wrapping", *Proceedings of Working Conference on Reverse Engineering (WCRE '97)* (IEEE Computer Society, 1997) 206–214.

79. H. M. Sneed, "Wrapping legacy COBOL programs behind an XML-interface", *Proceedings of Working Conference on Reverse Engineering (WCRE 2001)* (IEEE Computer Society, 2001) 189–197.

80. H. M. Sneed and E. Nyary, "Downsizing large application programs", *Proceedings of the International Conference on Software Maintenance (ICSM 2003)* (IEEE Computer Society, 1993) 110–119.

81. E. Stroulia, J. Thomson and G. Situ, "Constructing XML-speaking wrappers for WEB applications: Towards an interoperating WEB", *Proceedings of Working Conference*

on Reverse Engineering, Engineering (WCRE 2000) (IEEE Computer Society, 2000) 59–68.

82. P. Thiran and J. L. Hainaut, "Wrapper development for legacy data reuse", *Proceedings of Working Conference on Reverse Engineering (WCRE 2001)* (IEEE Computer Society, 2001) 198–207.

83. F. Tip, "A survey of program slicing techniques", *Journal of Programming Languages* **3**, no. 3 (1995) 121–189.

84. Transoft, *Product Family Enables E-Business and Enterprise Application Integration*, 2001, *http://www.transoft.com/news/adapter_announce.htm* (18 June 2004).

85. M. G. J. van den Brand, A. Sellink and C. Verhoef, "Control flow normalisation for COBOL/CICS legacy system", *Proceedings of the 2nd Euromicro Conference on Software Maintenance and Reengineering (CSMR '98)* (IEEE Computer Society, 1998) 11–19.

86. G. Villavicencio, "Formal program reversing by conditioned slicing", *Proceedings of Conference on Software Maintenance and Reengineering (CSMR 2003)* (IEEE Computer Society, 2003) 368–377.

87. Webster, Webster Dictionary, *http://www.webster-dictionary.org/definition/wrapper* (18 June 2004).

88. M. Weiser, "Program slicing", *IEEE Transactions on Software Engineering* **10**, no.4 (April 1984) 352–357.

89. T. A. Wiggerts, "Using clustering algorithms in legacy system remodularization", *Proceedings of Working Conference on Reverse Engineering (WCRE '97)* (IEEE Computer Society, 1997) 33–43.

90. B. Wu, D. Lawless, J. Bisbal *et al*, "The butterfly methodology: A gateway-free approach for migrating legacy information systems", *Proceedings of International Conference on Engineering of Complex Computer Systems (ICECCS '97)* (IEEE Computer Society, 1997) 200–205.

91. A. S. Yeh, D. R. Harris and H. B. Rubenstein, "Recovering abstract data types and object instances from a conventional procedural language", *Proceedings of Working Conference on Reverse Engineering (WCRE '95)* (IEEE Computer Society, 1995) 227–236.

PETRI NETS: A TUTORIAL

ALFS T. BERZTISS

University of Pittsburgh, Department of Computer Science
Pittsburgh, PA 15260, USA
E-mail: alpha@cs.pitt.edu

Petri nets are a powerful tool for visual representation of complex software engineering and knowledge engineering problems, and for analysis of their dynamic behavior. This survey consists mainly of practical examples, which include the use of time Petri nets. Petri nets have well-defined semantics, and can be used to interpret textual languages, particularly for communication and coordination. We explore one such application in detail. The nets can grow too large for human comprehension; some suggestions are given on how to deal with this problem. We also look at fuzzy reasoning based on Petri nets.

Keywords: Coordination, fuzzy reasoning, G-net, knowledge engineering, process control, Petri net, time Petri net.

1. Introduction

Petri nets were introduced in 1962 by Carl Adam Petri as a modification of finite automata — the nets were to simulate the tape of a Turing machine [1]. The extension of the basic idea in various directions has generated an immense amount of literature. At the same time their effect on software engineering practice has been negligible. To the author's knowledge, only one general software engineering text gives them serious consideration [2]. However, the activity diagrams of UML are very similar to Petri nets — this suggests that the concept can be made acceptable to practitioners (see [3] for the latest information on UML).

Why the resistance? First, there is the perception that Petri nets are a plaything of academics, and too theoretical to be of interest to practitioners. This objection can be overcome. The author has introduced Petri nets very successfully in undergraduate software engineering courses by starting with simple examples, and giving a formal definition only after an intuitive understanding of the concept and its uses has been reached. Unfortunately text books are not well suited for this approach. Petri nets are used to represent dynamic asynchronous processes, and it is difficult to show their evolution in time on a printed page.

Second, claims are made that for any non-trivial application the nets get too big for human comprehension, and that they cannot be decomposed. The total net can indeed become very large, and the asynchronous aspect does hinder decomposition to some extent, but with proper modular design, decomposition need not be excessively difficult.

Third, there are so many types of nets that a practitioner is at a loss to select the net that would best fit the current need. Here the response is that many of the types are of predominantly academic interest. By identifying the need to be satisfied, and identifying the type of net that best meets this need, the number of candidate nets becomes manageable.

Fourth, experiments show that visual representations, including Petri nets, do not necessarily lead to a better understanding of problems and their solutions than does text [4]. Our response is that this does indeed limit the usefulness of Petri nets for some people. The reason is a deep-seated preference for one or the other kind of representation, and some people are not comfortable with visual representations.

Our purpose is to respond to the first three of these objections. Section 2 shows some simple examples of the basic Petri net, and introduces essential terminology. It is deliberately simplistic — we want to give some idea of how students (and practitioners) can be made to accept Petri nets. Section 3 contains more complex examples, and introduces colored Petri nets. In Sec. 4, we look at time Petri nets. Section 5 is an examination of the decomposition issue. G-nets are introduced as one way of solving it. Section 6 considers the use of Petri nets in fuzzy reasoning. Section 7 is a brief summary.

At latest count, the Petri net bibliography maintained at the University of Hamburg contained 6,023 entries, and the bibliography does not even list publications in which Petri nets are not a main topic, such as [2]. Obviously we cannot survey all this material, and have to be very selective in what we do cover. We have chosen to emphasize Petri nets as a cognitive tool. This means that we will not be discussing analytical aspects of Petri nets, or specialized nets whose main purpose is to assist in analysis, such as stochastic Petri nets. All we can hope to achieve here is to raise an interest in Petri nets. Thus, our contribution is a tutorial rather than a state-of-the-art survey.

Early monographs on Petri nets by Peterson [5] and Reisig [6] are still useful. A recent 607-page compendium by Girault and Valk (with contributions by many others) [7] refers to more recent developments, but tends to be rather too abstract for practitioners, and shows numerous gaps — for example, the index has no entries for time Petri nets or fuzzy Petri nets. The best source of information is the 6,023-item bibliography [8]. An outstanding feature of this bibliography is that it supports keyword searches.

2. Petri Nets: Basic Concepts

A Petri net consists of *places*, *transitions*, and *arcs* that go from places to transitions and from transitions to places. In diagrams places are usually represented by circles and transitions by bars. In Fig. 1, we have five places ($P1, P2, P3, P4, P5$) and one transition (T). Places from which arcs lead into a transition are called the *input places* of the transition; places that are reached by arcs that originate at a transition

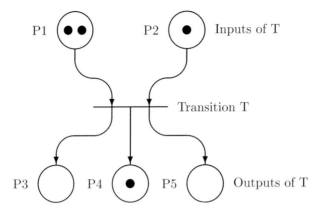

Fig. 1. A simple Petri net.

are its *output places*. In addition there are *tokens*, which are assigned to places. Such an assignment is called a *marking* of the net.

If we write the places in a fixed order, we can represent a state by writing down the counts of tokens in the places in this same order. In terms of Fig. 1, put the places in the order $\langle P1, P2, P3, P4, P5 \rangle$. The state as shown is then $\langle 2, 1, 0, 1, 0 \rangle$, or, if we do not expect token counts to reach 10, just 21010. Tokens can move through a Petri net, and this capability gives it a dynamic aspect. Whenever every input place of a transition contains at least one token, the transition is said to be *enabled*. An enabled transition may *fire*, and the result of a firing is that every input place of the transition loses one token, and every output place gains one token. The transition in Fig. 1 is enabled. When it fires its state changes from 21010 to 10121. Note that the total number of tokens after a firing does not need to be the same as that before firing. Here the count has increased by one.

One of the simplest uses of a Petri net is in the depiction of mutual exclusion from a shared resource. Suppose we have two processes, each making use of a resource, e.g. information relating to a bank account. One of the processes deals with deposits to the account, the other with withdrawals. If both processes can access the account balance at the same time, one can extract the balance and add to it, the other can extract the same balance and subtract from it. The resulting balance is then that amount that is reentered into the database last, meaning that the effect of one of the transactions is lost.

A mutual exclusion net is shown in Fig. 2. The two processes are represented by places $P2$ and $P4$, and the shared resource by the token in $P3$. Suppose $P2$ wants the resource. An access request is made by placing a token in $P1$. Now transition $T1$ is enabled and fires, and the state changes from 10100 to 01000. After $P2$ has finished with the resource, firing of $T2$ results in the state 00100. While the system is in state 01000, $P4$ may request the resource by placing a token in $P5$, producing state 01001, but, since $T3$ is not enabled, $P4$ has to wait until $P2$ has finished,

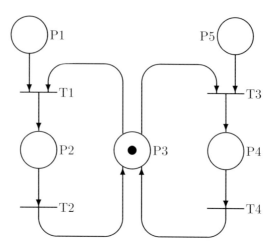

Fig. 2.   Mutual exclusion.

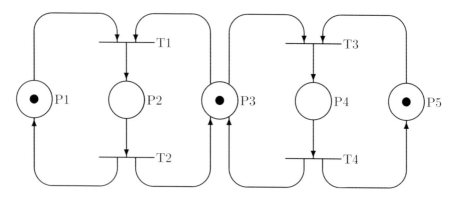

Fig. 3.   Mutual exclusion: Variant 2.

i.e., $T2$ has fired. The easiest way to see how a system represented by a Petri net evolves is to represent tokens by very small coins or buttons, and to move them around the drawing of the net.

Let us modify this example, to produce the drawing of Fig. 3. Instead of making access requests by placing tokens in $P1$ and $P5$, we let $P1$ and $P5$ make the request whenever the corresponding process ($P2$ or $P4$) does not already hold the resource. We start in state 10101, and supposing that $P2$ acquires the resource, the state becomes 01001. Again $P4$ is locked out until $P2$ finishes by firing $T2$. Note that the transition from 10101 can be to either 01001 or 10010, i.e., there is a degree of nondeterminacy. Moreover, although there is the assumption that an enabled transition will eventually fire, the actual time of firing is indeterminate.

We now modify the net of Fig. 3 to illustrate two additional concepts. Some external process deposits a token in $P6$ as a one-time event, and depending on where $P6$ is placed, we have either *starvation* or *deadlock*. Under starvation some section of the net becomes inaccessible. This is illustrated by Fig. 4. After $T3$ and $T4$ have fired, place $P4$ becomes inaccessible, but $T1$ and $T2$ can continue firing. In Fig. 5, let us fire $T3$, then $T4$, and then $T3$ again. The result is the state 100100. Since no transition is now enabled, this is a deadlock state.

Analysis of deadlock can be carried out by means of a *reachability graph*. Draw a box representing the start state. Recursively, for each state that has not yet been examined, determine the states that can be reached from it by a single transition, for each such state S, unless a box representing S already exists, draw a box, and draw an arc from the box representing the state being examined to the box representing S. Figure 6 is the reachability graph for the net of Fig. 5. Since there is no arc out of 100100, this is a deadlock state.

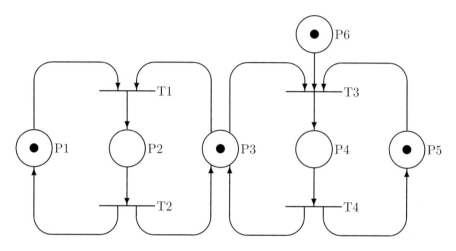

Fig. 4. Example of starvation.

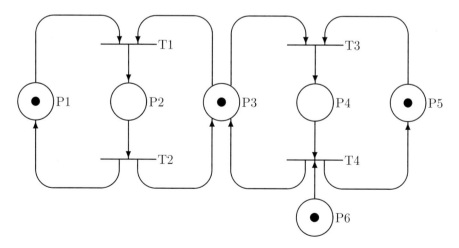

Fig. 5. Example of deadlock.

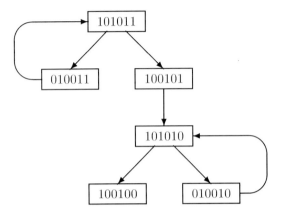

Fig. 6.   Reachability graph for the net of Fig. 5.

Besides deadlock and starvation, which, once established, are permanent, there is also fairness to consider. In terms of Fig. 3, a situation can arise in which $T1$ and $T2$ alone keep firing, although $T3$ and $T4$ are not permanently excluded. A fairness regime can be enforced as shown in Fig. 7, which represents a Petri net for the control of traffic lights at the intersection shown to the right of the net. The set of lights $L1$ controls the south-north traffic, and the set $L2$ controls east-west traffic. The token in X implements mutual exclusion, and thus prevents both sets of lights to be simultaneously green. The initial marking is as shown, with both sets showing red. Only rg2 can fire, which changes the lights in set $L2$ first to green, and then to amber. Transition ar2 returns a token to $R2$, but now only rg1 can fire, and the lights in set $L1$ go to green, amber, and back to red. Strict alternation between the firing sequences (rg2, ga2, ar2) and (rg1, ga1, ar1) is enforced by the set of places Y and Z. Without this mechanism one set of lights could keep circulating through green, amber, red, with the other set frozen at red. This example is taken from [9], but we have added fairness enforcement — Ref. [9] strongly advocates the use of Petri nets in the design of workflow systems.

At this point, we are ready for a formal definition of the concepts we have introduced informally.

A Petri net is the tuple $PN = \langle P, T, F \rangle$, where

> P is a set of *places*,
> T is a set of *transitions*,
> $F \subseteq (P \times T) \cup (T \times P)$ is a *flow relation*.

A *state* of a Petri net is the tuple

$$S = \langle P, T, F, m \rangle,$$

where m is a *marking*, $m \colon P \to NN$, and NN is the set of non-negative integers. More briefly, we say that m is the state. All the sets in this definition are finite.

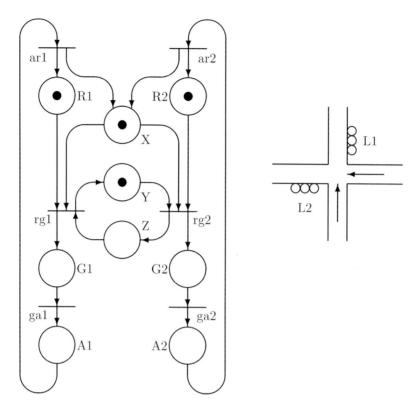

Fig. 7. Traffic light controller.

A transition t is *enabled* if $m(p) > 0$ for each place p such that $\langle p, t \rangle \in F$. An enabled transition t may *fire*. Let m_{pre} be the marking of *PN* before the firing, and m_{post} be the marking after the firing. The result of the firing:

$$\text{for each place } p \text{ such that } \langle p, t \rangle \in F, \ m_{post}(p) = m_{pre}(p) - 1,$$
$$\text{for each place } q \text{ such that } \langle t, q \rangle \in F, \ m_{post}(q) = m_{pre}(q) + 1.$$

For a given transition t, the sets $\{p|\ \langle p, t \rangle \in F\}$ and $\{q|\ \langle t, q \rangle \in F\}$ are, respectively, the input and output sets of t.

3. Examples of Petri Nets

3.1. *Bounded buffer*

Our first example relates to process control. Consider a system in which a process manufactures items, the items go into a warehouse, and are taken out of the warehouse by a second process. The warehouse has limited capacity, and we want to ensure that the first process does not continue manufacturing while the warehouse is filled to capacity. In Fig. 8, the first process is represented by $P1$, $P2$, $T1$, and the second by $P3$, $P4$, $T4$. Interaction with the warehouse is effected by $T2$, $P5$, $T3$.

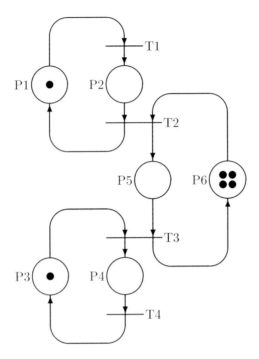

Fig. 8.   A bounded buffer net.

The warehouse capacity is the sum of tokens in $P5$ and $P6$, which in our case is four; initially all four tokens reside in $P6$. In general terms, we are dealing with a *bounded buffer*.

3.2. Order fulfillment

In most textbook examples of Petri nets tokens circulate indefinitely round and round. However, taking a cognitive view, instances of processes that have a definite beginning and end are easier to understand than a continuous process that subsumes the instances. But this requires some adjustment. For example, when the end of a process is reached, some places in the net may still hold tokens that have to be somehow eliminated. We borrow the "earthing" idea from electrical engineering: An earthed transaction fires and the tokens in its input places disappear (go to earth). Another possibility is that these tokens are handed over to another process.

In our next example, places that lead to no transitions are assumed to initiate new processes. We consider the fulfillment of a purchase order. This can be quite a complex problem, which we have analyzed at some length in [10]. We distinguish several different cases:

(1) If the entire order can be filled, it is assembled, the inventory database is adjusted, and the order is shipped. A possible problem is that the inventory database does not reflect the actual state of the inventory.

(2) If none of the order can be filled and the customer cancels the order, the order database is updated.

(3) If none of the order can be filled and the customer upholds the order, a shortage notice is sent to the factory, and the customer is given an expected delivery date.

(4) Partial shipment is possible, but the customer cancels the entire order. This is the same as Case 2, except that items reserved for this order are returned to general inventory.

(5) Partial shipment is possible, the customer accepts the partial shipment, but cancels the rest of the order. This is a combination of Cases 1 and 4.

(6) Partial shipment is possible, the customer accepts the partial shipment and upholds the order for the outstanding items. This is a combination of Cases 1 and 3.

(7) Partial shipment is possible, but the customer elects to wait until the entire order can be filled. This is essentially Case 1.

In addition, the customer may cancel an order fully or partially for reasons unrelated to inventory shortages. It is best to treat this as a separate process. Another refinement that could be included is the combination of several orders into a single shipment. The seven cases now allow us to construct a Petri net quite rapidly. The result is shown in Fig. 9. In this net places represent tasks, and we identify a transition with messages that are sent out by its input place and are intended for its output place or places.

An explanation of the tasks associated with the places of Fig. 9 are as below:

RI: Reserve inventory for the order. This task issues $T1$, which is a prompt to the warehouse personnel to make sure that the actual inventory corresponds to that indicated by the inventory database.

CA: Compare actual to expected inventory, and, if needed, adjust the inventory database. In case the inventory is insufficient to fill the order, issue $T2$, which is a prompt requiring that the customer be contacted for instructions. Otherwise issue $T3$, which is a signal telling the warehouse what is to be shipped, i.e., the shipping process is initiated (Case 1).

CR: Obtain customer response in case of shortages and update the order database accordingly. The customer response leads to one of five transitions: $T4$ results in initiation of the shipping process (Case 5); $T5$ initiates both the shipping and manufacturing processes (Case 6); $T6$ initiates the manufacturing process (Cases 3 and 7); $T7$ initiates a "release of reserved inventory" process (Case 4); $T8$ is process termination (Case 2).

Places Ship, MP, and RR stand for tasks that begin the corresponding processes. As with most complex processes, management has to consider different options, and it may be a good idea to present management with several nets representing the options. In Case 7, as represented by Fig. 9, reserved inventory remains reserved while the unavailable items are being manufactured; in the process shown in [10] the reserved inventory is released so that it can be used to fill some other order.

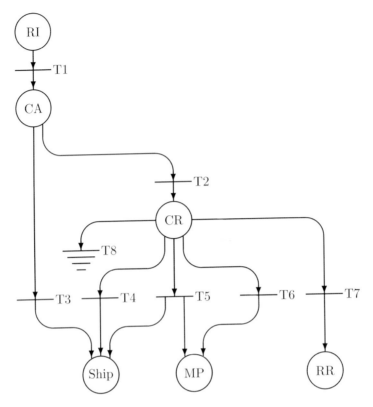

Fig. 9.   Filling of a purchase order.

3.3. *A manufacturing process*

Let us now consider place MP of Fig. 9, which initiates the manufacturing process. A shortage causes a token to be deposited in MP. We extend our concept of nets by assigning labels to tokens, and letting transitions carry out predicate tests on the labels. Thus, if n items of type T are required, the label is (T, n). A T-component determines which of the production lines of the manufacturing process is to be started by MP. For simplicity, we assume that there is only one type. Then, in Fig. 10, as part of task MP, n is reduced by 1, and while $n \geq 0$, the transaction so labeled deposits at each firing a token in place Source. The sequence of arcs from MP to the transition, and from the transition back to MP is known as a self-loop; note that some variants of Petri nets do not allow self-loops in order to simplify analysis of the nets.

Let us define the production process as the application of three machines A, B, and C. An item is first worked on by A, and then by B and C. Either B or C can be used first, which allows a degree of parallelism. When both B and C have worked on an item, it reaches X, which can represent a warehouse. To determine whether an item is ready to go into a warehouse we associate a counter with the

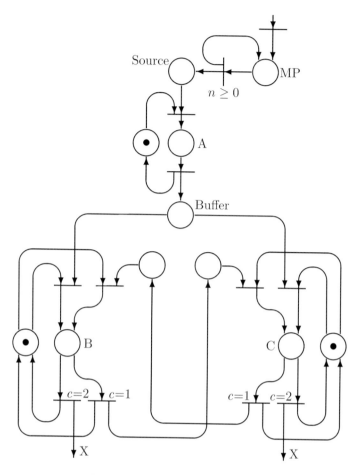

Fig. 10. A manufacturing process.

token representing the item. The value 0 is assigned to it at place A, and part of the tasks represented by B and C is to add 1 to the counter. When its value is 1, the item goes to the other machine; when it reaches 2, it goes to X. The purpose of the places holding tokens in the initial marking is to ensure that A, B, and C will always hold at most one token.

By attaching labels to tokens we have implemented a very simple version of a *colored* Petri net. The use of the term "colored" is a historical accident — the earliest nets used colored tokens. Actually great freedom is allowed in the selection of a data type for a label, but the labels of tokens that are to go to a particular place are all to be of the same (arbitrarily complex) data type. For a very detailed treatment of colored Petri nets, see [11–13].

One extension to the basic Petri net concept is to allow several arcs to join places and transitions. If there are three arcs going from place P to transition T, T cannot fire if P holds less than three tokens, and firing of T results in the loss of three tokens by P. Each output place of T gains as many tokens as there are arcs going from T to this place. In terms of a colored net, P would hold just one token with an integer-valued label, and a predicate associated with T would allow it to fire if the label were to have a value of at least 3.

It would seem that colored nets eliminate a need for multiple arcs, but this is not so. In a drawing the multiple arcs have a cognitive appeal. Moreover, if P were to hold five tokens, then, after the firing of T, it would still hold two tokens. In the case of a token "colored" with value 5, to achieve the same effect, we would have to find a way to send back to P a token with value 2. Multiple arcs do complicate the definition of a Petri net because the flow relation is no longer a set of ordered pairs, but a bag, i.e., a "container" in which multiple instances of the same element can occur, and their multiplicity is significant (for a brief introduction to the theory of bags, see Appendix A of [5]).

For an example of where the multiplicity is significant consider the evaluation of a submission to a journal. Suppose that three referees are required, that the five tokens in P represent five referees identified as suitable, and that firing of T represents selection of the three required referees. On firing T, three of the tokens leave P, but two remain. Then, if one of the three referees initially selected cannot for some reason do the work, we can go back to P and get a replacement.

4. Time Petri Nets

We noted earlier that Petri nets are associated with a certain degree of nondeterminism. With the marking as shown in Fig. 3, either of $T1$ and $T3$ can fire. This is referred to as a conflict situation. We can enforce a definite firing sequence, as in Fig. 7, but there is no obligation for an enabled transition to fire. With *time Petri nets* there is such an obligation. In a time Petri net each transition has two times associated with it, (a, b), and if the transition becomes enabled at time T, it must fire no earlier than $T + a$ and no later than $T + b$, unless it has become disenabled by the firing of some other transition. Ordinary Petri nets are a special case of time Petri nets in which all transitions are assumed to carry the time label $(0, \infty)$. We shall abbreviate a label (a, a) to just (a). Time Petri nets were introduced by Merlin and Farber [14]; Berthomieu and Diaz [15] describe analysis techniques for time Petri nets. For surveys of various approaches to time in Petri nets see [16,17].

Suppose that a transition marked (ta, tb) has just one input place, that this input place leads only to the transition under consideration, that a token reaches it at time $T1$ and another token reaches it at time $T2$, where $T2 < T1 + tb$. Then the transition has to fire at a time $t1$ within the time interval $(T1 + ta, T1 + tb)$, and again at a time $t2$ within $(T2 + ta, T2 + tb)$. Our interpretation permits $t2 < t1$, i.e., the transition due to the token that arrives last may be the first to fire. This is illustrated by Fig. 11, which shows a subnet at times $T = 0, 1, 2, 3$.

The lefthand net of Fig. 12 shows an alternative interpretation of the firing rule, as suggested in [16]. Suppose that place A has received two tokens at the same time $(T = 0)$, and that the transition fires at $T = 4$. Then, as regards the second token,

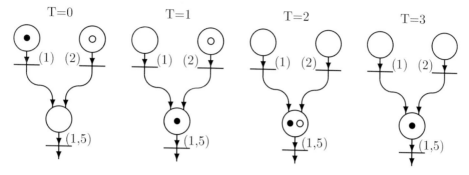

Fig. 11.   Firing sequence of a time Petri net.

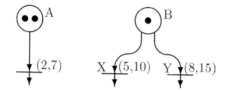

Fig. 12.   Problematic interpretations.

enabling power is only now assumed to begin. Consequently the second firing of the transition is to occur between $T = 6$ and $T = 11$. We consider the interpretation illustrated by Fig. 11 to be more natural than the sequential approach, and have adopted it here.

The righthand net of Fig. 12 shows another situation that could be interpreted in more than one way. Suppose place B receives a token at $T = 0$. Then, during the time period from $T = 5$ to $T = 8$ only X can fire, and from $T = 8$ up to $T = 10$ either X or Y can fire. But what happens at exactly $T = 10$ if neither has fired? Can Y now fire at some instant between $T = 10$ and $T = 15$, or must X fire at $T = 10$? Our firing rule states that an enabled transition must fire unless it has become disenabled. Hence X must fire, and the upper limit on Y is meaningless, i.e., the label should be $(8,10)$.

4.1. *Traffic lights revisited*

Our first example refines and simplifies the traffic light controller of Fig. 7. The use of time labels eliminates the need for places X, Y, and Z. Figure 13 shows the initial marking — the process is started by the firing of transition s.

We assumed that south-north traffic is heavier than east-west traffic. We therefore let the red-green-amber durations be 7–10–2 time units for $L1$ and 12–5–2 for $L2$. The markings on the transactions in Fig. 13 are to ensure this, and examination of how the markings change over time, as shown in Table 1, demonstrates that our aim has been achieved. Line 1 shows the marking just after the firing of transition s. $R1$ holds a token for 7 time units during which $L2$ goes through its green and amber phases. After amber has turned to red in $L2$, $R2$ holds a token

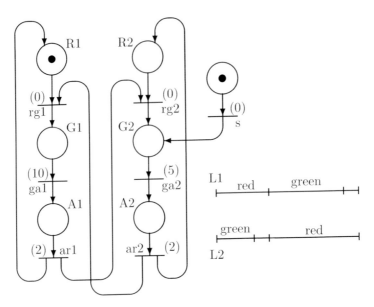

Fig. 13.   Traffic light controller: Version 2.

Table 1.   Transition history for net of Fig. 13.

Time	R1	G1	A1	R2	G2	A2
0	1	0	0	0	1	0
5	1	0	0	0	0	1
7	0	1	0	1	0	0
17	0	0	1	1	0	0
19	1	0	0	0	1	0

for 12 time units, allowing $L1$ to be green for 10 and amber for 2 units. At time 19, the marking is the same as in line 1, and a new cycle begins. Durations of the red phases do not explicitly appear in the time labels, but have to be deduced from durations of the green and amber phases for the opposite set of lights.

4.2. *Railroad crossing controller*

Our second example, shown in Fig. 14, is another traffic controller. It is to control a railroad crossing guarded by a gate. The problem of controlling the closing and opening of the gate is simple when we consider a single train [18]. In our example we allow for two trains that go in opposite directions and reach the crossing at about the same time. The first train to arrive causes the closing of the gate, but the difficulty lies in making sure that the gate remains closed until both trains have passed through the crossing area.

Actually, three problems have to be addressed. First, after the gate has been closed, the process that asked for the closing of the gate, and only this process, has to be told about this by setting an appropriate signal light. When there are two

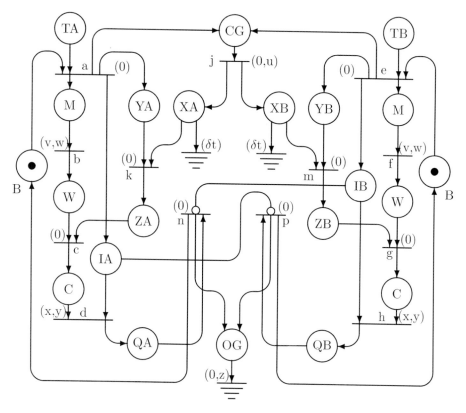

Fig. 14. Railroad crossing controller.

trains at the crossing, both will have requested closing of the gate, and both will get a signal when it is safe to proceed. But if there is only one train, the direction of this train has to be identified so that the signal goes to the right place. Second, while a train is in the gate area, no other train traveling in the same direction is to be allowed into the gate area. Third, once a train has passed through the gate area, it is to be prevented from opening the gate if a train going in the other direction is still in the gate area.

The gate area consists of three regions. In the first region the train, after having requested that the gate be closed, can still travel forward while the gate is being closed. However, at a point close to the gate it has to stop if the gate closing has not been completed. The third region is the actual gate that the train travels past.

We introduce four processes. Two relate to the trains, or, to be more precise, to sensors and signal boxes regulating the trains, and the other two see to the closing and opening of the gate, respectively. The problem is symmetrical, so we shall consider train TA alone. Its approach to the gate area is indicated by a token in place TA. Since there is a token in B, this causes transition a to fire. The purpose of B is to make sure that only one train traveling in the same direction as TA can be in the gate area at the same time. The firing results in placement of tokens in M, CG, IA, and YA. Place M stands for continuing movement of the train — it is estimated that it can travel for between v and w time units before it gets so close to the gate that it may have to go into a wait state (of course, we do not want the train to have to wait at all). During this time CG sees to the closing of the gate. This can take between zero time (if the gate is already closed) and u units. Firing of j puts tokens in XA and XB. Now, if YA holds a token, k fires, which places a token in ZA, and this allows TA to traverse the crossing. If CG got its token from the firing of e, k cannot fire, and the token in XA is earthed. The complex of places XA, YA, ZA (and XB, YB, ZB) is needed to solve the first problem discussed above, i.e., identification of the train that requested closing of the gate. (Why cannot we eliminate YA and ZA, and let the arc from XA go directly to transition, and similarly for YB, ZB, XB? But even if YA is needed, is ZA needed? If so, why?)

Suppose that TA is safely through the crossing, i.e., that d has fired. Now, as far as TA is concerned, the gate can be opened. But TB may just have arrived, and be in its state M. This is where IB comes into play: by the firing of e, place IB has received a token, and as long as h has not fired, this token prevents firing of n because there is an *inhibitor arc* going from IB to n. While IB holds a token, n cannot fire. Inhibitor arcs carry a small circle where a normal arc would have its arrowhead, and whereas tokens in the places from which normal arcs originate can enable transitions, tokens in places from which inhibitor arcs originate have the opposite effect. Inhibitor arcs are well suited for implementing our "last one through opens the gate" requirement. Place QA merely serves to satisfy the Petri net convention that an arc cannot go directly from one transition to another.

A distributed railroad control system is defined in [19] as a RAISE specification. It is an interesting project to define this system in terms of Petri nets.

4.3. *Semantics and time Petri nets*

Our third example is quite different. Its purpose is to show how time Petri nets can provide a textual formalism with semantics. We consider a software system as consisting of components that carry out the actual computations, and a coordination mechanism. We shall refer to a computational component as a transaction that converts an input assemblage x into an output $f(x)$. A transaction is initiated by a message sent out by the coordination component, and it obtains its inputs from the outside world, or a database, or as parameters carried by the initiating message. Acquisition of the input assemblage x can be spread out over time and geographical locations. This view is sufficiently general to cover localized, distributed, and mobile computing.

However, our primary interest is not in transactions, but in the coordination component, which we regard as a collection of actions. Actions are started by signals received from transactions or mechanical sensors, or by clocks, or by people, or by a combination of the above, and they invoke transactions. We shall represent software systems by time Petri nets. Intuitively we expect a one-to-one correspondence between transactions and places, and between actions and transitions. This works for transactions, but not for actions. Because of the complexity of today's systems, arbitrary complexity must be allowed for in the specification of actions, although in most applications very little of this power is needed. An action is thus represented not by a single transition, but by a Petri net that can reach considerable complexity.

Our experience has shown that textual representation of a complex action is easier to understand than the corresponding net, but text is often ambiguous, and, as we discuss in detail in [20], this is the case with the specification language looked at here. Components of the language are therefore provided with standard interpretation in terms of time Petri nets. An example of an action is:

> ACTION Example;
> @(p) ON(SigA(a,b)) IN(0,q) EXCEPTION(Exc) ::
> DELAY(x):
> (TrA(a,b), TrB(b));
> ENDACTION;

This action is initiated by a clock at time p. The action continues if signal SigA arrives no earlier than p and no later than $p + q$ — this is what the IN component checks: Unless the arrival of the signal is within the time interval $(0, q)$ with respect to p, an exceptional condition arises, and the action terminates by invoking exception handler Exc. Otherwise, after a delay of x time units, transactions TrA and TrB are started.

The syntax of the language for the specification of actions consists of seven productions expressed in BNF: Square brackets indicate that the item enclosed in the brackets is optional. If square brackets are followed by the symbol *, then the enclosed item may be present zero or more times; if followed by +, then the item must be present at least once. The symbol | indicates alternation, e.g. $A ::= B|C$ indicates that A may be rewritten as B or as C.

1. <Action>::   ACTION [<ActionId>];
           <Activator>:: [<ActPart>;]*
        ENDACTION;
2. <Activator>::=   ON<Sig> | ON(<Sig> [,<Sig>]+)OFF <TPart> |
           @<TPart> [ON(<Sig>) [<EPart>] |
           ON(<Sig>)IN <TPart>]
3. <TPart>::=   (<TimeExp> [,<TimeExp>]) [<EPart>]
4. <Sig>::=   <SigId> [(<Exp> [,<Exp>]*)]
5. <EPart>::=   EXCEPTION(<PrimAct>)
6. <ActPart>::=   [<Delay>]
           [<PrimAct> | (<PrimAct> [,<PrimAct>]*)]+
7. <Delay>::=   DELAY <TPart> [<EPart>]:

The example given above makes the syntax largely self-explanatory. The form of identifiers and expressions (ActionId, TimeExp, SigId, Exp) is left undefined. The PrimAct stands for a transaction, which may be an exception handling procedure, or an activator of a mechanical device, or a message sent to a human operator. The only component not used in the example is OFF. It becomes necessary when several conjoined signals are required, as in ON(SigA, SigB)OFF(15). If only one of the signals, say SigA, has arrived before a specified time (here 15 time units), then, to avoid an indefinite wait for the other signal, the action terminates by switching off SigA, and invoking an exception handler if one is provided.

We have modified time Petri nets by allowing clock readings to specify the time an action is to be initiated. In terms of the syntax, a TPart preceded by the symbol @ represents clock readings; otherwise the TPart has its conventional interpretation. Figure 15 provides a standard interpretation of the components of an action. Every action can be represented by a time Petri net composed of the subnets of Fig. 15. A broad arrow represents one or more arcs.

Case (i) corresponds to the first alternative of Production 2 — a signal starts an action. In Case (ii) several signals initiate an action, and this corresponds to the second alternative of Production 2. This is a synchronization mechanism: The action does not advance until all the signals have been raised. But if a signal does not get raised in the time period in which it is expected to be raised, the system freezes. To avoid this, the mandatory OFF is provided. After a time interval s, which is to be measured from when the first signal in the set is raised, all signals are switched off, and either an exception handler is invoked or the action aborts. Here as anywhere else the EPart is optional; the symbol E in Fig. 15 represents an exceptional situation, but an explicit exception handler need not be provided.

Case (ii) is complex, and its representation is merely schematic. The form of the net depends on the number of signals that are to be conjoined. In Fig. 16, we show the detailed net for two conjoined signals. In this net, place X is initially to hold a token. Suppose that a signal is raised first by the transaction represented by A. Then the transition that leads to P fires, removing the token from X, and we wait for the signal from B. If it arrives in time, i.e., before s time units are up, the action continues. If not, the exception transition fires. If the signal from B arrives first, the situation is symmetrically analogous.

Although the syntax allows an action to be initiated by conjoined signals, no conjoining is allowed for if initiation is by a clock. This keeps the syntax reasonably simple, without loss of generality. Conjoining in this case can be achieved by means of an auxiliary action initiated by the clock:

ACTION @(t):: TransA; ENDACTION;

TransA invokes a second action in which signals are conjoined:

ACTION ON(SigA, SigB)OFF(15):: TransB; ENDACTION;

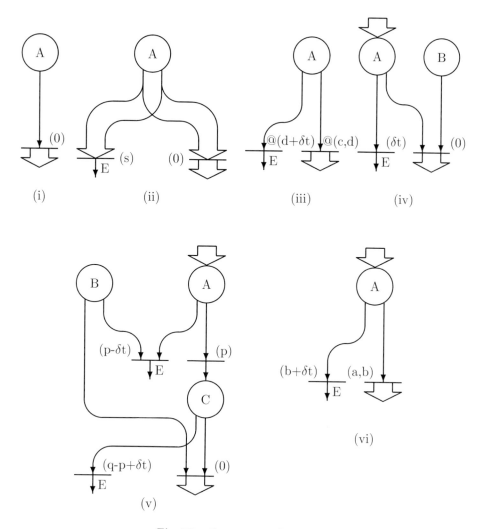

Fig. 15. Components of actions.

Signals are most likely to originate in transactions, but they can be sent out by sensors.

In Case (iii), the action is initiated by a clock or a person. If initiated by a clock, the setting would be $c = d$. If initiated by a person, a time period defined by two different clock readings can be stipulated. If the action has not been started at time d, an exception arises. Cases (iv) and (v) interpret the two optional components that can follow a clock-based initiation. In Case (iv) a signal has to be on at the time of initiation of the action — this signal is issued by a transaction represented by place B. If the signal is not on, we have an exception. In Case (v) we also require a signal to be on after the clock-based initiation, but not immediately. Rather, it should come on at a time within $(T + p, T + q)$, where T is the time at which the action is initiated.

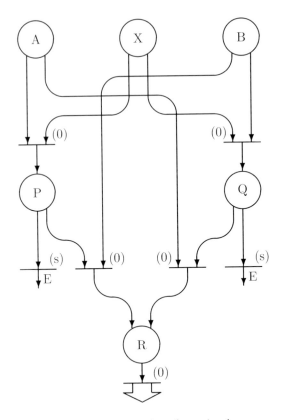

Fig. 16.   Conjunction of two signals.

Exceptional situations arise if the signal is already on at $T + p$, or has failed to come on by $T + q$. An example arises with package routing by means of destination gates. Suppose a bar code reader selects a gate for a package. The bar code reader also initiates the action. The gate should not open too early or too late. Here the signal is issued by the gate-opening mechanism at the time it opens the gate.

In the remaining case there is to be a delay of between a and b time units, and, as we noted earlier, a manager determines the precise length of the delay. An exception arises if the manager fails to resume the action before the delay time is exceeded.

Figure 17 shows the Petri net corresponding to our example of an action. It is built up from the components of Fig. 15 in a mechanical fashion. We leave it to the reader to identify the places and transitions that correspond to Cases (iii), (v), and (vi) of Fig. 15. The author finds the specification of the action as text easier to follow than the net of Fig. 17, but the net removes interpretation ambiguity. Moreover, the net representation allows the use of tools, such as the Tina toolbox, which supports both Petri and time Petri nets [21]. Such tools facilitate the analysis of complex systems consisting of numerous places and action-defining nets.

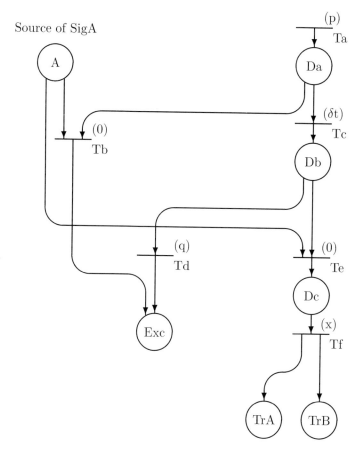

Fig. 17.   The net of an action.

There are other examples of where a representation has been transformed into some kind of Petri net in order to exploit its semantic soundness or analytic capability. In [18], a CSP-like specification language is translated into a Petri net to allow the use of Petri net analysis tools. In an investigation of fault trees the semantics of the fault tree formalism are provided by a high-level Petri net [22]. Information flow diagrams have been formalized in terms of Petri nets [23], and the data flow notation ESML has been similarly interpreted [24].

5. Decomposition of Petri Nets

There are two primary uses of Petri nets. One is to provide insight into the structure of complex asynchronous dynamic systems, and how the systems change over time. This is the cognitive aspect. The other is to determine from a Petri net representation of a system whether the behavior of the system is as expected. This is the analytical aspect. The high speed of modern computers and almost limitless memory allow the very largest nets that *arise in practice* to be analyzed. The emphasis is on practice because the equivalence of higher order Petri nets, such as time Petri nets, to Turing machines makes many properties of such nets formally undecidable. For example, since there does not exist a *general* algorithm that determines whether a Turing machine will eventually stop, there can be no *general* algorithm that detects deadlock in time Petri nets. But in particular cases of practical importance it is very likely that a solution can be found.

The cognitive aspect remains a problem. First, how are we to construct a Petri net for a very large system to begin with? Second, given the results of analysis, how are we to interpret them? Third, even if we ourselves come to understand our nets, how are we to convey our insights to others? Representation of Petri nets in a form that helps us understand them better is therefore very important.

The first step is to consider the topology of a drawing. We have followed a set of principles in designing the layout of the drawings in this chapter, but in the realization that in trying to satisfy one of the principles we may have to violate another. (1) Although some authors represent transitions by boxes, we prefer simple lines drawn horizontally. This makes it easier to differentiate between places and transitions. (2) An arc should enter a transition or place from above, and leave it from below. This helps to understand the flow of control in a net. (3) Labels on places and transitions are to be positioned close to the objects they relate to, and so reduce the possibility of misinterpretation. (4) Crossing of arcs is to be minimized. This also helps to understand the flow of control. (5) Rules 1–4 are to be disregarded whenever this makes it easier to interpret the net.

The next step is to try and reduce the size of the net. Two approaches have been taken in dealing with this. One is reduction or compression, the other is modularization. Under reduction, a simple place-transition-place sequence is reduced to a single place. Application of this to the net of Fig. 13 removes places $G1$ and $G2$, and transitions ga1 and ga2. The labels on ar1 and ar2 become (12) and (7), respectively. The other approach is to hide the inner workings of parts of the net, and use connectors to show how the parts are interconnected. Figure 18 shows the result of decomposition combined with compression applied to the net of Fig. 13.

As pointed out above, the power of modern computers has lessened the interest in reduction, which is a good outcome. In more complex reduction cases, because reduction has to preserve the property of interest for the analysis, different sets of reduction rules have to be developed for different types of nets and different properties of interest. This is particularly difficult for nets involving time — for a discussion, see [25]. Also, once a fault is found in a reduced net, there is little indication of why the original net possesses this fault.

Modularization encourages the use of standard components, which is a general trend in software engineering. For example, many applications use passwords or PINs. Password control is a fairly complicated process including timeouts, validity checks, restricted number of tries in case of invalid inputs, and, a restricted number of tries not just in the one session, but over a given time period, say 24 hours. Of course, in the implementation of password protection, the most efficient approach

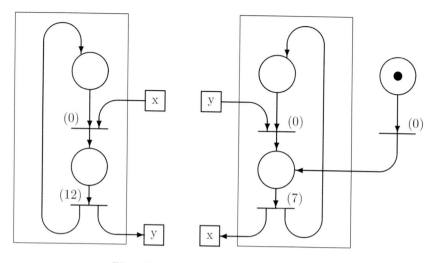

Fig. 18. Compressed and partitioned net.

is to reuse code, but a Petri net representation can be very useful in explaining this process.

Decomposition helps to understand even the most complex nets: Fig. 19 is the result of applying this technique to the railroad crossing example of Fig. 14.

An interesting approach to decomposition is provided by *G*-nets [26,27], which are an extension of Petri nets. The authors consider two kinds of knowledge, *F*-knowledge that refers to facts, and *I*-knowledge that refers to inference. *F*-knowledge is static, *I*-knowledge is dynamic. Both *F*-knowledge and *I*-knowledge need to be organized to show relationships between knowledge instances. A *G*-net representation allows the two types of knowledge to be organized by means of the same display format in a single system. Such a *G*-net system consists of individual *G*-nets, connected via *switch places*.

A *G*-net can be defined as the tuple $G = \langle P, T, u, I, O \rangle$, where P is a set of places, and T a set of transitions. Function u defines the initial marking of the net. Tokens in a *G*-net are colored. Functions I and O map from T, and determine the input and output behavior of a transition. The value of an $I(t)$ or $O(t)$ is a set of triples, where a triple consists of (a) the identifier of a place, (b) in $I(t)$ the number of tokens removed from this place and in $O(t)$ the number of tokens added to the place, and (c) the color of the tokens.

The meaning of a transition $t \in T$ is determined by the type of net. In a static net ontological relations are associated with the transitions, as shown in Fig. 20, which is taken from [26]. We have three objects, an armchair (AC), a highchair (HC), and a stool (S), located next to each other. The general class of the objects is indicated by an IS-A relation, their shapes by a "shape" relation, and their spatial arrangement by a "left-of" relation. We shall not consider static nets further here. Interested readers should refer to [26] for reasoning procedures on these nets. An inheritance procedure determines all properties of an object; a

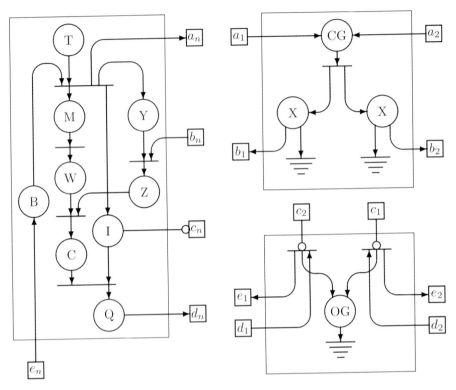

Fig. 19.   Crossing controller partitioned.

recognition procedure finds objects that stand in particular relationships with a
given set of objects.

The tokens of a dynamic net are colored white or black, and tokens can carry
additional information. In a dynamic net a predicate is associated with each transition. In most instances, the predicate is the constant "true". The purpose of the
predicates is analogous to the predicates associated with the counter c in Fig. 10.
A transition t is enabled if its input set contains the tokens required by $I(t)$, and
the predicate associated with t is true. The firing of t sends to each place in its
output set the tokens specified by $O(t)$. Consider place P in the output set. The
relevant triple in $O(t)$ contains either $(P, n, white)$, which adds n tokens to P, or
$(P, 1, black)$, which removes all tokens from P. Black tokens are created at a transition and are never part of a marking.

Black tokens can perform the same function as the earthing convention introduced in Sec. 3.3, the token counts in the I- and O-functions implement multiple
arcs, and the predicates associated with transitions can express timing constraints.
This means that G-nets are sufficiently powerful to allow the examples of Secs. 3
and 4.1 to be expressed in terms of them. However, it is not clear how to represent
inhibitor arcs, and thus arrive at a G-net design for the railroad crossing controller
of Sec. 4.2.

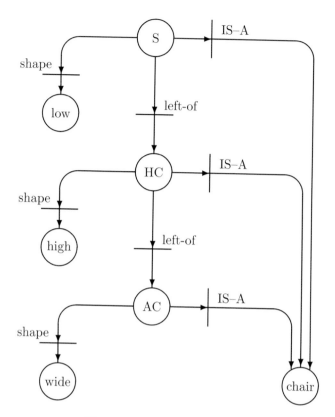

Fig. 20. An F-knowledge *G*-net.

Our interest in *G*-nets is largely motivated by the decomposition mechanism that they provide. Figure 21 shows the decomposition of the tasks of an editorial office. It follows Fig. 7 of [26], but has been somewhat streamlined. The example consists of three modules, represented by three *G*-nets. Individual *G*-nets are linked by means of switch places, which in Fig. 21 are represented by boxes — a box carries the identifier of the target module and of the entry place into this module.

Module: Editorial office. *P*1 extracts an incoming communication from a message queue, and selects a destination for it. If the communication is a submitted paper, *P*2 creates a new database entry for the paper, and *P*3 sends out an acknowledgement to the authors. Switch *Selection* then invokes three instances of the referee selection module, one for each of the three referees to be selected, and enters the selection module at its place *P*1. If the message is from a referee, switch *Decision* invokes the decision module, to be entered at its place *P*1.

Module: Referee selection. The referee selection module can be entered in three places, at *P*1, *P*2, and *P*4. The task at *P*1 selects a referee, inserts the referee particulars in the database, saves the current time T as a reference time, and fires *t*1. The task at *P*3 sends out the necessary materials to the referee. Places *P*2 and *P*4 implement delays. Transition *t*2 is to fire at a time $T + t_a$ unless a report

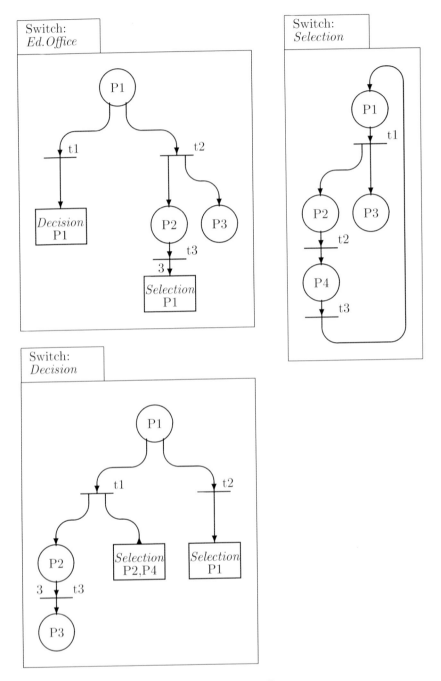

Fig. 21. Editorial office.

has been received before this time, which is made known by a black token being sent to $P2$. If $t2$ fires, then at $P4$ a reminder is sent out to the referee. If there has been a response to the reminder by time $T + t_b$, again indicated by a black token, all is fine; otherwise $t3$ fires, and a new referee is selected.

Module: Decision. Place $P1$ receives a referee's message. If it is an evaluation, then $t1$ fires, a token is sent to $P2$, and by means of the switch *Selection* black tokens are sent to both $P2$ and $P4$ in the selection module — their purpose is to remove tokens that might be in these places. The backward arrowhead shows that this is a black token operation. If the message is refusal by a referee to serve, then $t2$ fires, and switch *Selection* leads to the selection of a new referee. When three tokens have been accumulated in $P2$, transition $t3$ fires. The task at $P3$ evaluates the paper on the basis of the referees' reports, and sends the appropriate notification to the authors.

6. Petri Nets and Fuzzy Reasoning

Knowledge is often expressed in the form of if–then rules. For example, we could have "if it is cold then natural gas consumption increases", and "if natural gas consumption increases then the price of natural gas goes up". By *chaining* these two rules we find that coldness leads to a price increase. In general we have the production rule

$$\text{IF } p_j \text{ THEN } p_k,$$

and a knowledge base is a set of such rules, where p_j and p_k are predicates.

Often we are unsure about the level of truth of the predicates or about the validity of the production rule. Fuzzy sets have been used by numerous authors to represent and automate reasoning processes under such uncertainty. Here we shall examine the work of S.-M. Chen [28,29]. First some preliminaries about fuzziness (for a detailed exposition see [30]). If we know the exact temperature at a time and place, say $23°C$, this is a *crisp* value. But if we have no thermometer, and merely feel that it is warm, then we are dealing with a range of possible values. This is *fuzziness*, and it represents the uncertainty that arises from our lack of a precise temperature value, and the different perceptions by people of what is warm. Then, instead of the predicate "it is warm" being true (having value 1) or false (having value 0), our fuzzy predicate has a truth value in the range of real numbers $[0, 1]$.

In [28], a fuzzy Petri net is defined by adding components D, β, f, and α to the Petri net as defined in Sec. 2:

D is a set of propositions such that $|D| = |P|$;
$\beta: D \to P$ assigns a proposition to each place;
$f: T \to [0, 1]$ assigns a real value to each transition;
$\alpha: P \to [0, 1]$ assigns real values to places.

Actually $\alpha(p)$ is defined only when place p holds a token, i.e., it is associated with tokens, and it expresses a measure of the truth of the proposition associated with the place. As the marking of a net changes, so does α. Functions β and f do not change in time.

A fuzzy production rule IF d_1 THEN d_2 is modeled by places p_1 and p_2 representing propositions d_1 and d_2, and by a transition t from p_1 to p_2, which represents the IF–THEN. The value $f(t)$ indicates the belief in the validity of the production rule itself. Let p_1 hold a token such than $\alpha(p_1) = 0.80$. Place p_2 does not hold a token, so that $\alpha(p_2)$ is undefined. Let $f(t) = 0.90$. Then the firing of t removes the token from p_1 (and makes $\alpha(p_1)$ undefined), and places a token in p_2 with $\alpha(p_2) = 0.70 \times 0.90 = 0.63$, which stands for the truth value of d_2.

Composite production rules are illustrated by Fig. 22 for three cases. If the composite rule requires more than one transition, all the transitions have the same f-value. The effect of exercising (firing) of composite production rules is as follows:

(1) IF $\left(\bigwedge_{i=1}^{n} d_i\right)$ THEN d_r results in $\alpha(p_r) = min_{i=1}^{n} \alpha(p_i) \times f(t)$.
(2) IF d_r THEN $\left(\bigwedge_{i=1}^{n} d_i\right)$ results in $\alpha(p_i) = \alpha(p_r) \times f(t)$ for $i = 1, \ldots, n$.
(3) IF $\left(\bigvee_{i=1}^{n} d_i\right)$ THEN d_r implies n transitions and the evaluation rule is $\alpha(p_r) = max_{i=1}^{n} \alpha(p_i) \times f(t)$.
(4) IF d_r THEN $\left(\bigvee_{i=1}^{n} d_i\right)$ does not specify the flow of control in the net — rules of this type are not considered in [28].

Originally Case 2 was interpreted in [28] as a single transition branching out to n places, which intuitively seems to be the right choice. S.-K. Yu [31] pointed out that this results in formal difficulties, and introduced the form shown in Fig. 22. Individual IF–THEN rules that have the same antecedent take the same form as Case 2 in Fig. 22, but their f-values need not be identical. The output values for the cases shown in Fig. 22 are, respectively, 0.48, 0.49 in all three output places, and 0.56.

The model is refined in [29] by changing the values of f and α to *fuzzy numbers*. For example, the fuzzy condition "warm" can be represented by a triangular fuzzy number that rises from 0 at $18°C$ to 1 at $23°C$, and drops back to 0 at $28°C$. The model

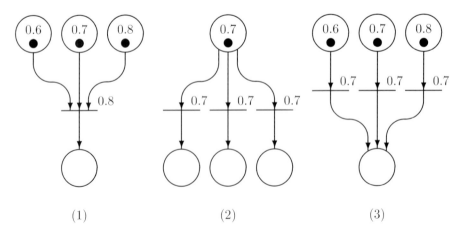

Fig. 22.   Composite production rules.

of [29] includes also a weight-function W, where $W(d_i)$ represents the importance assigned to proposition d_i relative to the other propositions in the scheme. The weighted fuzzy Petri net approach makes use of a fuzzy OR-operation. Its definition requires much deeper knowledge of fuzzy operations than we can assume or introduce here. For our example, we are therefore using the simpler model of [28].

Consider the following production rules, where C defines our confidence in the validity of a rule:

(1) IF d_1 THEN d_3 $(C = 0.90)$.
(2) IF d_1 THEN d_4 $(C = 0.85)$.
(3) IF $d_1 \wedge d_2$ THEN d_5 $(C = 0.90)$.
(4) IF d_3 THEN $d_6 \wedge d_8$ $(C = 0.95)$.
(5) IF d_4 THEN d_7 $(C = 0.80)$.
(6) IF d_4 THEN d_8 $(C = 0.80)$.
(7) IF d_5 THEN d_8 $(C = 0.90)$.
(8) IF d_8 THEN d_9 $(C = 0.90)$.

The system is represented by the fuzzy Petri net of Fig. 23 with the initial marking as shown. The values $\alpha(p_1)$ and $\alpha(p_2)$ are supplied by the user, as are the

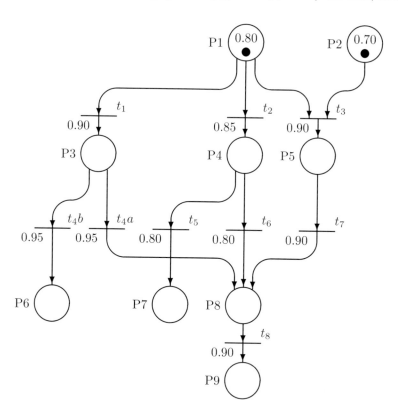

Fig. 23.   A fuzzy reasoning net.

values of function f (the C-values listed above). We want the value of $\alpha(p_9)$. In the first sequence of firings, we obtain $\alpha(p_3) = 0.72$, $\alpha(p_4) = 0.68$, and $\alpha(p_5) = 0.63$. Next, the firing of t_4 results in a contribution to $\alpha(p_8)$ of 0.68. It also gives $\alpha(p_6) = 0.68$, but, since our goal is a value for $\alpha(p_9)$, this is irrelevant, as is the result of firing t_5. The firing of t_6 contributes 0.54 to $\alpha(p_8)$, and the firing of t_7 gives 0.57. Then $\alpha(p_8)$ is the maximum of (0.68, 0.54, 0.57), namely 0.68. Finally, $\alpha(p_9) = \alpha(p_8) \times 0.9 = 0.61$.

7. Summary and Current Trends

As stated in the introduction, our purpose has been to point out the usefulness of Petri nets as a software engineering and knowledge engineering tool. We tried to convey our own view that Petri nets possess an immediate cognitive appeal, even charm. Some of our examples have been fairly complex, notably Fig. 14, but the problem that Fig. 14 represents is itself very complex, and we doubt that any other visual representation would give better insight into the problem, particularly after the problem has been decomposed as shown in Fig. 19.

Along the way we have introduced the main concepts that contribute to the power of Petri nets. We have looked in greater or lesser detail at basic Petri nets, colored Petri nets, time Petri nets, fuzzy Petri nets, and G-nets. With this repertoire it should be possible to deal with the representation of any software system that arises in practice. However, we often find it difficult to decide what type of net is best suited for a particular application. A taxonomy of the nets, and the identification of applications for which a particular class of nets provides the most effective representation would be an interesting research topic. But in this we should constantly be aware of individual preferences by people — a representation that suits one person need not be the best representation for another.

A methodology based on very simple principles, which was introduced as far back as 1962, can be regarded as mature. Nevertheless, some interesting developments are still arising. One is the consideration of spatial-temporal aspects in mobile computing. Although interest in the use of Petri nets for dealing with multimedia synchronization had already arisen in the mid-1990s, the integration of multimedia synchronization with mobile computing is fairly recent — for an example of such work, see [32]. Another development to note is work on a markup language for various types of Petri nets at the Humboldt University in Berlin [33]. Currently discussion focuses on what is general and what is specific. There is still uncertainty as to what "general" features must necessarily be included in the markup language, and what features are to be defined in separate Petri net type definitions.

Finally, a note to the authors of the work surveyed here. If I have misunderstood or misrepresented your work, please accept my apology for not having been more thorough in the study of your contributions.

References

1. C. A. Petri, *Kommunikation mit Automaten*, PhD Dissertation, University of Bonn (1962) (in German).
2. C. Ghezzi, M. Jazayeri and D. Mandrioli, *Fundamentals of Software Engineering* (Prentice Hall, 1991).
3. *http://www.omg.org/uml/*.
4. T. Menzies, "Evaluation issues for visual programming languages", *Handbook of Software Engineering and Knowledge Engineering: Emerging Technologies, Vol. 2* (World Scientific, 2002) 93–101.
5. J. L. Peterson, *Petri Net Theory and the Modeling of Systems* (Prentice-Hall, 1981).
6. W. Reisig, *Petri Nets — An Introduction* (Springer-Verlag, 1985).
7. C. Girault and R. Valk, *Petri Nets for Systems Engineering* (Springer, 2003).
8. *http://www.informatik.uni-hamburg.de/TGI/pnbib/index.html*.
9. W. v. d. Aalst and K. v. Hee, *Workflow Management: Models, Methods, and Systems* (MIT Press, 2002).
10. A. T. Berztiss, *Software Methods for Business Reengineering* (Springer, 1996).
11. K. Jensen, *Coloured Petri Nets: Basic Concepts, Vol. 1, 2nd edn.* (Springer, 1996).
12. K. Jensen, *Coloured Petri Nets: Analysis Methods, Vol. 2* (Springer, 1994).
13. K. Jensen, *Coloured Petri Nets: Practical Use, Vol. 3* (Springer, 1997).
14. P. Merlin and D. J. Farber, "Recoverability of communication protocols — Implications of a theoretical study", *IEEE Transactions on Communication* **COM-24** (1976) 1036–1043.
15. B. Berthomieu and M. Diaz, "Modeling and verification of time dependent systems using time Petri nets", *IEEE Transactions on Software Engineering* **17** (1991) 259–273.
16. C. Ghezzi, D. Mandrioli, S. Morasca and M. Pezze, "A unified high-level Petri net formalism for time-critical systems", *IEEE Transactions on Software Engineering* **17** (1991) 160–172.
17. D. Xu, Y. He and Y. Deng, "Compositional schedulability analysis of real-time systems using time Petri nets", *IEEE Transactions on Software Engineering* **28** (2002) 984–996.
18. K. M. Kavi, F. T. Sheldon and S. Reed, "Specification and analysis of real-time systems using CSP and Petri nets", *International Journal of Software Engineering and Knowledge Engineering* **6** (1996) 229–248.
19. A. E. Haxthausen and J. Peleska, "Formal development and verification of a distributed railway control system", *IEEE Transactions on Software Engineering* **26** (2000) 687–701.
20. A. T. Berztiss, "Time in modeling", *Information Modelling and Knowledge Bases XIII* (IOS Press, 2002) 184–200.
21. *http://www.laas.fr/tina*.
22. A. Bobbio, G. Franceschinis, R. Gaeta and L. Portinale, "Parametric fault tree for the dependability analysis of redundant systems and its high-level Petri net semantics", *IEEE Transactions on Software Engineering* **29** (2003) 270–287.
23. G. Lausen, "Modeling and analysis of the behavior of information systems", *IEEE Transactions on Software Engineering* **14** (1988) 1610–1620.
24. G. Richter and B. Maffeo, "Toward a rigorous interpretation of ESML — Extended Systems Modeling Language", *IEEE Transactions on Software Engineering* **19** (1993) 165–180.

25. E. Y. T. Juan, J. J. P. Tsai, T. Murata and Y. Zhou, "Reduction methods for real-time systems using delay time Petri nets", *IEEE Transactions on Software Engineering* **27** (2001) 422–448.

26. Y. Deng and S.-K. Chang, "A G-net model for knowledge representation and reasoning", *IEEE Transactions on Knowledge and Data Engineering* **2** (1990) 295–310.

27. Y. Deng and S.-K. Chang, "A framework for the modeling and prototyping of distributed information systems", *International Journal of Software Engineering and Knowledge Engineering* **1** (1991) 203–226.

28. S.-M. Chen, J.-S. Ke and J.-F. Chang, "Knowledge representation using fuzzy Petri nets", *IEEE Transactions on Knowledge and Data Engineering* **2** (1990) 311–319.

29. S.-M. Chen, "Weighted fuzzy reasoning using weighted fuzzy Petri nets", *IEEE Transactions on Knowledge and Data Engineering* **14** (2002) 386–397.

30. G. J. Klir and B. Yuan, *Fuzzy Sets and Fuzzy Logic* (Prentice Hall PTR, 1995).

31. S.-K. Yu, "Comments on "Knowledge representation using fuzzy Petri nets"", *IEEE Transactions on Knowledge and Data Engineering* **7** (1995) 190.

32. P.-Y. Hsu, Y.-B. Chang and Y.-L. Chen, "STRPN: A Petri-net approach for modeling spatial-temporal relations between moving multimedia objects", *IEEE Transactions on Software Engineering* **29** (2003) 63–76.

33. *http://www.informatik.hu-berlin.de/top/pnml/.*

PROGRAM SLICING

JENS KRINKE

Faculty of Electrical and Information Engineering,
FernUniversität in Hagen, 58084 Hagen, Germany
E-mail: Jens.Krinke@FernUni-Hagen.de

Program slicing is a technique to identify statements that may influence the computations of other statements. The original goal was to aid program understanding and debugging. Program slicing is now used as a base technique in other applications. Researchers in several areas of software engineering have suggested applications in program comprehension, software maintenance, reverse engineering and evolution, testing, and even verification. The following will give an overview of program slicing, including recent developments. This overview covers static as well as dynamic slicing. It contains a discussion of applications and basic approaches to compute slices, shows problems and their solutions, together with refinements of slicing.

Keywords: Program slicing, program dependence graph.

1. Introduction

Program slicing is a method for automatically decomposing programs by analyzing their data flow and control flow. Starting from a subset of a program's behavior, slicing reduces that program to a minimal form which still produces that behavior. The reduced program, called a "slice", is an independent program guaranteed to represent faithfully the original program within the domain of the specified subset of behavior.

Mark Weiser [115]

Program Slicing is a widely used technique for various aspects of software engineering. It basically answers the question "Which statements may affect the computation of a given statement?", something every programmer has asked. After Weiser's first publication in 1979, 25 years have passed and various approaches to compute slices have evolved. However, only recently have mature systems capable of slicing real-world systems become available. The availability of these systems makes it possible to fully explore and exploit the applications of slicing.

The original goal was to aid program understanding and debugging. Program slicing is now used as a base technique in other applications. Researchers in several areas of software engineering have suggested applications in program comprehension, software maintenance, reverse engineering and evolution, testing, and even verification. The following will give an overview of program slicing, including recent

1	read(n)		1	read(n)		1	
2	i := 1		2	i := 1		2	
3	s := 0		3			3	
4	p := 1		4	p := 1		4	p := 1
5	while (i <= n)		5	while (i <= n)		5	
6	s := s + i		6			6	
7	p := p * i		7	p := p * i		7	
8	i := i + 1		8	i := i + 1		8	
9	write(s)		9			9	
10	write(p)		10	write(p)		10	write(p)

(a) Original program	(b) Static Slice for (10, p)	(c) Dynamic Slice for (10, p, n = 0)

Fig. 1.   A program and two slices.

developments, thus complementing earlier works like Tip's excellent survey [107] and others [32, 52].

A slice extracts those statements from a program that potentially have an influence on a specific statement of interest, which is the slicing criterion. Consider the example in Fig. 1(a). This program computes the product p and the sum s of integer numbers up to a limit n. Let us assume that we are only interested in the computation of the product and its output in line 10. When we eliminate all statements that have no impact on the computation, we end up with the program shown in Fig. 1(b) that still computes the product correctly. This is called a *slice* for the *slicing criterion* "variable p in line 10". The process of computing a slice is called *slicing*. Because this slice is independent of the program's inputs and computes p correctly for all possible executions, it is called a *static* slice. If we are interested in the statements that have an impact on the criterion for a *specific* execution, we can compute a *dynamic* slice. A dynamic slice eliminates all statements of a program that have no impact on the slicing criterion for a specific execution as determined by the input for this execution. In Fig. 1(c), a dynamic slice is shown for the execution where the input to variable n is 0. Not only the complete loop has been deleted because the body is never executed, but also the input statement itself.

Originally, (static) slicing was defined by Weiser in 1979; he presented an approach to compute slices based on iterative data flow analysis [113, 115]. Another popular approach to slicing uses reachability analysis in program dependence graphs [36]. Program dependence graphs (PDGs) mainly consist of nodes representing the statements of a program, and control and data dependence edges, which is discussed in more detail in the next section. In PDGs, static slicing of programs can be computed by identifying the nodes that are reachable from the node corresponding to the criterion [36]. The underlying assumption is that all paths are *realizable*. This means that for every path a possible execution of the program exists that executes the statements in the same order. In the presence of procedures things get complicated. Paths are now considered realizable only if they obey the calling context (i.e. called procedures always return to the correct call site). This will be discussed in Sec. 4.3.

This chapter is restricted to slicing of imperative programs. However, this is not the only slice-able thing: There are other approaches to slicing of hierarchical state machines [55], web applications [99], class hierarchies [106], knowledge-based systems [111], logical programs [110], and hardware description languages [30]. Even binary executables can be sliced [65].

The rest of this chapter is structured as follows: The next section presents how slices are computed, followed by a discussion of some applications of slicing. Section 4 will present some problems of slicing and their solutions. Section 5 discusses graphical and textual visualization of slices. Section 6 presents refinements of slicing, including dynamic slicing. The chapter concludes with a presentation of available slicing tools.

2. Computing Slices

Weiser observed that programmers mentally build abstractions of a program during debugging. He formalized that process and defined slicing. He also presented an approach to compute (static) slices based on iterative data flow analysis [113, 115], which will be presented next. The other often used approach to slicing uses reachability analysis in program dependence graphs [36], presented afterwards. In the following, we will just use "slicing" for "static slicing". Dynamic slicing will be discussed in a dedicated section.

2.1. *Weiser-style slicing*

Weiser formally defined a slice as any subset of a program, that preserves a specific behavior with respect to a criterion. The criterion, also called the *slicing criterion*, is a pair $c = (s, V)$ consisting of a statement s and a subset V of the analyzed program's variables. A slice $S(c)$ of a program P on a slicing criterion c is any executable program P', where

- P' is obtained by deleting zero or more statements from P;
- whenever P halts on a given input I, P' will halt for that input; and
- P' will compute the same values as P for the variables of V on input I.

The most trivial (but irrelevant) slice of a program P is always the program P itself. Slices of interest are as small as possible: A slice $S(c)$ of a program P with respect to a criterion c is a *statement-minimal slice*, iff no other slice of P with respect to c with fewer statements exists. In general, it is undecidable if a slice $S(c)$ is statement-minimal. Weiser presented an approximation based on identifying relevant variables and statements, implemented as an iterative data flow analysis [115].

2.2. *Slicing program dependence graphs*

Ottenstein and Ottenstein [95] were the first who suggested the use of program dependence graphs to compute Weiser's slices. Program dependence graphs mainly consist of nodes representing the statements of a program and control and data dependence edges:

- *Control dependence* between two statement nodes exists if one statement controls the execution of the other.
- *Data dependence* between two statement nodes exists if a definition of a variable at one statement might reach the usage of the same variable at another statement.

An example PDG is shown in Fig. 2, where control dependence is drawn in dashed lines and data dependence in solid ones. In that figure, a slice is computed for the statement "`write(p)`". The statements "`s := 0`" and "`s := s+i`" have no direct or transitive influence on the criterion and are not part of the slice.

Slicing without procedures is trivial: Just find reachable nodes in the PDG [36]. The underlying assumption is that all paths are *realizable*. This means that a possible execution of the program exists for any path that executes the statements in the same order.

The (*backward*) *slice* $S(n)$ of a PDG at node n consists of all nodes on which n (transitively) depends:

$$S(n) = \{m \mid m \rightarrow^* n\}.$$

The node n is called the *slicing criterion*.

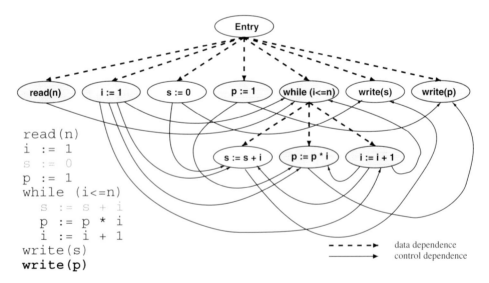

Fig. 2. A program dependence graph. The slice for the criterion "`write(p)`" is highlighted in the graph and in the source text.

This definition of a slice depends on a different slicing criterion than in Weiser-style slicing. Here, a criterion is a node in the program dependence graph, which identifies a statement together with the variable used in it. Therefore, these criteria are more restricted than Weiser-style criteria, where slices can be computed at statements for any set of variables. If a slice is to be computed at a node n for a variable that is not referenced at n, the program must be modified before analysis begins: A negligible use of that variable must be inserted at n.

While backward slicing identifies the statements that have an influence on the statement identified by the criterion, *forward slicing* identifies the statements that are influenced by the criterion:

The *forward slice* $S^F(n)$ of a PDG at node n consists of all nodes that (transitively) depend on n:

$$S^F(n) = \{m \mid n \to^* m\}.$$

In the presence of procedures, slicing is no longer trivial in PDGs. If the calling context is ignored, the analysis is *context-insensitive*, as a called procedure may return to call sites different to the site it has been called from. However, when the calling context is obeyed, the results will be much more precise. Paths along transitive dependences are now considered realizable only if they obey the calling context. Thus, slicing is *context-sensitive* if only realizable paths are traversed. Context-sensitive slicing is solvable efficiently — one has to generate summary edges at call sites [60]: Summary edges represent the transitive dependences of called procedures at call sites. How procedural programs are analyzed will be discussed in Sec. 4.

Bergeretti and Carré [15] presented an algorithm which is neither Weiser-style nor dependence graph based. Their algorithm uses the concept of information flow relations. Venkatesh [112] developed a denotational approach to slicing.

3. Applications of Slicing

Slicing has found its way into various applications. Currently, it is probably mostly used in the area of software maintenance and reengineering. In the following, some applications are presented to show the diversity.

3.1. *Debugging*

Debugging was the first application of program slicing: Weiser [114] realized that programmers mentally ignore statements that cannot have an influence on a statement revealing a bug. Program slicing computes this abstraction and allows to focus on potentially influencing statements. Dicing [85] can be used to focus even more, when additional statements with correct behavior can be identified. Dynamic slicing (discussed in Sec. 6) can be used to focus on relevant statements for one specific execution revealing a bug [4]. More work can be found in [38].

3.2. *Testing*

Program slicing can be used to divide a program into smaller programs specific to a test case [19]. For every test case, the statements that have no impact on the tested features can be sliced away. This reduces the time needed for regression testing because of two reasons: Firstly, the smaller programs execute faster, and secondly, only a subset of the test cases has to be repeated — all test cases can be ignored where no statement of the corresponding slice has been changed since the last regression test [13, 22, 46].

3.3. *Program differencing and integration*

Program *differencing* is the problem of finding differences between two programs (or between two versions of a program). Semantic differences can be found using program dependence graphs and slicing. Program *integration* is the problem of merging two program variants into a single program. With program dependence graphs it can be assured that differences between the variants have no conflicting influence on the shared program parts [57–59].

3.4. *Software maintenance*

If a change has to be applied to a program, forward slicing can be used to identify the potential impact of the change: The forward slice reveals the part of the program that is influenced by a criterion statement and therefore is affected by a modification to that statement. Decomposition slicing [39] uses variables instead of statements as criteria.

3.5. *Function extraction and restructuring*

Slicing can also be used for *function extraction* [80]: Extractable functions are identified by slices specified by a set of input variables, a set of output variables, and a final statement. *Function restructuring* separates a single function into independent ones; such independent parts can be identified by slicing [79].

3.6. *Cohesion measurement*

Ott *et al* [18, 94] use slicing to measure functional cohesion. They define data slices which are a combination of forward and backward slices. Such slices are computed for output parameters of functions and the amount of overlapping indicates weak or strong functional cohesion.

3.7. *Clone detection*

There exist two approaches that use dependence graphs and slicing to detect cloned (or duplicated) code. One approach [72] identifies similar code in programs based on finding similar subgraphs in program dependence graphs. It therefore considers not only the syntactic structure of programs but also the data flow within (as an abstraction of the semantics).

A very similar approach is presented in [66]. Starting from *every* pair of matching nodes, they construct isomorphic subgraphs for ideal clones that can be replaced by function calls automatically. Different from the first approach, they use heuristics to choose between alternatives and visit every node only once during subgraph construction.

3.8. *Software conformance certification*

Slicing can answer the question *"which statements have an influence on statement X?"*, but slicing cannot answer the question *"why statement Y influences statement X"*. Path conditions have been introduced by Snelting [104] as a way to validate software in measurement systems. Path conditions represent precise and necessary conditions for information flow between two program points. Constraint solvers can solve path conditions for the program's input variables. Solved path conditions may act as witnesses for safety violations such as an information flow between two program points of incompatible security level [77, 100].

3.9. *Other applications*

Slicing is used in model construction to slice away irrelevant code; transition system models are only built for the reduced code [54]. Slicing is also used to decompose tasks in real-time systems [40]. It has even been used for debugging and testing spreadsheets [96] or type checking programs [108].

4. Problems and Challenges in Slicing

Despite the fact that the basic principles of program slicing are fairly easy, the adaptation and implementation for real programming languages cause a series of challenges. Most implementations have been done for *C* or *C*-like languages. The following will present some general problems, which are slicing of programs with unstructured control flow, interprocedural, i.e., context-sensitive slicing, and slicing of concurrent programs.

4.1. *Unstructured control flow*

The original slicing algorithms assumed a language without jump statements. Such statements cause a small problem: Because the corresponding (correct) control flow graph (CFG) contains only a single outgoing edge, no other node can be control dependent on the jump statement, nor have these jump statements any outgoing data dependence. Therefore, a (backward) slice will never contain the jump statements. The exclusion of jump statements makes executable slices incorrect and non-executable slices difficult to comprehend. Various approaches exist to address this problem: Ball and Horwitz [11] augment the CFG by adding *non-executable* edges between the jump statement and the immediate following statement. This makes both the statements after the jump target and the one following the jump statement control dependent on the jump. During data dependence computation, the non-executable edges are ignored. The resulting program dependence graph can be sliced with the usual slicing algorithm, except that labels (the jump targets) are included in the slice if a jump to that label is in the slice.

The algorithm of Ball and Horwitz is similar to Choi and Ferrante's first algorithm presented in [29]. Their second algorithm computes a normal slice first (which does not include the jump statements), and then adds goto statements until the slice is correct. This algorithm produces slices that are more precise than slices from the first algorithm, but the additional gotos may not be part of the original program, and the computed slices may not match the definition of a slice. Agrawal [2] presents an algorithm which also adds jump statements to a normal slice in order to make it correct. However, the added statements are always part of the original program. Harman and Danicic present another algorithm [50], which is an extension of Agrawal's.

Kumar and Horwitz [78] present an improved algorithm based on the augmented control flow graph, and a modified definition of control dependence using both the augmented and the non-augmented control flow graph. They also present a modified definition of a slice based on *semantic effects*, which basically inverts the definition of a slice: A statement x of program P has a semantic effect on a statement y, iff a program P' exists, created by modifying or removing x from P, and some input I exists such that P and P' halt on I and produce different values for some variables used at y. However, such a slice may be a superset of a Weiser slice because according to their definition, a statement like "`x := x;`" has a semantic effect.

4.2. *Interprocedural slicing*

The problem within interprocedural slicing is the calling context. If the calling context is not obeyed, the computed slices will not be accurate. Consider the example in Fig. 3, which is the interprocedural version of the example from Fig. 1. When we compute the slice for variable p in line 10 again, without obeying the calling context, we are not able to delete a single line. Line 8 clearly has an impact, because variable i is increased. Thus, lines 11–13 have an impact, too, and must be included. But lines 11–13 also have an impact on line 6, which therefore also has to be included. As s is used there, line 3 must be included, too. However, if we use the calling context, we are able to distinguish the calls in lines 6 and 8. The call in line 6 only impacts line 6 and the call in line 8 only line 8. Thus, it is possible to omit lines 6 and 3 from the slice.

The extension of the PDG for *interprocedural programs* introduces more nodes and edges: For every procedure a *procedure dependence graph* is constructed, which

```
 1    read(n)
 2    i := 1
 3    s := 0
 4    p := 1
 5    while (i <= n)
 6       s := add(s, i)
 7       p := mul(p, i)
 8       i := add(i, 1)
 9    write(s)
10    write(p)
```

```
11    proc add(x, y)
12       z := x + y
13       return z
14
15    proc mul(x, y)
16       z := x * y
17       return z
```

Fig. 3.   An interprocedural program.

is basically a PDG with *formal-in* and *-out* nodes for every formal parameter of the procedure. A procedure call is represented by a *call* node and *actual-in* and *-out* nodes for each actual parameter. The call node is connected to the entry node by a *call* edge, the *actual-in* nodes are connected to their matching *formal-in* nodes via *parameter-in* edges and the *actual-out* nodes are connected to their matching *formal-out* nodes via *parameter-out* edges. Such a graph is called *Interprocedural Program Dependence Graph (IPDG)*. The *System Dependence Graph (SDG)* is an IPDG, where *summary edges* between actual-in and actual-out nodes have been added representing transitive dependence due to calls [60].

To slice programs with procedures, it is not enough to perform a reachability analysis on IPDGs or SDGs. The resulting slices are not accurate as the calling context is not preserved: The algorithm may traverse a parameter-in edge coming from a call site into a procedure, may traverse some edges there, and may finally traverse a parameter-out edge going to a different call site. The sequence of traversed edges (the path) is an *unrealizable path*: It is impossible for an execution that a called procedure does not return to its call site. We consider an interprocedural slice to be *precise* if all nodes included in the slice are reachable from the criterion by a *realizable* path.

The (*backward*) *slice* $S(n)$ of an IPDG $G = (N, E)$ at node $n \in N$ consists of all nodes on which n (transitively) depends via an interprocedurally realizable path:

$$S(n) = \{m \in N \mid m \to_R^* n\}.$$

Here, $m \to_R^* n$ denotes that there exists an interprocedurally realizable path from m to n.

These definitions cannot be used in an algorithm directly because it is impractical to check paths whether they are interprocedurally realizable. Accurate slices can be calculated with a modified algorithm on SDGs [60]: The benefit of SDGs is the presence of *summary* edges that represent transitive dependence due to calls. Summary edges can be used to identify actual-out nodes that are reachable from actual-in nodes by an interprocedurally realizable path through the called procedure without analyzing it. The idea of the slicing algorithm using summary edges [60,97] is first to slice from the criterion only ascending into calling procedures, and then to slice from all visited nodes only descending into called procedures.

The algorithm to compute summary edges in [60] is based on attributed grammars. A more efficient algorithm was presented in [97]. This algorithm starts on an IPDG without summary edges and checks for all pairs of formal-in and -out nodes, if a path in the dependence graph between the nodes exists and corresponds to a same-level realizable (matched) path in the control flow graph. If such a path exists, a summary edge between the corresponding actual-in and -out node is inserted. Because the insertion of summary edges will make more paths possible, the search iterates until a minimal fixed point is found. The algorithm only follows data dependence, control dependence and summary edges. Therefore, any path consisting of these edges must correspond to a same-level realizable path. This algorithm is basically of cubic complexity [97].

System-dependence-graph based slices are not executable because different call sites may have different parameters included in the slice. Binkley [21] shows how to extend slicing in system dependence graphs to produce executable slices.

System dependence graphs assume procedures to be single-entry-single-exit, which does not hold in the presence of exceptions or interprocedural jumps. Sinha *et al* [103] present *interprocedural control dependence* which occurs if a procedure can be left abnormally by an embedded halt statement. They extend the IPDG with corresponding edges and show how to compute slices within the extended graph [102].

Meanwhile, extensive evaluations of slicing algorithms have been done. For control-flow-graph based Weiser-style algorithms some data can be found in [9,87]. A preliminary evaluation of program-dependence-based algorithms has been conducted by Agrawal and Guo [1]. That study has been shown to be flawed in [73], which also contains a large evaluation of various slicing algorithms. Another comprehensive study is presented in [20]. These evaluations have shown that context-insensitive slicing is very imprecise in comparison with context-sensitive slicing. This shows that context-sensitive slicing is highly preferable because the loss of precision is not acceptable. A surprising result is that the simple context-insensitive slicing is *slower* than the more complex context-sensitive slicing. The reason is that the context-sensitive algorithm has to visit far fewer nodes during traversal due to its higher precision.

The effect of the precision of the underlying data flow analysis and points-to analysis has been studied in a series of works [8,24,83,87,101].

4.3. Object-oriented programs

Slicing of object-oriented programs is more complex than slicing of procedural languages because of virtual functions and the distinction of classes and objects.

Usually, virtual functions are handled like function pointers in C programs. All approaches to slice object-oriented programs are based on dependence graphs. Larsen and Harrold [81] have introduced the class dependence graph, which introduces *class member* edges and represents the class' members as formal parameters of the methods. The main challenge in the representation of object-oriented programs as dependence graphs is the representation of objects themselves, and how they are passed as parameters to methods. Tonella *et al* [109] use flow-insensitive pointer analysis to resolve the runtime types of objects. Thus, their approach is able to distinguish data members for different objects. Liang and Harrold [82] have extended the system dependence graph by representing the passed objects as polymorphic trees of members. This C++ targeted approach turned out to be insufficient for Java programs, and Hammer and Snelting [49] presented an improved approach to slice Java programs.

4.4. *Slicing of concurrent programs*

Müller-Olm has shown that precise context-sensitive slicing of concurrent programs is undecidable in general [88]. Therefore, one has to use conservative approximations to analyze and slice concurrent programs. There are many variations of the program dependence graph for threaded programs like parallel program graphs [26, 27, 34]. Most approaches to static or dynamic slicing of threaded programs are based on such dependence graphs.

Dynamic slicing of threaded or *concurrent* programs has been approached by different authors [28,34,42,64,68] and is surveyed in [107]. Probably the first approach for *static* slicing of threaded programs was the work of Cheng [26,27,117]. He introduced some dependences, which are needed for a variant of the PDG, the *program dependence net* (PDN). His *selection* dependence is a special kind of control dependence, and his *synchronization* dependence is basically control dependence resulting from the previously presented communication dependence. Cheng's *communication dependence* is a combination of data dependence and the presented communication dependence. Cheng defines slices simply based on graph reachability. The resulting slices are not precise, as they do not take into account that dependences between concurrently executed statements are not transitive. Therefore, the integration of his technique of slicing threaded programs into slicing threaded object-oriented programs [117] has the same problem.

The first precise approach [71] to slice concurrent programs uses a `cobegin/coend` model of concurrency. That approach has been improved in [90].

Almost all approaches are context-insensitive and ignore calling context. The only context-sensitive approach [74] models the calling context explicitly. Every concurrently executing thread is represented by its own calling context; the program's calling context is then a tuple of call strings which is propagated along the edges in PDGs (one tuple element for each thread).

There is a series of works that use static slicing of concurrent programs but treat interference transitively and accept the imprecision: [53] present the semantics of a simple multi-threaded language that contains synchronization statements similar to the JVM. For this language, they introduce and define additional types of dependence: Divergence dependence, synchronization dependence and ready dependence. In [86] Cheng's approach is applied to slice Promela for model checking purposes.

5. Visualization of Slices

The computed slices and the program dependence graph itself are results that should be presented to the user if not used in following analyses. As graphical presentations are often more intuitive than textual ones, a graphical visualization is desirable. However, experience shows that the graphical presentation is less helpful than expected, and a textual presentation is superior.

This section describes approaches and experiences with both graphical and textual visualization.

5.1. *Graphical visualization*

ChopShop [62] was an early tool to visualize slices and chops, based on highlighting text (in emacs) or laying out graphs (with dot and ghostview). It is reported that even the smallest chops result in huge graphs. Therefore, only an abstraction is visualized: Normal statements (assignments) are omitted, procedure calls of the same procedure are folded into a single node and connecting edges are attributed with data dependence information.

The CANTO environment [7] has a visualization tool PROVIS based on dot which can visualize PDGs (besides other graphs). Again, problems with excessively large graphs are reported, which are omitted by only visualizing the subgraph which is reachable from a chosen node via a limited number of edges.

In [12], the same problems with visualizing dependence graphs are reported and a decomposition approach is presented: Groups of nodes are collapsed into one node. The result is a hierarchy of groups, where every group is visualized independently. Three different decompositions are presented: The first decomposition is to group the nodes belonging to the same procedure together, the second is to group the nodes belonging to the same loop and the third is a combination of both. The result of the function decomposition is identical to the visualization of the call graph.

The VALSOFT slicing system [71] visualizes the slices in program dependence graphs procedure-by-procedure. The user is able to fold sets of nodes and to navigate along dependence edges. To enable a better comprehension, slices are simultaneously highlighted in the graphical and the textual, source-based view. An example visualization can be seen in Fig. 4, where a slice is visualized in the dependence graph and in source code by highlighting.

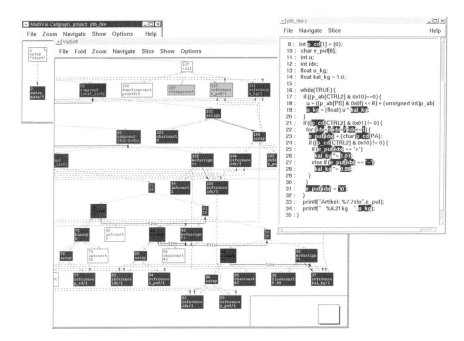

Fig. 4.   The VALSOFT graphical user interface.

5.2. *Textual visualization*

Every slicing tool visualizes its results directly in the source code. However, most tools are line based, highlighting only complete lines. CodeSurfer [6] has textual visualization with highlighting parts of lines, if there is more than one statement in a line. The textual visualization includes graphical elements like pop-ups for visualization and navigation along e.g. data and control dependence or calls. Such aids are necessary as a user cannot identify relevant dependences easily from source text alone. Such problems have also been identified by Ernst [35] and he suggested similar graphical aids. However, his tool, which is not restricted to highlighting complete lines, does not have such aids and offers depth-limited slicing instead.

Steindl's slicer for Oberon [105] also highlights only parts of lines, based on the individual lexical elements of the program. The VALSOFT slicing system [71] is able to highlight unrestricted sets of PDG nodes in the corresponding source text.

SeeSlice [10] is a more advanced tool for visualizing slices. Files and procedures are not presented through source code but with an abstraction representing characters as single pixels. Files and procedures that are not part of computed slices are folded, such that only a small box is left. Slices highlight the pixels corresponding to contained elements.

CodeSurfer [6] also has a project viewer, which has a tree-like structural visualization of the SDG. This is useful for seeing "hidden" nodes, such as nodes that do not correspond to any source text.

The visualization of slices in a graphical or textual representation has not yet reached the expected usability, and more abstract visualizations are needed like the ones presented in [76]. Some of the abstractions need refinements that make the computes slices focused to the users' requirements. Such refinements will be presented in the next section.

6. Refinements

25 years have passed after the first introduction of program slicing. Usually, inventions in computer science are adopted widely after around 10 years. Why are slicing techniques not easily available yet? William Griswold gave a talk at PASTE 2001 [45] on that topic: *Making Slicing Practical: The Final Mile.* He pointed out why slicing is still not widely used today. One of the main problems is that slicing "as-it-stands" is inadequate for essential software-engineering needs. Usually, slices are hard to understand. This is partly due to bad user interfaces (which can be resolved by adequate visualization and navigation aids as presented in the previous section), but mainly related to the problem that slicing "dumps" the results onto the user without any explanation. Griswold stated the need for "slice explainers" that answer the question why a statement is included in the slice, as well as the need for "filtering". This section will present such "filtering" approaches to slicing.

6.1. *Distance-limited slicing*

One of the problems in understanding a slice for a criterion is to decide why a specific statement is included in that slice and how strong the influence of that statement is onto the criterion. A slice cannot answer these questions as it does not contain any qualitative information. Probably the most important attribute is *locality*: Users are more interested in facts that are near the current point of interest than on those far away. A simple but very useful aid is to provide the user with navigation along the dependences: For a selected statement, show all statements that are directly dependent (or vice versa). Such navigation is central to the VALSOFT system [77] or to CodeSurfer [6].

A more general approach presented in [76] accomplishes locality in slicing by limiting the length of a path between the criterion and the reached statement. Using paths in program dependence graphs has an advantage over paths in control flow graphs: A statement having a direct influence on the criterion will be reached by a path with the length one, independent of the textual or control flow distance.

6.2. *Chopping*

Slicing identifies statements in a program that may influence a given statement (the slicing criterion), but it cannot answer the question why a specific statement is part of a slice. A more focused approach can help: Jackson and Rollins [62] introduced *Chopping*, which reveals the statements involved in a transitive dependence from one

```
1
2
3
4    p := 1
5
6
7      p := p * i
8
9
10   write(p)
```

Fig. 5. A chop from (4, p) to (10, p).

specific statement (the source criterion) to another (the target criterion). Consider again the example from Fig. 1. Assume that we are interested in how the assignment to variable p in line 4 has impact on the output of p in line 10. The computed chop in Fig. 5 reveals the involved statements are only lines 4, 7 and 10.

Chopping can be formulated and computed using PDGs. A chop for a chopping criterion (s, t) is the set of nodes that are part of an influence of the (source) node s onto the (target) node t. This is basically the set of nodes that lie on a path from s to t in the PDG.

The *chop* $C(s, t)$ of an IPDG $G = (N, E)$ from the source criterion $s \in N$ to the target criterion $t \in N$ consists of all nodes on which node t (transitively) depends via an interprocedurally realizable path from node s to node t:

$$C(s, t) = \{n \in N \mid p = s \rightarrow^*_R t \land p = \langle n_1, \ldots, n_l \rangle \land \exists i: n = n_i\}.$$

Jackson and Rollins restricted s and t to be in the same procedure and only traversed control dependence, data dependence and summary edges but not parameter or call edges. The resulting chop is called a *truncated same-level chop*; "truncated" because nodes of called procedures are not included. In [98], Reps and Rosay presented more variants of precise chopping. A *non-truncated* same-level chop is like the truncated chop but includes the nodes of called procedures. They also present truncated and non-truncated *non-same-level* chops (which they call *interprocedural*), where the nodes of the chopping criterion are allowed to be in different procedures.

Some additional chopping algorithms are presented in [73], which also contains the first evaluation (Reps and Rosay [98] only report limited experience).

6.3. *Barrier slicing and chopping*

The presented slicing and chopping techniques compute very fixed results where the user has no influence. However, during slicing and chopping a user might want to give additional restrictions or additional knowledge to the computation:

(1) A user might know that a certain data dependence cannot happen. Because the underlying data flow analysis is a conservative approximation, and the pointer analysis is imprecise, it might be clear to the user that a dependence found by the analysis cannot happen in reality. For example, the analysis assumes a dependence between a definition `a[i]=...` and a usage `...=a[j]` of an array, but the user discovers that `i` and `j` never have the same value. If such a dependence is removed from the dependence graph, the computed slice might be smaller.
(2) A user might want to exclude specific parts of the program that are of no interest for his purposes. For example, he might know that certain statement blocks are not executed during runs of interest; or he might want to ignore error handling or recovery code, when he is only interested in normal execution.
(3) During debugging, a slice might contain parts of the analyzed program that are known (or assumed) to be bug-free. These parts should be removed from the slice to make it more focused.

Both points have been tackled independently: For instance, the removal of dependences from the dependence graph by the user has been applied in Steindl's slicer [105]. The removal of parts from a slice has been presented by Lyle and Weiser [85] and is called *dicing*.

Another approach presented in [75] integrates both strategies into a new kind of slicing, called *barrier slicing*, where nodes (or edges) in the dependence graph are declared to be a *barrier* that transitive dependence is not allowed to pass. A barrier slice or chop is computed by not allowing the paths to contain nodes or edges of the barrier, because the presented approaches to compute slices and chops in dependence graphs all rely on realizable paths "$m \to_R^* n$" between nodes m and n.

6.4. *Dynamic slicing*

During debugging not all possible executions of a program are of interest. Usually, only one test case where a problem arises is in focus. Therefore, Korel and Laski have introduced *dynamic slicing* [69]: Dynamic slicing focuses on a single execution of a program instead of all possible executions like in Weiser's (static) slicing. The slicing criterion for a dynamic slice additionally specifies the (complete) input for the program. The criterion is now a triple $c = (I, s, V)$ consisting of the input I, a statement s and a subset V of the variables of the analyzed program. A *dynamic slice* $S(c)$ of a program P on a slicing criterion c is any executable program P', where

(1) P' is obtained by deleting zero or more statements from P,
(2) whenever P halts for the given input I, P' will halt for the input, and
(3) P' will compute the same values as P for the variables of V on input I.

Korel and Laski also presented an algorithm to compute dynamic slices based on the computation of sets of dynamic def-use relations (a variant of data dependences). However, the algorithm has been shown to be imprecise in [5]. The algorithm of Gopal [41], based on dynamic versions of information-flow relations [15], may compute non-terminating slices under certain loop conditions.

Agrawal and Horgan [5] have developed dynamic slicing on top of dependence graphs. They present four algorithms differing in precision and complexity:

(1) During execution of the program the nodes of the executed statements are marked. The approximate dynamic slice is then computed by doing a static slice on the node induced subgraph of the program's PDG.

(2) During execution, the dependence edges relating to the data and control dependences of the executed statements are marked. The approximate dynamic slice is done on the edge induced subgraph.

(3) For each execution of a statement a new node is generated. The data and control dependence of the executed statement to a certain execution of another statement generates an edge between the related node instances. The resulting graph is called *Dynamic Dependence Graph*. This algorithm is much more precise than the first two, however, its space requirement is much larger: In the worst case, it is equivalent to the amount of executed statements.

(4) To reduce the space requirement of the third algorithm, a reduction can be used that merges nodes with the same transitive dependences, resulting in a *Reduced Dynamic Dependence Graph*.

This work has been extended to *interprocedural* dynamic slicing in [3]. Kamkar's algorithms [63] are similar and focus on interprocedural dynamic slicing. An approach to interprocedural flowback analysis is presented in [28].

If the computed dynamic slices have to be executable, the use of unstructured control flow requires special treatment, like in static slicing. Algorithms for such circumstances have been developed by Korel [67] and Huynh [61].

To overcome the space requirements of dynamic dependence graphs, Goswami and Mall [43] have suggested to compute the graphs based on the paths between loop entries and exits. If the same path is traversed in a later iteration of the loop, the earlier execution of the path is ignored. Obviously, this produces incorrect dynamic slices: Consider a loop that contains two alternating paths A and B through the loop. Assume an execution where the loop is iterated at least four times, and the B path is executed at last; such an execution will be similar to ... $ABAB$. The suggested algorithm will now only consider AB as an execution and will omit dependences originating from statements in B going to statements in A.

A correct and efficient technique has been presented by Mund *et al* [89]: Their dynamic slicing algorithm uses the standard PDG where unstable edges are handled separately. Unstable edges are data dependence edges reaching the same target node, and additionally, their source nodes define the same variable. During execution the unstable edges are marked corresponding to which some of them has been executed lately and the dynamic slice for each node is updated accordingly. Its space complexity is $O(n^2)$ where n is the number of statements in the program. The authors claim that the time complexity is also $O(n^2)$, which is clearly wrong as it must be dependent on the number of executed statements N. Thus, the time complexity must be at least $O(nN)$.

Beszédes *et al* [17] have developed a technique that computes dynamic slices for each executed statement during execution. They employ a special representation, which combines control and data dependence. During execution, the presented algorithm keeps track of the points of the last definition for any used variable. An implementation of the algorithm is able to slice ANSI C including unstructured control flow and procedure calls.

Most dynamic slicing approaches require static analysis as a preprocessing phase where data and control dependences are computed and stored in an intermediate representation. In [116], this preprocessing phase is limited or even eliminated.

Dynamic slicing has been formalized based on natural semantics in [44]. This leads to a generic, language-independent dynamic slicing analysis, which can be instantiated for imperative, logic or functional languages.

Extensions for object-oriented programs are straightforward. Ohata *et al* [92] includes lightweight tracing information like tracing procedure calls [91]. Such an approach, called *hybrid slicing*, has been presented earlier by Gupta and Soffa [47].

Extensions to dynamic slicing for concurrent programs have been presented in [27, 34, 42, 64, 68].

Hall [48] has presented another form of dynamic slicing: *Simultaneous dynamic slicing*, where a dynamic slice for a set of inputs is computed. This is not just the union of the dynamic slices for each of the inputs, as the union may not result in a correct dynamic slice for an input [33]. Beszédes [16] uses unions of dynamic slices to approximate the minimal static slice.

Between static and dynamic slicing lies *quasi static slicing*, presented by Venkatesh [112], where only some of the input variables have a fixed value (as specified in the slicing criterion) and the others may vary like in static slicing. A generalization is *conditioned slicing* [25, 31]: The input variables are constrained by first order logic formula. A similar approach is *parametric program slicing*, presented by Field *et al* [37].

Surveys on dynamic slicing approaches can be found in [70, 107].

6.5. *Other refinements*

The SeeSlice slicing tool [10] already included some of the presented focusing and visualization techniques, e.g. the distance-limited slicing, visualizing distances, etc. The slicer of the CANTO environment [7] can be used in a stepping mode which is similar to distance-limited slicing: At each step the slice grows by considering one step of data or control dependence.

A *decomposition slice* [39] is basically a slice for a variable at all statements writing that variable. The decomposition slice is used to form a graph using the partial ordering induced by proper subset inclusion of the decomposition slices for all variables. Beck and Eichmann [14] use slicing to isolate statements of a module that influence an exported behavior. Their work uses *interface dependence graphs* and *interface slicing*.

Set operations on slices produce various variants: Chopping uses intersection of a backward and a forward slice. The intersection of two forward or two backward slices is called a *backbone slice*. Dicing [85] is the subtraction of two slices. However, set operations on slices need special attention because the union of two slices may not produce a valid slice [33].

Orso *et al* [93] present a slicing algorithm which augments edges with types, and restricts reachability onto a set of types, creating slices restricted to these types. Their algorithm needs to compute the summary edges specific to each slice. However, it only works for programs without recursion.

In *amorphous program slicing* [51], a slice is generated by any simplifying transformation, not only by statement deletion. Binkley [23] has shown how to compute amorphous slices with dependence graphs.

7. Available Systems

Most of the slicing systems had been research prototypes and were not available or vanished in the last years. Some comparative studies have been done to subsets of formerly available slicers [56]. None of these slicers is still available and to the author's knowledge, only the three following tools are available to the public.

7.1. *CodeSurfer*

The commercially available CodeSurfer [6] is the successor of the Wisconsin Program-Integration System. It is the most advanced, complete and stable slicing tool. Its primary target is program understanding of ANSI C programs.

It can visualize call graphs graphically; procedures are textually visualized. For better usability, other elements like variables or files can be browsed hierarchically. Programs can be sliced and chopped in various way. The main data structure is the system dependence graph of a program. CodeSurfer can be programmed using its scripting language (Scheme). The scripting has access to the complete dependence graphs through an API. Thus, CodeSurfer can be used as an infrastructure for other program analyses.

7.2. *Sprite*

Sprite is a slicing tool built on top of Icaria and Ponder [9,87]. Ponder is a language independent infrastructure to build tools for performing syntactic and semantic analyses of large software systems. Icaria is the language dependent component for ANSI C and contains the Sprite tool, which is able to slice ANSI C. It contains a textual visualization of slices and is able to do typical set operations on slices. The implemented slicing tool uses a Weiser-style algorithm via data flow analysis iterating over a control flow graph. All three tools are freely available.

7.3. *Unravel*

Unravel [84] is a prototype tool that can be used to evaluate ANSI C source code statically by using program slicing. In its target to evaluate high integrity software it is similar to the VALSOFT system [77]. However, it is limited to the computation of forward and backward slices, which can be combined using set operations. The implemented Weiser-style algorithm is based on data flow equations and control flow graphs.

References

1. G. Agrawal and L. Guo, "Evaluating explicitly context-sensitive program slicing", *Workshop on Program Analysis for Software Tools and Engineering* (2001) 6–12.
2. H. Agrawal, "On slicing programs with jump statements", *SIGPLAN Conference on Programming Language Design and Implementation* (1994) 302–312.
3. H. Agrawal, R. A. DeMillo and E. H. Spafford, "Dynamic slicing in the presence of unconstrained pointers", *Symposium on Testing, Analysis, and Verification* (1991) 60–73.
4. H. Agrawal, R. A. DeMillo and E. H. Spafford, "Debugging with dynamic slicing and backtracking", *Software, Practice and Experience* **23**, no. 6 (June 1993) 589–616.
5. H. Agrawal and J. R. Horgan, "Dynamic program slicing", *Proceedings of the ACM SIGPLAN '90 Conference on Programming Language Design and Implementation* (1990) 246–256.
6. P. Anderson and T. Teitelbaum, "Software inspection using codesurfer", *Workshop on Inspection in Software Engineering (CAV 2001)*, 2001.
7. G. Antoniol, R. Fiutem, G. Lutteri, P. Tonella, S. Zanfei and E. Merlo, "Program understanding and maintenance with the CANTO environment", *International Conference on Software Maintenance* (1997) 72–81.
8. D. C. Atkinson and W. G. Griswold, "Effective whole-program analysis in the presence of pointers", *Foundations of Software Engineering* (1998) 46–55.
9. D. C. Atkinson and W. G. Griswold, "Implementation techniques for efficient dataflow analysis of large programs", *Proceedings of the International Conference on Software Maintenance* (2001) 52–61.
10. T. Ball and S. G. Eick, "Visualizing program slices", *IEEE Symposium on Visual Languages* (1994) 288–295.
11. T. Ball and S. Horwitz, "Slicing programs with arbitrary control-flow", *Automated and Algorithmic Debugging* (1993) 206–222.
12. F. Balmas, "Displaying dependence graphs: A hierarchical approach", *Proceedings of the Eighth Working Conference on Reverse Engineering* (2001) 261–270.
13. S. Bates and S. Horwitz, "Incremental program testing using program dependence graphs", *Conference Record of the Twentieth ACM SIGPLAN-SIGACT Symposium on Principles of Programming Languages* (1993) 384–396.
14. J. Beck and D. Eichmann, "Program and interface slicing for reverse engineering", *IEEE/ACM 15th Conference on Software Engineering (ICSE'93)* (1993) 509–518.
15. J.-F. Bergeretti and B. A. Carré, "Information-flow and data-flow analysis of whileprograms", *ACM Transactions on Programming Languages and Systems* **7**, no. 1 (January 1985) 37–61.
16. Á. Beszédes, C. Faragó, Z. M. Szabó, J. Csirik and T. Gyimóthy, "Union slices for program maintenance", *International Conference on Software Maintenance (ICSM'02)* (2002) 12–21.

17. Á. Beszédes, T. Gergely, Z. M. Szabó, J. Csirik and T. Gyimothy, "Dynamic slicing method for maintenance of large C programs", *Proceedings of the Fifth Conference on Software Maintenance and Reengineering, CSMR 2001* (2001) 105–113.

18. J. M. Bieman and L. M. Ott, "Measuring functional cohesion", *IEEE Transactions on Software Engineering* **20**, no. 8 (August 1994) 644–657.

19. D. Binkley, "Using semantic differencing to reduce the cost of regression testing", *Proceedings of the International Conference on Software Maintenance* (1992) 41–50.

20. D. Binkley and M. Harman, "A large-scale empirical study of forward and backward static slice size and context sensitivity", *International Conference on Software Maintenance* (2003) 44–53.

21. D. Binkley, "Precise executable interprocedural slices", *ACM Letters on Programming Languages and Systems* **2**, no. 1–4 (1993) 31–45.

22. D. Binkley, "The application of program slicing to regression testing", *Information and Software Technology* **40**, no. 11–12 (1998) 583–594.

23. D. Binkley, "Computing amorphous program slices using dependence graphs and a data-flow model", *ACM Symposium on Applied Computing* (1999) 519–525.

24. D. W. Binkley and J. R. Lyle, "Application of the pointer state subgraph to static program slicing", *The Journal of Systems and Software* (1998) 17–27.

25. G. Canfora, A. Cimitile and A. De Lucia. "Conditioned program slicing", *Information and Software Technology* **40**, no. 11–12 (1998) 595–607.

26. J. Cheng. "Dependence analysis of parallel and distributed programs and its applications", *International Conference on Advances in Parallel and Distributed Computing*, 1997.

27. J. Cheng, "Slicing concurrent programs", *Automated and Algorithmic Debugging, 1st International Workshop, AADEBUG'93, Lecture Notes in Computer Science 749* (Springer, 1993) 223–240.

28. J.-D. Choi, B. Miller and R. Netzer, "Techniques for debugging parallel programs with flowback analysis", *ACM Transactions on Programming Languages and Systems* **13**, no. 4 (October 1991) 491–530.

29. J.-D. Choi and J. Ferrante, "Static slicing in the presence of goto statements", *ACM Transactions on Programming Languages and Systems* **16**, no. 4 (1994) 1097–1113.

30. E. M. Clarke, M. Fujita, S. P. Rajan, T. W. Reps, S. Shankar and T. Teitelbaum, "Program slicing of hardware description languages", *Conference on Correct Hardware Design and Verification Methods* (1999) 298–312.

31. S. Danicic, C. Fox, M. Harman and R. Hierons, "Consit: A conditioned program slicer", *International Conference on Software Maintenance* (2000) 216–226.

32. A. De Lucia, "Program slicing: Methods and applications", *IEEE Workshop on Source Code Analysis and Manipulation (SCAM 2001)*, 2001, Invited paper.

33. A. De Lucia, M. Harman, R. Hierons and J. Krinke, "Unions of slices are not slices", *7th European Conference on Software Maintenance and Reengineering*, 2003.

34. E. Duesterwald, R. Gupta and M. L. Soffa, "Distributed slicing and partial re-execution for distributed programs", *5th Workshop on Languages and Compilers for Parallel Computing, Lecture Notes in Computer Science 757* (Springer, 1992) 497–511.

35. M. D. Ernst, "Practical fine-grained static slicing of optimized code", Technical Report MSR-TR-94-14, Microsoft Research, Redmond, WA, July 1994.

36. J. Ferrante, K. J. Ottenstein and J. D. Warren, "The program dependence graph and its use in optimization", *ACM Transactions on Programming Languages and Systems* **9**, no. 3 (July 1987) 319–349.

37. J. Field, G. Ramalingam and F. Tip, "Parametric program slicing", *Conference Record of the 22nd ACM Symposium on Principles of Programming Languages* (1995) 379–392.

38. M. A. Francel and S. Rugaber, "The value of slicing while debugging", *Proceedings of the 7th International Workshop on Program Comprehension* (2001) 151–169.

39. K. B. Gallagher and J. R. Lyle, "Using program slicing in software maintenance", *IEEE Transactions on Software Engineering* **17**, no. 8 (1991) 751–761.

40. R. Gerber and S. Hong, "Slicing real-time programs for enhanced schedulability", *ACM Transactions on Programming Languages and Systems* **13**, no. 3 (1997) 525–555.

41. R. Gopal, "Dynamic program slicing based on dependence relations", *Conference on Software Maintenance* (1991) 191–200.

42. D. Goswami and R. Mall, "Dynamic slicing of concurrent programs," *High Performance Computing — HiPC 2000, 7th International Conference, Lecture Notes in Computer Science 1970* (2000) 15–26.

43. D. Goswami and R. Mall, "An efficient method for computing dynamic program slices", *Information Processing Letters* (2002) 111–117.

44. V. Gouranton and D. Le Metayer, "Dynamic slicing: A generic analysis based on a natural semantics format", *Journal of Logic and Computation* **9**, no. 6 (1999) 835–871.

45. W. G. Griswold, "Making slicing practical: The final mile", 2001. Invited Talk, PASTE'01.

46. R. Gupta, M. J. Harrold and M. L. Soffa, "An approach to regression testing using slicing", *Proceedings of the IEEE Conference on Software Maintenance* (1992) 299–308.

47. R. Gupta and M. L. Soffa, "Hybrid slicing: An approach for refining static slices using dynamic information", *Proceedings of SIGSOFT'95 Third ACM SIGSOFT Symposium on the Foundations of Software Engineering* (1995) 29–40.

48. R. J. Hall, "Automatic extraction of executable program subsets by simultaneous dynamic program slicing", *Automated Software Engineering* **2**, no. 1 (March 1995) 33–53.

49. C. Hammer and G. Snelting, "An improved slicer for Java", *Workshop on Program Analysis for Software Tools and Engineering (PASTE'04)*, 2004.

50. M. Harman and S. Danicic, "A new algorithm for slicing unstructured programs", *Journal of Software Maintenance* **10**, no. 6 (1998) 415–441.

51. M. Harman and S. Danicic, "Amorphous program slicing", *5th IEEE International Workshop on Program Comprehension (IWPC'97)* (1997) 70–79.

52. M. Harman and K. B. Gallagher, "Program slicing", *Information and Software Technology* **40**, no. 11–12 (1998) 577–581.

53. J. Hatcliff, J. C. Corbett, M. B. Dwyer, S. Sokolowski and H. Zheng, "A formal study of slicing for multi-threaded programs with JVM concurrency primitives", *Static Analysis Symposium, Lecture Notes in Computer Science 1694* (Springer, 1999) 1–18.

54. J. Hatcliff, M. B. Dwyer and H. Zheng, "Slicing software for model construction", *Higher-Order and Symbolic Computation* **13**, no. 4 (2000) 315–353.

55. M. P. E. Heimdahl and M. W. Whalen, "Reduction and slicing of hierarchical state machines", *Proceedings of the Sixth European Software Engineering Conference (ESEC/FSE 97)* (1997) 450–467.

56. T. Hoffner, M. Kamkar and P. Fritzson, "Evaluation of program slicing tools", *2nd International Workshop on Automated and Algorithmic Debugging (AADEBUG)* (1995) 51–69.

57. S. Horwitz and T. Reps, "Efficient comparison of program slices", *Acta Informatica* **28** (1991) 713–732.
58. S. Horwitz, "Identifying the semantic and textual differences between two versions of a program", *Proceedings of the ACM SIGPLAN '90 Conference on Programming Language Design and Implementation* (1990) 234–245.
59. S. Horwitz, J. Prins and T. Reps, "Integrating noninterfering versions of programs", *ACM Transactions on Programming Languages and Systems* **11**, no. 4 (July 1989) 345–387.
60. S. B. Horwitz, T. W. Reps and D. Binkley, "Interprocedural slicing using dependence graphs", *ACM Transactions on Programming Languages and Systems* **12**, no. 1 (January 1990) 26–60.
61. D. Huynh and Y. Song, "Forward computation of dynamic slicing in the presence of structured jump statements", *Proceedings of ISACC'97* (1997) 73–81.
62. D. Jackson and E. J. Rollins, "A new model of program dependences for reverse engineering", *Proceedings of the Second ACM SIGSOFT Symposium on Foundations of Software Engineering* (1994) 2–10.
63. M. Kamkar, P. Fritzson and N. Shahmerhi, "Three approaches to interprocedural dynamic slicing", *Microprocessing and Microprogramming* **38** (1993) 625–636.
64. M. Kamkar and P. Krajina, "Dynamic slicing of distributed programs", *International Conference on Software Maintenance* (1995) 222–231.
65. A. Kiss, J. Jasz, G. Lehotai and T. Gymothy, "Interprocedural slicing of binary executables", *Proceedings of the Third IEEE International Workshop on Source Code Analysis and Manipulation* (2003) 118–127.
66. R. Komondoor and S. Horwitz, "Using slicing to identify duplication in source code", *Eighth International Static Analysis Symposium (SAS), Lecture Notes in Computer Science 2126* (2001).
67. B. Korel, "Computation of dynamic slices for unstructured programs", *IEEE Transactions on Software Engineering* **23**, no. 1 (1997) 17–34.
68. B. Korel and R. Ferguson, "Dynamic slicing of distributed programs", *Applied Mathematics and Computer Science Journal* **2**, no. 2 (1992) 199–215.
69. B. Korel and J. Laski, "Dynamic program slicing", *Information Processing Letters* **29**, no. 3 (October 1988) 155–163.
70. B. Korel and J. Rilling, "Dynamic program slicing methods", *Information and Software Technology* **40**, no. 11–12 (1998) 647–659.
71. J. Krinke, "Static slicing of threaded programs", *Proceedings of the ACM SIGPLAN/SIGFSOFT Workshop on Program Analysis for Software Tools and Engineering (PASTE'98)* (ACM Press, 1998) 35–42, ACM SIGPLAN Notices 33(7).
72. J. Krinke, "Identifying similar code with program dependence graphs", *Proceedings of the Eighth Working Conference on Reverse Engineering* (2001) 301–309.
73. J. Krinke, "Evaluating context-sensitive slicing and chopping", *Proceedings of the International Conference on Software Maintenance* (2002) 22–31.
74. J. Krinke, "Context-sensitive slicing of concurrent programs", *Proceedings of the ESEC/FSE* (2003) 178–187.
75. J. Krinke, "Slicing, chopping, and path conditions with barriers", *Software Quality Journal* **12**, no. 4 (December 2004) 339–360.
76. J. Krinke, "Visualization of program dependence and slices", *Proceedings of the International Conference on Software Maintenance* (2004) 168–177.
77. J. Krinke and G. Snelting, "Validation of measurement software as an application of slicing and constraint solving", *Information and Software Technology* **40**, no. 11–12 (December 1998) 661–675.

78. S. Kumar and S. Horwitz, "Better slicing of programs with jumps and switches", *Proceedings of FASE 2002: Fundamental Approaches to Software Engineering, Lecture Notes in Computer Science 2306* (Springer, 2002) 96–112.

79. A. Lakhotia and J.-C. Deprez, "Restructuring programs by tucking statements into functions", *Information and Software Technology* **40**, no. 11–12 (1998) 677–690.

80. F. Lanubile and G. Visaggio, "Extracting reusable functions by flow graph-based program slicing", *IEEE Transactions on Software Engineering* **23**, no. 4 (April 1997) 246–259.

81. L. Larsen and M. J. Harrold, "Slicing object-oriented software", *18th International Conference on Software Engineering* (1996) 495–505.

82. D. Liang and M. J. Harrold, "Slicing objects using system dependence graphs", *Proceedings of the International Conference on Software Maintenance* (1998) 358–367.

83. D. Liang and M. J. Harrold, "Efficient points-to analysis for whole-program analysis", *Proceedings of the 7th European Software Engineering Conference and 7th ACM SIGSOFT Foundations of Software Engineering* (1999) 199–215.

84. J. Lyle and D. Wallace, "Using the unravel program slicing tool to evaluate high integrity software", *Proceedings of Software Quality Week*, 1997.

85. J. R. Lyle and M. Weiser, "Automatic program bug location by program slicing", *2nd International Conference on Computers and Applications* (1987) 877–882.

86. L. I. Millett and T. Teitelbaum, "Issues in slicing promela and its applications to model checking, protocol understanding, and simulation", *International Journal on Software Tools for Technology Transfer* **2**, no. 4 (2000) 343–349.

87. M. Mock, D. C. Atkinson, C. Chambers and S. J. Eggers, "Improving program slicing with dynamic points-to data", *Proceedings of the 10th International Symposium on the Foundations of Software Engineering*, 2002.

88. M. Müller-Olm and H. Seidl, "On optimal slicing of parallel programs", *STOC 2001 (33th ACM Symposium on Theory of Computing)* (2001) 647–656.

89. G. B. Mund, R. Mall and S. Sarkar, "An efficient dynamic program slicing technique", *Information and Software Technology* **44**, no. 2 (2002) 123–132.

90. M. G. Nanda and S. Ramesh, "Slicing concurrent programs", *International Conference on Software Testing and Analysis (ISSTA 2000)* (2000) 180–190.

91. A. Nishimatsu, M. Jihira, S. Kusumoto and K. Inoue, "Call-mark slicing: An efficient and economical way of reducing slice", *International Conference of Software Engineering* (1999) 422–431.

92. F. Ohata, K. Hirose, M. Fujii and K. Inoue, "A slicing method for object-oriented programs using lightweight dynamic information", *Proceedings of the 8th Asia-Pacific Software Engineering Conference*, 2001.

93. A. Orso, S. Sinha and M. J. Harrold, "Incremental slicing based on data-dependences types", *International Conference on Software Maintenance*, 2001.

94. L. M. Ott and J. M. Bieman, "Program slices as an abstraction for cohesion measurement", *Information and Software Technology* **40**, no. 11–12 (1998) 691–700.

95. K. J. Ottenstein and L. M. Ottenstein, "The program dependence graph in a software development environment", *Proceedings of the ACM SIGSOFT/SIGPLAN Software Engineering Symposium on Practical Software Development Environments, ACM SIGPLAN Notices* **19**, no. 5 (1984) 177–184.

96. J. Reichwein, G. Rothermel and M. M. Burnett, "Slicing spreadsheets: An integrated methodology for spreadsheet testing and debugging", *Conference on Domain Specific Languages* (1999) 25–38.

97. T. Reps, S. Horwitz, M. Sagiv and G. Rosay, "Speeding up slicing", *Proceedings of the ACM SIGSOFT '94 Symposium on the Foundations of Software Engineering* (1994) 11–20.

98. T. Reps and G. Rosay, "Precise interprocedural chopping", *Proceedings of the 3rd ACM Symposium on the Foundations of Software Engineering* (1995) 41–52.

99. F. Ricca and P. Tonella, "Web application slicing", *International Conference on Software Maintenance* (2001) 148–157.

100. T. Robschink and G. Snelting, "Efficient path conditions in dependence graphs", *Proceedings of the 24th International Conference of Software Engineering (ICSE)* (2002) 478–488.

101. M. Shapiro and S. Horwitz, "The effects of the precision of pointer analysis", *Proceedings from the 4th International Static Analysis Symposium, Lecture Notes in Computer Science 1302* (1997) 16–34.

102. S. Sinha, M. J. Harrold and G. Rothermel, "System-dependence-graph-based slicing of programs with arbitrary interprocedural control flow", *International Conference on Software Engineering* (1999) 432–441.

103. S. Sinha, M. J. Harrold and G. Rothermel, "Interprocedural control dependence", *ACM Transactions on Software Engineering and Methodology* **10**, no. 2 (2001) 209–254.

104. G. Snelting, "Combining slicing and constraint solving for validation of measurement software", *Static Analysis Symposium, Lecture Notes in Computer Science 1145* (Springer, 1996) 332–348.

105. C. Steindl, "Benefits of a data flow-aware programming environment", *Workshop on Program Analysis for Software Tools and Engineering (PASTE'99)*, 1999.

106. F. Tip, J-D Choi, J. Field and G. Ramalingam, "Slicing class hierarchies in C++", *Conference on Object-oriented Programming Systems, Languages and Applications* (1996) 179–197.

107. F. Tip, "A survey of program slicing techniques', *Journal of Programming Languages* **3**, no. 3 (September 1995).

108. F. Tip and T. B. Dinesh, "A slicing-based approach for locating type errors", *ACM Transactions on Software Engineering and Methodology* **10**, no. 1 (January 2001) 5–55.

109. P. Tonella, G. Antoniol, R. Fiutem and E. Merlo, "Flow insensitive C++ pointers and polymorphism analysis and its application to slicing", *Proceedings of the 19th International Conference on Software Engineering (ICSE '97)* (1997) 433–444.

110. W. W. Vasconcelos, "A flexible framework for dynamic and static slicing of logic programs", *Proceedings of PADL'99, Lecture Notes in Computers Science 1551* (1999) 259–274.

111. W. W. Vasconcelos and M. A. T. Aragao, "Slicing knowledge-based systems: Techniques and applications", *Knowledge Based Systems* **13**, no. 4 (2000).

112. G. A. Venkatesh, "The semantic approach to program slicing", *Proceedings of the ACM SIGPLAN '91 Conference on Programming Language Design and Implementation* (1991) 26–28.

113. M. Weiser, "Program slices: formal, psychological, and practical investigations of an automatic program abstraction method", PhD Thesis, University of Michigan, Ann Arbor (1979).

114. M. Weiser, "Programmers use slices when debugging", *Communications of the ACM* **25**, no. 7 (1982) 446–452.

115. M. Weiser, "Program slicing", *IEEE Transactions on Software Engineering* **10**, no. 4 (July 1984) 352–357.

116. X. Zhang, R. Gupta and Y. Zhang, "Precise dynamic slicing algorithms", *IEEE/ ACM International Conference on Software Engineering (ICSE)* (2003) 319–329.
117. J. Zhao, J. Cheng and K. Ushijima, "Static slicing of concurrent object-oriented programs", *Proceedings of the 20th IEEE Annual International Computer Software and Applications Conference* (1996) 312–320.

SIMULATION-BASED SOFTWARE PROCESS MODELING AND EVALUATION

OVE ARMBRUST*, THOMAS BERLAGE†, THOMAS HANNE‡, PATRICK LANG‡,
JÜRGEN MÜNCH*, HOLGER NEU*, STEFAN NICKEL‡, IOANA RUS§,
ALEX SARISHVILI‡, SASCHA VAN STOCKUM† and ANDREAS WIRSEN‡

*Fraunhofer IESE, Sauerwiesen 6,
67661 Kaiserslautern, Germany
E-mail: {armbrust, munch, neu}@iese.fraunhofer.de

†Fraunhofer FIT, Schloss Birlinghoven,
53754 Sankt Augustin, Germany
E-mail: {berlage, stockum}@fit.fraunhofer.de

‡Fraunhofer ITWM, Gottlieb-Daimler-Str., Geb. 49,
67663 Kaiserslautern, Germany
E-mail: {hanne, lang, nickel, sarishvili, wirsen}@itwm.fraunhofer.de

§Fraunhofer USA Center for Experimental Software Engineering,
College Park MD 20742-3290, USA
E-mail: irus@fc-md.umd.edu

Decision support for planning and improving software development projects is a crucial success factor. The special characteristics of software development aggregate these tasks in contrast to the planning of many other processes, such as production processes. Process simulation can be used to support decisions on process alternatives on the basis of existing knowledge. Thereby, new development knowledge can be gained faster and more cost effective.

This chapter gives a short introduction to experimental software engineering, describes simulation approaches within that area, and introduces a method for systematically developing discrete-event software process simulation models. Advanced simulation modeling techniques will point out key problems and possible solutions, including the use of visualization techniques for better simulation result interpretation.

Keywords: Software process modeling, data analysis, simulation, human resources, decision support, visualization, scheduling, optimization.

1. Introduction

Simulation is widely used in many sciences. For example, in molecular chemistry or biology, simulation helps to reduce costs by lowering the number of real experiments needed. In industrial contexts, simulation helps to lower costs, for example, in car construction, by replacing real crash tests with virtual ones.

---

*Corresponding author.

Experimental software engineering, as a profession that heavily involves experiments with the (cost-intensive) involvement of human subjects, is obviously very interested in using simulation. Here, simulation promises to save cost and time. As a rather young profession, (experimental) software engineering has only recently started to discover and use the benefits of simulation. When implemented, real experiments already yield good results, for example, in choosing a reading technique for inspections in a certain context. Still, the required experiments cost a lot of money, which companies naturally dislike, despite the benefits. But as in other professions, simulation or virtual experimentation can also be of assistance in software engineering.

In this chapter, we will give a short introduction to experimental software engineering, then describe discrete and continuous simulation approaches within that area, and introduce a method for systematically developing discrete-event software process simulation models. Advanced simulation modeling techniques such as the integration of empirical knowledge, the use of knowledge-discovery techniques, modeling human resources, optimization and visualization as well as the topic of model reuse will point out key problems and possible solutions.

The rest of the chapter is organized as follows. Section 2 introduces the underlying discipline of experimental software engineering. Section 3 gives an introduction to simulation approaches. Section 4 describes a method for systematically creating discrete-event simulation models. Section 5.1 explains the integration of empirical knowledge into simulation models, Sec. 5.2 the use of knowledge discovery techniques for use in simulation modeling. Human resource modeling is described in Sec. 5.3, visualization issues in Sec. 5.4, model reuse in Sec. 5.5, and optimization in Sec. 5.5. Section 5.6 explains optimization issues. Some conclusions are drawn in Sec. 6.

2. Experimental Software Engineering

Many efforts have been made in the field of software engineering in order to contribute to one goal: To develop software in a controlled manner so that quality, costs, and time needed can be predicted with high precision. Other goals include the overall reduction of development time and costs, and a general increase in product quality. No single best approach can be identified to achieve these goals, since software development is human-based and heavily depends on the context (such as organizational constraints, development methods, or personnel characteristics). Following Rombach *et al* [1], three different approaches to study the discipline of software engineering can be identified:

- the mathematical or formal methods approach,
- the system building approach,
- and the empirical studies approach.

Regarding the empirical approach, the word "empirical", derived from the Greek "empeirikós" (from "émpeiros" = experienced, skillful), means "drawn from experience". This suggests that data from the real world is analyzed in order to understand the connections and interrelations expressed in the measured data. This is an important issue in the empirical approach: The data must be measured somehow. Measuring empirical data is not trivial. On the contrary, many wrong decisions are based on incorrectly measured or interpreted data [2].

The aim of the empirical approach consists of two parts: Observing the real world correctly (with correct measurement and interpretation of the data measured), and coming to the right conclusions from the data measured. The latter concerns selection and usage of techniques, methods, and tools for software development as well as activities like resource allocation, staffing, and scheduling.

In order to improve software development performance, experimenting with changes to the current situation or alternatives is necessary. Generally, this is achieved by determining the current situation, then changing some parameters and evaluating the results. Evaluating a new technique across several projects, however, is difficult due to the different contexts. Additionally, whatever is proven by one experiment must not necessarily be true for other contexts [3].

Unfortunately, experimenting is a rather expensive way of gathering knowledge about a certain technique, method, or tool. The costs can be divided into two main parts.

First, the experiment itself must be conducted, that is, the experimental setup must be determined, the experiment needs to be prepared and carried out, the data must be analyzed, and the results evaluated. These are the obvious costs, which can be measured easily. Basili *et al* [4] estimate the costs for conducting an experiment to be at least $500 per subject per day.

The second part consists of risks (of delaying the delivery of a product, or using an immature technology). If a new technique is tested in a controlled experiment or a case study, for example, before it is used during development, this ensures that no immature or unsuitable technique is used in real life. Since software development is human-based, human subjects are needed for the experiment. During the experiment, they cannot carry out their normal tasks, which may result in delays, especially in time-critical projects. Competitors not carrying out experiments may be able to deliver earlier. These costs are not easily calculated. Still, in terms of product quality, delivery time, and person hours, using immature or unsuitable techniques is, in most cases, more expensive than experimenting.

3. Simulation and Experimental Software Engineering

Simulation is increasingly being used in software process modeling and analysis. After concentrating on static process modeling for a long time, software engineers are beginning to realize the benefits of modeling dynamic behavior and simulating process performance. These benefits can be seen, for instance, in the areas of strategic management of software development, operational process improvement, or training situations [5]. Depending on the respective purpose, the simulation focus ranges from lifecycle modeling (for long-term strategic simulation) to small parts of development, for example, a code inspection (for training purposes).

Three main benefits of software process simulation can be identified: Cost, time, and knowledge improvements. Cost improvements originate from the fact that conventional experiments are very costly. The people needed as experimental subjects are usually professional developers. This makes every experimentation hour expensive, since the subjects get paid while not immediately contributing to the company's earnings. Conducting a simulation instead of a real experiment saves these costs.

Time benefits can be expected from the fact that simulations can be run at (almost) any desired speed. While an experiment with a new project management technique may take months, the simulation may be sped up almost arbitrarily by simply having simulation time pass faster than real time. On the other hand, simulation time may be slowed down arbitrarily. This might be useful in a software engineering context when too much data is accumulated in too little time, and therefore cannot be analyzed properly. The time benefits result in shorter experimental cycles and accelerate learning about processes and technologies.

Knowledge benefits can be expected in two areas: New knowledge about the effects of technologies in different areas (e.g. performing replications in different contexts, such as having less experienced subjects) contributes to a better understanding of the software development process. Scenario-oriented training, for example, improves individual workforce capabilities. Using a simulation environment such as the one introduced in [6] enables the trainee to experience immediate feedback to his decisions: Their consequences do not occur months after the decision, but minutes. This way, the complex feedback loops can be better understood and mistakes can be made without endangering everyday business [7].

There are several simulation techniques available. Which one to choose depends on the model purpose. Two major approaches can be distinguished: The continuous approach and the discrete approach. A hybrid approach combines both, to overcome their specific disadvantages. In addition to that, there are several state- and rule-based approaches, as well as queuing models [8]. We will introduce the continuous approach and the discrete approach successively.

3.1. *Continuous simulation modeling*

In the early 1970s, the Club of Rome started an initiative to study the future of human activity on our planet [9]. A research group at the Massachusetts Institute of Technology (MIT) developed a societal model of the world. After a smaller-scale dynamic urban model, this was the first large continuous simulation model: The World Model [10].

Today, most continuous models are based on differential equations and/or iterations, which take several input variables for calculation and, in turn, supply output variables. The model itself consists of nodes connected through variables. The nodes may be instantaneous or non-instantaneous functions. Instantaneous functions present their output at the same time the input is available. Non-instantaneous functions take some time for their output to change after the input changes.

This approach of a network of functions allows simulating real processes continuously. An analogy would be the construction of mathematical functions (add, subtract, multiply, integrate) with analog components like resistors, spools, or condensers. Before computers became as powerful as they are today, this approach was the only way to solve that kind of equations in a reasonable time. Due to the continuous nature of the "solver", the result could be measured instantly.

Of course, simulating this continuous system on a computer is not possible due to the digital technology used. To cope with this, the state of the system is computed at very short intervals, thereby forming a sufficiently correct illusion of continuity. This iterative recalculating makes continuous models simulated on digital systems grow complex very quickly.

In the software engineering context, continuous simulation is used primarily for large-scale views of processes, like management of a complete development project, or strategic enterprise management. Dynamic modeling enables us to model feedback loops, which are very numerous and complex in software projects.

3.2. *Discrete simulation modeling*

The discrete approach shows parallels to the clocked operations car manufacturers use in their production, with cars moving through the factory. The basic assumption is that the modeled system changes its state only at discrete moments of time, as opposed to the continuous model. This way, every discrete state of the model is characterized by a vector containing all variables, and each step corresponds to a change in the vector.

To give an example, let us consider a production line at a car manufacturer. The production is described by a finite number of working steps: Each work unit has to be completed in a certain fixed or stochastically described amount of time. When that time is over, the car-to-be is moved to the next position, where another work unit is applied, or waits in a buffer until the next position is available. This way, the car moves through the complete factory in discrete steps.

Simulating this behavior is easy with the discrete approach. Each time a move is completed, a snapshot is taken of all the production units. In this snapshot, the state of all work units and products (cars) is recorded. At the next snapshot, all cars have moved to the next position. The effects of the variable values at time t

are considered at time $t + 1$. The real time that passes between two snapshots or simulation steps can be arbitrary, usually the next snapshot of all variables is calculated and then the simulation assigns the respective values. Since the time needed in the factory for completion of a production step is known (or determined from a stochastic distribution), the model describes reality appropriately. A finer time grid is certainly possible: Instead of viewing every clock step as one simulation step, the arrival at a work position and the departure can be used, thereby capturing work and transport time independently.

The discrete approach is used in software engineering as well. One important area is experimental software engineering, e.g. concerning inspections. Here, a discrete simulation can be used to describe the product flow, which characterizes typical software development activities. Possible simulation steps might be the start and completion of activities and lags, together with special events like (late) design changes. This enables discrete models to represent queues.

4. Systematically Creating Discrete-Event Software Process Simulation Models

This section describes a method for developing discrete simulation models. For the lack of space, only the most important steps are outlined with short descriptions. For a more comprehensive description of the method, please refer to [11] and [12]. The description in this chapter considers the development of a new simulation model without reusing or incorporating existing components. If reuse is considered (either incorporating existing components or developing for reuse), then the method has to be changed to address possible reuse of elements (see Sec. 5.4).

4.1. *Identification and specification of simulator requirements*

During the requirements activity, the purpose and the usage of the model have to be defined. The questions that the model will have to answer are determined and so is the data that will be needed to answer these questions. Sub-activities of the requirements specification are:

4.1.1. *Definition of the goals, questions, and the necessary metrics*

A goal/question/metrics (GQM) [13], [14] based approach for defining the goal and the needed measures seems appropriate. GQM can also be used to define and start an initial measurement program if needed.

The purpose, scope and level of detail for the model are described by the goal. The questions that the model should help to answer are formulated next. Afterwards, parameters (metrics) of the model (outputs) have to be defined. Once their values are known, the questions of interest can be answered in principle. Then those model input values have to be defined that are necessary for determining the output values. The input values should not be considered as final and non-changing after the requirements phase; during the analysis phase, they usually change.

4.1.2. *Definition of usage scenarios*

Define scenarios ("use cases") for using the model. For example, for answering the question: "How does the effectiveness of inspections affect the cost and schedule of the project?", a corresponding scenario would be: "All input parameters are kept constant and the parameter inspection effectiveness is given x different values between a minimum and a maximum value. The simulator is executed until a certain value for the number of defects per KLOC is achieved, and the values for cost and duration are examined for each of the cases." For traceability purposes, scenarios should be tracked to the questions they answer.

4.1.3. *Test case development*

Test cases can be developed in the requirements phase. They help to verify and validate the model and the resulting simulation.

4.1.4. *Requirements validation*

The customer (who can be a real customer, or plainly the stakeholder of the simulated process) has to be involved in this activity and agree with the content of the resulting model specification document. Changes can be made, but they have to be documented.

4.2. *Process analysis and specification*

The specification and analysis of the process that is to be modeled is one of the most important activities during the development of a simulation model.

We divide process analysis and specification into four sub-activities, as shown in Fig. 4.3-1: Analysis and creation of a static process model (group a), creation of the influence diagram for describing the relationships between parameters of the process (b), collection and analysis of empirical data for deriving the quantitative relationships (c), and quantification of the relationships (d). Figure 4.3-1 sketches the product flow of this activity, i.e., it describes which artifacts (document symbol) are used or created in each step (circle symbol).

4.3. *Analysis and creation of a static process model*

The software process to be modeled needs to be understood and documented. This requires that the representations (abstractions) of the process should be sufficiently intuitive for being understood by the customer and for constituting a communication vehicle between modeler and customer. These representations lead to a

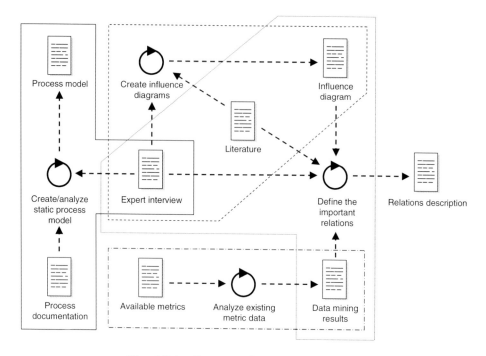

Fig. 4.3-1. Process analysis and specification.

common definition and understanding of the object of modeling (i.e., the software process), and a refinement of the problem to be modeled (initially formulated in the requirements specification activity). The created process model describes the artifacts used, the processes or activities performed, and the roles and tools involved. It shows which activities transform which artifacts and how the information flows through the process.

4.4. Creation of the influence diagram for describing the relationships between parameters of the process

For documenting the relationships between process parameters, we use influence diagrams. In the influence diagram, we start capturing the factors that influence the process. Influence factors are typically factors that change the result or behavior of the process. If these factors rise, they change the related factors. This is displayed by + and − at the arrows that depict the relationship.

When we draw the influence diagram, we should have in mind the inputs and outputs identified in the requirements phase. These inputs, and especially the outputs, have to be captured in the influence diagrams. Figure 4.4-1 presents an excerpt of a static process model and a corresponding influence diagram.

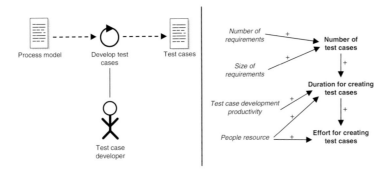

Fig. 4.4-1.   Static process model (left) and influence diagram (right).

4.5. *Collection and analysis of empirical data for deriving the quantitative relationships*

Depending on existing metrics, it is possible to use this metric data to calibrate the model. If a lack of data is identified, collecting data in the target organization during model development can fill this.

4.6. *Quantification of the relationships*

This is probably the hardest part of the analysis. Here, we have to quantify the relationships. Parameter types can be distinguished as follows:

Calibration parameters: For calibrating the model according to the organization, such as productivity values, learning, skills, and number of developers.

Project-specific input: For representing a specific project, such as number of test cases, modules, and size of the tasks.

Variable parameters: These are the parameters that are changed in order to record output variable behavior. In general, the variable parameters can be the same as the calibration parameters. The scenarios from the requirements or new scenarios determine the variable parameters during the model lifecycle.

Mathematical quantification is also done in this step. If historical metric data is available, it should be utilized, otherwise interviews with customers, experts, or bibliographic sources have to be used. The outputs of the process analysis and specification phase are:

- models (static, influence diagrams, and relationships) of the software development process,
- parameters that have to be simulated,
- measures (metrics) needed to be received from the real process, and
- a description of all the assumptions and decisions that are made during the analysis. The latter is useful for documenting the model for later maintenance and evolution.

Finally, several verification and validation steps must be performed here:

- The static model has to be validated against the requirements (to make sure it is within the scope, and also that it is complete for the goal stated in the requirements), and validated against the real process.
- The parameters in the influence diagram must be checked against the metrics for consistency, and the input and output variables of the requirements specification must also be checked.
- The relationships must be checked with respect to the influence diagram for completeness and consistency. All the factors of the influence diagram that influence the result have to be represented, for instance, by equations determining the relationships.

4.7. Model design

During this activity, the modeler develops the design of the model, which is independent of the implementation environment. The design is divided into different levels of detail, the high-level design and the detailed design.

4.7.1. High level design

Here, the surrounding infrastructure and the basic mechanisms describing how the input and output data is managed and represented are defined. Usually, the design comprises components like a database or a spreadsheet, a visualization component, and the simulation model itself, together with the information flows between them. The high level design is the latest point for deciding which type of simulation model should be created: System dynamics, discrete-event, or something else.

4.7.2. Detailed design

Here, the low level design of the simulation model is created. The designer has to decide on which activities have to be modeled (granularity, requirements, relationships), what the items are (granularity, requirements, relationships), and which attributes the items have. Additionally, the designer has to define the item flow in the model.

4.8. Implementation

During implementation, all the information and the design decisions are transferred into a simulation model. This activity in the development process heavily depends on the simulation tool or language used and is very similar to the implementation of a conventional software product.

4.9. *Validation and verification*

The model needs to be checked for its suitability about the purpose and the problems it should address, and to see if it sufficiently reflects reality (here the customer has to be involved).

Throughout the simulator development process, verification and validation should be performed after each activity. Furthermore, traceability between different products created during simulator development should be maintained to simplify model maintenance.

5. Advanced Simulation Modeling

In this section, we present some typical problems with simulation modeling, and possible solutions. First, we introduce a possible way to increase model validity by integrating empirical results. As an example, acquiring influence factors by knowledge extraction techniques is explained more thoroughly. Human resource modeling helps with considering personal and social aspects, and visualization techniques assist in interpreting simulation results. Reuse and optimization techniques lower the effort during modeling and when performing the modeled process.

5.1. *Increasing model validity: Integration of empirical studies*

Since one of the goals of software process simulation modeling is to gain knowledge about the real world, the model should comply with two requirements. First, the amount of information included in the model should be as small as possible to reduce model complexity. Second, sufficient information to answer the questions posed should be included. The second requirement is a hard one, i.e., if it is not met, the modeling goals cannot be reached. For example, a model that is to be used for calculating project costs needs information on effort for project activities; otherwise, no reliable prediction for project costs can be expected. The first requirement directly influences model complexity. The more information about the real world is included, the more complex the model becomes, with all known consequences for maintainability, usability, and understandability.

Many software process simulation models rely mainly on expert knowledge. Another way is the integration of empirical knowledge [15]. This can be done in three different ways.

- Empirical knowledge is used for the development and calibration of simulation models.
- Results from process simulations are used for planning, designing, and analyzing real experiments.
- Process simulation and real experiments are performed in parallel (i.e., online simulations).

Concerning model development and calibration, empirical data can be integrated virtually anywhere in the model. In fact, the creation of the influence diagrams explained in Sec. 4.4 can be supported quite well by empirical data. It may not always be completely clear which factor has which effect, but there are mathematical solutions that can assist with these problems, e.g. sophisticated data mining methods (see Sec. 5.2 for an example). When an initial model exists, calibrating the model using more empirical data, e.g. from replications of the experiment/study used for creating the influence diagram, is also possible. Another use of empirical knowledge might be to extend the model to aspects of reality that have not been modeled yet.

The integration of empirical knowledge also works in a reciprocal manner: Results from simulations can be used to scope real experiments. A simulation can predict where great changes in the result variables can be expected, and the real experiment can be designed to pay extra attention to these. This sort of decision support may also be used as a first stage for testing new technologies: Only candidates that prevail in the simulation are examined more closely. This obviously requires a sufficiently reliable simulation model.

Online simulations combine real experiments, usually for a small part of a more comprehensive process, with simulations taking care of the rest of the process. This way, not only the results from the experiment can be evaluated, but also their effects in a larger context. This provides an inexpensive scale-up for experiments. Another application would be training. Using simulation technology, e.g. the SimSE environment described in [6], the trainee can experience immediate feedback to decisions, without the lengthy delays and dangers that would occur in a real project.

This is only a short overview on the use of empirical knowledge in simulations. More detailed information can be found in [15].

5.2. Acquiring influence factors: Knowledge extraction in the software development process via additive nonlinear regression

Building a simulation model for the software development process requires the determination of input-output relationships for the different sub-processes. The basic information needed for building a simulation model is included in the qualitative process models, which provide a general understanding concerning the chronology of tasks, the flow, and the qualitative dependencies of objects. The simulation model can be built by following the control and flow diagram step by step. In this way, working units (WU) inside the simulation model with their related inputs and outputs, i.e., items, stuff, etc. are determined. Inside a working unit, the relationships between certain variables then have to be quantified by mathematical functions or logical rules. An influence diagram qualitatively describing the relationships in a working unit generally distinguishes between three types of variables:

- WU input variables, which do not depend on other variables.
- WU output variables, which do not affect other WU variables.
- Internal WU variables, which explain other WU variables and are also explained by them.

Based on the influence diagram, step by step one chooses each of the internal and output variables as the explained variable, and their corresponding predecessors as explaining variables. The related input-output relationships then have to be determined as a logical rule or a mathematical function. Possible methods for quantifying the qualitatively known input-output relationships are expert interviews, pragmatic models, stochastic analysis, and knowledge discovery techniques. The choice of the actual technique depends, of course, on the data or information available.

If sufficient measurement data is provided, an application of knowledge discovery techniques is possible. In a first step, these methods will be used for the quantification of the input-output relationships. Then, based on the identified mappings, new insight and knowledge for parts of the considered process can be extracted. Thus, the above mentioned knowledge discovery techniques can also be used for validating the simulation model. Based on simulation data, a simplified input-output mapping covering the complex dynamical dependencies of variables inside a WU could be determined. Analyzing this mapping, for example, by relevance measures, makes it possible to extract additional process knowledge.

Due to saturation effects, the influence of some of the input variables, like *skills of programmers or inspectors*, obviously is nonlinear. Therefore, it seems quite reasonable to use a nonlinear regression model. Here, we will consider an additive nonlinear regression model (AN). AN models are reasonable generalizations of classical linear models, since AN models conserve the interpretability property of linear models and, simultaneously, are able to reproduce certain nonlinearities in the data. It is also possible to interpret their partial derivatives. The importance of the partial derivatives lies in the relevance and sensitivity analysis.

The additive nonlinear regression function can be approximated by different methods. We believe that one appropriate technique are specially structured (blockwise) neural networks for the estimation of the AN model. In [16, 17], it was shown that fully connected neural networks are able to approximate arbitrary continuous functions with arbitrary accuracy. Furthermore, in [18], it was proven that neural networks are able to approximate the derivatives of regression functions. This result was assigned in [19] to block-wise neural networks as estimators for nonlinear additive, twice continuously differentiable regression functions and their derivatives. The network function consists of input and output weights for each unit in the hidden layer. These weights have to be estimated from given measurement data. One well-known method for performing this task is to minimize the mean squared error over a training set. The performance of the network is measured by the prediction mean squared error, which is estimated by cross validation [20].

Taking into account the special structure of the composite function of the AN model, which results from summing up d functions of mutually different real variables, a feed forward network with one hidden layer and with blockwise input to hidden layer connections seems to be convenient for its approximation. Figure 5.2-1 shows the topology and the mathematical description of a blocked neural network with d inputs and one output. In particular, each neuron in the hidden layer accepts

Blocked Neural Network Topology:

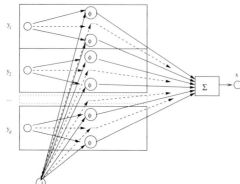

Network Function:

$$x_i = f(y_{1i}, \ldots, y_{di}, \Theta)$$

$$= \sum_{i=1}^{H(1)} v_i \phi(y_{1i} w_i + b_i) + \ldots$$

$$+ \sum_{i=H(d-1)+1}^{H(d)} v_i \phi(y_{di} w_i + b_i)$$

$$\phi(x) = \frac{e^x - e^{-x}}{e^x + e^{-x}}$$

$H(j) - H(j-1), \; \forall \; j = 2, \ldots, d:$
  number of neurons in block j

$H(d)$: total number of neurons in the
  hidden layer

Θ : vector of all neural
  network parameters

$w_j, j = 1 \ldots d:$ weights from the input to
  the hidden layer

$v_j, j = 1 \ldots d:$ weights from the hidden
  layer to the output layer

$b_j, j = 1 \ldots d:$ biases

Fig. 5.2-1. Topology and network function of a blocked neural network.

only one variable as input apart from the constant bias node. The trained neural network will be implemented in the model at the considered working unit for the considered variable of the influence diagram, to calculate the output for a given input during the simulation runs.

Now it will be shown that relevance measures calculated on the identified network function can be used to verify the correctness of modeling assumptions and further provide a deeper understanding of the dependencies in the software development process. The problem, which often occurs especially in modeling a software development process is that measurement data is not available for all input variables. The granularity of the model determines the minimal amount of measurement data needed for quantification, since all input and output variables of the underlying qualitative model should be used in this step. In the case of missing measurement data for one or more variables, one has to make further assumptions or skip these variables. Relevance measures in this case help to determine the impact of each input variable with respect to the output variable.

By considering the validation results and the corresponding relevance measure, one can easily verify whether the estimated functional dependencies describe the input-output relationship in a sufficient manner, if the impact of a skipped variable is too large. If a variable has only small relevance over its whole measurement range, it is redundant and thus can be skipped. Thus, based on measurement data, a relevance measure can also be used to validate the qualitative description of the dependencies given in the relevance diagrams, since the inputs for a node in the diagram are assumed to be non-redundant. Also, the size of the impact of every input variable for a given data set is available, and might give a manager new insight into the software development process under construction.

To define the relevance measures mathematically, we consider the following regression problem: $x_i = M(y_{1i}, \ldots, y_{di}) + \varepsilon_I$, $i \in [1, \ldots, N]$, where ε_i is independent identical $N(0, \sigma^2)$ distributed noise, the function $M \colon \mathbb{R}^d \to \mathbb{R}$ fulfills certain mathematical conditions. We now approximate the true regression function M with a neural network approximator:

$$\hat{x}_i = f_{nn}(y_{1i}, \ldots, y_{di}, \hat{\Theta}) + \varepsilon_i$$

and

$$\hat{\Theta} = \arg \min_{\Theta \in \Theta_H} \left(\sum_{i=1}^{N} (x_i - f_{nn}(y_{1i}, \ldots, y_{di}, \Theta))^2 \right)$$

where Θ_H is a compact subset of the parameter (weight) space. The most common measure of relevance is the average derivative (AD), since the average change in $\hat{x}$ for a very small perturbation $\delta y_j \to 0$ in the independent variables y_j is simply given by $AD(y_j) = \frac{1}{N} \sum_{i=1}^{N} \frac{\partial \hat{x}_i}{\partial y_{ji}}$, where $\hat{x}$ is the vector of estimated regression outputs. Additional important relevance measures are the coefficient of variation or the average elasticity.

In the case of a general nonlinear differentiable regression model, the computation of the relevance measures is also possible; however, in order to guarantee the interpretability of the results, further structural properties have to be fulfilled. For AN models, such as the blocked neural networks considered here, these properties hold, and therefore, the impacts of the single input variables can be estimated. In order to compute the relevance measures, the first partial derivatives of the trained network function with respect to each explaining variable have to be determined. For the sigmoid neuron activation function of the network, the partial derivatives (PD) are calculated via:

$$\frac{\partial f(y_1, \ldots, y_d, \Theta)}{\partial y_j} = \sum_{i=H(j-1)+1}^{H(j)} v_i (1 - \tanh^2(b_i + w_i y_j)) w_i, \quad j = 1, \ldots, d,$$

where $H(j)$ is defined as shown in Fig. 5.2-1. Obviously, the partial derivative explicitly depends only on the considered input, the influences of the other variables are comprised in the network parameters Θ. The PDs can already be used to analyze the impact of the input variables as shown in the following example:

The aim of the example was to identify the regression function between the input variables "effort", "inspected lines of code", and "total lines of code", and the output variable "major defects" on given measurement data. The left plot in Fig. 5.2-2 shows the used blocked neural network cross validation performance. The solid line in this plot is the measured number of detected major defects, and the dashed line

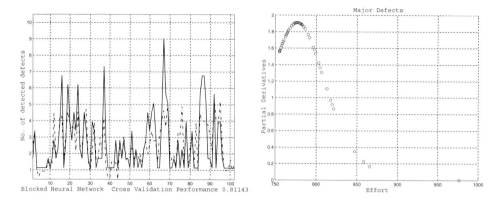

Fig. 5.2-2.   Performance plot and PD plot.

is the estimated number of the same variable. The estimated absolute mean error is ±0.8, i.e., one can expect that the neural network predicts in mean ±0.8 major defects per document incorrectly.

The right plot in Fig. 5.2-2 shows the PD plot for the variable "effort". One notices that for an actual effort in the range of 750 to 850 units, increasing the effort leads to a significant increase in the number of found defects. Obviously, the largest benefit for an increase in the working effort in terms of additional found major defects is obtained around 775 units. An increase in effort for documents with an actual value greater than 850 units will only lead to a slight increase in the number of found defects. Thus, based on the PD plot for the variable effort, and the known costs for each effort unit, a software manager can approximately determine the effort he would like to spend in the inspection. The distribution of the mean relevances of the input variables "effort", "inspected lines of code", and "total lines of code" to the output variable "detected number of major defects" is respectively: AD = [34 17 6]. This means that on average, the variable effort has the largest impact on the considered output.

Thus, AN models, especially the presented blocked neural network, are suitable for the quantification of the qualitative models based on measurement data and for an analysis of the determined mathematical equations in order to get a deeper insight into the input-output relationship by relevance analysis.

5.3. *Considering personal aspects: Human resource modeling*

5.3.1. *Skills*

When dealing with a detailed modeling of complex human-based processes, such as software development, there are various problems related to an adequate representation of persons (developers) involved in the processes. Until now, there are rather few established human-based models of software development processes. Occasionally, models appear to deal with human factors in an *ad hoc* way. Possibly, this is because of a lack of empirical data available for validating models. On the other hand, empirically proven results from psychology and other fields may be employed for reasonable (but still simple) models, for considering the most important effects related to software developers.

As a most common influence on software developers, experiences/skills and their changes during the process (learning/training) are considered. This is mostly done in an aggregated fashion, e.g. in the simulation models by [21–23]. Examples of modeling these effects on an individual basis can be found, e.g. in [24–26]. This allows presenting a more detailed view on individual skills and learning, thus also on the increase of knowledge in software development processes.

A typical assumption of a detailed modeling of humans is that specific skills determine personal productivities (i.e., the speed of work, see [27]), and the quality of work. This quality may be measured, for instance, by the number of defects produced during coding, or the number of defects found during inspection and testing. Since productivity-oriented and quality-oriented skills do not need to be the same for a person, or evolve synchronously, these two types of skill values may be distinguished in a model. Moreover, skills may be distinguished according to the type of work (e.g. coding, testing) and the domain of the application.

For ease of use, skill values may be calibrated on a non-dimensional [0, 1] interval. A skill value of about 0.5 is typical for an average developer, while a value near 1 characterizes an experienced or high performance developer. Multiplied with given values for maximum quality of work or maximum productivity (corresponding to skill values of 1), a person's actual defect (production, detection) rate and productivity can be determined.

5.3.2. *Learning*

One frequent approach to learning is that of a learning curve that describes the increase of productivities over time, or accumulates production (see e.g. [28]). For the case of software developers' skill values, a suitable model for the learning mechanism is that of the logistic growth model (see [29]). According to the pure logistic model, a minimum value of 0 and a maximum value of 1 is assumed with a continuous monotonic growth of the corresponding skill output variable (see Fig. 5.3-1).

Assuming small changes of time, Δt, the corresponding changes of the skill value can be described by

$$\Delta skill := f \Delta t \; skill(1 - skill)$$

where f is a learning factor specific to the particular skill, which depends on the institutional environment and personal factors not explicitly considered in the simulation model. Δt is the time used for an activity that involves the particular skill, thus the time elapsed since the last update of that skill. If an activity involves

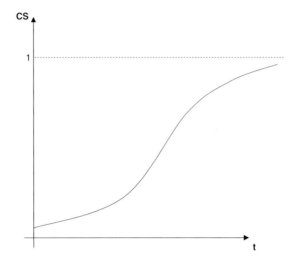

Fig. 5.3-1.   Logistic growth of skills.

several skills (e.g. phase-specific and domain-specific skills), all of them should be updated after finishing the activity. The factor f determines the steepness of the learning curve and thus the time needed to get from a low skill value to a high skill value. Therefore, it reflects the average learning capability of a software developing organization and depends, for instance, on the degree of re-usability of former artifacts.

5.3.3. *Time pressure, fatigue and boredom*

As another main effect on personal productivities, we discuss a time pressure model for capturing some motivational effects related to fatigue and boredom. Considering a standard level of workload and time pressure, it is assumed that an increase of time pressure first leads to an increase in productivity. For instance, people work in a more concentrated way, social activities are reduced, or voluntary overtime is done. This, however, can usually only be expected for a limited period of time and to some specific extent. Excessive time pressure leads to stress and negative motivation of personnel, coupled with a decrease of work performance to below the standard level.

On the other hand, insufficient time pressure results in underperformance of the staff, who may use extra time for extending social and other activities. Boredom due to low working requirements may decrease motivation and thus, productivity.

These effects are expressed in Fig. 5.3-2, which shows a time pressure factor, measured on a non-dimensional non-negative scale, and depending on the deviation x of planned time t^* to elapsed time t for the current activity, i.e., $x = t - t^*$. If the activity is behind schedule $(t > t^*)$, then first positive and later negative effects take place. If the fulfillment of the plan is easy $(t < t^*)$, boredom shows

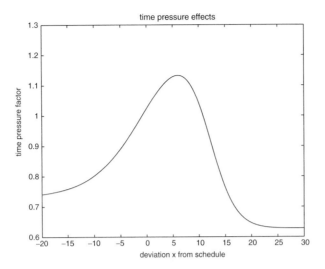

Fig. 5.3-2. Plan deviation and time pressure.

some negative effects. Such a relationship can be expressed by superimposing two logistic functions. The resulting function can be calibrated with the assumptions on the standard level ($tp = 1$) for a deviation $x = 0$, activation levels for extreme boredom, extreme backlog, and peak performance, the steepness of stepping inside these effects, and the mutual deferment of the effects. In Fig. 5.3-2, for instance, the boredom level is approximately 0.75, the overload level is approximately 0.63, the peak level 1.13, the steepness toward boredom level is smaller than towards overload level, and the deferment between these transitions is about 12 on the x-axis (which may be measured in working days). Note that the basic characteristics of the above function correspond to general assumptions on the psychological relationships between activation and performance according to ([30]).

The above approaches are just a few examples on how human impacts can be integrated into detailed simulation models of software development processes. A realistic modeling in that area, however, requires significant efforts in getting empirical information about the specific situation to be modeled. Convincing simulation models of human factors in software development processes are uncommon up to now, possibly exactly because of this lack of empirical data. Nonetheless, appropriate planning of the processes requires such information, and promises significant savings and other improvements (see Sec. 5.4 for more information).

5.4. *Interpreting simulation results: Visualization*

5.4.1. *Requirements*

Because software engineering consists of human and organizational processes, models of these processes will always be simplifications, and the nature and detail of valid models may vary considerably. Therefore, one of the requirements in simulating these models is that the structure of the model must be made explicit to the user (white box modeling), otherwise the resulting data cannot be used to influence decisions in the real world.

A second requirement is that because the models are still complex and have many parameters, a single view will not be sufficient to fully comprehend the simulation results. Instead, an interactive simulation cockpit is needed that can provide different views and perspectives and support decision-making as a result.

The most important variables in software engineering are resource usage (costs), time and quality. Decisions need to be justified as optimizing this set of result parameters by influencing input parameters such as scheduling (e.g. allocation of tasks to programmers) or sampling strategies (number and type of inspection meetings).

Finally, the simulation cockpit needs to support what-if analyses, i.e., varying input parameters while observing the effects as directly as possible. For cognitive reasons, it is highly beneficial if parameter variations result in animated changes in the result variables, as these directly map to active control mechanisms of the human brain.

There are three levels of detail in the visualization of simulation results.

- The *aggregate view*, summarizing the dependency of result variables on the input variables in terms of charts and diagrams. This view allows the user to quickly identify optimal points within the value range. However, as the simulation is often only qualitatively correct, the user does not understand the reason why the model behaves in this way.
- The *resource view*, summarizing the way resources are spent and thus giving an impression of where resources are wasted, and where they can be spent more effectively. This view level is described in more detail below. However, this view does not show the structure of the model or the individual rules employed.
- The *component view* that shows all details of the models, of the strategies and rules employed, and of the individual simulation runs. This level can be used to follow every detail, but is not able to convey action strategies to the user. This level is usually supported by the simulation tool (Fig. 5.4-1).

The visualization is coupled to the simulation tool via a database interface that is able to read out an event-based description of simulation runs. In principle, this interface can be coupled directly to the simulation, or it can read a batch of results from a set of simulation runs. The former approach allows the user to vary all parameters of the model, but the user has to wait for the simulation to finish. The latter approach provides a much quicker interactive response to changing the input parameters and observing the results, but all parameter combinations of possible interest need to be calculated in advance, which is expensive in time and space.

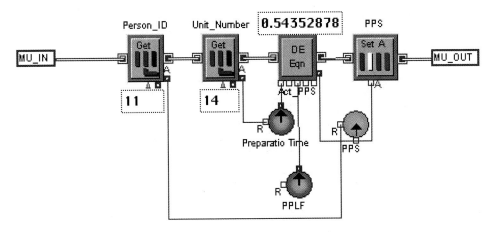

Fig. 5.4-1.   Detail view of the simulation model.

5.4.2. *Resource view*

The resource view (shown in Fig. 5.4-2) is a presentation of the three result variables *time* (along the x-axis), *relative cost* (along the y-axis) and *quality* (shown in colors). The x-axis encodes the simulation time of actual work spent (e.g. hours or days). The y-axis shows the resources employed from two perspectives: The manpower

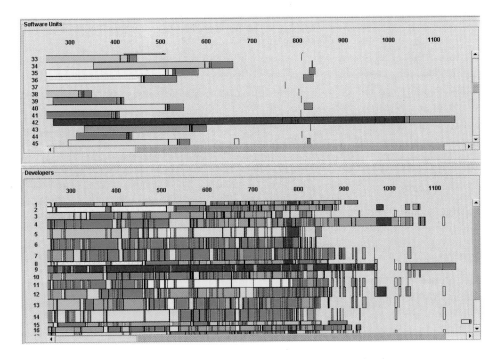

Fig. 5.4-2.   Resource view of a simulation result.

partitioned into persons (bottom), and the software partitioned into modules (top). The height of each resource should be roughly proportional to the cost of the resource, which can be the skill (and thus the salary level) of a programmer, or the complexity (and thus the labor intensity) of a module.

Every rectangle in the resource view shows a resource-consuming activity (such as programming or testing) with its start and ending time coming from the simulation run. As the height of the rectangle is roughly proportional to the relative cost, the area of the rectangle is roughly proportional to the total cost. While the filled areas signal costs, the amount of empty areas visualizes the effective use of time towards a delivery date.

It has to be noted that every activity occurs twice in the resource view: Once in the bottom area attached to the person conducting the activity, and once in the top area attached to the object being worked on. This dual appearance of each activity can be followed by highlighting an activity in one area and seeing it selected in the other area.

As a third dimension, quality variables (such as number of errors remaining) are visualized through color-coding the rectangles. In this way, the user can quickly assess the quality of the results and where it has been achieved (or not achieved). Homogeneity can also be observed.

Cognitively, the resource view employs human abilities to perceive relative sizes of objects presented together, to compare lengths in the same dimension, to distinguish between about 16 shades of intensity, to distinguish between foreground and background (colored versus gray or white) and to evaluate the relative frequency or frequency distribution of line patterns.

As a result, the resource view shows the important quality criteria for software engineering activities: The resource consumption, the effective use of available time, and the quality of the end products. These variables are not simply summarized into a single number, but from a discrete simulation. Particular causes can be spotted, such as critical modules, the effectiveness of scheduling, or time wasted on inspecting good quality modules.

5.4.3. *Studying cause-effect relationships*

A straightforward application for the simulation cockpit is to compare the results of two different simulation runs with different input parameters (e.g. with a different inspection or scheduling strategy). The two resource views can be shown side by side (in an appropriate scaling), and their relative effectiveness can be compared both globally (the total size of rectangles, their color density and their homogeneity) and locally (for outlier events such as large or colored or empty areas as well as for high-frequency, high-activity regions).

It is highly desirable to also study the effects of continuous input parameter manipulation on the resource view of the simulation. For that purpose, a representative set of input parameters can be pre-simulated, and each result can be stored as a data set of temporally ordered activities. The input values used can then be presented to the user as a slider or similar widget. While the user manipulates the widget and changes the input value, the corresponding resource view is shown. If the resource view display is fast enough, the result will be perceived as an animated transition.

Such an animated process allows the user to easily perceive not only the total cost, but also the nature of the change associated with the change of the input value. For example, the user would easily be able to spot reduced amount gaps, higher quality or quality being achieved earlier.

5.5. *Minimizing effort within modeling: Reuse*

5.5.1. *Introduction*

In the last years, many software process simulation models have been developed, using different simulation techniques and languages. The majority of these simulation models were developed from scratch, and development was *ad hoc*. Reuse of products is unsystematic and rarely employed. Reuse in simulation modeling usually occurred at the knowledge level, and was mostly accomplished by taking advantage of the modeler's own experience.

Reuse in software engineering resulted in the reduction of development and maintenance time and effort, and in improved software quality. We expect that for process modeling and simulation, the advantages of reuse will be similar.

5.5.2. *Reuse in process modeling simulation: What, when and how?*

What, when, and how to reuse elements of a simulation model during model development is not obvious or simple. There are many questions to be answered. We identified four main questions that can lead to structured solutions.

(1) What can be reused?

We identified different elements in the development process that can be subject to reuse:

(a) Requirements, environment, and scenarios for using simulation.
Often organizations have the same or similar problems regarding duration, effort, and quality, because these are usually the three main factors influencing the success of software development.

(b) Static process models or their components.
There are not so many different ways to organize certain base practices in software development, e.g. inspections, coding, or testing. For these components, predefined static descriptions can be created that could be transformed into the actual process description. A combination of these parts can lead to a process model that meets the scope of the problem under study.

(c) Influence diagrams or their components.

Influence diagrams qualitatively describe the relationships between process parameters. They usually include the relations between measurable variables (like size) or statistical values (productivity of a team or person), and the values that the model should predict, like effort or quality (e.g. defects per 1000 lines of code).

(d) Relations between process parameters.

The quantitative descriptions of relationships modeled in influence diagrams are represented as mathematical expressions that could be reused.

(e) Model design (patterns) [31].

For specific problems during modeling, such as how to represent activities, item flow, or resources, a pattern can help a novice modeler. These patterns are not necessarily specific for solving technical problems for only one simulation technique, but they can also describe proposed solutions for higher-level static or dynamic model descriptions.

(f) Executable model elements or components of executable models.

This type of information or models would correspond to a reuse of classes in software development. Models or components must be instantiated and parameterized with the input values for the specific problem.

Model elements in discrete event models could be compared to classes in software development. In fact, the simulation blocks of a discrete event model may be organized in libraries similar to class libraries. These simulation blocks can be combined to build more complex blocks for specific tasks. The blocks have input and output interfaces, and can form a hierarchy of sophisticated blocks.

Components are larger parts of simulation models, which are described with input/output interfaces and parameters. Depending on the definition, which has to be developed for the context of simulation models in general, discrete event model components can contain complete parts of a process (for example, an inspection). For components of models, we have to define the interfaces to enable reuse in other models. Also, a description is necessary to describe the properties and the interfaces of the component.

(g) Knowledge about model development, deployment, operation, and evolution methodology.

Not only pieces of artifacts can be reused, but also the knowledge acquired by the modelers as well as the methods they applied and that proved to be successful. In software development, the knowledge about the process is described with process models. If we document the process of developing a simulation model, then the description and the experience stored in the documentation can be reused. In the next step, we should identify typical modeling patterns and provide information on how to implement these in different modeling approaches. By describing these, we can support the process of simulation modeling.

(2) How to facilitate reuse?

How objects can be reused is really dependent on the type of the object. For example, executable simulation models or parts of them can be reused for other models that use the same modeling approach and the same language and environment. Obviously, complete simulation models can be reused if a similar software development process has to be modeled for simulation. If the software process that has to be modeled for simulation differs, the reuse of a complete simulation model is not appropriate.

For finding potential objects or parts of objects that we can reuse, we should follow a similar development method that produces the same artifacts during simulation model development. That makes it easier to identify reusable objects. Reuse can be done on different levels:

- by modularizing artifacts that are created during development, or
- by modularizing the model itself, or parts of it.

If the model itself will be based on modules, it is important to define standardized interfaces between the modules.

(3) When to look for elements for reuse?

We look for elements for reuse all the time, even if we do not do it knowingly [32]. The farther we are in the development process, the more concrete reuse objects we are looking for. The objects created more specific to (and dependent of) the simulation language or technique can be reused later in the development process. In the early stages of the development of a software process simulation model, the reuse of knowledge is more important than the explicit usage of modules developed in earlier projects.

(4) How to develop models for and with reuse?

This question is difficult to answer because often, simulation models are developed without using a well-defined method. At first, we have to adhere to a method for developing a simulation model with certain activities and artifacts that will be created. The first objects for reuse are artifacts and the knowledge captured in these artifacts. One possible method could start with a requirements definition for the model. The analysis has a high potential for reuse of knowledge and experience because here, the modeler has to understand the process and capture the important measures to fulfill the requirements. In the design and following implementation of the model, the objects for reuse become more and more concrete. During design, architectural patterns [33] can help to structure the model. The reuse of components can also be planned in the later design phase. More specific model elements or modeling patterns can support the implementation phase.

5.5.3. *Potential benefits of reuse in simulation modeling*

In [32], the authors describe the potentials and pitfalls for reuse in general in the software engineering domain. The benefits of reuse in software engineering are mainly a reduction of effort or gain in productivity for a particular project by reusing existing assets. With high quality assets, a gain in quality of the end product can be achieved, because more effort was spent in the development of the asset or the asset was more thoroughly debugged. Reusable assets can also reduce the development schedule and reduce the time-to-market.

The assets to be reused must first be developed and organized in libraries. Depending on the amount of information that is necessary to identify an asset for reuse, the likelihood of finding a matching asset decreases with an increasing amount of information. Also, the overhead necessary for developing, identifying, selecting, and adapting reusable assets and its costs are often not taken into account for a software reuse program. A poorly planned reuse program can cost more than it saves. The introduction of reuse also requires an organizational change.

In the context of simulation models, usually only isolated small teams or individuals are involved in the development of the model. Therefore, only the problem of finding a matching element for reuse can be considered to be an obstacle.

5.6. *Optimization of software development models*

5.6.1. *Introduction*

For simulation models, the problem frequently arises on how specific parameters of the model should be chosen (see, e.g. [34]). While the excerpt from reality to be represented specifies some of the parameters, there are others that can be chosen freely, and that influence the results and performance of the simulation model. Therefore, we are interested in finding optimal values for these parameters with respect to the model results. Mostly, such values are determined by systematic experiments or some trial and error approach. Only a few simulation tools are equipped with built-in optimization procedures for automatic determination of optimal parameters.

In the case of software development, even in detailed simulation models, one major requirement of modern project management is usually neglected: An efficient assignment of tasks to persons and the scheduling of tasks. For instance, in a model [35] based on the simulation tool Extend [36], the assignment of tasks to persons (e.g. items to be coded, items to be inspected) is done by a simple rule, namely in a first-come-first serve (FCFS) fashion. This means that items are treated in a given arbitrary order and the developers being available next become their authors. The assignment of coding and other software development tasks to people is relevant, since the duration of the project, i.e., the makespan, depends on this assignment and, in general, the time required for performing a task depends on a person's productivity, which is, for instance, influenced by his or her experience.

While assignment and scheduling usually refer to non-explicit parameters of a simulation model, there are others that require explicit determination. For instance, the quality of the process may depend on the extent of quality assuring techniques. Typical questions are, for instance: Should inspections be applied? Which documents should be inspected? How many persons should inspect a document?

Because of a dissatisfactory FCFS task assignment and the missing possibility of optimizing other planning parameters within a pure simulation model, we may reformulate a software development model with an associated combined assignment and parameter optimization problem.

5.6.2. *Multiobjective optimization*

Usually, in practice, there are several objectives to be considered at the same time. For a software development process (see, e.g. [21]), the following three objectives are frequently considered as the most important from a practical point of view: (a) The quality of the product measured by the eventual overall number of defects, td, of the documents produced during a project. (b) The duration, du, of the project (its makespan). (c) The costs or total effort, tc, of the project.

While the costs and number of defects can be determined once the model parameters (including persons assigned to specific tasks) are fixed, the calculation of the project duration requires the explicit generation of a schedule. In particular, dependencies on tasks have to be fixed. This, for instance, requires a commitment on which kinds of tasks may pre-empt (be pre-empted by) which other kinds of tasks. In the case of software development, we may assume that inspections tasks are done in an "interrupt fashion" such that waiting times for a synchronized start of the team do not occur. Interrupts for the inspection of other authors' documents are done "in between", where it is assumed that associated inspectors are immediately available when an item is completely coded. This assumption can be justified because inspection times are comparably small and, in practice, people usually have some alternative tasks for filling "waiting times".

The specific times of each task are calculated by constructing a schedule for all tasks to be done, i.e., a complete schedule for the software development project, which comprises several weeks or months. Based on this, the project duration, du, can simply be calculated by the maximum finishing time of the tasks.

The considered multiobjective optimization problem can then be formulated as

$$\text{"min"} \ (td(x), du(x), tc(x)) \tag{1}$$

for the decision variables x, which comprise the assignment of developers to tasks (coding, inspections, testing, ...), and the specification of other parameters (e.g. size of inspection teams). This problem is restricted by various constraints, which refer to the assignment (e.g. a person may not work as an author and inspector of the same document), define the temporal logic (working times for tasks), and specify the quality of results (effects of activities on the number of defects).

"*min*" in Eq. 1 means that each of the objectives should be minimized. Usually, the objectives can be considered to be conflicting, such that there exists no solution that optimizes all objectives at the same time. As a solution in the mathematical sense, generally the set of efficient solutions is considered. An efficient solution is an alternative for which there does not exist another one that is better in at least one objective without being weaker in any other objective, or formally: A multiobjective optimization problem is defined by

$$\text{“}min\text{”}\ f(x) \tag{2}$$

with $x \in A$ (set of feasible solutions) and $f\colon \mathbb{R}^n \to \mathbb{R}^q$ being a vector-valued objective function. For $x, y \in A$, the Pareto relation "$\leq$" is defined by

$$f(x) \leq f(y) := f_i(x) \leq f_i(y) \quad \text{for all } i \in \{1, \ldots, q\}$$

and

$$f_i(x) < f_i(y) \quad \text{for at least one } i \in \{1, \ldots, q\}. \tag{3}$$

The set of efficient (or Pareto-optimal) alternatives is then defined by:

$$E(A, f) := \{x \in A\colon \text{There does not exist } y \in A\colon f(y) \leq f(x)\}. \tag{4}$$

See [37] for more details on efficient sets.

Once the efficient set is determined, or a number of (almost) efficient solutions is calculated, then further methods may be applied to elicit preference information from the decision maker (the project manager), and for calculating some kind of compromise solution (see [38–41]). For instance, some interactive decision support may be applied for that purpose.

5.6.3. *Numerical results of optimizing a simulation model*

Evolutionary algorithms are one of the powerful techniques that can be used to optimize simulation models. These approaches are also especially useful for multiobjective optimization (see [42]). We have applied a multiobjective evolutionary algorithm for approximating the efficient set of a SD scheduling problem (see [41]). In Fig. 5.6-1, we have shown the results of applying an EA approach to planning inspections and scheduling staff with the above properties to a given test problem. For the populations of some selected generations, the values for two objective functions are represented in the 2-dimensional space for each combination of two objectives.

Note that the populations move from the upper right to the lower left region, which indicates an improvement of both objectives during time. The preserved bandwidth of objective values during the evolution reflects the fact that the objectives are conflicting. Therefore, an approximation of the efficient set consists of a diverse set of solutions.

As can be seen, there is continuing progress towards the minimization of the objectives and diversity of the solutions. For instance, considering the population of generation 1000 in Fig. 5.6-1, there are several solutions that are better with

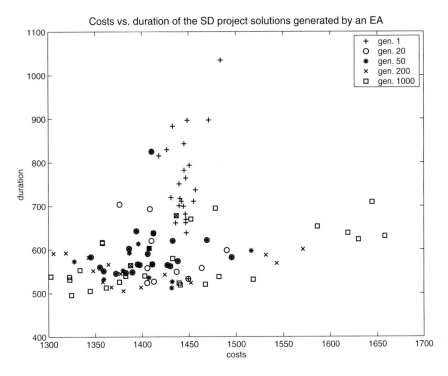

Fig. 5.6-1. Costs and durations in solutions of several generations.

respect to the duration and the costs, although there is no significant progress with respect to the best values in these objectives. Altogether, a more diverse population provides a better fundamental for decision-making. Of course, it is always possible (if desired) to decrease this scope, e.g. by applying aspiration levels for some or all of the objectives. On the other hand, it is possible to get a denser representation of the efficient set by increasing the population size, which, however, increases to computational effort.

Let us note that the computational requirements of optimizing a simulation model may be rather high. In our example, the execution of the multiobjective evolutionary algorithm with a population size of 30 and an evolution of 1000 generations requires about 6 hours on an 850 MHz computer. In that case, about 90% of the running time is required for evaluating the fitness function, i.e., calculating project schedules. On the other hand, the benefits of optimizing the schedules are significant. Depending on the characteristics of the specific project, on average, between 5% and 30% of improvements can be obtained in each of the objectives compared with a simple FCFS solution.

6. Conclusions

This chapter presented the idea of discrete-event simulation in software process modeling. After an overview of experimental software engineering, the possibilities of integrating simulation into the experimental context were explored. We further presented a method for systematically creating discrete-event software process simulation models. Finally, we explained situations that typically occur during modeling and when using the simulation model, and presented ideas such as the integration of empirical knowledge, the use of knowledge-discovery techniques, modeling human resources, optimization and visualization as well as the topic of model reuse to cope with these problems.

This short presentation does not claim to be exhaustive. It is intended to give an overview of simulation in software engineering, especially with respect to software process modeling. Determining the effects of processes for constructive purposes, as opposed to purely analytical intentions, is gaining importance within the research community. With respect to this, hybrid approaches look promising by combining the advantages of discrete-event and continuous simulation [43–45].

References

1. H. D. Rombach, V. R. Basili and R. W. Selby (ed.), "Experimental software engineering issues: A critical assessment and future directions", *International Workshop*, Dagstuhl Castle, Germany, *Lecture Notes in Computer Science* (Springer Verlag, 1993).
2. P. B. Ladkin, Report on the Accident to Airbus A320-211 Aircraft in Warsaw, 1994, *http://www.rvs.uni-bielefeld.de/publications/Incidents/DOCS/ComAndRep/Warsaw/warsaw-report.html*.
3. M. Joseph, "Software engineering: Theory, experiment, practice or performance", Research Report CS-RR-117, University of Warwick, UK (1988).
4. V. R. Basili, S. Green, O. Laitenberger, F. Lanubile, F. Shull, S. Sørumgård and M. V. Zelkowitz, "The empirical investigation of perspective-based reading", *Empirical Software Engineering*, no. 2, 1996.
5. M. I. Kellner, R. J. Madachay and D. M. Raffo, "Software process simulation modeling: Why? what? how?", *Journal of Systems and Software*, nos. 2–3, 1999.
6. E. O. Navarro, "SimSE — An educational software engineering simulation environment", 2002, *http://www.ics.uci.edu/~emilyo/SimSE/main.html*.
7. J. Münch and H. D. R. I. Rombach, "Creating an advanced software engineering laboratory by combining empirical studies with process simulation", *Proceedings of the International Workshop on Software Process Simulation and Modeling (ProSim)*, Portland, Oregon, USA, 2003.
8. R. L. Glass (ed.), *The Journal of Systems and Software — Special Issue on Process Simulation Modeling* (Elsevier Science Inc., 1999).
9. D. H. Meadows, D. L. Meadows, J. Randers and W. W. I. Behrens, "The Limits to Growth", 1972.
10. J. W. Forrester, "The beginning of system dynamics", *Banquet Talk at the International Meeting of the System Dynamics Society*, Stuttgart, Germany, 1989.
11. O. Armbrust, T. Berlage, T. Hanne, P. Lang, J. Münch, H. Neu, S. R. I. Nickel, A. Sarishvili, S. v. Stockum and A. Wirsen, "The SEV method for the simulation-based evaluation and improvement of software development processes", Fraunhofer Institut for Experimental Software Engineering (IESE), Kaiserslautern, Germany, 2003.
12. I. Rus, H. Neu and J. Münch, "A systematic methodology for developing discrete event simulation models of software development processes", 2003.

13. V. R. Basili and D. M. Weiss, "A methodology for collecting valid software engineering data", *IEEE Transactions on Software Engineering*, no. 6, 1984.

14. L. C. Briand, C. Differding and H. D. Rombach, "Practical guidelines for measurement-based process improvement", *Software Process: Improvement and Practice*, 1996.

15. O. Armbrust, "Using empirical knowledge for software process simulation: A practical example", Diploma Thesis, University of Kaiserslautern (2003).

16. K. Funahashi, "On the approximate realization of continuous mappings by neural networks", *Neural Networks*, no. 3, 1989.

17. K. Hornik, M. Stinchcombe and H. White, "Multilayer feedforward networks are universal approximators", *IEEE Neural Networks*, no. 5, 1989.

18. K. Hornik, M. Stinchcombe and H. White, "Universal approximation of an unknown mapping and its derivatives using multilayer feedforward networks", *IEEE Neural Networks*, 1990.

19. A. Sarishvili, "Neural network based lag selection for multivariate time series", University of Kaiserslautern, Germany (2002).

20. B. Efron and R. J. Tibshirani, *An Introduction to the Bootstrap* (Chapman & Hall, New York, USA, 1993).

21. T. Abdel-Hamid and S. E. Madnick, *Software Project Dynamics* (Prentice Hall, Englewood Cliffs, NJ, 1991).

22. J. D. Sterman, *Business Dynamics — Systems Thinking and Modeling for a Complex World* (McGraw-Hill, 2000).

23. I. Rus, "Modeling the impact on cost and schedule of software quality engineering practices", Arizona State University, Tempe, Arizona, USA (1998).

24. N. Hanakawa, S. Morisaki and K. Matsumoto, "A learning curve based simulation model for software development", *Proceedings of the 20th International Conference on Software Engineering (ICSE)*, Kyoto, Japan (1998) 350–359.

25. N. Hanakawa, K. Matsumoto and K. Torii, "A knowledge-based software process simulation model", *Annals of Software Engineering*, nos. 1–4, 2002.

26. A. M. Christie and M. J. Staley, "Organization and social simulation of a software requirements development process", *Software Process: Improvement and Practice*, 2000.

27. L. F. Johnson, "On measuring programmer team productivity", *Proceedings of the Canadian Conference on Electrical and Computer Engineering (CCECE)*, Waterloo, Ontario, Canada, 1998.

28. H. A. Kanter and T. J. Muscarello, "Learning (experience) curve theory: A tool for the systems development and software professional", Technical Report, 2000, *http://cobolreport.com/columnists/howard&tom/*.

29. M. I. Jordan, "Why the logistic function? A tutorial discussion on probabilities and neural networks", MIT Computational Cognitive Science Report 9503, 1995.

30. A. Welford, "On the nature of skill", ed. D. Legge, Harmondsworth (1970) 21–32.

31. E. Gamma, R. Helm, R. Johnson and J. Vlissides, *Design Patterns* (Addison-Wesley, 1995).

32. H. Mili, A. Mili, S. Yacoub and E. Addy, *Reuse-Based Software Engineering: Techniques, Organizations, and Measurement* (John Wiley & Sons, 2001).

33. F. Buschmann, R. Meunier, H. Rohnert, P. Sommerlad and M. Stal, *Pattern-Oriented Software Architecture* (John Wiley & Sons, 1996).

34. A. Gosvi, *Simulation-Based Optimization — Parametric Optimization Techniques and Reinforcement Learning* (Kluwer, 2003).

35. T. Hanne and S. Nickel, "Scheduling in software development using multi-objective evolutionary algorithms", *Proceedings of the 1st Multidisciplinary International Conference on Scheduling: Theory and Applications (MISTA)*, Nottingham, UK (2003) 438–465.

36. D. Krahl, "The extend simulation environment", *Proceedings of the Winter Simulation Conference (WSC)*, Arlington, Virginia, USA (2001) 214–225.

37. T. Gal, "On efficient sets in vector maximum problems — A brief survey", *European Journal of Operations Research*, 1986.

38. M. Zeleny, *Multiple Criteria Decision Making* (McGraw-Hill, 1982).

39. R. E. Steuer, *Multiple Criteria Optimization: Theory, Computation, and Application* (John Wiley & Sons, New York, 1986).

40. P. Vincke, *Multicriteria Decision-Aid* (John Wiley & Sons, Chichester, UK, 1992).

41. T. Hanne, *Intelligent Strategies for Meta Multiple Criteria Decision Making* (Kluwer Academic Publishers, 2001).

42. T. Hanne, "Global multi-objective optimization using evolutionary algorithms", *Journal on Heuristics*, no. 3, 2000.

43. P. Donzelli and G. Iazeolla, "Hybrid simulation modeling of the software process", *Journal of Systems and Software*, no. 3, 2001.

44. R. H. Martin and D. A. Raffo, "A model of the software development process using both continuous and discrete models", *Software Process: Improvement and Practice*, nos. 2–3, 2000.

45. R. H. Martin and D. A. Raffo, "Application of a hybrid process simulation model to a software development project", *Journal of Systems and Software*, no. 3, 2001.

SOFTWARE RELEASE PLANNING

GÜNTHER RUHE

University of Calgary, 2500 University Drive NW,
Calgary, AB T2N 1N4, Canada
E-mail: ruhe@ucalgary.ca

Incremental software development replaces monolithic-type development by offering a series of releases with additive functionality. To create optimal value under existing project constraints, the question is what should be done when? Release planning is giving the answer. It determines proper priorities and assigns features to releases. Comprehensive stakeholder involvement ensures a high degree of applicability of the results. The formal procedure of release planning is able to consider different criteria (urgency, importance) and to bring them together in a balanced way. Release planning is based on (estimates of) the implementation effort. In addition, constraints related to risk, individual resources necessary to implement the proposed features, money, or technological dependencies can be easily adopted into the release planning approach presented in this article.

Releases are known to be new versions of an evolving product. However, the idea of a release is not restricted to this, but can be applied to any type of periodic development where a release would correspond to an annual or quarterly time period. The special case of one release called prioritization is of even larger applicability wherever competing items have been selected under additional constraints.

An informal and later a formal problem description of the release planning problem is given. *Ad hoc* or just experience-based planning techniques are not able to accommodate size, complexity and the high degree of uncertainty of the problem. Plans generated in this way will typically result in unsatisfied customers, time and budget overruns, and a loss in market share. As a consequence of the analysis of the current state-of-the practice, we propose a more advanced approach based on the strengths of intelligent software engineering decision support.

Existing release planning methods and tool support are analyzed. An intelligent tool support called ReleasePlanner® is presented. The web-based tool is based on an iterative and evolutionary solution procedure and combines the computational strength of specialized optimization algorithms with the flexibility of intelligent decision support. It helps to generate and evaluate candidate solutions. As a final result, a small number of most promising alternative release plans are offered to the actual decision-maker. Special emphasis is on facilitating what-if scenarios and on supporting re-planning. Different usage scenarios and a case study project are presented. Practical experience from industrial application of ReleasePlanner® is included as well. Future directions of research are discussed.

Keywords: Software engineering decision support; incremental software development; requirements management; releases; feature engineering; stakeholder; optimization algorithms.

1. Introduction

Requirements management in general is concerned with the control of system requirements that are allocated to software to resolve issues before they are incorporated into the software project. It aims to accurately adjust plans and cost estimates as the requirements change, and to prioritize requirements according to their importance and their contribution to the final value of the product. There is very good reason to significantly improve the maturity of these processes. According to the Standish Group report [30], the three leading causes of quality and delivery problems in software projects are related to requirements management issues: Lack of adequate user input, incomplete requirements and specifications, and changing requirements specifications.

A software release is a collection of new and/or changed features that form a new product. Release planning for incremental software development assigns features to releases such that most important technical, resource, risk and budget constraints are met. Without good release planning 'critical' features are jammed into the release late in the cycle without removing features or adjusting dates. This might result in unsatisfied customers, time and budget overruns, and a loss in market share [22]. "Developing and releasing small increments of requirements, in order for customers to give feedback early, is a good way of finding out exactly what customers want, while assigning a low development effort" [7].

In this article, we focus on features as main characteristics of a release plan. Features are considered to be "a logical unit of behaviour that is specified by a set of functional and quality requirements" [15]. In other words, features are an abstraction from requirements that both customers and developers understand. Most of the topics discussed in this article are applicable to both the original requirements as well as to their aggregation into features. There is a growing recognition that features act as an important organizing concept within the problem domain and as a communication mechanism between users and developers [31]. They provide an efficient way to manage the complexity and size of requirements.

The concept of a feature is applicable and important for any software development paradigm. However, it is especially important for any type of incremental product development. Features are the "selling units" provided to the customer. Incremental development has many advantages over the traditional waterfall approach. First, prioritization of features ensures that the most important features are delivered first. This implies that benefits of the new system are realized earlier. Consequently, less important features are left until later and so, if the time or budget is not sufficient, the least important features are the ones most likely to be omitted. Second, customers receive an early version of the system and so are more likely to support the system and to provide feedback on it. Third, the schedule and cost for each delivery stage are easier to estimate due to smaller system size. This facilitates project management and control. Fourth, user feedback can be obtained at each stage and plans can be adjusted accordingly. Fifth, an incremental approach is sensitive to changes or additions to features.

Agile methods [9] have capitalized on the above advantages. In Extreme Programming [4], a software product is first described in terms of 'user stories'. These are informal descriptions of user requirements. In the planning process called 'Planning games', these stories are prioritized using the perceived value to the user and assigned to releases. Based on estimates of how long each story in an increment will take to implement, an iteration plan is developed for delivering that release. Each increment (or release) is a completed product of use to the customer. At any time, new stories may be added and incorporated into future releases. The whole planning procedure is mainly based on communication and the underlying assumption that the main stakeholders are physically present at the meeting. It is further assumed that they are able and willing to achieve a compromise of their typically conflicting opinions. However, planning games are unlikely to generate transparent release plan alternatives for larger problems. They are unable to address all the resource, technological or risk constraints in an appropriate manner.

This article is structured into eight sections. Following the introduction, an informal and later on a formal problem statement is presented in Section 2. A discussion of the relationship to other software disciplines and techniques is included in this part as well. Difficulties of the problem are presented to derive an appropriate understanding for its solution approach. Requirements prioritization and planning games techniques are presented in Section 4. Intelligent decision support for release planning as realized in the tool ReleasePlanner® is presented in Section 5. As a consequence of the degree of uncertainty, the problem size, and the problem complexity, we propose to rely on the synergy between computational strength and the experience and intelligence of the human decision maker. This is the guiding principle of the solution approach called EVOLVE* presented in this section. This includes the description of five usage scenarios for applying ReleasePlanner®. A case study project is given in Section 6. It is intended to illustrate the introduced concepts and procedures of both EVOLVE* and ReleasePlanner®. Practical experience in using the tool is reported in Section 7. Finally a summary and an outlook are given in Section 8.

2. Model Building and Problem Statement

2.1. *Informal problem statement and relation to other disciplines*

The requirements engineering process is a decision-rich problem solving activity [2]. One of the most prominent issues involved in incremental software development is to decide upon the most promising software release plans while taking into account diverse qualitative and quantitative project data. This is called release planning. The input for the release planning process is a set of features that are evolving due to changing user requirements and better problem understanding. Despite the obvious importance of the problem in current incremental and evolutionary development, it is poorly studied in the literature.

Release planning considers stakeholder priorities and different types of constraints. The output of the release planning process is a set of candidate assignments of features to releases. They are supposed to represent a good balance between stakeholder priorities and the shortage of resources. In each release, all the features are executed following one of the existing software development paradigms including analysis, system design, detailed design, implementation, component testing, system

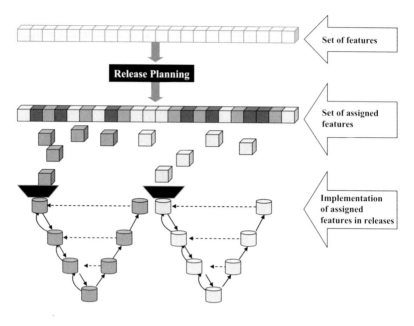

Fig. 1.   Process of planning and development of releases.

testing, and user testing. All the features are inputted into this process. As a result, a usable (release) product is provided. This fundamental procedure of planning and development of releases is illustrated in Fig. 1. In this case, release planning assigns features to release option 1 (next release), release option 2 (next + 1 release) or release option 3 (postponed). This is assumed to be a good compromise between short-term planning (just the next release) and planning of many releases ahead to time. Within each release development cycles, all features are passing the stages of a software development cycle. This cycle includes verification and validation activities at the different product stages (requirement, system design, component design, and code). At the end of this process, a release product is delivered. This principle can be easily extended to planning of more than two releases ahead.

Without any technological, resource, risk and financial constraints, all the features could be implemented in one release. However, the existence of all the constraints implies the questions: What comes first and why? The goal of release planning is to account for all these factors and to come up with suggestions for the most satisfactory release plans. There are two fundamental types of release planning problems: (i) release planning with pre-determined time interval for implementation, and (ii) planning with flexible intervals. In the second problem, you also decide about the length of the interval to implement all the assigned features. In this article, we will focus on release planning with pre-determined intervals.

Software release planning adds to two well-established disciplines of (incremental) software development: (i) requirements management, especially requirements prioritization, and (ii) software project planning and management. Defining the commonalities and differences between them helps to better understand release planning. Requirements management is the process of identifying, documenting, communicating, tracking and managing project requirements as well as changes to those requirements. As requirements are changing, or are becoming better understood, or new requirements are arising, requirements management is an ongoing activity.

Requirements prioritization is trying to determine the different degrees of priority. The problem of still delivering a large amount of features that are never used, and vice versa, not delivering those that are required, has (among others) to do with a lack of understanding and prioritization. As a feature has different relevant attributes (such as its functionality, inherent risk, effort of implementation) that contribute to the final judgement, requirements prioritization is a multi-attributive decision problem. Practically, most emphasis is on the provided functionality of the feature. Specifically, requirements prioritization is also a multi-person (multi-criteria) decision problem, as the prioritization is typically performed in a team-session. There is no clear description on how the different and conflicting opinions are actually negotiated. Software release planning as formulated later in this article extends prioritization in five directions:

- Release planning is based on a set of (representative and most important) stakeholders which can input priorities from a remote place (do not need to attend a physical meeting) via access to the web.
- There is a formal procedure to balance all the stakeholder priorities to determine an overall prioritization result. As part of that, the degree of importance of the different stakeholders can be varied.
- Release planning takes into account (estimates of) the implementation effort. In addition, it can also handle constraints related to risk, money, or technological dependencies.
- Release planning considers the time of implementation by assigning features to releases.
- The formal procedure of release planning is able to consider different criteria (urgency, importance) and to bring them together in a balanced way.

Software project planning and management is the art of balancing competing objectives, managing risk, and overcoming constraints to successfully deliver a product that meets the needs of both customers and the users. The planning stage is based on decisions about which features should be implemented in which release — as provided by release planning. In other words, release planning results are the input for the more detailed project planning and project management.

2.2. *Requirements, features and constraints*

Release planning is based on an evolving set of features and requirements. In this paper, we will formulate release planning related to features. Roughly speaking, features are composed of a set of (more fine-grained) requirements. The number of releases to be considered in advance may vary from case to case. We use "option k" for the assignment of a feature to release k. Because of the high degree of requirements volatility, it does not make sense to plan too many releases in advance. For this article (and without loss of generality), we will only consider two releases in advance. This is considered to be a good compromise of looking into the future while accepting the uncertainty and volatility of features. Consequently, as a result of release planning, each feature is assigned to exactly one of the three possible cases:

- next release (option 1);
- next but one release (option 2); or
- postponed or not (yet) considered for implementation (option 3).

Let $F = \{f_1, \ldots, f_n\}$ be the set of features to be assigned to releases. Whenever applicable without ambiguity, $\{1, 2, \ldots, n\}$ is used instead. As introduced above, release planning is distributing F into three categories: "next release" (option 1), "next but one release" (option 2), and "not yet decided" (option 3). Consequently, a release plan is characterized by a vector x of decision variables

(1) $x = (x(1), x(2), \ldots, x(n))$ with $x(j) = k$ if feature j is assigned to option k.

Assignment of features to releases cannot be done without considering the different types of dependencies between features. These dependencies are represented by relations defined on the product set $F * F$ of F. In [8], six different types of requirements dependencies were analyzed. From a release planning perspective, we formulate them below as six types of dependency between features. Some of them are illustrated by feature dependencies of a text processing system.

Type 1

i AND j if feature i requires feature j to function and vice versa.

If two features are in Type 1 relationship, then they must belong to the same release.

Example: "Copy" feature should be in the same release as the "Paste" feature.

Type 2

i FREQ j if feature i requires feature j to function, but not vice versa.

If two features are in Type 2 relationship, then i should not be implemented in an earlier release than j.

Example: The "Spelling and grammar" feature requires the "Dictionary" feature for the example text processing system.

Type 3

i TREQ j if implementation of feature i requires implementation of feature j.

If two features are in Type 3 relationship, then i should be implemented in the same release as j.

Example: Feature "Paste special in html format" is based on the implementation of the feature "html representation".

Type 4

i CVALUE j if feature i affects the value of feature j.

If two features are in Type 4 relationship, then the value of the two in combination is different from the additive value (non-additive value function) when applied in isolation.

Type 5

i ICOST j if feature i affects the implementation of feature j.

If two features are in Type 5 relationship, then the effort of the two in combination is different from the additive value (non-additive effort function).

Type 6

i IND j if feature i and feature j are independent, e.g. they are in none of the first five types of dependencies.

For the sake of simplicity, we assume that dependencies of Types 4 and 5 are handled by synthesizing these features into a new (integrated) one. To model the remaining types of dependencies, we introduce a directed graph $G(R) = (V(F), A(F))$ with a set of vertices $V(F)$ and a set of arcs $A(F)$. Feature i (not indexed) from a set of features F is represented by vertex set $i \in V(F)$. The set $A(F)$ of arcs is defined from dependencies of Type 1 to 3 as follows:

Type 1: i AND j implies $(i, j) \in A(F)$ and $(j, i) \in A(F)$

Type 2: i FREQ j implies $(i, j) \in A(F)$

Type 3: i TREQ j implies $(i, j) \in A(F)$.

With the graph $G(F) = (V(F), A(F))$, we can formulate dependency constraints as

(2) $(i, j) \in A(F)$ and $(j, i) \in A(F)$ for Type 1 dependency and $(i, j) \in A(F)$ for Type 2 and 3 dependency.

Release planning is impacted by a variety of constraints. These constraints can be related to different aspects such as effort, risk, or budget. The effort to implement a requirement is hard to estimate. For the easiest case, we assume an effort function, effort: $F \rightarrow R^+$ assigning to each feature an estimated positive effort for its implementation. As this effort is typically hard to predict, we assume that it is based on estimates such as the optimistic, the pessimistic and the most likely effort. For the sake of simplicity, we further assume an additive function for the implementation of set $A \subset F$.

Resources are an essential asset for planning of releases. Consideration of just "effort" is just a rough approximation and does not consider individual types of resources. For each release, we consider all necessary resources for performing the tasks assigned to this release. Definition of the actual resource types is done by the project manager. Example resource types are:

- Requirements specification
- Analysis and design
- Implementation
- Testing
- Money
- Risk.

Let's assume that R different resource types are considered to realize the different features. Not all resource types are necessarily needed for all features. We further assume resource capacity bounds ResourceBound(k, r) for the two releases to be planned and for all types of resources $r = 1, \ldots, R$. All feasible release plans have to fulfill the resource capacity constraints for release options 1 and 2, e.g.

(3) Resource$(k, r, x) := \sum_{x(i)=k} \text{resource}(i, r) \leq \text{ResourceBound}(k, r)$.
   For releases $k = 1, 2$ and for all resource types $r = 1, \ldots, R$.

In the same way, we can perform a risk evaluation for each feature. Risk estimation is used to address all the inherent uncertainty associated with the implementation of a certain feature. We employ a risk score as an abstraction of all risks associated with a given feature. These risks may refer to any event that potentially might negatively affect schedule, cost or quality in the final project results [26].

For each feature i, "risk" is an interval scaled function, risk: F $\rightarrow [0,1)$, where "0" means no risk at all and "1" stands for the highest risk. In what follows we assume that the risk assessment is done by expert judgment. We further assume, that the risk is independent from the assigned release. The objective of risk balancing is to avoid a concentration of too many risky features in the same release. The risk per release is supposed to be additive, and ResourceBound(k) denotes the upper bound for the acceptable risk for options $k = 1, 2$. This leads to constraints

(4) Risk$(k, x) := \sum_{x(i)=k} \text{risk}(i) \leq \text{ResourceBound } (k, r)$ for $k = 1, 2$.

In some cases, financial constraints are important as well (or even the most important constraint). From a purely monetary perspective, we assume an estimated financial effort required to realize feature i. For each feature i, "finance" is an interval scaled function, finance: $F \rightarrow R^+$ assigning to each feature an estimated amount of money for its implementation. As there is an available financial budget FinanceBound(k) for both the next two releases under consideration, all feasible release plans have to fulfill

(5) Finance $(k, x) := \sum_{x(i)=k} \text{finance}(i) \leq \text{FinanceBound}(k)$ for $k = 1, 2$.

With constraints as introduced above, we are able to define feasibility of release plans. A release plan x is called feasible if it fulfills all the model constraints (2)–(5). The set of all feasible release plans is denoted by X.

2.3. Stakeholder priorities

2.3.1. Stakeholder

One of the challenges of software development is to involve stakeholders in the requirements engineering process. System stakeholders in the area of software engineering are defined as "people or organizations who will be affected by the system and who have a direct or indirect influence on the system requirements". An approach for identification of stakeholders is addressed in [29].

Effectively solving the problem of release planning involves satisfying the needs of a diverse group of stakeholders. Stakeholder' examples are: user (novice, advanced, expert or other classifications of users), manager (project, product), developer, or sales representatives.

We assume q different stakeholders abbreviated by $S_1, S_2, \ldots, Sq$. Each stakeholder Sp is assigned a relative importance $\lambda_p \in (0, 1)$. The relative importance of all involved stakeholders is typically assigned by the project or product manager. If it is difficult to actually determine these weights, pair-wise comparison using the analytic hierarchy process [28] can be used as a support. We assume that stakeholder weights are normalized to one, i.e.,

(6) $\sum_{p=1,\ldots,q} \lambda_p = 1.$

2.3.2. Prioritization

The increasing focus on value creation as a result of software development implies the question of the impact on value for the different features or requirements. Typically, there are different and conflicting priorities between different (groups of) stakeholders. To determine the most attractive feature and product portfolio's, priorities have to be evaluated to the best knowledge available. There are different ways to evaluate the "priority" of a feature from a stakeholder perspective. For our purposes, we consider two dimensions of priority: A value-based, and an urgency-based prioritization. Value addresses the assumed impact on the value of the final product. Value here is considered to be independent of time. Urgency more addresses the time-to-market aspect, maybe, to reflect market needs and competitor analysis information. Intuitively, what we are trying to achieve is to assign features of high value and high urgency to first releases. We define two attributes for priority evaluation.

2.3.3. Value

Value-based software engineering can help to identify a process in which value-related decisions can be integrated into software engineering practices. Boehm and Huang [5] state that we can no longer afford to follow a value-neutral approach where

- software engineers treat every requirement, feature, use case, object, defect or other artefacts as of equal value;
- methods and practices are largely logical activities not primarily taking into account the creation of value;
- software engineers use earned-value systems to track project cost, schedule, but not stakeholder or business value;
- concerns are separated from software engineers' turning requirements into verified goals; and
- setting goals for improving productivity or correctness independent of stakeholder value considerations.

There is no easy and crisp definition of value. It can be (i) a fair return or equivalent in goods, services, or money, or (ii) the monetary worth of something, or (iii) relative worth, utility or importance. Without being more precise about the concrete meaning, we expressed "value" by a nine-point (ordinal) scale with increasing order of value corresponding to increasing value-based priority. The judgment of stakeholder S_p with regard to feature i is denoted by $\mathrm{value}(p, i)$ where $\mathrm{value}(p, i) \in \{1, 2, \ldots, 9\}$ represents the perceived value of the feature i for stakeholder S_p. We are using a nine-point scale of measurement which could be replaced by another (e.g. five-point) scale in dependence of the degree of knowledge about the subject. The higher the number, the higher the perceived value. As a guideline, we define

(7) $\mathrm{value}(p, i) = 1$ if feature i is of very low value

(8) $\mathrm{value}(p, i) = 3$ if feature i is of low value

(9) $\mathrm{value}(p, i) = 5$ if feature i is of moderate value

(10) $\mathrm{value}(p, i) = 7$ if feature i is of high value

(11) $\mathrm{value}(p, i) = 9$ if feature i is of extremely high value

All even numbers are defined as refinements in between the two adjacent odd values.

2.3.4. Urgency

We have introduced the three options on how to assign a feature to releases. Urgency addresses the degree of satisfaction with these three possible options from the individual stakeholder perspective. Urgency can be motivated by time-to-market of certain product features. For each feature i, the stakeholder S_p is asked to represent his/her satisfaction with the situation that feature i is assigned to option k $(k = 1, 2, 3)$. His/her judgment is expressed by $\mathrm{sat}(p, i, k) \in \{1, \ldots, 9\}$ with

(12) $\mathrm{Sat}(p, i) = (\mathrm{sat}(p, i, 1), \mathrm{sat}(p, i, 2), \mathrm{sat}(p, i, 3))$ for all features i and all stakeholder S_p;

(13) $\sum_{k=1,2,3} \mathrm{sat}(p, i, k) = 9$ for all features i and all stakeholder S_p.

The higher the number of votes (s)he assigns to option k, the more satisfied (s)he would be if the feature is put in the respective option. As a consequence, a urgency vote $\text{Sat}(p, i) = (9, 0, 0)$ expresses the highest possible urgency assigned by stakeholder S_p to feature i. Similarly, $\text{Sat}(p, i) = (5, 4, 0)$ describes a slight preference for assigning feature i to release 1 instead of release 2. Finally, $\text{Sat}(p, i) = (0, 0, 9)$ describes the maximum degree of uncertainty or non-urgency with respect to feature i from the perspective of stakeholder S_p.

2.4. *Objectives and formal problem statement*

The question of what actually constitutes a good release plan needs careful consideration. Intuitively, we are expecting most valued and most urgent features first. However, "most valued" and "most urgent" might refer to different features for different stakeholders. The user is expecting features that he or she would first need to get started. But there are different types of users such as novice, advanced and expert users having different types of expectations and preferences.

Potentially, there is a great variety of formally stated objective functions. Some example functions are discussed in [27]. We propose a function combining the individual stakeholder evaluations from the perspective of value and urgency in a multiplicative way. For each feature i, we introduce the weighted average priority $\text{WAP}(i, k)$ reflecting the product of the value and the urgency of stakeholders with respect to a fixed feature and a fixed option of assignment to releases.

Typically, not necessarily all stakeholders are able or comfortable to give their evaluation related to all features. A stakeholder S_p is called active with respect to feature i, if (s)he was assigned to provide an evaluation (and is called passive otherwise). The set of active stakeholders with respect to feature i is denoted by $P(i)$. For determining $\text{WAP}(i, k)$, the sum of all individual weighted products is divided by the sum of all active stakeholder weights.

Further flexibility is introduced by the possibility to vary importance of stakeholder weights λp and to weigh the importance ξ_1 and ξ_2 of release option 1 and release option 2, respectively. This yields the objective function $F(x)$ defined as

(14) $F(x) = \xi_1 \sum_{x(i)=1} \text{WAP}(i, 1) + \xi_2 \sum_{x(i)=2} \text{WAP}(i, 2)$ with

(15) $\text{WAP}(i, k) := [\sum_{p \in P(i)} \lambda_p \cdot \text{value}(p, i) \cdot \text{sat}(p, i, k)] / [\sum_{p \in P(i)} \lambda_p]$ for all features i and $k = 1$ and 2.

For a fixed vector λ of stakeholder weights and a fixed vector Bound of bounds, the release-planning problem $\text{RP}(\lambda, \xi, \text{Bound})$ becomes

(16) Maximize $F(x, \xi, \lambda, \text{Bound})$ subject to $x \in X$.

(16) represents a specialized integer programming problem. As described in [20], we will generate a set of alternative solutions having the additional property

of being maximally diversified in terms of the structural distance between all pairs of involved solutions. This solution set is typically small in terms of the number of solutions involved. Decision-making under incompleteness and uncertainty is supported by providing a qualified set of solution having the property of being maximally diversified. This increases the understanding of the possible range of solutions and improves the chance to offer a solution finally accepted by the decision-maker. From a solution set generated this way, the decision-maker can finally choose his or her most preferred solutions.

To perform what-if analysis or re-planning, a sequence $\{RP(\lambda^i, \xi^i, \text{Bound}^i)\}_{i=1,2,...}$ of problems with varying parameters λ^i, ξ^i and Bound^i is solved. Risk mitigation by investigating the impact of different risk levels for both releases is an important application of that. Another one comprises resource planning with changing levels of resource capacities.

3. Difficulties with Release Planning

Carlshamre [7] characterizes the release planning as "wicked" in the sense defined by [23]. That means that the objective is "to maximize the benefit", but it is difficult to give a measurable definition of "benefit". Wicked problems have no stopping rule in its solution procedure. The underlying model is "evolving": The more we study the problem, the more sophisticated the model becomes. Wicked problems have better or worse solutions, but no optimal one. Although we are approximating the reality, implicit and tacit judgment and knowledge will always influence the actual decisions. As a consequence of all these difficulties, we propose to rely on the synergy between computational strength and the experience and intelligence of the human decision maker as proposed by the paradigm of software engineering decision support [25].

Release planning is a very complex problem including different stakeholder perspectives, competing objectives and different types of constraints. Release planning is impacted by a huge number of inherent constraints. Most of the features are not independent from each other. Typically, there are precedence and/or coupling constraints between them that have to be satisfied. Furthermore, effort, resource, and budget constraints have to be fulfilled for each release. The overall goal is to find a relatively small set of "most promising" release plans such that the overall value and the degree of satisfaction of all the different stakeholders are maximized. The topic of investigation is uncertain and incomplete in its nature [27]:

- **Features are not well specified and understood**: There is usually no formal way to describe the features and requirements. Non-standard format of feature specification often leads to incomplete descriptions and makes it harder for stakeholders to properly understand and evaluate features and requirements.

- **Stakeholder involvement**: In most cases, stakeholders are not sufficiently involved in the planning process. This is especially true for the final users of the system. Often, stakeholders are unsure why certain plans were suggested. In the case of conflicting priorities, knowing the details of compromises and why they were made would be useful. All these issues add to the complexity of the problem at hand and if not handled properly, they create a huge possibility for project failures.
- **Change of features and requirements and other problem parameters**: Features and requirements always change as the project progresses. If a large number of features increase the complexity of the project, their dynamic nature can pose another challenge. Other parameters such as the number of stakeholders, their priorities, etc, also change with time — adding to the overall complexity.
- **Size and complexity of the problem**: Size and complexity are major problems for project managers when choosing release plans — some projects may have hundreds or even thousands of features. The size and complexity of the problem (known to be NP-complete), and the tendency for not involving all of the contributing factors, makes the problem prohibitively difficult to solve by individual judgment or trial and error type methods.
- **Uncertainty of data**: Meaningful data for release planning are hard to gather and/or uncertain. Specifically, estimates of the available effort, dependencies of features, and definition of preferences from the perspective of involved stakeholders are difficult to gauge.
- **Availability of data**: Different types of information are necessary for actually conducting release planning. Some of the required data are available from other information sources within the organization. Ideally, release planning is incorporated into existing Enterprise Resource Planning or other organizational information systems.
- **Constraints**: A project manager has to consider various constraints while allocating the features and requirements to various releases. Most frequently, these constraints are related to resources, schedule, budget or effort.
- **Unclear objectives**: "Good" release plans are hard to define at the beginning. There are competing objectives such as cost and benefit, time and quality, and it is unclear which target level should be achieved.
- **Efficiency and effectiveness of release planning**: Release plans have to be updated frequently due to changing project and organizational parameters. *Ad hoc* methods help determine solutions but are far behind objective demands.
- **Tool support**: Currently, only general-purpose tools for features management are available. Most of them do not focus on the characteristics of release planning.

4. Solution Methods and Techniques

4.1. *Requirements prioritization*

Prioritization, in general, answers the questions to classify objects according to their importance. This does not necessarily imply a complete ranking of all objects, but at least an assignment to classes like "Extremely important", "important", or "of moderate importance". Different scales are applicable according to the underlying degree of knowledge you have about the objects. Prioritization always assumes one or a collection of criteria to actually perform the process.

Karlsson *et al* [17] characterize a requirements prioritization session by three consecutive stages:

- Preparation: Structuring of the requirements according to the principles of the method to be applied. Provide all information available.
- Execution: Agreement on criteria between all team members. Decision makers do the actual prioritization with all the information available. In general, this step needs negotiation and re-iteration.
- Presentation: Final presentation of results to those involved in the process.

There are a number of existing approaches to requirements prioritization. The most important ones have been studied and compared in [17]. Among them are the analytic hierarchy process (AHP), binary search tree creation, greedy-type algorithms and other sorting-based methods. As a result of their evaluation, they concluded that AHP is the most promising approach. Most of those algorithms need $O(n^2)$ comparisons between the n requirements. This effort required soon becomes prohibitive for a larger number of requirements. In addition to that, none of the mentioned algorithms takes into account different stakeholder perspectives.

The Analytic Hierarchy Process (AHP) [28] is a systematic approach to elicit implicit preferences between different involved attributes. For the purpose of this investigation, AHP is applied to determine the importance of the various stakeholders from a business perspective. In addition, it is used to prioritize the different classes of requirements from the perspective of each stakeholder. The two preference schemata are combined to judge rank the importance of the different classes of requirements for the final business value of the software product. AHP assumes that the problem under investigation can be structured as an attributive hierarchy with at least three levels. At the first level, the overall goal is described. The second level is to describe the different competing criteria that are refining the overall goal of level 1. Finally, the third level is devoted to be used for the selection from competing alternatives. At each level of the hierarchy, a decision-maker performs a pair-wise comparison of actions or criteria. The result is an assessment of their contributions to each of the higher level nodes to which they are linked. The pair-wise comparison involves preference ratios (for alternatives) or importance ratios (for criteria).

Priority decisions become more complicated in the presence of stakeholders having different relative importance and different preferences. It becomes very hard in the presence of constraints about sequencing and coupling of requirements in various releases. Even more so if you are taking into account different resource types necessary for the implementation of requirements. None of the methods mentioned above can be applied under these circumstances.

4.2. *Planning games*

Amongst the informal approaches claiming to handle release-planning, one of the most well known ones is "planning games" as used in agile development [9]. The goal of this approach is to deliver maximum value to the customer in the least time possible. In half to one day long sessions, customers write story cards describing the features they want, while developers assign their estimates to those features. The customers then choose the most promising story cards for the next release by either setting a release date and adding the cards until the estimated total matches the release date, or selecting the highest value cards first and setting the release date based on the estimates given on them.

This simplistic approach works well in smaller projects. However, as the size and the complexity of the projects increases, the decisions involved in release planning become very complex. Various factors come into play, such as the presence of stakeholders having different relative importance and different preferences, the presence of constraints about sequencing and coupling of requirements in various releases, and the need to take into account resource allocation issues for implementing the requirements. Considering problems involving several hundreds of requirements and large number of widely scattered stakeholders, it becomes very hard to find appropriate solutions without intelligent support tools. The goal of such support is to account for all these factors in order to come up with a set of most promising release plans.

5. Intelligent Decision Support for Release Planning

5.1. *Evolutionary solution approach EVOLVE**

We have observed that the problem of release planning is extremely difficult because of its inherent uncertainty, size and complexity. It is unrealistic to expect that this problem can be completely solved through one iteration. Instead, our strategy is to try to gradually reduce the size and complexity of the problem and to increase the validity of the underlying model. Finally, we get a set of candidate solutions with reasonable size to be considered in depth by the decision makers.

The overall architecture of EVOLVE* is designed as an iterative and evolutionary procedure mediating between the real world problem of software release planning, the available tools of computational intelligence for handling explicit knowledge and crisp data, and the involvement of human intelligence for tackling tacit knowledge and fuzzy data. This is illustrated in Fig. 2.

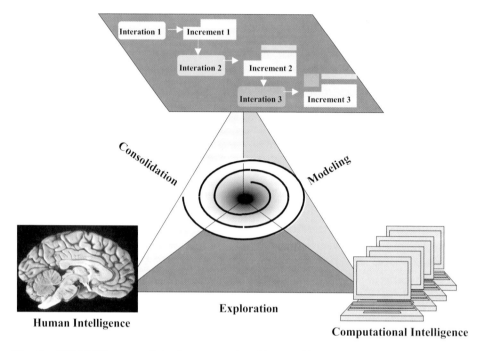

Fig. 2. EVOLVE* as a mediator between real problem world, computational intelligence based tools, and human intelligence.

The spiral curve describes the performance of EVOLVE*. At all iterations, three phases are passed:

- **Phase 1** — Modeling: Formal description of the (changing) real world to make it suitable for computational intelligence based solution techniques. This includes the definition of all decision variables, as well as their dependencies and constraints, and the description of what is, or contributes to, the "goodness" of a solution. Other data, such as stakeholder evaluation of all features, are also part of modeling.
- **Phase 2** — Exploration: Application of specialized optimization techniques to explore the solution space, to generate solution alternatives and to evaluate them according to the given criteria.
- **Phase 3** — Consolidation: Human decision maker is invited to investigate current solution alternatives. This contributes to the understanding of the problem and results in modifying parts of the underlying model or in some local decisions (e.g. pre-assigning some features to a release). Typically, these decisions reduce the size and complexity of the problem for the next iteration.

5.2. *Overview ReleasePlanner®*

ReleasePlanner® is a web-based tool suite (see www.releaseplanner.com for further details) that provides a flexible and web-based tool support for assigning requirements or features to releases such that most important risk, resource, and budget constraints are fulfilled. The tool was developed at the Laboratory for Software Engineering Decision Support (http://www.seng-decisionsupport.ucalgary.ca) at the University of Calgary. It can be used in different usage scenarios and aims to provide intelligent decision support for any kind of prioritization and iterative product development. It addresses the wicked character of the problem by an approach integrating computational and human intelligence.

ReleasePlanner® is based on a solution approach called EVOLVE* that combines the strength of specialized optimization algorithms with the flexibility of an iterative solution method. At all iterations, a specialized optimization algorithm are applied to determine the most promising solution alternatives. Main features of the tool are:

- Web-based tool that allows input and interaction even with remote stakeholders. This results in a much better chance to actually achieve high customer satisfaction with the products to be developed.
- Generation of a set of most promising alternative solutions. This allows to better approach inherent uncertainty and incompleteness of data as well as to allow decision-making including implicit human preferences.
- Compatibility with commercial tools addressing features management (as a prerequisite for using release planning) and project management (for actually planning and controlling the performance of the plan).
- Computational strength of its core optimization algorithms capable of solving even large scale problems in seconds.
- Applicability to a variety of usage scenarios. For further details on that, please compare Sec. 5.3.
- Modeling support is offered. As validated models are a mandatory prerequisite for meaningful results, different objectives (value maximization, optimal customer satisfaction), different schema of evaluation, and different types of constraints (effort, resource, precedence, finance, risk) can be included.
- Flexibility in granularity. ReleasePlanner® is able to work with different levels of abstraction. The lowest level is that of individual requirements, the highest level is (groups of) features.
- Supports scenario-based what-if analysis and re-planning.
- Portability: The tool can be used for different platforms and operating systems.

5.3. *Usage scenarios*

The decision support platform is widely applicable in planning and prioritization of software and hardware products and services. Releases are known to be new versions of an evolving product. However, the idea of a release is not restricted to this, but can be applied to any type of periodic development where a release would correspond to a milestone or to an annual or quarterly time period. The special case of one release known as prioritization is of even larger applicability wherever competing items have been selected under additional constraints.

In what follows, we will describe five usage scenarios for planning software releases. For each scenario, some background and the scenario output are given. For all scenarios, we assume an instance of the release planning problem (16) as an input. The overall planning information is secured and is only visible by the product (or project) manager. For all involved stakeholder, individual access to information is provided and controlled by the project manager.

Mismatch of customer satisfaction still with the functionality of the delivered software is one of the main reasons that software projects fail [30]. To achieve better customer satisfaction, their early involvement is crucial. In globally performing companies, stakeholders (including the different types of customer) are distributed all over the world. Using ReleasePlanner®, they can get easily access to the system to provide their urgency and value evaluation of the features assigned to them. This is a commonality for all the scenarios described in the following.

5.3.1. *Strategic planning and re-planning*

Background

Strategic planning (or road-mapping) addresses assignment of features to releases on a strategic level. The time interval of planning is typically several months. Preferably, total effort and risk constraints are considered to determine alternative release plans. The goal is to find an optimal balance between competing stakeholder priorities and bottleneck resources. Re-planning is applied either for assumed or actual changes of the problem parameters. Another direction of re-planning is to understand what has to be provided to achieve certain goals.

This scenario could be supported by any kind of collaborative environment. In the easiest case, this could be a teleconference. The product or project manager guides and moderates the process. The intelligence of the tool is the backbone for making proposals on how to balance the conflicting stakeholder interests.

Output

- Generation of a set of most promising alternative release plans.
- Comparison between strategic planning alternatives (maximally diversified).
- Reporting of complete planning information for further discussion and refinement of problem parameters.
- Trade-off analysis with respect to resource consumption, risk, and overall value creation.

5.3.2. *Operational planning and re-planning*

Background

Operational planning is a refinement of strategic planning. For the next release, a sequence of releases is defined for realizing the predefined features. Planning is devoted to main tasks for realizing the individual requirements. The planning is done for shorter time frames (weeks) resulting in the definition of which tasks are performed in which release. As for strategic planning, this scenario is aimed to better understand the impact of the different problem parameters.

Output

- Best operational planning alternatives refining strategic plan.
- Evaluation of operational feasibility of proposed strategic plan.
- Comparison between operational planning alternatives (maximally diversified).
- Reporting of complete planning information for further discussion and refinement of problem parameters.
- Trade-off analysis with respect to resource consumption, risk, and overall value creation.

5.3.3. *Resource planning and risk mitigation*

Background

This scenario emphasizes planning in terms of core resources, budgets and in terms of the anticipated risks of the features. Scenario playing here means to understand the impact of resource and budget shortages. In the same way, a comparison between the values achievable for different levels of accepted risks within a release is studied.

Output

Optimal strategies for resource planning and risk mitigation is dependent on varying project settings. In case of changed or added features, re-planning can easily be performed.

5.3.4. *Planning across projects*

Background

This scenario considers any of the questions discussed so far. The only difference is that the planning includes not only one product or project, but several. Organizations typically have more than one project running, and all the planning has to consider the proper balancing between them.

Output

The results are analogous to the first three scenarios with the extension of being applicable to the whole set of projects (instead of just one).

5.3.5. *Synchronization of releases*

Background

In the case of a product that is composed out of individual sub-products, release planning can be applied to different parts separately. For embedded software, these parts could be related to hardware, middle-ware and software components. In order to release a version of the whole product, all the releases of the sub-product have to be synchronized. Non-synchronized release plans would result in a situation where the delivery of the product is delayed whenever one of its inherent parts is delayed.

Output

Same principal output as above. Synchronized release plans provide optimal performance for the integrated product. All the release plans of the individual sub-products are adapted to achieve final synchronization.

6. Case Study

To illustrate solution approach EVOLVE* as presented above, we describe a case study project taken from the telecommunication domain. The usage scenario is "Strategic Planning and Re-Planning". To show the different stages of solution approach EVOVLE* and its implementation in ReleasePlanner, we perform two full iterations with all the three phases therein. This is fully in line with the paradigm of decision support aiming in the generation of most promising solution alternatives for the final human decision making. Because of the uncertainty of the data and the incompleteness of the problem understanding, this result can not be expected from performing only a single iteration without incorporating the human feedback from analyzing a first set of alternative solutions.

The trial strategic project encompasses 25 features clustered into five groups. The planning process is for the next two annual releases of the company XYZ's product development. Five out of the 25 features have already been pre-assigned to the first respectively second release. This is considered to be a predetermined decision outside the scope of the considered planning process.

Different (bottleneck) resources are required to implement the proposed features. Table 1 gives the list of all features and their estimated effort consumptions. In addition to that, the capacity bound for both releases are given for all resource types. The different resource types are:

- BTS Software Development.
- BTS Hardware Development.
- BSC/BSM Software Development.
- MTX Software Development.
- Testers.
- Documentation.
- Capital Requirement ($k).
- Risk (1 low risk, 10 high risk).

There are seven stakeholders participating in the evaluation process. They represent different types of customer organizations and different roles in the development process. Each stakeholder Sp is required to give his/her judgment with respect to

Table 1. List of all features and their estimated resource consumptions.

ID/Group	Feature	BTS Software Development	BTS Hardware Development	BSC/BSM Software Development	MTX Software Development	Testers	Documentation	Capital Requirement ($k)	Risk (1 low risk, 10 high risk)
1/A	16 sector, 12 carrier BTS	480	500	150	200	400	400	1500	10
2/A	China Feature 1	50	0	250	140	200	60	500	3
3/A	China Feature 2	60	10	120	120	190	40	200	5
4/A	China Feature 3	75	75	300	120	450	50	500	5
5/A	China Feature 4	0	0	100	450	400	50	0	3
6/A	China Feature 5	250	100	400	400	400	50	300	5
7/B	Common Feature 01	100	0	250	100	200	0	50	5
8/B	Common Feature 02	0	0	100	250	150	50	0	4
9/B	Common Feature 03	200	0	150	0	100	50	0	4
10/B	Common Feature 04	100	0	300	200	200	30	50	4
11/C	Cost Reduction of Transceiver	150	200	120	0	200	60	1000	5
12/F	Expand Memory on BTS Controller	75	120	10	0	75	20	200	3
13/F	FCC Out-of-Band Emissions	400	120	100	0	200	10	200	2
14/E	India BTS variant	575	420	400	200	250	200	750	4
15/E	India Market Entry Feature 1	200	100	250	250	250	100	500	6
16/E	India Market Entry Feature 2	0	0	300	250	250	100	300	4
17/E	India Market Entry Feature 3	100	100	150	100	300	25	1200	6
18/C	Next Generation BTS	450	350	375	125	500	200	150	9
19/D	Pole Mount Packaging	400	180	300	50	400	150	500	8
20/F	Software Quality Initiative	450	0	100	50	400	5	0	4
21/D	USEast Inc. Feature 1	100	0	500	200	400	100	0	3
22/D	USEast Inc. Feature 2	200	0	400	250	250	50	25	2
23/D	USEast Inc. Feature 3	400	0	600	500	500	200	100	4
24/D	USEast Inc. Feature 4	150	0	400	125	400	150	1000	8
25/D	USEast Inc. Feature 5	75	180	225	225	300	60	750	6
Bounds	Release 1	3000	1200	3600	2200	4000	1000	6000	120
Bounds	Release 2	3000	1200	3600	2200	4000	1000	5000	120

feature i by value(p, i) in the scale of 1 (lowest) to 9 (highest) as described in (7)–(11). The stakeholders are:

- USWest Inc.   (S_1 with weight of importance $\lambda_1 = 9$)
- Technical Director   (S_2 with weight of importance $\lambda_2 = 8$)
- SimpleCommunication   (S_3 with weight of importance $\lambda_3 = 6$)
- CanadaWest Inc.   (S_4 with weight of importance $\lambda_4 = 4$)
- North Communication   (S_5 with weight of importance $\lambda_5 = 6$)
- Asia Pacific Salesman   (S_6 with weight of importance $\lambda_6 = 3$)
- USEast Inc.   (S_7 with weight of importance $\lambda_7 = 3$).

Features are grouped, and there are individualized access rights which stakeholder is supposed to vote which group of features. Table 2 describes the different priorities of the stakeholders in terms of their urgency and perceived value. As it can be seen from there, certain stakeholders are assigned to just vote on specific groups. That also means that the stakeholders get access only to the descriptions of the assigned features. The rationale here is that this information is highly confidential between different types of customer organizations.

For the sake of simplicity, we assume just one coupling (Type 1) and one precedence constraint (Type 2) between features are defined. USEast Inc. Feature 1 is coupled to USEast Inc. Feature 2, i.e., they depend on each other and should be delivered in the same release. Analogously, China feature 1 must precede China feature 2, e.g. it does not make any sense to deliver China feature 2 before China feature 1. These constraints are handled as hard constraints for the generation of all release plan alternatives.

With all the parameters of the project defined (as the end of Phase Modeling of EVOLVE* as described in Fig. 2), the tool is now able to generate most promising solution alternatives. These alternatives are generated from a two-phased procedure. In the first step, we determine a set $X^0 \subset X$ of qualified alternative solutions. Typically, the cardinality of set X^0 is much lower than the cardinality of set X. In the second step, for a fixed cardinality L (determined by the decision-maker) we determine the L release plans out of X^0 that provide maximal diversity. The notion of diversity can be based on the "similarity" or "distance" between two solutions. Intuitively, the more two solutions are different, the more all the individual requirements are assigned to different releases. For two release plan solutions x, y from X, the degree of similarity can be represented by the Euclidean distance. The smaller the distance, the more similar the plans are.

Table 3 presents the five alternative solutions generated this way. They are supposed to be the most promising with respect to the original objectives. However, because of all the inherent uncertainty of data, it is not enough to exclusively look at the numerical values represented by the objective function performance. ReleasePlanner® is following the decision support paradigm and offers these alternative solutions in conjunction with options to further study their structure and to compare between them.

Table 2. Stakeholder voting.

ID/Group	USWest Inc. Urgency:	Value:	Tec. Director Urgency:	Value:	Simplecom. Urgency:	Value:	CanadaWest Inc. Urgency:	Value:	North Comm. Urgency:	Value:	Asia Pac. Sal. Urgency:	Value:	USEast Inc. Urgency:	Value:
1/A	(5, 4, 0)	5	(9, 0, 0)	9	(9, 0, 0)	9	(4, 5, 0)	5	No voting		(9, 0, 0)	9	No voting	
2/A	(9, 0, 0)	9	(9, 0, 0)	9	(8, 1, 0)	8	(9, 0, 0)	9	No voting		(9, 0, 0)	9	No voting	
3/A	(9, 0, 0)	9	(8, 1, 0)	8	(3, 6, 0)	6	(9, 0, 0)	9	No voting		(7, 2, 0)	7	No voting	
4/A	(4, 5, 0)	4	(0, 9, 0)	9	(8, 1, 0)	8	(0, 9, 0)	5	No voting		(7, 2, 0)	6	No voting	
5/A	(6, 3, 0)	6	(4, 5, 0)	5	(4, 5, 0)	5	(2, 7, 0)	7	No voting		(4, 5, 0)	5	No voting	
6/A	(7, 2, 0)	7	(2, 7, 0)	6	(2, 7, 0)	9	(3, 6, 0)	5	No voting		(3, 6, 0)	6	No voting	
7/B	(7, 2, 0)	6	(9, 0, 0)	9	(9, 0, 0)	9	(9, 0, 0)	9	(9, 0, 0)	9	(7, 2, 0)	7	(3, 3, 3)	1
8/B	(7, 2, 0)	6	(9, 0, 0)	9	(9, 0, 0)	9	(9, 0, 0)	9	(5, 0, 4)	6	(7, 2, 0)	6	(3, 3, 3)	1
9/B	(7, 2, 0)	7	(4, 5, 0)	4	(5, 4, 0)	9	(9, 0, 0)	9	(1, 6, 2)	4	(1, 1, 7)	1	(3, 3, 3)	1
10/B	(7, 2, 0)	7	(5, 4, 0)	5	(6, 3, 0)	9	(5, 4, 0)	5	(0, 0, 9)	1	(1, 1, 7)	1	(3, 3, 3)	1
11/C	(7, 2, 0)	7	(5, 4, 0)	5	(6, 3, 0)	6	(9, 0, 0)	9	No voting		No voting		No voting	
12/F	(7, 2, 0)	9	(5, 0, 4)	5	(6, 3, 0)	6	(9, 0, 0)	9	No voting		No voting		No voting	
13/F	(7, 2, 0)	7	(9, 0, 0)	9	(8, 1, 0)	9	(9, 0, 0)	9	No voting		No voting		No voting	
14/E	(7, 2, 0)	9	(5, 4, 0)	4	(2, 7, 0)	7	(2, 7, 0)	7	No voting		(2, 7, 0)	7	No voting	
15/E	(7, 2, 0)	6	(8, 1, 0)	8	(2, 7, 0)	7	(2, 2, 5)	2	No voting		(3, 6, 0)	9	No voting	
16/E	(7, 2, 0)	6	(7, 2, 0)	7	(2, 7, 0)	7	(2, 2, 5)	1	No voting		(3, 6, 0)	9	No voting	
17/E	(7, 2, 0)	7	(7, 2, 0)	7	(2, 7, 0)	7	(2, 2, 5)	2	No voting		(2, 7, 0)	5	No voting	
18/C	(7, 2, 0)	8	(8, 1, 0)	8	(8, 1, 0)	8	(2, 7, 0)	7	No voting		No voting		No voting	
19/D	(7, 2, 0)	5	(5, 4, 0)	5	(5, 4, 0)	7	(3, 6, 0)	6	No voting		No voting		(7, 2, 0)	7
20/F	(7, 2, 0)	9	(2, 7, 0)	7	(5, 4, 0)	5	(9, 0, 0)	9	No voting		No voting		No voting	
21/D	(7, 2, 0)	5	(7, 2, 0)	7	(9, 0, 0)	9	(9, 0, 0)	8	No voting		No voting		(7, 2, 0)	9
22/D	(7, 2, 0)	5	(7, 2, 0)	6	(9, 0, 0)	9	(9, 0, 0)	9	No voting		No voting		(7, 2, 0)	7
23/D	(7, 2, 0)	5	(6, 3, 0)	6	(9, 0, 0)	9	(9, 0, 0)	7	No voting		No voting		(8, 1, 0)	8
24/D	(7, 2, 0)	6	(4, 5, 0)	5	(5, 4, 0)	6	(1, 1, 7)	7	No voting		No voting		(7, 2, 0)	7
25/D	(7, 2, 0)	7	(2, 7, 0)	7	(4, 5, 0)	7	(2, 2, 5)	5	No voting		No voting		(0, 7, 2)	9

Table 3.   Structure of five alternative solutions generated in the first iteration.

Release Plan Alternative	Feature																								
	16 sector, 12 carrier BTS	China Feature 1	China Feature 2	China Feature 3	China Feature 4	China Feature 5	Common Feature 01	Common Feature 02	Common Feature 03	Common Feature 04	Cost Reduction of Transceiver	Expand Memory on BTS Controller	FCC Out-of-Band Emissions	India BTS Variant	India Market Entry Feature 1	India Market Entry Feature 2	India Market Entry Feature 3	Next Generation BTS	Pole Mount Packaging	Software Quality Initiative	USEast Inc. Feature 1	USEast Inc. Feature 2	USEast Inc. Feature 3	USEast Inc. Feature 4	USEast Inc. Feature 5
	1	2	3	4	5	6	7	8	9	10	11	12	13	14	15	16	17	18	19	20	21	22	23	24	25
1	3	1	1	2	2	2	1	1	2	2	1	1	1	2	1	3	2	1	2	2	1	1	2	1	1
2	3	1	1	2	2	2	1	1	1	1	1	1	1	2	2	2	1	1	2	1	1	1	1	2	2
3	3	1	1	2	2	2	1	1	1	2	1	1	1	2	3	2	2	1	2	1	1	1	1	1	2
4	2	1	1	2	2	2	1	1	2	2	1	1	1	3	2	2	2	1	2	1	1	1	1	3	2
5	2	1	1	2	2	2	1	1	1	2	1	1	1	3	2	1	1	1	3	1	1	1	1	2	2

In the consolidation phase, the human decision maker is supposed to study the appropriateness of the proposed solutions. There is the assumption that not everything can be explicitly described in the problem modeling, and that there is implicit knowledge and preferences that are influencing the choice of the final plan. We assume here that we want to generate plans with a lower level of anticipated risk (RiskBound(1) = 60 respectively RiskBound(2) = 80). In addition, we assume an increased budget for the first release (BudgetBound(1) = 8,000). Table 4 gives the final results from this replanning.

As a result from performing the update in the model, to further perform computations to generate a new set of most promising alternative solutions and from the human analysis standpoint, one most appropriate (and best understood) solution is selected. This is a qualified solution that is close to the maximum value. It need not necessarily be the one with the highest numerical value but with a high degree of confidence and satisfaction of the human decision maker.

Table 4.   Structure of five alternative solutions generated in the second iteration.

Release Plan Alternative	Feature																								
	16 sector, 12 carrier BTS	China Feature 1	China Feature 2	China Feature 3	China Feature 4	China Feature 5	Common Feature 01	Common Feature 02	Common Feature 03	Common Feature 04	Cost Reduction of Transceiver	Expand Memory on BTS Controller	FCC Out-of-Band Emissions	India BTS Variant	India Market Entry Feature 1	India Market Entry Feature 2	India Market Entry Feature 3	Next Generation BTS	Pole Mount Packaging	Software Quality Initiative	USEast Inc. Feature 1	USEast Inc. Feature 2	USEast Inc. Feature 3	USEast Inc. Feature 4	USEast Inc. Feature 5
	1	2	3	4	5	6	7	8	9	10	11	12	13	14	15	16	17	18	19	20	21	22	23	24	25
1	3	1	1	2	2	2	1	1	1	3	1	1	1	2	2	2	2	1	2	1	1	1	1	1	2
2	3	1	1	2	2	2	1	1	1	2	1	1	1	2	1	2	2	1	3	1	1	1	1	2	2
3	2	1	1	1	2	2	1	1	2	2	1	1	1	3	2	1	2	1	2	1	1	1	1	3	2
4	3	1	1	2	1	2	1	1	1	2	1	1	1	2	2	2	3	1	2	1	1	1	1	2	2
5	3	1	1	1	2	2	1	1	2	2	1	1	1	2	2	1	2	1	2	1	1	1	1	2	3

7. Release Planning at iGrafx

A typical scenario of performing release planning is described in [1]. Initially, iGrafx (a Product Group of Corel Inc.) releases were planned in an informal fashion using a Lotus Notes database of collated customer requirements. Records in the database were created for each distinct requirement received from customers (existing and prospective) and internal sources. In addition to title, description, and source, records included a priority ranking between 1 (high) and 4 (low). An effort field estimated the development time (in days) to complete requirements.

The Lotus Notes database was effective for providing a fast, simple, central storage of requirements available to program management (release planners) and software engineers (the developers). Lotus Notes was also good for creating a diverse set of reports and summaries to assist implementation. The planning process, however, was mostly *ad hoc*. Program management scanned the requirements attempting to identify the most commonly requested feature requests to add to the next release. The development team would then estimate how many requirements could be completed in the time allocated and the product plan would gradually come together. This process had several difficulties:

- Many requirement descriptions were not fully described.
- Stakeholders (other than program management) had no synchronized involvement in ranking.
- Coupling and precedence relationships between requirements were not formally defined.
- For many requirements, the effort was not defined early enough in the requirement selection process.
- Without a clear prioritization process, it was hard to achieve buy-in on the product plan.
- It was difficult to change the product plan when effort estimates changed or new "must-have" requirements arrived.

These planning deficiencies led to the discovery of ReleasePlanner®. Program management was quickly excited about the possibilities these new tools provided but software developers and other stakeholders were initially skeptical. They believed that ReleasePlanner® would only add unnecessary complexity to the release process. This negative perception has disappeared. Now there is universal agreement among the iGrafx team that ReleasePlanner® is improving the iGrafx product planning process and will deliver long-term value.

To date, we have run tests on a subset (about 250 requirements ranked by three stakeholders) of our database and the results are encouraging. For the first time, we are defining a plan that looks three releases into the future instead of only one (our past practice). In addition, we feel that the contents of each release are maximizing benefits to the stakeholders. Soon, we will define releases using the full set of 800 requirements ranked by seven stakeholders. Recently, other Corel product groups (e.g. XML Solutions and WordPerfect) have asked for information about the tool. They are keen to build on the experiences and success of the iGrafx team.

The application of ReleasePlanner® is helping the company to define a better product plan and providing the following benefits:

- Engineers are more careful to accurately estimate implementation effort. A good estimate is now required because the effort field directly determines release contents. In addition, by defining all precedence and couplings early in the planning process, the release contents are more certain and subject to fewer revisions.
- Requirement descriptions have improved. Stakeholders will not rank requirements with poorly written descriptions or will rank them lower. Poorly described requirements will probably not land in any release.
- Stakeholders are providing earlier and more valuable feedback. Before, stakeholders were asked for advice after the initial product plan was announced. Now, they are involved earlier and are more likely to endorse final release plans.
- Program Management can more easily identify and develop release themes that can later be used by marketing.
- Customers can be given a "road-map" of future plans extending beyond the next release.

8. Summary and Outlook

Release planning is an important and integral part of any type of incremental product development. There is a great variety of application scenarios about when and how to apply this process. Release planning is a wicked problem and needs ongoing effort. To make it successful, an organization has to understand their priorities and constraints. Depending on the maturity and specific needs, different scenarios with different constraints and objectives can be applied. In addition, the granularity of the planning process can be varied depending on the degree of certainty about all the data.

In this article, we have presented a formal description of release planning. This formal problem description is the cornerstone of an evolutionary solution approach that integrates human and computational intelligence in a proper way. We have further assumed that planning is always looking just two releases ahead, although the principal solution method can easily extended to other cases.

Release planning following EVOVLE* and using ReleasePlanner® has to be evaluated in terms of the added value generated. We foresee three directions of impact:

(i) Time savings for both the performing decision-maker (project or product manager) and the involved stakeholders. For both groups, time-consuming meeting can be replaced or at least reduced by using the proposed web-service.

(ii) The quality of the plans becomes better by the ability to include the complete portfolio of stakeholders. This also increases the likelihood to actually achieve higher customer satisfaction for the resulting release products.

(iii) Systematic planning addressing all important objectives and constraints allows higher probability of actually implementing the proposed features within time, budget and target quality.

The process of release planning is based on the ideas of constant learning and improvement derived from the Quality Improvement Paradigm (QIP). QIP is a methodological framework for goal-oriented systematic improvement. It was originally developed for (but is by no means restricted to) Software Engineering projects and organizations [3]. Since release planning strives to learn from, and improve projects at the organizational level, the QIP can guide the activities and goals of release planning [1]. QIP was designed to explicitly identify improvement goals, to capture relevant knowledge, and to evaluate and systematically reuse that knowledge. Therefore, a strong goal-orientation of the entire process as well as quality control of the captured knowledge is an important built-in feature of the QIP.

Release planning does not make sense if it is not done in coordination with other projects and process improvement efforts. Proper requirements management including the elicitation, specification, and analysis of requirements and features is an essential prerequisite for release planning. But it definitely adds value by analyzing the huge number of possible release strategies. It offers support in defining optimal or near-optimal release plans that can be taken as an input to finally decide in consideration of additional and implicit objectives and constraints.

Future research in release planning is going in different directions. Instead of having fixed release times, we could anticipate problems with flexible dates when a new release product is issued. Furthermore, the additivity with respect to effort, value or risk is not necessarily satisfied in the real world. Finally, the underlying release planning model should be extended to accommodate more general questions such as release planning for product lines or release planning for evolving systems.

Acknowledgement

The authors would like to thank the Alberta Informatics Circle of Research Excellence (iCORE) for its financial support of this research. Many thanks are due to Des Greer, Amandeep, An Ngo-The, Omalade Saliu, Pankaj Bhawnani, Pete Garrett, Sebastian Maurice, and Michael Richter for their collaboration and stimulating discussions. Kenny Tsang, Gregory Spiers, Erik Bauld, and David Goodladd, have contributed to the main parts of the implementation of EVOLVE*. The ongoing feedback of Mark Stanford from Corel iGrafx has helped us to better understand industrial needs in release planning.

References

1. Amandeep, G. Ruhe and M. Stanford, "Intelligent support for software release planning", *Proceedings PROFES'2004, Lecture Notes on Computer Science* **3009**, pp. 284–262.

2. A. Aurum and C. Wohlin, "The fundamental nature of requirement engineering activities as a decision-making process", *Information and Software Technology 2003* **45**, no. 14 (2003) 945–954.

3. V. Basili, G. Caldiera and D. Rombach, "Experience factory", eds. J. Marciniak, *Encyclopedia of Software Engineering* **1** (2001) 511–519.

4. K. Beck, *Extreme Programming Explained* (Addison Wesley, 2001).

5. B. Boehm and L. G. Huang, "Value-based software engineering: A case study", *IEEE Computer* (2003) 33–41.

6. B. Boehm and K. Sullivan, "Value-based software engineering", *ICSE 2003 Tutorial*, May 5, 2003.

7. P. Carlshamre, "Release planning in market-driven software product development: Provoking an understanding", *Requirements Engineering* **7** (2002) 139–151.

8. P. Carlshamre, K. Sandahk, M. Lindvall, B. Regnell and J. N. Dag, "An industrial survey of requirements interdependencies in software release planning", *Proceedings of the 5th IEEE International Symposium on Requirements Engineering* (2001) 84–91.

9. A. Cockburn, *Agile Software Development* (Pearson Education, 2002).

10. A. M. Davis, "The art of requirements triage", *IEEE Computer* **36**, no. 3 (March 2003) 42–49.

11. G. DeGregorio, "Enterprise-wide requirement & decision management", *Ninth Annual International Symposium of the International Council on System Engineering*, Brighton, England, June 6–10, 1999.

12. J. Favaro, "Managing requirements for business value", *IEEE Software* (March/April 2002) 22–24.

13. D. Greer and G. Ruhe, "Software release planning: An evolutionary and iterative approach" **46** (2004) 243–253.

14. P. Gruenbacher, "Collaborative requirement negotiation with easy winwin", *IEEE Software* (2000) 954–958.

15. J. van Gurp, J. Bosch and M. Svahnberg, "On the notion of variability in software product lines", *Proceedings of the IFIP Conference on Software Architecture* (IEEE Computer Society Press, 2001) 45–54.

16. H.-W. Jung, "Optimizing value and cost in requirements analysis", *IEEE Software* (1998) 74–78.

17. J. Karlsson, C. Wohlin and B. Regnell, "An evaluation of methods for prioritising software requirements", *Information and Software Technology* **39** (1998) 939–947.

18. L. Karlsson, B. Regnell, J. Karlsson and S. Olsson, "Post-release analysis of requirements selection quality — An industrial case study", *9th International Workshop on Requirements Engineering: Foundations for Software Quality (REFSQ'03)*, Klagenfurt, pp. 47–56.

19. J. Natt och Dag, B. Regnell, P. Carlshamre, M. Andersson and J. Karlsson, "Evaluating automated for requirements similarity analysis in market-driven development", *7th International Workshop on Requirements Engineering: Foundation for Software Quality*, June 4–5, 2001.

20. A. Ngo-The and G. Ruhe, "Maximally diversified solutions for software release planning", University of Calgary, Laboratory for Software Engineering Decision Support, Technical Report TR SEDS 10-2004.

21. B. Nuseibeh and S. Easterbrook, "Requirements engineering: A roadmap", *The Future of Software Engineering, ICSE 2000*, pp. 35–46.

22. D. Penny, "An estimation-based management framework for enhancive maintenance in commercial software products", *Proceedings in the International Conference on Software Maintenance* (2002) 122–130.

23. H. Rittel and M. Webber, "Planning problems are wicked problems", ed. N. Cross, *Developments in Design Methodology* (Wiley, Chichester, 1984) 135–144.

24. J. Robertson, S. Robertson, K. Orr and E. M. Bennatan, "Next practices in requirements engineering", Cutter Consortium, 2003.

25. G. Ruhe, "Software engineering decision support — A new paradigm for learning software organizations", *Proceedings Workshop on Learning Software Organizations* (Springer, 2003) 140–152.

26. G. Ruhe and D. Greer, "Quantitative studies in software release planning under risk and resource constraints", *Proceedings of the 2003 IEEE International Symposium on Empirical Software Engineering (ISESE 2003)*, pp. 262–271.

27. G. Ruhe and A. Ngo-The, "Hybrid intelligence in software release planning", *Journal of Hybrid Intelligent Systems* **1** (2004) 99–110.

28. T. L. Saaty, *The Analytic Hierarchy Process* (Wiley, New York, 1980).

29. H. Sharp, A. Finkelstein and G. Galal, "Stakeholder identification in the requirements engineering process", *Proceedings Tenth International Workshop on Database and Expert Systems Applications* (1999) 387–391.

30. Standish Group Research. "What are your requirements?", 2002, *http://www.standishgroup.com/*.

31. C. R. Turner, A. Fuggetta, L. Lavazza and A. L. Wolf, "A conceptual basis for feature engineering", *The Journal of Systems and Software* **49** (1999) 3–15.

SOFTWARE TRACEABILITY: A ROADMAP

GEORGE SPANOUDAKIS and ANDREA ZISMAN

Software Engineering Group,
Department of Computing, City University,
Northampton Square, EC1V 0HB, UK
Email: {gespan | a.zisman} @soi.city.ac.uk

Traceability of software artefacts has been recognized as an important factor for supporting various activities in the software system development process. In general, the objective of traceability is to improve the quality of software systems. More specifically, traceability information can be used to support the analysis of implications and integration of changes that occur in software systems; the maintenance and evolution of software systems; the reuse of software system components by identifying and comparing requirements of new and existing systems; the testing of software system components; and system inspection, by indicating alternatives and compromises made during development. Traceability enables system acceptance by allowing users to better understand the system and contributes to a clear and consistent system documentation.

Over the last few years, the software and system engineering communities have developed a large number of approaches and techniques to address various aspects of traceability. Research into software traceability has been mainly concerned with the study and definition of different types of traceability relations; support for the generation of traceability relations; development of architectures, tools, and environments for the representation and maintenance of traceability relations; and empirical investigations into organizational practices regarding the establishment and deployment of traceability relations in the software development life cycle. However, despite its importance and the work resulted from numerous years of research, empirical studies of traceability needs and practices in industrial organizations have indicated that traceability support is not always satisfactory. As a result, traceability is rarely established in existing industrial settings.

In this article, we present a roadmap of research and practices related to software traceability and identify issues that are still open for further research. Our roadmap is organized according to the main topics that have been the focus of software traceability research.

Keywords: Software traceability, traceability relations, representation and maintenance of traceability, deployment of traceability, software development process.

1. Introduction

Software traceability — that is the ability to relate artefacts created during the development of a software system to describe the system from different perspectives and levels of abstraction with each other, the stakeholders that have contributed to the creation of the artefacts, and the rationale that explains the form of the artefacts — has been recognized as a significant factor for any phase of a software system development and maintenance process [46], and contributes to the quality of the final product.

Typically, traceability relations denote *overlap, satisfiability, dependency, evolution, generalization/refinement, conflict* and *rationalization* associations between various software artefacts [51] (e.g. requirement specifications, software analysis, design, test models, source code), or *contribution relations* between software artefacts (typically requirement specifications) and the stakeholders that have contributed to their construction. Depending on whether traceability relations associate elements of the same artefact or elements of different artefacts, they can be distinguished into *vertical* and *horizontal* relations, respectively [36]. Another distinction is concerned with the notion of *pre-traceability* and *post-traceability* relations [26]. The former category includes relations between requirement specifications and the sources that have given rise to these specifications, i.e., the stakeholders that have expressed the views and needs which are reflected in them. The latter category includes relations between requirement specifications and artefacts that are created in subsequent stages of the software development life cycle.

Depending on their semantics, traceability relations present information that can be used in different ways in the software development life cycle. For instance, traceability relations may be used to support the assessment of the implications of changes in a system and the effective execution and integration of such changes during the development, maintenance, and evolution of a system. They may also be used to support various types of analysis that can establish whether a system meets its requirements (coverage and verification analysis), whether the requirements set for a system are those intended for it (validation). Furthermore, they may facilitate: (a) System testing by relating requirements with test models and indicating routes for demonstrating product compliance; (b) system inspection by helping inspection teams to identify alternatives and compromises made during development; and (c) system acceptance by allowing users to understand and trust specific choices that have been made about the design and implementation of a system. Finally, they may lead to the reuse of system components when these components are related to the requirements of existing systems that are similar to requirements of new systems [13].

Overall, as suggested by Lindval and Sandhal [36], the establishment of traceability relations makes the documentation of a system clear and consistent, and makes the process of maintaining the system less dependent on individual experts.

Many approaches have been proposed to support software traceability. Research into software traceability has been particularly concerned with:

(a) the study and definition of different types of traceability relations [16, 19, 23, 27, 31, 35, 36, 47, 50, 61];
(b) the provision of support for their generation [1, 4, 23, 39, 40, 44, 61];

(c) the development of architectures, tools and environments for the representation and maintenance of traceability relations [10, 11, 44, 55], and

(d) empirical investigations of organizational practices regarding the establishment and deployment of traceability relations during the software development life cycle [5, 8, 26, 36, 49, 51, 62].

However, despite the wide recognition of its importance and numerous years of research, effective traceability is still rarely established in contemporary industrial settings [5, 51]. This phenomenon may be attributed to the difficulty in automating the generation of traceability relations with clear and precise semantics that could, adequately and cost-effectively, support the types of analysis necessary to deliver the benefits of traceability outlined above. Typically, most of the existing approaches, environments and tools assume either that traceability relations should be identified manually (e.g. [10, 27, 47]), or offer traceability generation techniques which cannot identify relations with a rich semantic meaning (e.g. [1, 4, 40]). In the former case, the cost of identifying traceability relations manually clearly outweighs the expected benefits of traceability and makes organizations reluctant to enforce them, unless there is a regulatory reason for doing so. In the latter case, the lack of a clear and precise semantics make the asserted relations of little use and do not provide the benefits of using traceability as described above. Therefore, the relevant techniques are not widely adopted in industrial settings.

In this paper, we present a roadmap into the state of the art and practice in requirements traceability, discuss the main scientific and technological advances in this area, present the possible ways of establishing traceability that are available by current technology, and identify issues which require further research in this field. In the course of producing this roadmap, we have tried to be as objective and inclusive as possible. However, we may have not been entirely successful, as there is always a potential for missing out existing work and presenting approaches and techniques under the inevitable influence of personal perspectives and perceptions. To this end, our roadmap should be read in a critical way.

The rest of this article is organized as follows. In Sec. 2, we discuss the main types of traceability relations that have been proposed in the literature and suggest a classification for these types. In Sec. 3, we present the main approaches and techniques for generating traceability relations from manual, semi-automatic, and automatic perspectives. In Sec. 4, we outline the different approaches regarding the representation and maintenance of traceability relations in software development tools, and discuss the merit of each of these approaches. In Sec. 5, we discuss the various ways of using traceability relations in software development and maintenance settings, and present the implications that these ways have for other aspects of traceability, including the semantics of the deployed relations and requirements for their generation and maintenance. In Sec. 6, we present issues related to the semantics, establishment, representation and deployment of traceability relations which, in our view, are open to further research. Finally, in Sec. 7, we give a summary of the main findings of our roadmap.

2. Types of Traceability Relations

Stakeholders with different perspectives, goals and interests who are involved in software development may contribute to the capture and use of traceability information. Depending on their perceptions and needs, they may influence the selection of different types of traceability relations which are used in software development projects, and can establish project specific conventions for interpreting the meaning of such relations. As it has been suggested in [36, 51], existing approaches and tools for traceability support the representation of different types of relations between system artefacts but the interpretation of the semantics associated with a traceability relation depends on the stakeholders. Moreover, different stakeholders are interested in different types of relations. For example, end users may be interested in relations between requirements and design objects as a way of identifying design components generated by or satisfying requirements; designers may be interested in the same type of relations but as a way of identifying the constraints represented as requirements associated with a certain design object.

These phenomena are acknowledged by Dick [19] who has also stated that typically in industrial settings the semantics of traceability relations is very shallow and it is necessary to represent *deeper* and *richer* semantic traceability relations. Pinheiro and Goguen [44] have also asserted that traceability relations should have precise semantic definition to avoid the problem of culture-based interpretations. On the other hand, Bayer and Widen [6] suggested that in order to increase the use of traceability and, therefore, compensate for its cost, traceability relations should have a rich semantic meaning instead of being simple bi-directional referential relations.

In order to overcome the lack of standard semantic interpretations of traceability relations and establish meaningful forms of semantics for traceability relations, various researchers have proposed approaches, reference models, frameworks, and classifications incorporating different types of traceability relations [2, 19, 26, 35, 36, 40, 46, 51, 68, 78]. These classifications are based on different aspects of traceability. For instance, some classifications are based on the types of the related artefacts [22, 36, 46, 78], others are based on the use of traceability information in supporting different requirements management activities such as understanding, capture, tracking, evolution, and verification [19, 27, 51], or on impact analysis [68].

In general, traceability relations can be classified as *horizontal traceability* or *vertical traceability* relations [36].[a] The former type includes relations between different models, and the latter type includes relations between elements of the same model. Another classification focusing on requirements (*requirements traceability*) has been proposed in [46]. This classification includes 18 different types of

---

[a]In [9], the term "horizontal traceability" is defined as relations between models developed in one stage of the system development life cycle (the same model type), while the term "vertical traceability" is defined as relations between different models. However, in this paper, we adopt the definition given in [36].

traceability relations organized in five different groups. These groups are: (a) *Condition link group*, which includes relations between requirements and restrictions associated with them; (b) *content link group*, which includes relations that signify comparisons, contradictions, and conflicts between requirements; (c) *documentation link group*, which includes relations associating different types of software documents to a requirement; (d) *evolutionary link group*, which includes replacement relations between requirements (e.g. a requirement X has replaced a requirement Y in requirements document); and (e) *abstraction link group*, which includes relations representing abstractions like generalization and refinement between requirements.

In this paper, we organize the various types of traceability relations proposed in the literature into eight main groups namely: *dependency, generalization/refinement, evolution, satisfaction, overlap, conflicting, rationalization,* and *contribution* relations. These groups are described below. In our discussion about these groups, we use the term *element* in a general way to represent the different parts, entities, and objects in software artefacts that are traceable. Examples of these elements are stakeholders, requirements statements, design components (e.g. classes, states), code statements, test data, etc. It is worth noting that this classification is not orthogonal. Thus, two elements e_1 and e_2, in different or in the same software artefact can be related by more than one type of relations.

(a) *Dependency relations* — In this type of relations, an element $e1$ *depends on* an element $e2$, if the existence of $e1$ *relies on* the existence of $e2$, or if changes in $e2$ have to be reflected in $e1$. In [51], the authors proposed the use of dependency relations between different requirements, and between requirements and design elements. In their framework, dependency relations can be used to support requirements management, express dependency between system components for low-end users, and track compositions and hierarchies of elements. An application of this approach that supports the specification and evolution of workflow management systems by using dependencies between business process objects, decision objects, and workflow system objects has been proposed in [74]. Dependency relations are also suggested in [41] to support the management of variability in product and service families. In [68, 69], von Knethen *et al* suggested the use of dependency relations between documentation entities (e.g. textual requirements, use cases) and logical entities (e.g. function, tasks) to assist with fine-grained impact analysis. Other forms of dependency relations are found in Spanoudakis and Zisman *et al* [61, 78]. In this approach, dependency relations are called *requires-feature-in* relations and associate parts of use case specifications and customer requirements specifications. The *requires-feature-in* relations denote that a certain part of a use case cannot be realized without the existence of structural and functional features required by the requirement, or that one requirement depends on the existence of a feature required by another requirement. In Maletic *et al* [39], dependency relations are called *causal conformance* and are used between software documents to represent an implied ordering in the production of the related documents (e.g. bug reports cannot be produced before implementation report). In [27], dependency relations are called *developmental relations* and are used to describe the logical structure of development and provide tracing requirements through the artefacts generated during the other phases of the software development life cycle. In the *Software Information Base (SIB)*, that is an approach for building software repositories to support software reuse [14], dependency relations are realized as *correspondence* relations between requirements, design, and code artefacts. Dependency relations have also been used for requirements [2, 47], scenarios, code, and model elements [22], and to support the design and implementation of product lines [53].

   (b) *Generalization/Refinement relations* — This type of relations is used to identify how complex elements of a system can be broken down into components, how elements of a system can be combined to form other elements, and how an element can be refined by another element. In [46], these relations are classified as *abstraction links* and represent abstractions between trace requirements. In the case study developed in [51], generalization abstractions are seen as a special type of dependency relations. In [68, 69], *Generalization/Refinement* relations are used to represent logical entities at different levels of abstraction. Generalization/refinement relations are also used in the approach proposed in [74] to support associations between business process, decision, and workflow system objects. In [27], they are called *containment relations* and associate requirement artefacts that together form a composite artefact. Other approaches that use generalization/refinement relations are [35, 41, 44, 50].

   (c) *Evolution relations* — Relations of this type signify the evolution of elements of software artefacts. In this case, an element $e1$ *evolves_to* an element $e2$, if $e1$ has been replaced by $e2$ during the development, maintenance, or evolution of the system. In [46], the authors suggested that this type of relations should be used to associate requirements and use specializations of this type called *replace, based_on, formalize*, and *elaborate* relations. In [51], evolution relations specify process-related links that are used by high-end users to document the input-output relationship of actions leading from existing elements to new (or modified) elements and, therefore, identify the origins of the elements. In TOOR [44], evolution relations are called *replace* and *abandon* relations. A *replace* relation is used to signify that a requirement has changed. An *abandon* relation is used to signify that a requirement is unnecessary (i.e., it has been discarded). In [39], evolution relations are called *non-causal conformance* relations and are used to represent the fact that different documents, or their parts, conform to each other without necessarily having clear causality between them. An example of this case is related to the existence of multiple versions of the same documents. In Gotel and Finkelstein [27], evolution relations are called *temporal relations* and are used to associate requirement artefacts in order to represent the history of their development. In the Remap project [50], evolution relations between requirements are captured by using trace rules and are represented in a knowledge base. Evolution relations are also present in SIB [14] to signify *derivations* between requirements, design, and code artefacts.

(d) *Satisfiability relations* — In this type of relations, an element $e1$ *satisfies* an element $e2$, if $e1$ meets the expectation, needs, and desires of $e2$; or if $e1$ complies with a condition represented by $e2$. In [46], this type of relations is classified within the *condition link group*, which associates restrictions to requirements and contains *constraints* and *pre-condition* links. In [51], satisfiability relations have been proposed as associations between requirements and system components (e.g. design components) and are used to ensure that requirements are satisfied by a system. The satisfaction relations are product-related links, i.e., they describe properties of elements independent of how they were created. They are used to represent that requirements are satisfied by the system and to relate one or more requirements, design, implementation elements, and compliance verification procedures. In [2], satisfiability relations are specified between use cases. In [19], in order to allow rich traceability, two types of satisfiability relations have been proposed: (i) *Establishes relation*, a one-to-one relationship which represents links between main arguments of a system and the requirements satisfying these arguments, and (ii) *contributes relation*, a many-to-many relationship which represents links between arguments and requirements that contribute to the satisfaction of the arguments. In TOOR [44], requirements satisfiability is defined based on the notion of *derivation* and *refinement*: (a) If a requirement $r1$ is satisfied, its derived requirement $r2$ should also be satisfied; however, if a derived requirement $r2$ is satisfied, this does not mean that $r1$ is also satisfied; (b) if a requirement $r1$ refines a requirement $r2$, then satisfying $r2$ implies on satisfying $r1$. CORE [17] tool also supports satisfiability relations between design and requirements artefacts.

(e) *Overlap relations* — In this type of relations, an element $e1$ *overlaps* with an element $e2$, if $e1$ and $e2$ refer to common features of a system or its domain. In [61, 78], overlap relations are used between requirement statements, use cases, and analysis object models, while in 16 such relations are used between goal specifications represented in i^* models, use cases, and class diagrams. In the classification given in [46], an overlap relation is a documentation link that relates requirements with different types of documents such as test case, purpose, comment, background information, and examples. In [68, 69], overlap relations are called *representation* relations and represent relationships between document entities representing the same logical entity. The approach proposed in [22, 23] uses overlap relations between scenarios specifications and other model elements such as data flow, class, and use case diagrams. In PuLSE-BC (*Product Line Software Engineering Baselining and Customization* [6, 7]), potential traceability relations are defined based on overlaps of models that are identified based on name matching. The overlap relations between source code and requirements or manual documents proposed in [4, 40] are identified using probabilistic and vector space IR techniques. In [27], overlap relations are called *adopts relations* (a subtype of *connectivity* relation) and are used to associate requirement artefacts.

(f) *Conflict relations* — This type of relations signifies conflicts between two elements $e1$ and $e2$ (e.g. when two requirements conflict with each other). Conflict relations have been proposed in [2, 46, 51, 73, 79]. In [51], conflict relations are used to signify conflicts between requirements, components, and design elements, to define issues related to these elements, and to provide information that can help in resolving the conflicts and issues. This information is recorded by using specialized conflict resolution relations, namely *based_on*, *affect*, *resolve*, and *generate* relations between requirements artefacts and the rationale, decisions, alternatives, and assumptions associated with them. In [46], conflict relations are classified in the *content link group*. In [32, 79], conflicts are represented by *inconsistency* relations between requirements and design artefacts and are identified by using a goal-based approach. In this approach, inconsistency relations are established when similar goals cannot be achieved in two different specifications, or in parts of the same specification. Inconsistency relations between design artefacts are also used in [76].

(g) *Rationalization relations* — Relations of this type are used to represent and maintain the rationale behind the creation and evolution of elements, and decisions about the system at different levels of detail. In [51], rationalization relations are captured based on the history of actions of how elements are created. In [35], rationalization relations are expressed between traceable specifications (a software specification with different level of granularity such as document, model, diagram, use case, etc.) and a rationale specification (a document containing assumptions or alternatives to a traceable specification). Remap [50] also captures design rationale and represent them in a knowledge base. Rationalization relations are also found in [46, 54].

(h) *Contribution relations* — Relations of this type are used to represent associations between requirement artefacts and stakeholders that have *contributed* to the generation of the requirements. Contribution relations were initially proposed by Gotel and Finkelstein [27] to support requirements pre-traceability. Pre-traceability is the ability to relate a requirement (called "contribution") with the stakeholders that expressed it and/or contributed to its specification (called "contributors"). Their approach identifies three different types of contributors: (a) *principals* who motivate the production of artefacts are committed to what is expressed in the artefacts, and are responsible for the consequences of the artefacts for the system; (b) *authors*, who choose, formulate, and organize the content and structure of the information in the artefacts; and (c) *documentors*, who capture, record, or transcribe the information in the artefact.

Table 1 presents a summary of the various approaches for the different types of traceability relations that have been proposed in the literature and the types of the software artefacts that these types may interrelate. We also represent associations between the different types of artefacts and stakeholders. In this table, software artefacts, or their parts, are distinguished depending on the phase of the software development life cycle that they are created in. More specifically, we classify artefacts as: (a) requirements, (b) design, (c) code, and (d) others (e.g. goal documentation, test cases, rationale and purpose documentation, etc). The columns of the table represent the eight different types of traceability relations discussed

Table 1. Summary of the different types of traceability relations for different artefacts generated during various phases of the software development life cycle.

Rel. Type / Artefacts	Dependency	Generalization / Refinement	Evolution	Satisfiability	Overlap	Conflict	Rationalization	Contribution
Stakeholders — Requirements								Gotel et al [27]
Stakeholders — Design								
Stakeholders — Code								
Stakeholders — Other								
Requirements — Requirements	Alexander [2] Gotel et al [27] Pro-Art [47] Ramesh et al [51] Von Knethen et al [69] Rule-based tracer [78]	Gotel et al [27] Letelier [35] Mohan et al [41] TOOR [44] Remap [50] Pro-Art [47] Von Knethen et al [69]	SIB [14] Gotel et al [27] TOOR [44] Remap [50] Pro-Art [47]	Alexander [2] Dick [19] TOOR [44] Pro-Art [47]	Bayer et al [6] Egyed [22] Gotel et al [27] Rule-based tracer [61, 78]	Alexander [2] Pro-Art [47] Ramesh et al [51]	Letelier [35] Remap [50]	
Requirements — Design	SIB [14] Egyed [22] Ramesh et al [51]	Letelier [35] Remap [50]	Remap [50]	Ramesh et al [51] CORE [17]	Cysneiros et al [16] Egyed [22]	Kozlenkov & Zisman [32] Ramesh et al [51]	Letelier [35] Remap [50]	

Table 1. (*Continued*).

Rel. Type Artefacts	Dependency	Generalization Refinement	Evolution	Satisfiability	Overlap	Conflict	Rationalization	Contribution
Requirements — Code	Egyed [22] Maletic et al [39]		Maletic et al [39]	Ramesh et al [51]	Antoniol [4]			
Requirements — Other		Letelier [35] Mohan et al [41] TOOR [44]		Dick [19] Ramesh et al TOOR [44]	Cysneiros et al [16] Pro-Art [47]	Ramesh et al [51]	Letelier [35]	
Design — Design	Egyed [22], Von Knethen et al [69]	Von Knethen et al [69]		Ramesh et al [51]		Xlinkit [73] Zisman et al [79] Ramesh et al [51]		
Design — Code	SIB [14] Egyed [22], Maletic et al [39]	Letelier [35]	SIB [14] Maletic et al [39]	Ramesh et al [51]			Letelier [35]	
Design — Other		Letelier [35]		Ramesh et al [51]		Ramesh et al [51]	Letelier [35]	
Code — Code				Ramesh et al [51]				
Code — Other	Maletic et al [39]		Maletic et al [39]	Ramesh et al [51]				
Other — Other	Xu et al [74]	Letelier [35] Xu et al [74]		Ramesh et al [51]	Rule-based tracer [78]		Letelier [35]	

above, the rows represent combinations of different types of software artefacts, and the cells indicate the approaches that realize (in some form) the specific type of relation between the relevant types of artefacts. Empty cells in the table signify combinations of traceability relation and artefact types which, to the best of our knowledge, are not realized by any of the approaches that have been proposed in the literature.

From Table 1, it is clear that most of the existing approaches have proposed different types of traceability relations that relate requirements specifications [2, 6, 14, 19, 22, 27, 35, 41, 44, 47, 50, 51, 69, 78], and requirements with design specifications [14, 16, 17, 22, 35, 50, 51]. Some approaches have proposed traceability relations between code specifications and requirements and design artefacts [4, 22, 39, 51]. We attribute this to the fact that traceability was initially proposed to describe and follow the life of a requirement (i.e., *requirements traceability* [27]). In addition, the establishment of traceability relations involving code specifications and other software artefacts is not an easy task. It should also be noted that very few approaches support conflict [2, 32, 47, 51, 73, 79] and rationalization relations [35, 50] despite the importance of these types of relations. In addition, only one approach has focused on contribution relations between stakeholders and requirements [27] despite the fact that contribution relations are important to establish the source of the requirement and to identify stakeholders that should be consulted in the case of changes to these requirements.

The different types of traceability relations that have been proposed in the literature and the lack of a commonly agreed standard semantics for all these types do not provide confidence in the use of traceability techniques and do not facilitate the establishment of a common framework to allow the development of tools and techniques to support automatic (or semi-automatic) generation of these relations. In our view, the establishment of standardized definitions for different types of traceability relations are necessary to: (a) Assess the accuracy of established relations of these types in specific projects, and (b) develop tools and techniques to support the generation, maintenance and deployment of such relations.

As described in the beginning of this section, reference models have also been proposed to support semantic interpretation of traceability relations. Ramesh *et al* [51] have proposed the use of metamodels to support the representation of traceability information including types of different traceable elements and types of relations that may exist between these elements. The metamodel that they have proposed for this purpose is composed of entities and relationships that can be specialized and instantiated to represent traceability models used in specific organizations or projects. More specifically, their metamodel contains three types of entities. These are: (i) *Object entities*, that signify the conceptual elements which may be related by traceability relations (e.g. requirements, assumptions, designs, rationale, system components, etc.); (ii) *stakeholder entities*, that represent the agents involved in the system development and maintenance (e.g. project managers, system analysts designers, etc); and (iii) *source entities*, that represent the documentation of traceability information (e.g. requirements specifications, meeting minutes, designed documents, etc). The relationships in their metamodel associate object instances through *TRACES-TO* links, stakeholders and source instances through *MANAGES* links, source and objects instances through *DOCUMENTS* links, and stakeholders and objects or stakeholders and traceability links through *HAS-ROLES-IN* links. These relationships can be specialized depending on the application or the views of the stakeholders.

Applications and extensions of the traceability model and traceability links suggested in [51] have been proposed to assist in the specification and evolution of workflow management systems [68], identify common and variable requirements in product and service families [41], and assist software development process based on UML [35]. Another metamodel that supports capture of design rationale has been proposed in [50].

With regards to support for different types of traceability relations, the study reported in [51] shows that many CASE tools do not support the identification of satisfiability relations. This is due to the difficulty in automating the specifications of relations that can be identified based on existing relations (e.g. by transitivity) and deficiency in representing satisfying requirements as well as the degree of satisfaction. Dependency relations are also minimally supported by traceability tools and there is lack of precise characterization of dependency types and the strength of the relevant relations. On the other hand, software configuration management tools provide ways of representing and enacting evolution of coarse-grained artefacts, as well as notifying the users about changes. However, traceability tools only manage fine-grained objects. The study has also demonstrated that even experienced traceability users find it difficult to capture complex traceability information. The authors suggested that it is necessary to develop abstraction mechanisms to support different granularity and sophistication when performing traceability, inference services to support semantics of traceability link types and access to large amount of traceability information, formal and informal trace description, and mechanisms to define and enact model driven trace process.

3. Generation of Traceability

The majority of contemporary requirements engineering and traceability tools offer only limited support for traceability as they require users to create traceability relations manually. The manual creation of traceability is expected in numerous techniques and approaches including [1, 2, 5, 6, 19, 27, 44, 47] and tools (e.g. CORE [17], DOORS [64], PuLSE-BC [6], RDT [52], RTM [30], RETH [31]). As the manual creation of traceability relations is difficult, error-prone, time consuming and complex, despite the advantages that can be gained, effective traceability is rarely established manually unless there is a regulatory reason for doing so. To alleviate this problem, some approaches which support automatic or semi-automatic generation of traceability relations have been proposed (see [4, 12, 22, 29, 34, 40, 44, 47, 50, 61, 78]).

In the following, we describe the different approaches to the generation of traceability relations, grouped according to the level of automation that they offer. This level ranges from manual, to semi-automatic, and fully automatic generation. We also compare these approaches with respect to the level of effort that they require in establishing the traceability relations, the complexity of their use, the maturity of their development, and the precision of the relations that they can generate.

3.1. *Manual generation of traceability relations*

In this group of approaches, manual declaration of traceability relations is normally supported by visualization and display tool components, in which the documents to be traced are displayed and the users can identify the elements in the documents to be related in an easier way. Examples of this situation occur in tools like RETH [31], DOORS [64], RTM [30], RDT [52], and extensions of DOORS such as [2, 19]. The majority of these approaches claim to support (semi-)automatic traceability generation, since the relationships are identified manually, but the links between the elements being related are automatically generated by the supporting tool based on these relationships. However, in our opinion, these approaches are considered manual, as they expect the user to identify and mark the elements to be traced. In addition, some of these tools provide no support for defining the semantics of traceability relations in a declarative and enforceable axiomatic form (e.g. RETH [31], DOORS [64] and RTM [30]).

The approach in [1, 2] has been implemented on top of the requirements management tool DOORS [64] to allow generation and organization of traces into groups such as use cases and requirements, instead of having traces belonging only to atomic objects (individual requirements). Here traceability hyperlinks are created based on the manual specification of satisfiability, dependency, and conflict relations (see Sec. 2) between use cases and requirements, and fuzzy matching between use case names and references. The relationships are specified by the use of a special-purpose screen in which the users relate the names and object identifiers of groups of use cases and requirements. The HTML hyperlinks are constructed by the tool and can be visualized and navigated by using a web browser. The rich traceability approach proposed in [19] has also been implemented on top of DOORS [64]. It uses a rich traceability explorer tool to support visualization of the objects being traced and the traceability links.

In [27], the contribution relations (see Sec. 2) are manually defined in the artefacts, in an interactive way, and represented as hypertext mark-ups using the Standard Generalized Markup Language (SGML). A prototype tool has been developed to support visualizing and querying the artefacts stored in an online repository, agents, and relations; interactive definitions of traceability relations and agent details; and inference of agent capacities, social roles and commitments based on pre-defined rules.

The approach in [6] (PuLSE-BC) is still theoretical and tools to support automatic generation of *potential* traces between product family metamodels (e.g. views, models, and life cycle stages such as scoping, architectural, and implementation), based on name matching, have not yet been implemented.

Although the approaches in [2, 19] provide the users with advanced support for visualizing and navigating through the generated traceability relations, the effort to establish these relations is still high, especially when dealing with large and complex artefacts. The correctness of the traceability relations generated in [1, 2] relies on understanding the semantics of the relations by the users who identify them. And as this understanding can differ between the users involved in the process, different interpretations and inconsistencies may arise when referring to the relations.

3.2. *Semi-automatic generation of traceability relations*

In order to overcome the issues associated with the manual generation of traceability relations, some approaches have been proposed in which traceability relations are generated in a semi-automatic way. We organize the semi-automatic traceability generation approaches into two groups: (a) *Pre-defined link group*, that is concerned with the approaches in which traceability relations are generated based on some previous user-defined links [11, 12, 22, 23], and (b) *process-driven group*, that is concerned with the approaches in which traceability relations are generated as a result of the software development process [46, 47].

An example of a *pre-defined link* group approach has been proposed by Egyed and Gruenbacher [22, 23]. Egyed and Gruenbacher suggest the use of a rule-based scenario-driven approach to support the generation and validation of trace dependencies between scenarios, code, and model elements such as data flow, class, and use case diagrams. In this approach, traceability dependencies are generated and validated based on observed scenarios of the software system being developed, and on manually defined *hypothesized traces*, that link artefacts with these scenarios. Manually detected overlaps between scenarios and model elements of the system are represented as a footprint graph, which is normalized and refined. This footprint graph is used to support automatic generation and validation of new traceability links between model elements, model elements and code, and model elements and scenarios based on rules. The new trace dependencies are derived based on: (a) *Transitive reasoning* (i.e., if A depends on B and B depends on C, then A depends on C); and (b) *share used of common ground (code)* (i.e., the use of the criterion that if A and B depend on subsets of a common ground and these subsets overlap, then A depends on B). This approach has been validated on a library loan system and on a video-on-demand system [23].

In [11, 12], Cleland-Huang *et al* proposed an event-based approach to support generation of traceability links between requirements and performance models [12], and between non-functional requirements and design and code artefacts [11]. Similar to [22], in their approach fine-grained traceability links are dynamically generated during system maintenance and refinement based on user-defined links. These user-defined links are specified during inception, elaboration, and construction of the system. Their event-based technique supports dynamic trace generation based on invariant rules of design patterns which are used to identify critical components of classes.

PRO-ART [47] is an example of a process-driven approach in which traceability relations are generated as a result of creating, deleting, and modifying a product by using development tools (process execution environment). The development tools must ensure: (a) The recording of execution, input and output of each action related to the creation, deletion, and modification of a product in a trace repository, (b) generation of dependency links between two dependent objects, and (c) recording of the stakeholder performing the action and relationships between the action being executed and previous actions.

Although the above approaches may be considered an improvement when compared with the manual approaches, the identification of the initial user-defined links required by some of the approaches may still cause traceability to be error-prone, time consuming, and expensive. In addition, the tools that have been developed to support these approaches [12, 22] are prototypes implemented to illustrate and evaluate the approaches and not to be used in large-scale industrial settings. In the case of the process-driven approach, the generated traceability relations are dependent on the way that the system is developed.

3.3. *Automatic generation of traceability relations*

Recently, there have been proposals of approaches to support automatic generation of traceability relations. Some of these approaches use information retrieval (IR) techniques [4, 29, 40], others use traceability rules [50, 61, 78], special integrators [55], and inference axioms [45].

The use of information retrieval techniques to support generation of traceability relations has been proposed in [4, 29, 40]. In [4], a traceability relation is established between a requirement document and source code component, if the document matches a *query* specified as a list of identifiers extracted from the source code. Depending on the similarity between queries and documents, a ranked list of documents for each source code component is produced. Queries are matched with documents using *probabilistic* and *vector space* IR techniques. This approach is based on the assumption that the vocabulary of the source code identifier overlaps with various items of the requirements documents due to the fact that programmers normally choose names for their program items from the application-domain knowledge. This work has been reported to produce traceability relations at low levels of precision and reasonable levels of recall. It should be noted, however, that the relations produced by this approach can only represent overlap relations between elements in different system artefacts that refer to common features of a system.

Another approach that automates the generation of traceability relations using vector space IR techniques has been proposed in [29]. This approach attempts to reduce the number of missed and irrelevant traceability relations by using a classical vector IR model technique, and a classical vector IR model technique extended with the use of key-phrase lists or the use of thesauruses. The study has demonstrated that the use of a key-phrase list can improve the recall of the generated relations (fewer missed relations), but decreases their precision (i.e., it generates more irrelevant relations) when compared to classical vector IR techniques. It has also demonstrated that the use of a thesaurus outperforms in terms of recall and, sometimes, also in terms of precision the use of key-phrases.

The approach proposed in [39] is based on the use of *Latent Semantic Indexing* (LSI) to generate traceability links between system documentation (e.g. manual, requirements, design or test suites) and source code. This approach does not depend on the specification language used to produce the documentation of a system and the programming language used in the source code. It takes into consideration synonym terms since it uses linear combinations of terms as dimensions of the representation space. In this approach, a corpus is built based on pre-processing of the documents and source code. A traceability link between two documents is established when the semantic similarity measure of these documents is greater than a threshold. A comparison of this work with the work in [4] demonstrates that both recall and precision results are better in [40].

In the rule-base tracer proposed in [61, 77, 78], traceability relations between requirements statements, use cases, and analysis object models are automatically generated by using XML-based traceability rules. The rules are used to identify syntactically related terms in the requirements and use case documents with semantically related terms in an object model. The documents to be traced are represented in XML and the generated relations are represented as hyperlinks and expressed as an extension of Xlink [18]. The approach has been evaluated in case studies for a family of software-intensive TV systems and for a university course management system. The levels of recall and precision achieved by this approach in the reported case studies are promising: Recall and precision measures range between 50% and 95%. These results provide evidence of the ability of the approach to support automatic generation of traceability relations.

Another approach that supports the automatic generation of traceability relations between requirements and design artefacts based on *trace rules* has been proposed in the Remap project [50]. This approach also supports arbitrary chaining of rules in which the conclusion part of a rule can become part of the condition part of another rule. The generated traceability information is maintained in a knowledge base and may be used for further reasoning. An extension of Remap that allows the identification of commonality and variability traceability management in the development of e-service families (e.g. Internet, wireless and land-based telecommunication systems) between customer requirements and design artefacts has been proposed in [41].

In [55], Sherba *et al* have proposed an approach that allows the generation of new traceability relations based on relationship chaining. This approach uses special *integrators*, which can discover and create traceability relations between software artefacts and other previously defined relations. The new identified relations can be generated based on indirect and transitivity dependencies, complex dependencies containing more than one source or destination elements being related (anchors), intersection of anchors, or matching of pre-defined conditions between artefacts and/or relations. When more than one chaining option is available for certain documents, the user has to choose a specific chain of relation type. At the time of writing of this paper, this approach was still in the early stage of its development and no prototype tool was implemented.

In TOOR [44], traceability relations are defined and derived in terms of axioms. Based on these axioms, the tool allows automatic identification of traceability relations between requirements, design, and code specifications. TOOR also supports derivation of additional relations from the axiomatic definitions by transitivity, reflexivity, symmetry, extraction, and dependency. In addition, it allows users to define traceability relations manually.

It has to be appreciated that, although none of the above approaches can fully automate the generation of traceability relations, they have taken significant steps towards this direction. However, the achievement of acceptable levels of recall and precision that would increase the trustworthiness of the generated links is still missing. At the moment, there is no consensus of what could be considered as satisfactory recall and precision rates in industrial settings.

Also, existing approaches do not always deliver the relations that they can generate at adequate performance levels (see Sec. 6). It is also important to note that the majority of the developed approaches (e.g. [4, 29, 40]) have been implemented only as prototype tools and, therefore, they have not achieved a level of maturity required for large-scale use.

The approaches described in [44, 61] are easy to use once a complete set of traceability relation generation rules and axioms have been identified. This, however, is not always easy. As a way of addressing this problem, in [58], the authors have proposed a machine learning algorithm, which generates new traceability rules, based on examples of undetected traceability relations identified by the users.

4. Representation, Recording and Maintenance of Traceability Relations

The representation, recording and maintenance of traceability relations in different tools and environments are supported by a wide range of architectural approaches. These approaches can be distinguished into five main types, depending on the level of integration that they assume between the artefacts and traceability relations, and the representation framework that they use to store the artefacts and relations. These approaches are:

(a) the single centralized database approach;
(b) the software repository approach;
(c) the hypermedia approach;
(d) the mark-up approach; and
(e) the event-based approach

The main characteristics of each of these approaches and their merit in supporting traceability are discussed in the following. We also give examples of requirements management, CASE and traceability tools, and environments that realize each of the above approaches along with brief overviews of the ways in which they do it.

4.1. *Single centralized database approach*

In this approach, both the artefacts and the traceability relations that can be created between them are stored in a centralized database, which typically underpins the tool that is used to maintain the traceability relations. Most of the industrial requirement management tools that support traceability advocate this approach (e.g. DOORS [64], RTM [30]). Typically, these tools store the traceability relations between artefacts in an underlying relational database [51]. However, there are also tools based on object-oriented (e.g. TOOR [44]) or proprietary database technology.

The main benefit of using an underlying database is that the processing of the recorded relations can be based on extensive and efficient querying facilities that are available from this database. It has, however, to be appreciated that this approach makes it difficult to record and maintain traceability relations between artefacts which are not generated by the tool that manages the relations. To alleviate the problem of recording, some of the tools provide artefact importing and exporting capabilities (e.g. [30, 64]). Such facilities give some degree of flexibility, but are normally available only for artefacts created by other tools of the same vendor or by tools which operate on a common artefact representation framework (DOORS [64], for instance, provides import and export capabilities for artefacts which are constructed and managed by most of the popular CASE tools). It should be noted, however, that import and export facilities cannot support the effective maintenance of traceability relations between evolving artefacts, which are maintained by separate tools.

Furthermore, it has to be appreciated that, depending on the type of the underlying database, this approach may make it difficult to differentiate between different types of traceability relations. In tools which use relational or proprietary databases, for instance, it is difficult to define different types of relations and specify constraints for monitoring the integrity of the generated relations.

4.2. *Software repositories*

A second approach is to record traceability relations in a centralized software repository along with the artefacts that they relate [14, 46]. The main difference of this approach with the single database approach is that software repositories provide sufficient flexibility for defining schemas for storing a wide range of software artefacts and traceability relations between them. In addition, software repositories provide application programming interfaces (APIs) which implement data definition, querying, and management facilities that may be used to link them in client-server architectures with other tools which are used to construct the involved software artefacts.

The Software Information Base (SIB) [14] is an experimental repository system that can support the definition of complex semantic structures for holding information about artefacts and traceability relations at an infinite number of classification layers based on the data model of the conceptual modelling language TELOS. SIB defines traceability relation types that correspond to what in this paper has been termed as *dependency* and *evolution* relations. It also allows the definition of arbitrary additional types of traceability relations, and provides an API through which it may be connected as an information server to external tools.

PRO-ART [47] is a process centred requirements engineering environment which also advocates the software repository approach. PRO-ART assumes a process centred integration of tools that are used to create and maintain the involved software artefacts. More specifically, PRO-ART assumes the explicit specification of processes, which can create the involved artefacts. These processes are defined in terms of artefact creation, deletion, and modification actions. These actions are realized by different tools operating on the top of the underlying PRO-ART repository. Traceability relations in this environment are recorded as a by-product of executing such actions on the artefacts that they are meant to relate. For example, when a developer creates a textual rationale for an object class, PRO-ART automatically creates a *rationalization* relation between the class and the textual annotation. In PRO-ART, the text providing the rationale may be created by text editor that is different from the tool that was used to create the related class. However, by virtue of monitoring the enactment of an underlying process model, PRO-ART is able to identify the purpose of invoking the text editor and create the relevant rationalization relation. The main benefit of this process-centric approach is that it allows the definition of ways of capturing traceability relations as part of the software development processes and, thus, it can monitor or enforce the systematic capture of such relations (this need has been suggested by case studies — see [20], for example).

Overall, the software repository approach requires a heavy up-front tool integration effort to support traceability that may not be desirable, or feasible, in distributed software development settings. Furthermore, in realizations of this approach along the lines suggested by PRO-ART, additional effort is required for modelling the processes supported by the individual tools and their coordination of these processes in the context of a software development life-cycle model.

4.3. *The hypermedia approach*

To solve the problem of maintaining traceability relations as the artefacts that they associate evolve without having to integrate the relevant tools around a software repository, some tools advocate an approach based on *open hypermedia* architectures [71].

Sherba *et al* [55] have developed a traceability management, called *TraceM* that realizes this approach. *TraceM* is a research prototype system at an experimental development stage, which supports the recording, maintenance, and traversal of relations between software artefacts that are constructed by heterogeneous tools. *TraceM* stores traceability relations separately from the artefacts that they associate. A traceability relation in this system can be defined as an *n*-ary association between artefacts of different types, or their parts, by using metadata. These metadata specify: (i) The *types* of the artefacts associated by a relation, (ii) the *external tools* that create these artefacts, (iii) *transformers* that can be used to transform artefacts into the common representation framework of *TraceM*, and (iv) *integrators* which can be used to automatically discover and create the traceability relations. Metadata are also used to specify the types of stakeholders which may be interested in different types of traceability relations and the stages in a project when these relations are needed. Using a *scheduling service* that is provided by the system, developers can also specify the conditions for invoking artefact translators (e.g. a translator may be invoked any time when a new version of an artefact is created) and integrators. To take full advantage of its services (e.g. to navigate between artefacts using recorded traceability relations), developers have to integrate the external tools that are used for creating artefacts with *TraceM*. This integration is possible using standard techniques available in open hypermedia environments. In cases of artefacts which are created by non-integrated external tools, developers may use *TraceM* to record and view relations.

4.4. *The mark-up approach*

To enable traceability in widely distributed and heterogeneous software engineering settings, some systems advocate the use of representations of traceability relations using mark-up languages and store these relations separately from the artefacts that they associate.

Gotel and Finkelstein [27] have developed a toolkit that can be used to create and maintain *contribution* relations. This toolkit uses a combination of HTML and descriptive mark up representations to store different types of contribution relations between artefacts as hyperlinks (i.e., relations with hypertext trace anchors that can provide the required navigational capabilities). Maletic *et al* [39] have also developed a tool in which traceability relations are stored as "hyperlinks" of different types. These types specify the arity, directionality, and traversability of the relations.

STAR-Track [56] is a web-based requirements tracing tool that uses tagging mechanisms to represent traceability relations. The tags in *STAR-Track* can represent document elements or relations between these elements. Each tag is composed of a document identifier and a title. The tagging method used in this approach is quite simple: Users can either have the different sections in a document used as tags or define their own tags. The relations are denoted by the tag identifiers of the document elements related by them.

In the rule-based tracer described in [61, 78], both traceability relations and the artefacts that they relate are represented in XML. Traceability relations, however, are recorded separately from the artefacts they relate, and *XLink* elements [18] are used to indicate the parts of the artefacts these relations refer to. This system also incorporates *translators* that can transform textual artefacts from their original format into XML, and supports standardized XML representations for other types of models (e.g. XMI for object models). The rule-based tracer does not require any form of tool integration and, at its current state of development, provides only primitive support for maintaining traceability relations when artefacts are modified. In such cases, the modified artefacts have to be re-translated into XML and the tool embarks in a full rule-based analysis of their contents to identify the traceability relations, which remain valid or emerge after the changes.

4.5. *The event-based approach*

Except from the centralized software repository approach, in all other approaches explained above, it is difficult to ensure that traceability relations between artefacts will always be updated after modifications of these artefacts.

As a solution to this problem, Cleland-Huang *et al* [10] have developed an event-based traceability (EBT) server for recording and maintaining traceability relations between requirements documents and other software artefacts. This system is based on an event-notification mechanism that implements the *observer* pattern [25]. More specifically, the requirement documents can register their dependencies to other artefacts using the registry of the system. Following the registration of dependencies, their system monitors the artefacts and when any of them is modified, it notifies all the dependent requirements about the change. The requirement documents have responsibility for updating their contents, if necessary. This system can be used for maintaining *dependency* relations once they are identified. However, it provides no support for identifying them.

In terms of their support for interoperability, the event-based and mark-up approaches appear to be superior to centralized database and the software repository approaches. The latter, however, appear to be stronger in terms of performance and offer better data management facilities.

5. Deployment of Traceability

Traceability relations may be deployed in the development life cycle of a software system to support different development and maintenance activities, including:

(a) change impact analysis and management [12];
(b) system verification, validation, testing and standards compliance analysis [51];
(c) the reuse of software artefacts [69]; and
(d) software artefacts understanding [4, 40, 50, 51].

In the following, we overview ways in which traceability may support the above forms of analysis and discuss the main types of relations that can be used in these forms. We also discuss factors than can promote or prohibit the use of traceability in industrial settings as reported by relevant case studies [5, 49, 51].

5.1. *Traceability for change impact analysis and change management*

One of the primary drivers for establishing and maintaining traceability relations between different artefacts developed to document and implement software systems is the ability to use these relations during the entire life-cycle of a system in order to: (a) Establish the impact that potential changes in some part of the system may have in other parts (i.e., *change impact analysis*), and (b) make decisions about whether or not such changes should be introduced, and with what priority (i.e., *change management*).

The simplest form of analyzing the impact of a change in a given artefact (e.g. a requirement statement) is the identification of all the other artefacts that will be affected by the change (e.g. design artefacts and code). Primitive change impact analysis requires the provision of basic querying facilities to retrieve traceability relations of specific types that may also have specific values for the properties defined for these types. Most of the existing traceability tools and environments provide such querying facilities.

However, more complex forms of change impact analysis may also be desired in different settings. Examples of these forms are: (a) The classification of affected artefacts into different groups subject to the exact effect that the change will have on them, (b) the identification of side-effects that the change may have, and (c) the estimation of the cost of propagating the change. The delivery of such capabilities requires support for the composition of different traceability relations into *trace-paths*. These trace-paths can demonstrate how impact is propagated across artefacts that are not directly related. Compositions of traceability relations may be established by evaluating *regular expressions* [44], *deductive rules* [51], or *traceability rules* [61]. Some research prototypes provide such composition capabilities (e.g. TOOR [44], PRO-ART [47], and the rule-based tracer [61]). Most of the industrial traceability tools, however, can realize these capabilities only through the generation of appropriate scripts that can compute the required compositions. Support for the estimation of the cost of executing and integrating requested changes is provided at an inferior level. This is because the few cost estimation models (see [33], for example) that have been developed for this purpose cannot provide very precise cost predictions.

In certain cases, the assessment of the impact of a change may also require the execution of a simulation model to demonstrate the potential effects of the change. This kind of analysis requires not only the establishment of specific types of traceability relations between the artefacts to be changed and the simulation model that can demonstrate the effects of the change, but also the ability to propagate changed values across these relations, to inject changed values into the simulation model, and to execute the change. The EBT system [10] offers such capabilities and has been used to analyze the effect of requirement changes onto the performance of software systems by using dependency relations between requirements and performance simulation models [12].

Clearly, the accuracy of both simple and complex forms of impact analysis depends on the semantics, granularity and accuracy of the traceability relations, which are taken into account. Relations that are established by virtue of identifying references to common entities in different software artefacts may provide some evidence that a change could potentially have an impact on an artefact, but cannot establish this impact, or its nature, with certainty. Examples are the *overlap* relations between requirements and object-oriented analysis models identified in [61, 78], or between source code artefacts and manual pages or requirements identified by information retrieval techniques in [4, 40]. On the other hand, traceability relationships with a rich semantic content (e.g. the *dependency* relations in [51] or the *requires_execution_of* relations in [61]) can lead to more accurate impact analysis results.

The necessity of having traceability relations with rich semantics in order to be able to perform accurate impact analysis has been clearly identified by empirical studies [8, 36]. Empirical research has also indicated that the accuracy of impact predictions depends on the granularity of the entities, which are associated by traceability relations. As reported in [8], fine-grain relations that associate specific entities/parts within broad models and documentation result in more accurate results. Industrial case studies have also indicated that software developers are often reluctant to rely on traceability relations that have been produced automatically due to doubts about the correctness of such relations [36].

5.2. *Traceability for software validation, verification, testing and standards compliance*

Depending on their semantics, traceability relations can provide the basis for performing different types of analysis in order to ensure that a system implements the requirements desired by the stakeholders involved in its development (*validation*), verify that it satisfies certain properties and its specification (*verification*), test its individual components and the system as a whole, and assess its compliance with respect to existing standards.

Pre-traceability *contribution* relations, for instance, may be used to identify stakeholders and involve them in requirement validation activities [27]. The ability to verify the satisfaction of the specification of a system and its required properties also depends on the existence of traceability relations with appropriate semantics. Preliminary system verification, for instance, can be performed by consulting and/or composing *refinement, dependency* and *satisfiability* relations to establish whether all the requirements of a system have been allocated to specific design and/or source code components [42, 69]). Similarly, traceability relations may be used to check the existence of appropriate test cases for verifying different requirements and to retrieve such cases for further testing. The results of this preliminary verification analysis typically provide input to software inspection and auditing procedures [69]. They can also be correlated with the results of other forms of analysis, which may be carried out as part of the inspection and auditing procedures (e.g. functional simulations, textual and syntactic analysis of code, and standards auditing [42]). Traceability relations may also be used in system reviews concerned with the assessment of requirements and design models. Haumer *et al* [28], for instance, use *goal attainment* and *failure* pre-traceability relations between goal oriented requirement models and collections of observed cases of system usage encoded in multimedia (e.g. video and audio), in order to inform review activities which are concerned with the assessment of adequacy of these models.

Traceability relations have also been used in automated forms of verification analysis, which are aimed at assessing the consistency of different models of the same system [21]. Spanoudakis *et al* [59], for instance, present an approach that can be used to rewrite formal requirement specifications in order to express *overlap* relations known to hold between their parts and make them amenable to consistency checking using theorem proving. Techniques for detecting overlap relations between structural and behavioural object-oriented models of software systems, and deploying them for checking the consistency of these models with respect to specific consistency rules are also discussed in [60]. In [24], Fiutem and Antoniol extract design models from the source code of a system, detect *overlap* relations between these models and the original design models that had been developed prior to implementation by using string matching algorithms, and use these relations to verify the consistency of the implementation with the original design.

5.3. *Traceability for software reuse*

Researchers have widely acknowledged the potential of traceability relations in identifying reusable artefacts in the software development life-cycle [4, 14, 69]. These artefacts may be at different levels of abstraction (e.g. source code, design or requirement artefacts) and can be identified and reused through different scenarios, which require the existence of different types of traceability relations.

In the context of the *Software Information Base* [14] *dependency* traceability relations, called "correspondence" relations, are used to associate requirements specifications with design models, and design models with source code. These relations are established in the context of *application frames* which group artefacts of specific (or families of) software applications and must be asserted manually. Software engineers can follow these relations in order to locate concrete reusable artefacts in an application frame at low levels of abstraction (i.e., design and source code artefacts) once the possibility of reusing this frame (or parts of it) has been established. This possibility is established by assessing the similarity of application frame requirements with requirements for new systems. Similar approaches have been suggested in [19, 42]. In [42], reusable design elements are identified through *satisfiability, refinement* or *overlap* relations that connect them with events, pre-conditions, and post-conditions in use case models. Also, as suggested in [4], traceability relations between source code artefacts (e.g. functions in code libraries) and manual pages can help software engineers understand the functionality of the former and appreciate the possibilities of using (or re-using) them in specific contexts.

The traceability relations used in all the above approaches are *vertical relations* [36]. Different opportunities based on the deployment of *horizontal traceability relations* between requirement specifications are suggested in [2, 69]. The focus of the latter approach is the reuse of coarse-grain requirement specifications developed for families of software systems (or parts of these specifications) expressed as structured text. This process is termed "requirements recycling" and supports the production of a requirements specification document for a new member in a system family that shares features with existing members but may also introduce new features, or drop and modify some of the existing ones. Driven from change scenarios that incorporate feature introduction, modification and deletion requests, this approach first locates parts in existing requirement documents that refer to the required features. Then it uses *overlap, dependency,* and *refinement* traceability relations that involve these parts to identify other parts in the documentation that can also be recycled. The new requirement document is produced by copying and pasting the latter parts. However, while preparing the new document, the approach suggests the investigation of *overlap* relations in order to identify possible redundant parts that should be eliminated.

5.4. *Traceability for artefact understanding*

A significant driver for the generation of traceability relations is to use them in order to understand the artefacts that they involve in reference to the context in which they were created, or in reference to other artefacts related to them. This is particularly important in cases where the people who need to access, understand,

and maintain the artefacts are not those who contributed to their creation, a phenomenon that is typical in software maintenance.

The comprehension of source code artefacts is, for instance, one of the main objectives underpinning the generation of traceability relations between such artefacts and manual pages, requirement models [4, 38, 40] test cases, and system feature descriptions (e.g. *Software Reconnaissance technique* [71]), or design and domain analysis models [9]. The same objective of enabling code comprehension has driven the development of approaches which can trace components of programs generated by deductive synthesis (e.g. variable names, function calls) onto the specifications from which they were derived. These approaches (see [66], for example) use the formal proof that led to the generated program to construct *overlap* relations to parts of the specification that drove the derivation.

Similarly, the use of *rationalization relations* have been extensively suggested as a means of providing explanation about the form of requirement and design artefacts [28, 47, 50, 51]. Most of the traceability environments which support the recording of such relations (e.g. PRO-ART [47], REMAP [50]) record rationale based on variants of the IBIS model [13]. According to this model, artefact construction decisions can be represented in terms of the main *issues* that were considered in the construction process, the *arguments* that were articulated for these issues, and the *positions* taken by different stakeholders with regards to these issues. A slightly different approach is advocated in *EColabor* [62]. *EColabor* supports the recording of rationale for requirements specifications articulated around questions, answers, reasons, and commitments according to the *Inquiry Cycle* model using audio and video artefacts. *EColabor* provides support for fine-grain traceability relations between requirements specifications and segments of audio and video artefacts, and facilities monitoring of on-going discussions.

5.5. *Empirical studies of the use of traceability*

Empirical studies about the use of traceability in industrial organizations have confirmed its deployment for supporting the activities outlined in the preceding sections. They have also indicated significant differences in relevant practices, which are influenced by numerous environmental, organizational, and technical factors.

Based on the findings of a case study of 16 organizations in the US, Ramesh [49] has distinguished two different types of traceability users: The *low-end* and *high-end users*. Low-end users use traceability relations to allocate requirements to system components, inform system verification procedures, and manage changes in system development and maintenance life cycle. However, they do not view traceability as an important task in their development process and do not realize any form of "formal methodology" in their traceability practice. High-end users, on the other hand, are organizationally committed to traceability and tend to make extended use of it as part of its well-defined system development policies. Thus, they capture traceability relations between artefacts created in the entire life cycle of a system and relations between artefacts and rationale. They also tend to customize the tools that they use to provide better support for their traceability practices.

As indicated in other empirical studies [5], the main factor that prohibits the wide and effective use of traceability in industrial setting is the ability to establish traceability relations that could support the required forms of analysis in cost-effective ways. The diversity of the artefacts which are generated in the software development life-cycle and the lack of interoperability between the tools that are used to construct and manage them, make the capture of traceability relations expensive and create the perception that the benefits from establishing traceability are not justified. Additional costs also arise from the need to train users to use the relevant tools and platforms. This makes traceability a cumbersome task for short-term projects [5].

Finally, it should be noted that, since the accuracy of forms of analysis that deploy traceability relations depends on the correctness and completeness of these relations and these properties cannot be guaranteed for neither manually nor automatically generated traceability relations, users tend to be reluctant to use traceability relations in such forms of analysis. Empirical studies (e.g. [37]) have confirmed this tendency and suggest that in cases where there is access to experienced software engineers, organizations rely on them for certain forms of analysis (e.g. change impact) rather than deploying recorded traceability relations, despite the cost of this approach.

6. Open Research Issues

As discussed in the preceding sections, software traceability has been the focus of numerous as well as diverse research activities in the areas of software and systems engineering over the last 15 years. Numerous approaches tackling different aspects and issues of traceability have been proposed, and tools to support the establishment, maintenance and deployment of traceability during system development have been produced. However, despite these developments, empirical studies demonstrate that current technology does not provide sufficient support for traceability and, as a consequence, traceability is not widely adopted in industrial settings unless there is a regulatory reason for doing so [5, 49, 26, 51].

In the following, we discuss the main issues, which in our view prevent the widespread use of traceability in industrial settings and should be addressed by further research. Our discussion has been based on our study of the literature, the experience that we have gained from building systems to support traceability for industrial organizations [61, 78], and discussions that have taken place as part of the two international workshops on traceability that we have organized over the last two years, namely TEFSE 2002 [65] and TEFSE 2003 [66].

Evidently from Secs. 2 and 3, there are relatively few approaches that can automate the generation of traceability relations. With some exceptions, the relations that can be generated by these approaches do not have the strong semantic meaning required for the most important forms of analysis that can be based on traceability. Overlap relations, for instance, which can be automatically generated by existing approaches have a very general referential meaning and cannot support effectively significant forms of analysis such as change impact analysis. On the other hand, a close analysis of the reviewed approaches reveals that, with the exception of TOOR [44], none of them can support the generation of satisfiability relations which are important for analysis related to software verification. This problem becomes more significant in the case of relations that involve artefacts, which incorporate chunks of text such as requirement specifications, descriptions of rationale, and test cases. Most of the existing approaches assume that traceability relations involving artefacts of these types must be asserted manually and only a few of the reviewed approaches (i.e., [4, 40 and 61]) support the automatic generation of traceability relations involving them. Thus, as the manual assertion of traceability relations is labour intensive, traceability is rarely established unless there is a regulatory reason for doing so.

A possible way forward in the automatic generation of traceability relations could be the standardization of vocabularies that may be used to model systems in specific application domains. Another solution along the same direction could be based on the development of ontologies. Ontologies can provide formal specifications of common aspects of software systems and their domains (e.g. specifications of certain types of requirements in abstract forms). Thus, they can be used as a starting point for building system models with the precise semantic meaning that is required for the generation of traceability relations. For instance, requirement satisfiability relations could be established by reasoning about the satisfiability of the axiomatic definition of a requirement in ontology by other system artefacts such as design specifications.

Another problem related to the generation of traceability relations is the lack of mechanisms for verifying the correctness and completeness of these relations and, therefore, establishing the necessary degree of trust that is required for deploying them for further analysis with confidence. This is mainly an issue for approaches that automate the generation of such relations. At the moment, very few of these approaches provide mechanisms through which they could be tuned so as to achieve better performance in terms of correctness and completeness. A notable exception to this phenomenon is the rule base tracer discussed in [61]. This system uses historical assessments of automatically generated traceability relations provided by the users to compute degrees of confidence in the ability of its rules to generate correct relations for new sets of artefacts. These degrees of confidence can be used to de-activate and re-activate specific traceability rules if necessary [57]. It also uses machine learning techniques for generating traceability rule that could improve the levels of completeness that it achieves [58].

Clearly the levels of correctness and completeness which are required in different settings depend on the type of the involved traceability relations and the types of analysis that they are to be deployed for. In change impact analysis, for instance, it may be more desirable to have high completeness rather than correctness rates. On the other hand, in system verification and validation correctness seems to be more important. The development of clear guidelines for making decisions about performance criteria in specific settings and mechanisms for tuning different approaches, in order to achieve better performance are issues that need to be addressed by further research. It should be noted that mechanisms for verifying the correctness and completeness of traceability relations are necessary also for systems/approaches, which assume that such relations are asserted manually. This is because evidence from our empirical investigations has indicated that it is not unlikely to have different users suggesting different sets of relations for the same set of artefacts, depending on their interpretation of the contents of these artefacts.

In the absence of sufficient support for the automatic generation and verification of traceability relations, the cost of establishing traceability in industrial settings is high. Given this, the systematic and widespread adoption of traceability as part of software development processes would certainly require clear evidence about the potential benefits from its deployment. Current empirical research fails to provide hard quantitative evidence about these benefits and, to the best of our knowledge; methods that could be used to measure these benefits do not exist. Furthermore, although it has been argued that the adoption of traceability cannot be effective unless it is tailored to the needs of specific projects and organizations [20], there is little (if any at all) methodological support for identifying these needs and using them to inform traceability adoption and deployment strategies. The development of methodological support for this purpose should try to relate traceability establishment and deployment to the objectives of the involved organizations, the existing software development strategies, and the needs of the different types of stakeholders who are envisaged to make use of traceability (e.g. managers, developers, customers, auditors etc).

It should also be noted that the current level of tool support for traceability is one of the main reasons for its limited use in industrial settings. This is because most of the industrial tools and environments fail to provide support for all the types of artefacts that are constructed in the software development life-cycle, as well as all the types of traceability relations that may exist between these artefacts. Moreover, existing tools and environments do not interoperate with other tools, which are likely to be used in distributed and heterogeneous software development settings. Some research prototypes (e.g. EBT [10], and TraceM [55]) appear to address the interoperability problem. However, these tools do not adequately address the problem of automatic generation of traceability relations, and it is unclear whether they can achieve the data management effectiveness and robustness required in industrial settings. To this end, further research and development is required for delivering the right combination of capabilities.

7. Conclusions

In this article, we have presented a roadmap of the research and practical work that has been developed to support software system traceability. To produce this roadmap, we have reviewed and presented: (a) Different frameworks and classifications of traceability relations, (b) different approaches to the generation of traceability relations including manual, semi-automatic and automatic approaches, (c) different approaches to the representation, recording, and maintenance of traceability relations that underpin the architectural design and implementation of traceability tools and environments, and (d) different ways of deploying traceability relations in the software development process. Our review of the field has also identified issues that require further investigation by both the research and industrial communities which are also presented in the paper.

Our view is that the establishment and effective deployment of software traceability is very significant in the software development life cycle, and that existing approaches have made significant contributions to various aspects of traceability. However, it has to be appreciated that the provision of adequate support for traceability is not an easy task and given the current state of the art in this field, it cannot be claimed that holistic and effective support for traceability is available. As we discussed in Sec. 6, there is still a significant number of issues of traceability which are open to further research and need to be addressed adequately before traceability can be widely adopted in industrial settings and benefit system development processes.

References

1. I. Alexander, "Towards automatic traceability in industrial practice", *Proceedings of the 1st International Workshop on Traceability in Emerging Forms of Software Engineering (TEFSE 2002)*, Edinburgh, UK, September 2002.
2. I. Alexander, "SemiAutomatic tracing of requirement versions to use cases — Experience and challenges, *Proceedings of the 2nd International Workshop on Traceability in Emerging Forms of Software Engineering (TEFSE 2003)*, Canada, October 2003.
3. I. Alexander and F. Kiedaisch, "Towards recyclable system requirements", *Proceedings of the 9th Annual IEEE International Conference and Workshop on the Engineering of Computer-Based Systems* (2002) 9–17.
4. G. Antoniol, G. Canfora, G. Casazza, A. De Lucia and E. Merlo, "Recovering traceability links between code and documentation", *IEEE Transactions on Software Engineering* **28**, no. 10 (October 2002) 970–983.
5. P. Arkley, P. Mason and S. Riddle, "Position paper: Enabling traceability", *Proceedings of 1st International Workshop on Traceability in Emerging Forms of Software Engineering*, pp. 61–65, *http://www.soi.city.ac.uk/~zisman/traceworkshop.html*.
6. J. Bayer and T. Widen, "Introducing traceability to product lines", *Proceedings of the Software Product Family Engineering: 4th International Workshop, PFE 2002*, Bilbao, Spain, *Lecture Notes in Computer Science* (Springer-Verlag, ISSN:0302-9743).
7. J. Bayet, O. Flege, P. Knauber, R. Laqua, D. Muthig, K. Schmid, T. Widen and J. M. DeBaud, "PuLSE: A methodology to develop software product lines", *Symposium on Software Reusability*, May 1999.

8. A. Bianchi, A. R. Fasolino and G. Vissagio, "An exploratory case study of the maintenance effectiveness of traceability models" *Proceedings of 8th International Workshop on Program Comprehension (IWPC'00)*, Limerick, Ireland (June 2000) 149–159.

9. C. Boldyreff, E. L. Burd, R. M. Hather, M. Munro and E. J. Younger, "Greater understanding through maintainer driven traceability", *Proceedings of the 4th International Workshop on Program Comprehension (WPC'96)*, 1996.

10. J. Cleland-Huang, C. Chang and J. Wise, "Supporting event based traceability through high-level recognition of change events", *Proceedings of IEEE COMPSAC Conference*, Oxford, England, August 2002.

11. J. Cleland-Huang and D. Schmelzer, "Dynamic tracing non-functional requirements through design patter invariants", *Proceedings of the 2nd International Workshop on Traceability in Emerging Forms of Software Engineering (TEFSE 2003)*, Canada, October 2003.

12. J. Cleland-Huang, C. K. Chang, G. Sethi, K. Javvaji, H. Hu and J. Xia, "Automating speculative queries through event-based requirements traceability", *Proceedings of the IEEE Joint International Requirements Engineering Conference*, Essen, Germany, September 2002.

13. J. Conklin and M. Begeman, "gIBIS: A hypertext tool for exploratory policy discussion", *ACM Transactions on Office Information Systems*, no. 6 (October 1988) 303–331.

14. P. Constantopoulos, M. Jarke, Y. Mylopoulos and Y. Vassiliou, "The software information base: A server for reuse", *VLDB Journal* **4**, no. 1 (1995) 1–43.

15. W. Cyre and A. Thakar. "Generating validation feedback for automatic interpretation of requirements", *Formal Methods in System Design* (Kluwer, 1997).

16. G. Cysneiros, A. Zisman and G. Spanoudakis, "A traceability approach for i^* and UML models", *Proceedings of 2nd International Workshop on Software Engineering for Large-Scale Multi-Agent Systems — ICSE 2003*, May 2003.

17. CORE, *http://www.vtcorp.com*.

18. S. DeRose, E. Maler and D. Orchard, "XML linking language (XLink)", version 1.0, *http://www.w3.org/TR/2000/REC-xlink-20010627/*, World Wide Web Consortium.

19. J. Dick, "Rich traceability", *Proceedings of the 1st International Workshop on Traceability for Emerging Forms of Software Engineering (TEFSE'02)*, Edinburgh, UK, September 2002.

20. R. Dogmes and K. Pohl, "Adopting traceability environments to project-specific needs", *Communications of the ACM* **41**, no. 12 (1998) 55–62.

21. S. Easterbrook, J. Callahan and V. Wiels, "V & V through inconsistency tracking and analysis", *Proceedings of the 9th International Workshop on Software Specification and Design* (1998) 43–51.

22. A. Egyed, "A scenario-driven approach to trace dependency analysis", *IEEE Transactions on Software Engineering* **9**, no. 2, (February 2003).

23. A. Egyed and P. Gruenbacher, "Automatic requirements traceability: Beyond the record and replay paradigm", *Proceedings of the 17th IEEE International Conference on Automated Software Engineering (ASE)*, Edinburgh, UK, September 2002.

24. R. Fiutem and G. Antoniol, "Identifying design-code inconsistencies in object-oriented software: A case study", *Proceedings of International Conference on Software Maintenance* (March 1998) 94–103.

25. E. Gamma, R. Heml, R. Johnson and J. Vlissides, "Design patters: Elements of reusable object-oriented software", *Addison-Wesley Professional Computer Series*, 1st edn., ISBN 0201633612, 1995.

26. O. Gotel and A. Finkelstein, "An analysis of the requirements traceability problem", *Proceedings of the 1st International Conference in Requirements Engineering* (1994) 94–101.
27. O. Gotel and A. Finkelstein, "Contribution structures", *Proceedings of 2nd International Symposium on Requirements Engineering (RE '95)* (1995) 100–107.
28. P. Haumer, K. Pohl, K. Weidenhaupt and M. Jarke, "Improving reviews by extended traceability", *Proceedings of 32nd International Conference on System Sciences*, 1999.
29. J. H. Hayes, A. Dekhtyar and J. Osborne, "Improving requirements tracing via information retrieval", *Proceedings of the 11th IEEE International Requirements Engineering Conference*, Monterey Bay, 2003.
30. Integrated Chipware, RTM, *www.chipware.com*.
31. H. Kaindl, "The missing link in requirements engineering", *Software Engineering Notes* (June 1992) 498–510.
32. A. Kozlenkov and A. Zisman, "Are their design specifications consistent with our requirements?", *Proceedings of IEEE Joint International Requirements Engineering Conference — RE'02*, Essen, September 2002.
33. L. Lavazza and G. Valetto, "Requirements-based estimation of change costs", *Empirical Software Engineering — An International Journal* **5**, no. 3, (November 2000).
34. C. Lee, L. Guadagno and X. Jia, "An agile approach to capturing requirements traceability", *Proceedings of the 2nd International Workshop on Traceability in Emerging Forms of Software Engineering (TEFSE 2003)*, Canada, October 2003.
35. P. Letelier, "A framework for requirements traceability in UML-based projects", *Proceedings of the 1st International Workshop on Traceability for Emerging Forms of Software Engineering (TEFSE'02)*, Edinburgh, UK, September 2002.
36. M. Lindval and K. Sandahl, "Practical implications of traceability", *Software Practice and Experience* **26**, no. 10 (1996) 1161–1180.
37. M. Lindvall and K. Sandahl, "Traceability aspects of impact analysis in object oriented systems", *Software Maintenance: Research and Practice* **10**, no. 1 (1998) 37–57.
38. J. I. Maletic and A. Marcus, "Supporting program comprehension using semantic and structural information", *Proceedings of 23rd International Conference on Software Engineering*, Toronto, Canada (2001) 103–112.
39. J. I. Maletic, E. V. Munson, A. Marcus and T. N. Nguyen, "Using a hypertext model for traceability link conformance analysis", *Proceedings of the 2nd International Workshop on Traceability for Emerging Forms of Software Engineering (TEFSE'03)*, Canada, October 2003.
40. A. Marcus and J. I. Maletic, "Recovering documentation-to-source-code traceability links using latent semantic indexing", *Proceedings of 25th International Conference Software Engineering*, 2003.
41. K. Mohan and B. Ramesh, "Managing variability with traceability in product and service families", *Proceedings of the 35th Hawaii International Conference on System Sciences*, IEEE, 2002.
42. NASA, "Preferred reliability practices: Independent verification and validation of embedded software", *Practice No. PD-ED-1228*, Marshal Space Flight Centre.
43. E. Perez-Minana, T. Trew and P. Krause, "Issues on the composability of requirements specifications for a product family", *Proceedings of the 1st International Workshop on Traceability in Emerging Forms of Software Engineering* (September 2002) 47–53.
44. F. Pinheiro and J. Goguen, "An object-oriented tool for tracing requirements", *IEEE Software* (March 1996) 52–64.
45. F. Pinheiro, "Formal and informal aspects of requirements tracing", *Proceedings of 3rd Workshop on Requirements Engineering (III WER)*, Rio de Janeiro, Brazil, 2000.

46. K. Pohl, *Process-Centered Requirements Engineering* (John Wiley Research Science Press, 1996).
47. K. Pohl, PRO-ART: Enabling requirements pre-traceability, *Proceedings of the 2nd IEEE International. Conference on Requirements Engineering (ICRE 1996)* (1996).
48. K. Pohl *et al.*, "Product family development", *Dagstuhl Seminar Report No.304*, 2001, *http://www.dagstul.de/01161/report*.
49. B. Ramesh, "Factors influencing requirements traceability practice", *Communications of the ACM* **41**, no. 12 (1998) 37–44.
50. B. Ramesh and V. Dhar, "Supporting systems development using knowledge captured during requirements engineering", *IEEE Transactions in Software Engineering* (June 1992) 498–510.
51. B. Ramesh and M. Jarke, "Towards reference models for requirements traceability", *IEEE Transactions in Software Engineering* **27**, no. 1 (2001) 58–93.
52. RDT, *http://www.igatech.com/rdt/index.html*.
53. M. Riebisch and I. Philippow, "Evolution of product lines using traceability", *Proceedings of the Workshop on Engineering Complex Object-Oriented Systems for Evolution*, in conjunction with OOPSLA 2001, Tampa Bay, Florida, USA, October 2001.
54. J. Savolainen, "Tools for design rationale documentation in the development of a product family", *Proceedings of 1st Working IFIP Conference on Software Architecture*, San Antonio, Texas, 1999.
55. S. A. Sherba, K. M. Anderson and M. Faisal, "A framework for mapping traceability relationships", *Proceedings of the 2nd International Workshop on Traceability for Emerging Forms of Software Engineering (TEFSE 2003)*, Montreal, Canada, September 2003.
56. X. Song, B. Hasling, G. Mangla and B. Sherman, "Lessons learned from building a web-based requirements tracing system", *Proceedings of 3rd International Conference on Requirements Engineering* (1998) 41–50.
57. G. Spanoudakis, "Plausible and adaptive requirement traceability structures", *Proceedings of the 14th International Conference in Software Engineering and Knowledge Engineering*, Ischia, Italy (2002) 135–142.
58. G. Spanoudakis, A. Avilla Garcez and A. Zisman, "Revising rules to capture requirements traceability relations: A machine learning approach", *Proceedings of the 15th International Conference in Software Engineering and Knowledge Engineering (SEKE 2003)*, San Francisco, USA, July 2003.
59. G. Spanoudakis, A. Finkelstein and D. Till, "Overlaps in requirements engineering", *Automated Software Engineering Journal* **6**, no. 2 (1999) 171–198.
60. G. Spanoudakis and H. Kim, "Supporting the reconciliation of models of object behaviour", *International Journal of Software and Systems Modelling*, (2004) (to appear).
61. G. Spanoudakis, A. Zisman, E. Perez-Minana and P. Krause, "Rule-based generation of requirements traceability relations", *Journal of Systems and Software* **72**, no. 2 (2004) 105–127.
62. M. Strens and R. Sugden, "Change analysis: A step towards meeting the challenge of changing requirements", *Proceedings of the IEEE Symposium and Workshop on Engineering of Computer-Based Systems*, Fredrichshafen, Germany, March 1996.
63. K. Takahashi, C. Potts, V. Kumar, K. Ota and J. Smith, "Hypermedia support for collaboration in requirements analysis", *Proceedings of 2nd International Conference on Requirements Engineering* (1996) 31–40.
64. Teleologic, Teleologic DOORS, *www.teleologic.com/products/doors*.

65. G. Spanoudakis and A. Zisman, "Proceedings of the 1st international workshop on traceability in emerging forms of software engineering (organised in conjunction with the 17th IEEE International Conference on Automated Software Engineering)", eds. G. Spanoudakis, A. Zisman and E. Perez-Minana, September 2002.

66. G. Spanoudakis and A. Zisman, "Proceedings of the 2nd International workshop on traceability in emerging forms of software engineering (organised in conjunction with the 18th IEEE International Conference on Automated Software Engineering)", eds. G. Spanoudakis and A. Zisman, September 2003.

67. J. Van Baalen, P. Robinson, M. Lowry and T. Pressburger, "Explaining synthesized software", *Proceedings of the 13th IEEE Conference on Automated Software Engineering* (October 1998) 240–248.

68. A. Von Knethen, "Automatic change support based on a trace model", *Proceedings of the 1st International Workshop on Traceability in Emerging Forms of Software Engineering (TEFSE'02)*, Edinburgh, September 2002.

69. A. Von Knethen, B. Paech, F. Kiedaisch and F. Houdek, "Systematic requirements recycling through abstraction and traceability", *Proceedings of the IEEE International Requirements Engineering Conference*, Germany, September 2002.

70. R. Watkins and M. Neal, "Why and how of requirements tracing", *IEEE Software* (July 1994) 104–106.

71. E. Whitehead, "An architectural model for application integration in open hypermedia environments", *Proceeding of the 8th ACM Conference on Hypertext* (April 1997) 1–12.

72. N. Wilde and C. Casey, "Early field experience with the software reconnaissance technique for program comprehension", *Proceedings of the 1996 International Conference on Software Maintenance (ICSM '96)* (1996) 312–318.

73. Xlinkit, *http://www.systemwire.com/xlinkit.*

74. P. Xu and B. Ramesh, "Supporting workflow management systems with traceability", *Proceedings of the 35th Hawaii International Conference on System Sciences*, IEEE, 2002.

75. D. Zowghi and R. Offen, "A logical framework for modelling and reasoning about the evolution of requirements", *Proceedings of 3rd International Symposium on Requirements Engineering*, Annapolis, MD, January 1997.

76. A. Zisman, W. Emmerich and A. Finkelstein, "Using XML to build consistency rules for distributed specifications", *Proceedings of 10th International Workshop on Software Specification and Design — IWSSD-10*, San Diego, USA, November 2000.

77. A. Zisman, G. Spanoudakis, E. Perez-Minana and P. Krause, "Towards a traceability approach for product families requirements", *Proceedings of 3rd ICSE Workshop on Software Product Lines: Economics, Architectures, and Implications*, Orlando, USA, May 2002.

78. A. Zisman, G. Spanoudakis, E. Perez-Minana and P. Krause, "Tracing software requirements artefacts", *Proceedings of the 2003 International Conference on Software Engineering Research and Practice (SERP'03)*, Las Vegas, Nevada, USA, June 2003.

79. A. Zisman and A. Kozlenkov, "Consistency management of UML specifications", *Proceedings of 4th International Conference on Software Engineering, Artificial Intelligence, Networking, and Parallel/Distributed Computing (SNPD'03)*, Lübeck, Germany, October 2003.

SYSTEM DYNAMICS AND GOAL-ORIENTED MEASUREMENT: A HYBRID APPROACH

DIETMAR PFAHL*

*University of Calgary, Schulich School of Engineering,
Department of Electrical & Computer Engineering, ICT 540,
2500 University Drive NW, Calgary, Alberta T2N 1N4, Canada
E-mail: dpfahl@ucalgary.ca*

GÜNTHER RUHE

*University of Calgary, Laboratory for Software Engineering Decision Support,
2500 University Drive NW, Calgary, AB T2N 1N4, Canada
E-mail: ruhe@ucalgary.ca*

Goal-oriented measurement following the Goal/Question/Metric (GQM) approach is a well-defined and powerful tool in software management and decision-support. This chapter proposes the integration of GQM with a mature software process simulation approach, System Dynamics, in order to further enhance software managers' analytic, explorative, and decision-making capability. The proposed hybrid approach, which we denote "Dynamic GQM", overcomes limitations that exist if applying GQM and system dynamics in isolation. It offers a new dimension of support to managers and decision-makers by integrating traditional goal-oriented measurement and static modeling with the newly emerging paradigm of software process simulation and dynamic modeling. The hybrid approach is holistic by nature, i.e. it takes a global perspective on decision-making in contrast to the local perspective advocated by traditional GQM. The proposed approach combines individual GQM plans into one consistent model and adds time-dynamic behavior on top of it, thus offering a comprehensive view on what is actually happening in software projects.

Keywords: Dynamic GQM, goal-oriented measurement, hybrid modeling, software process simulation, System Dynamics.

1. Introduction

The process of software development and evolution is an ambitious undertaking. A huge number of individual steps and tasks are performed with a large number of involved resources. There are strong dependencies between the processes, and they are performed geographically distributed. From a decision-making perspective, all these activities are confronted with different objectives and constraints, with a huge number of variables under dynamically changing requirements, processes, actors, stakeholders, tools and techniques. Very often, this is combined with incomplete, imprecise, fuzzy or inconsistent information about all the involved artifacts, as well as with difficulties about the decision space and environment. This is illustrated

---

*Corresponding author.

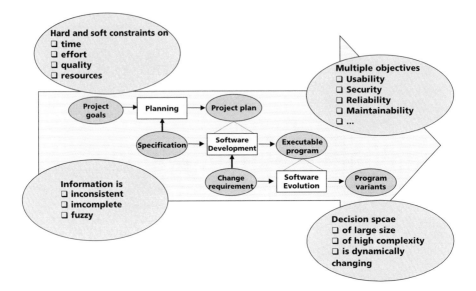

Fig. 1.   Issues in software engineering decision-making.

in Fig. 1 where a very coarse-grained model of software planning, development, and evolution is assumed. Nevertheless, making good decisions is of tremendous importance for developing software faster, cheaper and with better quality.

Currently, there is an increasing effort to not only measure or model certain aspects of the development processes, but to go further and integrate all available data, information, knowledge and experience with a sound methodology to provide the backbone for making good decisions. This mainly includes searching for all the objectives and constraints that influence a decision as well as elaborating the so-defined solution space for possible courses of action [18]. Valid models combined with valid empirical data are of crucial importance in this process.

This chapter aims at creating synergy from combining two powerful enabling techniques for software engineering decision support and software process improvement: the local, time-discrete measurement approach following the Goal/ Question/Metric (GQM) paradigm [2, 10, 21], and the global (holistic), time-continuous simulation approach following the System Dynamics (SD) method [7–9].

The purpose of the proposed hybrid approach is to enlarge the contributions of both methods when compared to its isolated application. In more detail, the purpose is to:

- Synchronize individual GQM models by putting them into a joint system perspective as suggested by SD.
- Enhance GQM by the dynamic features of SD.
- Incrementally increase the validity of both GQM and SD models by mutually reusing and validating models generated from GQM and SD.
- Integrate real world empirical results with experiments in a virtual world offered by SD.

The remainder of this chapter is structured as follows. Section 2 briefly sketches the main principles of goal-oriented measurement according to the GQM paradigm. Section 3 introduces the SD simulation modeling method. Section 4 lists limitations of both GQM and SD if applied separately. Section 5 presents the main advantages of combining GQM and SD in a hybrid measurement and simulation approach, i.e. "Dynamic GQM". Section 6 focuses on the complementary aspects of GQM measurement and SD simulation modelling and describes how they should be combined. Following the ideas outlined and described in previous sections, Sec. 7 illustrates the application of Dynamic GQM in the form of a case example. A brief discussion concludes the chapter.

2. Goal-Oriented Measurement (GQM)

Measurement is a technique that supports understanding, controlling, predicting, evaluating and improving software development processes and products. Goal-oriented measurement according to the Goal/Question/Metric (GQM) paradigm represents a systematic approach for tailoring and integrating the objectives of an organization into measurement goals and their stepwise refinement into measurable values (metrics). GQM focuses on a top-down approach for defining appropriate measures (metrics) and a bottom-up approach for analyzing and interpreting measurement results.

The GQM process is divided into several stages. After a pre-study, the first stage is to identify a set of measurement goals. After these goals have been set, questions that define the goals are derived. The purpose of the questions is to capture as many aspects of the measurement goal because they are necessary to cover it completely. The next step consists in specifying the metrics that need to be collected in order to answer the questions defined, and to track the conformance of development products and processes with respect to the defined measurement goals. Defined goals, questions and metrics are described in the GQM plan. The three layers (goals, questions, and metrics) of the GQM plan correspond to the following three levels:

- Conceptual level (Goal): The definition of the measurement goal specifies the object of measurement, the purpose of measurement, the quality model of interest, the role for which the measurement results are of interest (viewpoint), and the environment in which the measurement program occurs.
- Operational level (Question): A set of questions is used to define in a quantitative way the goal and to characterize the way the data will be interpreted. Questions try to characterize the object of measurement with respect to a selected quality issue and to describe either this quality issue from the selected point of view or the factors that may affect the quality issues.
- Quantitative level (Metric): A set of metrics — combined into a model — is associated with every question in order to answer the question in a quantitative way.

Two examples of GQM goal definitions follow below:

- *Analyze* the <product consisting of its intermediate work products, e.g. program code> (object) *for the purpose of* <understanding> (purpose) *with respect to* <inspection effectiveness> (quality focus) *from the point of view of* <a project-related role, e.g. project manager> (viewpoint) *in the context of* <project P of company XYZ> (environment).
- *Analyze* the <development process> (object) *for the purpose of* <evaluation> (purpose) *with respect to* <defect slippage> (quality focus) *from the point of view of* <a department-related role, e.g. process engineer> (viewpoint) *in the context of* <department A of company XYZ> (environment).

One technique for knowledge elicitation during measurement planning is the abstraction sheet [3, 5]. An abstraction sheet is structured into four sections (so-called quadrants). The first quadrant (Quality Focus) lists the set of indicators that shall be used to measure the quality aspect in the focus of interest (e.g. inspection effectiveness or defect slippage). The second quadrant (Variation Factors) lists the factors that are supposed to have an impact on the quality focus. The third quadrant (Baseline Hypotheses) contains hypotheses about possible values and/or distributions for the quality focus attributes defined in the first quadrant. Sometimes, this quadrant shows actual data measured in previous projects (serving as a baseline) as an estimate for the quality focus indicators. The fourth quadrant (Impact on Baseline Hypotheses) is used to set up hypotheses describing the impact of changes of the variation factors on the quality focus indicators (e.g. if variation factor x is lower than measured in the baseline project, then the product quality indicator y is expected to be higher).

Two GQM abstraction sheet examples related to the example GQM goal definitions introduced above are shown in Figs. 2 and 3.

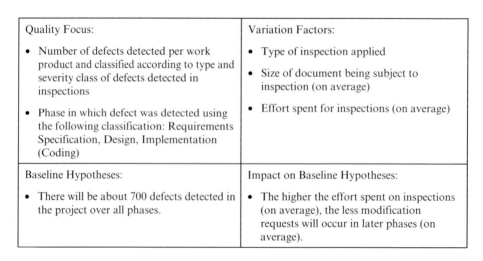

Quality Focus:	Variation Factors:
• Number of defects detected per work product and classified according to type and severity class of defects detected in inspections	• Type of inspection applied
	• Size of document being subject to inspection (on average)
• Phase in which defect was detected using the following classification: Requirements Specification, Design, Implementation (Coding)	• Effort spent for inspections (on average)
Baseline Hypotheses:	Impact on Baseline Hypotheses:
• There will be about 700 defects detected in the project over all phases.	• The higher the effort spent on inspections (on average), the less modification requests will occur in later phases (on average).

Fig. 2.   GQM abstraction sheet Example 1.

Quality Focus:	Variation Factors:
• Number of defects detected per work product and classified according to type and severity class of defects detected in inspections and tests • Phase in which defect was detected using the following classification: Requirements Specification, Design, Implementation (Coding), Test • Development phase in which the defect was inserted • Development phase in which the defect was corrected	• Type of inspection applied • Size of document being subject to inspection (on average) • Effort spent for inspections (on average) • Effort spent on testing (on average)
Baseline Hypotheses:	Impact on Baseline Hypotheses:
• About 60% of defects injected in previous phases will be detected during the current phase (in which inspection or testing is applied).	• The higher the effort spent on inspections and test (on average), the less corrections will occur in subsequent phases (on average).

Fig. 3. GQM abstraction sheet Example 2.

3. Process Simulation with System Dynamics

Simulation in general has the ability to study the behavior of complex processes and systems [6]. The continuous simulation method SD is a very powerful approach with a broad range of applications in complex social, managerial, economic or engineering systems. As soon as an SD simulation model exists that reproduces current or past behavior of reality, systematic variation of model parameters (i.e., sensitivity analysis or inclusion and exclusion of model structures) can help in understanding, controlling, and improving system behavior. SD modeling is supported by comprehensive tool support. The underlying paradigm of SD is Systems Thinking [20]. The essential step toward Systems Thinking is to recognize the presence of feedback mechanisms in the observed system. In Systems Thinking, the behavior of a system is considered as primarily being generated by the interaction of all the feedback loops over time.

In order to analyze — and eventually change — the behavior of observed objects in the real world, it is necessary to understand the important cause-effect relations of the factors that influence those variables that represent the observed behavior. In SD, these cause-effect relations are called base mechanisms. The union set of all base mechanisms is assumed to be the minimal set of cause-effect relations. This union set is able to explain the dynamic behavior described in the reference mode. The model describing all the base mechanisms is called a causal diagram.

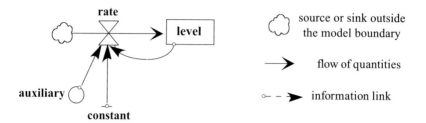

Fig. 4.   Schematic conventions of flow graphs.

In order to be able to run simulations, the causal diagram has to be transformed into a formal model. In SD, the formal model consists of a set of mathematical equations. SD model equations are separated into two groups: level equations and rate equations. This terminology of levels and rates is consistent with the flow-structure orientation introduced by Forrester together with schematic conventions invoking the image of fluid-like processes [8]. Using these conventions, SD model equations can be represented (and manipulated) graphically in the form of flow graphs. The basic ingredients of flow graphs are shown in Fig. 4.

The levels in an SD model describe the state of the system. They accumulate (or integrate) the results of action in the systems, an action being always materialized by flows in transit. The derivative of a level, or equivalently the rapidity at which it is changing, depends on its input and output flows. In SD tools, the computation of a level is approximated by a difference equation of the form:

$$\text{Level} \ (t + dt) = \text{Level} \ (t) + (\Sigma \ \text{input rates} - \Sigma \ \text{output rates}) \, dt. \qquad (1)$$

The rates are what change the values of levels. Their equations state how the available information is used in order to generate actions. A rate has four conceptual components: an observed condition is compared to a goal, and the discrepancy found is taken as the basis for action (flow) generation. The rate equation that formalizes this policy is an algebraic expression that depends only on levels and constant values. Auxiliary variables can be used for intermediate computation.

Under the name IMMoS (Integrated Measurement, Modeling and Simulation), an integrated framework for effective and efficient SD model development has been developed [13]. IMMoS combines four elements:

- Support for SD model goal definition.
- Process guidance for SD model development.
- Integration of static SE models (e.g. process, product, resource, and quality models) with SD models.
- Integration of SD modeling with goal–oriented measurement and process modeling.

Abdel-Hamid and Madnick were the first to introduce SD into the field of software engineering in the late 1980s [1]. Even though SD has provided an increasing number of applications in the software engineering domain since then (cf. [15, 16, 19] for compilations of process simulation examples), it is by no means suggested to be the new silver bullet technique for problem solving. Instead, it is important to clarify the underlying assumptions for SD modeling and simulation. Only if these assumptions hold, it is recommended to use the SD approach in a particular environment. The basic assumptions are:

- Problems under investigation are dynamic in nature and relate to systems with entities and attributes that are interconnected in loops of information feedback and circular causality.
- Sufficient maturity and stability of the software development processes in place in the organization.
- Availability of expertise for identification of base mechanisms and construction of causal diagrams.
- Availability of data for SD model calibration.

Finally, it should be noted that SD models add a new dimension to the traditional way of empirical learning and experimentation in software engineering [17, 22]. SD-based simulation is a very comprehensive tool in support of:

- Project management training.
- Process, project and risk analysis.
- Project planning.
- Exploration of process improvement opportunities.

More on the potentialities of SD-based process simulation for the purpose of learning and decision-support can be found in [14]. Benefits of combining process simulation with experimentation have been suggested by Münch *et al.* [11].

4. Limitations From the Isolated Application of GQM and SD

By applying GQM, information is identified that is relevant to solve specific problems (goals), and that can be represented in a practical, applicable and interpretable way. By applying SD, decision-making support for global and dynamically complex planning and improvement problems is provided. However, there are some limitations of both GQM and SD if used in isolation:

(L1) "Local" versus "Global"

GQM is "local" in the sense that always one goal is investigated in isolation.[a] For that purpose, other aspects and goals of the "global" software development projects are not taken into account. While it is important to understand certain aspects, it is hard to oversee its ramification for the whole system with its global objectives and constraints. It is not sufficient to improve certain parts of a system (to be "locally

---

[a] "Locality" in the context of the characterization of GQM versus SD mainly refers to the purpose, quality aspect, and viewpoint dimensions of a GQM goal and not so much to its object dimension, which actually can relate to a large project or process as a whole.

optimal") if this does not contribute and is not synchronized with all the remaining goals and constraints of software development and evolution ("globally optimal"). In contrast to GQM models, SD models typically capture mutual influence and feedback of many interrelated parameters, though on a rather abstract ("global") level, i.e., without offering means to analyze behavior of individual entities or attributes of entities.

(L2) "Static" versus "Dynamic"

GQM is static and thus unable to reflect changes that are due to interactions and feedback, causing change over time. What is missing to describe the dynamic changes in software development and evolution is a mechanism to integrate the GQM models that reflect the status of a system at discrete points in time. On the other hand, calibration of time-dynamic SD models requires information from various types of static quantitative models (descriptive, predictive, and evaluative), and thus could benefit from the outcomes of GQM measurement programs.

(L3) Synchronization with other existing GQM plans and models

Typically, when modeling an aspect of software development or evolution, this is interacting with existing models or experience formulated for other purposes. In the same way, several individual GQM plans are considered simultaneously. Unfortunately, there is no coordinating and integrating mechanism to model and describe the behavior of the overall system. This means that there is no mechanism to synchronize the GQM plan with other existing models of software development and evolution. An appropriate SD model could serve as a mechanism facilitating such synchronization.

(L4) Validity of GQM models

Development and validation of GQM models is a time-consuming and expensive process. Typically, from performing an individual measurement program, you learn about the current limitations of the model. Unfortunately, this process often takes too long and is too expensive. Again, a mechanism to check validity of GQM models from a system-theoretic perspective would be very useful to improve efficiency of measurement-based improvement processes.

(L5) Reuse of GQM plans

So far, reuse of GQM plans is exclusively considered from a perspective of reusing certain parts of the GQM template. However, there is a much larger potential of reuse if different models are considered simultaneously from a global/system-theoretic perspective. If time-dynamic problems are addressed, with using suited SD models as a unifying shell, certain GQM sub-models at the questions levels could be more easily reused, and a more comprehensive view on explanatory variables could be achieved.

(L6) Validity of SD models

Results from any simulation-based investigation, e.g. for the purpose of planning or exploration of improvement potentialities, are essentially based on the validity of the underlying models. However, there is no other way for checking the validity of SD models than conducting empirical investigations to compare real-word performance with virtual-world performance. GQM would be a good means for effective planning and efficient conducting of appropriate empirical investigations.

5. How to Overcome Current Limitations: "Dynamic GQM" — A Hybrid Approach

In what follows, we describe the framework of a hybrid and evolutionary approach. It combines goal-oriented measurement with SD-based modeling and simulation. The main idea is to guide and supplement goal-oriented measurement by a system-oriented modeling and simulation approach.

We consider software development from a system theoretic perspective and assume the existence of global (business) goals when studying systems. Starting from an initial understanding of the system under consideration, the most critical and worst understood parts of the overall system are most promising for candidates to make an in-depth investigation. This investigation can be done by designing and implementing a GQM-based measurement program with the goal derived from the subsystem under investigation. The results from this program are used to better understand system structure and system behavior at this point. This process can be iterated several times, where not only one measurement program needs to be considered at each step. The application of this interactive (between SD and GQM) and evolutionary (models, results, and insights are evolving and relying on each other) process results in

- a sequence of SD models with increasing accuracy and validity in describing reality,
- a sequence of GQM plans derived from the global improvement goal(s) and the perspective of the whole system,
- a means to incrementally improve the validity of both the SD models and the GQM models by checking their respective consistency,
- a sequence of reusing parts of both the SD models (information flow) and the GQM models (influencing variables on explanatory variables) for the respective other model,
- a method to combine the results of GQM with the power of SD to show how different individual/local goals fit together,
- a method that combines experiments in a virtual world by conducting simulation runs with experiments in a real world by performing goal-oriented measurement.

6. Complementary Elements of SD-Based Modeling and GQM-Based Measurement

SD-based modeling and simulation helps analyze real world problems that involve dynamic (time-dependent) behavior, while GQM-based measurement aims to quantitatively describe real world phenomena or develop (static) quantitative models for prediction or evaluation [5]. GQM-based measurement programs, i.e., the collected data and resulting (static) models, can be utilized at various stages of the SD modeling process. Four (informal) relationship patterns between SD-based modeling and GQM-based measurement can be identified (cf. [12, 13] for a more comprehensive discussion of relationships between process models, static quantitative models, and SD models).

The development and application of SD models involves the following modeling and simulation products:

- SD goal definition: Formally defines the problem to be analyzed; specifies scope, dynamic focus, purpose, user, and environment of the related SD model.
- SD reference mode: Describes current problematic or intended (improved) future dynamic behavior of interest; during SD modeling, the reference behavior serves for validating initial versions of the SD model.
- SD base mechanism: Describes a causal relationship between attributes of real-world entities; base mechanisms are graphically represented by directed arcs that connect one dependent with one or more independent variables; the impact of a dependent variable on the independent variable can be either positive or negative.
- SD causal diagram: Integrates the minimal set of SD base mechanisms that is able to reproduce the SD reference mode; this typically results in a directed graph with cycles (feedback loops).
- SD flow graph: Transforms the structural information contained in the SD causal diagram into a semi-formal graphical SD representation language; specifies the mathematical structure of the SD model (number, type and form of the mathematical equations).
- SD model equation: Defines an element of the SD flow graph (level, rate, constant, and auxiliary) in terms of a mathematical equation.
- SD simulation result: Comprises the outputs from simulation runs and their interpretation with respect to the SD goal definition.

Figure 5 sketches the relationship between the SD modeling and simulation products. It is important to note that SD modeling is a staged and highly iterative process that can roughly be described as a sequence of specification, design, implementation, execution and application activities. It should also be noted that there are two types of iteration loops, a global iteration loop that involves all SD modeling and simulation products and activities (from goal definition to problem solution), and a local iteration loop focusing on refinement and revision of the flow

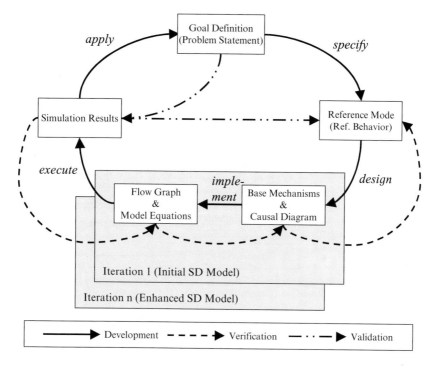

Fig. 5. SD modeling and simulation process.

graph and its associated model equations. Sometimes, local iterations may require a revision of the underlying causal diagram too.

The definition and performance of GQM-based measurement programs involves the following planning and measurement products:

- GQM goal definition: Formally defines the measurement goal; specifies object, quality focus, purpose, viewpoint, and environment of the related measurement program.
- GQM plan: Brakes down the GQM goal definition into questions, and defines measures (metrics) and (static) mathematical models needed to answer these questions.
- GQM abstraction sheet: Specifies types and scales of one dependent variable and associated independent variables (variation factors) for each (static) mathematical model; in addition, hypotheses are formulated with regards to the measurement results of the dependent variable and the impact of the variation factors.
- GQM measurement plan: Defines the roles, templates and tools involved in data collection activities; specifies the assignment of persons to roles, the logical synchronization of data collection activities with the software development process, and the schedule of data collection activities.
- GQM measurement result: Comprises the measurement data and their interpretation with respect to the GQM goal definition.

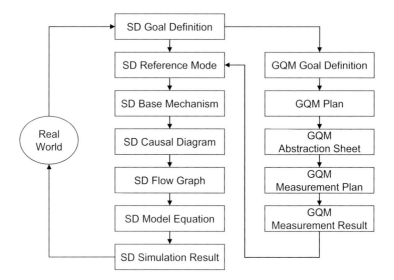

Fig. 6.   SD-GQM relationship pattern $P1$ ("time-series data").

Figure 6 shows relationship pattern $P1$ ("time-series data"). Descriptive models that plot quantitative data along the time-axis (time-series data) are a very useful means to precisely describe the dynamic behavior of those real-world entities/attributes that are in the focus of interest. The relevant set of these data plots defines the SD reference mode.

Figure 7 shows relationship pattern $P2$ ("simple predictive or evaluation model"). SD base mechanisms are those fundamental cause-effect relationships between real-world entities/attributes that are supposed to generate the reference behavior captured by the SD reference mode. Simple predictive or evaluation models describing the functional relationship between one dependent variable and one or more independent variables typically represent such cause-effect relationships. Because SD base mechanisms describe only qualitative cause-effect relationships, i.e., the exact form of the functional relationship is not yet needed, data analysis methods such as classification trees, rough sets, statistical correlation analysis or statistical testing can be sufficient to derive the required models from empirical data.

Figure 8 shows relationship pattern $P3$ ("hierarchically structured predictive or evaluation model"). GQM plans can be considered a means for hierarchically structuring predictive or evaluation models (nesting).

Figure 9 shows relationship pattern $P4$ ("parameter estimation and calibration"). The specification of SD model equations typically involves the reuse or development of quantitative models, i.e., descriptive, predictive or evaluation models. In order to derive the precise functional form, statistical parameter estimation techniques and methods such as regression analysis can be applied.

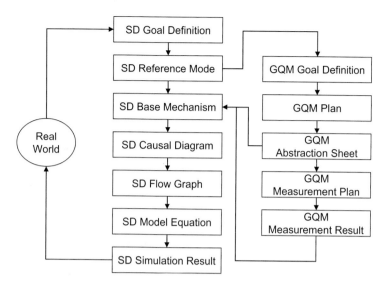

Fig. 7. SD-GQM relationship pattern $P2$ ("simple predictive or evaluation model").

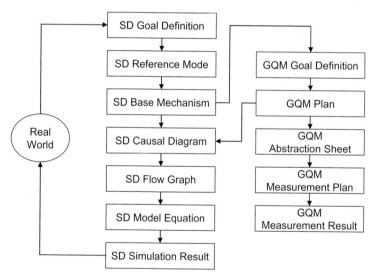

Fig. 8. SD-GQM relationship pattern $P3$ ("hierarchically structured predictive or evaluation model").

Recalling the SD modeling and simulation process as it was sketched in Sec. 6 (cf. Fig. 5), Fig. 10 shows where SD-GQM relationship patterns play a role in the global iteration loop (left-hand side). More specifically focusing on SD-GQM relationship pattern $P4$, the right-hand side of Fig. 10 shows how GQM measurement results (i.e., GQM models) are used in the local iteration loop.

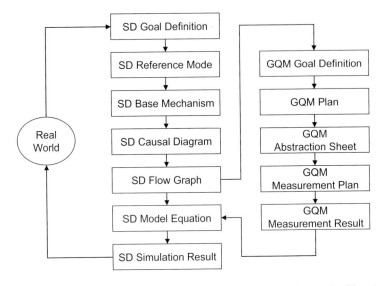

Fig. 9. SD-GQM relationship pattern $P4$ ("parameter estimation and calibration").

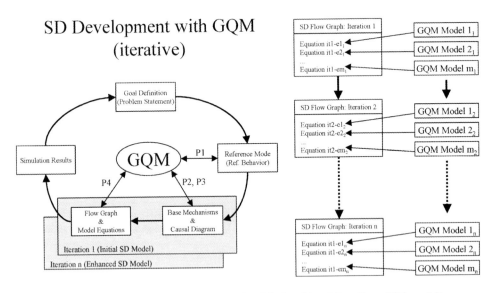

Fig. 10. SD-GQM relationship patterns in global and local iteration of SD modeling.

With the systematic integration of GQM modeling into SD modeling, simulation modeling according to SD can be interpreted as a dynamic expansion of the well-established GQM approach ("Dynamic GQM"). The following section illustrates with the help of an example how GQM measurement and SD simulation modeling can be smoothly integrated by exploiting the SD-GQM relationship patterns

*P*1 and *P*4. In order to keep the example short, we will not cover SD-GQM relationship patterns *P*2 and *P*3, which are used for identifying base mechanisms and
hierarchical structures among GQM models.

7. Integration of GQM and System Dynamics — An Example

In the following example, we assume the task to develop an SD simulation model
for the purpose of understanding and controlling software project dynamics that
are generated by trade-off effects between effort consumption, project duration, and
product quality ("magic triangle").

Following a top-down approach, a sequence of SD models is developed that
integrate at each development stage one or more GQM models. First, a sequence of
three SD models (SD_1*a*, SD_1*b*, SD_1*c*) is developed that illustrate the integration
of GQM models according to the various SD-GQM relationship patterns. The first
set of models focuses on the effort-duration trade-off only. In order to illustrate
how locally defined GQM models can be integrated into a SD model that covers all
trade-off relations comprised in the magic triangle, the development of a second set
SD models (SD_2*a*, SD_2*b*) is presented (cf. [1] for a more comprehensive SD model).

The purpose of SD models SD_1*a*, SD_1*b*, and SD_1*c* is to understand and control
the dynamics of software projects with regards to effort consumption and duration.

Exploiting SD-GQM relationship pattern *P*1 ("time-series data"), the SD reference mode, representing the typical project progress over time, is defined by GQM
model GQM_1 (cf. Fig. 11).

- GQM_1: Software product completion pattern over time (time-series
  data/S-shaped curve).

In order to define the SD base mechanisms and the SD causal diagram, the following
GQM models are used.

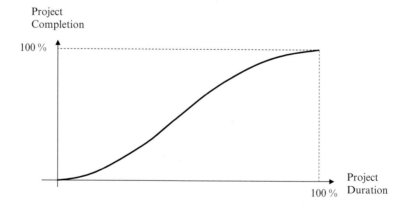

Fig. 11.   Product completion pattern (S-shaped).

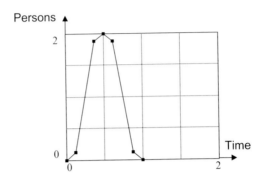

Fig. 12.   Typical manpower allocation pattern.

- GQM_2: Manpower allocation pattern over time (descriptive model — cf. Fig. 12).
- GQM_3: Effort — size dependency (simple predictive model/COCOMO [4]).

$$\text{Effort} = a * \text{Size}^{b} \qquad (2)$$

- GQM_4: Duration — effort — size dependency (hierarchically structured predictive model/COCOMO).

$$\text{Duration} = c * \text{Effort}^{d}. \qquad (3)$$

Eventually, GQM models GQM_2, GQM_3, and GQM_4 are used to define causal relationships and SD model equations. The stepwise integration of the GQM models into the initial SD model SD_1a (cf. Fig. 13) is shown in Figs. 15 (SD model SD_1b) and 17 (SD model SD_1c).

Characterization of SD model SD_1a (cf. Fig. 13):

- State variable: SW_Product.
- Input parameters: Number of requirements, duration, requirements to LOC transformation factor.

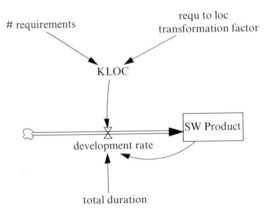

Fig. 13.   Initial SD model.

The initial SD model shown in Fig. 13 does not yet contain any model resulting from empirical analysis. It simply assumes that the development rate is calculated as follows:

$$\text{development\_rate} = \text{KLOC}/\text{total\_duration} \tag{4}$$

with

$$\text{KLOC} = \text{number\_of\_requirements} * \text{requirements\_to\_LOC\_transformation\_factor}. \tag{5}$$

The dynamic change of state variable SW_Product is determined by (Eq. 4) and the input variables. The simulation result of SD model SD_1*a* is shown in Fig. 14.

As the behavior pattern of SW Product does not show similarity to the *S*-shaped pattern of the reference behavior (cf. Fig. 11), model validity can be doubted. By including GQM model GQM_2, a more realistic behavior can be achieved (cf. Fig. 16).

Characterization of SD model SD_1*b* (cf. Fig. 15):

- State variable: SW Product.
- Input parameters: Number of requirements, total duration, requirements to LOC transformation factor.

By integrating GQM models GQM_3 and GQM_4 new causal relationships between product size, effort consumption and project duration are inserted into the SD model (cf. Fig. 17). This eliminates the need for having "duration" as model input.

Characterization of SD model SD_1*c* (cf. Fig. 17):

- State variable: SW Product.
- Input parameters: Number of requirements, requirements to LOC transformation factor.

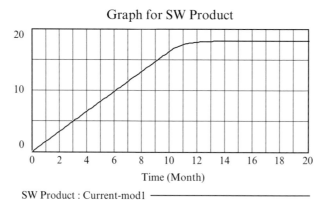

Fig. 14. Simulation output — development progress.

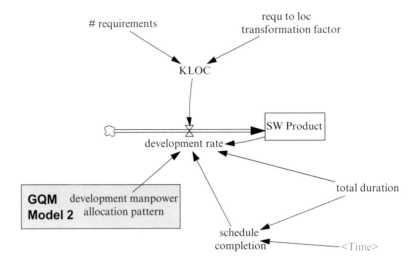

Fig. 15.   Initial SD model integrating GQM_2.

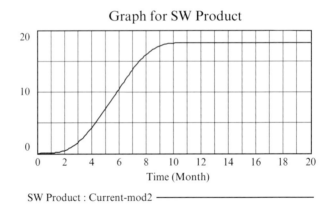

Fig. 16.   Simulation output — development progress.

In order to prepare for the inclusion of quality related aspects, and in particular the inclusion of quality assurance activities throughout all development phases, SD model SD_2a refines SD model SD_1c such that individual project phases (e.g. design, implementation, test) are explicitly represented.

Characterization of SD model SD_2a (cf. Fig. 18):

- State variables: SW Design, SW Code, SW Product.
- Input parameters: Number of requirements, requirements to design pages factor, requirements to LOC transformation factor.

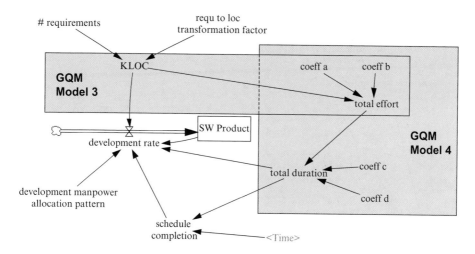

Fig. 17. Initial SD model integrating GQM_3 and GQM_4.

Integrated GQM models (selection):

- GQM_5: Phase specific manpower allocation patterns (descriptive model).
- GQM_6: Typical time overlap between phases (descriptive model).
- GQM_7: Typical effort split between phases (simple predictive model).

Figures 19 and 20 show simulation results generated by SD model SD_2a. The overlap between phases results from GQM model GQM_6. The various phase-specific manpower allocation patterns result from the combination of GQM models GQM_5, GQM_6, and GQM_7.

SD model SD_2b adds the defect generation-detection-correction coflow to the software design-implementation-test workflow of SD_2a, and thus integrates product quality aspects with effort and duration aspects of the project dynamics.

Characterization of SD model SD_2b (cf. Fig. 21):

- State variables: SW Design, SW Code, SW Product, Design Inspections, Design Defects Injected, Design Defects Detected, Design Defects Corrected, Code Inspections, Code Defects Injected, Code Defects Detected, Code Defects Corrected, Product Defects Detected, Product Defects Corrected.
- Input parameters: Number of requirements, requirements to design pages factor, requirements to LOC transformation factor, number of design inspections, number of code inspections.

Integrated GQM models (selection):

- GQM_8: Defect detection during design (simple predictive model).

$$\text{des\_insp\_eff} = f(\text{pages\_per\_insp}, \text{des\_defect\_density}) \tag{6}$$

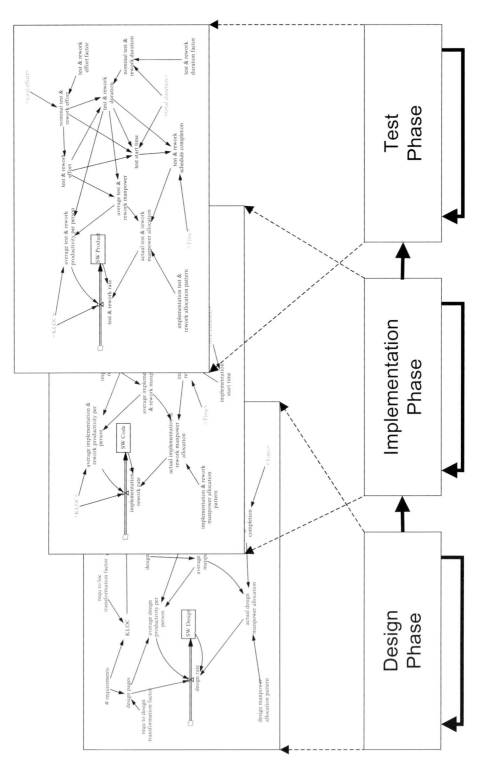

Fig. 18.   Refined SD model with separate design, implementation and test phases.

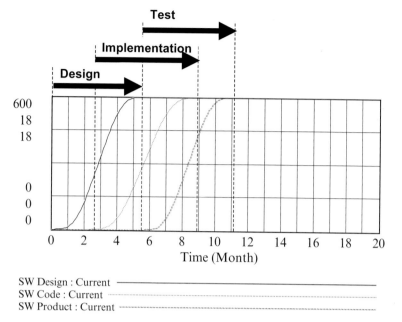

SW Design : Current ────────────────────
SW Code : Current ·······························
SW Product : Current ----------------------------

Fig. 19. Simulation output — design, code, and product development progress.

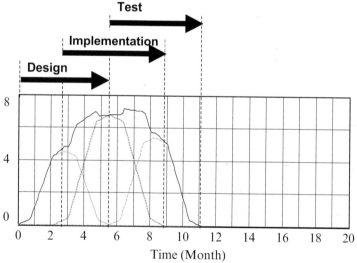

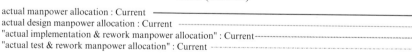

actual manpower allocation : Current ────────────────────
actual design manpower allocation : Current ·······························
"actual implementation & rework manpower allocation" : Current----------------
"actual test & rework manpower allocation" : Current -------------------------

Fig. 20. Simulation output — manpower allocation.

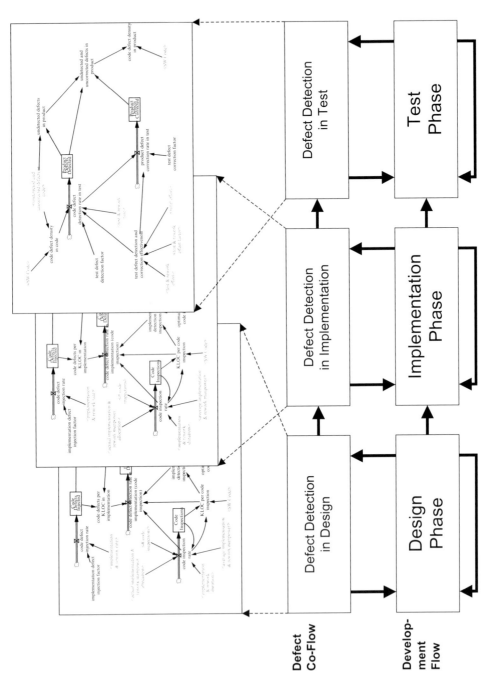

Fig. 21.   Refined SD model with defect coflow.

- GQM_9: Defect detection during implementation (simple predictive model).

$$\text{code\_insp\_eff} = f(\text{LOC\_per\_insp}, \text{code\_defect\_density}) \qquad (7)$$

- GQM_10: Defect detection during test (simple predictive model).

$$\text{test\_eff} = f(\text{test\_effort}, \text{code\_defect\_density}). \qquad (8)$$

Figures 22 and 23 show simulation results generated by SD model SD_2b. Figure 22 shows how the performance of code inspections during implementation affects the actual implementation and test manpower allocations. It can be seen, that there is a shift of effort from the test phase to the implementation phase if code inspections are conducted.

Figure 23 shows the effect of conducting code inspections on product quality. Product quality is expressed as the number of undetected defects. Observing the

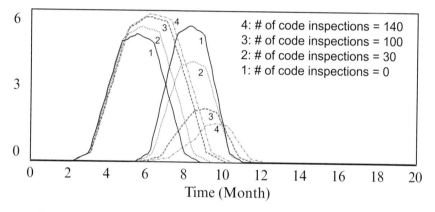

Fig. 22. Simulation output — actual manpower allocation for implementation and test phases.

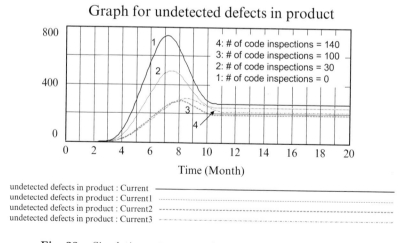

Fig. 23. Simulation output — undetected defects in the product.

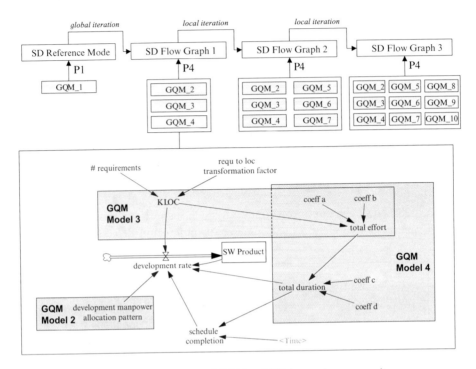

Fig. 24.   Integration of GQM and SD (example summary).

results of Cases 1–3, one can see that product quality increases with the number of code inspections. This is partly due to the fact that code inspection effectiveness depends on the average size of the code subject to inspection (in Case 3: ca. 180 LOC per inspection), as implied by GQM_9. On the other hand, it can be observed that the product quality in Case 4 (140 code inspections) is worse than in Case 3 (100 code inspections). This is due to the fact that the reduction of test effort has negative impact on test effectiveness, as implied by GQM_10. When the number of inspections is above a certain value, the negative effect on test effectiveness exceeds the positive effect of conducting more code inspections.

The example presented above gave some insight into the relationships between GQM products (i.e., GQM measurement results that are packaged into models) and SD modeling. Due to space limitations, only SD-GQM relationship patterns $P1$ and $P4$ (both are quantitative in nature) and their role in the global and local iteration loops of SD modeling were invoked. Figure 24 summarizes the most important aspects of the example indicating the type of iteration of SD modeling, affected SD products, invoked SD-GQM relationship patterns, and used GQM models.

8. Conclusion

In software development, we are typically encountered with situations of uncertainty, incompleteness, fuzziness or even inconsistency. We cannot expect reliable data of models for making any kind of decision related to products, processes, tools, or resources. We need an evolutionary, learning-based approach combined with an appropriate and sound methodology to enable intelligent decision support.

In this chapter, we proposed a new hybrid modeling approach called "Dynamic GQM". Its main purpose is to organize mutual interaction and support between sequences of models from System Dynamics simulation modeling and goal-oriented measurement following the GQM paradigm. The subsequent models are related to each other. Their increasing quality results from the supplementary character of the two types of models: System Dynamics addresses the behavior and performance of systems from a global perspective. In the same way, GQM is local in the sense that always one goal is investigated in isolation. From the integration of both types of models, new insights can be gained from experiments in both the real world and the virtual world (conducting simulation).

The benefits of "Dynamic GQM" are three-fold:

- It integrates and synchronizes individual GQM models from a global system perspective.
- It incrementally increases the validity of both GQM and SD models by mutually reusing and validating models generated from SD and GQM, respectively.
- It is a means to integrate real-world empirical results with experiments in a virtual world offered by SD.

The proposed approach was illustrated by the example of evolving models for trade-off analysis between effort, time, and quality. The principal example has shown that the isolated application of either one of the two approaches would not have been able to provide the same quality of models and meaningful insights.

Offering decision support based on vague and uncertain models is meaningless. Availability of reliable qualitative or quantitative data is needed for model description. Reflecting reality in terms of the underlying objectives and constraints is not an easy task, and it needs validation to do the "right things". Without an appropriate description of what are the main objectives, and how the different alternatives are restricted by resources, budget or effort constraints, the proposed support will not be applicable. Hybrid measurement and simulation contributes to the qualification of the support itself, as it can validate the proposed improvements in terms of more efficiency, effectiveness or transparency.

Future research should be devoted to further formalize "Dynamic GQM". This will lead to operational artifacts, rules and guidelines on how to proceed. Further effort will be devoted to provide tool support and to adapt and systematically evaluate the approach in industrial environments.

References

1. T. K. Abdel-Hamid, *Madnick SE, Software Projects Dynamics — An Integrated Approach* (Prentice-Hall, 1991).
2. V. R. Basili, G. Caldiera, H. D. Rombach and R. van Solingen, "Goal question metric paradigm", ed. J. J. Marciniak, *Encyclopedia of Software Engineering* **1** (John Wiley & Sons, 2001) 578–583.

3. A. Birk, R. van Solingen and J. Järvinen, "Business impact, benefit, and cost of applying GQM in industry. An in-depth, long-term investigation at Schlumberger RPS", *Proceedings of 5th International Symposium on Software Metrics (Metrics '98)*, Bethesda, MD, 20–21, November 1998 (IEEE Computer Society, 1998).
4. B. W. Boehm, *Software Engineering Economics* (Prentice Hall, 1981).
5. L. C. Briand, C. M. Differding and H. D. Rombach, "Practical guidelines for measurement-based process improvement", *Software Process Improvement and Practice* **2**(4) (1996) 253–280.
6. A. M. Christie, "Simulation: An enabling technology in software engineering", *CROSSTALK — The Journal of Defense Software Engineering* (April 1999) 2–7.
7. R. G. Coyle, *System Dynamics Modelling — A Practical Approach* (Chapman & Hall, 1996).
8. J. W. Forrester, *Industrial Dynamics* (Productivity Press, 1961).
9. R. Madachy, *Software Process Dynamics*, book to appear in 2005.
10. S. Morasca, "Software measurement", *Handbook of Software Engineering and Knowledge Engineering* **II** (2002).
11. J. Münch, H. D. Rombach and I. Rus, "Creating an advanced software engineering laboratory by combining empirical studies with process simulation", *Proceedings of 4th International Workshop on Process Simulation Modeling (ProSim'2003)*, Portland, USA, 2003.
12. D. Pfahl and G. Ruhe, "Goal-oriented measurement plus system dynamics — A hybrid and evolutionary approach", *Proceedings of 4th International Workshop on Process Simulation Modeling (ProSim'2003)*, Portland, USA, 2003.
13. D. Pfahl and G. Ruhe, "IMMoS: A methodology for integrated measurement, modelling and simulation", *Software Process Improvement and Practice* **7** (2002) 189–210.
14. D. Pfahl and G. Ruhe, "System dynamics as an enabling technology for learning in software organisations", *Proceedings of 13th International Conference on Software Engineering and Knowledge Engineering (SEKE'2001)*, Skokie, Knowledge Systems Institute (2001) 355–362.
15. D. M. Raffo, W. Harrison, M. I. Kellner, R. Madachy, R. Martin, W. Scacci and P. Wernick (eds.), *Special Issue on Software Process Simulation Modeling. Journal of Systems and Software* **46**(2/3) (1999).
16. D. M. Raffo and P. Wernick (eds.), *Special Issue on Software Process Simulation Modeling. Journal of Systems and Software* **59**(3) (2001).
17. G. Ruhe, "Learning software organizations", *Handbook of Software Engineering and Knowledge Engineering* **I** (2001).
18. G. Ruhe, "Software engineering decision support — A new paradigm for learning software organizations", *Advances in Learning Software Organization, Lecture Notes In Computer Science 2640* (Springer, 2003) 104–115.
19. W. Scacchi and D. Raffo (eds.), *Special Issue on Software Process Simulation Modeling. Software Process: Improvement and Practice* **7**(3/4) (2002).
20. P. Senge, *The Fifth Discipline — The Art & Practice of the Learning Organization* (New York, Doubleday, 1990).
21. R. van Solingen and E. Berghout, *The Goal/Question/Metric Method: A Practical Guide for Quality Improvement of Software Development* (McGraw-Hill, 1999).
22. R. van Solingen and E. Berghout, "On software engineering and learning theory", *Handbook of Software Engineering and Knowledge Engineering* **I** (2001).

TIME AND KNOWLEDGE MANAGEMENT IN E-LEARNING

SHI-KUO CHANG

Department of Computer Science, University of Pittsburgh,
Pittsburgh, PA 15260, USA
E-mail: chang@cs.pitt.edu

The chronobot is a device for time and knowledge exchange and management. It allows a group of people to exchange time and knowledge. This papers describes the basic concept of the chronobot, its mechanism for time/knowledge exchange and management, and its application to e-learning. Research issues are also discussed.

Keywords: Time management, knowledge management, e-learning, negotiation protocol, time exchange, knowledge exchange.

1. Introduction

The chronobot is a device for storing and borrowing time [2]. Using the chronobot one can borrow time from someone and return time to the same person or someone else. It is a convenient device for managing time.

The underlying premise of the chronobot is that there is a way to exchange time and knowledge. For example, one spends time to acquire knowledge and later uses this knowledge to save time. A group of people can also find some means to exchange time and knowledge. Thus, **the chronobot is a device to facilitate the exchange and management of time and knowledge**.

The chronobot is a logical extension of the Blog. While a BBS allows people to exchange individualized information, the BBS master seldom writes long articles himself/herself. In contrast the main idea of the Blog is that the Blog master actively contributes individualized knowledge. The chronobot further allows the exchange of individualized time and gives people greater freedom in time/knowledge management.

A natural application domain for the chronobot is e-learning, although we can think of many other interesting application domains for the chronobot. Indeed whenever we need to exchange time and knowledge, we can make good use of the chronobot.

2. Application Scenarios

In this section, we describe two examples of the chronobot for e-learning applications.

John is a teenager. His parents recently bought him a chronobot. When John wakes up in the morning, he has breakfast and then takes the bus to the school. On the bus John has some free time. So his chronobot says to John: "You know you have to write a big report on the eating habits of dinosaurs. Why don't you spend some time now to collect some information? There is a rock concert at Point Park tonight. If you get the report done early, maybe your mom will let you go to the rock concert!" (Fig. 1(a)).

John is excited about the rock concert and really wants to go, so he follows the chronobot's advice and puts in some effort to collect and organize information. After the second class period John again has some free time. Again, following the chronobot's advice, John puts in some time to get more pieces of information and label them according to the chronobot's suggestions (Fig. 1(b)).

But John's efforts later pay off. After John finishes school he turns to the chronobot who to his delight has already fused the knowledge together to form a rough draft of the report. John only has to do some editing and in less than twenty minutes the report is completed! But some critical facts need to be checked by John's teacher. So John goes to chronobot's virtual classroom to interact with his teacher, Ms. Newman (Fig. 1(c)).

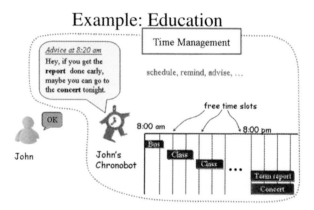

Fig. 1(a).   Time management by chronobot.

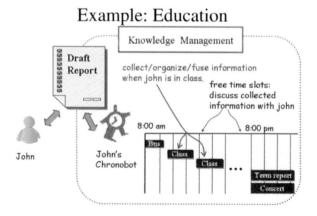

Fig. 1(b).   Knowledge management.

Example: Education

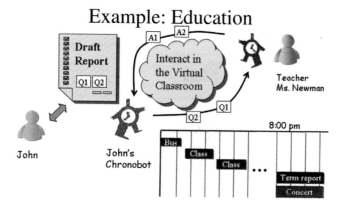

Fig. 1(c). Interact in the virtual classroom.

Example: Education

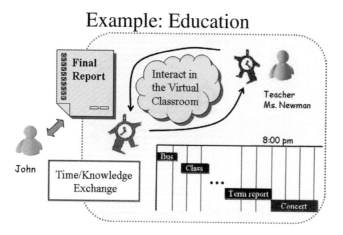

Fig. 1(d). Report completed on time.

In less than ten minutes, John gets all the answers from Ms. Newman. It is only 6.30 pm, and John proudly shows the finished report to his mother, who approves John's request for an outing [Fig. 1(d)]. So John happily goes to the rock concert with his buddies. If John does not have the chronobot, he would be stuck with the report writing task the entire evening and misses the rock concert!

The above example pretty much explains the usefulness of the chronobot. As another example, for a professional media artist George, the chronobot serves the same function of timely knowledge gathering. But it can be even more useful because unlike the teenager who is required to do his homework by himself, George has no such constraints and can rely upon the support from his coworkers. However there is no such thing as a free lunch. In order to ask his coworkers Suzie and Bill to share his workload, George has to put in efforts either in the past or in the future to help them. Because they trust George, at the present time when George needs help, Suzie and Bill will put in their efforts to help George [Fig. 2(a)].

Example: Team Working

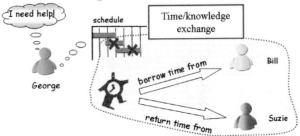

Fig. 2(a).   Time/knowledge exchange.

Example: Team Working

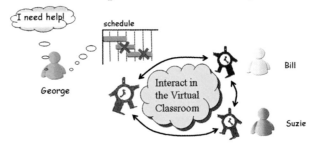

Fig. 2(b).   Interact in the virtual classroom.

Example: Team Working

Fig. 2(c).   Job is done.

Through their chronobots George, Suzie and Bill interact in the virtual classroom [Fig. 2(b)]. Their chronobots work independently to retrieve the knowledge previously organized by their respective masters, and then work together to fuse the knowledge into a format useful for George to put in the finishing touches [Fig. 2(c)].

3. Characteristics of the Chronobot

Based upon the above application scenarios we can derive some of the general characteristics of the chronobot (Fig. 3):

(1) The chronobot is a **time manager**. But it is not an ordinary time manager. It can be used to **manage not only one's own time, but also other people's time through time/knowledge exchange**. This is very important, because the unique concept of the chronobot is that **time and knowledge are exchangeable**. The chronobot can manage not only the present, but also the past and the future through suitable time/knowledge exchange protocols.

(2) The chronobot is also a **knowledge manager**. It can be used to store knowledge, organize knowledge, retrieve knowledge and **perform information fusion to produce new knowledge** [6]. Information fusion is the key concept. Without information fusion, the chronobot will not be as effective in managing knowledge and saving time.

(3) For e-learning and distance education applications, the chronobot offers a versatile **virtual classroom** that combines the functions of chat room, white board, and multimedia display. The learning materials, references and related information become a continuously expanding knowledge source or a Growing Book [5]. Evolutionary query processing provides query morphing and information fusion [6] capabilities to fully utilize this ever-changing knowledge source.

(4) Utilizing the time manager, the knowledge manager and the virtual classroom, the **chronobot can interactively provide timely knowledge to the end user**. This is the main characteristic of the chronobot. We often say *time is money*. We also say *knowledge is power*. If we can exchange time and knowledge, then these four entities — *time, money, knowledge and power* — *all become interchangeable!*

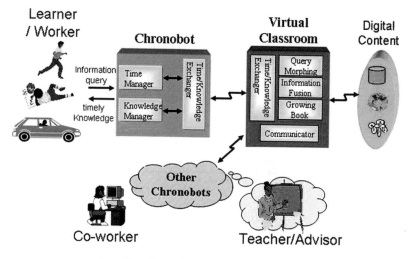

Fig. 3. Chronobot and virtual classroom.

4. From Experiences to Knowledge

Present-day e-learning systems are still too rigid and do not lend themselves easily to peer-to-peer learning. Since the chronobot is designed for time and knowledge exchange, the users are encouraged to exchange what they have learned. As illustrated in Fig. 3, the virtual classroom is where such exchanges actually take place. Thus, the chronobot equipped with the virtual classroom may circumvent the difficulty in supporting peer-to-peer e-learning.

Figure 4 illustrates the exchange of time and knowledge in the chronobot/virtual classroom (CVC) e-learning environment.

In Fig. 4, after a successful negotiation, the chronobot will send the *exchanged knowledge* to the virtual classroom where the actual learning takes place, i.e., one user will transfer the knowledge to another in the virtual classroom.

On the other hand the *experiential knowledge* extracted from user interactions in the virtual classroom will be tranferred to the chronobot so that the chronobot has better knowledge about the user characteristics and user preferences, i.e., the chronobot learns more about the user and stores such information into a User Profile.

We will call a learning session conducted in the virtual classroom a *learning session* or simply a *session*. We will call a transaction conducted by the chronobot a *time/knowledge exchange transaction* or simply a *transaction*.

The functions of the virtual classroom are illustrated in Fig. 5. The users (students and/or instructors) represented by emotive icons can join a virtual classroom to exchange information including text messages, web pages, sketches, and audio/video clips. The emotive icons express the feelings of a user in a learning session.

The virtual classroom is already in use at Knowledge Systems Institute (*www.ksi.edu*) in its distance learning classes. The next generation of virtual classroom can also be used to visualize the negotiation among the users in a time/knowledge exchange transaction. For example, the virtual classroom can display the state of a user's transaction such as creating a bid room, placing a bid, closing a bid room and so on. A user can override the state of a transaction to show an intended emotive icon for the learning session.

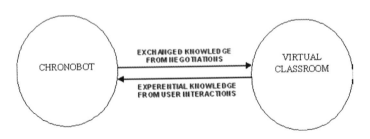

Fig. 4.   Chronobot and the virtual classroom.

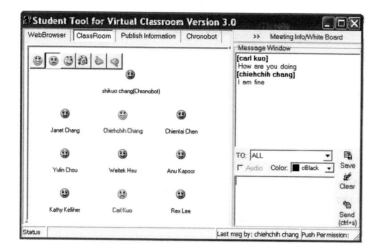

Fig. 5. An example of the virtual classroom.

5. The User Profile

Figure 6 illustrates the User Profile and the Relational Index, two important data structures for the chronobot/virtual classroom (CVC) system.

The User Profile is the physical realization of the User Model *UM*, which is an abstraction of the user's preferences and characteristics. The User Profile of a user u is a vector $\mathrm{P}(u) = (p_1(u), p_2(u), \ldots, p_n(u)) = (x_1, x_2, \ldots, x_n)$, where $p_i(u) = x_i$ is the ith attribute for the User Profile of the user u. An attribute may be part of an ontology, so the User Profile is a complex data structure.

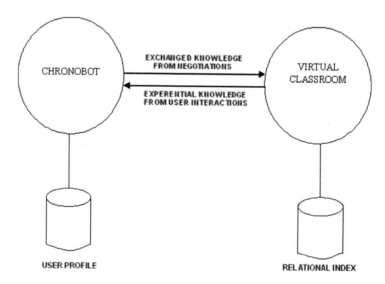

Fig. 6. User profile and relational index.

For example the User Profile for the media artist George can be as follows:

> (First_Name = George,
> Last_Name = Duncan,
> Profession = Media Artist,
> State = New York,
> Skills = {Media Design, Web Design})

When a user first registers for the CVC system, the user is asked to enter information such as personal data, areas of expertise and so on. The User Profile Manager provides a HTML front-end using which new users can register themselves with the system. During the registration, the User Profile Manager collects important information from the users such as the user id, name, address, credit card details, areas of experience, skill set, whether the user is an expert or not, the hourly rate, e-mail address and so on. The rationale behind having the credit card information is that if the user defaults, then his/her credit card is billed depending upon the number of hours defaulted.

The User Profile also provides a summary of the previous transactions/sessions, such as the number (and type) of time/knowledge exchange transactions completed by the user, the number (and type) of time/knowledge exchange transactions defaulted by the user, the number (and type) of learning sessions completed by the user, and the number (and type) of learning sessions defaulted by the user. This will provide valuable information for the chronobot to manage future time/knowledge exchange of the same user through negotiation protocols.

6. The Relational Index

The experiences accumulated in the virtual classroom are among the most valuable assets for further e-learning. In practice the experiences are the stored transcripts of the virtual classroom sessions. These transcripts are represented as XML documents. In fact we consider everything that is exchanged or recorded in the chronobot/virtual classroom system as some form of XML document.

As shown in Fig. 6, the Relational Index RI is built to support easy access of the accumulated learning experiences. The session transcripts (XML documents) are stored in an experience-base. The Relational Index is then constructed. It relates learning experiences to user preferences in the User Profile. For example, if $x_1, \ldots, x_n$ are keywords specified in the user profile, the Relational Index can be used to find u_j, the user most closely related to the specified keywords.

We can also use the Relational Index RI to relate users to keywords and/or users to users. In other words, RI is used to form an *association* in the information exchange process among users.

The RI is updated each time a new session transcript is created. The transcript is analyzed with respect to a set of pre-specified keywords $x_1, \ldots, x_n$. If a dialog of user u_j in the transcript involves a keyword x_k, we can store a new record

$[x_k; u_j; p]$ in RI where the frequency p is set to 1, or update p if such a record already exists. Similarly if a dialog between two users u_j and u_j in the transcript involves a keyword x_k, we can store a new record $[x_k; u_j; u_j; p]$ in RI where the frequency p is set to 1, or update p if such a record already exists.

For example, the transcript is as follows:

```
George: Do you think we need to add 3D graphics to the
presentation?
Suzie: No, I don't think so. But the layout can be improved.
George: That is good, because I still cannot find a person to do
3D graphics.
```

The pre-specified keywords set is:

$$\{\texttt{layout, graphics, 3D graphics}\}$$

The Relational Index, after the processing of the above transcript, contains the following records as well as other previously entered records:

```
[3D graphics; George; 2]
[3D graphics; George; Suzie; 1]
[layout; Suzie; 1]
[layout; George; Suzie; 1]
```

The Relational Index may contain records relating multiple (more than two) users or multiple (more than one) keywords. We can design the Relational Index to be as complex as is necessary for the intended application. However for practicality, it is important to keep it simple and manageable.

7. Self Model and Alien Model

As mentioned in previous sections, the User Profile is the physical realization of the User Model. In this section, we introduce a model for information exchange. This model was first described in [3]. One important feature of this model is that each user (or user agent, or agent) has a *self model* and an *alien model*. The self model is a model of oneself, and the alien model is a model of the other. This is the basis for any information exchange to take place.

Figure 7 illustrates how a user agent acquires experiences through direct engagement in actions, and the experiences are abstracted into knowledge in the knowledge acquisition process. Figure 8 illustrates how information is exchanged. Once the user agents have acquired experiences and abstracted them into the knowledge base, they may engage in information exchange activities through some negotiation protocols.

The information exchange process is further explained in Fig. 9, where the model for information exchange is illustrated. As mentioned above, the key feature of this

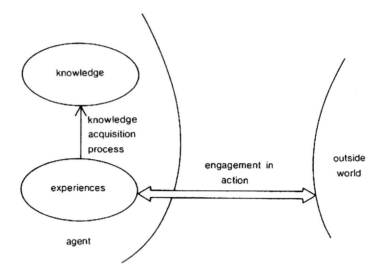

Fig. 7.   The knowledge acquisition process.

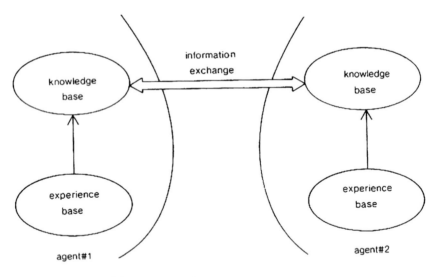

Fig. 8.   The information exchange process.

model is the (self-model, alien-model) pair. Each user agent has a self-model for itself, and also an alien-model for the other user agent. The encoder/decoder enables a user agent to engage in more complicated information exchange activities such as deception where the use of encoded message becomes necessary. The database stores the history of exchanged messages.

In the e-learning environment, we can have student and instructor as two basic types of users. They in turn may be a combination of *Information Collector, Provider, Analyzer, Filter, Creator* and *Annihilator* [3].

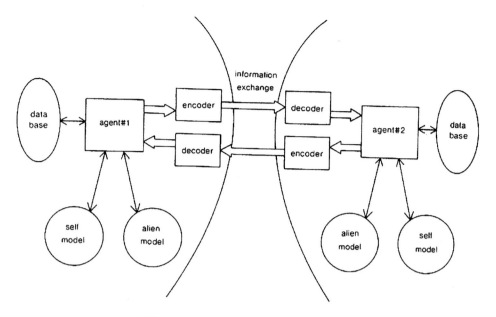

Fig. 9. The information exchange model.

8. The Negotiation Protocol

A *conversation* is the sequence of message exchanges among two or more user agents. A *protocol* is a conversation to enable interacting user agents to estimate respective models of alien user agents to achieve synergy, i.e., each user agent correctly estimates the alien model of the other user agent. If the user agents are of the same type, a protocol is often specified by a set of rules that governs the behavior of the user agents in the information exchange process.

The specific protocol that governs the information exchange for the Chronobot is explained in [7]. Its purpose is to estimate the alien models [3] to determine the most appropriate user agents for time/knowledge exchange and the acceptable exchange rate. Therefore, the chronobot's protocol governs the negotiation among the user agents in the bidding process for time/knowledge exchange.

9. Time and Knowledge Management

Time management for the chronobot differs from traditional time management in that all three ingredients — time, space and tasks — are considered in determining a time schedule. Therefore, time management and knowledge management are inseparable. In this section, we introduce the basic concepts.

A *time schedule* TS_v of an agent v is an assignment from the time line T to the state space S where each state is a pair (location, task). The agent may be a person, a project, a corporation, an institution and so on. In particular, a *life time schedule* LTS_u, or simply a *life*, is a time schedule of a person u where $LTS_u(t) = (\text{no-where, no-task})$ if $t \le t_{u-\text{birth}}$ or $t \ge t_{u-\text{death}}$.

Two locations are compatible if either both are real locations and they are close according to a distance measure, or both are virtual locations and they are compatible according to a location compatibility matrix. Two tasks are compatible if task$_1$ and task$_2$ are compatible according to a task compatibility ontology. Two states s_1 and s_2 are *compatible* if both locations and tasks are compatible.

A time schedule TS_v is *supported* by a life time schedule LTS_u in the interval $[t_a, t_b]$ if $TS_v(t)$ is compatible with $LTS_u(t)$ for any $t \in [t_a, t_b]$.

A time schedule TS_v is *feasible* in the interval $[t_a, t_b]$ with the support of G if for any sub-interval $[t_c, t_d]$ of $[t_a, t_b]$ there exists a $u \in G$ such that TS_v is *supported* by a life time schedule LTS_u in $[t_c, t_d]$. In practice, the sub-intervals are predefined time periods (see the Appendix). Finally a *life model* LM is an approach to generate a certain type of feasible life time schedules.

The Knowledge Manager checks the compatibility of time schedules and life time schedules with respect to a knowledge base containing information on location compatibility and task compatibility. A task may also have certain special characteristics such as: must-be-done-by-self, can-be-done-by-others, must-be-carried-out-at-certain-location, can-be-carried-out-anywhere, can-be-carried-out-in-virtual-locations and so on. Such task characteristics are also stored in the knowledge base and utilized by the Knowledge Manager in determining compatibility.

Supported by the Knowledge Manager, the Time Manager checks whether a time schedule is feasible. If it is not feasible, the Time Manager attempts to revise the time schedule and *out-source* certain tasks by revising the life time schedules of agents in G to make the revised schedules feasible.

When a time schedule is infeasible, it is sometimes possible to make it feasible by revising the schedule or absorbing certain tasks in the free time of a person. Therefore, it is not always necessary to outsource. Sometimes a task has explicit constraints so that it can only be done by oneself.

The Knowledge Manager makes sure certain tasks are compatible with certain persons by checking an ontology. The Time Manager can then automatically place a bid if the user has previously authorized the Time Manager to do so, or at least notify the user.

The following is an example of time/knowledge management using the concepts introduced above. The following small ontology for some related keywords can be part of a much larger ontology. However for practicality, we may want to refrain from using any ontology more complicated than a simple hierarchy:

```
Visual Art:
  Graphics:
    2D graphics
    3D graphics
    . . . . .
```

George is a media artist and his Life Time Schedule LTS for today is:

1–2 pm	2–3 pm	3–4 pm	4–5 pm
*	*	Gym	Gym
Do 2D graphics	Do 2D graphics	Jog	Jog

In George's schedule the asterisk indicates virtual space, i.e., George is willing to exchange time with someone to do graphics in a virtual space. Bill is willing to help and his Life Time Schedule LTS is:

1–2 pm	2–3 pm
*	*
Do graphics	Do graphics

According to the above ontology, "graphics" and "2D graphics" are compatible.

Therefore the two LTSs are also compatible, and Bill's LTS can support George's LTS. If Bill places a bid in the bidding room, the Bid Manager may grant him the bid provided that he is the most suitable bidder according to its QoB calculations.

If Bill has not entered a bid in the bidding room, George may still be able to find him using a Searcher supported by the Relational Index, which may contain a record such as the following due to prior interactions between Bill and George:

[visual design; Bill; George; 26]

In this case a larger ontology is needed to relate the two users.

10. Determination of the Exchange Rate

In the negotiation for time/knowledge exchange, if the two user agents feel their time has different value, it will become necessary for them to negotiate the exchange rate. In what follows, we describe a mechanism for the chronobots to assist them in determining the exchange rate.

We would like to express our terminology as follows, when we refer to agents, we refer to chronobot's user agents. For two agents agent u and agent v, each agent is characterized by attributes $(x_1, \ldots, x_n)$, and $(y_1, \ldots, y_n)$. For the two corresponding attributes x_i and y_i, the information distance measure is denoted by $d_i(x_i, y_i)$, where d_i is between 0 and 1 (a metric).

The exchange rate between agents u and v, is denoted as follows.

$$\text{Exchange (agent } u, \text{ agent } v) = e^{(1/\sum C_{ji} * d(x_{ji}, y_{ji}))}$$

where the summation is over all the terms $C_{ji} * d(x_{ji}, y_{ji})$, and C_{ji} is a scaling constant.

We now illustrate the concept by presenting an example. Let us assume that George and Bill are both media artists and the two agents' primary skill matches. Therefore $C_1 \, d_1(x_1, y_1) = 0$. If the primary skill does not match, $C_1 \, d_1(x_1, y_1)$

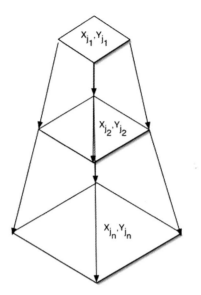

Fig. 10.   Determination of exchange rate.

becomes a big number. For instance, C_1 is 10,000 and d_1 is between 0 and 1, in this case close to 1. Then $C_1 \, d_1 \, (x_1, y_1)$ is close to 100,000 and the exchange rate is close to 1. No need to continue.

The two agent's familiarity with subject area also is comparable, so $C_2 \, d_2 \, (x_2, y_2) = 0$. If the familiarly does not match, then $C_2 \, d_2 \, (x_2, y_2)$ becomes a big number. For instance, C_2 is 1,000 and d_2 is between 0 and 1, in this case close to 1. Then $C_2 \, d_2 \, (x_2, y_2)$ is close to 1,000 and the exchange rate is close to 1. No need to continue either.

Finally, the two agents differ in secondary skill. Therefore $C_3 \, d_3 \, (x_3, y_3)$ is small and we have an exchange rate that reflects the difference in the two agents' secondary skill. Notice the index function takes care of the re-arrangement of the relative importance of the n attributes. The constants Cj are also important. They take care of the relative scaling of the various attributes. Figure 10 illustrates the determination of the exchange rate as a dynamic process of comparing different attributes to identify the ones that really matter. Once such attributes are identified, the users can negotiate to determine the exchange rate.

11. Scenario-Based Product Design

A prototype of the chronobot was implemented [8]. It does not yet possess all the features to fully realize the two scenarios described in Sec. 2, but it does possess the ability to negotiate time/knowledge exchange. For a demo, the reader is referred to our website: *chronobot.itri.org.tw*. A user such as Bill can decide whether to create a bid room, start a new bid or place a bid [Fig. 11(a)], then join a bid room [Fig. 11(b)] to place a bid.

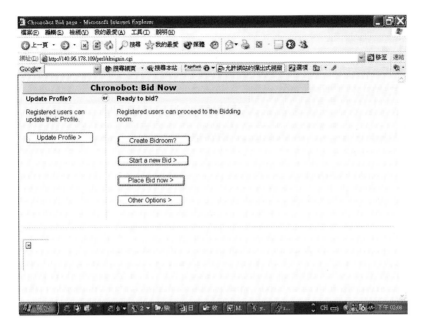

Fig. 11(a). User decides what to do.

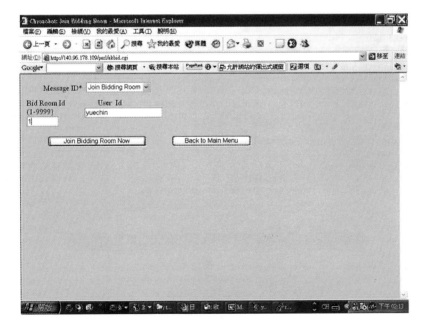

Fig. 11(b). User joins a bid room.

A scenario-based product design workshop was also conducted to identify *user models* as a basis for chronobot product design. The user models include a thirteen year old girl in junior high school, a twenty one year old college student, a twenty eight year old female SOHO worker, a forty five year old executive, and a sixty five year old retired lady. They all need to use chronobot for time/knowledge exchange. The user models have the following characteristics:

Junior High Student and College Student: peer group network; mobile phone e-learning modules; emphasis on peer group network.

Young SOHO Female: professional network; emphasis on quality of work, knowledge consistency and information security; a need to closely monitor exchanged work.

Middle Aged Executive: professional network; prediction; time management; emphasis on knowledge consistency and information security.

Senior Citizen: community network; exchange of time and knowledge within community; trading time to take care of one's relatives and for the future; avoiding fraud by using bidding constraints.

Efficient, reliable networking services and management are seen to be central to the success of the chronobot. Then we can consider technical solutions to information security, knowledge consistency, bidding constraints and prediction to give some intelligence to the chronobot.

12. System Architecture

In the scenario-based product design workshop additional system components are identified, including the context-aware workbot and the multi-sensor healthbot. The resulting conceptual architecture is shown in Fig. 12.

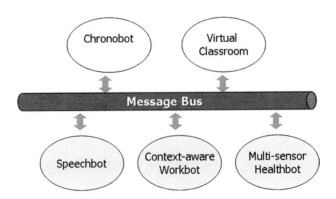

Fig. 12.   Conceptual architecture.

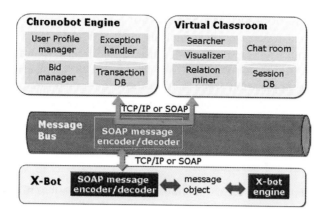

Fig. 13.   Chronobot system architecture.

The system architecture is shown in Fig. 13. It consists of the following components:

(1) A **User Profile Manager** to learn from (a) the *accumulated history of interaction sessions,* which are abstracted by the **Relation Miner** into the *Relational Index,* for example, about the preferences of users, and (b) the completed bidding transactions that are stored into the *transaction database* to be used, for example, in verifying the credibility and ability of users.

(2) A **Bid Manager** to perform **time management, knowledge management, negotiation**, and store *completed bidding transactions* into a *transaction database* to be abstracted into the *User Profile.* The Bid Manager handles the protocols such as the **negotiation protocol** and the **JIT protocol** (see Sec. 13), which may involve communication with the User Profile Manager, the Exception Handler and the virtual classroom. The Bid Manager also performs **user account management** to credit/debit user accounts.

(3) An **Exception Handler** to handle *failed bidding transactions* and store them into the transaction database, to be abstracted and stored into the User Profile.

(4) A **Message Bus (or Communication Server)** to encode, decode and manage all messages in the CVC system. (Messages are XML documents encoded into TCP/IP or SOAP format.)

(5) A **Visualizer** for the virtual classroom to display emotive icons, *FaceAlive icons,* as well as the *session state* and *transaction state* of all users.

(6) A **Searcher** with query morphing and information fusion [6] capabilities for the virtual classroom to search first the Relational Index and then the Internet for related users. The relevant information items, and other knowledge sources are integrated together according to user preference.

(7) A **Relation Miner** for the virtual classroom to construct the relational index from records in the *session database.*

(8) One or more **X-bots** such as a **Speech-bot** for speech input/output, a **Work-bot** for context-aware workflow analysis, and an **H-bot** for preventive health monitoring and health care through sensor-based information fusion.

For a specific application some of the above described components may be needed to implement it. Therefore, we can package the components to design chronobots for different application domains.

13. Just-in-Time e-Learning

One of our goals is to apply the chronobot to **just-in-time e-learning,** for example, to quickly amass e-learning resources in order to train the unemployed and socially disadvantaged so that they can acquire new skills quickly to qualify them for certain jobs. In JIT e-learning, a number of instructors each with certain skills volunteer to donate some time. When a client requires assistance, the volunteers use the chronobot to respond to the request. Since the client must acquire certain job skill by a certain date, sometimes one-on-one e-learning is the preferred solution.

A JIT e-learning model is needed to fit the job training into a specified time period. Adopting the time/knowledge management model introduced in Sec. 9, a job training schedule TS_v is *feasible* in the interval $[t_a, t_b]$ with the support of an instructor pool G if for any sub-interval (class period) $[t_c, t_d]$ of $[t_a, t_b]$ there exists an instructor $u \in G$ such that TS_v is *supported* by an instructor's life time schedule LTS_u in $[t_c, t_d]$.

In a client's life time schedule the sub-intervals (class periods) reserved for job training are subjected to *granularity constraints* such that each training sub-interval must be no less than the minimum allowable class period and no longer than the maximum allowable class period. Notice the time/knowledge management model specifically allows e-learning where both the client and the instructor can be in virtual locations.

The CVC system consisting of the chronobot and the virtual classroom can be used to deliver and manage JIT e-learning. The client later can return the time he or she owed by volunteering to be an instructor or a social worker.

Further experimental studies of the chronobot on JIT e-learning are under way at Taiwan's Industry Technologies Research Institute (ITRI) and Institute for Information Industry (III).

14. A Formal Model of the Chronobot

As explained in previous sections the methodology for time and knowledge exchange essentially consists of the following five steps: (1) **Identify** a slice of time or knowledge for exchange. (2) **Search** for exchange partner or partners. (3) **Perform** time or knowledge exchange through bidding and negotiation. (4) **Manage** the exchanged slice of time or knowledge. (5) **Evaluate** the results.

A chronobot agent u is defined as:

$$u = (P_u, RI_u, \text{Nego-}QoB_u, TS_u, KB_u, OP_u)$$

where P_u is user profile,
$\quad RI_u$ is relational index,
$\quad \text{Nego-}QoB_u$ is negotiation protocol according to quality of bid,
$\quad TS_u$ is time schedule,
$\quad KB_u$ is ontological knowledge-base and
$\quad OP_u$ is set of operations for agent u

The chronobot agents are characterized by hybrid-graphs and operations for the composition, decomposition and transform of hybrid-graphs. Pre- and post-conditions can be specified for these operations so that the operations, pre- and post-conditions together define the *patterns* for time/knowledge exchange.

15. Discussion

The main idea of the chronobot is the flexible allocation of one's time to achieve the best match for time exchange among different agents through negotiation. Such idea is gaining popularity in recent years due to advances in information technology. For example, at Nashoba Valley Medical Center registered nurses can bid on working shifts that have openings [1]. Chronobot will make this possible at the personal level so that everyone can open bids and place bids.

During the scenario-based design workshop the following technical issues are identified: information security, knowledge consistency, bidding constraints and prediction.

Information Security: Information security includes cryptography, prevention of plagiarism and security of intellectual property.

Bidding Constraints: Bidding constraints support the prevention of fraud and reckless user behavior so that no user can take advantage of other users. These are heuristic rules to specify the constraints, including integrity constraints, security constraints and domain specific constraints.

Knowledge Consistency: Knowledge consistency makes sure the knowledge items satisfy "common sense" constraints. It may depend upon the availability of the ontology for the application domain.

Prediction: Chronobot could have limited capability to give advice and predict the future. Just like the word processor may predict the complete word based upon the first few letters that the user types in, a chronobot may predict user's preference based upon the information the user enters. However, the user may always override a chronobot's prediction.

We are developing a methodology of query morphing for retrieving information from the accumulated user experiences utilizing an ontological knowledge base. A model to fuse information from different sources to dynamically construct the User Profile is also being developed. Last but not least, traveling information fusion agents or *adlets* [4] can be used by the Time Manager to find out who can take on certain tasks.

The concept of *time warp* [9] is in essence the **exchange of time with oneself**. In a *front-loaded career* a person may concentrate on one's career for the first twenty years of his/her professional life in order to have a second career for the next twenty years. Similarly in a *deferred life* a person may choose to have a career first and later consider marriage and child bearing. Such choices used to be difficult if not impossible to make, but now within the realm of possibility. In both cases, a life time schedule is supported by a rearranged life time schedule of the same person.

The flexible interweaving of career and living can be regarded as a limiting case of time travel. Instead of a sequential life model, a *non-sequential life model* is envisioned. This model is further explained in the author's sci-fi short story *The Matrix of Life* as well as other authors' sci-fi stories, where time and space are seemingly elastic and can be expanded, compressed, subdivided, transformed and warped. The chronobot can support and even help realize to a certain extent this life model. It may be the closest we can ever get to the classical notion of a time machine.

Acknowledgement

This research was supported in part by the Industry Technology Research Institute and the Institute for Information Industry of Taiwan. The figures were prepared respectively by Min-Hsin Sheng, Wei-Der Hsu and Ganesh Santhanakrishnan. The Virtual Classroom was designed by Xin Li and the Bid Manager implemented by Chirag Vaidya. Many other colleagues, too numerous to be named individually, contributed to this project and are hereby acknowledged.

Appendix: Time Scheduling Algorithms

In practice, to determine whether TS_v is feasible in the interval $[t_a, t_b]$ with the support of G, $[t_a, t_b]$ is divided into regular-sized time periods, and one can verify whether each time period is covered by at least one u in G. To construct a smaller support G, we first select the u in G covering the largest number of time periods, and then the next v in G covering the largest number of remaining time periods and so on, until all time periods are covered. Algorithms with other optimization objectives, such as maximizing runs of covered time periods by the same agent, can also be devised.

If every TS_v in a collection of time schedules $\mathbf{TS}_v$ is feasible in the interval $[t_a, t_b]$ with the support of G and no other proper subset of G, G is called the *minimum support* of the collection $\mathbf{TS}_v$. A virtual location is usually regarded as being compatible with any physical or virtual location. Thus a G consisting of a virtual expert in each field, i.e., an agent capable of handling only tasks of a certain type, is the minimum support for a collection of time schedules.

In the extreme case a "universal expert" or an "army of one" is the minimum support for any collection of time schedules. In practice, we can establish a virtual "help desk" manned by a group of instructors and/or teaching assistants in every virtual classroom to provide 24/7 assistance for all students.

References

1. D. Bushnell, an article in the *Boston Globe*, September 16, 2004. (Also available at: *www.boston.com/business/technology/articles/2004/09/16/software_enables_nurses_to_bid_for_extra_shifts/*).
2. Shi-Kuo Chang, *Nocturne*, a science fiction short story first published in Chinese in 1980; electronic version in English is available at: *http://jupiter.ksi.edu/~changsk/chronobot/nocturne.doc*.
3. S.-K. Chang, "A model for information exchange", *International Journal of Policy Analysis and Information Systems* **5**, no. 2 (1981) 67–93.
4. S.-K. Chang and T. Znati, "Adlet: An active document abstraction for multimedia information fusion," *IEEE Transactions on Knowledge and Data Engineering* (January/February 2001) 112–123.
5. S. Y. Shao and S.-K. Chang, "Management of the growing book as generalized objects", *Proceedings of 15th International Conference on Software Engineering and Knowledge Engineering*, San Francisco (July 1–3, 2003) 599–606.
6. S.-K. Chang, W. Dai, S. Hughes, P. S. Lakkavaram and X. Li, "Evolutionary query processing, fusion and visualization", *Proceedings of International Conference on Distributed Multimedia Systems*, San Francisco (September 20–22, 2003).
7. S.-K. Chang and G. Santhanakrishnan, "Chronobot: A time and knowledge exchange system for e-learning and distance education", *Proceedings of 2004 International Conference on Distributed Multimedia Systems*, Hotel Sofitel, San Francisco Bay (September 8–10, 2004).
8. S.-K. Chang, A. Kapoor, G. Santhanakrishnan and C. Vaidya, "The design and prototyping of the chronobot system for time and knowledge exchange", Technical Report, University of Pittsburgh, Pittsburgh, September 2004.
9. R. Florida, *The Rise of the Creative Class*, Basic Books (Perseus Books Group, 2002; new edition, 2004).

TOOL-BASED SOFTWARE PROJECT CONTROL

JÜRGEN MÜNCH* and JENS HEIDRICH†

Fraunhofer Institute for Experimental Software Engineering,
Sauerwiesen 6, 67661 Kaiserslautern, Germany
E-mails: *muench@iese.fraunhofer.de
†heidrich@iese.fraunhofer.de

Developing software and systems in a way that entails plannable project execution and predictable product quality requires the use of quantitative data for project control. In the context of software development, few techniques exist for supporting on-line monitoring, interpretation, and visualization of project data. This is caused particularly by the often insufficient use of such engineering principles as experience-based planning and plan-based execution in the software development domain. However, effective software project control requires integrated tool support for capturing, managing, analyzing, and storing data. In addition, advanced control approaches aim at providing purpose- and role-oriented information to all involved parties (e.g. project manager, quality assurer) during the execution of a project. This chapter introduces the concept of a so-called Software Project Control Center (SPCC), sketches a control-oriented software development model, and gives a representative overview of existing tool-based software control approaches from academia and practice. Finally, the different approaches are classified and compared with respect to a characterization schema that reflects important requirements from the viewpoint of practitioners.

Keywords: Software project control, software project control center, control tools, quality assurance, data interpretation, data visualization.

1. Introduction

The rapidly increasing importance of software in today's business and the high dependability on software in contexts such as critical systems demands answers on how software can be developed in a plannable way (i.e., matching time and budget constraints), whereby the resulting software product matches predefined functional and non-functional requirements (i.e., reliability). Outsourcing and global distribution of software development activities as well as the integrated development of systems with hardware and software components make predictable software project execution even more necessary. In addition, having repeatable processes for developing software variants within accurate time and cost estimations is gaining increasing importance. Modern cars, for instance, contain more than 50 software-based controllers. Missed delivery deadlines for such controller software can delay system integration significantly and lengthen the overall development; providing inadequate

---

*Corresponding author.

software quality can lead to expensive callbacks of thousands of vehicles. Many software development organizations still lack support for obtaining intellectual control over their software development projects and for determining the performance of their development processes and the quality of the produced products. Systematic support for detecting and reacting to critical project states in order to achieve planned goals is usually missing.

Software development based on engineering principles [13, 34] addresses these problems. It includes the definition of project goals, the development of explicit project plans based on experience [32], the execution of projects based on these plans, and the packaging of experience for future projects. The packaging step also includes the creation of explicit models (e.g. an effort baseline) from past project data in order to be reused and adapted while planning a new project. This feedback-cycle involves software engineering as well as knowledge engineering aspects.

One important means of engineering-style development is software project control. This comprises monitoring and analysis of actual product and process states, comparisons with planned values and the initiation of corrective actions during project execution. Measurement technology is needed to derive metrics for process and product characteristics, define target data values, and establish models for data comparisons and predictions.

In the mechanical production domain, so-called control rooms are a well-known instrument for engineers. A control room is a central node for all incoming information of a production process. It collects all incoming data (e.g. the current state of an assembly line) and visualizes them for control purposes. If there is a problem with the production process (e.g. a blocked assembly line), the user of the control room is informed and can handle the problem. Controlling in the software engineering domain requires an analogue approach that is tailored to the specifics of software processes (such as non-deterministic, concurrent, and distributed processes). A control room in the software engineering domain is a so-called Software Project Control Center (SPCC) [28]. Typical tasks of SPCCs such as distributed data collection, data storage, and data analysis suggest the use of tool-support for performing the tasks. Nowadays, systematic software project control is finding its way into practice. This is very often accelerated by organizational efforts to reach higher maturity of their software processes and practices.

It should be mentioned that software project control cannot only be used to monitor and adjust project performance during execution. The collected data can also be packaged (e.g. as predictive models) for future use and contribute to an improvement cycle spanning a series of projects. Additionally, data collection can be extended beyond the purpose of controlling. One example would be to perform a case study as part of a development project in order to determine the effects of process improvement.

This chapter is organized as follows: The next section gives a basic overview of software project control by means of a development model that integrates SPCCs into the software development cycle. Section 3 describes the scope of the discussed tool-based SPCC approaches. Section 4 introduces basic requirements for SPCCs. Section 5 discusses a set of tool-based SPCC approaches referring to the requirements. Section 6 illustrates some integrated SPCC techniques. Finally, Sec. 7 classifies the discussed approaches and highlights future research issues in this field.

2. Software Project Control

The activities around a software development project can be grouped into three basic phases. First, we consider activities related to project planning, including the basic characterization of the project itself, goal setting, such as setting measurement goals according to the Goal Question Metric (GQM) paradigm [1, 2, 5, 8, 10, 31, 36], and finally, selection of the right development process. Second, we consider activities related to project execution, including all development activities as well as project and quality management activities. Third, we consider activities related to know-how management, including activities for the analysis of project data, and packaging data in order to reuse them in future projects.[a]

Generally, project control can be defined as ensuring that project objectives are met by monitoring and measuring progress regularly to identify variances from plan so that corrective action can be taken when necessary [29]. Controlling is an activity that is basically applied during project execution, but has strong ties to planning and know-how management. Planning is the basis for controlling in order to be able to identify variances from plan. Know-how management is built upon controlling in order to be able to analyze the monitored and measured progress of the project and to package these data for future projects.

Sometimes controlling is defined as the pure monitoring and measurement process during project execution, and all corrective actions to bring the project back to plan, the so-called steering activities, are excluded. For this chapter, we want to include all such steering activities explicitly in our definition of the term "project control".

A Software Project Control Center (SPCC) supports project control and is defined as a means for process-accompanying interpretation and visualization of measurement data. An SPCC consists of a control architecture that clearly defines interfaces to its environment, and a set of underlying techniques and methods that allow for project control. Basically, an SPCC retrieves input data from the current project (e.g. goals, characteristics, baselines, and current measurement data) and generalized data from previous projects (e.g. quality, product, and process models), and produces a visualization of measurement data by using the incorporated techniques and methods to interpret the data accordingly. An SPCC is itself a kind of general control approach according to our definition and not necessarily

---

[a]All activities mentioned during the three phases cover the six project-related steps of the Quality Improvement Paradigm (QIP) [7].

tool-supported. But in order to fulfill control tasks like monitoring defect profiles, detecting abnormal effort deviations, cost estimation, and cause analysis of plan deviations, a certain amount of tool support is necessary and inevitable. Therefore, this chapter focuses on tool-supported software project control and highlights some approaches in this field.

SPCCs can be classified along two dimensions. First, the degree of variability and adaptability of used techniques and methods to control the project, which can vary from a strictly predefined set of built-in techniques and methods to a complete extensible and adaptable repository of techniques and methods. Second, the goal orientation of the produced views onto monitored measurement data, which can vary from one static view for each monitored project variable (like one chart for the project's effort) to a set of goal-oriented views, that is, views that depend on the previously defined measurement goals (like a set of charts covering all previously defined measurement goals).

The TAME (Tailoring a measurement environment) software development model [6, 7] acts as a basis for integrating an SPCC into a Software Engineering Environment (SEE). It makes all necessary control information available and comprises essential mechanisms for capturing and using software engineering experience. The TAME model has been a major source for the development of engineering-style methods like the Goal Question Metric (GQM) method and the Quality Improvement Paradigm (QIP) as well as the Experience Factory (EF) [3, 4, 12] organization. The model has been instantiated in several progressive software engineering environments, such as NASA-SEL [24] or MVP-E [9].

Figure 1 shows an integrated development model for SEEs based on the principles of the TAME model. It is used here to illustrate how an SPCC could be integrated into a software development organization and how it interacts with its environment. The development model distinguishes four different levels of abstraction: (1) roles, (2) services, (3) tools, and (4) information. The presented model exemplarily assigns several units to each of the four levels in order to illustrate the integration of an SPCC within a software development project. According to [28], we can describe the four levels as follows:

Roles: Different roles within a software development project use different services of the three basic phases of the project. For instance, the project planning group uses planning services in order to create a project plan, the development group uses technical services in order to develop products, the project management uses management services in order to control the project, and so on.

Services: This level incorporates services that support activities of the three basic project phases. (1) Project planning is done based on explicit project goals and characteristics. During planning, models (e.g. process models, product models) are instantiated and related in order to build a project representation with respect to the project's goals and characteristics. We distinguish initial planning, which refers to planning before the start of the project, from replanning, which addresses the systematic changing or detailing of the plan during project execution (eventually

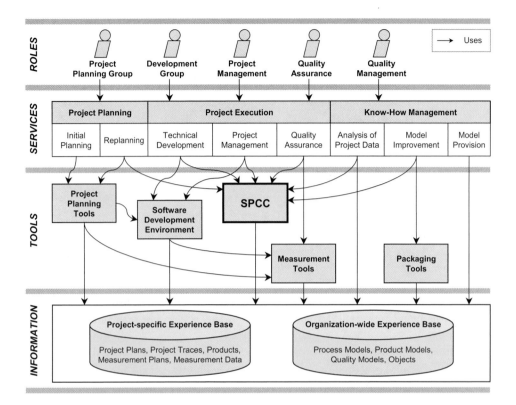

Fig. 1.   Software development model.

supported by an SPCC). (2) The services mainly needed for project execution can be divided into services for technical development of products, services for project management (including project control), and, finally, services for quality assurance. (3) Know-how management is used to analyze the collected project data in order to provide and improve existing models for future use.

Tools: A set of tools is able to provide some services completely (fully automated) or to support certain aspects of a service (human-based tool application). For instance, there exist tools to support project planning, to measure project data, to develop artifacts, or to package experience. The tools are invoked by services and use information resulting from other tools or from an experience base to perform their tasks. An SPCC tool supports roles such as project management, quality assurance, or development group (respectively corresponding services) by providing, processing, interpreting, and visualizing process-accompanying data for their specific needs and purposes. Thereby, it builds upon information stored in an Experience Base located in the last level of our development model.

Information: The fourth level addresses the information needed to perform a software development project, that is, information needed directly by services or needed by tools to support respective services. We assume that during project execution, measurement data is collected and validated. One task of the information level is to provide project-specific or organization-wide information during project execution in order to improve control over the project.

3. Scope of the Overview

This chapter presents an overview of selected tool-based approaches in the SPCC field. Existing surveys reside on a specific level of abstraction and present the work from a specific perspective. There are papers describing frameworks (e.g. [22]), papers describing methods and techniques (e.g. [38]), and papers describing tools (e.g. [17]). Typical perspectives found are improvement perspectives (e.g. learning organization, measurement programs), mathematical perspectives (e.g. model building), or empirical perspectives (e.g. data analysis and validation).

In this chapter, we define the scope in the following way: We focus on tool-supported approaches for online data interpretation and visualization in the context of software development (see Fig. 2). We consider the selected approaches for the overview as being representative of the work in this scope. For rendering the scope more precisely, we exclude several approaches.

First, we exclude approaches from other domains such as mechanical production processes (e.g. supervision of a coal power plant). The reason is that other domains have different characteristics and as a consequence, specific control approaches for these domains are not or not directly applicable for controlling software development. For instance, mechanical production processes are typically characterized by consistently identical production cycles, which are repeatedly performed in short time intervals. The small variance of mechanical production processes and the large

	Product-oriented Controlling	Process-oriented Controlling	Resource-oriented Controlling
Software Development Domain	X	X	
Business Domain	(X)	(X)	
Production Domain			

Fig. 2.   Scope of the overview.

quantity of data allows for completely different control and data analysis techniques and methods. In the area of business processes (e.g. accounting, acquisition), there exist a lot of control approaches (e.g. performance management with user-configured dashboards, which give the user the ability to view required information in a user-specific way). In contrast to software development processes, business processes are usually deterministic. However, approaches for controlling business processes are often used to control software development. For this reason, we picked up a typical approach from the business process domain for the overview and show the limitations of its use in the software development domain.

Second, we exclude solely resource-oriented approaches (such as attendance/absenteeism control, person-job matching, and performance appraisal) and solely product-oriented approaches (such as simple configuration control). The rationale behind this is that the quality of a developed software product and the efficiency of the corresponding process depend upon more than one dimension. Therefore, we only take approaches into account that have a wider view. That means, we only selected control approaches that at least consider process and product aspects.

Third, we exclude spreadsheet programs (e.g. Microsoft Excel), diagramming programs (e.g. Microsoft Visio), function plotting programs (e.g. gnuplot), and purely data monitoring-oriented approaches (e.g. the design and code metrics included in Borland Together). Spreadsheet programs can be used as front-end of an SPCC for measurement collection and validation. The familiarity of developers and managers with such tools might facilitate data collection procedures and, as a consequence, increase the acceptance of measurement activities. Diagramming and function plotting programs can be used as front-end of an SPCC. They can be used to turn data into diagrams and provide a variety of specialized diagram types. Purely data monitoring-oriented approaches can be used as one way to gain data for further SPCC interpretation and visualization activities.

This overview touches different abstraction levels because narrowing to only one level (e.g. only focusing on the tool level) would contradict our goal of providing a comprehensive overview of essential approaches for software project control centers. The description of the approaches focuses on the logical architecture to highlight the main components and their interaction. Additionally, selected techniques and methods in the context of the particular approach are sketched.

Most of the following approaches reside in the software development domain (in detail, Provence, Amadeus, Ginger2, SME, WebME, and PAMPA). One approach originates from the domain of business processes (namely, PPM) and is discussed here because it can be considered as a typical representative of existing business-oriented control tools.

In the following, we will concisely describe the intended use, the main idea, the logical architecture, and associated techniques, methods, and tools of each approach, where appropriate.

4. SPCC Requirements

In order to discuss the related tool-based approaches according to a unique schema, we will introduce some basic requirements for SPCCs. The description is organized as follows: At first, we will discuss requirements in the field of data collection; that is, requirements referring to distributed development, database access, and so on. Afterwards, we will treat data processing requirements; that is, requirements referring to the external and internal SPCC data processing functionality. Then, we will discuss requirements referring to data presentation, like abstraction and compression of data and viewpoint-oriented presentation.

4.1. *Data collection requirements*

The following section gives an overview of the requirements in the context of the overall SPCC data collection process; that is, it captures all requirements for incoming data.

R1: Support for reuse. All data of previous projects (like effort and error distributions) and organization wide experience (like quality models and qualitative experience) are potential reuse candidates. Project-specific data has to be adapted according to project goals and characteristics and models have to be instantiated in the context of the current project. This leads to a generic reuse architecture in which all used data are customized in correspondence to current project goals and characteristics. An SPCC should support such a generic reuse architecture.

R2: Support for distributed development. Software is increasingly developed at different distributed development locations. Each environment has its own way to collect data and to store them in a corresponding repository. An SPCC has to support distributed development and has to be able to integrate the data from different development environments into one single framework.

R3: Integration of measurement paradigms. There are several approaches to derive measurement plans for a project. One goal-oriented top-down approach is the already mentioned GQM method, which systematically derives questions from measurement goals and metrics from derived questions. An SPCC has to take into account of the measurement goals and plans and use them as an input for setting up the required SPCC functionality. So, an SPCC has to provide concepts in order to integrate an underlying measurement paradigm.

R4: Data validation capabilities. Incoming data have to be validated with respect to whether they make sense in a special (project) context or not. This includes, for instance, the range of incoming data. Furthermore, data from different distributed development locations have to be consistent in order to be integrated for further data processing. In general, an SPCC has to provide mechanisms for testing the validity of incoming data.

4.2. *Data processing requirements*

The following section gives an overview of requirements in the context of the SPCC data processing functionality.

R5: Provision of control techniques. We distinguish different usage purposes of an SPCC. For instance, an SPCC can be used to compare data with a corresponding baseline and detect deviations. For each purpose (or a group of purposes) a variety of possible techniques and methods exists. An SPCC has to provide a comprehensive pool of predefined techniques in order to control the project.

R6: Packaging of experience. In order to support organization-wide improvement paradigms, we need to integrate experiences, gained through the usage of an SPCC, into an experience base. This includes quantitative experience (e.g. an effort distribution) as well as qualitative experience (e.g. a list of retaliatory actions which has proofed to be useful if certain plan deviations occur). Therefore, an SPCC has to provide concepts in order to package experiences for further reuse.

R7: Variability. The applicability of a certain control technique often depends on the project's context and attributes (e.g. effort, number of defects, or design complexity) to control in this context. For instance, in order to apply Statistical Process Control the values of a controlled process attribute have to vary around an expected value. So, we'll probably need new methods and techniques if we introduce new project types, or new attributes to control. Therefore, an SPCC has to provide an extensible pool of techniques; that is, it has to be able to integrate new techniques.

R8: Adaptability. Every project differs in terms of project goals and characteristics (e.g. domain, programming language, or skills of developers). Therefore, all control techniques have to be adapted accordingly and an SPCC has to provide corresponding mechanisms to do so. Furthermore, it is possible, that certain project characteristics change during project execution. In this case, the applied control techniques have to be adapted to the new project characteristics dynamically.

4.3. Data visualization requirements

The following section gives an overview of requirements in the context of the SPCC data visualization process.

R9: Goal-oriented visualization. Different users of an SPCC (like a project manager, a quality assurance manager, a developer, or a tester) need different kinds of data visualizations. For instance, a project manager will probably need all data related to the state of the project, while a module designer will probably only need data about the design quality of a certain module. Therefore, an SPCC has to provide concepts for goal-oriented data visualization.

R10: Support for data compression/abstraction. SPCC users need data on different levels of abstraction at different points in time. For instance, a project manager needs an overview of the project's effort per project phase. If a plan deviation occurs in a certain phase, it is necessary to have a closer look at the effort data for all activities of this phase, and so on. A module designer, for instance, just needs design quality values for a certain module, while the system designer needs them for the whole software system. Generally, an SPCC has to provide mechanisms in order to present the processed data on different levels of abstraction.

R11: Provision of up-to-date information. In order to interpret the visualized data in the right way, you have to be sure that all displayed data are up-to-date. An SPCC has to guarantee this. This requires traceability among (1) the collected measurement data, (2) the way they are processed (by control techniques), and finally (3) the way they are visualized (for different users). Then, it is possible to trace the overall data flow, which allows for the interpretation of visualized data in the right way (e.g. in order to find causes for plan deviations).

5. Tool-Based Software Project Control Approaches

In the following, we discuss a set of tool-based approaches for software project control. First, we will briefly address the idea behind each approach and the field of application. Second, we will describe the architecture used to implement the approach. Third, we will discuss the requirements from Sec. 4. An overview of the latter is presented in Table 1. The discussion of requirements for each approach is organized into three parts. Part (a) mentions requirements fully supported by the approach, indicated by "Fully" in Table 1. Part (b) discusses requirements only partly supported; that is, the basic concepts are provided, but the integration is not fully addressed, indicated by "Partly" in Table 1. If necessary, Part (c) lists requirements not addressed by the corresponding approach, indicated by an empty cell in Table 1.

5.1. *Provence*

Idea: Provence [20] is a framework for project management. It informs managers about state changes of processes and products, and is able to generate reports of the project. Furthermore, it allows project managers to initiate dynamic replanning steps. The main idea behind Provence is an open and adaptable architecture. Most process-centered software development environments (SDEs) depend upon a monolithic structure; that is, they handle all tasks within the specific SDE. The component-based architecture of Provence allows the system to be flexible and facilitates integration into different organizations. Provence observes the development process, captures process and product data, answers queries about the current project state, and visualizes process transitions.

Architecture: The logical architecture of Provence consists of five components and is shown in Fig. 3. (1) A process server supports process transitions according to a specific process model. It generates specifications of requested events and registers those events at the event action engine. (2) The data management unit stores all relevant data of processes and products and allows the user to query the corresponding database. It is based on a pre-defined data model. (3) A smart file system detects changes of files caused, for instance, by tool invocation, and submits these events to the event action engine. (4) The event action engine collects all incoming events and informs the process server in case of previously registered events. (5) Finally, the visualizer is responsible for visualizing current process and product

Table 1. Overview of all discussed approaches.

Approach	R1	R2	R3	R4	R5	R6	R7	R8	R9	R10	R11
Provence	Partly	Partly		Partly	Fully	Partly	Fully	Fully		Partly	Fully
Amadeus		Fully	Partly	Partly	Fully	Fully	Partly	Partly	Partly	Partly	Fully
Ginger2	Fully		Partly	Partly	Fully	Fully		Partly	Partly		Partly
SME	Fully	Fully	Partly	Partly	Fully			Fully	Fully		Fully
WebME	Fully	Fully	Partly	Fully	Fully	Partly	Partly	Fully	Partly	Fully	Fully
PPM	Partly	Partly			Fully	Partly	Partly	Partly	Partly		Fully
PAMPA		Fully	Partly		Fully	Partly	Partly	Partly			Fully
SPCC Tech.	Partly	Fully	Partly	Fully	Fully	Partly	Fully	Fully	Fully	Fully	Fully

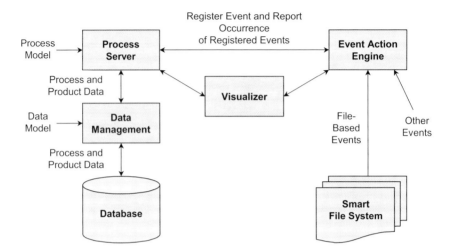

Fig. 3.   Logical architecture of Provence [20].

data. A prototypical instantiation of the Provence architecture uses existing tools to implement the five logical components of Fig. 3 (e.g. the process-centered SDE Marvel [19] is used as the process server).

Requirements: (a) Provence provides a set of standard control techniques in order to check for process conformance. The component-based architecture allows integration of alternative tools for each component. The visualizer guarantees an up-to-date view of process and project data. (b) Depending on the used tool-set it should be possible to support distributed software development and data validation mechanisms. Depending on the used visualizer data could be displayed on different levels of abstraction. (c) However, Provence provides no access capabilities to former project data or experience gained from former projects. It further provides no support to integrate existing measurement paradigms. Current project information cannot be packaged in order to be reused in future projects, and a static set of integrated standard queries for visualizing the project state is provided. Moreover, no mechanisms to support goal-oriented data visualization for different project roles and adaptation of applied analysis techniques are addressed.

5.2. *Amadeus*

Idea: Amadeus [30, 33] is a metric-based analysis and feedback system, and embedded into the process-centered SDE Arcadia. The goal is to integrate measurement into software development processes, and to establish analysis and feedback mechanisms by providing functions for interpreting different types of events. The main idea of the Amadeus system is to make measurement an active component during project execution. Amadeus is based on a script language that dynamically interprets process events, object state changes, and calendar time abstractions. These three events can be combined to form more complex ones. An Amadeus user defines (reusable) scripts to observe certain events. Events are kinds of triggers for user-dependent agents, which execute a number of actions, like collecting specific data items of the project. All collected data is analyzed either by humans or automatically. For instance, a method called classification tree analysis is used to classify components of a software system.

Architecture: The main part of the logical architecture (shown in Fig. 4) is a pro-active server, which interprets scripts and coordinates event observation and agent activation. Data integration frameworks allow for collecting data from processes, products, or personnel. The server does not distinguish between scripts generated by users, processes, or tools. A number of servers is able to run and interact (via scripts) at the same time. A server interacts with the evaluation component of an agent and coordinates tasks, where different agents participate. A client communicates with a server via dialog boxes. Both server and client have an associated expandable tool kit. The client's tool kit includes tools to define a script, and the server's tool kit includes tools as part of script interpretation (i.e., data collection and analysis tools). The user interacts with a so-called customizable goal palette that provides a summary of all available services and analysis processes. After selecting one process the system guides the user through the chosen technique.

Requirements: (a) The flexible server/client architecture allows Amadeus to support distributed software development. Client and server tool kits provide a set of standard techniques for project control and allow easy integration of new techniques and adaptation of existing ones for different projects. The user's goal palettes allow

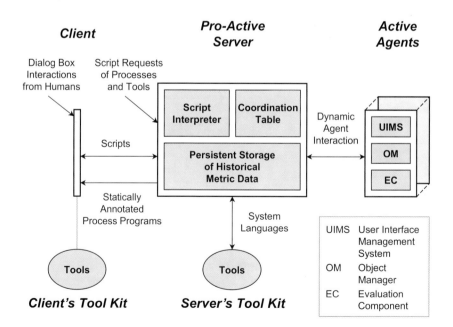

Fig. 4. Logical architecture of Amadeus [33].

an up-to-date view on gathered measurement data and analysis results. (b) Depending on the used techniques as part of the server and client tool kits accessing a reuse repository and packaging project experience should be possible. The same holds for data validation capabilities and integration of measurement paradigms. Amadeus users are individually supported by customizable goal palettes including available services and analysis processes. However, no user-dependent views of analysis results are addressed.

5.3. *Ginger2*

Idea: Ginger2 [40, 41] implements an environment for computer-aided empirical software engineering (CAESE). Torii *et al* present a framework that consists of three parts: (1) A life cycle model for empirical studies, (2) a coherent view of experiments through data collection models, and (3) an architecture that forms the basis of a CAESE system. The main idea is to center the experimental aspects of software development. Within a CAESE system, a software engineering problem is given, consisting of questions and hypotheses. The goal of the CAESE approach is to find knowledge about the given problem statement. Figure 5 illustrates the principal design of a CAESE environment. In that, the focus is more on conducting controlled experiments (so-called *in vitro* studies) and less on developing software products within a real software development project (so-called *in vivo* studies).

Architecture: The life cycle model of a CAESE environment consists of the following parts: The *needs analysis* unit is used to identify the problem, formulate

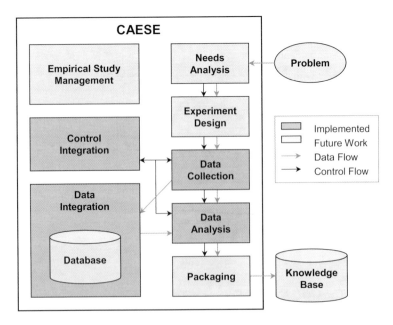

Fig. 5.   Logical architecture of Ginger2 [41].

goals and purpose of the study, and establish hypotheses. The *experiment design* unit determines how to enact the experiment (i.e., which participants are selected and which techniques, methods, and tools are used). The *data collection* unit gathers data according to the experiment design and a data collection model, which is used to collect data from different views. The *data analysis* unit analyzes the data according to the goals and purpose of the study. Finally, the *packaging* unit packages the problem statement and the analysis results into a knowledge base. In addition, there are some elements that support the units of the life cycle model: A *data integration* unit transforms data from the data collection unit according to the input type of the data analysis unit (e.g. making continuous data discrete). The *control integration* unit synchronizes the usage of different tools. Finally, the whole study is managed by the *empirical study management*. Ginger2 uses a multitude of techniques to collect data. Most of them are used to observe the behavior of the experiment participants. For instance, there are techniques to gather audio and video data of the experiment, data about mouse movements, keyboard inputs, and window movements, data about eye tracking, motion, and skin resistance of the participants, and finally, data about tool usage and program changes.[b]

Requirements: (a) The Ginger2 environment provides a set of standard techniques for gathering and analyzing measurement data and allows for packaging gathered knowledge in a knowledge base. The needs analysis unit allows for specifying goals and purposes of a study. (b) However, there is only limited integration of a measurement paradigm as well as mechanisms for data validation and goal-oriented visualization depending on the data collection and analysis units. The same holds for variability and adaptability of integrated techniques and methods. The focus of the Ginger2 system is on learning by means of controlled experiments. As a matter of fact, lots of analysis results are only available and used after project completion. (c) The lifecycle model does not address support for reuse and support for distributed development of software.

5.4. *SME*

Idea: The software management environment (SME) [16, 17] was developed within the software engineering laboratory (SEL) [21, 24] of the NASA Goddard space flight center (GSFC). The SME is a tool to provide experience, gathered by the SEL, to project managers. The usage of the SME presumes that software development takes place within a well defined management environment. Its basic functions are observation, comparison, prediction, analysis, assessment, planning, and control.

Architecture: The implementation of SME functions relies on information from previous projects, research results from studies of software development projects, and management rules, which are accessible via three separate databases. The

---

[b]The collection of data about tool usage and program changes is the main focus of the Ginger1 system [40].

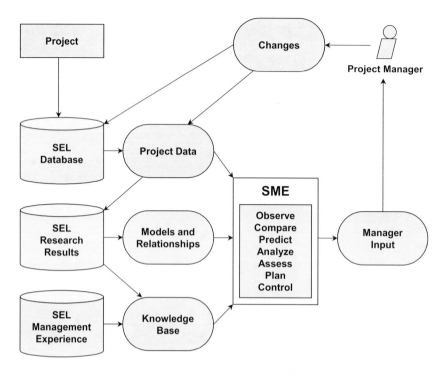

Fig. 6.   Logical architecture of the SME [16].

architecture is presented in Fig. 6. The *SEL database* includes information from previous projects, that is, subjective and objective process and product data, plans, and tool usages. The *SEL research results* database includes different models (such as growth or effort models) and relationships between certain parameters/attributes (described with quality models). Primarily, they are used to predict and assess attributes. The *SEL management experience* database includes the experience of managers in the form of rules within an expert system. They help inexperienced managers to analyze data and guide replanning activities. For instance, this database includes lists of errors and appropriate corrective actions. All these data are input for the SME, which performs the management functions above. These functions provide data for the project manager in order to support well-founded decision making. Experience gained during project execution may lead to changes of project data. This feedback mechanism enables SME to work with up-to-date information.

Requirements: (a) The SME provides access to different kinds of reuse repositories and supports packaging of project information. It further provides a set of standard management techniques covering different purposes (e.g. guidance). Integrated feedback mechanisms guarantee up-to-date project information. The goal-oriented visualization of gathered project data is mainly focused on the project manager. (b) SME supports a static set of collected measurement data corresponding to previously defined (static) measurement plan. However, mechanisms exist to adapt the SME to the needs of the currently performed project and to validate ingoing data. (c) Distributed development, different levels of abstraction for data visualization, as well as the enhancement of integrated techniques are not addressed.

5.5. *WebME*

Idea: WebME (web measurement environment) [37–39] is a web-based data visualization tool that is based on the SME approach. WebME enhances the capabilities of SME in terms of distributed development of software. While SME is concentrated on the development within a certain closed SDE, WebME supports the development at different locations with heterogeneous SDEs and provides appropriate data integration mechanisms. WebME uses a special script language, which is able to integrate information of different heterogeneous SDEs into one common view.

Architecture: The architecture is presented in Fig. 7. It consists of three layers. The *end-user applications* layer provides access to the WebME system via a web browser. A user specifies a query and gets an HTML response. This makes the architecture platform-independent and allows access from every location within the world wide web. The *mediating information servers* layer is the central processing layer. The query processor receives data from the web browser and transforms them to legal queries according to the WebME system. Vice versa, it transforms the answers of the WebME server to HTML pages and transmits them to the

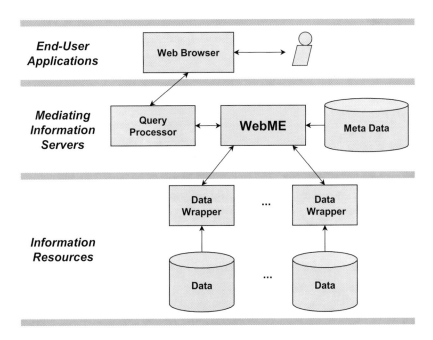

Fig. 7. Logical architecture of WebME [38].

web browser. To know which data of which host in which format is to be used, the WebME system needs appropriate meta data in the form of scripts. The *information resources* include a data wrapper for each development location of a distributed project. The data wrapper receives data from a local database and transmits them to the WebME system.

WebME uses the so-called *data definition language (DDL)* to specify scripts that describe which data of which host and in which format are to be used and how this data can be presented according to a certain query. A script processor transforms the scripts into measurement class and interface definitions, which can be processed by the WebME system to fill requests. A class represents a Software Development Environment, like NASA/SEL. Direct and indirect attributes can be assigned to each class by an appropriate DDL statement. Direct attributes are values of external databases (received via data wrappers). Therefore, we have to specify a name, a unit, an interval (e.g. a weekly data collection), a host, a port and a binary (which reads values from the external database) for each attribute. Indirect attributes are combinations of direct ones (e.g. the difference of two direct attributes).

Requirements: (a) WebME allows for accessing different kinds of data repositories and visualization of therein stored data. Distributed development is supported by its mediated architecture. It is further possible to validate ingoing data by specifying data units and collection intervals for each attribute. WebME provides a set of standard data collection and processing techniques via its script language and supports their adaptation. Moreover, it is possible to combine different attributes via these mechanisms and build kinds of abstraction levels. The web-based architecture guarantees accessibility and up-to-date project information. (b) The integration of measurement paradigms and goal-oriented data visualizations are only partly addressed by the script language. (c) Packaging mechanisms are not addressed by the logical architecture.

5.6. *PPM*

Idea: The process performance manager (PPM) is a tool to support the management of business processes and was developed by IDS Sheer AG [18]. The aim is (1) to guarantee compliance with activities and effort plans, (2) to identify weak points in process execution performance, (3) to optimize the business process by identifying improvement potential, and (4) to assess the achieved improvements on the business process. Therefore, it provides a basis for decision making within an organization. The idea of PPM is to close the feedback gap between business process specification and execution. PPM provides functions for observing and assessing the performance of a current business process, and for providing feedback about it. Furthermore, PPM is able to integrate existing (organization-specific) tools, and therefore, is able to present a common view across heterogeneous systems. *Key performance indicators (KPIs)* characterize a business process across different aggregation hierarchies. Through baseline specification, statistical analysis, and trend identification, PPM is able to identify deviations from baselines and to inform decision-makers.

Architecture: The architecture is shown in Fig. 8. Basically, it consists of four layers. (1) PPM is able to integrate existing source systems via an XML interface layer. An existing system accesses the PPM kernel, which runs as a server, via these adapters. (2) The PPM kernel layer includes a relational SQL database to store all relevant information of the source systems. In addition, the kernel includes a module to generate processes and compute the KPIs. (3) A user interface layer, which runs as a client, provides access to the PPM kernel and allows navigation of process data and visualization in the form of diagrams and tables. Therefore, a Java 2-compliant web browser is sufficient. (4) Finally, we have a layer with additional modules, like modules for process control, change management, analysis, and evaluation. The modules provide additional functionality to the PPM system.

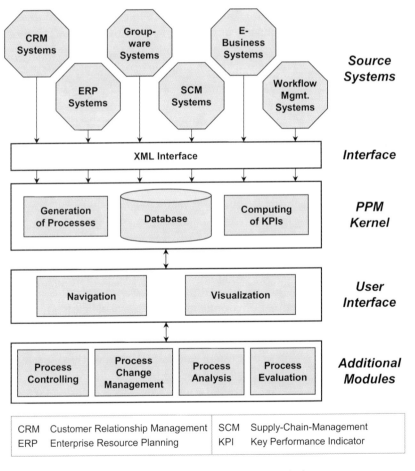

Fig. 8. Logical architecture of PPM [18].

Requirements: (a) The PPM system provides KPIs in order to assess the process performance and in addition a set of modules for further functionality, like process analysis. The system is adaptable to different projects through a variable XML adapter. Up-to-date project information is provided via a web browser. (b) PPM concentrates on business processes and does therefore not support distributed software development in particular, but the architecture provides concepts to access different, distributed data sources via its XML adapter. Support for data validation and packaging project experience depends on the integration of additional modules. The same holds for integrating data from a reuse repository and data visualization mechanisms. (c) However, integrating a measurement paradigm and support for different data abstraction levels are not addressed.

5.7. *PAMPA*

Idea: PAMPA (project attribute monitoring and prediction associate) [35] is a tool that is especially designed for data collection and visualization. It supports the work of a project manager by enhancing intellectual control over the software development project. PAMPA is integrated into a dual control and improvement cycle. It implements the project visualization stage, which consists of (1) data collection and (2) data analysis and prediction. This stage could easily be integrated into a control and improvement cycle of a particular project. Intelligent agents reduce the overhead of data collection. They replace manual and subjective data collection and analysis with objective procedures and allow a cost effective, automated solution for project control. Agents are responsible for data collection, data analysis, and report generation, and inform the project manager in case of plan deviations. Agents are generated by expert systems, which get their inputs from the PAMPA system.

Architecture: The basic architecture of PAMPA is shown in Fig. 9. Project information is stored in an object-oriented data management schema. PAMPA provides a set of predefined objects with relationships and attributes. The attributes correspond to measurement data or to nominal values of processes and products. They form the basis for further PAMPA functions. PAMPA uses Microsoft Windows and Office to visualize the collected data. In the area of data collection, several adjustments can be made to collect data from other environments, whereas visualization in the form of diagrams and tables and the generation of reports requires Microsoft Office.

Requirements: (a) PAMPA supports distributed software development and provides a set of control techniques through automated agents. Up-to-date information is provided through an MS Office front end. (b) PAMPA is integrated in a dual control and improvement cycle. However, mechanisms for integrating a measurement paradigm, packaging project data, or extending and adapting the set of applied control mechanisms are not fully addressed. (c) Concepts for accessing a reuse repository and data validation mechanisms are not addressed. The same holds for goal-oriented data visualization as well as data compression and abstraction mechanisms.

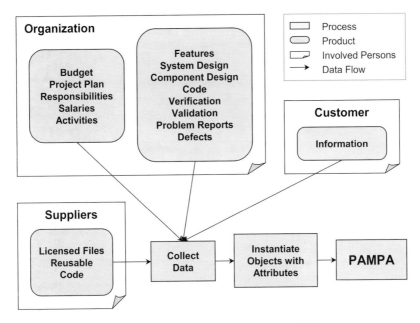

Fig. 9.   Logical architecture of PAMPA [35].

5.8. *SPCC technology*

Idea: The SPCC Technology approach was developed at the University of Kaiserslautern and the Fraunhofer Institute for Experimental Software Engineering (IESE) [14, 15]. The aim is to present the collected data in a goal-oriented way in order to optimize the measurement program and to effectively detect plan deviations. The benefits of this approach include (1) improvement of quality assurance and project control by providing a set of custom-made views on measurement data, (2) support of project management through early detection of plan deviations and proactive intervention, (3) support of distributed software development by means of a single point of control, (4) enhanced understanding of software processes and their improvement via measurement-based feedback, and (5) preventing information overload through custom-made views with different levels of abstraction.

Architecture: The architecture (see Fig. 10) is organized along three different layers. The information layer gathers all information that is essential for the basic functionality, for instance, measurement data from the current project, experiences from previous projects, and internal information, like all available purpose-oriented techniques and methods, the so-called SPCC functions. The functional layer performs all data processing activities, that is, it performs the currently used functions and composes role-oriented views. Finally, the application layer is responsible for all interactions with an user, that is, it provides the resulting information of the functional layer to a user and receives all incoming user requests. Each layer consists of several conceptual units, which provide the essential functionality.

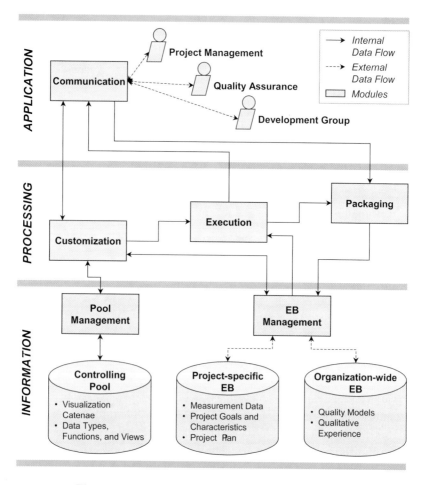

Fig. 10.   Logical architecture of SPCC Technology [28].

Pool Management: The pool management unit accesses an expandable and generic control pool, which stores all elements needed to support project control. The first type of elements are so-called functions, which are able to apply techniques and methods for several usage purposes, like monitoring, prediction, or guidance. In order to present the results of the functions according to a certain measurement goal, we need explicitly defined views, the second type of elements, of the processed data, such as one presentation suitable for the project manager, one for the quality assurer, and so on. Together, functions and views form a so-called visualization catena (VC). Functions process the measurement data, and views present the resulting information according to a certain measurement goal. The pool management unit is responsible for accessing the control pool, that is, it retrieves appropriate VC information and stores new, generalized functions and views in the corresponding sections of the control pool.

EB Management: As already mentioned, we need access to a twofold experience base (EB). One section provides project-specific information, like the measurement data of the current project, the project goals and characteristics, and the project plan. The other section provides organization-wide information, like quality models (e.g. as a basis for predicting measurement data) and qualitative experience (e.g. to guide project managers by providing a course of actions). The EB management unit organizes access to an experience base by providing mechanisms to access distributed data sources (in case of distributed development of software artifacts), validating incoming data, and integrating new experiences into the (organization-wide) EB. Therewith, the EB management unit provides all information necessary in order to perform the chosen functions.

Customization: The customization unit is the most complex conceptual unit. (1) At first, we have to initialize the EB; that is, we have to define all necessary data sources. (2) Afterwards, the pools are tailored to the project-specific needs; that is, we need to choose appropriate functions and views according to a certain usage or measurement goal (e.g. as part of a GQM plan). (3) Thereafter, we need to adapt the resulting three-layered visualization catena according to the project goals and characteristics. (4) Finally, if new functions or views are defined (e.g. by project administration), we need to generalize and integrate them into the respective pools for future usages.

Execution: The execution unit receives the chosen and adapted functions from the customization unit, determines input and output information, the function body, and the relationships with other functions. During execution of the chosen functions, the unit receives the respective input information from the EB management unit, respectively from a previously executed function. Furthermore, it receives the chosen and adapted views from the customization unit and determines the relationship between the views, and which function results have to be visualized by which view. All views are finally delivered to the user communication unit for device- or tool-specific visualization.

Packaging: The packaging unit summarizes all experiences gathered through the usage of SPCC Technology, generalizes them in order to be reused by future projects, and delivers them to the EB management unit for integration into the respective section of an experience base.

User Communication: First, the communication unit handles security issues, like the access granted to a specific user; that is, it permits a certain user to access the results of a certain set of functions, respectively a certain set of views. Second, it provides a graphical user interface (GUI) in order to customize the VC according to project goals and characteristics (via the customization unit). Third, it visualizes the views (delivered by the presentation unit) according to the chosen output interfaces.

The current SPCC Technology implementation covers the main aspects of the presented logical architecture with the exception of the packaging unit and a fully automated selection of functions and views according to a previously defined measurement goal. The control pool incorporates a set of control techniques and methods.

Requirements: (a) A user is able to access data and analysis results via the communication unit from different development locations. The formal VC definition allows for specifying explicit data validation rules. Moreover, a flexible and extendable pool of standard control techniques is provided and the specified VC is adaptable to different project contexts. A set of role-dependent views allows for goal-oriented data visualization and building up view hierarchies in order to visualize results of included data compression and abstraction mechanisms. The communication unit guarantees up-to-date information for every user. (b) A measurement paradigm (like GQM) can be used to formally derive a VC from measurement goals. However, currently no integrated mechanism is implemented. At present, the packaging module only exists conceptually; that is, data packaging depends on an SPCC function, which has to access a corresponding repository explicitly.

6. Integrated Techniques and Methods

In the following, we give a few samples of techniques and methods integrated into the previously mentioned tool-based software project control approaches. The presented techniques support different roles within a software development project. Some are more technical-oriented (e.g. Classification Tree Analysis) and some are more management-oriented (e.g. Dynamic Variables). The aim of this section is to get an impression of the variety of integrated techniques and methods.

6.1. *Classification tree analysis*

Classification tree analysis is a widely-used statistical method that is used in the context of Amadeus to identify error-prone software components on the basis of previous software releases [30]. According to the 80:20 rule, 20% of a software system cause 80% of costs (because of error-proneness). Before we can start to build a classification tree, we have to define a so-called target class, for instance, all components with more than n interface errors. After that, a recursive algorithm searches metrics to distinguish between components inside and outside the target class based upon components of previous software releases. Therefore, a special metric is chosen to classify the components appropriately. The metric itself is selected with a specific function, which is beyond the scope of this article. That is, the root of the classification tree contains all components to be classified, the nodes contain partly classified components, and finally, the leaves contain components that are either inside or outside the target class.

Figure 11 shows a classification tree example. The target class is defined by components with more than n interface errors. The first metric to classify the set of components is the number of data bindings (potential data exchanges via global variables). We get four different sets of components, namely, components with 0 to 3 data bindings, 4 to 5, 6 to 10, and more than 10 data bindings. Again, we select one

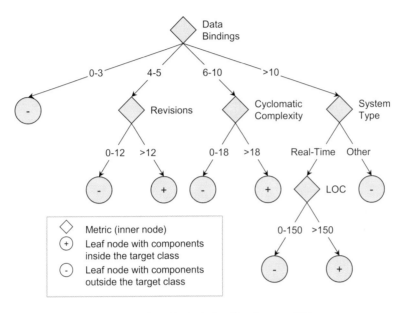

Fig. 11. Hypothetical classification tree [30].

metric for each node to partition the set of components within the node. This will be done until all components within one node are either inside or outside the target class. The first node contains all components with 0 to 3 data bindings. All these components are outside the target class and therefore, the termination criterion for this branch is met. The next node contains components inside and outside the target class. Therefore, we need another metric to classify them. The number of revisions is chosen to partition the set of components with 4 to 5 data bindings. According to Fig. 11, we get two sets that match the termination criterion for this branch of classification tree. All components with 0 to 12 revisions are outside the target class and all components with more than 12 revisions are inside the target class. The resulting classification tree is presented in Fig. 11. With this technique, error-prone or high-risk components can be identified and treated with more attention.

6.2. *Dynamic variables*

Doerflinger and Basili [11] describe the use of dynamic variables as a tool to monitor software development. The work was basically done in the context of the NASA SEL project and SME. The idea is to assume underlying relationships that are invariant between similar projects. These relationships are used to predict the behavior of projects with similar characteristics. A *baseline* of an observed variable (synonymous to an observed project attribute) is generated from measurement data of one or more completed projects in order to compare projects in progress to it. For instance, some projects with a representative productivity might be grouped to form a productivity baseline. The baseline is used to determine whether the project is in trouble or not. If the current values of a variable fall outside a *tolerance range* (i.e., the predetermined tolerable variation from the baseline), the project manager is alerted and has to determine the possible reasons for the failure.

To compare two similar projects, some points of time are needed to synchronize the comparison of variables. This can be *milestones*, such as the start or the end of a software development phase. But this is not the only crucial point. Variables, such as programmer hours and number of computer runs, are project dependent and therefore even hard to compare with other projects. We need to normalize the variables to compare values of different projects. The easiest way to create a project independent variable is to combine two dependent variables. The result is a relative measure, such as programmer hours per number of computer runs. Generally, there are two possibilities to express the time flow of a variable within a project. The first one is to measure the total number of events that have occurred from the beginning of the project up to the present (*cumulative*), and the second one is to measure the number of events that have occurred since the last measurement of the variable up to the present (*discrete*). For example, let us assume four development phases with respective efforts e_1 to e_4 for each phase. These four values represent a discrete measurement, because we measure the effort of each phase separately. The corresponding cumulative approach measures the whole effort from the beginning of the project, that is, we get a total effort of e_1, $e_1 + e_2$, $e_1 + e_2 + e_3$, and finally $e_1 + e_2 + e_3 + e_4$ after each of the four phases, respectively. Both ways offer different analysis aspects and conclusions.

The introduced method uses one table for each relative measure (i.e., for each project independent variable). This table lists possible interpretations/causes for deviations above or below a baseline of the measure. An example is shown in Table 2, which presents possible interpretations for the deviation of a measure called *programmer hours per computer run*. The table is divided into a row for deviations above and below an appropriate baseline of the measure. Each interpretation has two columns with cross references to tables of other measures, which are represented by numbers. A reference means that the corresponding interpretation is listed in the referenced tables as well. For instance, the interpretation *high complexity* is also listed in tables with numbers 1, 2, 4, 8, and 9 in row *above normal*.

Table 2.   Programmer hours per computer run [11].

Type	Interpretation	Above Normal	Below Normal
Above Normal	high complexity	$1, 2, 4, 8, 9$	
	modifications being made to recently transported code		9
	changes hard to isolate	$4, 8, 9$	
	changes hard to make	$4, 9$	
Below Normal	easy errors being fixed		$5, 9$
	error prone code	$3, 4, 5, 6$	$2, 8, 9$
	lots of testing		6

The method to determine most probable deviation causes is as follows: (1) Flag any measure outside an appropriate tolerance range. (2) Analyze the appropriate parts of the associated tables for each flagged measure. (3) Count overlaps of possible interpretations; that is, count the number of emergences of a certain interpretation in every flagged table. (4) Determine the most probable interpretation, that is, the interpretation with most overlaps. For instance, if n measures are outside the tolerance range (above or below normal), we have n corresponding lists with possible interpretations. Then, the number of overlaps for each interpretation is counted. If an interpretation I appears more often than an interpretation J, the former is more probable than the latter.

6.3. *Cluster analysis*

Li and Zelkowitz [23] describe the use of cluster analysis for extracting baselines from collected software development data. This data is either collected manually, such as effort data, error data, and subjective and objective facts about projects, or automatically, such as computer use, program static analysis, and source line counts. Each measure of a project is described by a so-called *measure pattern*, which is represented by a 15-dimensional vector composed of measurement values for 15 points of time. These points of time are assigned to four elementary software development phases: design, code/unit test, system test, and acceptance test (see axis of abscissae in Fig. 12). If you monitor a certain attribute (such as the number of modules changed) over several projects you get one measure pattern for each project. Then, we can build a so-called *measure model* by averaging the measurement values within one set of measure patterns by computing the average value for

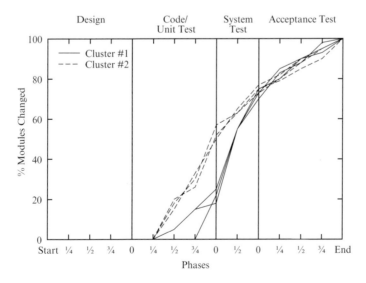

Fig. 12.   Clustering of six measure patterns for modules changed [23].

each point of time of our 15-dimensional vector. This measure model refers to the expected behavior of a certain attribute as a function of time. For instance, you have a set of n measure patterns, represented by 15-dimensional vectors $(p_{1,1}, \ldots, p_{1,15})$ to $(p_{n,1}, \ldots, p_{n,15})$. The measure model of this set is computed by:

$$(m_1, \ldots, m_{15}), \quad \text{where } m_i = \frac{p_{1,i} + \cdots + p_{n,i}}{n} \quad \text{for } i \in \{1, \ldots, 15\}.$$

Cluster analysis is a technique for finding groups in data that represent the same behavior. It is used to find similar measure patterns within collected data. The group of similar patterns is called a cluster. A *cluster model* is the measure model of all measure patterns within one cluster. A cluster consists of at least three measure patterns. Two patterns belong to the same cluster if their Euclidian distance is less than a certain threshold. In other words, each vector represents a point in a 15-dimensional space, and two points $P = (p_1, \ldots, p_{15})$ and $Q = (q_1, \ldots, q_{15})$ belong to the same cluster for a given ε if and only if:

$$\sqrt{(p_1 - q_1)^2 + \cdots + (p_{15} - q_{15})^2} < \varepsilon.$$

Figure 12 shows two clusters, built from the collected data for *modules changed* within six projects. Each measure pattern is represented by a line with 15 points. If the characterization vectors of these six projects were similar, they would be assigned to the same cluster in a static approach without computing their Euclidian distance. Cluster analysis allows us to build clusters for each considered variable of the six projects, which are based directly on the Euclidian distance of their measure models. Thus, two different clusters can be detected in Fig. 12. For a project in progress, a manager estimates the values of some variable to build an initial measure pattern. Bit by bit, estimates are replaced by real data as soon as they become available, and so the cluster model that is closest to the measure may change continuously. Furthermore, he is able to determine general characteristics for a new project within a given cluster from the common characteristics of old projects within the same cluster. Clustering can also be used to detect relationships among measures or projects. If the clusters of two variables (e.g. reported changes and reported errors) consist of the same projects, this implies a relationship between the two variables. Vice versa, if two projects are within the same clusters for a significant number of variables, this implies a relationship between the two projects.

6.4. Identification of trend changes

If a multitude of data points is available, the problem of making a decision based on collected project data is very difficult. The resulting scatter plot is hard to analyze and trend changes cannot be identified. Tesoriero and Zelkowitz [39] describe a method of smoothing data and identifying relevant trend changes. The basic idea is to compute the so-called *exponential moving average (EMA)* to smooth a given scatter plot. The method is adapted from the financial community and is used on sample data from NASA/SEL. Basically, the technique consists of three steps.

(1) At first, a smoothing technique is used to approximate the behavior of the data. Therefore, we use the EMA algorithm to smooth the scatter plot. The EMA value e_i at time x_i is computed by:

$$e_i = \left(1 - \frac{2}{N+1}\right) \cdot e_{i-1} + \frac{2}{N+1} \cdot y_i \quad \text{for } i \in \{1, \dots, 15\} \quad \text{and} \quad e_1 = y_1,$$

where y_i is the data value at x_i, $2/(N+1)$ is the smoothing constant, N is the number of points in the average, and n is the number of points in the scatter plot. The resulting 8-point EMA ($N = 8$) for an example scatter plot is presented in Fig. 13.

(2) After smoothing the scatter plot, we need to compute the extreme values of the resulting curve in order to identify trend changes of the original scatter plot. The smoothed scatter plot is continuous, but it is not differentiable. Therefore, another efficient way to compute the extreme values is chosen. The first step is to compute the so-called *instantaneous derivatives* or *delta values* of two consecutive points (x_{i-1}, e_{i-1}) and (x_i, e_i):

$$d_i = \frac{e_i - e_{i-1}}{x_i - x_{i-1}} \quad \text{for } i \in \{2, \dots, n\}.$$

The delta values are the input for a second invocation of the EMA algorithm, mentioned previously. The resulting curve is called the *signal line* and is presented in Fig. 13. It represents the average slope of the instantaneous derivatives for the

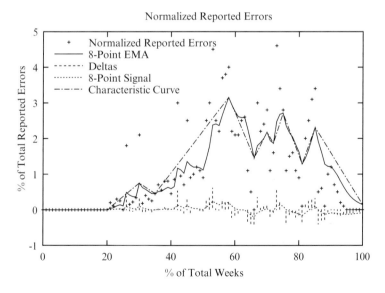

Fig. 13. Deltas, signal line and characteristic curve [39].

past N points. Therefore, if the signal line is zero in the neighborhood of x_i, you have a local maximum or minimum within the last N EMA values up to e_i. Such extreme values are called *pivot points*.

(3) The extreme values (called pivot points) of the smoothed scatter plot are the results of the second step of the algorithm. The last step is to connect each segment, defined by the pivot points, with a straight line. The resulting linear function is called *characteristic curve* and represents the major trends and trend changes of the original scatter plot (see Fig. 13).

6.5. *Sprint I control approach*

The Sprint I control approach [25–27] is a control technique used in the context of the SPCC Technology approach and built upon clustering algorithms to dynamically adapt the prediction of key project attributes during project execution. Sprint I is no pure control approach according to our definition because it predicts project attributes before project start and thus covers planning aspects as well. The prerequisite for a successful application of Sprint I to the currently performed project is that a software development organization has already performed a number of similar projects and measured at least one key attribute (e.g. effort per development phase) for each of these projects. Additionally, the context for each of these projects (i.e., the boundary conditions such as organizational, personal and technical constraints) needs to be characterized. The technique can be sketched as follows: First, the context-specific measurement data from former projects is analyzed in order to identify clusters. Based on the context of the project to be controlled, the technique selects a suitable cluster and uses its cluster curve (mean of all curves within a cluster) for predicting the attributes to be controlled. During the enactment of the project, the prediction is adapted based on actual project data. This leads to an empirical-based prediction and to flexibility for project and context changes.

The proposed control technique basically consists of five steps (see Fig. 14):

(1) Analysis. The first step of the technique analyzes the time-series of the measured attributes per completed project in order to get so-called characteristic curves of the attributes considered. A corresponding context is assigned to every characteristic curve, which represents the project environment that the curve originates from. A context description comprises all factors with a proven or assumed impact on the attribute values (such as people factors, technology factors, organizational factors, process factors).

(2) Clustering. For a certain attribute, clustering is used to identify groups of characteristic curves that belong together. These are, for instance, curves whose distance is less than a certain threshold. All characteristic curves within one cluster are averaged to get a model (the so-called cluster curve), which stands for the whole cluster. Again, a context is assigned to the aggregated curves based on a similarity analysis of the project contexts of the cluster.

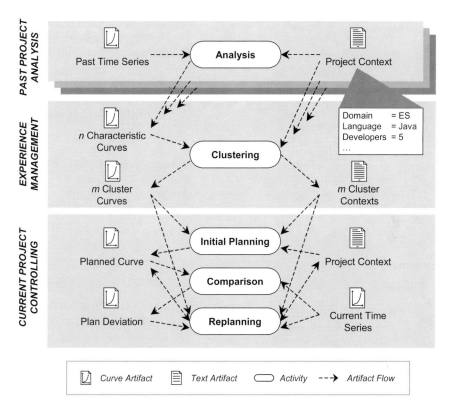

Fig. 14. SPRINT control approach.

(3) Initial Planning. During project planning, the relevant project attributes are estimated on the basis of cluster curves for the respective attributes of previous projects. At the beginning of the project, no actual data are available and therefore, context characteristics must be used in order to find a suitable cluster curve for the project attribute under consideration (see Fig. 1).

(4) Comparison. During the enactment of the project, the current values of an attribute are compared with the predicted values of the cluster curve. If a plan deviation occurs, the predicted values have to be adapted with respect to the new project situation. Therefore, the distance between the two curves has to be computed regularly. If the distance is above (or below) a most tolerable threshold, project management has to be informed in order to initiate dynamic replanning steps, and a new cluster curve has to be sought in order to make a new prediction.

(5) Replanning. In case of significant plan deviation, the causes for the deviation have to be determined. We basically distinguish three different cases: The first one is that the experience we used to build our prediction model was wrong. The second one is that the characteristics we assumed for our project were wrong (e.g. the experience of the developers was low instead of high). In this case, we have to adapt

the project context. The third case is that problems occur in the project that lead to a change of the characteristics of the project (e.g. technology changed). In all three cases, we can try to identify a new cluster curve within the set of computed clusters. Basically, there are three ways to choose a suitable cluster for prediction: The first one is matching the contexts of the actual project and the cluster curves (like step 3). The second possibility is to use the current data of a certain attribute, which has been measured during the enactment of the project up to the present, and match it with the cluster curves in order to find the best cluster curve for prediction. This is a dynamic assignment approach, which incorporates actual project behavior. The third option is to combine the static and dynamic approach to get a hybrid one. If both possibilities lead to different clusters, a set of exception handling strategies can be applied and reasons can be sought. Afterwards, step 4 is iterated and uses the adapted prediction in order to further control the project.

7. Summary and Conclusion

This chapter conceptually defined the term Software Project Control Center to support project control for software development projects and integrated an SPCC into the context of learning and improvement-oriented organizations. For doing so, we used the TAME model, which integrates measurement, support for model building, and support for project control and guidance. An SPCC is deployed during the execution of a software development project.

Selected existing approaches for SPCCs in the context of the described framework were sketched. For that, different abstraction levels for each approach were considered. In particular, techniques, methods, and tools were associated with each approach. The focus of the description was on the logical architecture. We included the PPM approach in the field of controlling and assessing business processes as a representative for an approach outside the software development domain. Figure 15

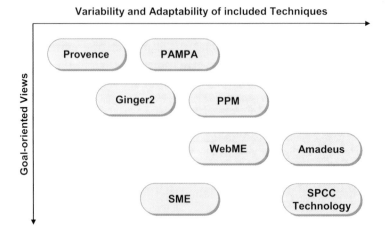

Fig. 15.   Overview of discussed approaches.

gives an overview of all discussed approaches and orders them according to the scheme mentioned in Sec. 2 on the basis of their descriptions in Sec. 5. The first dimension (the columns) describes the degree of variability of techniques and methods included; the second dimension (the rows) describes the goal-orientation of the produced views.

Existing approaches offer only partial solutions for SPCCs. Especially goal-oriented usages based on a flexible set of techniques and methods are not comprehensively supported. This leads to future research directions.

An important research issue is the development of a schema for adaptable SPCC techniques and methods, which effectively allows for purpose-driven usage of an SPCC in varying application contexts. Another research issue is the elicitation of information needs for involved roles and the development of mechanisms for generating adequate role-oriented visualizations of the project data. Both issues raise the question of an appropriate underlying logical architecture for an SPCC. The architecture should support (1) a variable and adaptable set of techniques and methods to provide the basic functionality, and (2) a goal-oriented presentation according to a certain usage goal of the SPCC. Furthermore, integration of popular visualization tools should be possible.

Another important research issue is the support of an SPCC for change management. When the goals or characteristics of a project change, the real processes react accordingly. Consequently, the control mechanisms, which should always reflect the real world situation, must be updated. This requires flexible mechanisms that allow for reacting to process variations. General problems exist in keeping data collection procedures consistent with the real processes, and managing partial backtracking of process tracks in the case of erroneous process performance. One open question is how to control process backtracking or online refinement during project execution, which is especially important for controlling "creative" process elements.

One long-term goal of engineering-style software development is to control and forecast the impact of process changes and adjustments on the quality of produced software artifacts and other important project goals. An SPCC can be seen as a valuable contribution towards reaching this goal.

Acknowledgements

We would like to thank Prof. Dr. Dieter Rombach from the Fraunhofer Institute for Experimental Software Engineering (IESE) for his valuable comments to this article, and Sonnhild Namingha from the Fraunhofer Institute for Experimental Software Engineering (IESE) and Marcus Ciolkowski from the University of Kaiserslautern for reviewing the first version of the article. Furthermore, we would like to thank the anonymous reviewers for their helpful comments on this article. This work was partly funded by the Deutsche Forschungsgemeinschaft as part of the Special Research Project SFB 501 "Development of Large Systems with Generic Methods" and the Federal Ministry of Education and Research (BMBF) as part of the project "Simulation-Based Evaluation and Improvement of Software Development Processes (SEV)".

References

1. V. R. Basili, "Software modeling and measurement: The goal/question/metric paradigm", Technical Report CS-TR-2956, Department of Computer Science, University of Maryland, College Park, MD, USA, 1992.
2. V. R. Basili, "Applying the goal/question/metric paradigm in the experience factory", *Software Quality Assurance and Measurement: A Worldwide Perspective*, Chap. 2 (International Thomson Publishing, London, UK, 1996).
3. V. R. Basili and G. Caldiera, "Methodological and architectural issues in the experience factory", *Proceedings of the Sixteenth Annual Software Engineering Workshop*, SEL-91-006, 1991.
4. V. R. Basili, G. Caldiera and H. D. Rombach, "The experience factory", *Encyclopedia of Software Engineering* **1** (1994) 469–476.
5. V. R. Basili, G. Caldiera and H. D. Rombach, "Goal question metric paradigm", *Encyclopedia of Software Engineering* **1** (1994) 528–532.
6. V. R. Basili and H. D. Rombach, "The TAME project: Towards improvement-oriented software environments", *IEEE Transactions on Software Engineering* **14**, no. 6 (1988) 758–773.
7. V. R. Basili and H. D. Rombach, "Support for comprehensive reuse", *Software Engineering Journal* **6**, no. 5 (1991) 303–316.
8. V. R. Basili and D. M. Weiss, "A methodology for collecting valid software engineering data", *IEEE Transactions on Software Engineering* **10**, no. 6 (1984) 728–738.
9. U. Becker, D. Hamann, J. Münch and M. Verlage, "MVP-E: A process modeling environment", *IEEE Software Process Newsletter* **10** (1997) 10–15.
10. L. C. Briand, C. Differding and H. D. Rombach, "Practical guidelines for measurement-based process improvement", *Software Process: Improvement and Practice* **2**, no. 4 (1996) 253–280.
11. C. W. Doerflinger and V. R. Basili, "Monitoring software development through dynamic variables", *Proceedings of IEEE Conference on Computer Software and Applications (COMPSAC)* (1983) 434–445.
12. R. L. Feldmann, J. Münch and S. Vorwieger, "Towards goal-oriented organizational learning: Representing and maintaining knowledge in an experience base", *Proceedings of the 10th International Conference on Software Engineering and Knowledge Engineering* (1998) 236–245.
13. W. W. Gibbs, "Software's chronic chrisis", *Scientific American* (September 1994) 86–95.
14. J. Heidrich and M. Soto, "Using measurement data for project control", *Proceedings of the Second International Symposium on Empirical Software Engineering*, Rome (October 2003) 9–10.
15. J. Heidrich, "Effective data interpretation and presentation in software projects", Technical Report 05/2003, Sonderforschungsbereich 501, University of Kaiserslautern, 2003.
16. R. Hendrick, D. Kistler and J. Valett, "Software Management Environment (SME) — Concepts and architecture (Revision 1)", NASA Goddard Space Flight Center Code 551, Software Engineering Laboratory Series Report SEL-89-103, Greenbelt, MD, USA, 1992.

17. R. Hendrick, D. Kistler and J. Valett, "Software Management Environment (SME) — Components and algorithms", NASA Goddard Space Flight Center, Software Engineering Laboratory Series Report SEL-94-001, Greenbelt, MD, USA, 1994.
18. IDS Scheer AG, "Optimieren Sie Ihre Prozess Performance — Process Performance Manager®", IDS Scheer AG, White Paper, 2000.
19. G. E. Kaiser, N. S. Barghouti and M. H. Sokolsky, "Preliminary experience with process modeling in the marvel software development environment kernel", *Proceedings of the 23rd Annual Hawaii International Conference on System Sciences* **II** (IEEE Computer Society Press, January 1990) 131–140.
20. B. Krishnamurthy and N. S. Barghouti, "Provence: A process visualization and enactment environment", *Proceedings of the 4th European Software Engineering Conference, Lecture Notes in Computer Science 717* (Springer, Heidelberg, Germany, 1993) 451–465.
21. L. Landis, F. McGarry, S. Waligora, R. Pajerski, M. Stark, R. Kester, T. McDermott and J. Miller, "Managers handbook for software development — Revision 1", NASA Goddard Space Flight Center Code 552, Software Engineering Laboratory Series Report SEL-84-101, Greenbelt, MD, USA, 1990.
22. C. M. Lott, "Process and measurement support in SEEs", *ACM Software Engineering Notes* **18**, no. 4 (1993) 83–93.
23. N. R. Li and M. V. Zelkowitz, "An information model for use in software management estimation and prediction", *Proceedings of the 2nd International Conference on Information and Knowledge Management* (1993) 481–489.
24. F. McGarry, R. Pajerski, G. Page, S. Waligora, V. R. Basili and M. V. Zelkowitz, "An overview of the software engineering laboratory", Software Engineering Laboratory Series Report SEL-94-005, Greenbelt, MD, USA, 1994.
25. J. Münch, J. Heidrich and A. Daskowska, "A practical way to use clustering and context knowledge for software project planning", *Proceedings of the 15th International Conference on Software Engineering and Knowledge Engineering, SEKE 2003)*, San Francisco, USA, July 1–3, 2003, 377–384.
26. J. Münch and J. Heidrich, "Using cluster curves to control software development projects", *Proceedings of the First International Symposium on Empirical Software Engineering*, Nara **II** (2002) 13–14.
27. J. Münch and J. Heidrich, "Context-driven software project estimation", *Proceedings of the Second International Symposium on Empirical Software Engineering*, Rome **II** (2003) 15–16.
28. J. Münch and J. Heidrich, "Software project control centers: Concepts and approaches", *Journal of Systems and Software* **70**, no. 1 (Elsevier, 2003).
29. Project Management Institute, "A guide to the Project Management Body of Knowledge (PMBOKÆ Guide) 2000 Edition", Project Management Institute, Four Campus Boulevard, Newtown Square, PA 19073–3299 USA, 2000.
30. A. A. Porter and R. W. Selby, "Empirically guided software development using metric-based classification trees", *IEEE Software* **7**, no. 2 (1990) 46–54.
31. H. D. Rombach, "Practical benefits of goal-oriented measurement", *Software Reliability and Metrics* (1991) 217–235.
32. H. D. Rombach and M. Verlage, "Directions in software process research", *Advances in Computers* **41** (1995) 1–63.
33. R. W. Selby, A. A. Porter, D. C. Schmidt and J. Berney, "Metric-driven analysis and feedback systems for enabling empirically guided software development", *Proceedings of the 13th International Conference on Software Engineering* (1991) 288–298.

34. M. Shaw, "Prospects for an engineering discipline of software", *IEEE Software* **7**, no. 6 (1990) 15–24.

35. D. B. Simmons, N. C. Ellis, H. Fujihara and W. Kuo, *Software Measurement — A Visualization Toolkit for Project Control and Process Improvement* (Prentice Hall Inc, New Jersey, USA, 1998).

36. R. van Solingen and E. Berghout, *The Goal/Question/Metric Method, A Practical Method for Quality Improvement of Software Development* (McGraw-Hill, UK, 1999).

37. R. Tesoriero and M. V. Zelkowitz, "The Web Measurement Environment (WebME): A tool for combining and modeling distributed data", *Proceedings of the 22nd Annual Software Engineering Workshop (SEW)*, 1997.

38. R. Tesoriero and M. V. Zelkowitz, "A model of noisy software engineering data (Status Report)", *International Conference on Software Engineering* (1998) 461–464.

39. R. Tesoriero and M. V. Zelkowitz, "A web-based tool for data analysis and presentation", *IEEE Internet Computing* **2**, no. 5 (1998) 63–69.

40. K. Torii, K. Matsumoto and S. Kusumoto, "GINGER: A quantitative analysis environment for improving programmer performance", Technical Report, Graduate School of Information Science, Nara Institute of Science and Technology, 8916-5 Takayama, Ikoma, Nara 630-01, Japan, 1995.

41. K. Torii, K. Matsumoto, K. Nakakoji, Y. Takada, S. Takada and K. Shima, "Ginger2: An environment for computer-aided empirical software engineering", *IEEE Transactions on Software Engineering* **25**, no. 4 (1999) 474–492.

INDEX

access control, 31, 33, 39–42, 54
accountability, 32, 33, 38, 58
additive nonlinear regression, 344, 345
agency, 66, 67, 72
agent-oriented modeling, 63, 122, 123
  active object, 123
  agent, 122–124
  agent-class diagram, 123
agile process, 93, 96, 99, 100
Amadeus, 483, 487–490, 500
amorphous program slicing, 325
antivirus software, 37, 49
architectural description, 119, 120, 124,
  130, 134, 135, 144, 145
  architectural style, 126, 127, 129, 131,
    133, 145
  architecture description language
    (ADL), 120, 125, 128–134, 137,
    140, 141, 143, 144
  component, 124–132, 134–136, 138–140,
    142, 143
  connector, 125–128, 130–132, 134–136,
    138, 140, 142, 143
  constraints, 122, 126, 127, 129,
    131–134, 140, 143
  glue, 126, 128, 135
  interface, 120, 122, 124–126, 128–130,
    133, 135, 138–142, 145
  port, 124–126, 138, 143
  role, 126, 135, 138
  systems, 126–128, 134
assurance, 32, 33
attack, 31–40, 43, 44, 46, 47, 51–54, 57–59
audit, 42, 43
authentication, 31–33, 36–40, 45–47, 53,
  56, 58
authorization, 33, 37–39, 41, 42, 58
autonomic computing, 64
autonomous software, 63–65, 67–69, 72,
  76, 80, 81
autonomy
  matrix, 65, 67, 68, 78

  orientation, 64, 81
  specification, 63–65, 68, 76, 81
  status, 66–68, 75–78, 80
  transformation loop, 65, 76, 77
availability, 32–34, 37, 38, 42, 43, 53

backbone slice, 325
backward slice, 310, 312, 313, 315, 325,
  326
bag, 286
barrier slicing, 321, 322

calling context, 309, 311, 314, 315, 317
capability, 68, 70, 76, 78, 80, 88
  of organizations, 95, 97–99, 101, 107,
    112–115
capability maturity models, 85, 87, 88,
  100
chop, 321, 322
chopping, 320, 321, 325
classification tree analysis, 500
classifier, 218–223
clone detection, 312
cluster analysis, 503, 504
CMM, 85, 88, 89, 93, 100, 110, 114, 115
  adjunct models, 97
  and extreme programming, 99
  capability-based, 104
  domain-related, 104
  for e-commerce, 99, 104
  for formal specification, 104, 105, 107
  for information systems, 85, 104, 109
  for knowledge management, 89, 97,
    104, 112
  for requirements engineering, 85, 93,
    96, 104–106
  for requirements quality, 104
  for reuse, 96, 100, 104
  for small organizations, 98, 114
  for software, 87
  generic, 85, 88, 92

phase-related, 104
process, 85, 88, 92
process-based, 104
purposes of, 88
Taiji, 100
tailored models, 96, 97
CMMI, 88–90, 97, 99–102, 113–115
continuous, 89, 100, 101, 104
process areas, 100, 102
product suite, 100
sources of, 100
staged, 89, 100, 102
transition from SW–CMM, 113
cohesion measurement, 312
commitment, 68, 69, 74–76, 80
component-based software engineering
(CBSE), 124
component-object based software
architecture (COSA), 136
Computation Independent Model (CIM),
210
confidentiality, 32–38, 40, 42, 43, 45–47,
52, 53, 58
context-insensitive, 311, 316, 317
context-sensitive, 311, 313, 316, 317
continuous simulation, 334, 336, 337, 362
control, 64–68, 73, 77, 80
control and data dependence edges, 308,
310
control dependence, 310, 313, 314, 316,
317, 319, 321, 323, 324
control tools, 477, 483
countermeasure, 31, 32, 38, 53, 59
cryptography, 31, 44–46, 58

daily build, 99
DARPA Agent Markup Language
(DAML+OIL), 208
data dependence, 308, 310, 313, 314,
316–318, 321–324
data interpretation, 477, 482
data visualization, 477, 485, 488, 493, 494,
496, 500
debugging, 307, 309, 311, 313, 322
decomposition slice, 324
decomposition slicing, 312
dependency, 68, 71–73, 77, 78, 81
description logics, 178, 180, 198
design patterns, 151, 153, 154, 167, 169,
171, 172

dicing, 311, 322, 325
discrete-event simulation, 334, 361
distance-limited slicing, 320, 324
domain ontologies, 203
dynamic dependence graph, 323
dynamic GQM, 429, 431, 437, 442, 453
dynamic slice, 308, 322–324
dynamic slicing, 307, 309, 311, 317,
322–324
dynamic variables, 500, 501

e-learning, 455, 459, 460, 462, 464, 470,
472, 474
empirical studies, 334, 343
expectation, 63, 68, 70, 74, 75, 77, 78, 80,
81
Experience Factory (EF), 480
experimental software engineering,
333–335, 338, 361
experiments, 333–336, 343, 344, 358
extreme programming, 98, 99

feature engineering, 365
firewall, 47, 48
forward slice, 311, 312, 325
forward slicing, 311, 312
function extraction, 312
function restructuring, 312
functional architecture, 217, 223
fuzzy reasoning, 301

G-net, 297–299, 304
decomposition, 299
editorial office, 299, 300
Ginger2, 483, 487, 490, 491
Goal Question Metric (GQM), 479, 480
goal-oriented measurement, 429, 431, 437,
453
goal/question/metrics (GQM), 338
GOOD OLD AI, 204
GQM method, 484
GQM plan, 499
GUI reimplementation, 234, 243, 244

horizontal consistency, 178, 179
human resource modeling, 334, 343, 348
hybrid modeling, 429, 453

identification of trend changes, 504
if–then rule, 301
incremental software development, 365–368
individuals, 209, 220, 221, 223–228
instance layers, 211
integrity, 32–34, 36–38, 40, 42, 43, 45, 46, 49, 50, 52, 53
inter-consistency, 178
interface dependence graphs, 325
interface slicing, 325
interprocedural control dependence, 316
interprocedural program dependence graph (IPDG), 315
interprocedural slicing, 314
intra-consistency, 178
intrusion detection, 31, 32, 42–44

key process areas (KPA), 88, 90–94, 97–99, 101–104, 106–110, 112, 114
knowledge exchange, 455, 458–460, 462, 465, 467, 468, 470
knowledge management, 455, 456, 465, 466, 471, 472
knowledge representation, 204, 205
knowledge sharing, 203, 204

legacy systems, 233–242, 244–252, 257, 264, 268, 269

mappings, 213, 216
MDA-based languages, 213
measurement, 478–480, 482–484, 486, 488, 490–494, 496–503, 506, 508
measurement process, 479
Meta-Object Facility (MOF), 204, 210
metamodeling, 205, 211–215, 217, 218, 223, 228
metamodeling constructs, 217, 218
mobile agent, 31, 32, 50–59
mobile computing, 31, 32, 50, 59
Model Driven Architecture (MDA), 203, 204, 210, 212
Model-View-Controller design pattern, 233, 234, 241, 242, 244, 253, 261, 268
motivation, 68, 69, 72, 74, 76, 79, 80
multi-agent architectures, 151, 152

multi-layer Web-based architecture, 233, 240
MVP-E, 480

negotiation protocol, 455, 462, 463, 465, 471
non-decomposable, 233, 234, 239–241, 246–248, 252, 255, 257, 264, 268, 269
non-repudiation, 32, 33, 38, 46, 56, 58

object-oriented modeling, 119, 120, 122, 130, 131, 134, 135, 144, 145
    attributes, 120, 121
    class, 120–122, 140
    message calls, 120, 121
    methods, 120–122, 128, 130, 140
    object (instance), 120
    object constraint language (OCL), 122, 130, 133
    object-orientation, 120, 121, 130, 131, 135, 136
    object-oriented programming, 120, 123, 131
    objects, 121
    unified modeling language (UML), 119, 122, 123, 130–135, 144, 145
ontological engineering, 203–205, 213–215, 228
ontological layers, 211, 212
ontologies, 203–210, 213, 215–217, 223, 228
ontology building tools, 206
ontology classes, 219, 221, 224, 225
Ontology Definition Metamodel, 203, 216, 217, 228
ontology development tools, 206, 207
Ontology Inference Layer (OIL), 208
ontology metamodel, 204, 214
ontology properties, 214, 220, 226, 227
Ontology UML Profile (OUP), 203, 204, 216, 217, 223–228
operational mechanisms, 135
    compositionality, 142
    inheritance, 137–140
    instantiation, 137, 140
    refinement, 142, 143
    subtyping, 137–140
    supertyping, 138

templates, 140
traceability, 143
optimization, 333, 334, 343, 358–360, 362
optimization algorithms, 365, 381
orders fulfillment, 86, 282
organizational styles, 1–6, 14, 24, 25, 27
OWL DL, 209, 217
OWL Full, 209, 217
OWL Lite, 209

PAMPA, 483, 487, 496, 497
password control, 296
path conditions, 313
people CMM, 97
perspective of observation, 68
    external, 64, 68, 71, 73, 74, 76, 78–80
    internal, 66, 68–72, 74, 75, 78, 79
Petri net, 43, 55, 275–278, 280–287,
    290–292, 294–297, 301, 303, 304
    and fuzzy reasoning, 301
    and turing machines, 296
    and turning machines, 296
    arc, 276
    bibliography, 276
    colored, 285
    conflict in, 286
    deadlock, 278–280, 296
    decidability, 296
    decomposition, 295
    fairness, 280
    flow relation, 280
    for a manufacturing process, 284
    for bounded buffer, 281
    for mutual exclusion, 277, 280
    for order fulfillment, 282
    for railroad crossing, 288
    for referee selection, 286
    for traffic lights, 280, 287
    inhibitor arc, 290
    input place, 276
    marking, 280
    markup language, 304
    modularization, 296
    output place, 277
    place, 276
    reachability graph, 279
    reduction, 296
    representation of, 296, 304
    starvation, 278
    state, 280

    token, 277
    transition, 276
Petri nets
    and semantics, 290
Platform Independent Model (PIM), 210
Platform Specific Model (PSM), 210
PPM, 483, 487, 494–496, 508
procedure dependence graph, 314
process coordination, 290
process modeling, 333, 335, 355, 361, 362
production system, 196, 197
program dependence graph (PDG), 307,
    308, 310–315, 317–321, 323
program differencing, 312
program integration, 312, 325
program slicing, 307, 311–313, 320, 324,
    326
project management, 480, 481, 486, 497,
    507
properties, 121, 126
property, 209, 213–215, 218–223, 226, 227
property problem, 214
protégé, 213–215
Provence, 483, 486–488

quality assurance, 477, 481, 485, 497
Quality Improvement Paradigm (QIP),
    479, 480

range of activity, 69
    deliberative, 68–71, 78
    normative, 68, 70, 74, 77, 79, 80
    performative, 68–71, 73, 78
RDF Schema (RDFS), 208, 209, 213–216
RE–CMM, 104, 106, 110
realizable, 308–311, 315, 316
realizable path, 311, 315, 316, 321, 322
regression testing, 312
releases, 365–377, 379–384, 386, 389, 390
requirements development, 94, 103, 108
requirements engineering, 1, 3, 26
requirements management, 90, 91, 93, 94,
    102, 106, 110, 365, 366, 368, 369, 391
resource, 205, 208, 209, 218, 221, 222, 226
Resource Description Framework (RDF),
    208
rete algorithm, 196

reuse, 334, 338, 343, 355–358, 362
reverse engineering, 233, 234, 236, 237, 240, 241, 243, 268

security, 31, 32
semantic consistency, 178–180, 182, 183, 198
semantic web, 203–210, 215, 216, 222, 228
semantic web languages, 206, 207, 213–215
semantic web tools, 206
shuttle project, 95
simulation, 333–339, 342–346, 349, 351–362
simulation modeling, 333, 334, 336, 337, 343, 355, 356, 358
slice, 307–318, 320, 322–325
slicing, 307–309
slicing criterion, 308–311, 320, 322, 324
SME, 483, 487, 491–493, 501
Software Acquisition CMM, 97
software architecture, 120, 126, 130, 131, 133, 134, 137, 138, 143, 144
    4+1 view model, 134
    component-based software architecture (CBSA), 120, 144
    component-object based software architecture (COSA), 129, 135, 140, 141, 144, 145
    object based software architecture (OBSA), 120, 144
software conformance certification, 313
software development project, 479
software engineering decision support, 365, 376, 381
software migration, 233, 235
software process simulation, 333, 336, 338, 343, 355, 357, 362, 429
software process types, 85–88, 92, 93, 96, 98, 104, 105, 107, 113
software processes, 478, 497
software project control, 477–480, 486, 500
Software Project Control Center (SPCC), 477–479, 483, 508
software traceability, 395, 396, 413, 421, 424
SPCC technology, 497–499, 506
Sprint I control approach, 506

stakeholder, 369–373, 389–391
statement, 205, 209, 211, 223, 227, 228
statement-minimal slice, 309
static slicing, 308, 309, 317, 318, 322–324
styles, 143
SW–CMM, 87–91, 94–104, 106, 110, 113–115
    appraisals problems, 113, 114
    evaluation, 113
    levels of, 87, 88, 90, 95
syntactic consistency, 178, 179, 185, 198
system dependence graph (SDG), 315–317, 325
system dynamics, 429, 430, 433, 443, 453
system is decomposable, 233, 234, 239, 241, 242, 245, 257, 264, 268, 269

tailoring a measurement environment (TAME), 480
Team Software Process, 96, 97
time exchange, 455, 458–460, 462, 465, 467, 468, 470, 472
time management, 455, 456, 465, 466, 470–472
time petri net, 286
Tina tools, 294

UML
    activity diagrams, 275
UML CASE tools, 211, 216
UML metamodel, 211, 212, 214
UML Profiles, 204, 210, 212, 213, 216

vertical consistency, 178, 179
visualization, 333, 334, 342, 343, 351, 352, 362, 477, 479, 482, 483, 485, 491, 492, 494–496, 498, 499, 509

Web Ontology Language (OWL), 208, 209, 217
WebME, 483, 487, 493, 494
Weiser-style slicing, 309, 311
wrapping, 234, 236, 238–241, 243, 244, 246, 268

XDD clause, 186, 190, 194
XDD description, 186, 190, 194

XML, 203–209, 211, 213, 214, 216
XML Declarative Description (XDD)
   theory, 178, 186, 190
XML expression, 178, 186, 190, 191

XML Metadata Interchange (XMI), 204
XML Metadata Interchange (XMI)
   format, 178, 186
XSLT, 213–217